ARNOLD READERS IN HISTORY

TITLES IN THE
ARNOLD READERS IN HISTORY SERIES

THE IMPACT OF THE ENGLISH REFORMATION 1500–1640

Edited by PETER MARSHALL

Lecturer in History, University of Warwick

A member of the Hodder Headline Group
LONDON • NEW YORK • SYDNEY • AUCKLAND

First published in Great Britain in 1997 by
Arnold, a member of the Hodder Headline Group,
338 Euston Road, London NW1 3BH
175 Fifth Avenue, New York, NY 10010

Distributed exclusively in the USA by
St Martin's Press, Inc.
175 Fifth Avenue, New York, NY 10010

British Library Cataloguing in Publication Data
A catalogue record for this book is available from the British Library

Library of Congress Cataloging-in-Publication Data
The impact of the English Reformation, 1500–1640 / edited by
Peter Marshall.
p.   cm. – (Arnold readers in history)
Includes bibliographical references and index.
ISBN 0–340–67708–2 (hardback). – ISBN 0–340–67709–0 (pbk.)
1. Reformation–England.   2. England–Church history–16th
century.   3. England–Church history–17th century.   I. Marshall,
Peter.   II. Series
BR375.I55   1997
274.2'06–dc21   96–37853
CIP

ISBN 0 340 677090 (Pb)
ISBN 0 340 677082 (Hb)

Typeset in 10/12pt Sabon by J&L Composition Ltd, Filey, North Yorkshire
Printed and bound in Great Britain by J.W. Arrowsmith, Bristol.

Contents

Preface

As an object of academic investigation and a focus of sometimes fierce scholarly debate, the 'English Reformation' has been growing over recent years in more senses than one. Since the mid-1970s a series of self-styled 'revisionist' attacks on what were perceived to be prevailing orthodoxies has helped to re-invigorate the subject at both sixth form and undergraduate level. At the same time, Reformation historians are allowing themselves an ever more generous interpretation of the chronological bounds of their subject, to the extent that academic conferences convened under the 'English Reformation' label are now as likely to bring forth papers on seventeenth-century topics as on sixteenth-century ones. Moreover, historians of the Reformation are increasingly prepared to accept that they have something to learn from other disciplines and are turning, for example, to the study of iconography or the techniques of textual criticism.

The historiography of the English Reformation is not, or not yet, as unmanageable in its scope and volume as that of the French Revolution has already become, and that of the English Civil War threatens to become. Nonetheless, it can be difficult for students, and indeed their teachers, to orientate themselves amidst a welter of recent books and articles, some of which can seem arcane, introspective or self-referential to the non-specialist. The intentions of this volume are to direct students to examples of significant recent (1980s and early 1990s) work on the Reformation changes in England, and to draw attention to some patterns, methodologies and particular concerns in current scholarship, without in any sense seeking to impose a false framework, either of consensus or of conflict, which the authors represented might themselves reject.

No collection of a dozen articles can lay claim to be entirely representative of historical approaches to its subject, let alone to be comprehensive in its thematic coverage. Important aspects of the impact of the Reformation (for example, the dissolution of the religious houses) are little touched upon in the pages that follow, and there are a number of important and productive Reformation historians whose work, for reasons of space, is not represented here. The principles underlying selection are, inevitably, to some extent subjective ones, reflecting the editor's own assessment of what is interesting and important in the field in which he works. Certain criteria for exclusion and inclusion have, however, been consciously applied. In the first place, the stress upon the 'impact' of the Reformation is not intended to denigrate the world of high policy and its formulation as unimportant, but it does reflect a perception that students may gain a familiarity with the essential aspects of the 'political Reformation' from a variety of fairly accessible secondary works. It also underlines the increasing awareness among scholars that religious change had to be enacted, negotiated, accepted or rejected at all levels of English society, and not merely be decided upon at the centre. Second, it was decided that no overtly historiographical pieces should be included, though there have been a number of enlightening recent essays of this type.[1] Each of the chapters below represents substantive original research, to which it is important that students should have access, though at the same time care has been taken to ensure that each piece locates itself within a context of wider issues and debates. Finally, the chronological span of the chapters, which range from the first decades of the sixteenth century to the eve of the English Civil War, reflects a conviction that, in trying to understand the Reformation as a crucial and transforming episode in the history of English culture and religion, it makes little sense to cut the story off at some point in the second half of the sixteenth century, as most textbook accounts still do.

The structure of this book attempts to break up England's 'long Reformation' into manageable and conceptually meaningful parts, though readers will find that there is a degree of overlap between the readings in different sections, in terms both of themes raised and of chronological range. Section 1 focuses largely on the nature and extent of grass-roots enthusiasm for religious change in the half-century before the accession of Elizabeth, the period now usually referred to as the 'early Reformation'. Section 2 offers various perspectives on the implementation of officially sanctioned reform in the localities from the 1530s to the last years of Elizabeth, focusing on the role of central and local authorities in enacting or reversing 'Reformation', and the reaction of local communities to these processes. The third Section is intended to survey recent discussions of how Reformation had affected the religious sensibilities and attitudes of the English people by the last decades of the sixteenth and first decades of the seventeenth century: in what sense had England become a 'Protestant nation'? How much continuity remained with the Catholic past?

Note

1 See C. Haigh, 'The Recent Historiography of the English Reformation', in C. Haigh ed., *The English Reformation Revised* (Cambridge, Cambridge University Press, 1987), pp. 19–33; D. MacCulloch, 'The Myth of the English Reformation', *Journal of British Studies*, 30 (1991), pp. 1–19; W.I.P. Hazlett, 'Settlements: the British Isles', in T.A. Brady *et al.*, eds, *Handbook of European History 1400–1600* (Leiden, Brill, 1995), II pp. 455–69; P. Collinson, 'The English Reformation 1945–1995', in M. Bentley, ed., *The Writing of History* (London, Routledge, forthcoming).

Acknowledgements

I am grateful to Christopher Wheeler for encouraging me to undertake this volume, and for steering me calmly through its preparation. Thanks are due also to those scholars who took the trouble to discuss the proposal with me, in particular Susan Brigden, Eamon Duffy and Andrew Foster, and to Patrick Collinson, who kindly sent me a draft of an important bibliographical essay in advance of its publication. I am especially indebted to my colleagues at Warwick, Bernard Capp and Steve Hindle, who at short notice read a draft of the Introduction and made many helpful suggestions. As always, I must thank my wife, Ali Marshall, for her forbearance and support.

The editor and publisher would also like to thank the following for permission to use copyright material in this volume:

Blackwell Publishers for Christopher Harper-Bill, 'Dean Colet's convocation sermon and the pre-Reformation Church in England', from *History*, 32 (1988), pp. 191–210; *Archiv für Reformationsgeschichte* and Mrs Margaret Woffenden for J.F. Davis, 'Lollardy and the Reformation in England', from *Archiv für Reformationsgeschichte*, 73 (1982), pp. 217–36; Oxford University Press for Susan Brigden, 'Youth and the English Reformation', from *Past and Present*, 95 (1982), pp. 37–67; *Archiv für Reformationsgeschichte* for A.G. Dickens, 'The early expansion of Protestantism in England, 1520–1558', from *Archiv für Reformationsgeschichte*, 78 (1987), pp. 187–221, previously reprinted in A.G. Dickens, *Late Monasticism and the Reformation* (London, Hambledon Press, 1994), pp. 101–32; the Southern History Society for Robert Whiting, '"For the health of my soul": prayers for the dead in the Tudor south-west', from *Southern History*, 5 (1983), pp. 68–94; Cambridge University Press and the author for Ronald Hutton, 'The local impact of the Tudor Reformations', from C. Haigh, ed. *The English Reformation Revised* (Cambridge, Cambridge University Press, 1987), pp. 114–38; the Board of the Medieval Institute, Western Michigan University for Margaret Aston, 'Iconoclasm in England:

official and clandestine', from Clifford Davidson and Ann Eljenholm Nichols, eds *Iconoclasm vs. Art and Drama* (Kalamazoo, Medieval Institute Publications, 1989) pp. 47–91, previously reprinted in Margaret Aston, *Faith and Fire: Popular and Unpopular Religion, 1350–1600* (London, Hambledon Press, 1993), pp. 261–90; Yale University Press and the author for Eamon Duffy, 'Mary', from Eamon Duffy, *The Stripping of the Altars: Traditional Religion in England 1400–1580* (New Haven and London, Yale University Press, 1992), pp. 524–64; Macmillan Press Ltd for Christopher Haigh, 'The Church of England, the Catholics and the people', from C. Haigh, ed. *The Reign of Elizabeth I* (Basingstoke, Macmillan, 1984), pp. 195–219; Macmillan Press Ltd for Judith Maltby, '"By this book": parishioners, the Prayer Book and the established Church', from Kenneth Fincham, ed. *The Early Stuart Church* (Basingstoke, Macmillan, 1993), pp. 115–37; the University of Reading and the author for Patrick Collinson, 'From iconoclasm to iconophobia: the cultural impact of the Second English Reformation' (The Stenton Lecture 1985, University of Reading, 1986); Cambridge University Press and the author for Tessa Watt, 'Piety in the pedlar's pack: continuity and change, 1578–1630', from M. Spufford, ed. *The World of Rural Dissenters 1520–1725* (Cambridge, Cambridge University Press, 1995), pp. 235–72.

Introduction

Most current scholarly interest in the impact of the English Reformation can be traced directly, or by a remove or two, to the appearance some thirty years ago of A.G. Dickens's magisterial survey, *The English Reformation* (1964). At the time of its publication, the conventional approach to the subject was embedded in a somewhat ossified historiographical tradition that was content to epitomize the course of the Reformation in England simply as an 'act of state'. By contrast, Dickens attempted to complement the familiar political narrative with a strong 'socio-biographical' emphasis which stressed the autonomous contribution of individual reformers, and the considerable potential of Protestantism to make converts, often in advance of, or in opposition to, official government policy. Informing Dickens's approach was the familiarity with and respect for the local archival sources he had demonstrated in his first book, *Lollards and Protestants in the Diocese of York* (1959). The sheer volume of such sources held in English local record offices – wills, church court records, parish accounts – is unparalleled in Europe, and Dickens's lead in utilizing them for more than merely antiquarian purposes continues to be followed by generations of research students. More than any other development in post-war Reformation historiography, this has transformed our understanding of the topic.

Ironically, it was from such an intensive local study that the beginnings of what has come to be termed a 'revisionist' approach to the study of the English Reformation emerged in the mid-1970s. Christopher Haigh's *Reformation and Resistance in Tudor Lancashire* (1975) argued that in that north-western county pre-Reformation Catholicism was thriving and popular, Protestantism was able to make few converts, and resistance to the imposition of the Reformation continued, with a considerable degree of success, into Elizabeth's reign and beyond. Subsequently, Haigh developed his argument for other parts of the country in a series of important articles (*see* Reading 9). He has also contributed a recent general survey, which, though it modifies some of his earlier pronouncements, maintains the overall thesis.[1] In the interim, the revisionist case had been bolstered in a published set of lectures by J.J. Scarisbrick, hitherto best known as the biographer of Henry VIII. Scarisbrick's epigrammatic opening has become the familiar motto of revisionist historiography: 'on the whole, English men and women did not want the Reformation and most of them were slow to accept it when it came'.[2] Further (to some minds, definitive) confirmation of the thesis came in a 'best-seller' of the early 1990s, Eamon Duffy's *The Stripping of the Altars*.[3] Duffy devotes the first part of a lengthy book to a sensitive and sympathetic evocation of the laity's involvement in and commitment to orthodox religion in the century before the break with Rome; the second part is a poignant account of the, as it seems, inexplicable devastation wrought upon that world by government action from the late 1530s onwards.

It is fair to state that revisionist scholarship on the English Reformation has essentially set itself a negative explanatory goal: to demonstrate that the conventional 'Whiggish' or (in an unkind formulation of Haigh's) 'Dickensian' version cannot be sustained by the evidence – there was no particular reason for the great mass of the people to be alienated from or dissatisfied with the teachings, worship and institutions of the Catholic Church. In so far as revisionists tackle the 'causes' of the English Reformation, the emphasis tends to be on political contingency, or the agency of particular interest groups. Some aspects of their case are now gaining wide acceptance. Despite a valiant rearguard action by A.G. Dickens, most historians are becoming sceptical about the existence of 'anticlericalism' as a ubiquitous and potentially explosive phenomenon in late medieval society (*see* Reading 1).[4] That endemic tension between the clergy and sections of the laity is more likely to have accompanied than to have precipitated Reformation changes is generally admitted, even by scholars like Susan Brigden, who discern a considerable populist potential in early Protestantism (*see* Reading 3). Other facets of the revisionists' argument remain more contentious, in particular their assessment of the tradition of late medieval dissent known as Lollardy. While Duffy, Haigh and Scarisbrick would concur in regarding Lollardy as a 'disparate, dispersed, undangerous movement', other scholars have discerned in it organizational sophistication and theological depth (*see* Reading 2). The most substantial recent study accords Lollardy the status of a 'premature Reformation'.[5]

It would, however, be misleading to present 'revisionist' historians of the English Reformation as constituting a unified, internally coherent historiographical 'party'. While they might share a generally positive assessment of the pre-Reformation Church, very different views are possible on the extent to which traditional Catholic piety was to hold up under conditions of official disapproval, some scholars stressing its resilience, others its vulnerability and relatively rapid collapse (*see* Readings 5,

6, 9). If we lay aside for the moment the (admittedly important) exception represented by the Pilgrimage of Grace, accounting for the quite extra-ordinary level of popular acquiescence in the face of change remains a problem for those historians convinced that the reforms initiated by Henry, Edward and Elizabeth were almost universally resented in the parishes. In discussing the abolition of the chantries in 1547, one modern commentator suggests that it may have struck contemporaries much as we should view 'the forcible closure of all hospices for the terminally ill'.[6] Its successful execution was thus testimony to the efficiency and ruthlessness of Tudor government (*see* Readings 5, 6). The nature and spirit of popular 'com-pliance' with the Reformation is still a thoroughly vexed question, though it may be that continuing painstaking work on local sources will take us some way towards a more nuanced understanding of the issue that does not involve attributing everything to the mesmerism exercised by an all-powerful Tudor state. A recent study of Tudor parish accounts, for exam-ple, points to the considerable success of some local communities in concealing from the authorities communal resources threatened with seizure.[7] An ever-increasing sophistication in the analysis and classification of Tudor wills suggests that thoroughly conservative religious sentiments could be encoded within apparently 'neutral' or 'reformist' statements of belief.[8] Moreover, as Margaret Aston makes clear (Reading 7), officially inspired iconoclasm could encounter significant local opposition, to the extent that the authorities were sometimes compelled to proceed in a 'clandestine' manner. Further enlightenment may come with the growing recognition that within particular local communities, religious change was not just externally and arbitrarily 'imposed', but mediated, negotiated, or (in a word which is seen to have considerable interpretative potential) 'brokered'. The 'brokers' of the English Reformation were those local men of standing (including parish clergy and churchwardens) who bore the primary responsibility for the implementation of government direc-tives, but who can hardly be seen without significant qualification as agents of the state, and who must have placed considerable value on the good opinion of their neighbours. Further exploration of this theme may start to produce convincing answers to some of the awkward questions posed by the revisionists, though as yet the topic awaits a fully conceptualized and comprehensive articulation, which could have been included in this collection.[9]

The influential position which revisionism now holds in approaches to the English Reformation has not been achieved without generating some heat. The fact that several prominent revisionist historians – Jack Scaris-brick, Eamon Duffy, Richard Rex – are practising Roman Catholics has led some observers to bewail the emergence of a 'new confessionalism' in approaches to the study of the English Reformation. (Christopher Haigh has taken some pains to point out that he is not a Catholic.[10]) If this is 'confessionalism' it is arguably not so new: Dickens's *English Reformation* can be thought in many respects to represent a quintessentially 'Anglican' account of what Patrick Collinson has called 'the birthpangs of Protestant England'. It may also be the case that some historians professing no religious faith have been inclined to take a more 'functionalist' view of the significance of early modern religion.[11] In this sensitive area it may be more charitable, as well as more honest, to accept that in the postmodern world which we all inhabit no one is in a position to pretend to a total neo-Rankean objectivity about the past 'as it actually was', and that diversity of committed perspectives can enrich our understanding of the religious change which took place in this period.

One of the most salutary results of revisionism has been its formulation of an interpretative scheme to which, consciously or unconsciously, virtually all students of the English Reformation find themselves compelled to refer. In an article first published in 1982, Christopher Haigh suggested that the progress of the Reformation in England could be considered under four headings: Reformation 'from above', 'from below', 'rapid Reformation' and 'slow Reformation'. Studies of the Reformation could therefore be classified with a label from each of the sets of paired opposites, depending on the historian's assessment of the pace of reform, and of whether the primary momentum for change came from government directive or from grass-roots initiative.[12] While a number of historians might protest about precisely where they have been plotted on Haigh's 'matrix' (*see* Reading 4), its conceptual utility has been widely recognized. Some critics might, however, object that the polarity of 'from above' and 'from below' posits too rigid a dichotomy: from the 1530s onwards the progress of reform implied a symbiosis between state action and private enterprise (*see* Reading 7).

The perception that, in Haigh's terms, the real impact of the English Reformation was 'slow' rather than 'rapid' is gradually winning wide acceptance, but the crucial question remains: how slow is slow? A recent (1996) conference in London on the theme of 'the Long Reformation' excited considerable enthusiasm among historians of the English Reformation, but produced no consensus on what its terminal date might be. Increasingly, the confines of an indeterminate and contested 'periodization' are coming to shape approaches to the English Reformation, and assessments of its 'success' or 'failure'. The issue is further complicated by those unspoken yet still largely prescriptive rules of demarcation that regulate the study of history at virtually all levels: when (if at all) does an investigation of 'the impact of the Reformation' have to become a study of 'the causes of the English Civil War' (the subject of a companion volume in this series)?

Such a question did not present itself to A.G. Dickens when he published his *English Reformation* in 1964. Dickens brought his narrative to a conclusion with the Elizabethan settlement, appending a brief discussion of the 'residual problems' of recusancy and Puritanism. In the second edition of 1989, Dickens saw no necessity to expand the scope of the work. Unsurprisingly, Christopher Haigh has taken Dickens to task for implying that 1559 was 'end of story',[13] but it may be significant that Haigh draws his own recent textbook account to a close in the 1580s. There is now a substantial body of opinion which holds that it was precisely from this decade onwards that Protestantism in a more than formal sense began to make substantial inroads on a national scale. An important county study by Diarmaid MacCulloch has demonstrated that in Suffolk (considered by Dickens a precociously Protestant area) it was not until the second half of the 1580s that the godly Protestant gentry were able finally to defeat their conservative rivals and assert unchallenged control of the county administration.[14] Moreover, if we take the view (one clearly held by a large number of contemporaries) that a properly trained and motivated Protestant parish clergy were the essential agents for bringing Reformation to the people, the later Elizabethan decades can look more like a point of departure than of culmination. A uniformly graduate ministry remained an aspiration rather than a reality until at least the 1620s, and even then the quality of much of the profession left a great deal to be desired.[15] It is important to recognize also that the success of Protestant evangelism, and the availability of the evangelizers, seems to have remained highly disproportionate across different regions both of highland and lowland England well into the seventeenth century. In terms of susceptibility to the Protestant message, the regional disparities noted by Dickens for the Henrician and Edwardian periods (*see* Reading 4) may have been no less apparent a half-century later. The continuing production of careful local studies (many of them doctoral theses in the first instance) is doing much to flesh out this picture; in the interim we can accept the broad pattern of a more receptive south and east, and a more resistant north and west without endorsing a crudely reductionist geographical determinism about the matter.

More than any other historian of his generation, Patrick Collinson has encouraged us to regard the Elizabethan and early Stuart periods as an essential part of the Reformation 'process', and to see that the attempts of an army of godly ministers and lecturers to inculcate a truer understanding of the Protestant message must constitute the 'real' Reformation, the fleshing-out of the skeleton released from the cupboard by the settlement of 1559.[16] Most particularly, Collinson has transformed our understanding of 'Puritanism', a phenomenon we can no longer view as an 'opposition party', the symmetrical counterpart of Catholic recusancy, but rather as a set of attitudes and impulses making for 'further Reformation' which was situated close to the mainstream of contemporary Protestantism. The work of Collinson, and of scholars such as Peter Lake and Nicholas Tyacke who have broadly endorsed his interpretation,[17] has left us in little doubt just how 'Protestant' the Elizabethan and Jacobean Church was, and has done much to demolish the idea that there was any such thing as 'Anglicanism' much before the middle of the seventeenth century (*see* Reading 11).

Collinson would not, however, suppose that the late sixteenth-century Reformation made progress in precisely the way the 'godly' would have wished. In a recent article, he has suggested that in the reign of Elizabeth accommodation to the reformed faith must have proceeded by a kind of 'twin-track': on the one hand, 'the almost imperceptible penetration of the language of Bible and Prayer Book as heard and absorbed in parish worship by a majority of the population'; on the other, a 'more deliberate, active, instructed response' to godly preaching and first-hand Bible reading.[18] Some similar sense of duality seems to inform Christopher Haigh's characteristically memorable observation that by the last years of the sixteenth century clerical efforts had succeeded in creating 'a Protestant nation, but not a nation of Protestants'.[19] Much of the most interesting and innovative recent work on the 'acculturation' of Protestantism from the Elizabethan period has addressed itself in one way or another to aspects of this apparent paradox (*see* Readings 9–12).

The consensus of recent research leaves us in little doubt that by the early seventeenth century England was certainly a 'Protestant nation' in the sense that its national culture had become profoundly anti-Catholic. Decades of exposure to Foxe's *Book of Martyrs* punctuated by the crises of 1570 (papal excommunication of Elizabeth), 1588 (Armada), 1605 (Gunpowder Plot) and 1623 (Charles's abortive courtship of the Spanish Infanta) had fed a virulently xenophobic anti-popery. For centuries this would remain a vital force in English cultural and political life, certainly potent enough to defeat the hopes of James II in 1688. There appears to have been a sense in which anti-Catholicism could itself become the vital constitutive element of an English Protestant identity, positing the existence of a stereotypically evil 'Other' against which the integrity of the English Church could be vindicated.[20] It has recently been argued that the abandonment of a common and consensual anti-Catholic rhetoric by Charles, Laud and his 'Arminian' allies in the 1630s played no small part in the breakdown of trust and confidence in the political and ecclesiastical establishment which was an essential precondition for civil war.[21] At the same time, David Cressy's evocatively entitled *Bonfires and Bells* has enriched our understanding of the potential of popular anti-Catholicism to contribute to a new Protestant national consciousness. In England, the Reformation did not merely prune back radically the traditional calendar, with its saints' days and festivals; it overlaid it with a series of new national and patriotic festivities: for example, bell-ringing to commemorate the accession of Queen Elizabeth, bonfires to celebrate the unmasking of the Gunpowder Plot.[22]

It must have required little understanding of the doctrines of justification and election to participate enthusiastically in the calendrical festivities which Cressy describes, yet the extent to which many of those who did so can meaningfully be classified as 'Protestants' is a question which continues to vex historians, much as it vexed clerical commentators at the time (*see* Readings 9 and 10). Should we attempt to gauge Protestant commitment in a concrete and definable way, in terms of knowledge and understanding of official formulae? Or was it something which proceeded more organically through society, an untidy fusion of esteem for the English liturgy, anti-popish sentiment, and acknowledgement of the centrality of scripture? English historians could take note here of parallel debates on the impact of the Lutheran Reformation in Germany. From a study of Protestant educational methods and catechizing, Gerald Strauss has argued that Lutheranism was remarkably unsuccessful in making a real impression among the mass of the people.[23] By contrast, Robert Scribner has claimed to identify by the early seventeenth century a vibrant and confessionally aware popular Lutheranism, albeit one employing 'images and elements from pre-Reformation religious culture' which might have appalled Luther himself.[24]

In the English context, the points of intersection between Protestant ways of thinking and a more durable 'popular culture' have been further explored by a number of historians demonstrating an ever-increasing sophistication in the expounding and decoding of contemporary texts. Peter Lake has examined the lurid genre of 'murder pamphlets', productions which clearly fed a popular demand for titillation and sensationalism, but were at the same time often suffused with characteristically Protestant notions of divine providence and predestination.[25] Alexandra Walsham has similarly discerned a Protestant appropriation of ideas about God's providence in a number of anti-Catholic tracts and (*pace* Collinson, Reading 11) *pictures* of the Jacobean period. She concludes suggestively that both anti-popery and providentialism might have provided 'a region of ideological common ground' between the more self-consciously godly and the mass of the people.[26] Particularly influential in recent years has been Tessa Watt's exploration of the world of religious 'cheap print' in the century before the Civil War.[27] Watt concludes that Protestant teaching made considerable progress in penetrating the consciousness of the lower orders, but that it did so by modifying rather than by extirpating traditional religious concerns and forms of representation (*see* Reading 12).

Characteristic of all these 'post-revisionist' approaches to the impact of the Reformation has been an insistence that within a generation or two the Reformation was instrumental in effecting decisive changes in English cultural life, changes that affected all social classes. Paradoxically, though, such success owed much to continuities with the past, and an accommodation to traditional and enduring preoccupations and patterns of thought:

'the Church of England was to be a nursery in which the masses were gently weaned, not roughly snatched from popery.'[28] In so far as they are polemically conceived, such approaches have as their target two related historiographical traditions. First, they seek to modify the revisionist 'hard line' associated with Christopher Haigh, that popular conservatism was too deeply entrenched and the Reformation message too inherently demanding and unattractive for it to have made much impact below the level of the élite. Second, they take issue with the model suggested by some early modern social historians that zealous, committed Protestantism appealed fairly exclusively to ruling groups in society, who recognized its potential as an ideology for moral regulation and social control. Elizabethan and early Stuart society, particularly rural society, thus became characterized by a deep cultural fissure: on the one hand, a godly social élite committed to the 'Reformation of Manners'; on the other, a largely irreverent 'popular culture', whose focal points were the alehouse and the maypole rather than the pulpit or catechism class.[29] Arguably, such assessments have been inclined to take too much at face value the complaint literature produced by 'Puritan' critics, who tended to dismiss as 'ungodly' all those who did not share their values and assumptions. An important development in recent approaches to the study of Elizabethan and early Stuart religion has been a more systematic attempt to investigate the degree of religious commitment of the 'conformist' majority, whom the godly tended to view with disdain (*see* Reading 10). Here historians have been able to make some progress in establishing levels of church attendance and the (sometimes surprisingly high) degree of participation in Easter communion, but the extent to which conformity habitually went beyond the 'mere' or 'nominal' to be imbued with a profound spirituality of its own remains highly problematic.[30]

It will have become apparent that many of the most fruitful lines of inquiry into the English Reformation are now concentrated in the later end of the period. This is a trend that seems likely to continue as historians pursue the ramifications of a 'Protestantization' process well into the seventeenth century. Here, of course, the investigation acquires an added piquancy from its proximity to, and inter-penetration of, a well-established debate about the role of religion in fomenting the English Civil War.[31] In addition, the adjacency of an English 'golden age' of literature is likely to prove a considerable inducement to Reformation scholars, as the walls separating scholarly disciplines are increasingly breached, and as historians become less squeamish about adopting a systematic approach to the literary study of texts. As historians are belatedly recognizing (or rediscovering), not the least important of such texts in late Tudor and early Stuart England was the Bible itself – this was a society that appears to have been saturated with the language and imagery of scripture, a circumstance which differentiates it markedly from that of a century before and which was to be of the utmost significance for the future cultural development of England.[32]

By comparison with the later period, the early Reformation, or more precisely the early Reformation movement, looks in danger of falling into neglect, despite the continuing production of significant works such as Susan Brigden's study of the Reformation in London, or Diarmaid MacCulloch's biography of Thomas Cranmer.[33] In part, this may be due to the increased richness of sources for the later period, facilitating a methodological approach to the 'social history of religion' which is the favoured perspective of many current scholars. It may reflect also a feeling that much of the revisionist case for the strength and vitality of the pre-Reformation Church is now so firmly established that further work will do little more than confirm it in its essentials. It is unlikely (though not inconceivable) that future scholars will attempt to revive a version of the early Reformation that portrays large numbers of lay men and women thankfully abandoning an arid and oppressive Catholicism for the pure spiritual water of reformed faith. Yet interpretative flash-points remain. One such, as we have seen, is the nature and potential of Lollardy. Another is the significance of the Marian attempt to restore Catholicism in 1553–8. Could the Reformation in England have been stopped permanently in its tracks in this period? It is to be hoped that someone will take up Eamon Duffy's challenge (*see* Reading 8) and attempt to write a comprehensive religious history of the reign. More broadly, a thorough and convincing account of early English Protestantism up to and including the reign of Edward VI remains a major desideratum. Its author will need to display historical and theological expertise in equal measure, and probably linguistic skills as well, for in spite of a common tendency to regard the Reformation in England as fundamentally *sui generis*, students of pre-Elizabethan Protestantism are increasingly observing its European dimension and international-mindedness.[34] It must be thought questionable also just how long most historians will remain satisfied with interpretations of the English Reformation which (bar the obligatory preliminary survey) often display relatively little curiosity about events prior to Henry VIII's summoning of the Reformation Parliament in 1529. It ought in theory to be possible to discern long-term significance or disruptive potential in intellectual, social and religious developments within the pre-Reformation Church, while at the same time recognizing the strength and adaptability of late medieval Catholicism, and without seeking to resurrect a Whiggish teleology of religious change.

It might be objected that as the chronology of the English Reformation is increasingly stretched, so its usefulness an an organizing concept consequently declines. It is remarkable that the most recent general study has even questioned whether such a thing as *the* English Reformation ever took place. Christopher Haigh's subject is *English Reformations* – a series of discontinuous and parallel 'reformations' in sixteenth-century England, with short-term political, rather than long-term socio-religious, causes.[35] The structure of this collection might be thought to imply, though it does not necessarily seek to assert, a more unitive process.

I hope that the bringing together of these essays will help students to determine for themselves whether or not 'the English Reformation' actually happened, and if it did, what significance we should attach to it as a formative episode in our history.

Notes

1 C. Haigh, *English Reformations: Religion, Politics, and Society under the Tudors* (Oxford, Oxford University Press, 1993).
2 J.J. Scarisbrick, *The Reformation and the English People* (Oxford, Oxford University Press, 1984), p. 1.
3 E. Duffy, *The Stripping of the Altars: Traditional Religion in England 1400–1580* (New Haven and London, Yale University Press, 1992).
4 C. Haigh, 'Anticlericalism and the English Reformation', *History*, 68 (1983), pp. 391–407; A.G. Dickens, 'The Shape of Anticlericalism and the English Reformation', in E.I. Kouri and T. Scott, eds *Politics and Society in Reformation Europe* (Basingstoke, Macmillan, 1987), pp. 379–410; P. Marshall, *The Catholic Priesthood and the English Reformation* (Oxford, Oxford University Press, 1994).
5 Scarisbrick, *Reformation and the English People*, p. 46; A. Hudson, *The Premature Reformation: Wycliffite Texts and Lollard History* (Oxford, Oxford University Press, 1988).
6 P. Collinson, 'England', in B. Scribner, R. Porter and M. Teich, eds *The Reformation in National Context* (Cambridge, Cambridge University Press, 1994), p. 88.
7 B. Kümin, *The Shaping of a Community: the Rise and Reformation of the English Parish c.1400–1560* (Aldershot, Scolar Press, 1996), pp. 210–12.
8 Duffy, *Stripping of the Altars*, ch. 15; C. Litzenberger, 'Local Responses to Changes in Religious Policy Based on Evidence from Gloucestershire Wills (1540–1580)', *Continuity and Change*, 8 (1993), pp. 417–39.
9 The concept of 'brokerage' was first discussed in the early modern English context by C. Holmes, *Seventeenth-Century Lincolnshire* (Lincoln, 1980), ch. 5. See also suggestive remarks in P. Collinson, '*De Republica Anglorum*: Or, History with the Politics Put Back', in P. Collinson, *Elizabethan Essays* (London, 1994), pp. 1–29, and K. Wrightson, 'The Politics of the Parish in Early Modern England', in P. Griffiths, A. Fox and S. Hindle, eds *The Experience of Authority in Early Modern England* (Basingstoke, 1996), pp. 25–31.
10 Haigh, *English Reformations*, pp. vii–viii.
11 See, for example, Keith Thomas's magisterial *Religion and the Decline of Magic* (London, Weidenfeld & Nicolson, 1971).
12 C. Haigh, 'The recent historiography of the English Reformation', *Historical Journal*, 25 (1982), pp. 995–1007, reprinted in C. Haigh, ed. *The English Reformation Revised* (Cambridge, Cambridge University Press, 1987), pp. 19–33.
13 Haigh, *English Reformations*, p. 16.
14 D. MacCulloch, *Suffolk and the Tudors: Politics and Religion in an English County 1500–1600* (Oxford, Oxford University Press, 1986), pp. 218–19.
15 D. MacCulloch, *The Later Reformation in England 1547–1603* (Basingstoke, Macmillan, 1990), p. 115; P. Collinson, *The Religion of Protestants: The Church in English Society 1559–1625* (Oxford, Oxford University Press, 1982), p. 93.
16 P. Collinson, *The Elizabethan Puritan Movement* (London, Cape, 1967); *Religion of Protestants*; *Godly People: Essays on English Protestantism and Puritanism*

(London, Hambledon Press, 1983); *The Birthpangs of Protestant England: Religious and Cultural Change in the Sixteenth and Seventeenth Centuries* (Basingstoke, Macmillan, 1988)

17 N. Tyacke, *Anti-Calvinists. The Rise of English Arminianism c. 1590–1640* (Oxford, Oxford University Press, 1979); P. Lake, *Moderate Puritans and the Elizabethan Church* (Cambridge, Cambridge University Press, 1982); *Anglicans and Puritans? Presbyterianism and English Conformist Thought from Whitgift to Hooker* (London, Allen & Unwin, 1988)

18 P. Collinson, 'William Shakespeare's Religious Inheritance and Environment', in P. Collinson, *Elizabethan Essays*, p. 228.

19 Haigh, *English Reformations*, p. 280.

20 P. Lake, 'Antipopery: the Structure of a Prejudice', in R. Cust and A. Hughes, eds *Conflict in Early Stuart England: Studies in Religion and Politics 1603–1642* (London, Longman, 1989), pp. 72–106.

21 A. Milton, *Catholic and Reformed: the Roman and Protestant Churches in English Protestant Thought, 1600–1640* (Cambridge, Cambridge University Press, 1995).

22 D. Cressy, *Bonfires and Bells: National Memory and the Protestant Calendar in Elizabethan and Stuart England* (London, Weidenfeld & Nicolson, 1989).

23 G. Strauss, 'Success and Failure in the German Reformation', *Past and Present*, 67 (1975), pp. 30–63; *Luther's House of Learning* (Baltimore, John Hopkins University Press, 1978).

24 R. Scribner, 'Incombustible Luther: the Image of the Reformer in Early Modern Germany', in R. Scribner's *Popular Culture and Popular Movements in Reformation Germany* (London, Hambledon Press, 1987), pp. 323–53.

25 P. Lake, 'Deeds against Nature: Cheap Print, Protestantism and Murder in Early Seventeenth-Century England', in K. Sharpe and P. Lake, eds *Culture and Politics in Early Stuart England* (Basingstoke, Macmillan, 1994), pp. 257–83.

26 A. Walsham, "The Fatall Vesper": Providentialism and Anti-Popery in Late Jacobean London', *Past and Present*, 144 (1994), pp. 36–87.

27 T. Watt, *Cheap Print and Popular Piety 1550–1640* (Cambridge, Cambridge University Press, 1991).

28 A. Walsham, *Church Papists: Catholicism, Conformity and Confessional Polemic in Early Modern England* (Woodbridge, Boydell Press, 1993), p. 17.

29 This approach has been particularly associated with an influential local study by K. Wrightson and D. Levine, *Poverty and Piety in an English Village: Terling, 1525–1700* (London, Academic Press, 1979). See also Wrightson's *English Society 1580–1680* (London, Hutchinson Press, 1982), ch. 7.

30 J.P. Bolton, 'The Limits of Formal Religion: the Administration of Holy Communion in Late Elizabethan and Early Stuart London', *London Journal*, 10 (1984), pp. 135–54; M. Spufford, 'Can We Count the "Godly" and the "Conformable" in the Seventeenth Century', *Journal of Ecclesiastical History*, 36 (1985). The work of Martin Ingram has been particularly valuable in elucidating these themes: *Church Courts, Sex and Marriage in England, 1570–1642* (Cambridge, Cambridge University Press, 1987), ch. 3; 'From Reformation to Toleration: Popular Religious Cultures in England, 1540–1690', in T. Harris, ed. *Popular Culture in England c.1500–1850* (Basingstoke, Macmillan, 1995), pp. 95–123; 'Puritans and the Church Courts, 1560–1640', in C. Durston and J. Eales, eds. *The Culture of English Puritanism 1560–1700* (Basingstoke, Macmillan, 1996), pp. 58–91.

31 The literature here is extensive; for a useful conspectus, see A. Hughes, *The Causes of the English Civil War* (Basingstoke, Macmillan, 1991), ch. 2.

32 See a forthcoming study by Ian Green, provisionally entitled *Print and Protestantism in Early Modern England*; C. Hill, *The English Bible and the Seventeenth-Century Revolution* (London, Allen Lane, 1993).

33 S. Brigden, *London and the Reformation* (Oxford, Clarendon Press, 1989); D. MacCulloch, *Thomas Cranmer: a Life* (New Haven and London, Yale University Press, 1996).

34 This is characteristic of MacCulloch, *Cranmer*, and of A. Pettegree, *Marian Protestantism: Six Studies* (Aldershot, Scolar Press, 1996).

35 Haigh, *English Reformations*, pp. 12–21.

SECTION

I

ORIGINS

Commentary

To devote a section to an investigation of the 'origins' of the English Reformation might be thought in some quarters to complicate the issue unnecessarily: instead of seeking to elucidate patterns of long-term causation, historians should recognize that the Reformation in England originated in the marital difficulties of Henry VIII (see Reading 1). In one sense this is incontrovertibly the case, and few historians would now seriously contend that the English Reformation represented from the outset an inevitable mass popular protest against the 'corruption' of the late medieval Church. As the readings which follow indicate, however, it is still possible for scholars to take crucially different views on the extent to which 'traditional religion' (the formulation is Eamon Duffy's) was able to meet the spiritual and social needs of all the English people, both before and in the decades after Henry's break with Rome. In this context, therefore, 'origins' may be understood as referring to the achievements and potential of Protestantism or (more accurately) 'evangelical reform' in attracting committed adherents in the period before a Protestant polity was established at the accession of Elizabeth.

Revisionist historians who have emphasized popular satisfaction with the pre-Reformation Church have sometimes been accused of explaining why the Reformation didn't happen. The charge cannot fairly be levelled at Christopher Harper-Bill, who is a medievalist rather than a Reformation specialist, and therefore to some extent exonerated from responsibility for having to explain the Reformation. Nonetheless, his contribution is overtly supportive of the revisionist reassessment of pre-Reformation Catholicism, sketched out by Christopher Haigh and Jack Scarisbrick, and subsequently massively elaborated by Eamon Duffy. Like them, Harper-Bill is dismissive of the utility of 'anticlericalism' as an indicator of lay dissatisfaction with the Church, contending that overall the clergy were performing well and that outbursts like Colet's sermon of 1512 need to be read as part of a well-worn genre of prophetic admonition, rather than as objective social comment. Such conclusions have been broadly endorsed by other late medieval historians such as R.N. Swanson and J.A.F. Thomson.[1] Harper-Bill does recognize structural weaknesses and jurisdictional conflict within the higher reaches of the Church, though this perception may be more useful in accounting for the relative lack of episcopal opposition to the take-over mounted by Henry VIII, than for explaining grass-roots disenchantment with the sacramental worship and traditional devotions of Catholicism.

While Harper-Bill raises the issue of Lollardy only to minimize its significance, J.F. Davis's contribution in this section takes much more seriously the importance of principled doctrinal dissent within the pre-Reformation Catholic Church. More perhaps than any other English historian, Davis fits into the 'Haigh matrix' as a proponent of an early Reformation 'from below'. Davis is not unique in emphasizing the vitality and strength of early sixteenth-century Lollardy. Indeed, since his article was written, important new research has done much to illuminate the surprising prominence and high social status of Lollards within some communities. But while historians following in the tradition of A.G. Dickens might seek to represent Lollardy as a 'spring-board' or 'seed-bed' for the English Reformation, a ready-made group of potential sympathizers who fairly rapidly accommodated themselves to the more vibrant doctrinal currents flowing from the continent, Davis attributes to the Lollard tradition a considerably greater two-fold significance. In the first place, far from being easily assimilated into mainstream Protestantism, Lollardy persisted in some places as a radical separatist tradition, later to connect with 'anabaptist' tendencies and cause headaches for the Protestant Church authorities. Second, and paradoxically, Lollard ideas might also have been decisive in shaping the doctrinal development of English Protestantism itself, in particular its marked proclivity towards a sacramentarian, 'Swiss' view of the nature of the eucharist, which was very far removed from the real presence doctrine espoused by Martin Luther. Much of this is controversial, and it has signally failed to convince those historians who remain persuaded that Davis's approach tends inexorably to impose a false cohesion and unity of purpose on a rag-bag of dissidents and deviants who had little in common but the misfortune that landed them in the church courts. Nonetheless, it is at the very least suggestive, as Diarmaid MacCulloch has recently pointed out, that those features which might be regarded as most characteristic of mature English Protestantism – hostility to the real presence, detestation of images and a kind of 'moral legalism' – all bear some affinity to persistently recorded Lollard concerns.[3]

As Susan Brigden's article demonstrates (see Reading 3), a Lollard background was by no means a precondition for showing interest in reforming doctrine. While Harper-Bill attributes active hostility to the old order only to a 'tiny minority of influential men', Brigden contends that, in the capital at least, early Protestantism fulfilled its potential as 'a revolutionary movement', with a particular appeal to the disaffected youth. In the inflexible economic conditions of early sixteenth-century London, where opportunities for youth were limited by craft regulations and by statute, the rejection of priestly authority, as mediated through the confessional and the mass, seems almost analagous to the rejection of parental authority, or the authority of masters. Brigden's portrayal of early Protestantism as in large measure a religion of novelty and protest with a populist character it was later to lose (see Reading 11), cautions us against too rigid a typology of religious positions in the early part of the English Reformation: confessional identities had not yet hardened and Londoners could be drawn to employ the rhetoric of 'reform' for a variety of motives, not all of them purely spiritual.

In the final contribution in this section A.G. Dickens complements Brigden's study of London with a broad national survey. At the outset Dickens makes clear his frustration at being cast as the straw man of revisionist attacks, and denies holding to any simplistic conception of quick 'Reformation from below'. Nonetheless, his article explicitly sets out to establish the central contention of his classic study, *The English Reformation*, namely that by the end of Edward VI's reign Protestantism had become so firmly established across large swathes of England that its progress could not be permanently arrested or reversed. As befits a historian who was in many ways the pioneer of the local study of the Reformation, Dickens draws upon a host of local studies to establish a topography of precocious Protestant advance. His resultant impression of a 'great crescent' of areas receptive to the reformers has now gained wide currency, and indeed it is fair to state that the real point at issue between Dickens and his revisionist critics is not so much in which parts of England Protestantism first made gains, but how numerically significant such gains were at any point in the first half of the century. Here both the methodology and taxonomies Dickens has brought to his statistical analysis of large numbers of wills remain highly contentious (see also Reading 5). The search for an exact percentage of the English people who had embraced Protestantism in the reigns of Henry and Edward is, of course, a chimerical one, and Dickens is not so foolish as to attempt it. Nonetheless, a certain fascination with 'number-crunching' has informed the Haigh–Dickens debate.[4] It may well be that most Tudor historians are coming to accept, pace Dickens, that before the reign of Elizabeth English Protestants were not only a small minority of the population, but a small minority in nearly every place where they were to be found. This, however, should not deceive us into regarding them as insignificant. In tracing the interests and connections of early English Protestants, their local importance and relations with their neighbours, their patterns of conversion, and the well-springs of their dissatisfaction with traditional orthodoxy, much work remains to be done.

Notes

1 R.N. Swanson, *Church and Society in Late Medieval England* (Oxford, Basil Blackwell, 1989); J.A.F. Thomson, *The Early Tudor Church and Society 1485–1529* (London, Longman, 1993).
2 See in particular A. Hope, 'Lollardy: the Stone the Builders Rejected?', in P. Lake and M. Dowling, eds *Protestantism and the National Church in Sixteenth Century England* (London, Croom Helm, 1987), pp. 1–37; D. Plumb, 'The Social and Economic Status of the Later Lollards', in M. Spufford, ed. *The World of Rural Dissenters 1520–1725* (Cambridge, Cambridge University Press, 1995), pp. 103–31.
3 D. MacCulloch, 'England', in A. Pettegree, ed. *The Early Reformation in Europe* (Cambridge, Cambridge University Press, 1992), pp. 172–3.
4 See Haigh, *English Reformations*, pp. 198–9.

1

Dean Colet's convocation sermon and the pre-Reformation Church in England

CHRISTOPHER HARPER-BILL

John Colet's convocation sermon of February 1512,[1] an impassioned plea for the reform of the church, long provided one of the main texts for critical evaluation of the late medieval church in England, culminating in the magisterial survey of Professor Dickens, published in 1964.[2] Gradually, however, the traditional view of the Reformation as a popular reaction against a moribund church has been undermined by a series of regional studies, most recently and significantly, because of the huge size of the diocese and its position in the heartland of England, by Mrs Bowker's work on Lincoln.[3] It is gratifying for a medievalist to find his Tudor colleagues rejecting the picture of the pre-Reformation church which has permeated popular consciousness – a sad tale of decline and decay, stagnation and superstition, a squalid world in which the only light was provided by humanists, who were ignored, and by Lollards, who were persecuted. Much attention has been devoted in the past quarter-century to the ecclesiastical history of late medieval England, and many historians have, through specialised study of various topics and localities, come to doubt that the church was at worst corrupt and at best ineffective, probably generally unpopular and certainly incapable of attracting any great loyalty. The aim of this paper is to test the strictures of Colet's sermon against the evidence produced by recent research, and to attempt a more realistic review of the state of the *ecclesia Anglicana* in the early Tudor period.

Colet's main attack was launched on the covetousness and secularity manifested by all levels of clergy. There was a mad rush to obtain rich benefices and a ruthless determination to maximise their revenues. The clergy were sycophantic to lay potentates, constantly occupied in secular business and totally ensnared by mundane concerns. No new legislation was necessary to remedy this situation, merely the conscientious enforcement of existing canon law. If through its observance the clerical order conducted itself in a godly fashion, the people would follow suit; the good example of the priesthood would be more effective than any sanctions. Tithes and offerings would then be easily gathered from a grateful flock,

Reprinted from *History,* 73 (1988).

and the clergy would no longer be dragged before secular judges, to the derogation of the liberties of the church.

There is nothing radically new in Colet's analysis. That covetousness was the major disfigurement of the church at all levels had been a theme of satirical but profoundly serious criticism since at least the late eleventh century, as Professor Yunck demonstrated when tracing *The Lineage of Lady Meed*, that personification of avarice in Langland's *Vision of Piers Plowman*.[4] A glance through the indices of G.R. Owst's volumes on medieval English sermons will produce countless examples, from the thirteenth to the fifteenth century, of the castigation from the pulpit of the abuses and laxity alleged by Colet – hawking and hunting, lavish banquets and extravagant dress.[5]

To support his view that the evil life of priests was a greater danger to the church than the false preaching of heretics Colet cited St Bernard of Clairvaux – the only authority later than Pope Gregory the Great to whom he refers in the sermon. Colet had a very elevated view of the clerical order: 'the dignity of priests . . . is greater than either the king's or emperor's; it is equal with the dignity of angels'. This was the doctrine of the papal reformers of the late eleventh century, who had sought to elevate the priesthood as a separate and superior estate, the directive force in Christian society.[6] Just like St Bernard, writing in the mid-twelfth century, Colet was unable to forgive those unworthy priests who jeopardised this ideal. As St Bernard had lamented the manner in which 'we seek our own and, envying and provoking one another, we are stirred to hatred, aroused in injuries, excited to arguments . . . we are oppressed by the stronger and we in turn oppress those who are weaker',[7] so Colet remarked 'how much greediness and appetite of honour is nowadays in men of the church. How run they, yea, almost out of breath, from one benefice to the other, from the less to the more, from the lower to the higher.' There is marked similarity between St Bernard's condemnation of the venality of the church courts of his day and Colet's assault on the judicial profiteering and litigiousness of early sixteenth-century England. Whatever else, then, the Convocation sermon of 1512 cannot be used to demonstrate any sudden decline in the state of the church in the early Tudor period.

It is apposite to examine briefly John Colet's personal circumstances.[8] If intellectually he adhered to an elevated 'Gregorian' view of the clerical order, his background was that of a prosperous London mercer's family. The Mercers' Company in the early sixteenth century was not uncritical of the contemporary church, even if its members remained fiercely orthodox. There is, of course, no incompatibility between an idealistic view of the clerical order and fierce criticism of its aberrant members. Colet's attack on the church courts is echoed by the Mercers' response to the mayor and aldermen's request for legislative proposals to set before Parliament in 1529 to have in remembrance how the king's poor subjects, principally of London, have been polled and robbed without reason or conscience by the ordinaries in probating of testaments and taking of mortuaries, and also vexed and troubled by citations with cursing one day and absolving the next, and all this for money.[9]

It is impossible to determine to what extent the dean of St Paul's was influenced by the opinions of his own social group, or how far the corporate view of the Mercers was formulated by the preaching of one of their own who had attained exalted status within the church. Yet certainly in 1487 Archbishop Morton had recognised the danger which stemmed from radical sermons to the laity, particularly at Paul's Cross, in which the church and ecclesiastical dignitaries were violently criticised, and he exhorted preachers to denounce malefactors to him in private, so that scandal might be avoided.[10]

John Colet, moreover, had not faced the struggle for a benefice experienced by so many of his contemporaries. In 1512 he attacked simony, sycophancy to lay lords and non-residence. As a young man he had been fortunate in that his family possessed the gift of livings. In 1485, aged about 20, he was presented by his cousin to the church of Dennington, in Suffolk. From 1493 to 1496 he was studying on the continent and was rector of two or three English churches. In 1499, while he was lecturing at Oxford, Dennington was served by a parochial chaplain who was also vicar of nearby Ashby, where he was denounced for neglect of chancel and vicarage.[11] In 1512 Colet still held Dennington and was also dean of St Paul's, treasurer of Chichester and a canon of York and Salisbury. This accumulation of lucrative benefices was not abnormal; it was the time-honoured means of providing for the intellectual élite of the medieval church, be they employed in scholarship, ecclesiastical administration or royal government. Among such privileged clerics, Colet was far from unique in expending his surplus income on the foundation of a notable educational establishment. Colet did not appreciate that the system which fostered him also supported many other worthy men whose talents lay in other fields. Pluralism and non-residence were apparently justifiable when they provided sustenance for an innovatory Biblical scholar, but reprehensible when utilised to provide for the king's clerical administrators. It is arguable that Colet, like Pope Gregory VII or Thomas Becket centuries before, envisaged an unrealistic separation between the church and the world. Yet just as in 1179 the appointment of three bishops as Henry II's chief justices could be defended by the assertion that they would improve the quality of judgment,[12] so now many of those privileged and pluralist clerks staffed the increasingly busy equitable law courts of the crown, tempering the rigour of the law with the notions of merciful justice learned in the canon law schools.[13] Such men fulfilled as useful a social role as the revolutionary theologian.

In his analysis of the state of the church in 1512 Colet devoted remarkably little attention to two aspects of religious life which have preoccupied modern historians. First, it is notable how little time in his sermon was devoted to the religious orders. They should withdraw from the world and should dedicate themselves to prayer and fasting, to the chastening of their flesh and the observance of their Rule. Colet was echoing arguments which had been advanced in England since the early twelfth century.[14] In Colet's time neither monks, canons nor mendicants exercised the influence on the church at large to which they had aspired in their pristine days. This was probably inevitable, for no order could hope to perpetuate the radical reforming zeal of its founding fathers.[15] Certainly the late medieval English church was burdened with the debris of an earlier age, that period after the Conquest when the conventional gesture of piety for so many lords, however minor, had been to found a religious house. Many such poorly endowed communities staggered on with diminished numbers from generation to generation.[16] It is easy enough to criticise the state of late medieval monasticism, the pious lamenting a supposed decline from the spiritual heights, the more worldly caustically contrasting practice and ideals. Such an approach is unjustified, both because visitation records, which provide the bulk of the material on which judgments can be based, concentrate on abuses and ignore normality,[17] and because there is no comparable body of evidence from the twelfth century, although fragmented references give hints of scandals in that century as reprehensible as any in the later middle ages.[18]

The overall impression must be that the religious orders in late medieval England were not characterised by gross moral turpitude, but that there are countless indications that in most houses there was little spiritual dynamism, for which there is little evidence even in well-regulated houses presided over by able administrators, such as Prior Wessington at Durham in the early fifteenth century or Abbot Islip at Westminster after 1500 – but exactly the same could be said of Bury St Edmunds under Abbot Samson in the late twelfth century.[19] In general the Benedictines showed themselves no more amenable to the reforming efforts of King Henry V in 1421 and of Cardinal Wolsey in 1520 than to those of Pope Innocent III in 1215.[20] The crucial difference may be that in the fifteenth century the religious observance of increasing numbers of literate laypeople was of greatly enhanced quality, and that they were far more discriminating in their view of monasticism.[21] In the early twelfth century Heloise, in her assertion that the monastic Rule added nothing to the duties of a faithful Christian save the vow of chastity, was a voice crying in the wilderness.[22] In the fifteenth century this claim might find many echoes. The Lady Margaret Beaufort, an informed and humane innovator in matters of religion and education, nevertheless continued to patronise the ancient Benedictine houses of Westminster, Durham, Thorney and Crowland.[23] There are signs of vitality at Glastonbury on the very eve of the dissolution and of efforts at regeneration from the late fifteenth century in the English Cistercian communities.[24] The Observant Franciscans were introduced under the aegis of Edward IV and Henry VII, but far greater influence was exercised by Henry V's twin foundations of Bridgettines at Syon and Carthusians at Sheen. Their importance lies not so much in the courageous resistance of their inmates to the tyranny of Henry VIII as in the fact that for over a century they fulfilled the aim of their founder by acting as an exemplar of the religious life for pious layfolk, disseminating devotional works directed towards those who wished to attempt the imitation of Christ while remaining in the world.[25]

There were many religious houses which invited dissolution. The precedent had been provided by the closure of the multitude of alien priories, suspect because of their French connections, whose estates had financed the foundation of many academic colleges. Bishop Alcock of Ely was content in 1496 that the decayed house of nuns at Cambridge should be suppressed in order to endow Jesus College, and Wolsey dissolved a plethora of priories to provide for his colleges at Ipswich and Oxford.[26] Few can have regretted their passing. If Syon, Sheen and the other Carthusian houses stood at the centre of important spiritual developments which touched the lives of those most aware of the obligations of the Christian faith, and if a great abbey such as Westminster served most adequately as an exemplar of the stately grandeur of traditional religion and as a mausoleum for the great, very many monasteries had ceased to have much relevance to the religious life of the English people. There was probably little overt hostility. The local gentry would cheerfully dine or hunt with a monastic superior and associate with him in the business of the shire.[27] The greatest indictment of late medieval monasticism in England is, perhaps, that in an age when the demand for intercessory prayer for the souls of the dead had apparently expanded, those classes who had for centuries been the main benefactors of religious houses which had been founded primarily to fulfil this function now undramatically but *en masse* eschewed their spiritual ministrations and sought salvation through the establishment of chantries and obits in parish churches.

If Colet lingered little over the monastic order, he lamented the existence of heretics, but did not regard them as the greatest threat to the church. His view ran counter to that of many diocesan bishops, who in 1511–12 conducted a major purge to root out Lollardy.[28] The dean's assessment of the situation was, however, probably correct. John Wyclif had attracted much support in the late fourteenth century when he lambasted the pope, exalted the power of the king and demanded disendowment, until his eucharistic heresy impugned the validity of his arguments and lost him powerful support.[29] The abortive rising of Sir John Oldcastle in 1414 had provided irrefutable confirmation of the bishops' assertion that heresy and sedition were inextricably inter-related and ensured that the church would henceforth have the whole-hearted support of the secular arm in the eradication of the sect.

Much recent work by Dr Aston and Dr Hudson has emphasised the coherence of Lollard doctrines and teaching, the emphasis on literacy, the production of a corpus of vernacular writings and the establishment of a sophisticated and radical political theology.[30] All these examples of religious and intellectual vivacity are drawn, however, from the decades around 1400. By the 1430s all this had been lost under the pressure of concerted persecution. The Lollards had been driven underground and deprived of their natural leadership, and their theology became increasingly garbled and derivative. The intellectual content of Lollardy was re-established only in the 1520s, when English Lutherans gratefully discovered insular precedents for many of their newly acquired ideas and hastened to print these evidences of their native antecedents. All the tracts thus published were, however, at least 100 years old. The recent description of Lollardy in the early sixteenth century as a simple non-sacerdotal, non-sacramental protest which cannot be fully distinguished from pre-Christian survivals,[31] or the view that the history of Lollardy after 1414 has no more coherence than the history of any other felony,[32] are perhaps overstated reactions against that concentration upon the heretics which has stemmed from so much recent and distinguished work. There can, nevertheless, be no doubt that crudity and simplicity are frequent characteristics of the beliefs of Lollards examined by the ecclesiastical authorities in the later fifteenth and early sixteenth centuries. Moreover, as recently remarked, more persons petitioned the court of Rome for indults and dispensations in any one year than were executed for heresy in the whole course of the fifteenth century.[33] The main impact of Lollardy after 1414 was negative; the threat which it had posed in the early years made the hierarchy excessively cautious. It has been well argued that Henry V's bishops made a constructive effort to foster orthodox lay piety within the church as a counter to Lollardy.[34] Nevertheless Bishop Reginald Pecock was condemned, at least in part, because he attempted to refute heresy in the English language; Colet was accused of unorthodox doctrine because of his criticism of the contemporary church; and whereas in Germany the efforts of the orthodox Brethren of the Common Life resulted in the lay use of vernacular Gospels, in England Lollard advocacy of translation resulted in its prohibition.[35]

Reformation, urged Colet, must originate with the bishops, whom he clearly thought were not providing adequate leadership for the church. There must, above all, be canonical election of bishops, who should then reside in their dioceses and should divorce themselves from all secular preoccupations and ambitions, as an example to their clergy. Episcopal appointment was, of course, effectively the prerogative of the crown; canonical election and papal provision were mere formalities.[36] This was nothing new in the Tudor age, for the royal initiative had gone almost unchallenged since before the Norman Conquest, except for a brief interval in the reign of Henry III. It would be a brave cathedral chapter which risked the consequences of royal *malevolentia* by insisting on the freedom conceded to the English church in a series of royal charters. By the fifteenth century papal provision to bishoprics had long been the norm, yet in England the new bishop before his installation renounced clauses in the bull of provision considered prejudicial to the king's regality. Yet if Colet abhorred the appointment of prelates by the secular power, it may be doubted if free election or papal provision, both of which processes could be influenced by factors unconnected with religion, would have produced better bishops. There were in England between the Conquest and the Reformation remarkably few scandalous members of the episcopal bench. Among all the civil servants, Henry II could appoint St Hugh of Lincoln and Henry VII advance St John Fisher to Rochester. Fisher, because of his resistance to subsequent royal policies, has become something of a cult figure, coupled with St Thomas More as an illustration of the hidden potential of the unreformed church, which on the continent was to bear fruit in the Counter-Reformation.[37]

In 1512, however, it is doubtful if, to an impartial observer, Fisher would have appeared an exceptional figure among the bishops, for they were a distinguished body of men, the equal, it may be suggested, of Thomas Becket's colleagues, who are generally acknowledged to have constituted the finest episcopal bench in twelfth-century Europe.[38] Amongst them was Richard Fox, who while keeper of the privy seal ensured the efficient administration of his diocese and after his retirement from court devoted himself unflaggingly to the beneficent government of the see of Winchester; the large archive pertaining to his episcopate provides ample evidence of his concern.[39] Over Norwich there presided Richard Nix, a peppery ecclesiastic perhaps, reacting strongly to obstacles placed in his way by the local influence of Sir James Hobart, the attorney-general, and threatening to treat as heretics any who utilised the statute of *Praemunire*, but nevertheless vigorous and resident in his diocese, exercising the craft which he had learned as Fox's vicar-general.[40] From the circle of the Lady Margaret Beaufort, that power-house of late medieval spirituality and learning, came Hugh Oldham of Exeter and William Smith of Lincoln.[41] The latter was president of the Council of the Marches until 1512, but was obviously concerned about the clash of obligations, and even when burdened by secular responsibilities visited his diocese and administered it personally on a number of occasions.[42] After his appointment to the same presidency of 1512, Bishop Geoffrey Blythe of Coventry and

Lichfield continued to supervise an efficient diocesan administration.[43] At Chichester Robert Sherborne thoroughly overhauled the machinery of diocesan government and sought by regular visitation to improve the standards of pastoral ministry.[44] The performance of other less conspicuous members of the episcopate was far from discreditable.

Many of these bishops have left ample records of their visitatorial activities, in the diocese of Chichester, Coventry and Lichfield, Norwich and Winchester, while Archbishop Warham, although he was Chancellor of England, a few months before Colet's onslaught had conducted a personal visitation of the religious houses and most of the rural deaneries of his diocese of Canterbury.[45] It is a commonplace that in the later middle ages the episcopal office was dominated by lawyers, yet in 1512 five of the English bishops were doctors of theology.[46] It is even more significant that some of the best diocesan bishops had been trained as lawyers.[47] The episcopate also had a good record as benefactors of education at a time when the main object of new foundations was to provide a training ground for an educated clergy.[48] Fox was founder of Corpus Christi College, Oxford, William Smith was co-founder of Brasenose and endowed two grammar schools, Oldham was prominent in the establishment of Manchester grammar school, and Fisher acted as the Lady Margaret's adjutant in the foundation of Christ's and St John's colleges at Cambridge.[49] Many other bishops, perhaps the majority, made substantial benefactions, in money or books, to educational institutions.

It is notable that on every occasion when a late medieval prelate has been subjected to detailed scrutiny he has emerged from the process with an enhanced reputation. Professor Haines's studies of John Carpenter of Worcester and William Gray of Ely, for example, have revealed extremely conscientious diocesan bishops.[50] Thomas Langton, despite his close involvement in Richard III's government, was extremely active in his diocese of Salisbury from 1485 to 1493.[51] Archbishop Morton, despite his preoccupation with affairs of state, did not fail to superintend the conscientious pursuit of reform within the province of Canterbury, after the manner of Archbishop Hubert Walter in the late twelfth century.[52] More work is needed on early Tudor bishops, but where this has been accomplished the picture which has emerged has been creditable, as at Lincoln under Atwater and Longland, or at Ely under the energetic direction of Nicholas West, again significantly one of Fox's diocesan officials before his elevation.[53]

Colet's charge of non-residence can in very many cases be disproved, but it might be thought almost irrelevant. In three dioceses in 1512 even sporadic residence was impossible, for Archbishop Bainbridge of York was the king's permanent representative at Rome, while two sees were held by Italians resident at the papal curia.[54] Yet there is absolutely no evidence of neglect in the diocese of Bath and Wells, whose bishop was

Adriano Castellesi, formerly papal collector in England. During his continual absence the diocese was administered by Master Roger Church, who as a senior member of Morton's staff at Canterbury had temporarily governed several vacant sees and had acquired a wide range of experience. Castellesi's register reveals his conscientious activity as vicar-general.[55] Sacramental functions of the bishop were fulfilled by suffragans. In the west country Thomas Cornish, a Hospitaler and bishop of Tenos *in partibus infidelium*, was extremely active between 1486 and 1513 in the dioceses of Wells and Exeter, and Morton's suffragan at Canterbury was prior of the city's Franciscan convent.[56] It is doubtful if children confirmed, priests ordained or parishioners whose church was dedicated by such men felt any sense of spiritual deprivation.

The courts through which the diocesans and their officials operated attracted from Colet vituperation which foreshadowed the complaints detailed in the Commons' Supplication against the Ordinaries. They visited vexation upon the people by excessive charges for probate and the canon law was enforced only when it resulted in profit; every day new means of extracting money were invented. The filth of courts must be eliminated, thundered the dean. Any punishment imposed by the church courts was, of course, almost certainly resented by the malefactor, and all fees charged by any court are a matter of complaint. Nevertheless, recent studies of these tribunals in the closing decades of the medieval period, whether of individual courts or of specific categories of business, indicate that the judges were in general both efficient and humane and that the whole machinery of ecclesiastical jurisdiction fulfilled a useful social function.[57] The majority of office cases concerned offences against the church's moral code, but there are many indications that denunciations during visitation were prompted by resentment of the breach of social conventions rather than by indignation that the law of the church had been flouted.[58] The trend in almost all dioceses was to impose upon the adulterer or fornicator a monetary penalty rather than the more humiliating forms of public penance, and there was general concern to match the punishment to the financial resources of the guilty party. In the early sixteenth century, however, the aggressively respectable citizens of London ceased to be satisfied with such mild castigation as was imposed by judges whose academic training had taught them to temper justice with mercy, and preferred to resort to the city courts, presided over by men of their own sort, eager to make a public spectacle in the pillory of the sexual transgressor.[59]

The majority of the cases heard in the courts of the archdeacons and bishops' commissaries were, however, instance business, suits brought by plaintiffs in matters such as defamation, and most particularly breach of faith, that is, broken contracts. The rapid decline in such business is obvious in the early sixteenth century, but this is probably due less to

dissatisfaction with the ecclesiastical courts than to the extension of the
jurisdiction of the common law courts to embrace oral contracts, the
expansion of the equitable jurisdiction of Chancery and the greater efficiency of the urban courts. In London, for example, the city's Court of
Requests was established in 1518 to deal with these categories of business.

The other main preoccupation of the church courts was, of course, the
probate of testaments, which accounts for 41 per cent of the business in the
archdeacons' and commissary courts in Lincoln diocese.[60] Once again,
evidence from Winchester, Norwich, Lincoln, London and Chichester
dioceses indicates that there were few abuses. The only criticism generally
valid must be that the scribal fee bore heavily on the estates of the poorest
testators, which otherwise were exempted from charges. It was certainly
not the poor whom the Commons sought to help in 1532. In short, the
evidence relating to office, instance, and probate jurisdiction from all the
court books which have been studied in recent years supports the assertion
of the Ordinaries in that same year: that there were, of course, isolated
instances of malpractice, rare abuses, occasional mistakes, but this was far
from the norm.[61] In general, it seems that the ecclesiastical courts
responded to the needs of society while seeking to temper the most
vengeful instincts of local communities and individual litigants.

It would be facile, of course, to claim that all members of the clerical
order fulfilled the very high standards outlined by canon law or by manuals
of pastoral theology. Yet of most of the charges which Colet laid against
the parochial clergy the vast majority may be acquitted.[62] Those who
actually served the parishes were, it seems, little employed in secular
business, save for the necessity of augmenting their income by the exploitation of their glebe, and perhaps by the duties of chaplaincy to the local
squire. It has recently been shown that, in Bristol at least, service to an
individual family in chantry foundations was of tremendous benefit to the
parish as a whole.[63] Simony did occasionally occur, committed by non-
residents in search of lucrative benefices, but when detected was vigorously
prosecuted – Archbishop Warham had launched a drive against simoniacs
in 1509.[64] Pensions to resigning incumbents have often been regarded as a
concealed form of simony, but Langton's Salisbury register indicates that
from most parish churches only a very small pension was granted, barely
sufficient to support a retired priest and certainly of little interest to the
careerist seeking to accumulate substantial income.[65] Colet's censure of
vicars and parochial chaplains, who often bore the brunt of pastoral work,
is particularly prejudiced. These he described as foolish, unsuitable and
interested only in profit. All recent work suggests that such men were little
different in educational and moral standards from the generality of resident rectors, and far from being grasping, the majority of such priests, in
the inflationary conditions of the early sixteenth century, found it extremely difficult to eke out a living and fulfil their traditional obligations of

hospitality and charity.[66] Colet wrote as a privileged graduate; his desire that men like himself should serve in the parishes, which was the implication of his attack on non-residence and pluralism, would, if fulfilled, have resulted in a further decrease in the expectations of a benefice, or even clerical employment, for priests who were not 'sublime and literate persons', but who were adequately equipped, both by education and social background, to exercise satisfactorily the spiritual and social functions of a rural curate.[67] Colet's sermons may have had a great impact on the educated laity of London, but one may wonder what impression they would have made on the peasants of Dennington, had he ever served the cure in person. Perhaps academic historians, like the dean, have been too inclined to see the needs of the late medieval layman solely from the viewpoint of the consumer of those devotional works flooding from the new printing presses, rather than that of the rural masses for whom the liturgy of the church served, on one very significant level, to punctuate the rhythm of the agricultural year. Bishops such as Fox and Longland were reformers whose responsibilities included the oversight of countless country parishes; they were probably more realistic in appreciating that these communities might be competently served by priests fully integrated within their structure, while other highly educated clergy were more usefully employed in extra-parochial business.

Visitation records do not present a particularly sombre picture of the lower clergy. Mrs Bowker's work on Bishop Atwater's visitations in the huge diocese of Lincoln between 1514 and 1521 shows that few priests failed to fulfil their obligations to celebrate mass and recite the office, to hear confessions and to visit the sick. There was no general neglect of pastoral and liturgical duties, even if many priests would have had difficulty in explaining the rationale of abstract points of theology, for the exposition of which there would have been little demand in most rural communities. Certainly it is impossible to establish any correlation between the keeping of suspect women and disregard for the social and religious functions of the priestly office. The vast majority of the clergy appear to have been acceptable to their parishioners, despite inevitable occasional friction over tithes and other dues, exacerbated by the general economic conditions of the early sixteenth century.[68] There were few signs of anticlericalism in the countryside or in small provincial towns.[69]

In Suffolk in 1499, out of 478 parishes visited, only 38 rectors and two vicars were reported to be non-resident. Many of these had good reasons for their absence – study or diocesan administration. More significantly, only six of these parishes were not regularly served by other clergy. Serious defects of learning or behaviour were detected in only eight incumbents.[70] In the diocese of Canterbury in 1511, from more than 260 parishes only 29 beneficed clergy were reported or noted as absentees.[71] Six were licensed to be non-resident, seven rectors resided in nearby parishes, but in two of these cases the churchwardens specifically stated that the church was well served. Four were absent temporarily on the king's business. One incumbent was deprived, two resigned as a result of the visitation. In 14 parishes at most was any significant dissatisfaction with the local clergy expressed. There was certainly a need for supervision and for enforcement, but this was not lacking, and it appears that neither in Suffolk in 1499 nor in Kent in 1511 nor in the diocese of Lincoln in the early sixteenth century were there Augean stables to be cleansed. It is, of course, possible to isolate cases of drunkenness, addiction to field sports, and sexual immorality among the parish clergy, but for each such instance one may cite the example of an incumbent or parochial chaplain who after years of service entered Syon or Sheen in order to perfect his own spiritual life, or who on his death left his possessions to the church which he had served for decades, or to the poor of the parish.

This review of the large amount of specialised work on various aspects of the history of the English church in the century before the Reformation suggests that previous unfavourable judgments on the performance of that institution should be at least modified, if not reversed. The majority of bishops were learned, able and conscientious. They were aided by a corps of efficient adminstrators, acting through a network of courts which have been shown to have been neither tardy nor oppressive. Concentration on normality, rather than on isolated eye-catching abuses, transforms our view of the parochial clergy. Increasing provision was made for their education, and if those who were most able seldom served the parishes which provided part of their living, and few only resided in their cathedral prebends, divine service was in almost all cases conducted by competent deputies. Indeed, in the rural parish a curate less sublime and literate might have greater capacity for the important social role of pacification. Despite the crippling fear of heresy, many prelates had encouraged the development of lay initiative within orthodox religion. There were few signs of disease or sterility. This reassessment of the state of the late medieval church, of course, makes it more difficult to explain why the English Reformation occurred. What follows is not an attempt to answer this imponderable question, but merely to suggest some contributory factors relating to the structure and public image of the English church in the half-century before 1529.

First, the higher clergy were dependent upon the crown. Although it has been argued above that clerical service to the civil government was socially and politically beneficial and that it did not, as Colet suggested, adversely effect the pastoral role of the church nor create scandal, nevertheless the long-established habit of obedience and service made it less likely that the natural leaders of the English clergy would react quickly or strongly enough to novel royal policies after 1529. The control of the crown had been firmly exercised at least since the tenth century, and it has recently been cogently argued that it was greatly strengthened in the reign of Henry V, who led an extraordinarily able team of bishops in a programme of liturgical reform designed to create religious unity within a national church, and 'acted as supreme governor of the Church of England in all but name'.[72] In a reassessment of Henry VII's religious policy it has been suggested that the traditional view of a king meticulously but utterly conventionally pious should be amended to take account of his perceptive use of politico-theological propaganda; Henry envisaged 'his mission as being closely bound up with a renewal of the religious authority of kingship'.[73] On a more mundane level the crown exercised extensive ecclesiastical patronage, and there was much overlap and interaction between the higher echelons of ecclesiastical and civil administrations. The church was dependent on the machinery of royal government for the apprehension of excommunicates and the burning of heretics. The crown itself delimited the boundary between the two jurisdictions by the issue of writs of prohibition. The clergy were accustomed to the payment of taxes to the crown; in the early Tudor period roughly two and a half times more was paid in regular taxation alone to the royal Exchequer as was rendered in various dues to Rome.[74] Perhaps the most notable manifestation of royal control was that from 1435 to the Reformation the Convocation of Canterbury, designed for the discussion and propagation of reform, met almost always in response to a royal writ stressing the urgency of financial subvention from the clergy; indeed, 1510 was the only exception to this pattern. Certainly matters of religion were discussed, but normally as an appendage to bargaining over taxation.[75] Colet was certainly justified in his impassioned plea in 1512 that this Convocation should actually discuss the state of the church.

The second factor is the influence of the city of London, not so much because the capital provided cover for heretics, so that London became the centre of interchange between residual Lollards and innovative Lutherans, but because the metropolis was the habitat of a multitude of common lawyers, jealous of the church's jurisdiction, whose influence radiated outwards into their own localities;[76] because the complexity of commercial incomes accorded ill with the traditional system of tithing designed for a rural society, and this made endemic friction almost inevitable,[77] because the citizens saw the prelates ensconced in their opulent London houses, where they did appear as politicians and royal servants rather than pastors, however diligent they might be in their own dioceses; because Londoners provided an audience for impassioned debates about clerical rights and privileges, such as the Carmelite attacks on the rights of the parish clergy to tithes in the 1460s, or Henry Standish's assault on benefit of clergy in 1515;[78] because London attracted to itself the least worthy of the lower clergy, that very small minority in the country as a whole who sought to evade their responsibilities – three of the non-resident incumbents in

Suffolk in 1499 were reported to be there.[79] In 1487 Archbishop Morton
had rebuked a group of London clergy for their frequenting of taverns and
in the same year the provincial assembly, concerned about radical sermons
preached in London, lamented the perennial hostility of the laity.[80] In the
context of the capital, though not of the country at large, it is possible that
the situation was correctly assessed, and of course, in the early Tudor
period as now, the influence of the capital over the realm was disproportionate. Colet reflected the criticisms of educated Londoners, but like most
inhabitants of the metropolis he failed to take account of the regions and
to appreciate that in the countryside, as in many provincial towns, the
church and the clergy were in large measure fulfilling the needs of their
flocks.[81]

On 11 July 1495 a crowd of curious bystanders at St Paul's witnessed an
extraordinary spectacle. The officials of the bishop of London, who was
engaged in a bitter dispute with the archbishop of Canterbury concerning
probate jurisdiction, posted on the cathedral doors a copy of a citation of
the archbishop to Rome; they refused to allow Morton's servants to
examine this, and announced publicly that he had been excommunicated.[82]
This unedifying scene links public opinion in London with the last factor
here to be considered, the divisions *within* the church in the 50 years before
the Reformation. Hamilton Thomson, in his splendid survey of the late
medieval church, stressed the prevailing calm of the ecclesiastical politics
of the age.[83] The stability which is suggested by the loquacious and
repetitive entries in so many fifteenth-century episcopal registers may,
however, be deceptive. Historians of the central middle ages have come
to appreciate that it is simplistic to treat the church as a single, huge,
united corporation. They have become increasingly conscious of numerous
tensions and divisions, between Benedictines and new orders, between
religious communities and bishops, between suffragans and metropolitans.
The interests of a particular church, of York, of Lincoln, or Bangor, were
of greater significance even to ardent reformers than loyalty to the abstrac-
tion of a universal church headed by Rome or to the *ecclesia Anglicana*.
The late medieval church in England was not a monolithic structure, and
conflicts which had never been satisfactorily resolved in an earlier period
were now resurrected with renewed bitterness. Archbishop Morton's assertion of the customs and prerogative of the church of Canterbury, for
example, was as strenuous as that of Lanfranc, Becket or Pecham; it
provoked furious resistance from his suffragans and from exempt religious
orders and houses which saw a threat to their customary privileges.

A perusal of the *Calendar of Papal Registers* of the fifteenth century will
provide evidence of very many minor jurisdictional disputes, which were
still fought out at the court of Rome.[84] The main issues, however, were the
struggle between the exempt religious and the diocesan bishops, and the
probate dispute which soured the relationship between Canterbury and its

suffragans. These conflicts dominated the Convocation of 1512, from which Dean Colet had hoped for so much constructive discussion of reform. There was an appeal to the pope against the friars, and more particularly against the Hospitallers, who, it was argued, robbed prelates of their rights and priests of their livelihood, and whose conduct led to heresy, schism and contempt for all authority.[85] Equally serious was the appeal to Rome by the bishops against the alleged abuse by Archbishop Warham of the prerogative probate rights of the church of Canterbury. The king's attempts to mediate, at the pope's request, were not successful, and Canterbury's prerogative jurisdiction continued for a few years more to cause resentment among the hierarchy, until indignation was redirected against the novel claims of Wolsey's legatine court.[86]

These tensions within the higher echelons of the English church had unfortunate consequences. They militated against cohesion on what was, potentially, a very fine bench of bishops, cancelling out factors which should have made for unity. Archbishop Morton and Bishop Hill of London, for example, were both loyal servants of Henry VII, but association in the royal service did not prevent a very bitter dispute between them.[87] Their joint interests as patrons of the new learning did not deter Bishops Fox and Oldham from leading the assault on Archbishop Warham in 1512. It was, moreover, impossible for any prelate to exercise his authority decisively in any controverted matter without unleashing an interminable series of appeals. Just as Morton's attempt to dislodge the unworthy abbot of St Albans in 1490 was frustrated, despite his papal commission to reform exempt houses, and his *sede vacante* jurisdiction was challenged in an appeal by the monks of Winchester, so the archbishop himself successfully impeded Bishop Hill's attempt to depose the notorious prior of Holy Trinity Aldgate, not because he believed in his innocence, but because in his removal the jurisdiction of the Court of Canterbury had been flouted.[88] Any attempt at reform was liable to be frustrated by manipulation of the technicalities of the legal system. Prolonged litigation between institutions with a permanent corporate existence, moreover, left a legacy of bitterness and suspicion.

Dean Colet certainly appreciated this situation, condemning 'this mad and raging contention of ordinaries'. The jurisdictional conflicts within the English church were not, of course, the direct cause of the Reformation, but they did vitiate attempts at internal reform of corporate bodies, they made the church susceptible to criticism by the educated laity of the court circle and of London, in whose view these battles were normally fought out, and they contributed to a lack of united leadership in a period of crisis. However worthy were the bishops as individuals, however committed to the implementation of effective pastoral ministry within their dioceses, they proved incapable of working as a united body. The tensions within the hierarchy were not created, but merely exacerbated, by Wolsey's distortion of the traditional constitutional structure of the English church. Yet the centralisation of authority within a 'national' church was probably the most effective means of achieving reform, as was demonstrated by Cardinal Ximenes in contemporary Spain. Wolsey's efforts perhaps lacked credibility because of the irregularity of his own position, but similar measures had been attempted before, particularly by Morton, with no greater success. The privileges of exemption and the complicated judicial machinery of appeals to Rome hampered effective executive action. Those reforms which were necessary might have been achieved by the centralisation of all ecclesiastical authority in the hands of one prelate, able to suppress minor convents and even decayed major houses while preserving the integrity of the monastic order, and to eliminate those vain and frustratory appeals which circumscribed all attempts to implement judicial decisions and which consumed enormous time and energy whenever the least significant right of any ecclesiastical corporation was threatened. It was a proportion of the monasteries and collegiate churches, rather than the parochial clergy, which invited reform, but which possessed the income and influence to resist.

A picture of the English church at the close of the middle ages might be painted which is far from depressing. The church militant in England in the early sixteenth century was functioning as effectively as at most periods of its history, even if, inevitably, it fell far short of the ideal of the church triumphant. Most of the lower clergy were fulfilling the needs of the majority of their parishioners. Bishops administered their dioceses effectively, either in person or through very capable deputies. There was, of course, room for improvement, and there was need for reform of those corporate bodies which were the lumber of the past, fortresses of prayer which had long since ceased to provide spiritual defence for the English people and which had become entrenched in privileges designed to protect their autonomy in a hostile world in which their inmates had served as the warriors of Christ, but which were now irrelevant and harmful in a society far more thoroughly Christianised than that of the eleventh century. Their existence provided ammunition for that tiny minority of influential men at court, in London and in the legal profession who for doctrinal or professional reasons had a vested interest in the destruction of the old order. Yet ultimately even these bastions of outdated privilege might have been reinvigorated, as on the continent, by the increased influence of new, reformed and streamlined religious orders. When all qualifications have been made, we must return to Henry VIII's matrimonial problems and financial needs as the ultimate cause of the Reformation in England. Political expediency provided the gate by which a few wolves might enter into the sheepfold – but then very few wolves are needed to destroy a healthy flock.

Notes

1 The sermon will be found most conveniently in *English Historical Documents* V *1485–1588* edited by C.H. Williams (London, 1967), pp. 652–60, where it is reprinted from J.H. Lupton, *Life of John Colet* (London, 1887), appendix C, pp. 293–304. For a useful discussion of the sermon in the context of Colet's theology, see H.C. Porter, 'The Gloomy Dean and the Law', in G.V. Bennett and J.D. Walsh (eds), *Essays in Modern English Church History in Honour of Norman Sykes* (London, 1966), pp. 18–43. This article perhaps places rather too much emphasis on the singular circumstances of the Hunne case. Cf. J.B. Trapp, 'John Colet and the *Hierarchies of the Ps-Dionysius*', S[tudies in] C[hurch] H[istory], xvii, 1981 pp. 127–48.

2 A.G. Dickens, *The English Reformation* (London, 1964); see especially pp. 45, 64–5, 90.

3 M. Bowker, *The Secular Clergy in the Diocese of Lincoln, 1495–1520* (Cambridge, 1968); *The Henrician Reformation: the Diocese of Lincoln under John Longland, 1521–47* (Cambridge, 1981).

4 J.A. Yunck, *The Lineage of Lady Meed: the Development of Medieval Venality Satire* (Notre Dame, 1963).

5 G.R. Owst, *Preaching in Medieval England: an Introduction to the Sermon Manuscripts of the Period c.1350–1450* (Cambridge, 1926); *Literature and Pulpit in Medieval England* (Cambridge, 1933).

6 Among many works on this period, see especially G. Tellenbach, *Church, State and Christian Society at the Time of the Investiture Contest*, translated by R.F. Bennett (Oxford, 1940), and R.W. Southern, *Western Society and the Church in the Middle Ages* (Harmondsworth, 1970), pp. 36–41. For an eleventh-century statement of views on the priesthood echoed by Colet, see Pope Gregory VII's letter to Bishop Herman of Metz, 1081, in B. Tierney (ed), *The Crisis of Church and State, 1050–1300* (Englewood Cliffs, NJ, 1964), pp. 66–73.

7 Bernard of Clairvaux, *Five Books on Consideration: Advice to a Pope*, translated by J.D. Anderson and E.T. Kennan (Cistercian Fathers Series, XXXVII, Kalamazoo, 1976), p. 84. The whole treatise, written 1148–53, is permeated by fierce criticism of avarice and litigiousness.

8 For a convenient synopsis of Colet's career, see A.B. Emden, *A Biographical Register of the University of Oxford to AD 1500* (Oxford, 1957), pp. 462–64.

9 Cited from Mercers' Company Acts of Court, fo. 25v, by H. Miller, 'London and Parliament in the Reign of Henry VIII', *Bulletin of the Institute of Historical Research*, 1962, xxxv, p. 144.

10 C. Harper-Bill (ed), *Register of John Morton, Archbishop of Canterbury 1486–1500* C[anterbury] and Y[ork] S[ociety], 1987, LXXV, no. 91.

11 C. Harper-Bill, 'A Late Medieval Visitation: the Diocese of Norwich in 1499', *Proceedings of the Suffolk Institute of Archaeology and History*, 1977, xxxiv, p. 44.

12 C.R. Cheney, *From Becket to Langton* (Manchester, 1956), pp. 22–4.

13 N. Pronay, 'The Chancellor, the Chancery and the Council at the End of the Fifteenth Century', in H. Hearder and H.R. Loyn (eds), *British Government and Administration: Studies Presented to S.B. Chrimes* (Cardiff, 1974), pp. 87–103.

14 D. Nicholl, *Thurstan Archbishop of York, 1114–40* (York, 1964), pp. 187–91.

15 For the internal transformation of religious orders, see J. Leclercq, 'A Sociological Approach to the History of a Religious Order', in M.B. Pennington (ed), *The Cistercian Spirit: a Symposium* (Shannon, 1969), pp. 136–43. For the orders in early sixteenth-century England, M.D. Knowles, *The Religious Orders in England*, III (Cambridge, 1971).

16 J.C. Dickinson, 'Early Suppressions of English Houses of Austin Canons', in V. Ruffer and A.J. Taylor (eds), *Medieval Studies Presented to Rose Graham* (Oxford, 1950), pp. 54–77.

17 For visitation material see especially A.H. Thompson (ed), *Visitations in the Diocese of Lincoln, 1517–31* (L[incoln] R[ecord] S[ociety], 1940–47), XXXIII, XXXV, XXXVII; A. Jessopp (ed), *Visitations of the Diocese of Norwich*,

AD 1492–1532 (Camden Society, ns XLIII, 1888); P. Heath (ed), *Bishop Geoffrey Blythe's Visitations, c.*1515–1525 (Staffordshire Record Society, fourth series, 1973, Vol vii).

18 For a spectacular twelfth-century scandal, see G. Constable, 'Aelred of Rievaulx and the Nun of Watton: an Episode in the Early History of the Gilbertine Order', in D. Baker (ed), *Medieval Women* (Oxford, 1978), pp. 205–26. See also nine letters of St Bernard relating to apostate monks – a problem well documented in fifteenth-century visitation records in B.S. James (ed), *The Letters of Bernard of Clairvaux* (London, 1953), nos. 58, 73, 82, 86, 102, 362, 432, 445, 448; cf. C. Harper-Bill, 'Monastic Apostasy in Late Medieval England', *J[ournal of] E[cclesiastical] H[istory]*, 1981, xxxii, pp. 1–18.

19 R.B. Dobson, *Durham Priory, 1400–1450* (Cambridge, 1973); Knowles, *Religious Orders*, III, pp. 96–9; H.E. Butler (ed), *The Chronicle of Jocelin of Brakelond* (London, 1949).

20 Knowles, *Religious Orders*, I, pp. 9–27; II, pp. 175–84; III, pp. 159–60; Southern, *Western Society*, pp. 236–37.

21 For lay religion, see F.R.H. Du Boulay, *An Age of Ambition: English Society in the Later Middle Ages* (London, 1970), pp. 143–59. Among many recent articles, for a characteristically challenging interpretation see C. Richmond, 'Religion and the Fifteenth-century English Gentleman', in R.B. Dobson (ed), *The Church, Politics and Patronage in the Fifteenth Century* (Gloucester, 1984), pp. 193–208.

22 B. Radice (ed), *The Letters of Abelard and Heloise* (Harmondsworth, 1974), p. 164.

23 M.G. Underwood, 'Politics and Piety in the Household of Lady Margaret Beaufort', *JEH*, 1987, xxxviii, pp. 39–52.

24 R.W. Dunning, 'Revival at Glastonbury, 1530–39', *SCH*, 1977, xiv, pp. 213–22; D. Baker, 'Old Wine in New Bottles: Attitudes to Reform in Fifteenth-century England', *SCH*, 1977, xiv, pp. 193–211.

25 J. Catto, 'Religious Change under Henry V', in G.L. Harriss (ed), *Henry V: the Practice of Kingship* (Oxford, 1985), pp. 97–115. R. Lovatt argues that the *Imitatio Christi* of Thomas à Kempis was restricted to a very narrow circulation in 'The Imitation of Christ in Later Medieval England', *Transactions of the Royal Historical Society*, fifth series, 1968, xviii, pp. 97–212, but the argument of Catto may be thought more convincing.

26 D. Knowles and R.N. Hadcock, *Medieval Religious Houses, England and Wales* (second edition, London, 1971), pp. 83–95, *passim*, pp. 257, 452.

27 For recent studies of the religion of the gentry see M.G.A. Vale, *Piety, Charity and Literacy among the Yorkshire Gentry, 1370–1480* (York, 1976); N. Saul, 'The Religious Sympathies of the Gentry in Gloucestershire, 1200–1500', *Transactions of the Bristol and Gloucestershire Archaeological Society*, 1980, xcviii, pp. 99–112; P.W. Fleming, 'Charity, Faith and the Gentry of Kent, 1422–1529', in A.J. Pollard (ed), *Property and Politics: Essays in Late Medieval English History* (Gloucester, 1984), pp. 36–58.

28 J.A.F. Thompson, *The Later Lollards, 1414–1520* (Oxford, 1965), pp. 87, 136, 162, 185, 198; J. Fines, 'Heresy Trials in the Diocese of Coventry and Lichfield, 1511–12', *JEH*, 1963, xiv, pp. 160–74.

29 Of many studies, see most conveniently K.B. McFarlane, *John Wycliffe and the Beginnings of English Nonconformity* (London, 1952), and most recently A. Kenny (ed), *Wyclif in his Times* (Oxford, 1986).

30 M. Aston, *Lollards and Reformers: Images and Literacy in Late Medieval Religion* (London, 1984); A. Hudson, *Lollards and their Books* (London, 1985).

31 J.J. Scarisbrick, *The Reformation and the English People* (Oxford, 1984), p. 46.

32 Catto, 'Religious Change', p. 114.

33 J.A.F Thomson, 'The Well of Grace: Englishmen and Rome in the Fifteenth Century', in Dobson (ed), *Church, Politics and Patronage*, p. 114.

34 Catto, 'Religious Change'.

35 Hudson, *Lollards*, pp. 158–60; Lupton, *John Colet*, pp. 202–5; M. Deanesly, *The Lollard Bible* (Cambridge, 1920), especially p. 373.

36 F.R.H. Du Boulay, 'The Fifteenth Century', in C.H. Lawrence (ed), *The English*

Church and the Papacy in the Middle Ages (London, 1965), pp. 224–27; A. Hamilton Thompson, *The English Clergy and their Organisation in the Late Middle Ages* (Oxford, 1947), pp. 1–39; R.G. Davies, 'The Episcopate', in C.H. Clough (ed), *Profession, Vocation and Culture in Late Medieval England* (Liverpool, 1982), pp. 51–89.

37 See especially E.E. Reynolds, *St John Fisher* (London, 1955).

38 M.D. Knowles, *The Episcopal Colleagues of Archbishop Thomas Becket* (Cambridge, 1951), pp. 155–56.

39 M.P. Howden (ed), *The Register of Richard Fox, Lord Bishop of Durham 1494–1501* (Surtees Society, 1932), pp. xxxvii–lvi.

40 Emden, *Biographical Register*, pp. 1381–82; R.L. Storey, *Diocesan Administration in Fifteenth-century England* (second edition, York, 1972), p. 30.

41 Emden, *Biographical Register*, pp. 1396–97, 1721–22.

42 Bowker, *Secular Clergy*, pp. 14–18.

43 Heath, *Blythe's Visitations*, p. xiv.

44 S. Lander, 'Church Courts and the Reformation in the Diocese of Chichester', in R. O'Day and F. Heal (eds), *Continuity and Change: Personnel and Administration of the Church in England, 1500–1642* (Leicester, 1976), pp. 215–37.

45 See note 17; K.L. Wood-Legh (ed), *Kentish Visitations of Archbishop William Warham and his Deputies, 1511–12* (Kent Records, 1984, V xxiv).

46 Audley of Salisbury, Blythe of Lichfield, Fisher of Rochester, Fitzjames of London, Mayhew of Hereford.

47 For example, Warham, Fox and Nix.

48 For fifteenth-century bishops, see J.T. Rosenthal, 'Lancastrian Bishops and Educational Benefaction', in C.M. Barron and C. Harper-Bill (eds), *The Church in Pre-Reformation Society* (Woodbridge, 1985), pp. 199–211; H. Jewell, 'English Bishops as Educational Benefactors in the Late Fifteenth Century', in Dobson (ed), *Church, Politics and Patronage*, pp. 146–67.

49 Emden, *Biological Register*, pp. 716–17, 1397, 1721–22; M.G. Underwood, 'The Lady Margaret and her Cambridge Connections', *Sixteenth-Century Journal*, 1982, xiii, pp. 67–81.

50 R.M. Haines, 'Aspects of the Episcopate of John Carpenter, Bishop of Worcester 1444–76', *JEH*, 1968, xix, pp. 11–40; 'The Practice and Problems of a Fifteenth-century English Bishop: the Episcopate of William Gray', *Medieval Studies*, 1972, xxxiv, pp. 435–61.

51 D.P. Wright (ed), *The Register of Thomas Langton, Bishop of Salisbury 1485–93* (CYS, 1985, lxxiv).

52 C. Harper-Bill, 'Archbishop John Morton and the Province of Canterbury, 1486–1500', *JEH*, 1978, xxix, pp. 1–21; cf. C.R. Cheney, *Hubert Walter* (London, 1967).

53 Bowker, *Secular Clergy*; F. Heal, 'The Parish Clergy and the Reformation in the Diocese of Ely', *Proceedings of the Cambridgeshire Archaeological Society*, 1975, lxvi, pp. 142–51.

54 W.E. Wilkie, *The Cardinal Protectors of England* (Cambridge, 1974), pp. 23–5, 31, 40–1.

55 C., Harper-Bill, 'The *Familia*, Administrators and Patronage of Archbishop John Morton', *Journal of Religious History*, 1979, x, pp. 240–42; H. Maxwell Lyte (ed), *The Registers of Oliver King and Hadrian de Castello, Bishops of Bath and Wells 1496–1518* (Somerset Record Society, 1939, Vol liv).

56 *Handbook of British Chronology* (third edition, London, 1986), p. 286.

57 B.L. Woodcock, *Medieval Ecclesiastical Courts in the Diocese of Canterbury* (Oxford, 1952); M. Bowker (ed), *An Episcopal Court Book for the Diocese of Lincoln, 1514–1520* (LRS, 1966, Vol lxi); R.H. Helmholz, *Marriage Litigation in Medieval England* (Cambridge, 1975); E.M. Elvey (ed), *The Courts of the Archdeaconry of Buckingham, 1483–1523* (Buckinghamshire Record Society, 1975, Vol xix); R. Houlbrooke, *Church Courts and the People during the English Reformation, 1520–1570* (Oxford, 1979).

58 A.J. Kettle, 'City and Close: Lichfield in the Century before the Reformation', in

Barron and Harper-Bill (eds), *Church in Pre-Reformation Society*, pp. 164–69; Harper-Bill, 'Late Medieval Visitation', pp. 37–41.

59 For this and following remarks on London courts, see R.M. Wunderli, *London Church Courts and Society on the Eve of the Reformation* (Cambridge, MA, 1981).

60 M. Bowker, 'Some Archdeacons' Court Books and the Commons' Supplication against the Ordinaries', in D.A. Bullough and R.L. Storey (eds), *The Study of Medieval Records* (Oxford, 1971), p. 291.

61 H. Gee and W.J. Hardy (eds), *Documents Illustrative of English Church History* (London, 1896), pp. 155–70; cf. Bowker, 'Archdeacons' Court Books', pp. 312–14.

62 For a perceptive, critical yet generally sympathetic treatment, see P. Heath, *The English Parish Clergy on the Eve of the Reformation* (London, 1969).

63 C. Burgess, '"For the Increase of Divine Service": Chantries in the Parish in Later Medieval Bristol', *JEH*, 1985, xxxvi, pp. 46–65.

64 A.T. Bannister (ed), *Registrum Ricardi Mayew Episcopi Herefordensis AD MLIV–MLXVI* (CYS, 1921), xxvii, pp. 107–8.

65 Wright (ed), *Langton's Register*, pp. xix-xxi.

66 P. Heath, *Medieval Clerical Accounts* (York, 1964), pp. 12–25; M.L. Zell, 'Economic Problems of the Parochial Clergy in the Sixteenth Century', in R. O'Day and F. Heal (eds), *Princes and Paupers in the English Church* (London, 1981), pp. 19–43. A modification of this view is offered by J. Pound, 'Clerical Poverty in Early Sixteenth-century England: Some East Anglian Evidence', *JEH*, 1986, xxxvii, pp. 199–296, but much more work needs to be done before Zell's view for the country as a whole should be modified.

67 For contemporary emphasis on moral worth rather than academic learning, see R.M. Haines, 'The Education of the English Clergy during the Later Middle Ages', *Canadian Journal of History*, 1969, iv, p. 16; for the latest, enhanced view of the educational opportunities offered to potential clergy, see J.A.H. Moran, *The Growth of English Schooling, 1340–1548: Learning, Literacy and Laicisation in Pre-Reformation York Diocese* (Princeton, 1985).

68 Bowker, *Secular Clergy*, pp. 85–154.

69 That this was the situation nationally is vigorously asserted by C. Haigh, 'Anti-clericalism and the English Reformation', *History*, 1983, lxviii, pp. 391–407.

70 Harper-Bill, 'Late Medieval Visitation', pp. 41–5.

71 Wood-Legh (ed), *Warham's Visitations*, *passim*; see index. Heath, *Parish Clergy*, notes 37 absentees.

72 Catto, 'Religious Change', p. 115. This article reinforces the argument of a neglected paper, D. Hay, 'The Church of England in the Later Middle Ages', *History*, 1968, liii, pp. 35–50.

73 A. Goodman, 'Henry VII and Christian Renewal', *SCH*, 1981, xvii, pp. 115–25.

74 J.J. Scarisbrick, 'Clerical Taxation in England, 1485–1547', *JEH*, 1961, xii, pp. 41–54.

75 E.W. Kemp, *Counsel and Consent* (London, 1961), p. 147.

76 For them, see E.W. Ives, 'The Common Lawyers', in Clough (ed), *Profession*, pp. 181–217.

77 Wunderli, *London Church Courts*, pp. 108–13; J.A.F. Thomson, 'Tithe Disputes in Later Medieval London', *English Historical Review*, 1963, lxxviii, pp. 1–17; S.E. Brigden, 'Tithe Controversy in Reformation London', *JEH*, 1981, xxxii, pp. 285–301.

78 F.R.H. Du Boulay, 'The Quarrel between the Carmelite Friars and the Secular Clergy of London, 1464–68', *JEH*, 1955, vi, pp. 151–74; Knowles, *Religious Orders*, III, pp. 53–5.

79 Harper-Bill, 'Late Medieval Visitation', p. 42.

80 *Register of John Morton*, no. 92.

81 For the satisfactory relationship in a large provincial town, see N.P. Tanner, *The Church in late Medieval Norwich, 1370–1532* (Toronto, 1984).

82 *Register of John Morton*, no. 196.

83 Hamilton Thompson, *English Clergy*, p. 1.

84 For examples, see *Calendar of Entries in the Papal Registers relating to Great*

Britain and Ireland: Papal Letters (14 vols, 1894–1961), *1431–47*, pp. 244–45, 259,
544–45; 1447–55, p. 45; *1458–71*, pp. 486–87.
85 *Register of Richard Mayew*, pp. 50–2.
86 C.J. Kitching, 'The Prerogative Court of Canterbury from Warham to Whitgift', in
O'Day and Heal (eds), *Continuity and Change*, pp. 191–213.
87 C. Harper-Bill, 'Bishop Richard Hill and the Court of Canterbury, 1494–96',
Guildhall Studies in London History, 1977, iii, pp. 1–12.
88 Harper-Bill, 'Richard Hill'; *Register of John Morton*, nos. 221–66; M.D. Knowles,
'The Case of St Albans Abbey in 1490', *JEH*, 1952, iii, pp. 144–58.

2

Lollardy and the Reformation in England

J.F. DAVIS

Whether Lollardy had an effect upon the English Reformation rather
depends upon what one takes the Reformation to have consisted of. There
is a strong tradition in English historiography to regard the Reformation
as an act of state.[1] This has received recent confirmation by C. Cross, who
writes that 'In one fundamental respect the Henrician Reformation must
still be seen as a naked act of State.'[2] She regards the Reformation acts as
providing unity to the elements of reform. However, the disparate aims of
Erastians, sacramentarians, Lollards and Anabaptists after 1534 hardly
support this view. I prefer to see the Henrician acts as a jurisdictional
breach with Rome which would never have occurred had Charles V not
been in possession of the papacy of Clement VII and if Catherine of Aragon
had not been Charles's aunt. Other monarchs had received papal dispensa-
tion to divorce and re-marry for dynastic purposes but Henry was denied
this facility by political circumstances. Everywhere else in Europe, reform
is viewed as religious change and I see no reason why this should not be
so in England. A.G. Dickens has stressed that the history of the Reformation in England should have less to do with government acts and more with
local evidence of religious change.[3] However, he rather goes back on this
judgement in his later work on the English Reformation, calling Lollard
revival in the sixteenth century 'the Abortive Reformation', implying that
the Reformation acts brought about the successful Reformation.[4] In his
consummate study of the enforcement of the breach with Rome and the
Royal Supremacy by Thomas Cromwell, G.R. Elton subtitles his book
'The Enforcement of the Reformation in the Age of Thomas Cromwell',

Reprinted from *Archiv für Reformationsgeschichte*, 73 (1982).

but tacitly admits in a note that there was 'a political Reformation'.[5] Although some Lollards were anti-papal there were few reformers in the years 1531–33 who shared their views, and the so-called Reformation acts can hardly be seen as having been religiously inspired. In fact, the Reformation acts were accompanied by a religious reaction. On 3 March, probably in 1527, Edward Crome, Hugh Latimer, and Thomas Bynley were excommunicated, and subsequently tried for heresy.[6] These trials, from 1527 to 1532, marked the end of that period of evangelical preaching that can be best described as a period of English Evangelism. The classic work on the subject under discussion, *Lollardy and the Reformation in England* by J. Gairdner, reached some anomalous conclusions. Gairdner took a pessimistic view of the reign of Henry VIII and saw Lollardy as the black conspiracy that rent the seamless garment of medieval Christendom in England. He believed that Lollardy revived when encouraged by Henry in the interests of the divorce. He took an exaggerated view of the political content of Lollardy, terming the Edwardian period 'Lollardy in Power'. On the level of religious beliefs, Gairdner minimized the role of Lollardy: he asserted that Lollard ideas 'mingled with, and domineered over the Reformation, though they did not bring it on'.[7]

The resolution of the problem of whether the Reformation was political or religious in England seems plain enough. The first anticlerical moves were not religiously inspired and were accompanied by a religious reaction. There is, however, a grain of truth in the assertion that the Reformation was an act of state in so far as there was relief for those who opposed the papacy. On 22 March 1531 Chapuys wrote to Charles V describing the trial of Edward Crome. Detained by the bishops, Crome appealed to be heard before the king, who subsequently declared that one of Crome's articles of heresy, that the pope was not head of the church, 'was quite certain and true'. Crome was allowed to go home under the protection of the Boleyns, under whose patronage he had gained the London cure of St Anthony's, although this did not stop the king from requiring him to recant his Evangelism.[8] thereafter, between 1533 and 1536, the Henrician acts of state were underwritten by such Erastian reformers as Cranmer, Barnes and Latimer, who preached the royal supremacy together with attacks on idolatry and superstitions connected with the saints. However, the mass of sacramentarian heretics, Lollard and others, found no relief from the Reformation statutes. If the Reformation in England was an act of state then Lollardy could have had little to do with it. It is this traditional interpretation of the Reformation by English historians that has caused the role of Lollardy to be seriously underestimated. If, as is surely more tenable, the English Reformation was really a process of religious change that gradually spread upwards from Lollard artisans and merchants, to academic reformers of Evangelism and Erastianism, and then to the aristocracy, Lollardy was a profound influence on the English Reformation.

Gairdner was surely wrong in assigning a political role to Lollardy, which monarchy and aristocracy equally detested until they too adopted a sacramentarian view of the eucharist in the reign of Edward VI. He was also wrong in assuming that Lollard ideas did not contribute to reform.

The first indication of the serious contribution of Lollardy to the English Reformation comes in the resilience of its nomenclature. The term Lollard crops up in the records from the beginning of the sixteenth century until 1556. On 14 April 1526, Bishop John Fisher of Rochester prosecuted William Smith, butcher of Gravesend, for offences that led him to be called 'Lollardus'. Smith was guilty of eating meat at Easter, of neglecting his Easter rites, and of having refued to pay the customary oblation to his parish priest.[9] On the face of it, Smith does not seem to be much of a Lollard, but the bishop may have had further information. In the same year, and in the same place, Paul Lomely abjured a typical Lollard view of the eucharist: 'That these prestis makith us to beleve that the syngynge brede they holde over there heedes is god and it is butt a cake.'[10] Religious conservatives in the reign of Henry VIII often called the king, his Council, and Thomas Cromwell 'Lollards' for having introduced measures against pilgrimages, abused images, feast days and offerings to images.[11] These truly reforming measures were brought about by Cromwell, a self-confessed Lutheran, and others like Cranmer and Robert Barnes. Together with the Ten Articles, which reduced the sacraments by implication from seven to three, they are still partly politically inspired rather than religiously so, since they paved the way for a diplomatic understanding with the League of Schmalkalden. Finally, on 8 February 1556, two parishioners of West Barsham in Norfolk, together with another from neighbouring Great Snoring, were indicted for eating meat on fast days and labelled as adherents of 'Lollardy'.[12]

Next, there is the purely circumstantial evidence that Lollardy professed the whole gamut of opinions that were later to be adopted by the Reformation from anti-papalism to crude doctrines of the celestial flesh of Christ. The most enduring tenet of Lollardy was the denial of the real presence and of transubstantiation, derived from Wyclif's own realist thought. The basic and most usual form of this was that material bread remained after the words of consecration. The complexity of Lollard sacramentarian thought, however, was considerable and covers nearly all subsequent developments. This is demonstrated in Lollard confessions in trials in the diocese of Coventry and Lichfield in the years 1511–12. Some Lollards were simply sceptical of current doctrines of the eucharist: 'May a priste make god to daie & ete hym & doo likewise to morowe.' Others deprecated the mercenary character of the mass: 'it is a pretty falshod of the pristes to buy a c. cakes for a peny and sell them ageyn for two ob.' Thomas Bowen had a book that expressed the common Lollard assertion that the eucharist was a commemorative service only, 'oblationem

spiritualem in memoriam passionis Christi.' Again, Thomas Abell heard
at a meeting that he attended,

> that god made man & not man god / as the Carpenter doth make the
> howse & not the howse the carpenter. And that he shuld take it as a
> token or a remembraunce of cristes passion & not as the very body of
> criyste.

The future Zwinglian and Anglican position that the elements were a
signification or representation of Christ's body is also prefigured. John
Blumstone was reported as having said 'that the hoste consecrate was not
the very body of our lorde but a figur'.[13] As early as 1428, Thoma Fougeler
was accused of this advanced position: 'The sacrament of the aulter ys but
a figure or a shadowe in comparison to the present body of god.'[14] Yet
more sophisticated positions were confessed by two priests of Salisbury
diocese in 1499. John Whitehorne, rector of Letcombe Basset, had held
that 'pure brede' remained in the eucharist and that the body of Christ was
ascended into heaven and remained there till domesday – a common
Lollard assertion that was later taken over by Protestantism, as we shall
see. Also taken over by the English reformers was his next arugment, that
the bread instituted by Christ was really God's Word,

> for the Worde ys god / and god is the Worde / As in the begynyng of
> Saint Johannus gospell / And therefor whoosoever Resceive devoutly
> goddis word he Resceyveth the verey body of christe.[15]

This theology is repeated in an opinion of John Pykas, an Essex Lollard, in
1528, 'that the body of Christ was in the Word and not in the bread; that
God is in the Word, and the Word is in God, and God and the Word
cannot be departed.'[16]

After sacramentarianism, by far the most common Lollard doctrines
were those against the veneration of images, and the practice of pilgrimages. Both these positions derived from Wyclif's fear of idolatry. In
1493, Thomas Deny of Waltham Abbey had said that offerings to images
were idolatry. Other Lollard positions were that there is no purgatory, that
confession to a layman or to one's conscience is as good as confession to a
priest, that every layman is a priest, and that is is better to pray in the
fields than at church. There was a puritanical streak in some Lollards, who
opposed singing, ringing of bells and organs. Perhaps significant for the
future was Lollard anti-papalism. One Lollard held that the pope was the
Antichrist, the churchmen his disciples, and the churches synagogues. The
most common form of this belief was that the successors of Peter only had
the power of loosing and binding if their lives were as blameless as Peter's
was. Or, as William Graunger of Gloucester expressed it in 1448, that the
best man alive in the world was the pope. Other Lollard tenets with a
modern ring about them were that prayer is no good if said in a language

not understood, that baptism is as good in a ditch as in a font, that baptism is not needed for the children of Christian parents, and that Lollards would be allowed to preach without let in the future.[17] This is a selected list of Lollard tenets that were later to be taken up by Protestants and Radicals. Other Lollard opinions were eccentric and individual and did not last.

The persecution of Lollards on a hitherto unprecedented scale proves to be the background to the English Reformation in the early sixteenth century. These mass abjurations, known as *magna abjurata*, occurred in a number of places: under Bishop Fitzjames of London in 1510 and 1518; under Bishop Blythe of Coventry and Lichfield in 1511–12; under Archbishop Warham in 1511; under Bishop Smith of Lincoln in 1506–7; under Bishop Tunstall in 1527–28; and under Bishop Longland of Lincoln in 1521.[18] As in the case of the Albigensians in southern France, these enclaves of heresy in Kent, Berkshire, Essex, the Midlands and London provided traditions of anti-authoritarianism and anti-sacerdotalism from which later Protestants profited. We can be more specific in saying that definite traditions of dissent can be perceived in these areas, springing from Lollardy itself. The first of these traditions to be investigated is that existing in the textile villages of south-west Kent. In 1428, an official of Archbishop Chichele tried to apprehend some twenty-one Lollard suspects who were led by William White, chaplain of Tenterden. In fact, these Lollards made a migration to another textile-producing area north of the River Waveney in Norfolk. The original villages from which they had come were Tenterden, Romney, Woodchurch, Staplehurst, Benenden, Halden, Cranbrook, Wittersham and Rolvenden.[19] Other cases arise from this area in the course of the fifteenth century, and in 1511 Archbishop Warham again forced Lollards to abjure in Benenden, Tenterden and Cranbrook. A feature of these Kentish trials was their extreme sacramentarian character, all seven sacraments being called into question, an indication that Kent was the home of radical heresy.[20] Cranbrook has the most enduring tradition of dissent and was the home of one of Tyndale's agents, Richard Harmon. In 1528, Thomas Davy of Cranbrook wrote to Harmon complaining that 'no man in England may speak of the New Testatment on pain of bearing a faggot'.[21] On 3 June 1539, a commission from Thomas Cromwell to Archbishop Cranmer ordered the investigation of sacramentarians in various places, one of them being Cranbrook.[22] In the Marian period, commissioners of the queen sat at Cranbrook to try heresy, and in Archdeacon Harpesfield's visitation of 1555 three from the town suspected of heresy were ordered to be apprehended.[23] In Elizabethan times, Cranbrook was a noted centre of Puritanism, of conventicles, and of those who desired further reformation.[24] It may be questioned whether this Kentish tradition of dissent was just a heretical conclave that attracted other heresies, or whether Lollardy had an enduring effect here. From the evidence of the trials of John Philpot of Tenterden in 1556 it does appear that Lollardy actually lingered on and provided an enduring sacramentarian strain that goes counter, for example, to Lutheranism. The possibility is that Lollardy contributed to the English Reformation a sacramentarian sectarianism that is purely native in character. Philpot did not believe in the Catholic church but 'christes congregation'. His eucharistic thought combines all the Lollard positions:

> that in the blessed sacrament of the Aulter under the formes of bread and wyne there is not the verie bodie and bloud of our Saviour Jesu Christ in substaunce but onlie a token signe and a Remembraunce therof, and that the verrie bodie and bloud of christ is onelie in heaven and no where ells.

He further believed that the eucharist should be ministered in English and in both kinds. He denied papal supremacy and maintained that faith and works must be inseparable for them to justify a man.[25] This last conclusion goes against solifidianism and relfects the Lollards' affection for the Epistle of James that was so distasteful to Luther. It appears that Lollardy was probably to turn into Puritanism in so far as its radical character was likely to press for further reformation, based on conventicles and congregations rather than upon the established church.[26] It is likely that Lollard congregations later coalesced with the 'hotter' sort of Protestants to produce further reformation. In 1554, Farrar, Coverdale, Hooper, Bradford, Philpot, Crome, and Saunders signed to eight articles demanding the necessity of scriptural authority, the necessity of founding the church on the same, and for the sacraments to be founded upon Christ's institution.[27] The Calvinistic elements of Puritanism came rather later.

Another Kentish tradition of heresy exists in the diocese of Rochester, situated in the towns and villages along the River Medway. This tradition has an unusual continental connection with the heresy of the Free Spirit, possibly because the Medway provided a route for ideas, and perhaps books. On 9 October 1431, Thomas Hellis of Brenchley abjured a number of articles akin to the Free Spirit heresy: that a priest in sin may not consecrate the elements; that however much a man persists in sin he shall not be damned; that adultery is no sin but a private transaction and a common solace; and that men and women are hypocrites when they perform public devotions, particularly women who fast before the Holy Nativity and Pentecost and who afterwards receive absolution and communion. Hellis reckoned that these women were fit to be 'rebuked as evylleverys and to be withdrawe fro the devocion and luve of god'. Lollard conventicles are mentioned at West Malling in 1425, at Hadlow in 1431, and at Tonbridge in 1496. The last represented more usual Lollardy, Christopher Payn abjuring on 8 April 1496, and confessing that he had been a Lollard for five or six years, and that he had held meetings in his house. They discussed certain heretical books which contained Lollard doctrines: that there is no purgatory except in this world; that priests have no power to consecrate Christ's body; and 'that all the werkis of holy chirch be nought'. The Free Spirit influence returns in the heresy of John Moress, weaver of Rochester, in 1505. The denigration of the role of Christ and the elevation of the sinless superman is an enduring feature of this influence. Moress believed that Christ did not die in perfect charity, since he pardoned one thief and not the other. He also believed that Christ took no flesh from Mary. In 1525, the prior of a Rochester hospital abjured opinions combining Lollardy and a superficial Lutheranism that can be best described as Evangelism. In 1528, a schoolmaster of Tonbridge was charged with having brought a copy of Tyndale's *New Testament* into the Rochester cloister. Another example of the Free Spirit heresy comes as late as 1532, when John Dissenger, a joiner, confessed his heresy that included among other things the opinion that Christ was 'a wroth and a angry fellow and did naught in casting down the poor man's goods in the Temple'.[28] Of the Marian martyrs of Rochester, two came from Tonbridge and one from Rochester itself. One of these betrayed a narrow biblicism in refusing to recognize the church as her mother – it not being in the scriptures.[29] This Rochester tradition is perhaps of little importance but is illustrative of how a radical form of Lollardy could endure until 1532, adding eccentricity to the story of English reform.

More material is the London tradition of dissent in the north-west sector of the city comprising the wards of Coleman Street, Cripplegate, Cordwainer and Cheap. This was yet another cloth centre, including many trade and company halls for the sale of wool. It was in William Parche-myner's house in the parish of St Sepulchre that Oldcastle lay concealed after his abortive rising in 1414. A major conventicle met in the house of John Claydon, skinner, in the same quarter.[30] Parishes in this area connected with Lollardy in the years 1476 to 1499 are St Michael Bassishaw, St Dunstan's in the West, St Mildred's Poultry, St Peter the Poor, St Michael Quern, St Sepulchre's, St Andrew's Cornhill, and St Peter Cheap.[31] The *magna abjurata* conducted by Bishop Tunstall of London in 1528 discovered that the main sustainer of the Lollard calls in London, Berkshire and Essex was John Hacker, 'of Coleman Street in London, water bearer'.[32] The London conventicles of the period were all close proximity to Coleman Street. Early reforming circles gathered in the same area of the city. The distribution of heretical books to the universities was organized from All Saints Honey Lane, and the Cambridge reformers took up pulpits here: Richard Bayfield at St Vedast, Edward Crome at St Antholin's, Thomas Arthur at St Mary Woolchurch, and Hugh Latimer at St Mary Abchurch. Reforming congregations gathered in a warehouse in Bow Lane in 1532, and this same street was used by the Marian underground Protestants in 1555.[33] Again, the connection with Puritanism is strong, since the leaders of that movement in London, John Field, Thomas Wilcox and Robert

Crowley, held cures in the same quarter of the city, in particular, the benefices of St Giles Cripplegate and All Hallows Honey Lane.[34]

Another local tradition of dissent springing from Lollardy is to be found in northern Essex. In extent, this ran inland from Colchester to Thaxted, with a north–south area from the Suffolk border of the Stour Valley to the textile villages of central Essex, such as Witham and Coggeshall. Essex made the largest contribution to the Oldcastle rebellion, and there were a number of burnings in Colchester in the first half of the fifteenth century.[35] There was a Lollard conventicle at Saffron Walden in 1466, and in 1528, John Hacker's Lollard connections were strong at Colchester itself, at Steeple Bumpstead, and at Boxstead. In 1528, the Colchester Lollard, John Pykas, had learnt his heresies from Wycliffite scriptures and from Tyndale's *New Testament*. Despite the Lutheran prologues of the latter, he still taught the old Lollard sacramentarianism that bread and wine remained after consecration of the elements.[36] In the Marian period, the queen's Council busied themselves with measures against seditious preaching and conventicles at Stoke-by-Nayland, and at Colchester.[37] One of the most revealing documents of the whole Reformation is a confession of faith found upon Robert Wade in 1555. It was produced in the Stour Valley that was to be the home of the notable Puritan meeting, the Dedham classis. This confession is mainly an exposition of the text, 'Chryste oure pascall lambe is offred up for us', and is a statement of Wade's faith in the eucharist. Wade rejected the view that the eucharist was a bare sign and goes on to place it firmly in the context of the Passover feast. It is just this kind of scriptural reasoning that made Puritanism an on-going reformation. Wade had developed beyond Lollardy but still owed much to its biblicism.[38]

Another well-defined tradition of dissent that contained a strong Lollard content is to be found at Bristol. The academic Wycliffite, William Taylor, was to be found there in 1420, and there are prosecutions for Lollardy in Bristol in the course of the fifteenth century. One of these was John Younge, chaplain of the parish of the Holy Cross of the Temple, who denied the pope to be vicar of Christ on earth, among other things.[39] In the years 1498 to 1501, there were prosecutions in the Redcliffe area of the city, when two weavers held views against the worship of images and the real presence. In 1511, a Birmingham man admitted to knowing Bristol Lollards, their chief doctrine being that 'the sacrament of thaltar is not the very body of our Lorde but materiall brede'. Hugh Latimer preached against the veneration of saints, especially the Virgin, pilgrimages and shrines in the city and caused a furore there. He maintained reforming preachers there when bishop of Worcester. Bristol was one of the places noted for sacramentarians in the 1539 commission against the same already mentioned. Lollard sacramentarianism crops up in the opinions of the Marian martyrs in Bristol. William Saxton, weaver of Bristol, was condemned in 1556 for holding that 'the sacrament was a sign of a holy thing: also he denied that the flesh and blood of Christ is there after the words of consecration.' Richard Sharpe, weaver of Redcliffe, tried on 9 March 1556, denied the real presence and called the host an idol. This assertion of idolatry in the mass looks like an extension of the Lollard fears of idolatry in the worship of images that probably stems from John Frith's eucharistic thought. In 1533, Frith maintained that the host was not to be worshipped. At the time he was in touch with Lollard circles and seems to have had a profound effect upon them.[40] Another Bristol martyr, Thomas Hale, shoemaker, also called the mass an idol. Another, Thomas Benion, weaver, was burnt in 1557 for saying 'there is nothing but bread in the sacrament'. It looks as if Lollardy existed in Marian Bristol and survived to provide the lowly, textile artisans of the Marion persecution there.[41]

Another textile-producing city that contributed martyrs under Mary was Coventry. The city was a centre of Lollardy in the fifteenth century, was well represented in the persecution held by Bishop Blythe in 1511–12, and was later a centre of Puritanism.[42] A lesser tradition is to be found in the worsted-producing areas of Norfolk along the valleys of the Bure and Waveney. Flourishing conventicles were found there in the years 1428 to 1431 by Bishop Alnwick of Norwich, and there were isolated cases in the rest of the fifteenth century. Agitation against images was strong at Aylsham in the sixteenth century.[43] Not only do these traditions of dissent indicate that Lollardy fathered reform, but that it actually lingered on in congregations and in pockets of sacramentarianism. Lollardy provided some of the impetus for further reformation along scriptural lines in opposition to the dregs of popery that Puritanism saw in the established church. Worth noting also is the socio-economic element in these traditions: they were all areas of the textile industry in England.[44] Undoubtedly, the textile industry was providential to Lollardy in so far as the weavers and the rest occupied a new, independent stance, in medieval and early modern society. They lived in gathered communities, linked by the trade in wool and cloth which could provide access to the circulation of books and ideas, and were frequently visited by middlemen. Lollardy partly bequeathed this socio-economic connection to reform and Protestantism in such places as Hadleigh in Suffolk, the cure of Rowland Taylor; in the more conservative north, towns like Leeds, Dewsbury, and Manchester provided footholds for Protestantism among textile communities.

A more direct contribution to the Reformation was made by that organized wing of Lollardy that is known as the Christian Brethren. The existence of the Christian Brethren has been noted, but their full import not yet fully grasped.[45] Medieval Lollardy had its manuscript production, a rudimentary priesthood, knightly patronage, and widespread contacts, sometimes kept together by letters.[46] However, in the early sixteenth century, a more solid organisation seems to have evolved among some Lollards, usually with middle-class components; it had printing presses for the publication of books and the disbursement of money for officials in the various cells of the organizaiton. These cells are hinted at by the names Lollards called each other: 'brother in Christ', 'the known men', and 'the just-fast men'. The first indication of the Christian Brethren comes in the *magna abjurata* of 1528, when some of John Hacker's contacts in London seem to have more than temporary links with others of their own kind. John Stacy and Lawrence Maxwell, leading members of the Tilers' and Bricklayers' Company, regularly travelled abroad to visit other brethren.[47] The first solid evidence of a cell of these Christian Brethren comes in 1531 in a letter to that arch-conservative, the duke of Norfolk, from Edmund Knyvet. Knyvet was much exercised about illegal assemblies in the Suffolk clothing town of Mendlesham. An unwilling informant had revealed that there had been meetings in various houses ranging from one hundred to twenty in number, 'for a ghostly purpose to be done by us Christian brothers and sisters'. They had elected a 'shadow cabinet' of municipal officers, including a mayor, a shrieve, a lord, and a bailiff, and had gathered together money for their use. One of the Mendelsham brothers had been set in the stocks for attacking the local curate. He had come to the curate claiming that he was fit to be entered into the parish book of those that had been granted absolution, since he had declared his sins to God directly and received His absoltuion. This reflects the Lollard dis-regard for auricular confession.[48] Heresy at Mendlesham re-occurs in the records. Sometime after 1531, the local persecutor of heretics in Suffolk complained to the duke of Suffolk that the vicar of Mendelsham had caused a scandal in the county by bringing his wife and children home to his vicarage. This act was accompanied by the claim that the king knew of his marriage and this supposed immunity had prevented the bishop from taking action.[49] In 1555, William Whiting of Mendelsham abjured an article of heresy, that the eucharist was an idol. It appears that the same Tyrrel family was actively persecuting, as appeared in the letter to the duke of Suffolk about the vicar of Mendelsham, since Sir John Tyrrel had forced twenty-one persons to flee his attentions from the same town of Mendlesham.[50]

More revealing information is forthcoming from a report of Sebastian Newdygate in 1531. He was one of the Carthusians who were to suffer in 1535. For the present he was informing someone of activities against the eucharist. Thomas Keyle, mercer of London, had unwisely told Newdygate of 'Augmentations of christen brethren of his sorte' paid to clerks in the city of London, which were sent all over the realm. There were also auditors to keep account of the money so raised and used. Three priests, Sir George Parker, Pathmore, and Mershall, together with Thomas Keyle and Shreve, a barber surgeon, held views against the real presence: 'that the Sacrament

of the Awtor after the consecration is nother body not blode but remay-
neth brede and wyne as did before.' There can be no doubt as to the
Lollard provenance of these men. The priest, Pathmore, could be Thomas
Patmore, graduate of Oxford in 1510, and MA of Cambridge in 1515. He
was the son of Henry Patmore, draper of London, and became rector of
Much Hadham, Hertfordshire, between 1515 and 1531. In 1531 he was
charge with having communicated with Luther in Wittenberg, and with
having celebrated the marriage of his curate, Simon Smith, fellow of
Gonville Hall, to his maidservant, Joan Benmore. She was connected
with 'the Bell' in New Fish Street, home of William Mason, a tailor
who was a member of John Hacker's Lollard connection in London.[51]
George Bull, one of Patmore's parishioners, believed the incongruous story
told him by the rector concerning a local well that sprang from the bones
of Wyclif.[52] Patmore himself held traditional Lollard views against the
veneration of saints and images, holding that for centuries the truth of
scripture had been lost. If the connection between the Christian Brethren
and Thomas Patmore is correct, we have a peculiarly eclectic Lollardy here
that was bent on reform of whatever stripe.

This possibility that the Christian Brethren was an eclectic reforming
agency will gain further support shortly; its basic, Lollard, character,
however, is certain. Returning to Newdygate's report, he further asked
Sir George Parker how the king and lords of the realm viewed his sacramentarianism? Parker replied that they were hot against it, especially the
king himself, the dukes of Norfolk and Suffolk, and the marquis of Exeter.
When asked how he would overcome this, Parker replied that they already
had 2000 books against the sacrament in circulation, together with books
on other subjects, 'affirmyng that yf it were ones in the commons hedes
thei wolde have no further care'.[53] This can perhaps be seen as one of the
most revolutionary statements of Tudor history – a clear indication of the
fact that reformation was designed to work in opposition to government. It
is instructive to compare this heretical edition of 2000 with other heretical
books in circulation. Sometime in the chancellorship of More, John Tyndale, William's brother, and Thomas Patmore, merchant – perhaps the
man already met as rector of Much Hadham after 1531 – were charged in
Star Chamber with having spent £1850.10d on purchasing Tyndale's *New
Testament* and other books. Assuming that the majority of these books
were New Testaments, at a wholesale price of 9d a testament,[54] this works
out conservatively at 50,000 books.[55] On 14 June 1527, Bishop Nix wrote
to Archbishop Warham congratulating him on spending £516.9s.4d on
buying up Tyndale's *New Testament* 'with and without glosses'.[56] Adding
to this the 300 testaments that were offered to Robert Necton by a Dutch-
man in 1527,[57] we have a further 14 500 books, making a total of at least
64 000 of Tyndale's *New Testament* in circulation among a population of
three and a half million. We might compare this with two million

published copies of Luther's German Bible. Besides the Tyndale *New Testament*, the Christian Brethren's contribution appears modest. However, it appears that Stacy and Maxwell enabled Robert Bayfield to become an agent for Tyndale in England, and if Thomas Patmore was an agent too, and if A.G. Dickens is right in thinking that Tyndale's merchant patron Humphrey Monmouth was a member of the Christian Brethren, the Brethren had much to do with the distribution of New Testaments.[58]

The next indication of the activity of the Christian Brethren comes in the diocese of Salisbury in 1541. Bishop Capon and Charles Bulkeley wrote 'unto yor good lordshyppes' (probably the king's Council) that the conservative opponent of Latimer in the West Country, William Hubbardine, at St Edmund's church in Salisbury, had preached against psychopannychism. This doctrine of the death or sleep of the soul pending the general resurrection was an enduring feature of the Radical Reformation that had also been adopted by Carlstadt and Luther himself. The following Sunday, the priest of St Edmund's, John Forsett, declared in contradiction that 'sowlye slepe a slepe', further declaring that Luther was a good man and better than Hubbardine, and that if he (Forsett) was put to penance he would not say Our Lady's Psalter. After Forsett's sermon, some of Salisbury were dismayed and affirmed that Forsett and others met together and read doubtful books. Further light was shed on these activities by a letter from Erley to Mister Mathewe and Mister Downes, the last being an upholsterer of Cornhill in London. From this letter it appears that one Sooham of London 'ys A comen messenger and Also A reader of newe bookes from town to town to suche persones as be of that Secte'. Sooham was supported by money collected secretly from among the confederates. This is a revealing instance of how heretical literature was read to gathered companies, so that reforming ideas could circulate even if the hearers were illiterate. The informants of the sect had also found Lutheran books in the possession of John Byrdeler, namely 'A booke of the Germagne Confessyon' and *The Apocalypse* of Philip Melanchthon. The last had been edited by Richard Taverner and printed *cum privilegio* in 1539; it contained the doctrine of consubstantiation which the informants found to be 'false and heretycall'. Another letter to the same persons requested news of those who favoured the word of God, and desired something in rhyme 'to gyve currage unto lytle chyldr to rede the word of god'. It appears that that time-honoured Protestant institution, the Sunday School, was already coming into being.[59] By 1541, the Christian Brethren appear to have involved the English people in Lutheranism in their eclectic espousal of reforming literature.

Another probable publisher of the Christian Brethren was John Gough. He reprinted Wycliffite tracts and supplied Thomas Garret with Tyndale's *New Testament* and Latin texts for his heretical book trade in the universities.[60] Later, together with another Lollard publisher, John Mayler, grocer of London, he published the works of Thomas Becon, many of which were dedicated to the Kentish aristocracy.[61] The enduring Lollard character of the Christian Brethren is attested by the indictment of Mayler under the Six Articles. He had called the eucharist 'the baken god' and added, in the form of hearsay Lutheranism so common to Lollardy, that the mass was called 'the mysse' abroad because 'all is amisse in it'.[62] That some cells of the Christian Brethren survived into the Marian period is suggested by an article in the trial of John Fishecocke of Headcorn in Kent in 1556: 'he will not comunicate with an advouterer / nor a covetous parson / that first was a brother in christ neyther will he pray with him nether salute him.'[63] The Christian Brethren emerge from the records as a Lollard association that sustained cells throughout the country and played a vital part in the distribution of reforming literature. Especially, they aided the spread of Tyndale's *New Testament*, proved eclectic in their choice of works, and helped to bring about the conversion of the English aristocracy to reform. There is one hint that the Christian Brethren may have occasionally evolved into Anabaptism. In 1548, John Champnes of Stratford-le-Bow confessed his mainly Libertine heresy and acknowledged in one of his articles 'that that was the most principall of our markid mans doctrine' to believe that there was a spirit given to man to keep him always righteous.[64] Champnes had published a book full of his doctrines, and it is possible that the name 'markid man' denoted an off-shoot of the Christian Brethren. One Lollard who did make the transition from Lollardy to the Radical Reformation was Joan Boucher, as we shall relate shortly.

So far we have examined some of the indirect and direct contributions of Lollardy to the English Reformation. It remains to be seen, on the level of ideas, how Lollardy contributed to the successive stages of religious change: English Evangelism from 1525 to 1533; Erastianism and Sectarianism from 1533 to 1547; Edwardine Protestantism; the Protestant opposition under Mary, and the growth of sectarianism. The concept of English Evangelism is a somewhat new idea in English history. The preaching of men like Thomas Bylney, Thomas Arthur, Hugh Latimer and Edward Crome can be compared with European Evangelism in the Spain of Juan de Valdés, in the Naples of Julia Gonzaga and Vittoria Colonna, in the French diocese of Meaux under Bishop Briçonnet and Jacques Lefèvre d'Etaples, in Zwingli's Zurich from 1519 to 1523, and in Strassburg under Matthew Zell and others. All these places saw the march of evangelical reform whilst still in communion with Rome. They saw the impact of Luther upon otherwise orthodox circles that produced an emphasis upon faith and grace. New doctrines of faith emerged. In the south, Cardinal Seripando championed double justification at the Council of Trent, while in England the emphasis was upon the object of faith, the all-sufficiency of Christ. English Evangelism postulated faith in the mediation of Christ alone, a doctrine that was often couched in Lollard terms: faith in Christ rather than in the saints. Evangelism elevated the authority of scripture over the church, stressed the preaching of the Gospel rather than sacraments and ceremonies, and was an eclectic movement, sensitive to medieval heresies and Erasmianism. It was with Evangelism that Lollard ideas gained respectability in academic circles. While the Cambridge reformers are often called Protestants and Lutherans, upon closer inspection they turn out to have been much occupied with the traditional Lollard invective against the saints. Can these preachers really be called Protestants when they did not question the Catholic doctrines of the eucharist? Surely, we can only talk of Protestants in England after a fully reformed set of dogmas had been promulgated and accepted under Edward VI. Further, there was a reaction to Luther, but it was in the form of vague doctrines of faith of Evangelism rather than in fully blown solifidianism.

An early case of Evangelism was that of Thomas Batman, prior of the hospital of St Bartholomew in Rochester. He was charged with being a Lutheran but his heresies were mainly Lollard: 'diversos errores et opiniones Lutheri viz de non veneracione sanctorum in ecclesias / eciam sanctorum in celo'. His second article of 1524 was that all men generally approve of Lutheranism. His third depicts the heart of Evangelism, that he puts all his faith in God and not in the saints. His second abjuration on 4 February 1525 was in similar fashion. Still branded a Lutheran, his mainly Lollard opinion remained: 'that no man shuld offer to sayntes nor worship them but only god'. His hearsay Lutheranism included the recommendations that priests should marry – as they did abroad – and priests should minister in both kinds.[65]

The major figure in English Evangelism was Thomas Bynley, and his joint trial with Thomas Arthur of 1527–28 reveals the heart of the movement. There has been considerable controversy over the Lollard articles of his abjuration, since it is strange that a leading acaedmic reformer should have been so much involved with the heresy of clothworkers and other artisans. However, Sir Thomas More was in no doubt as to Bylney's heresy: 'that we should do no worship to images, nor pray to the saints, nor go on pilgrimages'.[66] More was indeed a hostile witness but he was a realist and well acquainted with English reform. Further, Lollards attested that they had heard Bylney preach against the saints. Bylney's abjuration contained articles against the saints, together with Lollard anti-papalism: that no man can inherit the position of Peter unless he shows like purity of life. His reaction to Luther was simple, that no man may merit by his own deeds.[67] The Lollard content of Evangelism is to be found in the trials of the heretical book agents: Robert Bayfield in 1528; Geoffrey Lome; and Thomas Garret.[68] How these academics, ex-monks and clergy came to adopt Lollard opinions is not quite clear. One important piece of evidence suggests that they were actively involved in Lollard groups. Steeple Bumpstead appears to have been a meeting place for Lollards and Cambridge men. One of the clergy there was known as 'Sir Arthur', probably Thomas Arthur the Cambridge reformer. Miles Coverdale, another prominent Cambridge man, was active here. A prominent figure at Steeple Bumpstead was the curate of the place, Richard Fox. Fox actively persuaded his parishioners to take a commemorative view of the eucharist, used the pseudo-Wycliffite tract *The Wicket*, and declaimed against the veneration of images. Fox and Coverdale persuaded a friar to believe aganst the saints by getting him to read Erasmus's *Colloquies*, and the latter converted him to a sacramentarian position on the eucharist by his preaching. Fox appears to have been a throw-back to the Lollard chaplain of former times. The importance of the Steeple Bumpstead coterie is to be seen in this cooperation of Cambridge men and Lollards like John Tyball and Thomas Hilles.[69]

In 1531, Edward Crome and Hugh Latimer were made to recant articles of heresy that included the Lollard invective against the saints, and so the days of Evangelism grew to a close.[70] Most of the former preachers of Evangelism now adopted an Erastian position after making an uneasy compromise. The Erastian way is illustrated by a directive to preachers of 1534. Every preacher was to declaim against papal supremacy, declare the validity of the king's marriage, and declare the injustice of Rome. They were to omit any reference to certain doctrines, or to preach neither for nor against them, for one year. These doctrines were purgatory, honouring of saints, clerical marriage, justification by faith, pilgrimages, and miracles. Sometimes, the Erastians found their compromise difficult to keep. One of those who found it so was Thomas Becon. He had been an agent of the royal supremacy under Cromwell, but was forced to recant in 1543 for certain indiscretions. One of his articles was that saints are not to be prayed for, indicating that when the Erastians did fall into disfavour, it was because they espoused Lollard doctrines.[71] To the left of the Erastians were the sacramentarians, who continued to espouse Lollard doctrines. A number of Lollards were indicted under the Six Articles, showing that Lollard sacramentarianism was an enduring feature of the English Reformation. For example, in 1541, John Athee was indicted for words against the real presence: 'that he wolde not beleave in that thinge that the knave preest made meanyng the sacramente of Thaltar nor in that that Longes wyf selleth, but he wolde beleave in godd that ys in heyyn'. He had added, 'so he mighte doo yf he wolde putt into yt a chekyns Legge meanyng the Sacramente of thaltare'.[72] Athee was a bitmaker of Stroud Green in Middlesex – a typical Lollard artisan. In the same year, Robert Wisdom, a sacramentarian colleague of Becon's, abjured articles of heresy, one of which was the Lollard assertion that saints should not be venerated or prayed to.[73]

In the years 1541 to 1546, it was not only Lollard artisans who were indicted for sacramentarianism; ex-bishops, a parliamentarian, courtiers, gentry, and the well-born Ann Askew were also caught in the web of the Six Articles. In 1543, it was rumoured in Kent that Archbishop Cranmer had given a lecture in which he described the eucharist as a similitude. Ideas that the eucharist was a figure of Christ had been current in the south for some time,[74] and it is likely that Lollardy played some part in this triumphant march of sacramentarian influence. Cranmer and his comissary in Canterbury protected prominent Lollards from the rigours of the law.[75] Given the intricacies of Lutheran and Zwinglian influence, it remains likely that Lollard precedents aided the spread of the new doctrines.

Turning to the trials of Protestant preachers under Mary, it is no surprise to find that they had taken over the language of Lollardy. To be sure, the Edwardine settlement was opposed by crude sacramentarianism that was Lollard in tone, but when it came to the point Edwardine Protestants had adopted Lollard arguments about the eucharist. John Hooper held the stark Lollard opinion that material bread and wine remained in the eucharist. John Rogers reverted to the old Lollard assertion that the church of Rome was the church of Antichrist, and held to the Lollard arguments about the eucharist, including the one that said that Christ was in heaven above. Rowland Taylor uttered similar Lollard views: that bread and wine remained in the eucharist, that the natural body of Christ is above, and that Christ's body cannot be in two places at once.[76] Humbler Protestants in Norfolk also displayed Lollard eucharistic opinions in their trials. These Lollard opinions of the eucharist are to be found throughout the diocese of Norwich under Mary. In 1555, Robert Bayock, weaver of Stoke-by-Nayland, held that the eucharist was but a figure or remembrance of Christ's passion. Hugo Cowper of Wixoe, husbandman, believed that the body of Christ is above and not in the eucharist. William Abraham, shoemaker of Bury St Edmunds, used the most common argument, that after the consecration the eucharist remains bread and wine.[77] The probability is that many of these artisans were Lollards who had prospered under Edwardine religion, while men like Rowland Taylor probably had contact with Lollard brotherhoods that survived in textile-producing towns like Hadleigh. One other contribution that Lollardy made was to the growth of the Radical Reformation in England. We have already come across the Lollard belief that the Virgin was but a sack to put Christ in, and this is accompanied by other versions of the celestial flesh doctrine such as that the Virgin is like a saffron bag, or a pudding when the meat was out. Joan Bocher was accused of Lollardy in 1528, became a notable sacramentarian in Kent in 1543, and was finally burnt under Edward for holding the full-blown Anabaptist view that Christ took no flesh of the Virgin.[78] In conclusion, it can be seen that Lollard ideas contributed to the English Reformation on the level of both bishops and artisans, and that Lollard brotherhoods persisted to form a basis for Puritanism later on.

Notes

1 C. Hill: *Puritanism and Revolution* (1958), 32.
2 C. Cross: *Church and People 1450–1660*, 53.
3 A.G. Dickens: *Lollards and Protestants in the Diocese of York 1509–1558* (1959), 1.
4 A.G. Dickens: *The English Reformation* (1964), 22–37.
5 G.R. Elton: *Policy and Police* (1972), 266n.
6 P.R.O., C.C. 306, 38.
7 J. Gairdner: *Lollardy and the Reformation in England* (1908), i, 100, 278, 307, 322.
8 *Letters and Papers, Foreign and Domestic, of the Reign of Henry VIII*, ed. J.S. Brewer, J. Gairdner, R.H. Brodie (1862–1932), v, 148.
9 Kent Record Office, Act Book, DRb/Pa/8, fo. 120r.
10 Rochester Diocesan Registry, Rochester Registers, iv, Register Fisher, fo. 133r.
11 Elton, *Policy and Police*, 356.
12 Norfolk and Norwich Record Office, Norfolk Quarter Sessions, Box 4, unfol.
13 J. Fines: 'Heresy Trials in the Diocese of Coventry and Lichfield 1511–12', *Journal of Ecclesiastical History*, xv (no. 2), (1963), 166–167.
14 P.R.O., State Papers 1, 113, xi, fo. 108v.
15 Lambeth Palace Library, Register Morton, fo. 104r.
16 *Letters and Papers*, iv (ii), 4150 (3).
17 J.A.F. Thomson: *The Later Lollards, 1414–1520* (1965) 35, 37, 40, 41, 64, 76, 134, 246–247, 250.
18 Dickens, *Lollards and Protestants*, 8.
19 *Register of Henry Chichele*, ed. E.F. Jacob (Canterbury and York Society, 1943), iii, 85, 108: iv, 203.
20 Lambeth Palace Library, Register Warham, fos. 159r–175v.
21 *Victoria County History, Kent*, ii (1974), 63–65.
22 Lambeth Palace Library, Register Cranmer, fo. 68r.
23 *Harpesfield's Visitation 1557*, ed. L.E. Whatmore (Catholic Record Society, 1950–51), i, 183.
24 P. Collinson: *The Elizabethan Puritan Movement* (1967), 96, 140, 266, 380.
25 British Library, Harleian 421, fos. 92r–93r.
26 Collinson, *Puritan Movement*, 36.
27 C.D. Cremeans: *The Reception of Calvinistic Thought in England* (Illinois Studies in Social Science, xxxi, 1949), 34.
28 Rochester Diocesan Registry, Rochester Registers, iii, Register Langdon, fos. 31r, 93v, 94r; iv, Register Savage, fo. 16v; Register Fisher, fos. 41v, 127r; Kent Record Office, Act Book 1526–1535, DRb/Pa/9, fos. 101v–103r; E.E. Reynolds: *Saint John Fisher* (1955), 120.
29 John Foxe: *Acts and Monuments*, ed. G. Townsend and R.S. Cattley (1837–1839), viii; 318–321.
30 Thomson, *Later Lollards*, 140–142.
31 W. Hale: *A Series of Precedents* (1847), 1, 2, 4, 5, 8, 12, 13, 60, 67, 69.
32 Foxe, *Acts and Monuments*, iv, 582.
33 *The Diary of Henry Machyn*, ed. J.G. Nichols (Camden Society xlii, 1848), 79; Foxe, *Acts and Monuments*, viii, 444.
34 Collinson, *Puritan Movement*, 84–86.
35 Thomson, *Later Lollards*, 119, 121.
36 *Letters and Papers*, iv (ii), 4029 (2).
37 *Acts of the Privy Council of England*, ed. J.R. Dasent (1890–1907), iv, 383, 395.
38 British Library, Harleian 421, fos. 209r–212r.
39 Thomson, *Later Lollards*, 25, 37.

40 Guildhall Library, Register Stokesley, 5391/11, fo. 71r.
41 K.G. Powell: *The Marian Martyrs and the Reformation in Bristol* (Bristol Branch of the Historical Association, 1972), 4, 5, 6, 9, 10, 11, 13.
42 Thomson, *Later Lollards*, 100; Collinson, *Puritan Movement*, 153.
43 Thomson, *Later Lollards*, 136; *Letters and Papers*, xii (i), 1316.
44 J.F. Davis: 'Lollard Survival and the Textile Industry in the South-east of England', *Studies in Church History*, iii (1966).
45 Dickens, *The English Reformation*, 70.
46 Cross, *Church and People 1450–1660*, 21–30.
47 Dickens, *The English Reformation*, 28.
48 *Letters and Papers*, v, 186.
49 British Library, Cotton Titus B VIII, fo. 151r.
50 British Library, Harleian 421, fo. 175r; Foxe, *Acts and Monuments*, vii, 158.
51 Foxe, *Acts and Monuments*, v, 36.
52 Foxe, *Acts and Monuments*, v, 34.
53 P.R.O. State Papers 1, 237, fo. 78r.
54 *Letters and Papers*, iv (ii), 4030.
55 British Library, Harleian 425, fo. 15r.
56 British Library, Vitellius B IX, fo. 131r.
57 *Letters and Papers*, iv (ii), 4030.
58 Dickens, *The English Reformation*, 70–71; Foxe, *Acts and Monuments*, iv, 680–682.
59 P.R.O. Star Chamber, 2/34/28.
60 Dickens, *The English Reformation*, 37, 76.
61 D.S. Bailey: *Thomas Becon and the Reformation in England* (1952), 5–16, 18–22; J.K. McConica: *English Humanists and Reformation Politics* (1965), 219–220; D.B. Knox: *The Doctrine of Faith in the Reign of Henry VIII* (1961), 250–253.
62 *Letters and Papers*, Addenda, i, 1463 (19).
63 British Library, Harleian 421, fo. 101v.
64 Lambeth Palace Library, Register Cranmer, fo. 71r.
65 Kent Record Office, Act Book 1523–1526, DRb/Pa/8, fo. 62r; Rochester Diocesan Registry, Rochester Registers iv, Register Fisher, fo. 127r.
66 Thomas More: *Dialogue Concerning Tyndale*, ed. W.E. Campbell (1927), 13.
67 Guildhall Library, Register Tunstall, 9531/10, fo. 135r.
68 Foxe, *Acts and Monuments*, iv, 680–682; Guildhall Library, Register Tunstall, fos. 137r–137v.
69 *Letters and Papers*, iv (ii), 4218, 4254 (1).
70 *Letters and Papers*, vii, 464.
71 Guildhall Library, Register Bonner, i, 9531/12, fo. 43v.
72 Guildhall Library, Register Thirlby, fo. 254r.
73 Guildhall Library, Register Bonner, i, fo. 43r.
74 British Library, Cotton Cleopatra E. V, fo. 397r.
75 *Letters and Papers*, xvii (ii), 546.
76 British Library, Harleian 421, fos. 37r, 40r, 41v.
77 British Library, Harleian 421, fos. 186r, 186v.
78 *Letters and Papers*, iv (ii), 4242 (3): xvii (ii), 546; Lambeth Palace Library, Register Cranmer, fo. 75r.

3

Youth and the English Reformation

SUSAN BRIGDEN

Sir Thomas More blamed the Reformation upon a conspiracy, a conspiracy in which 'lewde laddys' took concerted action to spread their heresy.[1] Catholic opponents of reform thought the younger generation eager to discard the faith of their fathers and easily won to the new ideas. There is nothing in the world older than the proclivity of one generation to reject the beliefs and mores of the last and for the elder generation to despair of rebellious youth,[2] but were young people really at the vanguard of the English Reformation? Since there were vastly more young people than old in early modern England, where perhaps half the population was under twenty,[3] it proves nothing to show that very many young people were won early to the new faith; rather it remains to explain whether Protestantism was the creed of youth and whether young people played a distinctive part in its passage.

Third of the Seven Ages of Man is adolescence, and it is this stage of life which is considered here.[4] Adolescence was thought to last between the ages of fifteen and twenty-five, and was marked at its beginning by one rite of passage – confirmation – and at its end by another – marriage.[5] This was recognized above all as an age which must be ruled, for 'lusty Iuventus youthe' was by nature ignorant, ill-disciplined and savage.[6] Ascham thought the age between seventeen and twenty-seven 'the most dangerous tyme of all a man's life, and most slipperie to stay well in'.[7] Children were not invariably regarded as innocent, as Christ had seen them;[8] rather, tainted by the Fall, they were 'propere and readye, without any teacher, to take and embrace vice, unthriftines and al maner noughtinesse'.[9] Six-teenth-century theologians and pedagogues, whether Catholic or Reformed, perceived the young as wild, headstrong and passionate, ever seeking to shock by rioting, swearing or unbridled sensuality.[10] This was a society in which the young were allowed no authority: the prevailing ideal was gerontocratic, for only the old had *gravitas* and wisdom enough to rule.[11] For young men to command was against the 'law of nature':[12] they must obey until they had achieved mastery of their baser desires. Only at the age of twenty-four were men deemed ready, for example, to be ordained to the priesthood or emancipated from apprenticeship.[13] Protes-tantism, with its doctrine of the priesthood of all believers, in attacking

Reprinted from *Past and Present*, 95 (1982).

the paternalistic authority of the priesthood and undermining the heads of
Catholic households, might appeal to young people seeking independence
and spiritual liberation: so, at least, the Reformation's opponents feared
and made play upon in their propaganda.

Catholic preachers and writers who sought, retrospectively, to explain
the pernicious spread of heresy invariably blamed the rebellious 'younger
and carnall sorte', and excoriated apostate Catholics for 'credityng the
merie conceytes of these yonglinges'.[14] It was, of course, easy to convince
the reactionary by attacking radical youth, to discredit the movement by
ascribing all responsibility to the habitually anarchic, but propaganda only
works if it plays upon real suspicions or desires. In January 1547, when
Edward VI's imminent accession augured a Protestant ascendancy, John
Feckenham gave a desperate sermon. He inveighed against the 'youthe of
England', whose upbringing showed the lamentable contemporary decline
'from pryde to lechery, from lechery to thefte, and from thefte to heresie'.[15]
To these defenders of the Catholic church the motives behind young
people's wilful adherence to the new faith were patently obvious: that
they found in the doctrines of Protestantism the perfect excuse and legiti-
mation for their natural tendency to disobedience, to follow their baser
instincts. Protestantism allowed sexual licence, it was said, and licence to
turn upside down the established order.[16] Everyone in a position of authority over the young was now scorned. Children would make 'a mery mockery
of their parents', and say:

> My father is an old doting foole and will fast upon the fryday; my
> mother goeth alwayes mumblinge on her beades. But you shall se me
> of another sorte, I warraunt you. For I will neuer folowe no suche
> superstitious folye; nor walke in the papisticall pathes of my par-
> ents.[17]

The clergy could no longer command respect, and 'disobedience to magistrates and aged men was at no tyme more practised'.[18] Such insubordination led to anarchy: apprentices and servants became 'not only odiouse to
the worlde but also unthriftye to their masters, and in maner became
masters themselves'.[19] All this subversion proceeded from adolescents'
new preoccupation with Scripture, it was said. The young and the poor
– those with little present stake in society – would interpret the Bible as
they wished and find in it what they looked for: the excuse for liberty and
equality. For the conservatives, 'parasite libertye' lay at the root of the
allegiance to Protestantism and all the consequent disaffection.[20] All this
was propaganda. For the reality behind the charges we look to the
reasons why young people might abandon the old faith for the new,
albeit reasons different for every one who did so.

I

Youthful religious doubt was nothing new. Even Pope Gregory VII had questioned central doctrines in his youth. Doubt would commonly assail the younger members of the religious orders as they came to tackle theology for the first time, especially within those orders, like the Dominicans, which existed to combine orthodox piety with advanced learning. The devil was known to challenge the convictions of the young, particularly of novices, for they were the most vulnerable, feeling themselves the first in the world to be racked by such doubt.[21] Catholic writers on the eve of the Reformation were much concerned with the problem of scrupulosity, the over-exacting conscience which would allow no redemption for the soul in sin.[22] Not surprisingly, young intellectuals suffered such spiritual torment most acutely, and Luther's crisis of faith was shared by countless others at the Reformation.[23] The 'fall into heresie' of William Roper, while a pupil at the inns of court, 'did growe of a scruple of his owne conscience, for lacke of grace and better knowledge'. With 'immoderate fasting and many prayers', Roper 'did werye himselfe euen *usque ad taedium* [until sick at heart]', till finally he found comfort in the Lutheran doctrines of justification and grace.[24] At Cambridge, Thomas Bliney, while in his early twenties, discovered the answer to his agonizing search for atonement and salvation through his humanist study of Scripture. He told how:

> I chanced upon this sentence of St. Paul . . . 'It is a true saying, and worthy of all men to be embraced, that Christ Jesus came into the world to save sinners; of whom I am the chief and principal'. This one sentence, through God's instruction and inward working . . . did so exhilarate my heart, being before wounded with the guilt of my sins, and being almost in despair, that immediately I felt a marvellous comfort and quietness, insomuch 'that my bruised bones leaped for joy'.[25]

Bilney was of the third generation of humanists, which Lewis Spitz described: the first generation had been pioneers, rediscovering classical learning; the second generation, while making advances in scholarship, was concerned also to contrast the ideal Christian life with the flawed contemporary reality; the third had a more radical vision, determined to reform a society which their elders had simply criticized.[26] Bilney's testament of faith is the most unequivocal of the early reformers' revelations of the spiritual reasons for rejecting the old religion for the saving Protestant message of justification by faith alone. More accused 'the false subtyle iugler the deuyll' of teaching 'these younge iuglers hys scolers, Luther, Huskyn, and Tyndale . . . to iugle awaye . . . the bylefe of all grace'.[27] It was not for doctrines of salvation alone that the reformers abandoned Catholicism, for their sermons were often marked more by attacks upon the materialism of the Catholic church, its multiplicity of laws and the corruption of its clergy than by the expounding of Scripture.[28] Yet the freedom to find the truth through the Bible alone had evident appeal for impatient young university converts, like Dr Sands, who averred: 'I know my years young, and my learning small; it is enough to know Christ crucified, and he hath learned nothing, that seeth not the great blasphemy that is in popery.'[29]

England's first Protestant evangelists – Cranmer, Latimer, Becon, Bale, Frith, Arthur, Garret, Joye, Bilney, Crome, Lambert, Hilsey and many others – were converted at the universities, chiefly at Cambridge.[30] In one way the age of people when they came to Protestantism may be seen as less material than the time or place in which they heard the new ideas, for to be in Cambridge in the 1520s, where a 'climate of heresy' existed, was to make men susceptible to conversion. Many of the first reformers were certainly not particularly young: Cranmer was already thirty by the time he was converted, Latimer, Tyndale and Hilsey were in their thirties, and one of the staunchest defenders of the sect was Dr Forman, who as Master of Queen's College was certainly among the establishment.[31] Yet it was usually the undergraduates and younger dons who were won to the new faith, to the alarm of elder dons. Bishop Longland had good reason to fear the 'corruption of yougeth' at Cardinal College, Oxford.[32] The presumption of young Protestants combating old doctors of theology is evident in literary imagery and in reality. More was incensed by 'good yong father Fryth whych now sodaynly commeth forth so sagely, that .iii. olde men, my brother Rastell, the bysshoppe of Rochester & I, matched wyth father Fryth alone, be now but very babys'; and Dr Jeffrey rebuked young Julius Palmer: 'Thou art but a beardless boy, start up yesterday out of the schools; and darest thou presume to offer disputation, or to encounter with a doctor?'[33]

Forces of conservatism were very strong, not least because for elders to apostatize would be to admit a lifetime of error and virtual redundancy. Dr John London, Warden of New College, Oxford, and arch-conservative, was appalled to discover in 1534 that his undergraduate nephew Edward had been writing anti-papal tracts and infecting London's own college with heresy, especially since London had just been smugly boasting with Gardiner of Oxford's stalwart orthodoxy. Calling Edward before him, London urged him to return to grace, to be chastened by his mother's grief, and to remember that 'hetherto ther was neuer heretycke off alle owar kyne . . . that owar forfathers awncyent wellernyd and holy mene culde not haue erryd thes many hunderyth yeres'.[34] Appeals to tradition and conformity did nothing to restrain young intellectuals from looking for the religious truth as they saw it, nor to prevent those who looked to the new faith for less than spiritual reasons.

Religious conversion occurs for reasons individual and personal: only if spiritual autobiographies of all Protestant converts existed would the motives and age of the convert be revealed. They do not, but from one young man's testimony of his discovery of the new faith general themes appear. In 1532 Richard Hilles, apprentice to a London merchant-taylor, wrote beseeching Thomas Cromwell for protection, and described how:

> on a certayne Sonday at after non when I was idell I thought that I wolde . . . goo abowt some good thyng to kepe me from idelnes, and then I remembryd that a good honest yong man dyd ones requyre me to shew hym my mynde in how I dyd understand that part off Sancte James pystell that sayd how Abraham was iustiffyed by workes.

Hilles did write a tract upon that subject: this was heresy and, during Lord Chancellor More and Bishop Stokesley's persecution, folly, as his masters pointed out, calling him 'opynatyffe'. He said 'they askyd me yff I thought myselffe wyser than all other men, and I answeryd that I countyd myselffe all togyther noughte, and the worde of god to be very truthe'.[35] Hilles's determined apostasy confirmed all the elder generation's perennial fears: of the arrogance of youth in thinking that it asked questions never asked before, and provided answers better than those of men older and wiser; that the devil made work for idle hands; that the consorting of young men together could only mean trouble.

II

There were many reasons for young people to be more than usually frustrated and disaffected in the early sixteenth century, and looking for a cause and salvation. The Reformation came at a time of chronic social and economic instability, and where there was economic distress in a society which favoured age the young would suffer most. The cause of Protestantism and the cause of the poor were soon associated – an allegiance seen as malignant by conservatives, who feared social disruption – but religion transcended the usual barriers of rank and wealth, and the new faith drew adherents from across the social spectrum.[36] Yet there were powerful reasons – social and economic as well as spiritual – why young people should have been particularly attracted to reform. From a study of London (in the section which follows), where the new doctrines of the Reformation were first and most fervently spread, and where there were more young people than anywhere else in England, such reasons might appear.

The first cause of instability and hardship in the early sixteenth century was the vast rise in population. London grew – almost pathologically, contemporaries thought – from a city of around 60 000 in 1500 to one of about 200 000 by 1600, overspilling its ancient walls.[37] To the capital there was 'great resorte and confluence', for London had always drawn its population from the rest of England and from Europe.[38] Of seventy-nine deponents before a London commissary court between 1537 and 1544 only ten had been born in London, and this was not untypical.[39] Adolescents were the most restless, the most untrammelled of the population, and the most evidently on the move.[40] Young people streamed to the metropolis in search of their fortunes, and maybe for freedom from the constraints of their country communities.[41] Those who sought a craft came from all over the realm to be apprenticed. G.D. Ramsay has analysed the origins of 1088 young men admitted to the freedom of the city in the period 1551–3 and found that less than a quarter (244) were from the city, only 80 from the Home Counties, and the rest from much futher afield, including 168 from Yorkshire.[42] Young men and women also came to serve the growing numbers of nobility and gentry who were congregating in the capital.[43] Most difficult to chart, and most subversive, were the vagrant poor, overwhelmingly children, adolescents and young adults, who flooded the city and in the end made of London a paupers' graveyard.[44]

The streets of London were not paved with gold for these immigrants. The vastly rising population put enormous pressure on the medieval gild, parish and ward structure of the city, let alone upon the supply of food and housing.[45] The craft gilds of London had long controlled not only the economic life of the capital, but social and political life also, since only membership of one of the seventy-five or so companies conferred the freedom of the city, and with it civic privilege.[46] The craft system was the only path to social status in the political and economic cartel of London, and it was essentially gerontocratic.[47] The medieval gilds, with independent craft masters producing in small workshops, had so ordered matters that the apprentices bound to the master to learn the trade, and the journeymen, waiting to set up their own establishments, had the expectation of being masters and freemen themselves – in time. But the frequent city and company orders by the mid-sixteenth century that masters should not take on more than two apprentices, and the penalties imposed, suggest that the number of apprentices was growing too fast. From about the turn of the sixteenth century, mastership could no longer be the expectation of every apprentice and journeyman.[48] As the gilds became ever more oligarchical a significant, but as yet little understood, organizational change occurred within them: the yeomanry or junior branch emerged in competition with the livery, the ruling senior members of the gild.[49] There were frequent clashes between the 'young men' or 'bachelors' and the liveries, as in the serious crises in the Shermen's Company in 1510 and 1518, within the Goldsmiths' Company in 1529 and in the Saddlers' Company in the 1540s, and this is evidence of a wider dissatisfaction.[50]

The mounting burden of population upon an inflexible economy had the effect of holding back youth, as Keith Thomas has shown. For if economic opportunites were to be limited, then those who held authority would monopolize them.[51] In London in 1556 young people were barred from competing with their elders by delaying their freedom from apprenticeship until the age of twenty-four, and the Statute of Artificers of 1563 expressly protected 'aged artificers' and 'ancient householders'.[52] Linked with the frustration of being denied economic independence was another: apprentices were forbidden to marry.[53] The extension of apprenticeship meant the extension of bachelorhood. The London ordinance of 1556 made a Malthusian attempt to end the 'greate povertye, peniurye and lacke of liuinge', which debilitated the city and stemmed from the 'ouer hastie maryages and over sone settyng upp of householdes of and by the youthe . . . which have comonly usyd . . . to marye themselves as sone as euer they come owte of their apprentyshode, be they never so yonge and unskilful'.[54] Although the age of marriage was late anyway, such restrictions can hardly have been popular, and the presence of so many unsettled young men added to the instability of the city.

The youth of London were known to be politically unstable and easy to rally to a cause. In the capital news travelled quickly and young men would soon band together. Evil May Day was far from the first or the last youth riot in early modern England, but it was the most serious. The trouble began early in 1517 when one John Lincoln stirred 'younge and euell disposed people' to be 'reuenged on the merchaunt straungiers'. Wolsey, fearing rebellion among 'young and ryotous people', commanded the city rulers to maintain the peace, and it was thought best to 'kepe the younge men asonder'. But when an alderman, finding 'two young men in chepe plaiynge at Buckelers, and a great company of younge men lokynge on them', attempted to arrest them, they resisted 'and cryed prentyses and clubbes'. The following day a thousand rioted, and most of the prisoners taken were 'poore prentises' and 'yongelinges'.[55] A similar rising by apprentices against aliens was only narrowly averted in 1529, and young Londoners continued to be obsessively suspicious of foreigners.[56] John Bradford sought to rouse young people to the Protestant cause, and did so by warning them of the Spaniards' designs 'not to have one lyving that hath byn born these xx years; but either to dryve them into forren realmes, or ells to make them slaves lyke the Mores, or ells to destroy them at home'.[57] So, as Philip II's 'retynew and harbengers came ryding thorugh London' in January 1554, 'the boyes pelted at theym with snowballes; so hatfull was the sight of ther coming into theym'.[58]

Young people had their heroes, and were likely to follow those whose interests were very different from those the crown and the stability of the realm required. The duke of Somerset had the dubious political advantage of having the partisanship of many of the young and poor of London; dubious precisely because this support would in itself alienate the political orders. Somerset's popular following seems to have derived largely from his supposed sympathy for reform: during the coup which brought the

Protector down in October 1551 John Cardmaker, an inflammatory Protestant preacher, urged the people to stand by the duke lest the advances for the Reformation be lost, for 'thow he had a falle he was not undone'.[59] Indeed in April 1551, so it was alleged, Somerset conspired to raise the Londoners: the plan was to call 'the earl of Warwick to a bankett with the marques of Northampton & divers other to cutte off their hedes'. Mr. Partridge 'shuld raise London and take the greate seale with the prentis of London'. The government forces were to be 'assauted by two thousand footmen' of Mr Vane, and by the 'idle people' who took the duke's part. If Somerset were to be overtaken he would run through the city and 'crie libertye, libertye to raise the prentises'.[60] Somerset's planned coup was never to be executed, but the source of his allegiance and the charges whereby his opponents chose to topple him reveal the importance of apprentices in London politics, especially opposition politics.[61]

London apprentices would continue to present a spectre of instability. In June 1595 the mayor feared that 'the great disorder of multitudes of rebellious apprentices . . . shall not be suppressed until some of them be punished according to the martiall lawe'.[62] The radicalism of London apprentices continued into the seventeenth century, when they acted together to petition parliament, and beyond.[63] At any sign of general disaffection the city's first precaution was always to order a curfew for apprentices and servants, to close the alehouses where they would loiter with intent. During the Reformation, orders for the supervision of young people were frequent; especially so in Mary's reign, when young people had common cause – persecuted Protestantism – and common enemies – the priesthood and the Spaniards.[64]

The constant alarm of the authorities at the association of young people, and fear of what they might do, suggests that they were regarded as a separate order. Adolescents departing their homes in country villages and finding themselves uprooted in the metropolis, unused to its ways, may well have felt more of a sense of solidarity with others in their own condition and less of a sense of deference to their superiors.[65] So at least the development of a distinctive apprentice literature might suggest.[66] Adrift from their families, adolescents would look for new associations and find the gang. Apprentices ideally lived with their masters as they would with their own families, promising obedience, and not to run away, in return for being taught a trade and being given their keep. Bequests for apprentices in the wills of city masters reveal how well this paternalistic system might work, how little it was questioned, but there were, naturally enough, common reports of apprentices running away or otherwise disobeying their masters, of masters having to answer for their apprentices' good behaviour[67] and, conversely, of unsatisfactory masters exploiting and maltreating their apprentices.[68] The Reformation brought new causes for discord: apprentices began to neglect their work in order to attend Protestant sermons or read Protestant tracts; would 'talke muche of the scripture, goodes worde, and yet wyll not learne therof to be obedient and gentle vnto theyr maysters'.[69] In 1546 Richard Wilmot, an eighteen-year-old apprentice, and his young friend were voluble supporters of Dr Crome in his refusal to recant his sacramentarian sermons: for this they were whipped, and Wilmot's angry master threatened to confiscate and burn his books.[70] With the new faith had come new opportunites and excuses for disobedience.

Adolescents were most turbulent in their play. In their traditional misrule, when normal social behaviour was abrogated and the rules in relations reversed, young people might make their feelings felt in a society in which they had no authority. Lords of Misrule were chosen at Christmas and piped around the parish, free to do as they would.[71] In 1524 this *carte blanche* was recognized officially when a Master of Misrule in London was pardoned for murder.[72] London schoolboys had their special games: 'disorderly in the open street', the 'pigs' of St Anthony's school would challenge the 'pigeons' of St Paul's with '"Salue tu quoque, placet tibi mecum disputare, placet? [Greetings to you, you would like to dispute with me, would you?]", and so proceeding from this to questions in Grammar, they vsually fall from wordes to blowes'.[73] Pupils at the inns of court would riot, and schoolboys 'bar out' their masters.[74] The London apprentices too had their traditions: they chanted rhymes when Bow Bell was rung late, they pulled down the brothels on Shrove Tuesday.[75] Youthful high spirits and the desire to humiliate unpopular elders did not find expression in London in the creation of organized youth groups, such as the Abbot of Gaiety and his Good Children of Lyon and others studied by Natalie Zemon Davis, yet in the 'rough music' which punished marital quarrellers, adulterers and cuckolds by publicly shaming them, adolescents played a leading part. The apprentices of a goldsmith 'misusyd' their master in February 1558 'by makyng a horned head upon his dore sett betwene the lettres of his name and other lyke villanyes'.[76] New sport was to be provided by the Reformation: not without reason did More liken Tyndale to an 'abbote of mysrule in a Christemas game'.[77]

In its many holidays and festivals the Catholic church had given to the young games and a chance for misrule. On Childermass Day in the festival of the Boy Bishop a child would dress as a bishop, preach a sermon and parade around the parish;[78] Lent would be ushered in on Ash Wednesday by boys throwing at cocks or at the effigy of 'Jack-a-Lent'.[79] Many of the Catholic holy days coincided with pagan festivals – Midsummer Day became the feast of the Nativity of St John the Baptist, and when Easter fell on 24 April May Day was followed immediately by Hock Monday and Hock Tuesday – and the danger was that their spirits would become confused also.[80] The Protestants were to attack many of the cherished festivals of the Catholic church as pagan, which they were, and as soon as they were empowered to excise them from the liturgical year they did so. Holy days, processions and games were outlawed early by the Edwardian regime, and young people must have felt their loss most, for they had provided, at the least, a chance for insolent behaviour.[81] In May 1547 many 'light persones beyng mennes servantes' were punished for assembling themselves in the traditional way 'in a may game', and in 1549 masters were commanded to keep 'servauntes and youth' from joining May games, interludes or gatherings on holy days.[82] Yet although the Reformation did restrict the religious resources available for holidays and for distintive gatherings of young people, in other ways reform had a special appeal and clear role for the young, ways that did not have all to do with Protestant teaching.

III

The reasons for turning away from Catholicism to Protestantism were diverse: for some it was enough to discover spiritual salvation in the new doctrines of grace, for others the appeal lay rather in liberation from oppressive authority, spiritual or secular. Even before the Reformation many in the church and in secular society were growing impatient with those who had the power to reform, but never did so – the elders in whom alone authority was vested. John Colet exhorted his 'reverend fathers' in the Convocation of 1511 'to the endeavour of reformation of the church's estate', although concerned that it was 'unmeet, yea and almost malapert, that I, a servant, should counsel my lords, that I, a son, should teach you, my fathers'[83] (albeit his radicalism was hardly that of youth, and his filial piety a convention). The new faith had never meant to challenge the social order, to question deference; indeed, its theologians insisted upon obedi-ence to divinely ordained superiors.[84] Tyndale even changed 'this worde preste, into this worde senyour'.[85] Yet Protestants soon came to attack paternal authority: the priesthood as 'ghostly fathers' to 'ghostly children', the Pope and fathers of Catholic households. The doctrine of the priest-hood of all believers could provoke irreverence to the dignitaries of the old faith. In the *Dialogue or Conversation between a Father and his Son*, published in Erfurt in 1523, the son, newly out of Wittenberg, challenged the priestly monopoly of spiritual truth, the priesthood as sole repository of divine authority: 'Oho, father, I too am a priest and consecrated. Christ says so, Matthew 5: You are the salt of the earth. He does not say "The priests are"; no, "you are". I also can absolve as well as any priest or monk'.[86] Much the same would be said by the young radicals of the English Reformation.

Two sacraments of the Catholic church held the people in thrall, and gave the priesthood its particular authority: the mass and confession.[87] To deny them was to reject priestly authority, and to deny clerical power was to vitiate the potency of the sacraments. At the Reformation it was the miracle of transubstantiation which the Protestants attacked most vehemently and were prepared to die for denying. The mass had been so central that it seemed impossible for anyone nurtured in Catholicism to pronounce the nature of the divine presence therein a matter of uncertainty, let alone indifference.[88] Yet it may have been that young people, being imbued less long with the doctrine, were more free to question it. More insisted that 'euery chylde that is of competent age / hath herde þt god gyueth by hys holy ordynaunce . . . grace wyth all his .vii. sacramentes',[89] but quite when that age of spiritual discretion was, and whether children attended church and observed the miracle before they partook of the mass themselves, are important problems, as yet unsolved. Charles Phythian-Adams wondered whether children attended church at all before confirmation.[90] If young people were indeed only exposed to the sacrament of the altar at the age of confirmation, then those who were rejecting it at the Reformation were not spurning in adolescence what they had accepted in childhood, in the way of modern adolescents, but rather objecting to it *de novo*.[91] Seventeen-year-old William Mauldon foresaw 'by the spirit' even in 1540, 'when the mass most flourished, altars with the sacrament thereof being in their most high veneration', that the mass would be put down.[92]

Attacks upon the sacrament of the altar became ever more common in the 1530s and 1540s, and it was very often young people who were found reviling the mass. Denial of priestly power to perform the miracle was one reason for its repudiation: 'the newe sorte' would taunt 'Nowe, Syr John, where fynde you your Masse in scripture, or who gaue you auctorite to make god?'[93] Young people died among the first Protestant martyrs for their sacramentarianism: under Henry VIII, John Porter, 'that gentyll and godlye yonge manne', Richard Mekins, 'a poore symple ladd of 17 yeres of age', Andrew Huet, a London apprentice of twenty-four, John Frith, Anne Askew and others went to the stake.[94] Some, like John Warne, a clothworker's servant of twenty and 'pestilent heretyque & ranke sacramentarye', who was before the court of aldermen and privy council in 1546, and John Davis, a blind boy of twelve from Gloucester, narrowly escaped, Warne only to be martyred under Mary.[95] During Edward VI's reign, when 'Mother Messe' was officially denounced, attacks upon the sacrament were rife, but only punished when too rowdy and disruptive. On Corpus Christi day in 1548, the most sacred of festivals, two boys and a girl dared to profane the sacrament of the altar at their London parish church, and that September a boy of thirteen or fourteen, Charles Tylby, was whipped naked, for 'att the tyme of the elevacon of the blessed sacrament . . . he dvd cast his cap att yt'.[96] The priest at St Peter Paul's Wharf reprimanded Cheseborow's young son for 'playing the boy in the quyer' and 'prophanyng'.[97] As we shall see, many of the Marian martyrs for Protestantism were young, but their adherence to reform was of a different spirit, for they were conformist, dying for repudiating the mass which they had been brought up to believe idolatrous.

The Catholic priesthood had long held great power over the laity in confession and absolution, because every Christian who had reached the age of discretion was to confess at least once a year.[98] How often people did confess is a matter for speculation, but it is more than likely that fathers and masters, who absconded themselves, would insist that their young charges attend.[99] Medieval confessional manuals were full of advice regarding youthful failings. So vehement and widespread were attacks upon auricular confession at the Reformation that it seemed as if it was almost a reason in itself for abandoning the old faith.[100] With Protestantism came the absolute denial of the priestly power to bind and loose; as young John Staunton, servant to a Lutheran merchant, challenged his old confessor, George Rowland:

> Sur, there ys one thynge in my stommack which grevyth my conscyence very sore, and that is by reason of a sermon that I herd heyre yesterdaye of master Latimer sayng that no man of hym selffe had authoryte to for gyue synnes and . . . therfor I am in dought whether I shall haue remyshon of my synnes of you or not.[101]

More radical yet was to claim a direct relationship with God. In 1536 a boy of twenty, one of the 'Christian Brethren' of Mendlesham, Suffolk, peremptorily told his curate, 'I come to desyer you to set my name in yor boke þt I am shryuen and forgeuen of godd, for this mornyng I spake with hym soo þt I know myself assoylyd [absolved]'.[102]

Priestly authority was further challenged when the laity left their clergy behind them in knowledge of Scripture and theology. The educated Catholic laity, dissatisfied with parish clergy too arrogant or ignorant to instruct them,[103] could and did read orthodox devotional tracts, like Richard Whitford's *Werke for Housholders* (1530), in which they were urged to 'gather your neyghbours aboute you on the holy day, specially the yong sorte & rede them this poore lesson'.[104] Scriptural knowledge did not necessarily have anything to do with literacy or education, for the godly could know God's word 'by the spirit', but increased educational opportunity in the early sixteenth century stimulated theological study. The more that the laity learnt for themselves the more impatient they grew with their clergy. Bishop Foxe warned the episcopate in 1534 that 'The lay people do now know the holy Scripture better than many of us; . . . moreover, they have so opened these controversies by their writings, that women and children may wonder at the blindness and falsehood that have been hitherto.'[105] In 1538 Master Laburne addressed his parish at St Benet Gracechurch, 'raylyng against yong wittes' there, who had gone to hear Latimer preach and now denied the power of saints and their images. 'St. Austen', Laburne pointed out, had 'landed in the yle of Thannet bryngyng with hym a crosse of wod and a picture of Christ, in whyche tyme, he sayd, that he was sure that then so wyse men were as now be'. To which the 'yong wittes' knowingly objected that St Augustine was the 'legate of a reprobate master the pope'. Moreover, Laburne gravely embarrassed himself when he sought to show that St Paul had failed to prove predestination, for, compared with his audience, he 'lacked Scripture', and losing himself in his argument, was driven to end, 'O, the inestymable power of God'.[106]

Some young Protestants showed their contempt for priests much more aggressively. Anticlericalism is commonly said to have been rife and the harbinger of the Reformation, yet even in London it was not until the late 1540s, when Protestant doctrines undermining the status and function of the priesthood had taken hold, that attacks upon the clergy were really widespread. Closer investigation reveals, not surprisingly, that it was usually young people who were the aggressors. In 1543, as he walked through the city, Sir William Gravesend was 'lewdely sett uppon and evell entreted' by a band of 'prenteses and mennes servantes which had played at fute ball'.[107] This attack seems to have been unprovoked, and in this way typical: simply the priestly dress and shaven crown were enough to stir this juvenile impudence. In 1546 a prophecy-monger predicted that 'within this twelve moneth ye shall see that every boye in the streat shall spytte in the preystes faces and hurl stones at them':[108] sure enough, in November 1547 the Edwardian government found it necessary to issue a proclamation ordering serving-men and apprentices not to 'use such insolence and evil demeanour towards priests as reviling, tossing of them, taking violently their cappes and tippets from them'.[109] Mocking priests became the favourite pastime of London boys during Mary's reign: a 'lytle boye' had his crown 'shorne lyke a pryest' by an apprentice, and it is not hard to guess who might have been responsible for dressing a dead cat like a massing priest in April 1554.[110] When Rowland Taylor, the martyr, was forced to don Catholic vestments he postured and jested, 'If I were in Cheap, should I not have boys enough to laugh at these apish toys, and toying trumpery?'[111]

Attacks upon priests became legion as the Reformation progressed: although in part youthful pranks, they were more than simply anti-authoritarian delinquency, for they invariably took place during some Catholic service, sermon or procession, and were directed against the conservative clerical hierarchy. That Bonner was persistently insulted by juvenile opponents, for example, is suggested by Foxe's tale of the bishop's furious and supposedly unprovoked assault upon a group of boys bathing in the Thames.[112] John Hale was whipped in June 1555 because he 'malycyously and scornefully did laye a puddynge in one of the prestes of Powles necke in cheapesyde as he was goyng in generall processyon', and threw another at Bonner.[113] Other assaults were more serious: 'a desperate ladde strake at the preste' celebrating mass at St Margaret Westminster and almost killed him, and Friar Peto nearly died from a stone thrown at him.[114] The restored monks provided new targets. While leading Catholic clerics were jeered at by irreverent young radicals, especially during periods of reaction, the Protestant evangelists were their heroes, as we shall see. Such as Crome, Latimer and Cardmaker would gather crowds of young devotees – apparently the same crowds that Watson, Weston and Gardiner had to be protected from.[115]

The conflict between radical youth and elderly conservatism was very evident at the inns of court, where Protestantism spread early among the young members, despite all the efforts of the senior benchers to repress it.[116] The relentlessness of Sir Thomas More's interrogation of James Bainham in 1532 stemmed not only from Bainham's obduracy in refusing to name the gentlemen of the inns of court already 'infected', but also from More's horror that heresy had touched even his own family, for William Roper had apostatized, to be saved only by More's prayers.[117] Some of the most fervent proselytizers of Protestantism – Simon Fish, James Bainham, John Bradford, Thomas Sampson, Bartlet Green – were members of the inns of court, and there Anne Askew came to consort with the like-minded.[118] So too, among the elder benchers, were some of the Reformation's sternest critics – Judge Shelley, who lambasted Robert Barnes, and Sir Anthony Fitzherbert, who vowed that neither he nor any of his family should ever profit from the Dissolution.[119] But even young renegades would often become conservative professional lawyers in time: Chief Justice Sir Roger Cholmely did so, and counselled young men before him for 'misorders'

> in yougth, I was, as you ar now: and I had twelue feloes like unto my self, but not one of them came to a good ende. And therefore, folow not my example in yougth, but folow my councell in aige.[120]

Young Protestants would also be found rebelling against reactionary parents. It may be that the 'dark corners of the land' remained unconverted to the Word because the elder generation were left behind, hostile and unresponsive to religious change, while their young people departed for London and the towns to exert a radical influence there. Once they had left home we usually know nothing of their links with their families, but some lost their families too as they abandoned the old faith. Intransigent Catholic parents might cast out their cuckoo Protestant offspring, as Julius Palmer's mother did when he confessed that he did not believe as his father and 'all our forefathers have done':

> 'If thou be at that point', saith she, 'I require thee to depart from my house and out of my sight, and never take me more for thy mother

hereafter. As for money and goods I have none of thine, thy father bequeathed nought for heretics: faggots I have to burn thee.'[121]

Some Protestant children were eager to win their elders to the Word – Nicholas Sheterden wrote to his mother before his martyrdom pleading with her to 'consider your own soul's health is offered you; do not cast it off: we have not long time here'[122] – and some, like Roger Holland and Robert Plumpton, were successful.[123]

IV

The early Reformation was a revolutionary movement, Protestantism a fifth column within the English church. Young converts to the new creed were the prime movers in its passage, activists in spreading the heresy, and had an impact quite out of proportion to the influence they otherwise had in society. Meeting in secret conventicles to expound the Gospel, watching illicit interludes with a Protestant message, singing heretical ballads, posting bells and spreading forbidden literature all well suited the fraternal and subversive mentality of unsettled young people. As sedition as well as heresy, such activities were doubly dangerous. Sir Thomas More was fearful of the determination of 'lewde laddys' to infiltrate their heresy and of their turbulence (doubtless remembering his impotence to halt the Evil May Day riots while under-sheriff of London).[124] When one child in More's household, taught 'vngracyouse heresye' by George Joye, began to instruct another child in error, More had him whipped, for his aim was always to prevent the corruption of youth, and to 'make almost euery boy able to perceyue the false folly' of the new doctrine.[125] Gardiner was incensed by Richard Hilles's proselytizing in 1540, and accused him of trying 'to draw . . . all men after you, (especially foolish boys, and young men like yourself)', of denying the right thinking of his parents, 'grave and prudent persons'.[126] Young 'brethren' would meet together in conventicles to expound Scripture, those who could read instructing those who could not, and would save to buy copies of forbidden works[127] Protestant apprentices were soon entering the book trade, and young book agents operating.[128] The brethren supported each other under persecution: evangelical vigilantes sprang the faithful from prison, as they did Andrew Huet and George Constantine, and the London apprentices relayed messages and gathered money for Anne Askew while she was in Newgate.[129] Young men were among the most daring of the 'gospellers', who expounded the Bible from the pulpits and disrupted services with 'brabbling of the New Testament'.[130]

The early Protestants were determined that the Word should go forth at whatever risk. William Roper was not content to 'whisper' the new doctrine 'in hugger mugger, but thirsted very sore . . . to diuulge it, and thought himselfe very able so to doo, and it were euen at Paules Crosse';[131]

not that John the Baptist had bidden 'euery boye go forth and take hym selfe for an apostle and go preche', as More remarked sourly.[132] Just as Protestantism spread first among an educated élite, so it would be spread by them, and university-trained theologians with the 'ytche of preaching' were the great evangelists of the Reformation. Many left academe for a wider arena, and came above all to the capital.[133] Some stayed at the universities to convert new generations of undergraduates, and one of the great grudges of the conservatives was that the Dissolution had pulled down 'C prynsly howsys . . . puttyng owte godly, lernyd & devoyte men that sarvyd God daye and nyghte, and thurte yn ther plase a sorte of lowsye boyes'.[134] Others became schoolmasters: William Tyndale taught in the West Country;[135] Geoffrey Lome, porter at St Anthony's, More's old school, abjured in 1528 for 'advauncing the Lutheran sect' by circulating forbidden works;[136] John Lambert spent most of the 1530s teaching Latin and Greek in London;[137] Thomas Harding, while a master at Winchester College, introduced a receptive John Louthe to Frith's *Purgatorye*, and Julius Palmer taught at Reading.[138] The education of youth was recognized to be of paramount importance: a radical sectary, John Erley, pleaded in 1540 for 'some godly mater in ryme or mytre to geve currage to litle children to read the word of God',[139] and catechisms were produced by both sides. Protestants became tutors to the children of the gentry; some in houses where there was sympathy for their faith, like Cobbe, who was 'cherisshed as a jewell' in Stephen Vaughan's household,[140] and others where it was feared that the tutor would make the pupil 'lyke hymselfe, too good a Latinyste and too great an heretyke'.[141] Success for the movement would come when they won the next generation, especially the children of the ruling orders.[142] The most dazzling child convert was, of course, Edward VI, who, like the boy king Josiah, would crush the 'preestes and prophetes of Baall'.[143]

Preaching, for impatient evangelical Protestants, was the way by which men's minds might be illuminated by the Word, which had been hidden from them for a millennium by men 'angered to lose their glorye and give it to Christ'.[144] Sermons had not been a popular spectator sport before the Reformation, unless some friar preached, but when the 'prechers of novelties' would give 'iii sermonis in a daye' large audiences would gather to listen.[145] The evangelists, many once friars themselves, assumed the traditional role of the friars in opposition to covetous secular clergy, and borrowed Lollard invective against the worldliness of the church.[146] While many must have found these attacks upon the old piety they held dearest quite unpalatable, and stayed away,[147] there was one section of society which apparently flocked to hear – the young. There was always the problem of keeping young people in towns off the streets and at work: in principle they were to work as long as there was light to see, but in practice there was much loitering on street corners, consorting in alehouses, playing football and forbidden card games, and watching seditious interludes.[148] To encourage idle youth to listen to edifying sermons was a worthy Protestant aim – in 1551 at St Benet Gracechurch there was 'a lecture for seruantes on the Mondayes'[149] – but might have disturbing consequences. Beyond surmise that young people with time on their hands might join the crowds which attended sermons – perhaps to listen, perhaps to jeer – there is evidence of the authorities' alarm that they were doing so. In 1548 there was 'moche contraversy and moche besynes in Powlles every sonday, and syttyng in the churche, and of none that were honest persons, but boyes and persons of lyttylle reputacyon'.[150] To prevent such dissension all sermons were halted by proclamation in December 1548, and an order was given by the Mercers' Company that every householder 'shall loke to his apprentices or other servauntes that they do not ronne to Poules a gasynge or gapynge as they have ben wonte to do heretofore for because that theire shall be noo sermondes ther yet a whyle'.[151]

Why should young people so eagerly attend these sermons, even the tirades of the conservatives as well as the exhortations of the Protestants? Some were, of course, sincerely delighted to hear Scripture expounded by the reformers; Richard Mekins was certainly won to the new faith by Robert Barnes, and Huet by John Frith; Dr Crome gathered a circle of supporters, and many spoke of the charismatic Latimer.[152] If the reformers were, moreover, preaching a message of social as well as spiritual egalitarianism from the Gospel, then the young and dispossessed might find a special inspiration in their preaching.[153] Many probably enjoyed the spectacle of seeing images destroyed, or the battles waged in the pulpits between radical and reactionary clergy, which became acrimonious and even ludicrous, as when Hubberdine, dancing in rage against Latimer, fell through the pulpit.[154] Young Protestants would go along to hear the old church pilloried during periods of reaction, to revile the papists, especially if conservative preachers gratified them by singling them out for special criticism.[155] In Mary's reign their disapproval was volubly expressed: when Dr Bourne preached at Paul's Cross there was a 'gret up-rore and showtyng at ys sermon, as yt [were] lyke madpepull, watt yonge pepell and woman [as] ever was hard, as herle-borle, and castyng up of capes'.[156] A 'stripling' was whipped about London in November 1555, as an example for others, for speaking against 'the byshop that dyd pryche the Sonday a-for'.[157] When many were gathered together their opposition was dangerous, and Catholic clerics who preached in the first month of Mary's reign took their lives in their hands. At a sermon by Dr Watson on 20 August 1553 one hundred and twenty armed men 'stode aboute the crosse wt their halberds to garde the preacher and to apprehend them that wolde strive', and that month the mayor gave special orders that no servants should attend the Paul's Cross sermons or carry weapons.[158] Whether these young audiences attacked conservatives for sport, whether through outraged conviction, will always be uncertain. Adolescents would anyway be more likely to heckle and jeer than their elders, who would prefer more sedate forms of opposition, but the fact that their taunts were always reserved for popish preachers, and the reformers never thus maltreated, reveals their sympathies.

If Protestantism had taken away holidays as pagan it gave in return the chance for young people to congregate for other sport. The most violent of new sixteenth-century pastimes was iconoclasm. As reform spread so did reckless image-breaking, and in England, as in France and the Netherlands, it seems that it was the young who were the statue smashers[159] When the Rood of Grace of Boxley Abbey was publicly exposed as a fraud by Latimer it was left to the 'rude people and boyes' to smash; again, in 1547, a mechanical image of Christ was destroyed by 'boyes'.[160] The pupils of Bodmin free school had a special game: emulating the partisanship of their elders they banded into two factions, for the new religion and for the old, each with its captain. They fought fiercely until one boy managed to blow up a calf with gunpowder, the master whipped offenders and the division was ended.[161] In March 1554 three hundred children gathered in Finsbury Fields, 'divided up into two bands and fought at the quarrel of the Queen against Wyatt'.[162] It is natural for children to imitate in sport the conflicts they see in society, but there is a suspicion that some of these childish games were stage-managed by those old enough to know better: in the wake of rebellion they were dangerously unsettling. A 'yonge mayden' playing 'the byrde that spake in the wall' in Aldersgate Street, again in March 1554, drew huge crowds by responding to such leading questions as 'What is the masse?' with the correct Protestant answer, 'Idolatry'. But she had been 'procured to do that feat' by one Drakes and others, who gave her a whistle.[163] It is possible that children were led to their apparently spontaneous zeal against popish idolatry by their elders. The iconoclasm at Rouen in 1562, allegedly initiated by children, seems to have been master-minded by men who wished for more drastic reform than they were prepared openly to espouse,[164] and modern terrorist organizations, whether in the Congo or in Ulster, are known deliberately to exploit their junior members by sending them into the front line of the fighting.[165] But even so, children may soon become accustomed to violence and join in the conflict of their own accord. When a boy in present-day Northern Ireland was asked whether boys were being paid by older men to throw stones at British soldiers, he laughed and said that they did it for nothing.[166] This boy was of a generation brought up during the 'troubles', knowing nothing other than sectarian conflict: so it was for a generation of English children growing up Protestant in the 'progress time' in the south-east to abhor papistry. With the Marian reaction these young Protestants would become involved in a protest movement of a different kind.

V

Any stance of radical youth and reactionary age in one generation was likely to be turned about within another as each succeeding generation rebelled against the prevailing mores. Protestantism was changed from orthodoxy to outlawed heresy on Mary's accession, and the Protestant younger generation found themselves unwitting rebels; their rebellion now not wilful apostasy, but their refusal to conform and their campaign to thwart the popish establishment. Any one aged less than twenty on Mary's accession could never have known England under papal authority, and no one reaching the age of confirmation during Edward's reign would ever have received the mass, officially at least.[167] John Bradford's warning in 1554 of the invasion of implacable Spanish papists foresaw a massacre of all those under twenty: 'For we wer borne out of the fayth, and so, saye they, we shall dye'.[168] The Venetian ambassador claimed in 1557 that there were no Catholics in England under the age of thirty-five, for anyone younger could know only heresy and schism[169] This was true in law, if not in fact. Cardinal Pole lamented 'youthe browght up in a contrarye trade' never knowing the true faith:[170] a whole generation had to be converted if the country was to be properly restored to the Catholic fold. Bonner and Pole recognized how essential was education, but how difficult too, for the young, 'of late daies . . . nouseled with . . . pernicious euil doctrine', would not soon forget it 'as the new vessel long doth kepe the sent or savoure of the first liquore wherwith it was seasoned'.[171] But a policy of gentle edification and catechism was given little chance, for any would-be ecclesiastical educators were turned persecutors by government fiat, and more importantly, the bishops found the young resolutely resistant.

Forced now to choose between disobedience to God and to the queen, many young Protestants remained loyal to the faith and would not accommodate their consciences. At first their interrogators were sympathetic to their confusion, offering endless chances for recantation, offering even to set up an apprentice in mastership if he were circumspect.[172] Bishop Bird pleaded with Haukes, 'Ye are a young man, and I would not wish you to go too far, but learn of your elders to bear somewhat'.[173] But, as Roger Holland admitted, 'Youth delighteth in vanity', and few would be persuaded to emulate the worldly mutability of perjured ecclesiastical officials who adapted themselves to shifting religious policy; like Thomas Drowry, a blind boy, asked by Dr Williams:

Chancellor: Then thou art a heretic, and shalt be burned. But who hath taught thee this heresy?

Thomas: You, master chancellor . . . You said, the sacrament was to be received spiritually by faith, and not carnally and really, as the papists have heretofore taught.

Chancellor: Then do as I have done, and thou shalt live as I do, and escape burning.[174]

But Drowry would not; nor would others. Calling them 'peevish boy', 'stout boyly heretic' and 'malapert', the bishops sent intransigent Protestants to the flames.[175]

The Marian martyrs were very often young.[176] Philip Hughes pointed out that thirty-eight of the of the fifty-two martyrs whose ages he ascertained had not reached fourteen, the age of spiritual discretion, until after the break with Rome, and were thus not properly apostate, as the nation was, for they had never renounced Catholicism.[177] The Marian interrogators sought to discover what the faith of the accused had been at the age of fourteen, in order to discover whether or not they were responsible for their heresy.[178] Although some were young enough never to have been Catholic – like Joan Warne, who 'from the time that she was eleven years of age, she hath misliked the sacrifice of the mass', and Joan Horns, who 'being a xi years of age began to learn the faith set forth in King Edward's days'[179] – they were martyred nonetheless.

The martyrdom of young people provided dangerous propaganda against the persecuting regime and powerful inspiration for fellow Protestants. Their heroic resistance to the forces of Antichrist and constancy in suffering were a vindication for the righteousness of the cause, for 'ex ore infantium &c [out of the mouths of babes . . .]'.[180] Young brethren once again formed a fifth column against persecution, as the previous generation had done in the 1520s, meeting in clandestine congregations, spreading subversive literatue and protecting those on the run from arrest.[181] As the band of martyrs suffered, their young supporters would gather at the stake to strengthen them in their resolve. John Tooley died a hero – not only Protestant but anti-Spanish – as three hundred stood by. Reading from a pamphlet, 'Beware of Antichrist', he dropped it, and an apprentice in a blue coat dashed up to retrieve it for him.[182] So great were the crowds which gathered for the fires in Smithfield to watch their brethren's ends, and such the government's unpopularity because of them,[183] that orders were given to the mayor and sheriffs in London on 14 January 1556 that no householder was to 'suffre any of his apprentices or other servants to be abrode' at the time of the burnings, and that anyone 'comforting, aiding or praysing thoffenders' be arrested.[184] But on 22 January a new order had to be issued 'over nyght that no yong folke' should attend the burnings, for that morning at Smithfield 'the grettest [number] was as has byne sene at shyche a time'.[185] The tradition of martyrdom and of secret conventicles would inspire Elizabethan Puritans for the next generation.

Young people had played a moving part in the reception of Protestantism and were at the vanguard of the English Reformation, but any pattern of age and religious allegiance would change with time. The zealous

Protestant innovators of Henry VIII's reign were likely to become the staunch conservative Anglicans of Elizabeth's, for prudence would come with age even to such as Richard Hilles. To be a youthful Protestant in the 1520s, when the faith was new and outlawed, was to be a revolutionary: a generation later Protestantism was the orthodoxy, young Protestants then conventional rather than disobedient, and the rebels not the reformers but whose who looked to the restoration of the old faith, which now had the appeal of exotic and forbidden fruit. Once Catholicism became an evangelical faith young disciples were at the forefront of the mission; like the apprentices 'enticed from their maisters to goe . . . into Italy to cardynall poole' in 1551;[186] like those who went to Louvain 'to make forts in that university against the open truth of Christ's gospel', or later fled to the capital of the Elizabethan mission at Douai.[187]

Notes

1 St Thomas More, *The Apology*, ed. J.B. Trapp, in *The Complete Works of St. Thomas More*, ix (Yale edn., New Haven, CT 1979), pp. 11, 153–63.
2 See, for example, a Mesopotamian hymn in H. Frankfort, *Before Philosophy: An Essay on Speculative Thought in the Ancient Near East* (London, 1971 edn.), p. 217.
3 D.V. Glass and D.E.C. Eversley (eds.), *Population in History: Essays in Historical Demography* (London, 1965), pp. 207, 212.
4 Balliol College Library, Oxford, MS. 304, fo. 102. For the literary *topos* of Youth, see *Two Tudor Interludes: Youth and Hick Scorner*, ed. I. Lancashire (The Revels Plays, Manchester and Baltimore, 1980), pp. 49, 90, n. 203.
5 I follow the definition of youth used by contemporaries, and by C. Phythian-Adams in his *The Desolation of a City: Coventry and the Urban Crisis of the Late Middle Ages* (Cambridge, 1979), pp. 83–6; N.Z. Davis, 'The Reasons of Misrule', in her *Society and Culture in Early Modern France* (London, 1975), p. 108; S.R. Smith, 'Religion and the Conception of Youth in Seventeenth-Century England', *Hist. Childhood Quart.*, ii (1974–5), p. 495. See P. Ariès, *Centuries of Childhood: A Social History of Family Life*, trans. R. Baldick (New York, 1962). Children were confirmed in the pre-Reformation church at the age of seven or even earlier, to Protestant disgust, but at the Reformation the age of confirmation was delayed: William Tyndale, *An Answer to Sir Thomas More's Dialogue*, ed. H. Walter (Parker Soc. [xxxviii], Cambridge, 1850), pp. 71–2; K.V. Thomas, *Religion and the Decline of Magic: Studies in Popular Beliefs in Sixteenth and Seventeenth Century England* (London, 1971), pp. 56–7. See p. 65 above. For the age of marriage in early modern England, see J. Hajnal, 'European Marriage Patterns in Perspective', in Glass and Eversley (eds.), *Population in History*, pp. 101–43; Phythian-Adams, *Desolation of a City*, pp. 84–5.
6 John Longland, *A Sermonde Made before the Kynge, at Grenewiche, vpon Good Frydaye* (London, 1538, S.T.C. 16796), cited in J.W. Blench, *Preaching in England in the Late Fifteenth and Sixteenth Centuries* (Oxford, 1964), p. 234; G. Strauss, *Luther's House of Learning: Indoctrination of the Young in the German Reformation* (Baltimore and London, 1978), ch. 5; S. Thrupp, *The Merchant Class of Medieval London, 1300–1500* (Ann Arbor, MI, 1962 edn.), pp. 164–8; Thomas Elyot, *The Education or Bringinge up of Children, Translated out of Plutarche* (London [1535?], S.T.C. 20057), sig. Fi'.
7 Roger Ascham, *The Scholemaster* (London, 1570, S.T.C. 832), sig. Fi.ᵛ
8 Mark x.14–15; 'Sermon of the Child Bishop, Pronownsyd by John Stubs, Querester, on Childermasse Day at Glocester, 1558', ed. J.G. Nichols, in *Camden*

Miscellany, vii (Camden Soc., new ser., xiv, London, 1875), p. 29; Strauss, *Luther's House of Learning,* pp. 91–2, 99.

9 Edmund Bonner, *An Honeste Godlye Instruction for Bringing Vp of Children* (London, 1555, S.T.C. 3281), sig. Aii; Miles Huggarde, *The Displaying of the Protestantes* (London, 1555, S.T.C. 13557), sig. Lv.

10 Richard Whitford, *A Werke for Housholders, or for Them that Haue the Gydynge or Gouernaunce of Any Cōpany* (London, 1530, S.T.C. 25422), sigs. B^v, Ciiii^v, Dii–iiii; Ascham, *Scholemaster,* sig. Fiii; Sir Thomas Elyot, *The Boke Named the Gouernour* (London, 1531, S.T.C. 7635), cited in *English Historical Documents,* v, *1485–1558,* ed. C.H. Williams (London, 1967), pp. 1046–7.

11 K.V. Thomas, 'Age and Authority in Early Modern England', *Proc. Brit. Acad.,* lxii (1976), pp. 1–46.

12 Tyndale, *Answer to Sir Thomas More's Dialogue,* p. 18.

13 The ages of men as they entered the priesthood are rarely given, but of the seventy-three men who were admitted as deacons in the diocese of London during Ridley's episcopate we know the ages of sixteen: five were over forty (one was sixty-seven), ten in their thirties, and only one under thiry: Guildhall Lib., London, MS. 9535/I, fos. 1–13^v. For the age of emancipation from apprenticeship, see note 52.

14 William Peryn, *Thre Godlye and Notable Sermons, of the Sacrament of the Aulter* (London, 1546, S.T.C. 19785.5), sig. Aii; Huggarde, *Displaying of the Protestantes,* Preface.

15 Public Record Office (hereafter P.R.O), S.P. 1/228, fos. 55–6, in *Letters and Papers, Henry VIII,* xxi (2), no. 710, pp. 370–1.

16 See, for example, St Thomas More, *The Confutation of Tyndale's Answer,* ed. L.A. Schuster *et al.,* in *The Complete Works of St. Thomas More,* viii(1) (Yale edn., New Haven, 1973), p. 451.

17 John Christopherson, *An Exhortacion to All Menne to Take Hede and Beware of Rebellion* (London, 1554, S.T.C. 5207), sig. Tii^v, cited in Thomas, 'Age and Authority in Early Modern England', p. 45. See also, Huggarde, *Displaying of the Protestantes,* sig. Lvi.

18 Huggarde, *Displaying of the Protestantes,* sig. Lv^v.

19 Huggarde, *Displaying of the Protestantes,* sig. Lvii.

20 Huggarde, *Displaying of the Protestantes,* sig. Oiiii; R.H. Pogson, 'Reginald Pole and the Priorities of Government in Mary Tudor's Church', *Hist. Jl.,* xviii (1975), p. 9.

21 A. Murray, 'Was Religious Doubt Regarded as a Sin in the Middle Ages?' (lecture delivered at Harvard University in December 1979).

22 J. Rhodes describes the writings of Erasmus, Bonde and Whitford on scrupulosity in her 'Private Devotion in England on the Eve of the Reformation' (Univ. of Durham PhD thesis, 1974), pp. 134 ff.

23 H. Moller, 'Youth as a Force in the Modern World', *Comp. Studies in Soc. and Hist.,* x (1967–8), pp. 237–60. For an exercise in psycho-history, see E. Erikson, *Young Man Luther: A Study in Psycho-Analysis and History* (New York, 1959). This line of study is not followed in this essay. However, Steven Smith acutely suggested that if young people were to suffer an 'identity crisis', then in the sixteenth and seventeenth centuries this was likely to be about religion: Smith, 'Religion and the Conception of Youth in Seventeenth-Century England', pp. 508–12.

24 *Harpsfield's Life of More,* ed. E.V. Hitchcock (Early English Text Soc., original ser., clxxxvi, London, 1932), pp. 85–6.

25 John Foxe, *Acts and Monuments,* ed. G. Townsend and S.R. Cattley, 8 vols. (London, 1837–41), iv, p. 635; *Dictionary of National Biography.*

26 L.W. Spitz, 'The Third Generation of German Renaissance Humanists', in A.R. Lewis (ed.), *Aspects of the Renaissance: A Symposium* (Austin, TX, and London, 1967), pp. 105–21.

27 More, *Confutation of Tyndale's Answer,* ed. Schuster *et al.,* p. 206.

28 Guildhall Lib., MS. 9531/10, fos. 129–36; Foxe, *Acts and Monuments,* iv, pp. 625–8. See S.E. Ozment, *The Reformation in the Cities: The Appeal of Protestantism*

to Sixteenth-Century Germany and Switzerland (New Haven and London, 1975), pp. 56 ff.

29 Foxe, *Acts and Monuments*, viii, p. 594.

30 H.C. Porter, *Reformation and Reaction in Tudor Cambridge* (Cambridge, 1958).

31 Foxe, *Acts and Monuments*, viii, p. 4; P.R.O., S.P. 1/47, fos. 107–10; Brit. Lib., Harleian MS. 421, fo. 19, in *Letters and Papers, Henry VIII*, iv (2), no. 4175, pp. 1844–6; E.G. Rupp, *The Making of the English Protestant Tradition* (Cambridge, 1947), pp. 19–20, 195–202.

32 P.R.O., S.P. 1/47, fo. 54, in *Letters and Papers, Henry VIII*, iv (2), no. 4004, pp. 1778–9.

33 More, *Confutation of Tyndale's Answer*, ed. Schuster *et al.*, p. 35; Foxe, *Acts and Monuments*, viii, p. 215.

34 P.R.O., S.P. 6/6, fo. 94, in *Letters and Papers, Henry VIII*, vii, no. 146, pp. 54–5. For other New College Protestants, see *Narratives of the Days of the Reformation*, ed. J.G. Nichols (Camden Soc., old ser., lxxvii, London, 1859), pp. 32–5, 55. See also Foxe's account of the death of Randall in 1531: Foxe, *Acts and Movements*, iv, p. 694.

35 P.R.O., S.P. 1/74, fos. 107–8, in *Letters and Papers, Henry VIII*, vi, no. 99, p. 39. Many London apprentices were probably literate by the sixteenth century. As early as 1469 the Goldsmiths' Company had insisted that young men apprenticed to them should be able to read and write: T.F. Reddaway and L.E.M. Walker, *The Early History of the Goldsmiths' Company, 1327–1509* (London, 1975), pp. 261–2. The apprentices' book of signed oaths of the Barber Surgeons' Company shows that they could at least sign their own names: Guildhall Lib., MS. 1698/1. Of deponents before a London commissary court, 1489–97, 41 per cent were described as *literatus* – strikingly close to Sir Thomas More's estimate of popular literacy: Guildhall Lib., MS. 9065.

36 N.Z. Davis, 'Strikes and Salvation at Lyon', in her *Society and Culture in Early Modern France*, pp. 1–16; my 'Popular Disturbance and the Fall of Thomas Cromwell and the Reformers, 1539–40', *Hist. Jl.* xxiv (1981), pp. 257–78.

37 R. Finlay, *Population and Metropolis: The Demography of London, 1580–1650* (Cambridge, 1981); E.A. Wrigley, 'A Simple Model of London's Importance in Changing English Society and Economy, 1650–1750', in P. Abrams and E.A. Wrigley (eds.), *Towns in Societies* (Cambridge, 1978), p. 215; P. Corfield, 'Urban Development in England and Wales in the Sixteenth and Seventeenth Centuries', in D. Coleman and A. John (eds.), *Trade, Government and Economy in Pre-Industrial Britain* (London, 1976).

38 More, *Apology*, ed. Trapp, p. 116.

39 Guildhall Lib., MS. 9065/1A (deposition book in testamentary causes). Some 42.4 per cent of deponents before the same court between 1489 and 1497 had been in their current homes for less than five years: Guildhall Lib., MS. 9065.

40 P. Clark, 'The Migrant in Kentish Towns, 1580–1640', in P. Clark and P. Slack (eds.), *Crisis and Order in English Towns, 1500–1700* (London, 1972), pp. 124, 134–5; Thomas, 'Age and Authority in Early Modern England', p. 14.

41 P. Burke, 'Popular Culture in Seventeenth-Century London', *London Jl.*, iii (1977), pp. 158–9; see P.R.O., C. 1/349/57, C. 1/1351/1, C. 1/1504/6.

42 G.D. Ramsay, 'The Recruitment and Fortunes of Some London Freemen in the Mid-sixteenth Century', *Econ. Hist. Rev.*, 2nd ser., xxxi (1978), pp. 528–9; J. Wareing, 'Changes in the Geographical Distribution of the Recruitment of Apprentices to the London Companies, 1486–1750', *Jl. Hist Geog.*, vi (1980), pp. 241–9. S. Rappaport, 'Social Structure and Mobility in Sixteenth-Century London', *London Journal*, x (1984), pp. 107–34.

43 F.J. Fisher, 'The Development of London as a Centre of Conspicuous Consumption in the Sixteenth and Seventeenth Centuries', *Trans. Roy. Hist. Soc.*, 4th ser., xxx (1947), pp. 37–50; Burke, 'Popular Culture in Seventeenth-Century London', p. 158; Corporation of London Records Office (hereafter C.L.R.O.), Repertory 13, fo. 120ᵛ.

44 A.L. Beier, 'Vagrants and the Social Order in Elizabethan England', *Past and Present*, no. 64 (Aug. 1974), pp. 9–10. The London records for the early sixteenth

century do not generally give the ages of vagrants apprehended. In times of plague, such as November 1543 and February 1555, the parish clerks were ordered to report weekly to their aldermen the number of children in their parishes, and the number of people who died there; C.L.R.O, Journal 15, fo. 61ᵛ, Repertory 11, fo. 258. For the problems of estimating the vagrant population, see Corfield, 'Urban Development in England and Wales', p. 246 n. 53.

45 The insupportable demand for housing, and the consequent abuses of dividing houses into tenements and rack-renting, perturbed both social critics and the authorities: P.R.O., S.P. 2/M, fos. 199–200, in *Letters and Papers, Henry VIII*, v, no. 1788, p. 734; Robert Crowley, 'The Way to Wealth', in his *Select Works*, ed. J.M. Cowper (Early English Text Soc., extra ser., xv, 1872), p. 133; Thomas Lever, *A Sermon Preached at Pauls Cross, the .xiiii. Day of December, Anno .M.D.L.* (London, 1551, S.T.C. 15546.3); C.L.R.O., Journal 15, fo. 203; F.A. Youngs, *The Proclamations of the Tudor Queens* (Cambridge, 1976), pp. 170–4. The parish structure of London in the sixteenth century had been established by the twelfth century, but the churches were no longer able to contain all their parishioners, nor their clergy able to serve them: see, for example, P.R.O., E. 301/89, fo. 3ᵛ; C.L.R.O., Letter Book P, fo. 220ᵛ; John Stow, *Survey of London*, ed. C.L. Kingsford, 2 vols. (Oxford, 1908), i, p. 127; C.N.L. Brooke and G. Keir, *London, 800–1200: The Shaping of a City* (London, 1974), pp. 122–47.

46 The best analyses of London gild organization remain G. Unwin, *The Gilds and Companies of London*, 4th edn. (London, 1963); G. Unwin, *Industrial Organization in the Sixteenth and Seventeenth Centuries* (Oxford, 1904); also W.H. Herbert, *A History of the Twelve Great Livery Companies of the City of London*, 2 vols. (London, 1837). Seventy-five London crafts were listed in the early sixteenth century: Balliol College, Oxford, MS. 354, fo. 107ᵛ.

47 *Tudor Economic Documents*, ed. R.H. Tawney and E. Power, 3 vols. (London, 1924), i, pp. 356–7. For the *cursus honorum* in London politics, see F.F. Foster, *The Politics of Stability: A Portrait of the Rulers in Elizabethan London* (London, 1977), ch. 4. A comparable gerontocracy in Coventry is described in Phythian-Adams, *Desolation of a City*, pp. 93, 114–15, 122, 124, 153, 273–4.

48 See, for example, C.L.R.O., Repertory 12, fos. 57ᵛ, 99, 369, 528, Repertory 13, fos. 20, 24, 36ᵛ, 105ᵛ; Guildhall Lib., MS. 7090/1, fo. 50ᵛ (Pewterers' Company), MS. 11588/1, fos. 7, 9, 12ᵛ (Grocers' Company), MS. 5177/1, fo. 34 (Bakers' Company); Mercers' Company, London, Acts of Court, fo. ccxlviᵛ; Clothworkers' Company, London, Court Book i, fos. 198ᵛ, 205, 242ᵛ, 254ᵛ, 257; Goldsmiths' Company, London, Court Book K, fo. 34ᵛ. Aliens were utterly forbidden to indenture apprentices upon pain of disenfranchisement: *Tudor Economic Documents*, ed. Tawney and Power, i, pp. 293–5; C.L.R.O., Journal 15, fo. 383ᵛ, Journal 16, fo. 253ᵛ.

49 This development is insufficiently understood, but see Unwin, *Gilds and Companies of London*, pp. 223–31; Unwin, *Industrial Organization*, pp. 41 ff.; S. Rappaport, 'The Yeomanry in the London Cloth Industry during the Tudor Period' (Columbia Univ. MA Thesis, 1974). For the establishment of the yeomanry within the Barber Surgeons Company, see Guildhall Lib., MS. 5257/1, fo. 15. It should be noted that 'young man' was coming to mean little more than 'junior' or 'inferior': Phythian-Adams, *Desolation of a City*, p. 274.

50 C.L.R.O., Repertory 2, fos. 96ᵛ, 105, 200ᵛ, 213, 236ᵛ, Repertory 4, fo. 71 (Shermen's Company); *Tudor Economic Documents*, ed. Tawney and Power, i, pp. 110–13; M. and V. Pearl, 'A Revolt in 1529 by Yeomen against the Wardens of the Goldsmiths' Company', *The Review* [The Worshipful Company of Goldsmiths] (May 1980), pp. 23–7; C.L.R.O., Repertory 12, fos. 176, 178ᵛ 179ᵛ, 209 (Saddlers' Company), Repertory 13, fo. 105 (Bakers' Company).

51 Thomas, 'Age and Authority in Early Modern England', pp. 12–14. A similar age barrier operated in the inns of court: R.M. Fisher, 'Reform, Repression and Unrest at the Inns of Court, 1518–1558', *Hist. Jl.*, xx (1977), p. 785.

52 C.L.R.O., Journal 17, fo. 3ᵛ; Thomas, 'Age and Authority in Early Modern England', p. 13.

53 There were penalties imposed upon masters who allowed their apprentices to

marry: see, for example, C.L.R.O., Repertory 12, fo. 311, Repertory 13, fo. 101, Journal 15, fo. 327^v; Mercers' Company, Acts of Court, fo. cclxv^v.

54 C.L.R.O., Journal 17, fo. 3.

55 Edward Hall, *The Union of the Two Noble and Illustre Families of Lancastre and Yorke*, ed. H. Ellis (London, 1809), pp. 586–91; More, *Apology*, ed. Trapp, p. 156; *Chronicle of the Grey Friars of London*, ed. J.G. Nichols (Camden Soc., old ser., liii, London, 1852), p. 30; C.L.R.O., Repertory 3, fos. 141^v, 142–4^v, 145, 164^v.

56 *Calendar of State Papers, Venetian*, iv, no 569, p. 240.

57 John Strype, *Ecclesiastical Memorials, Relating Chiefly to Religion, and the Reformation of It . . . under King Henry VIII, King Edward VI and Queen Mary*, 6 vols. (Oxford, 1822), iii pt. 2, p. 347.

58 *The Chronicle of Queen Jane, and of Two Years of Queen Mary*, ed. J.G. Nichols (Camden Soc., ist ser., xlviii, London, 1850), p. 34.

59 *Chronicle of the Grey Friars*, ed. Nichols, p. 64; Brit. Lib., Stowe MS. 142, fo. 16; P.R.O., S.P. 10/9, fo. 113.

60 Brit. Lib., Cotton MS. Nero, C, x, fos. 44–5; P.R.O., K.B. 8/19, m. 27; C.L.R.O., Repertory 12, fos. 326, 327.

61 In October 1551 the Mercers' Company gave orders than no one should discuss 'the Kynges affayres nor concernynge the Ducke of Somersettes captivitie': Mercers' Company, Act of Court, fo. ccli. There are witnesses to the unusual distress at his execution: Brit. Lib., Cotton Cat. iv. 17; Brit. Lib., Harleian MS. 353, fo. 121^v; Charles Wriothesley, *A Chronicle of England during the Reigns of the Tudors, from A.D. 1485 to 1559*, ed. W.D. Hamilton, 2 vols. (Camden Soc., new ser., xi, xx, London, 1875–7), ii, p. 65; John Stow, *Annales, or a Generall Chronicle of England*, ed. E. Howes (London, 1631), p. 607.

62 Brit. Lib., Lansdowne MS. lxxviii, fo. 160.

63 S.R. Smith, 'The Apprentices' Parliament of 1647', *History Today*, xxii (Aug. 1972); S.R. Smith, 'The London Apprentices as Seventeenth-Century Adolescents', *Past and Present*, no. 61 (Nov. 1973), p. 157; G. Holmes, 'The Sacheverell Riots: The Crowd and the Church in Early Eighteenth-Century London', *Past and Present*, no. 72 (Aug. 1976), pp. 73–4.

64 See, for example, C.L.R.O., Repertory 3, fos. 223–4, Repertory 4, fo. 71, Repertory 12, fos. 90^v, 98, 108^v, 150^v, 271^v, Repertory 13, fos. 67^v, 72, 119^v, 131, Journal 15, fo. 240^v, Journal 16, fos. 15^v, 17^v, 258, 261^v, 367; *Acts of the Privy Council of England*, ed. J.R. Dasent, 32 vols. (London, 1890–1907), iv, p. 317; Mercers' Company, Acts of Court, fos. ccxxiiii, ccxxxi–ccxxxii; Clothworkers' Company, Court Book 1, fo. 247^v; Goldsmiths' Company, Court Book 1, fo. 181; Foxe, *Acts and Monuments*, vi, p. 392; *Calendar of Patent Rolls, Edward VI*, iv, pp. 197, 287; *Calendar of Patent Rolls, Philip and Mary*, i, pp. 383–4, 387, and ii, pp. 24, 79, 146.

65 Burke, 'Popular Culture in Seventeenth-Century London', p. 159; P.R.O., C.1/349/57, C.1/1351/1, C.1/1504/6; Smith, 'London Apprentices as Seventeenth-Century Adolescents', pp. 155–7; R. Trexler, 'Ritual in Florence: Adolescents and Salvation in the Renaissance', in C. Trinkaus and H.A. Oberman (eds.), *The Pursuit of Holiness in Late Medieval and Renaissance Religion* (Studies in Medieval and Renaissance Thought, x, Leiden, 1974), pp. 200–64.

66 *Songs and Ballads Relative to the London Prentices*, ed. C. Makay (Percy Soc., i, London, 1840); Smith, 'London Apprentices as Seventeenth-Century Adolescents', pp. 154–5; L.S. O'Connell, 'The Elizabethan Bourgeois Hero-Tale: Aspects of Adolescent Social Consciousness', in B.C. Malament (ed.), *After the Reformation: Essays in Honour of J.H. Hexter* (Manchester, 1980), pp. 267–90.

67 For provision for apprentices in wills, see, for example, Guildhall Lib., MS. 9171/12, fos. 2^v, 5, 7, 9, 12, 18, 31, 51^v, 72^v, 87, 95^v, 111^v, 127, 137, 139, 150, 152^v, MS. 9171/13, fos. 1, 3^v, 30, 46, 86^v, 89, 97^v. For a few among many examples of such disobedience, see C.L.R.O., Journal 15, fos. 10, 59, 198–99^v, Repertory 13, fo. 127; P.R.O., C.1/1293/23–4; Clothworkers' Company, Court Book 1, fo. 195; Goldsmiths' Company, Court Book K, fos. 11, 31, 51.

68 See, for example, P.R.O., C.1/296/70; Court of Requests, 2/v/211; C.L.R.O.,

Repertory 12, fo. 512^v; Bodleian Lib., Oxford, Gougth MS., London, 10, fo. 3^v; Clothworkers' Company, Court Book 1, fos. 196^v, 247^v.

69 William Scott, *Two Notable Sermones Lately Preached at Pauls Crosse* (London, 1546), sig. Hiv^v, cited in Blench, *Preaching in England in the Late Fifteenth and Sixteenth Centuries*, p. 243. Miles Huggarde sarcastically described how 'Jack prentise was called in for his testament' at the Islington congregation: Huggarde, *Displaying of the Protestantes*, sig. Piii.

70 Foxe, *Acts and Monuments*, viii, pp. 518–20. For Crome's offending sermon, see Brit. Lib., Harleian MS. 425, fos. 65–6, in *Letters and Papers, Henry VIII*, xvi, no. 814, p. 394.

71 See the curate of Harwich's strictures against the misrule in his parish, and descriptions of the disorder: P.R.O., S.P. 1/99, fos. 203^v–4^v, in *Letters and Papers, Henry VIII*, ix, no. 1059, pp. 364–5. Davis, *Society and Culture in Early Modern England*, p. 17; C. Phythian-Adams, *Local History and Folklore: A New Framework* (London, 1975), pp. 23, 26–7.

72 *Letters and Papers, Henry VIII*, iv (1), no. 390 (30), p. 170.

73 Stow, *Survey of London*, i, p. 75; Wriothesley, *Chronicle of England during the Reigns of the Tudors*, ii, p. 130.

74 K.V. Thomas, *Rule and Misrule in the Schools of Early Modern England* (Reading, 1976); Fisher, 'Reform, Repression and Unrest at the Inns of Court', pp. 783–5. During the 1549 rebellions benchers at the inns were ordered to keep their 'companyes quietly governed': C.L.R.O. Repertory 12, fo. 108^v.

75 Stow, *Survey of London*, i, pp. 255–6; Burke, 'Popular Culture in Seventeenth-Century London', pp. 144–5.

76 Goldsmiths' Company, Court Book K, fos. 31, 35; Davis, 'Reasons of Misrule', pp. 97–123. Thomas also found moral purpose in schoolchildren's play: Thomas, *Rule and Misrule in the Schools of Early Modern England*, pp. 32 ff.

77 More, *Confutation of Tyndale's Answer*, ed. Schuster *et al.*, p. 42.

78 'Sermon of the Child Bishop', ed. Nichols; R.L. de Molen, '*Pueri Christi imitatio*: The Festival of the Boy Bishop in Tudor England', *Moreana*, xlv (1975), pp. 17–28. See Dean Colet's statutes for the foundations of St Paul's School: *English Historical Documents*, v, *1485–1558*, ed. Williams, p. 1043. The festival, abolished by Henry VIII, was restored by Mary: Foxe, *Acts and Monuments*, viii, pp. 222, 579.

79 Phythian-Adams, *Local History and Folklore*, pp. 27–8; Foxe, *Acts and Monuments*, vi, pp. 32, 35.

80 More, *Confutation of Tyndale's Answer*, ed. Schuster *et al.*, p. 5; Phythian-Adams, *Local History and Folklore* pp. 27–8.

81 For confusion over the keeping of holidays, see *Chronicle of the Grey Friars of London*, ed. Nichols, p. 59. For insolence and misrule in Catholic festivals on the Continent, see, for example, D. Nicholls, 'Inertia and Reform in the Pre-Tridentine French Church: The Response to Protestantism in the Diocese of Rouen, 1520–62', *Jl. Eccles. Hist.*, xxxii (1981), pp. 193–4; R.W. Scribner, *For the Sake of Simple Folk: Popular Propaganda for the German Reformation* (Cambridge Studies in Oral and Literate Culture, Cambridge, 1981), p. 68.

82 C.L.R.O., Repertory 11, fo. 350, Repertory 12, fo. 90^v.

83 *English Historical Documents*, v, *1485–1558*, ed. Williams, p. 652.

84 William Tyndale, *The Obediēce of a Christen Man, and How Christē Rulers Ought to Governe* ([Antwerp], 1528, S.T.C., 24446); Foxe, *Acts and Monuments*, viii, p. 475.

85 More, *Confutation of Tyndales's Answer*, ed. Schuster *et al.*, pp. 144, 182.

86 Cited in A.G. Dickens, *The German Nation and Martin Luther* (London, 1974), p. 130.

87 C.W. Dugmore, *The Mass and the English Reformers* (London, 1958); F. Clark, *Eucharistic Sacrifice and the Reformation* (London, 1960); Thomas, *Religion and the Decline of Magic*, pp. 33–6.

88 People had questioned the miracle before: Murray, 'Was Religious Doubt Regarded as a Sin in the Middle Ages?'

89 More, *Confutation of Tyndale's Answer*, ed. Schuster *et al.*, p. 148.

90 Phythian-Adams, *Desolation of a City*, p. 83 n. 16. Evidence for the age of spiritual discretion is confusing: the Marian clergy thought fourteen the age at which knowledge and conviction in matters of faith might be assumed (Foxe, *Acts and Monuments*, vi, pp. 730, 738), but in March 1554 the mayor and aldermen of London ordered householders to ensure that everyone over twelve did their spiritual duty at Easter (Foxe, *Acts and Monuments*, vi, p. 43).

91 I am grateful to Professor Patrick Collinson for this point. There is some evidence of children attending church: they were, for example, accused of unruly behaviour during services: 'Sermon of the Child Bishop', ed. Nichols, pp. 24–5; Huggarde, *Displaying of the Protestantes*, sigs. Lv-v^v. Schoolmasters were ordered in 1554 to 'instruct their children, so as they may be able to answer the priest at the Mass, and so help the priest to Mass, as has been accustomed': *Documents Illustrative of English Church History*, ed. H. Gee and W.H. Hardy (London, 1896), p. 383.

92 Foxe, *Acts and Monuments*, viii, p. 580.

93 Christopherson, *Exhortation to All Menne*, sig. Tiiii.

94 John Bale, *Yet a Course at the Romyshe Foxe, Compyled by J. Harryson* (Zurich, 1543, S.T.C. 1309), sigs. Cviii^v, Fi; Foxe, *Acts and Monuments*, v, pp. 14–18, 441–2, 451–2, 537–50; More, *Apology*, ed. Trapp, pp. 122, 124–5.

95 C.L.R.O., Repertory 11, fo. 300; *Acts of the Privy Council*, i, pp. 494–5; *Narratives of the Days of the Reformation*, ed. Nichols, pp. 60–8.

96 C.L.R.O., Repertory 11, fos, 464^v, 495^v. For the importance of the Corpus Christi festival, the one especially reviled by the Protestants, see 'John Bon and Master Parson', in *Tudor Tracts 1532–1558*, ed. A.F. Pollard (Westminster, 1903), p. 161; A.N. Galpern, *The Religions of the People in Sixteenth-Century Champagne* (Cambridge, MA, 1976), pp. 16–17, 71–8, 158–9; N.Z. Davis, 'The Rites of Violence', in her *Society and Culture in Early Modern France*, pp. 165–72; P. Benedict, *Rouen during the Wars of Religion* (Cambridge Studies in Early Modern History, Cambridge, 1981), pp. 61, 63, 67.

97 Greater London Records Office (hereafter G.L.R.O.), DL/C/209, fos. 50–2.

98 T.N. Tentler, *Sin and Confession on the Eve of the Reformation* (Princeton, 1977), pp. 70 ff.

99 Whitford, *Werke for Housholders*, sigs. Fii–iiii. In 1554 Bishop Bonner insisted upon the mandatory confession at Lent; those who were refusing to attend were 'giving thereby a pernicious and evil example to the younger sort': Foxe, *Acts and Monuments*, vi, p. 426. Masters could certainly stop their servants and apprentices from attending confession at the Reformation: presumably the reverse was true before: Foxe, *Acts and Monuments*, v, p. 445; G.L.R.O., DL/C/614, fos. 22^v, 26^v, 48^v, 50, 59^v, 60^v.

100 Ozment, *Reformation in the Cities*, pp. 23–32.

101 P.R.O., S.P. 1/102, fo. 73, in *Letters and Papers*, x, no. 346, p. 130; G.R. Elton, *Policy and Police: The Enforcement of the Reformation in the Age of Thomas Cromwell* (Cambridge, 1973), pp. 27–30. Rowland was sixty-one: Guildhall Lib., MS. 9065 A1, fo. 38^v.

102 P.R.O., S.P. 1/65, fo. 203, in *Letters and Papers, Henry VIII*, v, no. 186, p. 89.

103 For an example of arrogance, see Henry Gold's warning against sermons as throwing pearls before swine: P.R.O., S.P. 1/83, fos. 147–8, in *Letters and Papers, Henry VIII*, vii, no. 523 (4), p. 209. A. Murray, *Reason and Society in the Middle Ages* (Oxford, 1978), pp. 244–51.

104 Whitford, *Werke for Housholders*, sig. Bi.

105 Foxe, *Acts and Monuments*, v, p. 382.

106 P.R.O., E. 36/120, fos. 107–8; P.R.O., S.P. 1/132, fo. 218, in *Letters and Papers, Henry VIII*, xiii (1), nos. 1111 (1 & 2), pp. 406–7. See *English Historical Documents*,v, 1485–1558, ed. Williams, p. 653.

107 C.L.R.O., Journal 15, fo. 9.

108 P.R.O., S.P. 1/220, fo. 68, in *Letters and Papers, Henry VIII*, xxi (1), no. 1027, pp. 513–15.

109 *Tudor Royal Proclamations*, ed. P.L. Hughes and J.F. Larkin, 3 vols. (New Haven, 1964–9), i, no. 292. The command was repeated in December 1553: Clothworkers' Company, Court Book I, fo. 250; Goldsmiths' Company, Court Book 1, fo. 188.

110 C.L.R.O., Repertory 13, fo. 157. For the case of the cat with the shaven crown, see C.L.R.O., Journal 16, fo. 287ᵛ, Repertory 13, fo. 147; *The Diary of Henry Machyn, Citizen and Merchant-Taylor of London, from A.D. 1550 to A.D. 1563*, ed. J.G. Nichols (Camden Soc., old ser., xlii, London, 1848), pp. 59–60. The culprits were never found: Huggarde, *Displaying of the Protestantes*, sig. Oviiiᵛ.

111 Foxe, *Acts and Monuments*, vi, p. 691.

112 Foxe, *Acts and Monuments*, v, p. 526.

113 C.L.R.O., Repertory 13, fo. 291ᵛ. For other instances of juvenile anticlericism, see C.L.R.O., Repertory 13, fos. 127, 335. For a sacrilegious 'procession of priests and bishops' at the court of Edward VI, see *Calendar of State Papers, Spanish*, x, p. 444.

114 Huggarde, *Displaying of the Protestantes*, sigs Miiiiᵛ-v; *Acts of the Privy Council*, v, p. 169; C.L.R.O., Repertory 13, fo. 335.

115 See pp. 61–3, 65–7, 70–1 above. Gardiner was especially hated: see Wriothesley, *Chronicle of England during the Reigns of the Tudors*, i, p. 215; *Calendar of State Papers, Spanish*, xi, nos. 174, 253, 256; xiii, no. 73, p. 62.

116 The clash between youth and age as a reason for disruption in the inns is signalled in Fisher, 'Reform, Repression and Unrest at the Inns of Court', pp. 800–1.

117 Foxe, *Acts and Monuments*, iv, p. 698; see p. 57 above.

118 Foxe, *Acts and Monuments*, iv, pp. 657, 697–706; v, pp. 444, 540; vii, p. 731; *Plumpton Correspondence*, ed. Thomas Stapleton (Camden Soc., old ser., iv, London, 1839), pp. 231–5; C.A. Haigh, *Reformation and Resistance in Tudor Lancashire* (Cambridge, 1975), p. 161.

119 P.R.O., S.P. 1/239, fo. 83, in *Letters and Papers, Henry VIII*, Addenda (1), no. 953, p. 334; R.M. Fisher, 'The Inns of Court and the Reformation, 1530–1580' (Univ. of Cambridge PhD thesis, 1974), p. 120; Elton, *Policy and Police*, pp. 32–3, 378–9.

120 Ascham, *Scholemaster*, sig. Giiᵛ.

121 Foxe, *Acts and Monuments*, viii, p. 209. See also Palmer's encounter with Sir Robert Abridges, who was in 'the eleventh hour' of his old age: Foxe, *Acts and Monuments*, viii, p. 217. The Puritan Laurence Chadderton was likewise spurned by his father, and John Bradford grieved his mother: Haigh, *Reformation and Resistance in Tudor Lancashire*, p. 167.

122 Foxe, *Acts and Monuments*, vii, p. 314.

123 Foxe, *Acts and Monuments*, viii, p. 474; A.G. Dickens, *Lollards and Protestants in the Diocese of York, 1509–1558* (Oxford, 1959), pp. 131–7; Chrisopherson, *Exhortacion to All Menne*, sig. Tii.

124 More, *Apology*, ed. Trapp, p. 156.

125 More, *Apology*, ed. Trapp, pp. 117–18. The boy's name was Dick Purser: More, *Apology*, ed. Trapp, p. 366.

126 *Original Letters Relative to the English Reformation*, ed. H. Robinson, 2 vols. (Parker Soc. [xxiii, xxviii], Cambridge, 1846–7), i, p. 232.

127 C.L.R.O., Repertory 11, fos. 158–60; P.R.O., Star Chamber, 2/34/28 ii; Foxe, *Acts and Monuments*, v, p. 446; vii, p. 287; viii, pp. 247, 522.

128 C.L.R.O., Repertory 11, fo. 160; Strype, *Ecclesiastical Memorials*, i (2), p. 64; P.R.O., S.P. 1/47, fos. 10–11, in *Letters and Papers, Henry VIII*, iv (2), no. 3962; Foxe, *Acts and Monuments*, v, p. 38; vi, p. 561; *Acts of the Privy Council*, vi, p. 124.

129 More, *Apology*, ed. Trapp, pp. 90–1, 119, 121, 156–7; Foxe, *Acts and Monuments*, v, pp. 16–18, 452, 547. See also p. 74 above.

130 Bale, *Yet a Course at the Romyshe Foxe*, sigs 1i, Mv; C.L.R.O., Repertory 11, fo. 117ᵛ; Henry Brinklow, 'The Complaynt of Roderych Mors', ed. J.M. Cowper (Early English Text Soc., extra ser., xxii, London, 1874), p. 54; Huggarde, *Displaying of the Protestantes*, sig Lviiiᵛ.

131 *Harpsfield's Life of More*, ed. Hitchcock, p. 84.

132 More, *Confutation of Tyndale's Answer*, ed. Schuster *et al.*, p. 122.

133 For the preaching campaign in the capital, see my 'The Early Reformation in

London, 1522–1547' (Univ. of Cambridge PhD thesis, 1979), pp. 99–101, 108–9, 153–63. See the account of the spread of Protestantism in Lancashire through the missions of university evangelicals in Haigh, *Reformation and Resistance in Tudor Lancashire*, pp. 163–77.

134 *Narratives of the Days of the Reformation*, ed. Nichols, pp. 182–3. Complaints against students are perennial: Brit. Lib., Egerton MS. 2623, fo. 9.

135 W. Mozley, *William Tyndale* (London, 1937), pp. 22 ff.; Foxe, *Acts and Monuments*, v, p. 115.

136 Guildhall Lib., MS. 9531/10, fos. 136^v–137^v.

137 Foxe, *Acts and Monuments*, v, pp. 225–6.

138 *Narratives of the Days of the Reformation*, ed. Nichols, pp. 55, 98 ff.; Foxe, *Acts and Monuments*, viii, pp. 201 ff. The book was one of the most influential of the English Reformation: John Frith, *A Disputacion of Purgatorye Mede by Iohan Frith which is Deuided into Thre Bokes* (London, 1533, S.T.C. 11388).

139 P.R.O., Star Chamber, 2/34.28 ii.

140 P.R.O., S.P. 1/208, fo. 39^v, in *Letters and Papers, Henry VIII*, xx (2), no. 416. During the heresy drive of 1546 Vaughan was no longer able to protect his tutor, and Cobbe fled into exile: *Letters and Papers, Henry VIII*, xxi (1), no. 1494, pp. 745–6; xxi (2), no. 52, p. 22.

141 *Narratives of the Days of the Reformation*, ed. Nichols, p. 46.

142 Christopherson, *Exhortacion to All Menne*, sig. Aai; William Turner, *The Huntyng of the Romyshe Vuolfe* (Emden[1555?], S.T.C. 24356), Preface.

143 John Champneys, *The Haruest Is at Hand wherin the Tares Shall Be Bound and Brent* (London, 1548, S.T.C. 4956), sig. Avii.

144 P.R.O., S.P. 1/105, fo. 104, in *Letters and Papers, Henry VIII*, xi, no. 138, pp. 56–7.

145 P.R.O., S.P. 1/99, fo. 104, in *Letters and Papers, Henry VIII*, ix, no. 1059, pp. 364–5. There were, reportedly, ten thousand people at an incendiary sermon Latimer gave on 22 May 1538: Wriothesley, *Chronicle of England during the Reigns of the Tudors*, ed. Hamilton, i, p. 81.

146 See, for example, Rowland Phillips's account of the reformist preaching in the capital from 1534: P.R.O., S.P. 1/123, fos. 125–8, in *Letters and Papers, Henry VIII*, xii (2), no. 361, pp. 144–5.

147 *Narratives of the Days of the Reformation*, ed. Nichols, p. 23.

148 K.V. Thomas, 'Work and Leisure in Pre-Industrial England', *Past and Present*, no. 29 (Dec. 1964), pp. 50–62; Phythian-Adams, *Desolation of a City*, pp. 74–9. For interludes, see C.L.R.O., Repertory 12, fos. 99, 162^v; Strype, *Ecclesiastical Memorials*, iii (2) pp. 22–3; my 'The Early Reformation in London', ch. 8 (iv). For youthful misdemeanours, see, for example, C.L.R.O., Repertory 10, fo. 174^v, Repertory 11, fos. 350, 388^v, 409, Repertory 12, fos. 54, 90^v, 98, 368^v, 377^v, Repertory 13, fos. 6–7, 131^v–2, Journal 15, fo. 311^v.

149 Guildhall Lib., MS. 1568/1, p. 34; see pp. 66–7 above.

150 *Chronicle of the Grey Friars of London*, ed. Nichols, p. 56.

151 Mercers' Company, Acts of Court, fo. ccxxiiii, cited in D. Hoak, *The King's Council in the Reign of Edward VI* (Cambridge, 1976), p. 215.

152 *Original Letters Relative to the English Reformation*, ed. Robinson, i, p. 208; P.R.O., S.P. 3/13, fo. 14, in *Letters and Papers, Henry VIII*, ix, no. 583, pp. 193–4; *Acts of the Privy Council*, i, pp. 418–19; *Chronicle of the Grey Friars of London*, ed. Nichols, pp. 50, 56; Foxe, *Acts and Monuments*, v, pp. 441–2; viii, pp. 518–20.

153 See my 'Popular Disturbance and the Fall of Thomas Cromwell and the Reformers', pp. 270–2.

154 Foxe, *Acts and Monuments*, vii, p. 478; Elton, *Policy and Police*, ch. 1.

155 See pp. 55–6 above.

156 *Diary of Henry Machyn*, ed. Nichols, p. 41.

157 *Diary of Henry Machyn*, ed. Nichols, pp. 97–8. Richard Grafton, *Grafton's Chronicle*, or History of England, ed. H. Ellis (London, 1809), p. 536; *Acts of the Privy Council*, iv, p. 317.

158 Brit. Lib., Harleian MS. 353, fos. 141, 143; Wriothesley, *Chronicle of England*

during the Reigns of the Tudors, ed. Hamilton, ii, pp. 99–100; Guildhall Lib., MS. 5177, fo. 89ᵛ (Bakers' Company); Foxe, *Acts and Monuments*, vi, p. 538.

159 P. Mack Crew, *Calvinist Preaching and Iconoclasm in the Netherlands, 1544–1569* (Cambridge Studies in Early Modern History, Cambridge, 1978), p. 166; Davis, 'The Rites of Violence', p. 183.

160 Wriothesley, *Chronicle of England during the Reigns of the Tudors*, ed. Hamilton, i, pp. 74–6; ii, p. 1.

161 A.L. Rowse, *Tudor Cornwall*, 2nd edn. (London, 1969), p. 262.

162 C.L.R.O., Repertory 13, fo. 131; *Calendar of State Papers, Spanish*, xii, p. 146; *Chronicle of Queen Jane*, ed. Nichols, p. 67. Children would re-enact the battle of Sedgemoor every year: T.B. Macaulay, *History of England from the Accession of James II*, 4 vols. (Everyman edn., London, 1906), i, p. 460.

163 *Calendar of State Papers, Spanish*, xii, pp. 154–5; Wriothesley, *Chronicle of England during the Reigns of the Tudors*, ed. Hamilton, ii, pp. 117–18; *Diary of Henry Machyn*, ed. Nichols, p. 58; Huggarde, *Displaying of the Protestantes*, sigs. Oviiᵛ–viii. See also the men accused of 'maintaining their boys to sing a song against the sacrament of the altar' in 1540: Foxe, *Acts and Monuments*, v, p. 445. Young people were particularly suspect during Wyatt's rebellion: C.L.R.O., Repertory 13, fo. 113. In its aftermath an apprentice was in trouble for spreading rumours that Wyatt had cleared Princess Elizabeth from complicity in the conspiracy: Foxe, *Acts and Monuments*, vi, p. 431; C.L.R.O., Repertory 13, fos. 153, 155; *Chronicle of Queen Jane*, ed. Nichols, p. 75.

164 Benedict, *Rouen during the Wars of Religion*, p. 98.

165 M. Fraser, *Children in Conflict*, 2nd edn. (Harmondworth, 1969), pp. 152–3.

166 Fraser, *Children in Conflict*, pp. 16–17.

167 Philip Hughes was the first historian to make this point: P. Hughes, *The Reformation in England*, 3 vols. (London, 1950–4), ii, pp. 289–93.

168 Strype, *Ecclesiastical Memorials*, iii (2), p. 347. Bradford was, in fact, born *circa* 1510 himself: *Dictionary of National Biography*.

169 *Calendar of State Papers, Venetian*, vi, no. 884, pp. 1074–5.

170 Strype, *Ecclesiastical Memorials*, iii (2), pp. 497 ff.

171 Bonner, *An Honeste, Godlye Instruction*, sig. Aii. For the Catholic programme of re-education, see G.M.V. Alexander, 'Bonner and the Marian Persecutions', *History*, lx (1975), pp. 386 ff.; Pogson, 'Reginald Pole and the Priorities of Government in Mary Tudor's Church'.

172 Foxe, *Acts and Monuments*, vi, p. 727.

173 Foxe, *Acts and Monuments*, vii, pp. 104–5; see also pp. 44, 101.

174 Foxe, *Acts and Monuments*, viii, pp. 145, 467; see also, Foxe, *Acts and Monuments*, vii, pp. 119, 353; viii, p. 161.

175 Foxe, *Acts and Monuments*, vii, pp. 111, 151; viii, pp. 157, 477, 483.

176 Of those whose tribulations Foxe records, and whose ages can be discovered, at least eight were certainly twenty or under – William Hunter (19), John Leaf (19), Joan Horns, George Searles (20), Robert Purcas (20), Elizabeth Folkes (20), Rose Allin (20), Thomas Hinshaw (19 or 20): Foxe, *Acts and Monuments*, v, p. 722; vii, p. 192; viii, pp. 142, 153, 387, 391, 483. Still more were described as 'lad', 'boy', 'young maid' or 'young man': Foxe, *Acts and Monuments*, vii, pp. 328, 750; viii, pp. 142, 144, 153, 157, 489, 506, 511. A further twenty who suffered were still in their twenties – John Warne (29), Thomas Haukes, John Launder (25), Patrick Pachingham (21), George Tankerfield (27 or 28), John Went (27), John Tudson (27), Barlet Green (25), William Halliwell (24), Ralph Jackson (24), Laurence Pernam (22), Lyon Cawch (28), John Routh (26), Agnes George (26), Adam Foster (26), Julius Palmer (24), Thomas Moor (24), Joan Waste (22) and Jeffrey Hurst and Roger Holland: Foxe, *Acts and Monuments*, vii, pp. 80, 101, 323, 332, 343, 717, 738, 747–8; viii, pp. 153, 158, 217, 242, 247, 473, 562. Seventeen more were under forty: Foxe, *Acts and Monuments*, vii, pp. 86, 746; viii, pp. 152–3, 160, 333, 386, 427, 462–3, 493. Apprentices and servants were commonly scourged for their obdurate heresy: Foxe, *Acts and Monuments*, viii, pp. 426, 483, 521–2, 524, 525.

177 Hughes, *Reformation in England*, ii, pp. 289–91

178 Foxe, *Acts and Monuments*, vi, pp. 730, 738; vii, p. 716.
179 Foxe, *Acts and Monuments*, vii, p. 717; viii, p. 142.
180 Foxe, *Acts and Monuments*, viii, p. 215. For Catholic fears of the potent legacy of martyrdom, see, *inter alia*, Christopherson, *Exhortation to All Menne*, sig. 1ii^v; Huggarde, *Displaying of the Protestantes*, sigs. Gviii, Pv^v.
181 See, for example, Foxe, *Acts and Monuments*, vi, pp. 561, 723; vii, p. 287; viii, pp. 214, 460, 474, 483, 521–4, 549.
182 Foxe, *Acts and Monuments*, vii, pp. 90 ff.
183 For reports of the unpopularity of the burnings, see *Calendar of State Papers, Spanish*, xiii, nos. 148, 161, pp. 138–9, 148; *Calendar of State Papers, Venetian*, vi, no. 116, pp. 93–4; both cited in D.M. Loades, *The Reign of Mary Tudor* (London, 1979), pp. 330, 334, 446–7.
184 *Acts of the Privy Council*, v, p. 224; see also, Strype, *Ecclesiastical Memorials*, iii (2), p. 501; Foxe, *Acts and Monuments*, vi, pp. 728, 740.
185 *Diary of Henry Machyn*, ed. Nichols, pp. 90–1, 99–100; C.L.R.O., Repertory 13, fo. 400^v.
186 C.L.R.O., Repertory 12, fo. 342.
187 Foxe, *Acts and Monuments*, viii, p. 649; J. Bossy, *The English Catholic Community, 1570–1850* (London, 1975), ch. 1; Haigh, *Reformation and Resistance in Tudor Lancashire*, pp. 258, 278–9, 311.

4

The early expansion of Protestantism in England, 1520–1558

A.G. DICKENS

The timing of the English Reformation

The present essay concerns the strength, expansion and geographical distribution of Protestant convictions among the English people during the early Reformation period, the thirty-eight years which separate the first incursion of Lutheranism from the accession of Elizabeth. To some extent it will react against the conclusions attained recently by certain original and respected scholars such as Dr Christopher Haigh and Professor Jack Scarisbrick, who envisage a very slow growth of the movement, sometimes suggesting that, apart from very limited areas of the south-east and certain large towns elsewhere, few English people became convinced Protestants during this early period.[1] Without setting forth much local evidence, they insist that English society did not want the Reformation and remained substantially Catholic until the new beliefs captured many areas in the middle decades of Elizabeth. In 1983 Dr Haigh referred to the area-studies

Reprinted from *Archiv für Reformationsgeschichte*, 78 (1987).

summarised in my own book *The English Reformation*, published in 1964 and now recently (1989) updated by reference to more recent researches:

> And in the area of enquiry which Dickens drew to our attention, the progress of religious change at the popular level, the Dickens picture has been substantially redrawn. From the area studies which sought to chart the pace of reform in the provinces, only Kent has appeared to give unequivocal support for a rapid and popular Reformation while Cambridgeshire, Cornwall, Gloucester, Lancashire, Norfolk, Suffolk, Sussex and York city have yielded at best only small pockets of advanced opinion and a general impression of conservative attachment until the reign of Elizabeth.[2]

More recently Dr Haigh has enlarged somewhat upon this picture, rightly suggesting a differentiation between the towns and the countryside, but then taking snapshots of several counties, from some of which I still find myself bound to differ.

> Though there is a substantial body of opinion, led by Professors Dickens and Elton, which holds that Protestantism spread rapidly in early Tudor England, there is a growing 'slow Reformation' school, composed partly of historians who have conducted local studies of religious change. Protestantism did make early progress in towns such as Bristol, Colchester, Coventry, Ipswich and London, but elsewhere, and especially in the countryside, the reformist breakthrough came much later. In Cambridgeshire, Cornwall, Gloucestershire, Lancashire, Lincolnshire, Norfolk, Suffolk, Sussex, and Yorkshire, the Protestant Reformation was an Elizabethan (and often mid-Elizabethan) event.[3]

In more general terms Professor Scarisbrick appears to accept this scheme, stressing (with good reason) the survival of the parish fraternities and other forms of Catholic piety until the Edwardian dissolutions.[4]

With less justification, he does not proceed to analyse either the slow development of popular Protestantism between 1530 and 1547, or its much swifter, more ascertainable development under Edward VI. He attaches no positive significance to Protestant resistance and martyrdom during the Marian persecution, that crucial episode to which he devotes only seven words in his book *The Reformation and the English People*.[5] My differences from Dr Haigh are somewhat more complicated, though less wholesale than he appears to suppose. For many decades I have been agreeing with the view that Protestantism always had to fight hard, and that throughout some considerable parts of the realm Catholic beliefs did in fact maintain their preponderance until the middle decades of Elizabeth and beyond. From the early 1930s to the late 1940s I worked mainly upon reactionary rebellions and Elizabethan Catholic recusancy, the forces in strong opposition to the Reformation. This early preoccupation has remained explicit in my later works. In 1959 I remarked that the ethos of Anglicanism was not widely understood before the period of Hooker, and that Puritanism had to struggle for a following until the late Elizabethan period.[6] In 1964 I stressed the 'gradual consolidation' of the Anglican church under Elizabeth and its slowness to convert remote areas, adding that the growth of new movements during the seventeenth century 'might almost be regarded as a second English Reformation'. I also drew attention to the role of Elizabethan Puritanism in converting the so-called 'dark corners of the land'.[7] In view of such oft-repeated conclusions I remain at a loss to understand why Dr Haigh continues at such frequent intervals to label me as a champion of quick and easy 'Reformation from below'.

In fairness it must be added that I have also maintained a converse yet wholly compatible proposition. I believe in territorial diversity, and that one should carefully study regional contrasts before venturing upon generalisations concerning the realm as a whole. I applaud Dr Haigh when he concludes his historiographical review (n. 1) with the words 'we must show the past in all its variety and irreducible complexity, no matter how far art has to be sacrificed to accuracy'. Yet having widely surveyed the evidence so far presented, I still conclude that by 1553 Protestantism had already become a formidable and seemingly ineradicable phenomenon in fairly large and very populous areas of marked political importance. After all, the regions of England were not of equal influence upon the history of the nation; and the seat of government could not be transferred to Lancashire or the centre of the economy to Wales. Where was this heartland of the early Protestant movement? As I shall shortly demonstrate, it was far more extensive than Kent; it embraced all the coastal counties from Norfolk to Sussex and had sizeable westward extensions. The heart of this heartland was of course London. Moreover, the remainder of the country did not in 1553 consist wholly of what the Puritans regarded as the 'dark corners' of the land. Much of it represented what might be called intermediate or mixed areas, in which the new beliefs had already spread widely rather than intensively, yet where they cannot be adequately characterised as 'small pockets' of Protestantism.

Thus in regard to several specific areas my scheme does show some radical differences from that of Dr Haigh, while overall I take the inherent vitality and expansive achievements of pre-Elizabethan Protestantism far more seriously than either he or Professor Scarisbrick. I cannot imagine, for example, how Dr Haigh can bring himself to class Suffolk – by any criteria one of the three or four most heavily converted counties in England – along with Lancashire, Lincolnshire and Cornwall in a 'conservative' group. Likewise the view of Sussex as a highly conservative county may have been deduced from Professor R.B. Manning's emphasis upon the strong group of Catholic gentry there in Elizabethan times. Yet this later spectacle far from obliterates the weighty and varied evidence more recently produced by M.J. Kitch and G.J. Mayhew, and shows a heavy infiltration of Protestantism in Edwardian East Sussex. Indeed the thirty-five local Marian martyrs burned in Sussex should have prepared us for these later discoveries.[8] Again, both Gloucestershire and Norfolk have also been differentiated from the conservative counties by Ralph Houlbrooke, Elaine Sheppard, Ken Powell and others.[9] Least of all can I understand Dr Haigh's omission of Essex from the above passages, since here we are enormously well informed regarding a county which rivalled even Kent in the intensity of its popular convictions, despite the small but resolute group of local gentry who helped their diocesan Bishop Bonner to carry out the Marian reaction.[10] It is nevertheless true that neither Dr Haigh's minimal picture of pre-Elizabethan Protestantism nor my own more expansionist view can be proved outright by precise statistics. For the most part our broader conclusions must perforce consist of probabilities, though often strong probabilities – rather than fully demonstrable facts. This irritating situation one can only explain by a rapid glance at the nature of our source-materials for the period 1530–1558.

The major sources and their limitations

Of course it would be easy to begin with some much simpler rejoinders. For example, Dr Haigh elsewhere regards puritanical Elizabethan clergy as producing an anticlericalism among the laity far more violent than any experienced by the pre-Reformation clergy.[11] If this be the case, one finds it difficult to see how the Puritans accomplished even a partial conversion at a time when the people are alleged to have hated them and their teachings so strongly. Again, if England really remained 'a Catholic country' in the autumn of 1558, does this not make a mad gambler or else an imperceptive fool of William Cecil, who within a year of that date ventured to erect a fully fledged Protestant settlement in England? Revisions which imply a caricature of this most cautious of ministers must surely be in need of reconsideration. Though these may be judged rather more than debating points, the problems of religion in Tudor society nevertheless demand far more fundamental approaches. We need above all to attack the local history of the Reformation in detail and to explore its regional aspects with sensitive antennae. These situations cannot, however, be appreciated without grasping the grave limitations which beset our sources. Their coverage, at first sight so voluminous and revealing, is nevertheless far too meagre to allow us to minimise the early Reformation by reference to what they do not tell us.[12] The demonstrable incompleteness of these sources should forbid such arguments from negative evidence and compel us to beware of all overconfident generalisation. After all, during these decades we have nothing remotely resembling a contemporary census of early Protestants or a poll of religious opinions. There can be little prospect of establishing tolerably hard statistics concerning the number of these people, or even the rough percentage of the English population which at any stage they attained. When Dr Haigh offers 'a general impression of conservative attachment', he will surely permit others to offer some general impressions of a more varied and complex character.

The strength and the limitations of our sources can best be ascertained by reference to the valuable *Biographical Register of Early English Protestants, 1525–1558*, laboriously compiled by Dr John Fines.[13] It contains names and biographies of some 3000 persons collected from printed and manuscript sources and will doubtless be somewhat enlarged by future research. Whence exactly does such a compilation derive its data? As ever John Foxe's *Acts and Monuments* remains the most prolific source of supply, though Foxe himself was conscious of the large gaps in his information. Ecclesiastical archives, especially bishops' registers and the surviving act books of the church courts, have also yielded the names of many persons suspected or convicted of Protestant heresies. Governmental records such as the Domestic State Papers prove less broadly fruitful, since they naturally say more about Catholic dissidents, who were regarded under both Henry VIII and Edward VI as actual or potential enemies of the state. Conversely under Mary, the complete and fully printed Acts of the Privy Council are distinctly informative on Protestant activism, which the Council sought day by day to suppress. The roughly 800 Protestants who went into exile during Mary's reign – nearly 500 of them traced in British and continental sources by Miss Garrett[14] – have also contributed materially to John Fines's *Register*. So too have a number of miscellaneous narratives, diaries and memoirs, together with the various collections of letters by the martyrs and other notable Protestants.[15]

That the Fines *Register* will prove an invaluable instrument for social historians of religion one cannot doubt, yet its uses as a means of assessing the total extent of the movement must be limited because – for various reasons I shall shortly explain – there must have been large numbers of more or less convinced Protestants who without much difficulty managed to keep outside all the records. Most essentially the *Register* must be a list of the persecuted minority of the Protestants, the risk-takers, activists, martyrs, exiles, the people who got into trouble and consequently into the official archives and the martyrologies. We can arrive at no statistical hypotheses, no multipliers enabling us to enlarge these 3000 names into an acceptable estimate of England's total Protestant population. Indeed, we cannot seriously attempt this feat even in regard to those individual towns or counties where information is most plentiful. Any sort of quantitative thinking on this aspect of the movement must be attended by a host of complications. Let us briefly observe six main factors which make our information about early Protestantism so incomplete, and thus so incapable of supporting negative deductions and arguments minimising the extent of the movement.

1. The loss of ecclesiastical archives has been severe, especially in regard to court books likely to have contained proceedings against numerous heretics. The gaps have been most closely recognised in the cases of our most voluminous diocesan collections, such as those of Lincoln, York, Norwich and London.[16] In some places the actual compilation of records seems to have become less efficient from about 1547, the year when Protestantism appears to have begun its strongest period of advance. For example, the writer's recovery of information from two brief Peterborough act books (which have strayed into the Northamptonshire Record Office) has virtually doubled our previous factual knowledge about Henrician Protestantism in Northamptonshire and Rutland.[17] Likewise Dr Houlbrooke remarks that his surviving archdeaconry court book (Sudbury, November 1544 to July 1546) shows how much valuable evidence of the spread of dissent has been lost through the disappearance of the other books in that series.[18] Yet again Dr Margaret Bowker's long enumeration of the multiple gaps at Lincoln illustrates a similar situation upon a very large scale.[19]

2. Despite the devotees who believed that God would mitigate their sufferings at the stake, and that their reward would be incalculable and immediate, ordinary people of this period are unlikely to have ignored the prospect of extreme physical pain. The element of fear and the natural urge to survive and avoid notoriety must have operated to keep the vast majority of Protestants out of the fire – and so in most cases out of the records. Convicted heretics were normally granted one recantation, after which a second conviction in the ecclesiastical court meant the delivery of a defendant to the sheriff for burning. Thus martyrdom became a voluntary calling for heroes and heroines only. For humble prisoners who lacked the means to placate their gaolers, even a stretch in a Tudor prison could prove a harrowing trial of their steadfastness, especially if they were manacled for long periods. To the 58 Henrician martyrs and the 291 Marian martyrs we should add at least 40 people who died in prison.[20] Needless to say, these figures, though forming a phenomenon unique in English history, can have constituted but a tiny minority of the Protestant body during the early decades.

3. Quite apart from these severe physical and mental deterrents, the English population was far from dividing itself neatly into convinced Protestants and convinced Catholics. In the reign of Mary the letters and speeches of the heroes denounce their unheroic followers who saved themselves by pretending to be Catholics, while still known to their close associates as Protestants at heart. The martyr Ralph Allerton told Bishop Bonner that in England there were not two but three religions, 'and the

third is a neuter, being indifferent – that is to say, observing all things that are commanded outwardly, as though he were of your [i.e. Bonner's] part, his heart being set wholly against the same'.[21] The more famous martyr John Bradford wrote to his friend Richard Hopkins at Coventry, bewailing the fact that less than a tenth of their body was daring to persevere. These 'maungye mongrelles' the temporisers 'pretend outwardly popery, goyng to Masse with the papistes and tarying with them personallye at theyr anti-christian and idolatrous servyce, but wyth their harts (say they) and wyth theyr spirites they serve the Lorde'.[22] The Venetian residents in Marian London, Soranzo, Surian and Michiele, all agree with the Habsburg agent Renard that the English obeyed Mary out of fear and would probably lapse after her time.[23] These foreign observers, we must add, probably knew little about conservative public opinion in areas distant from the capital. Their picture of unwilling submission and outward compliance is no doubt also influenced by the thousands of heretical foreigners in London, who normally hastened to recant when confronted by charges of heresy. So far as concerns the natives, Foxe is likely enough to have understated the frequency of recantations for obvious reasons: though basically honest, he cannot have wanted to blur his sharp impressions of heroism.

4. The body of 'neuters' was swollen not merely by terror but by a secular spirit. Contemporary moralists and church officials often com-plained that many of the people cared little for any sort of religion and 'roistered' in the alehouses even during the times of divine service.[24] That Tudor towns and villages contained convivial as well as pietist groups cannot be doubted, even though religious problems also appear to have been frequently discussed in public houses. In fact we learn that in London, Colchester and elsewhere the inns sheltered 'underground' Protestant con-gregations as well as roisterers.[25] It is also probable that most of the small, close-knit communities conspired to profess ignorance when interrogated concerning their own members suspected of heresy,[26] an attitude which must have restricted actual testimony against local suspects.

5. A further important deprivation of evidence has arisen from the fact that most of the Marian bishops, diocesan chancellors and local gentry failed to institute rigorous enquiries and prosecutions, or at most selected a few ringleaders. Such methods have apparently reduced the record in those counties like Sussex and Gloucestershire where the recorded offen-ders now occur mostly by ones and twos per village. This would suggest a minimising illusion, since under Tudor social conditions it seems highly improbable that most actual offenders were solitaries, thinly spread over the countryside. Yet further distortions occurred because John Foxe patently received better reports from some areas than from others. He strove to obtain reliable local knowledge, but under the conditions of that day could not produce a uniform efficiency among his correspondents, some of whom may have felt a certain need for caution even after Mary's

death. On the other hand the Marian Council and its commissioners were apparently less concerned to produce an even persecution than to spur on the church officials in those areas – such as the dioceses of London and Canterbury – where they knew heresy to be rampant. All in all, it was actual persecution which meant documentation, yet the irregularities of governmental pressure and episcopal zeal – quite apart from the notoriously uneven distribution of Protestantism itself – mean that we cannot accurately estimate and compare local situations from evidence of such varying quality.

6. Moreover, there is ample reason to suppose that numerous Protestant groups existed in places unmentioned by Foxe, by ecclesiastical records, or indeed by any of the standard, coherent sources of information. Quite often we detect such groups only through the fortuitous survival of personal letters or other detached and fleeting documents, which in any less fortunate instances must long since have perished. For example, only a letter from the militant wheelwright John Clement has revealed the existence of three otherwise unrecorded groups at Nutfield, Merstham and Chaldon, all near Redhill in Surrey.[27] Likewise without the preservation of Thomas Hancock's valuable manuscript, relating his turbulent encounters as a missionary at Salisbury, Poole and Southampton, we should know extremely little about the strong Protestant parties at the latter two places.[28] So far as I am aware, our knowledge of the iconoclasm in 1547 at Portsmouth now depends upon a letter by Stephen Gardiner, yet in this case it was one of those which fell into the hands of Foxe and was printed in the *Acts and Monuments*.[29] Yet again, our knowledge that Lyme Regis was a notoriously Protestant town, and financially penalised as such by Queen Mary, depends upon one reliable document: a retrospective memorandum written as late as 1586 by Sir Francis Walsingham.[30] Another 'lucky' survivor is the manuscript letter of 1562 from William Ramsey, 'minister' of Chard in Somerset, to his former parishioners at South Molton near Exmoor, to whom he had preached the gospel 'even in a perilous time'.[31] It contains a tribute to Sir John Chichester, who fought 'for the defence of his naturall countrye agaynst the tyranny of the Spaniards and superstition of the romishe Antichriste'. The letter also lists thirteen names, some of them gentry, from this otherwise unrecorded group in the then flourishing North Devon cloth town. Given some preachers, Ramsey believed that Devon would show itself fully ripe for conversion.

The perils of judging from negative evidence become lurid when we realise how few local events and situations can ever have been recorded in an age with no real equivalent to the newspaper, and how impermanent personal correspondence has always been. Only when armed with a realistic view of the extant sources, of their defective coverage and their silences, should we assess the local development of the English Reformation.

On this basis certain of Dr Haigh's summary judgements seem to me reasonable, while others, for reasons I shall explain, run counter to the probabilities. While he has more than once wisely discounted the value of arguments based on negative evidence, as a vigorous campaigner for a 'small' early Reformation, he inevitably runs into danger of using arguments ultimately based on such grounds. Quite recently, for example, he criticised an alleged slenderness of the materials used by Dr J.F. Davis: 'But even in the south-east of England, heresy appears to have been a restricted phenomenon: case after case from the same few parishes, and heretics under interrogation revealed the same few names, with little indication of wider support.'[32] Yet in the three counties chiefly described by Dr Davis a much larger cast was in fact treading the stage – even in our fragmentary records. Between 1525 and 1559 the Fines *Register* has the names of 263 heretics for Kent, 209 for Suffolk and 304 for Essex. These 776 known persons come from more than 200 parishes and if my foregoing arguments stand, they represent only the visible tip of a very large Protestant iceberg. Again, we should not be influenced subconsciously by the highly populated landscapes of our own day, since England then contained about one-fifteenth of its present population. In this near-vacuum preachers as effective as Latimer, Bradford or Knox could within a few weeks have modified the balance of opinion in a small county. Likewise a heterodox congregation of forty people could have deeply influenced religious change in a typical market town with an adult population of only three or four hundred.

Where did Protestantism most readily take root?

So far as concerns the role of the largest towns, Dr Haigh's emphasis appears wholly justified. England's five most populous provincial cities of that day, each likely to have contained from ten to twelve thousand inhabitants, were Norwich, Bristol, Coventry, York and Newcastle upon Tyne. In the first three of these, Protestantism appears strong by 1558. At York, with its relatively huge and influential clerical population, the movement remained weak compared with its success in neighbouring Hull, a maritime and merchant-dominated place, about half the size of York, where the few clergy were closely controlled by the civic oligarchs.[33] Newcastle lay within a frontier zone little touched by the new beliefs, which were just being introduced by Bernard Gilpin. The city itself began its conversion under the preachers John Knox and John Rough, who nevertheless moved south before the onset of the Marian reaction.[34]

Even so, to close the urban list with these places, or even with Colchester, Ipswich and the other major towns correctly cited by Dr Haigh, would restrict the picture, since without any doubt another special *locus classicus* of early English Protestantism was the minor urban or near-urban community: the smallish weaving town, the even smaller market town, the large, semi-industrialised village. Foxe was well supported by the evidence when he chose Hadleigh in Suffolk as the prime exemplar of a godly Reformation community. Urged on by its rector Rowland Taylor, both its men and its women studied the Scriptures, so 'that the whole town seemed rather a university of the learned, than a town of cloth-making or labouring people'.[35] In the mid-Tudor years, other places of similar size seem also recognisably proto-Puritan. To take only three counties, those with at least a few documented Protestants may be listed as follows. In Kent were Cranbrook, Ashford, Faversham, Staplehurst, Pluckley, Maidstone, Tenterden, Tonbridge, Lenham, Ulcombe. In Essex we note Bocking, Coggeshall, Steeple Bumpstead, Great Bentley, Billericay, Horkesley, Dedham. In Suffolk the list would include Hadleigh, Bury St Edmunds, East Bergholt, Mendlesham, Winston, Stoke by Clare and Stoke by Nayland. Numerous similar places existed in Gloucestershire, Wiltshire and other parts of southern England.[36] In the North they appear far more rarely, the most obvious example being Halifax, which resembled Cranbrook as a spacious industrial parish containing various subsidiary villages.[37] Nearly all the places listed above were cloth towns: many of them had until quite recent years contained Lollard congregations while some were destined to become notable centres of Puritanism. The long association of textile operatives with religious radicalism, and also the local tenacity of a broadly radical spirit have both been noted by Dr J.F. Davis and others.[38] Attention has also been given to Newbury in Berkshire as furnishing a textbook example of consistent radicalism extending all the way from Lollardy to the nineteenth century.[39]

The degree to which early English Protestantism depended upon travellers abroad, foreign visitors and the import of foreign books, has become another familiar topic of modern Reformation history. Historians have often cited the irate remark made as early as 1530 by Bishop Nix of Norwich, when he complained of being 'accombred' by people who studied heretical books in English, adding that the gentlemen and commonalty 'be not greatly infected, but merchants and such that hath their abiding not far from the sea'.[40] In subsequent years ample evidence supports the truth of this observation. To the big towns and the cloth towns we must add English ports of all sizes, and of these, few of any significance along the eastern and southern coasts fail to reveal a Protestant presence between 1530 and 1558. Beginning with Hull and moving southward, this presence is recorded at Boston, King's Lynn, Yarmouth, Dunwich, Aldeburgh, Orford, Ipswich, Harwich, Dovercourt, Gravesend and Dartford. In the extended port of London, English and foreign businessmen, sailors, ship-builders and publicans formed a heretical *demi-monde* over which the church exercised a very tenuous authority. Within the city such a society appears in the intramural areas around London Bridge, Queenhithe, Thames Street and

Billingsgate. Yet probably the greater part of it flourished further east: in St Katherine's, Wapping, Ratcliff and Limehouse, together with Southwark, Rotherhithe and Deptford on the opposite bank of the Thames.[41] South of the estuary in Kent there were early Protestants at Rochester, Faversham, Birchington, Sandwich, Dover and Hythe.

At this point on the list, let us not overlook Calais, which until its loss in January 1558 was an English port-town with a large body of Protestants, well over fifty being actually named by Dr Fines.[42] Along the south coast of England smaller lists appear at Rye, Winchelsea, Hastings, Brighton, Hove, Chichester, Portsmouth, Southampton, Poole, Lyme Regis, Exmouth and Exeter. This provisional list of ports does not arise from exhaustive local researches, and will doubtless be extended. For example, it has only recently emerged from a close examination of the manuscript archives of Boston, Lynn and Yarmouth that on the death of Edward VI, the councils of these towns decided to back the Dudleys and Lady Jane Grey. When the East Anglian squires rallied around Mary, the councils of the three ports hastily conformed, partially erasing their earlier decisions from the record.[43]

I shall now briefly survey the more debatable regions of England, saying little about those where the essentials are generally agreed, and without unnecessarily duplicating the relevant and still viable summation of the early advances of Protestantism by Professor Palliser,[44] which should be read alongside the following pages. I shall not be so contentious as to dispute all Dr Haigh's verdicts. There can be no doubt that he is justified in placing Cornwall, Lancashire and even Lincolnshire among the slow developers. Wanting to be offensive, Henry VIII upbraided the Lincolnshire rebels of 1536 as 'the rude commons of one shire, and that one of the most brute and beestelie of the hole realme'.[45] With the broad Humber to the north and the broader fens to the south, it was subject to a topographical isolation almost rivalling that of Lancashire. This feature applied less to the more southerly shires within the huge diocese of Lincoln, which latter embraced most of the east Midlands from the Humber to the Thames. Though Dr Margaret Bowker has supplied such valuable information on Bishop Longland's successful struggle against a mainly Lollard resistance,[46] the development of Protestantism after his death in 1547 has not yet been closely analysed. Though most parts of the diocese were distinctly slow to adopt new ideas, it should not be dismissed in purely negative terms, especially when we recall the depletion of its ecclesiastical records after 1547, and the fact that little pertinacious and revealing persecution occurred. Including Northamptonshire, detached in 1541 to form the new diocese of Peterborough, I have located – and again without prolonged seeking – activist Protestant groups in rather more places than might be expected, notably at Horncastle, Boston, Grimsthorpe, Northampton, Oakham, Oundle, St Martin's parish in Leicester, Gaddesby, Amersham, St Neots and probably at Lincoln, Stamford, Grantham,

Bedford, and St Ives.[47] One need scarcely add that Reformers became numerous in Oxford at the southern extremity of the Lincoln diocese: likewise just over its eastern boundary at Cambridge and certain neighbouring villages in the diocese of Ely.[48] Perhaps some of these groups were small and transient, yet there remains every likelihood that many others existed yet left no distinct trace in the relatively meagre records. For example, many of the scattered individuals detected in 1556 by Cardinal Pole's visitation are likely to have had local confederates who escaped charges.[49] Certainly this visitation bears every sign of a rapid and superficial inquiry which cannot have plumbed the depths of evasive and collusive heresy. Among her Marian exiles, Dr Garrett biographed numerous persons who fled from the diocese of Lincoln and went abroad, most of them being gentry, clergy, students and members of the middle order of society. Many of these came from Lincolnshire itself, where the Henrician martyr Anne Askew had a remarkably large circle of kinsfolk and admirers. At Grimsthorpe the widowed duchess of Suffolk, herself soon to become a prominent exile, enlisted the support of Latimer and other notable Edwardian preachers.[50] Admittedly, even these many occurrences across so large an area fail to create any impressive spectacle of religious change, but in view of the defective sources it can no longer be suggested that the diocese of Lincoln remained a wholly conservative area or failed to participate in the Protestant expansion from 1547.

From this unsensational scene, we move across the Midlands to their south-western areas, where the Cotswolds extend southward to the Avon and the Bristol Channel. Though not to the same degree as Kent, Essex and Suffolk, Gloucestershire proved receptive to the Reformation. The situation there was not fully appreciated until 1971–73, when my former associate Ken Powell described it in three clear and searching essays.[51] These have changed our view of the religious history of that county and prompted historians in search of the popular Reformation to cease gazing too exclusively upon south-eastern England. The rather spectacular manifestation of Protestantism at Bristol had tended to obscure its diffusion throughout the many towns and villages long since made prosperous by sheep-farming and the cloth-trade; places like Wotton, Dursley, Tetbury, Chipping Campden, Stroud, Stonehouse, Newent, Lydney, Tewkesbury and Gloucester itself.[52] Not so many decades earlier Lollardy had spread across the country and into the industrial Forest of Dean, but from the mid-1530s the expansion of Lutheran ideas had obvious debts to Latimer's preaching and to the labours of people like Richard Webb, the busy distributor of Protestant books in Bristol.[53] By way of a climax there came in 1551 the appointment of the Zürich-trained Hooper to the new see of Gloucester, followed by his vigorous assault upon a parish clergy as yet ignorant of the new biblical theology, and in many cases of the most basic documents of Christianity. Despite his angular disciplinary zeal, Hooper maintained good relations with the civic authorities of Gloucester and also with the common people, who gathered in great numbers to deplore his execution for heresy.[54]

Regarding the role of the great port of Bristol as a gateway to this region, caution might be advisable until we know more, if only because Bristol traded almost wholly with Catholic countries. It might prove more fruitful to examine the purely English connections of merchants, trades-men and craftsmen in Bristol, and to associate Gloucestershire in general with its landward neighbours Wiltshire and Berkshire, which, after the surrender of Dorset in 1541 to the new diocese of Bristol, remained to form that of Salisbury.[55] Berkshire reached up into the Thames Valley, through which it may have received its main stimulus from London and the south-east, as it had done in the days of Lollard missionising. By the same token Berkshire touched Oxford, where the new religion became strong around the mid-century. Yet again, both Wiltshire and Berkshire resembled Glou-cestershire in their dependence upon the clothiers, whose mobility and social coherence helped them to propagate Reformation doctrines. The activism of this otherwise neglected area has been usefully chronicled by Mr I.T. Shield in an unpublished thesis of 1960, which deserves more attention than it has received. Not a few of the grandchildren of the pious West-Country builders, patrons and parishioners of 'wool churches' embraced Protestant ideas without waiting for safe times. Apart from the Gloucestershire martyrs, eleven other leaders suffered execution at Wind-sor, Salisbury, Devizes and at the productive cloth town of Bradford on Avon. Under Mary some seven more burnings followed at Salisbury, Col-lingbourne and the former Lollard metropolis of Newbury.[56] One of these latter victims was Julins [*sic*] Palmer, the schoolmaster at Reading and a former fellow of Magdalen, that notably Protestant college in Edwardian Oxford. As befitted this career, Palmer's views appear exceptionally humane for that day, since he maintained that 'no man ought to be put to death for matter of religion'.[57] Even the cathedral city of Salisbury did not lack a fairly numerous group of Protestants. When the diocesan chancellor narrowly predeceased Queen Mary, considerable numbers of people were awaiting examination by him on charges of heresy. In fact certain of those in prison at Salisbury were not released by the Elizabethan government until 31 December 1558.[58]

Apart from Bristol, Gloucestershire, Coventry and a few lesser places in Warwickshire and Staffordshire, religious changes came very gradually in the western Midlands and along the Welsh Marches. In Coventry, it is true, the new beliefs vigorously invaded even the ruling civic hierarchy and occasioned some martyrdoms, together with the expulsion and replace-ment of a heretical mayor by the Marian government.[59] Once a city of demonstrative piety, yet also an important Lollard centre, Coventry always held great importance for the Reformers. Writing to Bullinger in July 1560,

Thomas Lever recalled it as a place where there had always been 'great numbers zealous for the evangelical truth'. He then describes the burnings and banishments. Returning there shortly after Elizabeth's accession, Lever had found 'that vast numbers in this place were in the habit of frequenting the public preaching of the Gospel', and so he had consented to settle in Coventry with his family and to serve as one of its preachers.[60] It can be safely assumed that this marked propensity was not suddenly created between Elizabeth's accession and July 1560.

In other parts of Warwickshire the cautious Protestants were probably numerous, at all events among the people who appear here as substantial testators. An analysis of about 600 Warwickshire wills proved in the prerogative court of Canterbury shows that during the reign of Edward VI the number in that well-off class, who deliberately omitted the hitherto almost universal formulae indicating saint-worship, exceeded the traditionalist Catholic wills by nearly three to one. Naturally, under the Marian reaction many such testators nervously reverted to the traditional forms, yet even then the number of traditional wills does not much exceed that of the Protestant type.[61]

While the Tudor religious history of Staffordshire, Shropshire, Derbyshire and Cheshire has not yet been exhaustively investigated, it has been shown that the literary and devotional culture of that region remained on the whole conservative and slow-moving until and beyond the accession of Elizabeth.[62] Certainly, however, some locally sensitive enquiries need to be conducted within such areas, which were by no means homogeneous in spirit. So far, for example, we have been content to regard Lichfield as a quiet, backward-looking cathedral city,[63] yet to stage a local revision one need go no further than Foxe's *Acts and Monuments*, supported by items from his manuscript collection now in British Library, MS Harley 421. The more spectacular episodes occurred at Lichfield in the reign of Mary: they affected not only the population of the city but a number of people in the neighbouring places, especially within the nearby northern tip of Warwickshire. As usual, a local persecution reveals the facts.[64] Ralph Baines, a Catholic exile under Edward VI and a professor of Hebrew at Paris, returned to England at the accession of Mary and in November 1554 was consecrated as bishop of Lichfield and Coventry. Along with his chancellor Anthony Draycot – another energetic Marian regarded by Foxe as notably cruel – Bishop Baines took strong action in September 1556 by compelling various Lichfield people to do penance as heretics. Joyce Lewis, daughter of a squire at Tixall and wife of another at Mancetter, refused. She was spared for a year, but only to be condemned and burned at Lichfield in September 1557. At her execution many members of the large crowd joined in drinking with her and showing other marked sings of admiration. There and then her numerous backers joined in open prayers for the abolition of the mass and 'papistry'. Even the officiating sheriff, Nicholas Bird, cried 'Amen' with the rest, while an unsympathetic priest compiled a list of the main demonstrators, many of whom (including Bird) were afterwards arrested and forced to do public penance. From the records of the transactions we derive the actual names of about sixty local Protestants, mostly from Lichfield itself. The other local martyr also came from the gentry. He was Robert Glover, who took his MA at Cambridge and inherited considerable lands at Baxterly and elsewhere. Having been examined at length by Bishop Baines at both Lichfield and Coventry, he was burned at the latter in September 1555. His younger brothers John and William Glover both suffered severe persecution; John, well known to Foxe, being an introspective Puritan who often despaired of his own salvation. Foxe also observes that John Glover had become the chief spiritual adviser to the martyr Joyce Lewis.

Another member of this group was Latimer's Swiss-born secretary Augustine Bernher, who comforted Robert Glover on the eve of his execution and accompanied Mrs Lewis on the way to the stake. Yet another friend of the Glovers was that well-known propagandist Thomas Becon, who wrote a first-hand account of early Protestantism in Warwickshire, Staffordshire and Derbyshire, which in regard to religious progress he graded in that order.[65] Foxe explains that behind the whole group there stood the major missionary and martyr Laurence Saunders, the original inspirer of Joyce Lewis, a close accociate of the Glovers and in his last days the author of a long letter addressed 'To the professors of the Gospel and true doctrine of our Saviour Jesus Christ in the town of Lichfield'.[66] Under Edward VI Saunders had in fact been employed as a Reader in Lichfield Cathedral. Further back still, Dr John Old, translator of the *Paraphrases* of Erasmus and chaplain to Walter Devereux, Lord Ferrers (d. 1558), had survived charges of heresy during the last years of Henry VIII and had retired to Staffordshire, where he entertained Thomas Becon and Robert Wisdom. Having briefly served as a canon at both Lichfield (1551) and Hereford (1552), Old fled in 1554 to Frankfurt.[67] Despite all these local personalities and activities, the materials at present available show scarcely any evidence of Protestant confederacies in the Staffordshire towns, apart from Lichfield.

The annals of early Protestantism in Shropshire are much slighter, though as early as May 1528 Richard Cotton, curate of Atcham near Shrewsbury, abjured his heresies in Lichfield Cathedral.[68] He had been accused of reading Lutheran books and holding frequent disputations and conversations with disciples of the Lutheran sect 'and mainly with a certain George Constantine in the towns of Whitchurch and Atcham'. This reference is to Tyndale's well-known agent, who at Antwerp had been assisting the Reformer to set forth his edition of the New Testament and to prepare tracts for despatch to England. After further jouneys to and from Antwerp, Constantine was caught and imprisoned in 1530 by the Lord

Chancellor, Sir Thomas More. While it is of interest to see Constantine operating so far from his usual spheres of activity in the south-east, we cannot suppose that he made much impact on the staid clergy of the west Midlands, where even towns such as Shrewsbury and Hereford show so little evidence of religious change. There remained local differences. Unlike rural Worcestershire, the city of Worcester had its early Protestants and at no stage can be regarded as a stronghold of Catholicism.[69] By contrast, from a denunciatory letter written by Bishop Scory in 1561,[70] it emerges that the clergy and people of Hereford were still offering open resistance to the new Anglican Settlement: this must have been one of the English towns least impressed by Reformation propaganda.

Meanwhile across the Welsh border the initial barriers against the Reformation look even more formidable: bad communications, a relative lack of towns, a poorly educated parish clergy, an almost total lack of printed books in the Welsh language and a suspicion of religious ideas mediated through England.[71] Over and beyond these factors, the case of Wales differed radically from that of any English region. Its rich and still largely oral poetic tradition had many champions and practitioners even after the disappearance of those former patrons, the heads of religious houses. Moreover some educated Welshmen, such as Sir John Price and William Salesbury, keenly admired Erasmus: they backed concepts of biblical humanism and church reform coming from that source rather than from Luther. They managed to attract some Welsh disciples emancipated from mere peasant conservatism, from fear of clerical persecution and even from advanced Protestant theology. In 1538 and 1542 at least two of the Welsh bishops ordered their clergy to administer religious instruction in the vernacular, both Welsh and English, while in 1551 Salesbury took an important step by publishing his Welsh translations of the scriptural passages included in the Anglican Prayer Book of 1549. A few poets even wrote in that language in order to promote Protestant beliefs. Conversely, though most Welshmen came to terms with the Elizabethan government, a considerable body of Catholic literature arose from Welsh recusants during the last decade of the century.[72]

However debatable some of Dr Haigh's general theories may appear, it would be difficult to overpraise his authoritative work on the Reformation in Lancashire: it remains the most comprehensive and scholarly survey of any English region in Tudor times.[73] He describes a shire largely isolated between the Pennines and the Irish Sea. It contained a high proportion of uncultivated land, especially in the northern area, with their wild, spacious fields, moors and mosses. Apart from the south-eastern places around Manchester, it was then industrially underdeveloped, seldom visited by the great, and managed by the conservative Stanleys, earls of Derby, not by the Council in the North. Lancashire was then on the way to nowhere of great consequence – apart from Ireland. Many enterprising young people went away to work in London and seldom returned.

Under Edward VI two devoted Protestant clerics, born Lancastrians and destined to martyrdom, conducted preaching tours. John Bradford visited Manchester, Ashton-under-Lyne, Prestwich, Bolton, Bury, Wigan, Eccles, Middleton, Radcliffe and Liverpool. George Marsh is said to have visited Deane, Eccles, Bolton, Bury and many other parts of the diocese of Chester.[74] Judging from this list they probably made little impact outside a radius of eight or ten miles from the centre of Manchester. They and the few lay zealots, like Geoffrey Hurst and Roger Holland,[75] found an exceptionally resistant clergy and people, with a reputation for rough manners and licentiousness. Many were prepared to denounce even local heretics, yet few appreciated theological issues. A number made wills attempting to combine Lutheran justification by faith with saint-worship and other Catholic principles.[76] This primitive conservatism lingered until the advent of Jesuits and seminary priests during Elizabeth's later years, by which time Puritanism was also initiating that process whereby Lancashire became a museum of Protestant sects as well as the most heavily Catholic county of the realm.[77]

East of the Pennines we find this intensely provincial history by no means closely mirrored. Though late Elizabethan Yorkshire preserved several limited Catholic enclaves, its social and economic situation had long differed from the Lancashire model.[78] It had maintained direct sea-going contacts with the Continent for centuries. Alongside a few advanced squires and clerics, Yorkshire developed some major pockets of early Protestantism, as at Hull, Leeds and Halifax, while even conservative York did not wholly lack devotees, some of them from continental backgrounds.[79]

In the far south-west of England, modern research is indicating situations more varied than that impression of uniform religious reaction one would derive from Frances Rose-Troup's classic narrative, *The Western Rebellion of 1549*. By far the most detailed analysis of religious change among the people is that by Dr Robert Whiting, who concludes that the Henrician and Edwardian changes rapidly shattered the old pieties, and that modern historians have indeed exaggerated the elements of religious resistance in mid-Tudor Devon and Cornwall. While Catholicism revived only with the coming of the seminarists, the general popularising of Anglicanism also occurred during the reign of Elizabeth.[80] Though the majority of the western rebels doubtless followed their priests in demanding a return in religion to the last years of Henry VIII – though not to the Papal Supremacy – the old label 'Prayer Book Rebellion' ignores a well-documented complex of secular discontents in the south-west. Professor Youings has recently displayed the striking elements of a class war, though one directed especially against the Carews and other families identified with the entire new order in both church and state. Only a few gentry joined the rebels, some like the Pomeroys figuring as staunch Catholics even while they were organising extensive purchases of secularised chantry lands. Confronted by the rebel host, the civic leaders of Exeter, divided in religion, stood wholly and consistently united in their determination to maintain the defence of their city. Everywhere economic motives were openly displayed by the rebels, who resented the pressure of inflation and detested the poll-tax recently imposed upon sheep and woollen cloth.[81] Yet another economic element with political and religious over-tones lay in the near future. In the later years of Mary, the sea-going gentry of those counties, led by the Killigrews, began their long history of piracy and war directed against the trade of Portugal and Spain. The now familiar combination of maritime aggression and Protestantism had already come to birth, long before the exploits of Hawkins and Drake.[82] That Cornwall, still largely Celtic-speaking, must be classed among the slower movers goes without saying, yet any claim that is was uniformly Catholic and 'medi-eval' until after 1558 would remain a simplification. It can be challenged by several references to Protestant opinion, not least by that oddly revealing anecdote told by the Cornish antiquary Richard Carew.[83] In 1548 the boys of Bodmin School divided themselves into two fighting factions, called the Old Religion and the New Religion. With unchanging membership and under two captains, they carried this partisanship into all their activities. The climax arrived when one of them converted a candlestick into a gun, which he charged and fired, killing a calf. Whereupon, concludes our author, 'the owner complained, the master whipped and the division ended'. Such an event could scarcely have occurred had not adult religious partisanships already existed at Bodmin, which in the following year was to furnish many rebels.

Through discoveries and eliminations we are now close to defining the heartland of the English Reformation, the area wherein society was deeply permeated by Protestant doctrines before the accession of Elizabeth. It should certainly not be envisaged as consisting merely of London and Kent: rather should we think in terms of a great crescent running from Norwich down to Hove and beyond. Its most intensive sections were Suffolk, Essex, London and Kent. Despite the strength of Protestantism in Norwich and the long tally of martyrs in East Sussex, the two extremities of this crescent may have been somewhat less intensively involved. Yet in addition a western offshoot ran up the Thames Valley embracing not only the old Lollard centres in Buckinghamshire but also places in Oxfordshire and Berkshire, thus linking the crescent with the Protestant communities in Gloucestershire and Wiltshire. The Thames Valley has not yet been fully investigated, but some plain evidence was recorded by the Princess Eliza-beth's custodian Sir Henry Bedingfield, who made direct enquiries about the local religious situation when in May 1554 he conducted his charge on a leisurely journey from the Tower of London to Woodstock.[84] These enquiries Bedingfield was bound to make, since one of his main functions lay in preventing Protestants and other disaffected persons from communicating with the popular princess, whom he shows to have been besieged by fervent good wishes and gifts everywhere along the route: at Eton, Wycombe, Wheatley, Stanton St John, Islip and Kidlington. He considered that while the Oxfordshire men were reliable,[85] those between London and that county 'were not good and whole in matters of religion': they firmly backed the former abolition of papal authority, though otherwise they showed themselves as loyal subjects.

At Wooburn in Buckinghamshire the party was shown the way by one Chrisopher Cooke, a husbandman whom Sir Henry found 'a very Protestant'. Cooke soon divulged that 'the most part' of the people there and at Wycombe were also of the same opinion, having been encouraged by Francis Russell – soon to become second earl of Bedford – 'and certayn other gentlemen off his secte'.[86] Now about twenty-seven years of age, Francis resided at Amersham and had actually served as a remarkably youthful Member of Parliament for Buckinghamshire in 1545 and 1547. Imbibing Protestantism since his early days at Cambridge, he became friendly with many notorious adherents of that persuasion, including Edward Underhill, John Bradford and Thomas Becon.[87] Detained briefly in the Fleet prison on Mary's accession, Francis covertly admired the rebel Wyatt. He inherited his father's vast estates in 1555, including Chenies in Buckinghamshire and Woburn Abbey, not far distant in Bedfordshire; but he immediately gained permission to travel abroad, visiting Zürich and gaining the friendship of Bullinger. Undoubtedly mid-Thames Protestantism owed not a little to this powerful figure, who represented so great an expansion of the Russell heritage. Yet there were older local roots, especially the strong Lollard tradition repressed by Longland not many years earlier. This doubtless connects with the popular acclaim received by John Knox, when he boldly continued to preach at Amersham for some time after Mary's accession.[88] The few remaining districts of the south-east appear to have been far less affected than those already mentioned: for example, the inland areas of the diocese of Winchester, comprising most of Hampshire and Surrey, where, in the depleted episcopal records, little beyond a sparse succession of heretics and martyrs may be documented from 1530 onward.[89] So much for our geographical survey, which has said little about the relatively undisputed areas, such as London and Kent at the Protestant extreme, or conversely those little-affected north-western counties, Cheshire, Derbyshire, Westmorland and Cumberland, which seem even more isolated than Lancashire itself.

It need scarcely be added that such a survey of early Protestant expansion would achieve more significance were it accompanied by an objective survey of Catholicism among the English people during this same period, *c.* 1530–58. In what senses was the old religion developing under the stresses of the Henrician and Edwardian state reformations? Was Catholic belief and observance in temporary decay? Had it fallen into the danger implied by Thomas More at his trial: the deprivation of its international sustenance?[90] Did the people 'of both religions' really 'detest the Pope', as the Venetian envoy Daniel Barbaro, a future Patriarch of Aquileia, reported from England in 1551?[91] Did the hapless Mary Tudor succeed in fusing Spanish Inquisition with Roman papacy in the popular mind? How do we explain the collapse in 1559 of the hitherto conservative parish clergy? Why, apart from crass self-interest, did the great majority of them conform so readily to the Elizabethan Settlement? On these mid-Tudor Catholic problems the evidence may prove somewhat rarefied, yet it seems strange that so very few historians have seriously attempted to explore in close detail this tract of religious history, the importance of which now seems so obvious.[92]

Continuing research: the study of wills

Can we hope to extend our present imprecise notions as to the relative strengths of the Protestant and non-Protestant populations at the various stages of the period 1530–58, and in particular counties and towns? Here our only hope of progress seems to lie in a mass study of the many thousands of contemporary wills extant in ecclesiastical archives and probate registries. Already begun in certain places, this task needs to be pursued with caution, and without the expectation that refined statistics will emerge. Yet provided they are used in considerable numbers, wills seem broadly acceptable as indicating trends of opinion. While individual testators quite frequently outline Protestant doctrines or give other direct evidence of religious beliefs, a mass survey must attach special importance to the pious preambles with which almost all wills of the period commence. Traditional Catholic wills begin with the testator leaving his soul to the company of the saints in heaven, while Protestant-type wills naturally discard this practice and show the testator bequeathing his soul to God or to Christ. In view of the still huge popularity of the saint-cults on the eve of the Reformation, a real significance can be attached to this differentiation, even though we certainly cannot presume that every will corresponds precisely with the personal religious standpoint of the testator. It is known that parish priests and notaries often gave advice on such points. The former, and perhaps most of the latter, were people of conservative views, and if their pressures did in fact distort the pictue, this would be by enhancing the prevalence of traditionalist, Catholic wills. Of course, a much stronger influence in the same direction must spring from the fact that most testators were elderly people, since it is certain that the new doctrines appealed far less to them than to their younger contemporaries.[93] Again, it seems likely that Tudor testators, most of whom made their wills in the close anticipation of death, acted out of conscience. Whatever prohibitions may have operated back in 1530 to menace the validity of Protestant wills,[94] the government of Edward VI does not seem to have seriously threatened to disqualify Catholic wills. Moreover, poor peasants and craftsmen seldom made formal wills: our testators were mostly people of some standing, likely to have their own ideas, well able to find a congenial notary, and in short quite likely to resist manipulation in either direction. All these factors considered, it would seem defensible to use wills in the mass with reasonable confidence that they will roughly indicate trends of opinion in their various localities. Yet for the above reasons they should by no means exaggerate the strength of Protestant opinion. The fact that so many come from the middling groups of society should not greatly disturb the balance, since Protestantism cannot possibly be dismissed as a middle-class phenomenon.[95]

Thirty years ago, after an already long acquaintanceship with the great collections of manuscript wills at York, I advocated the examination of wills under these restricted assumptions, and with the proviso that we should at all costs avoid presenting the results with statistical pedantry.[96] Since then a number of scholars have pursued such enquiries in regard to various counties and towns, though classifying them under somewhat differing schemes. It has now become possible to make a provisional statement on the results so far obtained. The available localities are varied and together they may constitute a fairly representative sample of the country as a whole. The counties include Kent, East Sussex, Yorkshire, Warwickshire, Lincolnshire and Nottinghamshire, together with the archdeaconry of Northampton and the urban communities of York, Hull, Leeds and Norwich.[97] The trends indicated in these various areas have a good deal in common. As Professor Scarisbrick discovered after reading very numerous early wills, the great majority continued to make traditional bequests to the church throughout the 1530s.[98] In the above group of places, apart from London and Kent, signs of change are indeed by no means common until around 1545, while the notable period of Protestant advance occupies the whole of Edward VI's reign. Soon after the accession of Mary there occurs a predictable decline of Protestant forms, though nowhere does this partial reversion restore the Henrician situation. Then in 1559–60 a swift resurgence of Protestantism supports my conjecture that many crypto-Protestants, doubtless accompanied by mere opportunists, emerged into the open as soon as it became safe to do so.

As one would anticipate, such fluctuations occur at somewhat later dates and lower numerical levels in Yorkshire, Lincolnshire and other conservative areas, as compared with 'advanced' Kent, where we observe already an annual increase in Protestant-type wills from 1532 to 1542. By the years 1542–46 about half the Kent wills were showing Protestant inclinations, which then heavily predominated throughout Edwardian years, and even – though in lesser degree – under Mary. As elsewhere, the Protestant figures in Kent rise dramatically in 1559–60. In East Sussex such signs are rare until 1545, though a steep increase appears in 1547–8, and by 1549–53 threatens to overwhelm the old forms. Though in Sussex, probably as a result of the sharp local persecution, traditional wills prevailed by 1556–58, a considerable Protestant core survived and the normal reversal occurred from 1559. In Northamptonshire the slower tempo is noticeable. Even under Edward VI over half the testators retain the traditional forms, while about one-third reject the saints and one-sixth retain more decisive signs of Catholic belief. By contrast, the city of Norwich shows early inclinations towards change. There the first new-style wills occur in 1535: by 1544–45 over half the wills are Protestant, and by 1553 only about 5 per cent remain traditional. The Catholic figures revive after 1533, but over the whole Marian reign they still constitute less than 40 per cent of the whole.

In Yorkshire a high proportion of the numerous extant wills remain in manuscript: I have assessed 750 of them dated from 1538 to 1558, but this figure is far from exhausting the surviving deposit of Yorkshire wills; it needs to be amplified and to be split regionally, since patterns were far from uniform over so large and varied a territory. Yet somewhat to my surprise, I found that more than a third of these wills rescinded the saints, while for the years 1547 to 1553 there occurred 139 traditional wills, as opposed to 153 of Protestant type, with 31 'neutral'. Under Mary only one Protestant martyr suffered in a population which I take to have approached a quarter of a million:[99] hence the emotional temperature presumably remained far lower than in south-eastern England. About one-third of the Yorkshire Marian wills I examined had Protestant affinities, yet I remain somewhat sceptical regarding the representative character of this figure in a still broadly conservative area.

Throughout all these groups of wills the local evidence on religious opinion corresponds to a reassuring extent with the miscellaneous information derived from other sources. It attests not only the advanced situation of Kent but also some of the more localised situations, such as the Protestant tenor of belief at mercantile Leeds and Hull, as compared with the conservative, clerical ethos of York. Future progress with these admittedly rough and ready indicators may perhaps produce some surprises, yet so far the results strongly argue that we must not take lightly the substantial advances made by the English Reformation before 1558. They also clearly indicate that neither Lancashire at one extreme nor Kent at the other should be accepted as a national norm. Yet, statistics and maps apart, the present writer comes away from all these sources with the distinct impression that, by the advent of Elizabeth, Protestantism had not only surmounted the harshest threat to its survival but had for the time being attained a greater psychological vitality and cohesion in English society than had the cause of conservative Catholicism. At all events this impression would seem fully applicable to the large south-eastern heart-land and its westward extensions, the regions which by mere area comprised less than half England, though constituting the wealthiest, most populous and best-educated portion of the realm. Seventeen years ago, and before such indications were less obvious than they have since become, Geoffrey Elton was guided by a sure instinct when he wrote: 'But the fact is that by 1553 England was almost certainly nearer to being a Protestant country than to anything else; unless that fact is recognized, what follows becomes incomprehensible.'[100] All the same, Dr Haigh's interventions seem to me acceptable insofar as they demonstrated that Lancashire, and in varying measure several other counties, by no means corresponded with this formula, large sections of their people retaining Catholic sympathies in 1559 and for some decades thereafter.

Some residual problems

In conclusion I desire to set the record straight regarding some general issues which have arisen directly from the problems discussed in the foregoing pages. As already remarked, some readers may have derived the impression that I hold a simplistic belief in 'Reformation from below', as distinct from 'Reformation from above', as an act of state.[101] Writing fifty or even thirty years ago, I certainly did hope to modify the excessive preoccupation of English historians with the statute book, with the mechanisms of church and state, with the top people who manipulated both. It then seemed high time to reiterate that, in England as elsewhere, the Reformation also involved personal conversions and convictions. In particular, should modern observers become too coolly enlightened to perceive the supreme propaganda value of martyrdom, they would lose contact not only with the Tudor mind, but with all Christian history. Even so, our modern concern with popular religion and grass-roots mentalities must not for a moment be suffered to obliterate our interest in the familiar theme of 'Reformation from above'. The greater part of my book *The English Reformation* did in fact continue to treat this old theme in detail, since 'from above' and 'from below' remain inseparable and equally essential elements of the story. After all, even the Henrician government abolished the monastic life, brutally despoiled the saints' shrines, forbade 'superstitious' cults, provided English Bibles in the churches and allowed Cranmer to experiment with a vernacular liturgy. Such masterful acts of state powerfully affected, though they never totally dictated, popular belief and opinion. Their continuance and expansion by the Edwardian government gave Protestant convictions the necessary breathing space to attain that degree of recruitment, integration and confidence needed to survive the Marian counter-assault, which must still be regarded as the major crisis of the Reformation in England.

Finally I should explain that this present essay does not seek to reestablish some 'Whiggish' orthodoxy regarding the speed and extent of the Protestantizing of English society. Rather does it seek to avoid all such simplistic, overarching theories in favour of humbler tasks, in particular the clarifying of the differentials between the various regions of England and the defining of a prime geographical focus of Protestantism which accords with the imperfect data and makes sense of the Elizabethan *dénouement*. The former of these tasks seems to me as important as the latter. If one seriously maintained, for example, that in regard to pre-Elizabethan Protestantism Lancashire and Gloucestershire stood approximately on the same level, then one's broader conclusions would at once be in danger of distortion. Of course, 'Whig history' has deeper implications. Yet the label is by no means so readily applicable to the sixteenth as to the seventeenth century. Moreover its present coding has become unduly complex. It nowadays suggests that the Whig under observation has given up research and lost interest in the advances made by younger scholars. Advanced in years, no longer fashionable, he has been left high and dry by the recent spectacular advances of brilliant young revisionists. More generally, it also means that he shows suspicious signs of being Protestant and patriotic, or even, in the most acute cases, that he believes the course of English history to have been 'inevitable' and always guided 'for the best' by forces resembling divine providence. While the present writer and not a few of his contemporaries must leave these charges to the verdict of posterity, let us at least hope we are found guiltless of Bishop Aylmer's notorious belief that 'God is English'. As applied to complex historical changes, I have never been able to attach any clear or useful meaning to the word 'inevitable'. Yet I also believe that our primary task is to examine the history which actually happened, rather than to create cardboard opponents or to fabricate those alternative scenarios which, given a little more luck, might have attained reality.

In the Old Whig *versus* Tory Revisionist controversy on the early English Reformation, a major debate is still provided by the alleged 'failure' of Mary Tudor, that highly significant climax of our story which may form a brief but by no means irrelevant coda to this essay, if only because one must not leave the impression that the religious issue dominated all else. Was there indeed anything 'inevitable' about the collapse of Mary's aspirations? Had she lived another twenty or even ten years, would not the English Reformation have become − as the father of Tory Revisionism, Hilaire Belloc maintained − 'an abortive and forgotten episode?'[102] Given the queen's continuing survival, would not England have entered upon a new politico-religious course, avoiding the 'sterile' religious divisions of

the seventeenth and eighteenth centuries? One must fear that such specu-
lations will produce little more than debating-club superficialities. The
contending factors cannot be computerised, and all our verdicts may tend
overmuch to lie at the mercy of our prejudices. Yet, if we must indulge in
this shadow-boxing, it may well be that moderate Whig attitudes will
appear more respectful toward the evidence than those of their romantic
opponents. Again, offered an imaginary choice, it might be reasonable
enough, at least on secular grounds, to prefer the courses which our
history has actually followed. After all, on what rational grounds could
we envisage a beneficent outcome of Queen Mary's survival? After that
first triumph of legitimism in 1553, she was soon surrounded by a complex
of harsh problems: English antipathy toward Spain, an aggressive king of
France, a defensive suspicion among the buyers of former church properties, a shortage of funds and an even greater shortage of realistic counsel-
lors. There remained two overriding disasters. One of these was that
mistaken view of the English heresy – shared in later years by Cardinal
Allen – that the heretics consisted of a few pockets of small tradesmen
readily destructible by tuition and combustion. Yet the supreme irony came
from continental Europe: the poisonous hatred felt by Pope Paul IV for
Spain, a hatred which in itself was to make Mary's two shining ideals
wholly incompatible. This formidable complex demanded a consummate
politician with an astute sense of priorities, but Mary was no sort of
politician and suffered from a mental fibrosis almost unique among our
former rulers. Her sorrowful memories, her 'nerves', her romantic admiration for her mother's country swamped her natural intelligence. The deep
elements of pathos in her plight demand that blend of sympathy and
critical insight recently shown by historians such as Professor Loades and
Dr R.H. Pogson.[103] Thanks to such scholars, we now understand the
problems she set Reginald Pole far more deeply than we did twenty years
ago. Yet even in terms of Mary's own ideals, the reign must still be judged
not merely a huge failure, but one likely to have become more monumental
with every succeeding year. Attacking every problem with the aid of prejudices and dogmas, Mary could display no flexibility even when her most
esteemed advisers, the Emperor Charles and King Philip, enjoined caution.
Today we cannot credibly envisage her as an Arminian in the making, as a
potential Anglo-Catholic with fair prospects of uniting the nation, still
less as a liberal Roman Catholic, who might eventually have granted
freedom of worship at least to the more moderate of her Protestant
subjects. Such a step we cannot imagine her ever taking, yet if our present
contentions are justified, nothing short of this would have been likely to
solve her problem.

Whatever the balance between their religious and their secular opinions,
the English became ever more restive throughout the reign. The Privy
Council records give the impression that few English governments have

become more widely beset by disaffection and plotting. This inauspicious atmosphere prevailed to the end. By Mary's last year the supply of martyrs showed no sign of diminishing, and her further survival would surely have meant more exiles, more burnings, more conspiracies, very possibly even civil warfare on the subsequent Dutch and French models. People did not need to be rabid Protestants in order to reject such a persecution, while a government so burdened both by its own miscalculations and its un-deserved misfortunes could not afford so divisive a luxury. Less acceptably still, the English people – presently ranged alongside Philip's oppressed Netherlandish subjects – became conscious of the need to resist the intru-sion of Habsburg hegemony and Spanish Inquisition into north-western Europe. Meanwhile Mary surrounded herself with notable Spanish experts on the eradication of heresy.[104] In short she collided not merely with Protestantism but with a more powerful force: the endemic and instinctive nationalism so obviously on the upgrowth in England ever since the four-teenth century. Granted that legitimist monarchical sentiment had also prospered under the Tudors, it nevertheless remained far from proof against identification with an unpopular foreign dynasty or against disasters in foreign policy so ignominious as the loss of Calais. We are hence fully entitled to ask whether Mary's Catholicism could ever, under such aus-pices, have become an English Catholicism. Were not English political life and religious culture already diverging violently from those of Spain? At all events, a historian should not be dismissed as a Protestant Whig or a complacent chauvinist because he finds it hard to discern any tolerable outcome from a hypothetical prolongation of the Marian experiment.

Notes

1 C. Haigh, 'The Recent Historiography of the English Reformation', *Historical Journal*, xxv (1982), pp. 995–1007, and other works cited below, notes 2, 3, 11, 12; J.J. Scarisbrick, *The Reformation and the English People* (Oxford, 1984), especially p. 137.
2 *English Historical Review* xcviii (1983) p. 371.
3 C. Haigh (ed.), *The Reign of Elizabeth I* (London, 1984) p. 196.
4 Scarisbrick, *The Reformation and the English People*, ch.2.
5 Scarisbrick, *The Reformation and the English People*, p. 136.
6 A.G. Dickens, *Lollards and Protestants in the Diocese of York* (Oxford, 1959), p. 251. For analogous statements in 1941 and 1957 see my *Reformation Studies* (London, 1982), pp. 156–57, 182.
7 A.G. Dickens, *The English Reformation* (London, 1964), pp. 308, 318, 336–37.
8 R.B. Manning, *Religion and Society in Elizabethan Sussex* (Leicester, 1969), ch. 3, 12; for Kitch and Mayhew see respectively notes 9 and 97, below. E.T. Stoneham, *Sussex Martyrs of the Reformation* (3rd ed, Burgess Hill, 1967) shows that, with two or three exceptions, they were manual workers from sixteen places in East Sussex.
9 Foxe's main passages on Suffolk are in *Acts and Monuments* [hereafter *A.&M.*] (ed. S.R. Cattley, London, 1937–41), viii, pp. 145–48, 424–27. He has also much on Lollardy there: *A.&M.*, iii, pp. 584–600. The most important record-sources are

treated by R.A. Houlbrooke, 'Persecution of Heresy and Protestantism in the Diocese of Norwich under Henry VIII', *Norfolk Archaeology*, xxxv (1973) and in his *Church Courts and the People during the English Reformation* (Oxford, 1979), ch. 8, especially pp. 222–42. Compare Foxe's own statement: 'Many other, yea a great multitude were persecuted in Suffolke also, whych for that I lack their names, I omyt at this time.' This passage was removed from the editions of the *Acts and Monuments* after that of 1563, but restored in J. Pratt's edition of 1877, vol. viii, app. vi (unpaginated). On Sussex see M.J. Kitch, 'The Reformation in Sussex', *Studies in Sussex Church History*, ed. M.J. Kitch (London, 1981), pp. 77–98; G.J. Mayhew (note 97, below). On Norfolk see Houlbrooke, 'Persecution of Heresy' and Elaine Sheppard (note 97, below). Gloucestershire is more fully treated in this present essay; see notes 49–52, below.

10 J.E. Oxley, *The Reformation in Essex* (Manchester, 1965), ch. ix, x, describes the main personalities and martyrs, but does not bring out the volume of early Protestantism in that county. Dr Fines's *Register* (note 13, below) names 304 early Essex Protestants, including some thirty-nine martyrs. On other local features see D.M. Loades, 'The Essex Inquisitions of 1556', *Bulletin of the Institute of Historical Research*, xxxv (1962), pp. 87–97.

11 C. Haigh, 'Puritan Evangelism in the Reign of Elizabeth I', *English Historical Review*, xcii (1977), pp. 30–58.

12 Dr Haigh has warned against this tendency: *Reformation and Resistance in Tudor Lancashire* (Cambridge, 1975), pp. 76–77; 'Recent Historiography', pp. 1002–3; yet see note 32 below.

13 A provisional first volume (A-C) was published at Sutton Courtenay, 1980. Part 2 (D-Z) is now published by the West Sussex Institute of Higher Education.

14 Christina H. Garrett, *The Marian Exiles: A Study in the Origins of Elizabethan Puritanism* (Cambridge, 1938); see on the total figures, pp. 30–32, 40–41, where Foxe's estimate of 800 is well supported by the extant data.

15 Note especially, J.G. Nichols (ed.), *Narratives of the Days of the Reformation* (Camden Society, first series, lxxvii, 1859); and E. Bickersteth (ed.), *The Letters of the Martyrs* (London, 1837) from the original edition by Miles Coverdale, *Certain most Godly Letters, etc.* (London, 1564; *Short Title Catalogue*, 5886).

16 Many London act books, especially for the reign of Mary, are now missing. On Norwich and Lincoln, see below, notes 18 and 19. On York, see Dickens, *Lollards and Protestants*, pp. 240–42.

17 'Early Protestantism and the Church in Northamptonshire', in Dickens, *Late Monasticism and the Reformation* (London, 1994), pp. 134–49.

18 Houlbrooke, 'Persecution of Heresy', p. 311.

19 Margaret Bowker, *The Henrician Reformation: The Diocese of Lincoln under John Longland, 1521–1547* (Cambridge, 1981), p. 181.

20 For statistics on the Marian martyrs, see e.g., J.H. Blunt, *The Reformation of the Church of England* (London, 1896), ii, pp. 220–24; H.E. Malden, 'Notes on the Local Progress of Protestantism in England', *Transactions of the Royal Historical Society*, new series, ii (1885), pp. 61–76. Blunt, *Reformation of the Church of England*, pp. 275–78, comments on belief in deliverance from pain.

21 Foxe, *A.&M.*, viii, p. 407.

22 A. Townsend (ed.), *Writings of John Bradford . . . Sermons, Meditations, etc* (Parker Society, Cambridge, 1848), p. 390.

23 *Calendar of State Papers, Venice*, v, pp. 346, 356; vi (pt. 1), p. 94; vi (pt. 2), pp. 1018, 1074–75; *Calendar of Letters . . . between England and Spain*, xiii, pp. 139–40.

24 Moralist attacks on alehouses by, e.g., Fisher, Cranmer, Crowley and Christopherson preceded those by Elizabethan Puritans. See also P. Clark, 'The Alehouse and the Alternative Society', D. Pennington and K. Thomas (eds), *Puritans and Revolutionaries* (Oxford, 1978), pp. 61–67. Bishop Bonner forbade his flock to visit alehouses, go hawking or hide at home in service-time, Gina Alexander, 'Bonner and the Marian Persecution', *History*, lx (1975), p. 387. Compare the licensing statutes, 5 and 6 Edward VI, cap. 25 and 2 and 3 Philip and Mary, cap. 9. Towns also

could prohibit drinking in service-time, e.g. in 1555 at Coventry, *The Coventy Leet Book*, pt. 3, *Early English Text Society, Original Series*, 138 (1909), p. 812.

25 On the inns used in London see Dickens, *The English Reformation*, pp. 274–75; on those in Colchester and London, Foxe, *A.&M.*, viii, pp. 382–93, *passim*, and W. Wilkinson: *A Confutation of certaine Articles Delivered unto the Familye of Love* (London, 1579; *Short Title Catalogue*, 25665).

26 Compare Houlbrooke, 'Persecution of Heresy', p. 311.

27 J. Strype, *Ecclesiastical Memorials* (Oxford, 1822) iii (pt 2), p. 434. In 1556 Clements also wrote a long confession of faith (Strype, *Ecclesiastical Memorials*, pp. 446–67) and died in the King's Bench prison (Foxe, *A.&M.*, viii, p. 151).

28 Printed in Nichols (ed.), *Narratives*, pp. 71–84.

29 Foxe, *A.&M.*, vi, pp. 26–28; compare J.A. Muller (ed.), *The Letters of Stephen Gardiner* (Cambridge, 1933), pp. 272–76.

30 BL, MS Harley 368, fo. 124, quoted in J. Hutchins, *History and Antiquities of . . . Dorset* (Westminster, 1863), ii, p. 46.

31 BL, MS Lansdowne, 377, fos 8v–28v; compare P. Collinson, *The Elizabethan Puritan Movement* (London, 1967), p. 21.

32 *English Historical Review*, ci (1986), pp. 489–90. J.F. Davis, *Heresy and the Reform in the South East of England, 1520–1559* (1983) added much more than this criticism would suggest.

33 M. Claire Cross, the two articles cited in note 79, below; D.M. Palliser, *The Reformation in York* (Borthwick Institute, York, 1971), p. 32.

34 R. Howell, *Newcastle upon Tyne and the Puritan Revolution* (Oxford, 1967), pp. 63–82. Victoria County History, *Warwickshire*, ii (1908), pp. 33–38 gives the main references for the Marian persecution at Coventry; on its striking earlier Tudor Lollardy, see Foxe, *A.&M.*, iv, pp. 133–35, 557–58, together with the recent discoveries by J. Fines, 'Heresy Trials in the Diocese of Coventry and Lichfield', *Journal of Ecclesiastical History*, xv (1963), pp. 160–74; G.R. Elton, *Policy and Police* (Cambridge, 1972), pp. 133–35. On John Rough in northern England, see Dickens, *Lollards and Protestants*, pp. 197–99.

35 Foxe, *A.&M.*, vi, pp. 676–78. The relative size of such villages is sometimes surprising. For example, the Chantry Surveys give Coggeshall 1000 communicants, Oxley, *The Reformation in Essex*, p. 153, which could make its *total* population a fifth of the size of that given for our largest provincial towns.

36 On Suffolk, see note 9, above; on Wiltshire and Berkshire, see I.T. Shield, 'The Reformation in the Diocese of Salisbury, 1547–1562' (unpublished Oxford BLitt thesis, 1960), *passim*, especially ch. 7.

37 Dickens, *Lollards and Protestants*, pp. 216–18, 225–26, 247–48.

38 J.F. Davis, 'Lollard Survival and the Textile Industry in the South-East of England', *Studies in Church History*, ed. G.J. Cuming, iii (1966), pp. 191–201. Bishop Hooper claimed that in Essex and Kent a number of such workers were continental immigrants, who imported sectarian ideas, Blunt, *The Reformation of the Church of England*, ii, pp. 225–26.

39 C.G. Durston, 'Wild as Colts Untamed; Radicalism in the Newbury Area', *Southern History*, vi (1984), pp. 36–52.

40 *Letters and Papers of Henry VIII*, iv (pt. 3), no. 6385, from BL, MS Cotton Cleop. E. v. 360.

41 R.E.G. and E.F. Kirk (eds), *Returns of Aliens . . . in the City and Suburbs of London, Proceedings, Huguenot Society*, x, pt. 1 (1900), *passim*: A. Pettegree, 'The Foreign Population of London in 1549', *Proceedings, Huguenot Society*, xxxiv (1984), pp. 141–46. On London see J.W. Martin, 'The Protestant Underground Congregations of Mary's Reign', *Journal of Ecclesiastical History*, xxxv (1984), pp. 519–38. On the general situation see also Irene Scouloudi, 'Alien Immigration into and Alien Communities in London, 1558–1640', *Proceedings, Huguenot Society*, xvi (1938), pp. 1–23.

42 See Lord Lisle's report, 30 May 1539, with its vivid acount of the Protestant faction in Calais in Muriel St Clare Byrne (ed.), *The Lisle Letters* (Chicago and London, 1981), v, pp. 510–11.

43 R. Tittler and Susan L. Battley, 'The Local Community and the Crown in 1553: The Accession of Mary Tudor Revisited', *Bulletin of the Institute of Historical Research*, lvii (1984), pp. 131–39.

44 D.M. Palliser, 'Popular Reactions to the Reformation during the Years of Uncertainty', Felicity Heal and Rosemary O'Day (eds), *Church and Society in England: Henry VIII to James I* (London, 1977), pp. 35–56.

45 *State Papers of Henry VIII*, i (London, 1830), p. 463. On the isolation of Lincolnshire, see J.W.F. Hill, *Tudor and Stuart Lincoln* (Cambridge, 1956), pp. 1–4. As late as 1569 a group of Lincolnshire gentry wrote to Philip II expressing their continuing allegiance to him. J.A. Froude, *History of England* (London, 1870), ix, pp. 159–62.

46 Bowker, *The Henrician Reformation*, especially pp. 57–64, 166–85.

47 For Northampton, Oakham and Oundle, see article cited in note 17, above; for Boston, article in note 43, above; for Horncastle, *Letters and Papers of Henry VIII*, xiv (2), no. 214. The cases from Leicester and Gaddesby occur in Lincoln Archives Office, Vj. 13, fos 158b and 162b: compare Foxe, *A.&M.*, viii, p. 242. On Latimer's preaching visits to Grimsthorpe in 1552, see G.E. Corrie (ed.), *Sermons by Hugh Latimer* (Parker Society, 1844), pp. 326, 447. For Latimer's sermon at Stamford in 1550, see Corrie (ed.), *Sermons by Hugh Latimer*, p. 282 and compare *Short Title Catalogue*, no. 15293. On the Leicester martyr Thomas Moore, see Foxe, *A.&M.*, viii, p. 242. For serious iconoclasm at St Neots, see *Acts of the Privy Council*, ii, pp. 140–41 (23 Oct. 1547). For St Ives, see Strype, *Ecclesiastical Memorials*, iii, pt. 2, p. 392, and *Calendar of State Papers, Domestic, 1547–1580*, p. 17, no. 21. On Knox's preaching in 1553 before large congregations at the Lollard centre of Amersham, see T. M'Crie, *The Life of John Knox* (London, 1847), p. 67, and D. Laing (ed.), *The Works of John Knox* (6 vols, Edinburgh, 1846–64), iii, pp. 307–8: on Bedford, Strype, *Ecclesiastical Memorials*, iii, pt. 2, p. 390 and Joyce Godber, *History of Bedfordshire* (Bedford, 1969), p. 187. For further cases from Lincoln, Grantham, Harlaxton, Ponton, etc., see R.B. Walker, 'A History of the Reformation in the Archdeaconries of Lincoln and Stow, 1534–94' (unpublished Liverpool PhD thesis, 1959), and by the same author, 'Reformation and Reaction in the County of Lincoln, 1547–1558', *Lincolnshire Architectural and Archaeological Society, Reports and Papers*, new series, ix (1961), pp. 49–62; G.A.J. Hodgett, *Tudor Lincolnshire* (Lincoln, 1975), ch. 11. Of the 351 Marian exiles whose places of origin are given by Garrett, at least forty-seven came from the diocese of Lincoln, nineteen of them from Lincolnshire. Dr Fines's *Register* recovers only about 150 names for the diocese, of whom thirty-four came from Lincolnshire.

48 Margaret Spufford, *Contrasting Communities: English Villagers in the Sixteenth and Seventeenth Centuries* (Cambridge, 1974), pp. 334–44.

49 Strype, *Ecclesiastical Memorials*, iii, pt. 2, pp. 389–413.

50 On the relationships of Anne Askew see D. Wilson, *A Tudor Tapestry* (London, 1972), but the circle seems to extend ever more widely, and is still being intensively researched. The patronage of Charles Brandon, duke of Suffolk (d. 1545) and of his young duchess Katherine included the prominent Reformer Alexander Seton. Some others, though by no means all his appointees, were 'advanced' clerics.

51 K.G. Powell, 'The Beginnings of Protestantism in Gloucestershire', *Transactions, Bristol and Gloucestershire Archaeological Society*, xc (1971), pp. 141–57; Powell, 'The Social Background to the Reformation in Gloucestershire', *Transactions, Bristol and Gloucestershire Archaelogical Society*, xcii (1973), pp. 96–120; Powell, *The Marian Martyrs and the Reformation in Bristol* (Bristol Branch, Historical Association, 1972).

52 Dr Fines's *Register* has only sixty-four named early Protestants in Gloucestershire. Of these about forty are distributed across twenty parishes, the rest being in Gloucester and Bristol, which latter obviously contained numerous Protestants outside these lists.

53 Richard Webb was reported to More (as Lord Chancellor) for scattering 'pestilent' books in the streets and leaving them on doorsteps. See T. More, *The Confutation of Tyndale's Answer*, Complete Works, Yale edition, viii, pt. 2, pp. 813–15. Webb

was later one of Foxe's informants; see Powell, 'The Beginnings of Protestantism', p. 143.

54 F.D. Price, 'Gloucester Diocese under Bishop Hooper', *Transactions of the Bristol and Gloucestershire Archaeological Society*, lx (1939), p. 147.

55 The subsequent passage is largely derived from Shield 'Reformation in the Diocese of Salisbury'.

56 'Reformation in the Diocese of Salisbury', pp. 211–24. On Newbury, see note 37, above.

57 On Palmer, see Shield, 'Reformation in the Diocese of Salisbury', pp. 213–33 *passim*; Nichols (ed.), *Narratives*, pp. 85–131.

58 *Acts of the Privy Council*, vii, pp. 34–35.

59 VCH, *Warwickshire*, iii (1908), pp. 33–34 gives main references.

60 H. Robinson (ed.), *The Zurich Letters* (Parker Society, 1842), pp. 86–87.

61 This survey was made by a research student some years ago; it has not yet been checked or printed.

62 For this region see Imogen Luxton, 'The Reformation and Popular Culture', Heal and O'Day (eds), *Church and Society in England*, pp. 57–77.

63 The best background account is in P. Heath, 'Staffordshire Towns and the Reformation', *North Staffordshire Journal of Field Studies*, xix (1979), pp. 1–21.

64 The subsequent passage is based upon Foxe, *A.&M.*, viii, pp. 255–56, 401–5, 429. Compare BL, MS Harley, fos 69, 73, 78. Joyce Lewis, Robert Glover, Laurence Saunders, Anthony Draycot, Augustine Bernher and Bishop Baines are all in the *Dictionary of National Biography*. The detail on the Glover family is mainly in Foxe, *A.&M.*, vii, pp. 384–402. Baines and Draycot were active in the case of the blind martyr of Derby, Joan Waste (Foxe, *A.&M*, viii, pp. 247–50).

65 Thomas Becon, *The Jewel of Joy*, J. Ayre (ed.), *The Catechisms of Thomas Becon, etc.* (Parker Society, 1844), pp. 418–76.

66 Bickersteth (ed.), *Letters of the Martyrs*, p. 39. Note also his letter to the Glovers in Foxe, *A.&M.*, vi, p. 635.

67 John Old, an educated priest who took part in the translation of Erasmus's Paraphrases, sheltered Thomas Becon and Robert Wisdom in 1543. As chaplain to Lord Ferrers, he probably converted his master's son, Richard Devereux. Summoned by the Privy Council in 1546, he temporized, but then held benifices under Edward VI, being a canon of Hereford before fleeing to Frankfurt in 1554. The *Dictionary of National Biography* account is corrected in *Bulletin of the Institute of Historical Research*, xxi (1946), p. 83.

68 J. Fines, 'A Incident of the Reformation in Shropshire', *Transactions of the Shropshire Archaelogical Society*, lvii (1961–64), pp. 166–8; Haigh, *Reformation and Resistance in Tudor Lancashire*, pp. 76–79, gives further references on heresy in the diocese of Lichfield.

69 A.D. Dyer, *The City of Worcester in the Sixteenth Century* (Leicester, 1973), pp. 237–39.

70 *Calendar of State Papers Domestic, Elizabeth 1547–1580*, p. 183, no. 24; compare M.D. Lobel (ed.), *Historic Towns of the British Isles* (London, 1969), i, p. 9.

71 My brief comments on Wales are based on three works by Glanmor Williams, *Welsh Reformation Essays* (Cardiff, 1967); 'Wales and the Reformation', *Transactions of the Honourable Society of Cymmrodorion* (1966, pt. i), pp. 108–33; 'Religion and Welsh Literature in the Age of the Reformation', *Proceedings of the British Academy*, lxix (1983), pp. 371–408. Given more space, one would like to add here the revealing story of the Welsh fisherman-martyr Rawlins White (Foxe, *A.&M.*, vii, pp. 28–33).

72 Williams, 'Religion and Welsh Literature', pp. 383–89.

73 Haigh, *Reformation and Resistance*; for Bradford and Marsh, see ch. 10–12 *passim*; for Hurst, pp. 85, 172–73, 187–92, 208; for Holland, pp. 46, 50, 161, 190, 193. On reputed immorality, index *s.u.*, and on traditional piety, ch. 5, 11, 12.

74 VCH, *Lancashire*, ii, pp. 47–49.

75 See note 73, above.

76 Haigh, *Reformation and Resistance*, p. 194. On the Catholic resistance to Elizabeth, ch. 14–19.

77 The modern religious history of the county is well summarised by W.A. Shaw in VCH *Lancashire*, ii, pp 68–96.

78 Dickens, *Lollards and Protestants*, pp. 1–7.

79 Dickens, *Lollards and Protestants*, index *s.v.* Halifax, Hull, Leeds, Beverley; M. Claire Cross, 'The Development of Protestantism in Leeds and Hull, 1520–1640: The Evidence from Wills', *Northern History,* xviii (1982), pp. 230–38; M. Claire Cross, 'Parochial Structure and the Dissemination of Protestantism . . . A Tale of Two Cities', D. Baker (ed.), *Studies in Church History,* xvi (London, 1979), pp. 269–78.

80 R. Whiting, 'The Reformation in the South-West of England' (unpublished Exeter PhD thesis, 1977). Note especially pp. 293–8, 'The Impact of the Reformation'. *The Western Rebellion of 1549* (London, 1913) nevertheless remains a mine of information. A.L. Rowse based upon it an excellent account in *Tudor Cornwall* (London, 1941), ch. 11.

81 The social-economic aspects are ably discussed in Joyce Youings, 'The South-Western Rebellion of 1549', *Southern History,* i (1979), pp. 99–122.

82 On Cornish Protestantism and the activities of the seamen, see Rowse, *Tudor Cornwall*, ch. 12, 15.

83 F.E. Halliday (ed.), *Richard Carew of Antony: The Survey of Cornwall* (London, 1953), pp. 196–97. Carew first published the work in 1602.

84 BL, MS Add. 34563, ed. C.R. Manning, *Norfolk Archaeology,* iv (1855), p. 133–231.

85 Note in this context A.V. Woodman, 'The Buckinghamshire and Oxfordshire Rising of 1549', *Oxoniensia*, xxii (1957), pp. 78–84.

86 Manning, *Norfolk Archaeology,* p. 150. The derogatory term 'sect' comes of course from Bedingfield himself.

87 On Francis Russell and his Protestant associates, such as Becon, Bradford and Underhill, see Garrett, *Marian Exiles*, pp. 275–77; Foxe, *A.&M.*, vi, p. 537; vii, pp. 218–19. For Lord Russell's standing among them see Bradford's letter, Bickersteth (ed.), *The Letters of the Martyrs*, pp. 213–15; Nichols (ed.), *Narratives*, pp. 146–46.

88 On Knox's mission see note 47, above.

89 Houlbrooke, *Church Courts* has much information on the conservative diocese of Winchester; see also VCH, *Hampshire*, ii, pp. 66–75. On the stubborn citizens of Winchester, note Bishop Horne's letter of January 1562 in *State Papers Domestic, Elizabeth*, xxi, no. 7. The main Protestant hero is Archdeacon John Philpot (Foxe, *A.&M.*, vi, 396ff; vii pp. 605–714; viii, pp. 171–73), and the horror story that of Thomas Bembridge (*A.&M.*, viii, pp. 490–92; *Acts of the Privy Council*, vii, p. 361).

90 I refer to More's declaration at his trial, R.W. Chambers, *Thomas More* (Peregrine edn., 1963), pp. 325–26.

91 *Calendar of State Papers, Venice*, v, p. 346.

92 The arguments for a strong, continuous Catholic survival are well put by C. Haigh, 'The Continuity of Catholicism in the English Reformation', *Past and Present*, xciii (1981), pp. 37–69. This view is supported by Scarisbrick, *The Reformation and the English People*, ch. 7. On spontaneous revival under Mary, see D.M. Loades, *The Reign of Mary Tudor* (London, 1979), pp. 351–52.

93 Susan Brigden, 'Youth and the English Reformation', *Past and Present*, xcv (1982), pp. 37–67 (*see* Reading 3, above). The present writer can corroborate this revealing article from still further evidence.

94 Note the case (1531) of William Tracy's Protestant will and the attempt to invalidate it by a charge of heresy, Dickens, *English Reformation*, p. 96. Grafton then publicised the will in the 1550 edition of Edward Hall's chronicle, *The Union of the Two Noble Families*, fol. cci.

95 Despite the probability that Protestant clerics and prominent laymen ran a much greater risk of being reported and charged, working-class people remain far more numerous in J. Fines's *Register* and in the lists of martyrs.

96 Dickens, *Lollards and Protestants*, pp. 171–72.

97 P. Clark, *English Provincial Society from the Reformation to the Revolution: Religion, Politics and Society in Kent, 1500–1640* (Hassocks, 1977), pp. 41,

58–60, 76–77, 100, 102, 152, 420 (notes 72–73); G.J. Mayhew, 'The Progress of the Reformation in East Sussex 1530–1559: The Evidence from Wills', *Southern History*, v (1983), pp. 38–67; Mayhew, *Tudor Rye* (Falmer, 1987); Dickens, *Lollards and Protestants*, pp. 171–72, 215–18, 220–21; D. Wilson, *A Tudor Tapestry* (London, 1972), p. 260; W.J. Sheils, *The Puritans in the Diocese of Peterborough (Northamptonshire Record Society*, xxx, 1979), pp. 15–18; Palliser, *The Reformation in York*, p. 32; Claire Cross, 'Parochial Structure', *passim*; Claire Cross, 'The Development of Protestantism in Leeds and Hull', *passim*; Elaine Sheppard, 'The Reformation and the Citizens of Norwich', *Norfolk Archaeology*, xxxviii (1983), pp. 44–58. In addition note the smaller groups of wills cited by Margaret Spufford, *Contrasting Communities*, and by Haigh, *Reformation and Resistance*, pp. 68–71, 82, 194, 220–21, 227; these latter concern the numerous Lancashire wills printed by the Chetham Society and elsewhere. It should finally be noted that Dr Susan Brigden in her unpublished Cambridge PhD thesis (1977), 'The Early Reformation in London', pp. 333–48, also finds wills important as an index to religious change in London.

98 'There was certainly an upsurge of Protestant wills, with a full-blown non-Catholic preamble and absence of traditional religious legacies, in London from the mid-1530s', Scarisbrick, *Reformation and the English People*, p. 6. On methodology see M.L. Zell, 'The Use of Religious Preambles as a Measure of Religious Belief in the Sixteenth Century', *Bulletin of the Institute of Historical Research*, 1 (1977), pp. 246–49.

99 See my rough yet convergent calculations for Yorkshire, c. 1600, in *Reformation Studies* (London, 1980), p. 193.

100 G.R. Elton, *Reform and Reformation: England 1509–1558* (London, 1977), p. 371.

101 Haigh, 'Recent Historiography', and elsewhere.

102 H. Belloc, preface to G. Constant, *The Reformation in England*, i, *The English Schism* (London, 1939), p. ix.

103 R.H. Pogson, 'Revival and Reform in Mary Tudor's Church: A Question of Money', *Journal of Ecclesiastical History*, xxv (1974), pp. 249–65; Pogson, 'Reginald Pole and the Priorities of Government in Mary Tudor's Church', *Historical Journal*, xviii (1975), pp. 3–21; Pogson, 'The Legacy of the Schism: Confusion, Continuity and Change in the Marian Clergy', Jennifer Loach and R. Tittler (eds.), *The Mid-Tudor Polity, c. 1540–1560* (London, 1980), pp. 116–36.

104 On Bartolomé Carranza, Pedro de Soto and Alonso à Castro, see Blunt, *The Reformation of the Church of England*, ii, pp. 249–58, and numerous references in Loades, *Reign of Mary Tudor*.

SECTION
II

IMPLEMENTATION

Commentary

The readings in this section explore in various ways the mechanics and the consequences of officially inspired attempts to reform religious practice in the parishes of England, over the period from the last decade of Henry VIII's reign to the middle years of Elizabeth. 'Implementation' here implies a fairly complex structural dynamic, as it is becoming increasingly clear that the success of reforming or counter-reforming programmes in the localities relied not so much upon simple governmental fiat as upon the co-operation of a number of central and local authorities, from the council at Whitehall, via the diocesan bishops and leading county gentry to the parish clergy, churchwardens and humble parishioners in the parishes. The parameters of that co-operation, and the nature of the acquiescence or 'consent' of the laity to sometimes drastic change are important themes of the chapters which follow.

Robert Whiting has been labelled a 'revisionist' historian of the Reformation, but in contrast to the arch-revisionist, Christopher Haigh, he argues for an early and decisive impact of government policy in undermining popular religious practices which appear to have been thriving up to the very eve of Henry's break with Rome. Whiting's evidence, presented in Reading 5, a companion article and a substantial monograph,[1] has made a particular impression because the area he has studied (the south-western counties of Devon and Cornwall) is far from the seat of government and might reasonably be supposed to have evinced little spontaneous enthusiasm for new reforming ideas. His thesis that popular reactions to reform were characterized typically by passivity and conformity in the face of a powerful and awe-inspiring Tudor state is an attractive one, in so far as it allows us to square the circle which has perplexed Reformation historians: the paradox of a thriving and popular pre-Reformation piety which appears to have done little to attempt to preserve itself in the face of official hostility. Doubts have been expressed, however, as to whether wills are really such a straightforward guide to changing popular *mentalité* as Whiting seems to imply,[2] and not all commentators have been convinced by his attempts to minimize the significance of the South-Western Rebellion of 1549, or by his somewhat monolithic conception of the Tudor state. Whiting's detailed regional study does, however, receive broad support from the national survey of Tudor churchwardens' accounts undertaken by Ronald Hutton (Reading 6), which concurs with the assessment that as early as Henry's reign, official policy had succeeded in inflicting irreversible blows on a previously flourishing popular religion, and popular religious culture.

In contrast to Whiting and Hutton, who remain content with a fairly 'top-down' paradigm, Margaret Aston in Reading 7 stresses the interaction of 'official' and 'unofficial' agencies in implementing religious reform, an approach that does much to demonstrate the absurdity of seeking to preserve the Reformation as 'act of state' and the Reformation as 'spiritual movement' as distinct conceptual models. Aston's work on iconoclasm has done much to illuminate the motivation behind the often ferocious campaigns to destroy statues and rood-lofts, to white-wash walls, to purge the English Church of its 'idolatrous' past. This is a theme in which most leading 'revisionist' historians have evinced relatively little interest.[3]

Revisionism has, however, helped bring to centre-stage again what had long been a rather neglected field of Reformation studies. Eamon Duffy's chapter on the reign of Mary is perhaps the most controversial part of his much-debated book, *The Stripping of the Altars*. Though areas of broad consensus are beginning to emerge in other areas of English Reformation historiography – on the relative vitality of the pre-Reformation Church, for example, or the relative slowness of Protestant evangelism to make a real impact nationally – such a degree of consensus has signally failed to characterize approaches to the Marian period, where even the chapter headings have proved contentious: 'reaction', 'restoration' or 'counter-Reformation'?[4] Historians who would normally resist the temptation to play with counter-factual propositions are almost inexorably drawn to them in the case of Mary: if Mary had ruled as long as Elizabeth, if Mary had had a son by Philip, would the Reformation movement in England have been stamped out as thoroughly and permanently as it was later to be in Bavaria or Austria? The question represents more than idle parlour-game speculation, but goes to the heart of radically divergent assessments of the vitality, diffusion and potential of English Protestantism by 1553 (compare Dickens's remarks at the conclusion of Reading 4). In contrast to Whiting and Hutton, who stress the irreparable damage that had been done to the cult of saints, belief in purgatory and the ideals of monasticism by Mary's accession, and thus the very considerable difficulties her government faced, Duffy makes the intriguing case that the authors of Marian policy were not simply looking to the past and that they consciously promoted a newer, 'counter-Reformation' style of devotion. Duffy's emphasis on the success of the campaign to restore Catholic worship and furnishings in the parishes supports the observation of Whiting and Hutton that Tudor governments were remarkably effective in ensuring compliance with their will in the localities, though he does not make the point as explicitly as they do. This arguably strengthens the case for the potential of Marian Catholicism in the longer term, but renders more problematic Duffy's contention that the Marian restoration must have enjoyed widespread and enthusiastic popular support. Duffy himself might accept that a full history of Marian religion would need to pay considerably more attention to the significance of the martyrs and of Protestant resistance than is apparent here.

Common to all the chapters in this section is a great imponderable: what effect did a cumulative process of proscription, iconoclasm and destruction, and a bewildering inconsistency of government policy over the mid-Tudor decades have in terms of eradicating or undermining traditional certainties, patterns of devotion and habits of thought? Despite the valuable work that has been done on 'non-élite' sources such as churchwardens' accounts and wills, these are questions that can never be illuminated in any straightforward statistical way. Aston (like a number of recent historians of the continental Reformation) addresses directly the psychological impact of official iconoclasm on those who witnessed it: to remove or destroy long-venerated images may have been to undermine or destroy their miraculous power, and must have been intended to do so, a process Aston calls 'credal engineering'. Whiting goes further in asserting that the old religion fairly rapidly lost its emotional hold on the people, but that the void was filled by confusion, cynicism and anticlericalism rather than by commitment to Protestantism. Of all the authors represented in this section, Duffy is most resistant to accepting a significant 'erosion of Catholic feeling' by the 1550s, but he too accepts that government policies of the preceding years may have shaken confidence in traditional devotion. The differences here may be ones of the time-scale involved and of detailed reading of the evidence, rather than of basic interpretation. There is a growing recognition (and this may well have been a perception shared by the reformers themselves) that the implementation of religious reform in England was a two-stage process: the people had to be 'de-catholicized' before they could be 'protestantized'. On this reading the destructiveness, the apparent negativity, of much of the government's activity over the mid-Tudor decades was far from being mindless. How easy it would be to inculcate an understanding of reformed doctrine into a population severed from so many of its ties to the past is, however, another question, one that will be considered more closely in Section III.

Notes

1 R. Whiting, 'Abominable Idols: Images and Image-breaking under Henry VIII', *Journal of Ecclesiastical History*, 33 (1982), pp. 30–47; *The Blind Devotion of the People: Popular Religion and the English Reformation* (Cambridge, Cambridge University Press, 1989).
2 See, in particular, Duffy, *Stripping of the Altars*, ch. 15; C. Litzenberger, 'Local Responses to Changes in Religious Policy Based on Evidence from Gloucestershire Wills (1540–1580)', *Continuity and Change*, 8 (1993), pp. 417–39.
3 See also M. Aston, *England's Iconoclasts I: Laws against Images* (Oxford, Clarendon Press, 1988), and a number of the articles in her *Faith and Fire: Popular and Unpopular Religion, 1350–1600* (London, Hambledon Press, 1993).
4 Compare Haigh, *English Reformations*, ch. 12; D. Loades, *The Reign of Mary Tudor* (2nd ed., London, Longman, 1991), ch. 8.

5

'For the health of my soul': prayers for the dead in the Tudor south-west

ROBERT WHITING

How was the 'average man' affected by the Reformation? After more than four centuries, the answers given to this apparently simple question are in fact diverse and often conflicting. Some historians have emphasized the element of change. Professor Dickens, for example, has claimed to discern a fundamental re-orientation of religious attitudes, even in supposedly conservative areas like Yorkshire and Nottinghamshire.[1] Other writers, however, particularly in recent years, have maintained that the implementation of reform was frequently restricted and delayed. In Lancashire, for example, Dr Haigh has argued that religious change was seriously obstructed by a combination of official weakness and local resistance.[2] The precise popular impact of the Reformation remains, in short, highly problematic.

In a previous examination of the Henrician campaign against images, the present author adduced evidence to suggest that the local enforcement of religious change may have been markedly more effective than recent historians have usually allowed.[3] The following study represents an extension of the investigation into a second and even more crucial area of reform: the assault upon prayers for the dead. Was the traditional popular devotion to such practices effectively eradicted during the Reformation decades? Or was it able, in reality, to survive substantially intact? Seeking answers to these questions, the present examination focuses upon the English south-west, a region which possesses a valuable range of sources – including wills, and an unusually rich collection of churchwardens' accounts – for the study of religious development at the popular level. Chronologically, however, this investigation is wider than its predecessor, extending from the decades immediately preceding the Reformation, through the upheavals under Henry VIII, Edward VI and Mary, and on to the establishment of official Protestantism under Elizabeth I.

I

'Orate pro animabus Katharine Burlas, Nicholai Burlas, et Johannis Vyvyan, qui istam fenestram fecerunt fieri.' Thus pleads an early Tudor

Reprinted from *Southern History,* 5 (1983).

window – which also portrays the donors themselves – in the parish church of St Neot.[4] A similar inscription, in English, is still to be seen on the exterior of the church at Cullompton. It reminds us that John Lane and his wife founded one of the chapels in 1526, and asks us to say a *Pater Noster* and *Ave* for them, their children, and their friends; it also expresses the hope that God will have mercy on their souls and finally bring them to glory. Even more explicit were the texts formerly to be seen in the chapel founded by another prosperous merchant, John Greenway, at Tiverton in 1517. 'O that the Lord may / Grant unto John Greenway / Good fortune and grace / And in Heaven a place.' 'Of your charity, pray for the souls of John and Joan Greenway, his wife . . . and for their fathers and mothers, and for their friends and their lovers. On them Jesu have mercy. Amen. Of your charity, say *Pater Noster* and *Ave*.'[5]

The prayers thus requested supposedly speeded souls through the purifying torments of Purgatory and into the eternal blessedness of Heaven. Pre-Reformation worshippers at Exeter Cathedral were indeed bidden to pray 'for all the souls [that] bideth the mercy of God in the bitter pains of Purgatory: that God, of his mercy, the sooner deliver them through your devoted prayers'.[6] It was therefore inevitable that intercessions should lie close to the very heart of the popular religion. They began within hours of the death itself. Until the 1530s, parsons of Down St Mary would visit the corpse of each newly deceased parishioner in his own house, 'where they were wont to say *dirige* and other prayers, with the neighbours of the dead man, for the souls of all such corpses'.[7] Further prayers attended the burial: '*hic roget sacerdos orare pro anima defuncti*', instructs a late medieval service-book discovered at Coldridge.[8] But these were merely the initial stages of a highly organized intercessory process which might continue for months, years or even generations after the body had been laid to rest. Wills, churchwardens' accounts and chantry certificates leave no doubt that on the very eve of the Reformation, an overwhelming multiplicity of 'masses', '*diriges*', 'trentals', 'obits', 'mind-days', 'anniversaries' and similar rites were still being celebrated throughout the region on behalf of the dead. 'There is no day', the heretic Thomas Benet reportedly complained to the clergy at Exeter in 1531, 'but ye say divers masses for souls in feigned Purgatory.'[9]

Nor were these merely the endowment of earlier generations. Wealthier members of the laity continued to invest substantial sums in such intercessions for themselves, their families and their friends. In 30 wills made by Cornish or Devonian laypeople, from below the level of the gentry, between 1520 and 1529, prayers or masses were endowed in no less than 21 (70%).[10] Some prayers were to be said by fellow laymen. John Trotte, founding an almshouse at Cullompton in 1523, required its inmates to pray for his and certain other souls, while Joan Tackle, at Honiton in 1528, left 4*d* to each householder in the town to pray for her. John Greenway, arranging his burial in his superb new chapel at Tiverton in 1529, sought to ensure grateful prayers for his soul by ordering a dole of £20 and a dinner for the poor; and more money and food were to be distributed at his 'month's mind'.[11] Most intercessions, however, were entrusted to the acknowledged specialists. Friars were specified in 5 of the 21 wills. Nicholas Ennis of Luxulyan left 10s each to the friaries at Bodmin and Truro in 1522, in return for trentals for his soul, while at Exeter in 1523 John Bridgeman gave 53s.4d to the Franciscans for a perpetual obit. William Sellick of Tiverton bequeathed 10s in 1524 to 'all the houses of friars within Devonshire', for trentals on behalf of his soul, and in 1529 Gilbert Rugge of Widecombe left 2s to the Exeter Francisans. In the same year John Greenway of Tiverton left 40s to the Dominicans of Exeter, 'to the intent that the friars there being shall devoutly say and sing four trentals for my soul and all Christian souls, immediately after my decease'; and he ordered similar trentals from the Franciscans at Exeter, and from the Franciscans and Dominicans at Plymouth.[12]

Even more frequently hired for such intercessory purposes were the secular priests. It was such a priest that John Hugh of Branscombe, for example, required to 'pray for my soul' in 1521. Another priest was hired by Nicholas Ennis of Luxulyan in 1522 'to pray for the soul of an old woman which lost her purse with 2s 8d therein; that I found when I was young, and did never recompense her'. In 1526 Thomas Hamlyn of Totnes arranged annual intercessions in his parish church: the vicar, Lady priest and parish clerk were to say '*placebo* and *dirige* with *lauds*', perform a requiem mass, and pray for his and certain other souls. In 1529 John Greenway endowed a priest to pray and sing for his soul for seven years in his new chapel at Tiverton, while another merchant, John Lane, endowed a priest for the new chapel of Our Lady at Cullompton. Lane also donated a total of £33.6s.8d to no less than 100 neighbouring churches – on condition that they enter him on their bede-rolls, 'to pray for me in their pulpits'.[13]

Even laymen incapable of financing individual intercession found prayers and masses available on a communal basis. A relatively modest offering procured the addition of a name to the parochial bede-roll. Such receipts appear frequently in the accounts of pre-Reformation churchwardens, together with payments to priests for reciting rolls from the pulpit. Even more attractive was the membership of a religious gild. This privilege was sometimes restricted to a specific trade: thus the fraternity of the Holy Trinity at Helston in 1517 was for local cobblers. Most groups, however, seem to have drawn support and finance from a variety of occupations within the parish. The gild of St Katherine at Chagford – which may have operated from a house still standing near the church – received income from parishioners' gifts, as well as from the local sale of its sheep and wool. The gild of the High Cross at Stratton (whose accounts commence in 1512) was financed by fees, gifts and a yearly Ale, while the gilds at North Petherwin drew revenue from the sale of bread and ale.[14] Although such groups differed in composition and in organization, their primary function seems everywhere to have been similar. This was the hastening of departed members through the 'bitter pains of Purgatory'.

Many, like the High Cross at Stratton, began by arranging their members' burial, often with knell, cross and tapers. Most also maintained their own bede-roll. At Stratton, most years between 1512 and 1530 saw local people buying places on the High Cross roll, which the vicar would recite regularly. Thus in 1527 Alison Pudner paid 6s.8d 'for her husband's grave, and to set him apon the bede-roll', while Robert Hecket gave a piece of pottery worth 10s 'for to set three names apon the bede-roll'. Such rolls actually survive among the early sixteenth-century accounts for North Petherwin. Folio 38v, for instance, begins with an exhortation to pray for the deceased brothers and sisters of St Michael's gild, and then lists their names. Usually, moreover, the fraternity hired a priest to celebrate at a particular altar in the parish church. Masses for departed brothers and sisters of the Holy Trinity were performed in Helston church, each surviving member reciting a Lady Psalter on their behalf. St Katherine at Chagford hired priests and organized obits, including an anniversary for its departed on the morrow of St Katherine; and Stratton's High Cross maintained its own chantry-priest, as well as paying the vicar to perform perpetual obits. Even in smaller communities, like North Petherwin, gilds arranged *dirige* and mass for their dead. On occasion the rites organized by such groups were impressively elaborate. At Lostwithiel in the reign of Henry VIII, St George's gild held an annual parade along the main street. One member, riding on horseback and attended by mounted followers, was dressed as St George himself, with armour, crown, sceptre and sword. At the church he was received by the priest, and escorted inside to hear a *dirige* in the gild's chapel; then the whole company retired to a local house, for their customary feast.[15]

The continuing popularity of such groups is attested by their very number on the eve of the Reformation. Several of the 20 or so 'stores' at Ashburton, for example, were certainly associated with altars, and chapels were dedicated to Our Lady, St John, Sts Katherine and Margaret, St Thomas and St Nicholas. Chagford boasted not only St Katherine but also the Blessed Virgin, St Antony, St George, St Nicholas, St Lawrence, St Eligius, the Name of Jesus, and Young Men. There were about nine groups at Stratton, and about ten at Camborne: several of the latter were dedicated to local saints like Ia, Winwaloe and Meriasek, and at least four arranged *diriges*. Numerous such groups operated even in relatively small communities like Morebath, South Tawton, Winkleigh, Antony and North Petherwin. At both Antony and North Petherwin they totalled about 11, those in the latter parish being named after St Nicholas, St

Patern, St George, St Michael, St Luke, St Thomas, St John, St Christopher, Allhallows, Our Lady and the Trinity.[16] The persistence of popular support for such gilds is confirmed, moreover, by the 30 surviving wills from 1520–9. Bequests to them appear in 17 (57%). Some testators left money, like the 3s.4d donated by John Hart at Bovey Tracey in 1520; other contributions were in kind, like the sheep given by Christopher Stephen of Highbray in 1524. At Totnes in 1526 Thomas Hamlyn bequeathed money to five groups in the parish church; and to one, dedicated to Our Lady of Pity, he left also the income from certain land, requiring its priest to pray for him and his family. In the same year a merchant of South Molton, Thomas Leigh, not only ordered an annual *dirige* and mass from a local gild of the High Cross, but also gave 12d each to seven groups in the parish church, as well as money, cloth and timber 'to the building of the chantry-house belonging to the gild of the Trinity'.[17]

The available evidence can thus leave little doubt that, on the very eve of the religious upheavals, the traditional apparatus of intercession continued to play a vital role in the lives of individuals and of communities throughout the south-west. It was a central and flourishing feature of popular piety that was soon to encounter hostility from the reforming regimes.

II

The next problem is to evaluate the impact of the Henrician Reformation upon such intercessions. Did the policies decreed by Henry VIII, Cromwell and Cranmer in 1529–47 actually initiate significant changes in the pattern of popular practice? Or did official decrees, in reality, pass over the heads of the average man? The evidence required for the formulation of answers to these crucial questions is to be sought in the four major indices of religious change that survive from the Henrician years. These are wills, legal records, chantry certificates, and the accounts of church- and gild-wardens.

Wills, at first sight, might appear to indicate that popular enthusiasm for intercessions sustained little substantial damage from the Henrician Reformation. In 1536, for example, Joan Bidwell of Shobrooke arranged her registration on a local bede-roll, 'to be continually prayed for, for ever'; she also ordered a trental and required a priest 'to sing and pray for my soul, my friends' souls, and for all the souls departed, abiding the mercy of God; and that to be done in Shobrooke church'. In 1540 Robert Hone arranged an elaborate burial at Ottery St Mary, complete with psalter, knell and black-clothed mourners, and a gift of 1d to the spectators to pray for his soul. He also ordered obits and a place on their bede-rolls ('there to be prayed for, amongst the brothers') from fraternities at South Molton and Cullompton, and other masses including a trental, 'with masses, fasting, and prayers, after the old customable usage'. He even forgave his debtors on the condition that they pray for him, and left his god-children 12*d* each 'to say a *Pater Noster, Ave,* and Creed, praying for my soul'. Gilbert Kirk of Exeter similarly left 4*d* to each householder in the parish of St Mary Arches in 1546, 'to pray to Our Lord God to have mercy on my soul and all Christian souls'.[18]

A closer examination of the wills, however, suggests that in significant respects the traditional patterns were already beginning to change. The most obvious disruption occurred in 1536–9, when the suppression of religious houses brought to a sudden end the intercessions endowed within them by laymen. As late as 1534–5 Robert Hooker of Exeter had arranged for the local Dominicans and Franciscans to say a trental for his and certain other souls, and John Flood of Topsham had commissioned a trental, for 10*s*, from the Exeter Franciscans.[19] But such endowments declined as the government's hostility to religious orders became increasingly explicit. They appear in only 1 of the 22 wills from 1536–9 – when John Forde of Ashburton ordered trentals from friaries at Exeter and Plymouth in April 1538[20] – and disappear totally from West-Country wills thereafter. Even more significant is the evidence relating to religious gilds. Bequests to these still appear in 11 of the 19 wills from 1530–5 (58%). John Brown of Uffculme, for instance, left a silver chalice, a mass-book, a bell, cruets and vestments to a local fraternity of Our Lady in 1535.[21] Such bequests, however, are found in only 10 of the 22 wills from 1536–9 (45%); and for 1540–6 the figure falls to 19 of 69 (28%). These statistics would suggest that investment in intercessory gilds may have been in decline from as early as the 1530s.

Most notable of all, however, is the apparent change in the overall volume of intercessory endowment. Prayers and masses had been arranged in 21 of the 30 wills from 1520–9 (70%). Of the 41 wills from 1530–9, by contrast, they were endowed in only 21 (51%); and of the 69 wills from 1540–6, in no more than 23 (33%). Despite their relatively small number, the surviving wills would therefore seem to indicate a marked decline in intercessory investment from the onset of the Henrician Reformation. Such a modification of the established patterns of piety is rendered the more significant by the inherent probability that most testators, being of above-average age, were slower to abandon traditional religion than were the young and the middle-aged. In sources relating to a wider range of age-groups, the signs of incipient change are even more strikingly apparent.

One such source is the legal record. In the Consistory Court, and in central courts like Chancery and Star Chamber, several cases of a type rare in 1500–29 indicate that devotion to the traditional apparatus of interces-sion was beginning to wane. As early as 1530, at Cullompton, several local men (headed by the More family) reportedly occupied the chapel erected only four years previously by John Lane. Lane had intended a chantry-priest to celebrate there; the intruders outraged his widow by using it for their burials instead. Similar disruption occurred at Exeter, where property had formerly been bequeathed to the parish churches of St Kerrian and St Martin for the maintenance of intercessory prayers and masses. In 1533–8 Richard Drewe prevented their continuance by appropriating the income for his own use. At about the same time, Edward Thorn of Sheepwash was detaining certain deeds, so as to hinder the collection of a rent which maintained intercessions in the parish church at Silverton. A comparable situation arose at Shillingford, where land had once been granted to the dean and chapter of Exeter on condition that they kept an obit in the cathedral and prayed for their benefactor's soul. In 1537–8 the land was appropriated by John Blackaller, one of Exeter's leading citizens. He refused to allow the clergy their rent, to the inevitable detriment of the customary obit.[22]

In 1538–44 there was similar disruption at Holsworthy, Marwood and South Petherwin. Land had been given to maintain a priest who served the gild and altar of St Katherine at Holsworthy; but the donor's heir now detained its deeds, preventing its use for the original pious ends. Richard Frear similarly claimed land at Clayhanger which, according to a local priest, belonged to St Katherine's chantry at Marwood. Again, land used by a gild of Jesus at South Petherwin to hire a priest – who sang 'Jesus masses' in the parish church – was now claimed by John Blackmore. By 1544–7 such attitudes were no longer uncommon. At Halberton, for example, Christopher Sampford and John Warren reportedly dismissed a stipendiary priest from his post, 'commanding him to depart, saying to him that he should serve there no longer'. At Davidstow, the local constable John Jelley persuaded the parishioners to sell certain oxen, the hiring-out of which had maintained a priest 'to the laud and praise of Almighty God'. He then kept the proceeds for himself. At Aveton Giffard, in about 1547, a local man claimed land which (according to other parishioners) belonged in fact to a neighbouring chantry.[23]

Internal dissensions as well as external assaults are revealed by the legal records. At Zeal Monachorum, money belonging to the stores of St John and St Katherine was dishonestly retained in 1534. In the same year, the responsibilities of gild-wardenship were refused by a parishioner at Crediton. At Cullompton in 1538–44 the members of the gild of St John not only quarreled with their stipendiary priest, but also argued bitterly amongst themselves, the Mores claiming pre-eminence on account of their benefactions. At Yealmpton in 1544, Nicholas Thorning refused to return rings and money worth over £16 that had been entrusted to his care by the store of Our Lady. They had originally been collected for 'divers good and godly purposes and intents' within the parish church.[24] Evidence of this nature serves to strengthen the impression that between 1530 and 1547, enthusiasm for intercessory institutions experienced a significant decline.

Further light upon developing attitudes is provided by the chantry-certificates of the Henrician and Edwardian commissioners. These reveal that, on the eve of their suppression, many chantries were already in serious decay. At Creed, for example, land once donated for the maintenance of a priest to celebrate 'Jesus masses' had been 'conveyed from the churchwardens of long time'; a house belonging to a chantry at Helston was in ruins; and an obit at St Winnow had been discontinued. A hospital at Kingsteignton had a chapel in which the five poor inmates were supposed to hear divine service; but it now lacked ornaments, jewels, plate, goods and chattels, 'for that it hath not been maintained according to the will of the founder'. Property given to maintain a chantry-priest in the parish church at South Petherwin had been in dispute, and 'a great part of the issues of the said lands' was thus 'expended in the suit of the same'.[25]

Most of the disruption seems to have occurred in the last years of Henry's reign. An endowment at Truro had maintained a priest to pray for the founder and his family; but it ended in the early 1540s, the mills which provided its income being allowed to decay. In about 1543 a chantry at Bampton, founded by Humphrey Calwoodley in about 1521, was dissolved by Michael Mallett; he discharged the incumbent and assumed the property for himself. John Trotte's almshouse at Cullompton, the inhabitants of which had prayed for the founder's soul since its establishment in about 1523, was dissolved by his own sons in about 1544 – an act symbolizing the attitude frequently adopted by this generation towards the piety of its fathers. It was similarly in about 1544 that land originally given to maintain obits at Looe was employed by the townsmen to finance the repair of their bridge. The commissioners also reported that a chantry on the 'isle of Laman' now lacked all equipment and property, 'for that the service in the chapel hath of late discontinued'.[26] The certificates thus confirm that devotion to intercessions was often in decline several years before the advent of a Protestant regime.

The final source of evidence is the account of the church- or gild-warden. This, too, provides indications of change. At the parish church of St John's Bow in Exeter, for example, annual payments for 'obits of St Gregory' were recorded in the accounts until 1535–6 – but then ceased altogether. Payments to a priest in the parish church at Ashburton, for the celebration of mass at an altar dedicated to Our Lady, similarly ended after 1536–7; and several gilds made their last appearance in the Ashburton accounts in 1537–9. The gild of St Antony at Chagford, which organized masses on St Antony's Day, disappeared from the accounts after 1536–7, at which date a gild of St Nicholas in the same town seems also to have ended. The accounts of a group at St Thomas-by-Launceston, dedicated to the Blessed Virgin and maintaining its own bede-roll, similarly ceased in 1537. Two 'stores' at Broadhempston, named after St Christopher and Our Lady, apparently ended after 1539. In the same year, no less than four groups – dedicated to St Antony, St Sidwell, St Sunday and Our Lady – seem to have disappeared from the parish church at Morebath.[27]

A gild of St Eligius at Chagford seems to have ended in about 1540; and several of the groups recorded in the Camborne accounts up to 1540 – notably 'Yea', 'Gwynwala', 'Nyales', 'Bastyen', and 'Jane and Margaret' – are conspicuously absent thereafter. 'Our Lady Holmadons' at Stratton apparently suspended operations after 1541–2 – when, in fact, John Mock was paid 'for drawing down of Our Lady chapel'. Another group dedicated to Mary, at Woodbury, appears to have dissolved in 1542–3, when its goods were transferred to the central wardens. At North Petherwin, the last account for St George's gild is dated 1543; and no accounts from the 1540s exist for several gilds known to have operated here in previous years. Similarly suggestive absences occur in the accounts for Ashburton and South Tawton.[28] Allowance being made for the incompleteness of some account-sequences, it is again difficult to avoid the conclusion that inter- cessory institutions were frequently disappearing several years before the arrival of official Protestantism in 1547. The accounts confirm also that even the surviving groups did not necessarily continue to flourish. They record (for example) that gild-wardenship was refused at Morebath in 1536, and that many of the gilds at Antony in the last years of Henry VIII were owed money by local men: these proved so slow to repay that the 'Six Men' of the parish began to threaten legal action. The accounts show also that bede-rolls were still recited, and new names occasionally added; but the particularly full records of Stratton's High Cross group reveal a decline in enrolments from 1540. There was but one name added in 1541, 1542, 1544 and 1546, and one in 1540, 1543 or 1545.[29]

The combined testimony of wills, legal records, chantry-certificates and wardens' accounts can thus leave little doubt about changing attitudes to the traditional apparatus of intercession. Between 1530 and 1547 the decline in popular enthusiasm appears to have been both widespread and rapid. The study of prayers for the dead – like the study of image- veneration – renders it difficult to maintain the thesis that the Henrician Reformation passed 'over the head' of the average man. On the contrary, it appears probable that fundamental changes in his religious activity were initiated in these tumultuous years.

If a decline in enthusiasm for intercessions can be asserted with relative confidence, the factors behind this trend are less immediately apparent. In most cases, nevertheless, it appears to have been non-ideological in origin, and to have represented an essentially pragmatic response to the unam- biguously hostile activities of the government and of the local gentry.

The intentions of the government became increasingly clear from 1529, when the acceptance of stipends for singing masses for the dead was restricted by statute.[30] The suppression of religious houses in 1536–9, moreover, not only ended lay-endowed intercessions within them, but also publicized governmental doubts about the efficacy of any prayer or mass for the dead. 'The founding of monastries argued Purgatory to be', observed Latimer; 'so the putting of them down argueth it not to be'.[31] Even more disturbing were the statute of 1545, which threatened to transfer the property of chantry foundations to the Exchequer, and the associated activities of the chantry commissioners – 'the king's visitors for the church lands', whom the churchwardens of Woodbury (for example) had to meet in 1545–6.[32] The expectations of an imminent dissolution that were inevitably aroused by such developments can only have served to undermine popular confidence in intercessory institutions, discouraging new investment and stimulating the diversion of existing endowments to essentially secular ends.

At the same time, the population of the south-west saw chantries come under increasing attack from members of the gentry. Motivated more often by material interest than by Protestant conviction, this development can be traced to the earliest years of the Reformation. In 1529–32 the deeds of a Trinity gild at Exeter were detained by Charles Coplestone, and an annuity maintaining a chantry-priest at Tretherf was appropriated by the founder's son. A stipendiary chaplaincy at Thornbury was dissolved by a gentleman named Specott in about 1531; property at St Winnow, granted by William Casely to maintain an obit, was reclaimed by his heirs in about 1537; and at Colyford, in the early 1540s, Robert Stowford refused to pay the chantry-priest more than half his stipend. Another gentleman, meanwhile, claimed land at Lansallos that had maintained the performance of obits, while chantries at Halberton and Colebrooke were dissolved by members of the gentry in about 1545.[33] The example thus set by his social superiors must have eroded even further the confidence of the average man in the traditional organs of intercession.

III

Intercessory institutions had thus already lost much of their vitality when, after the accession of Edward VI, they were subjected to an official assault unprecedented in rigour and in scope. By the Act of 1547, all properties, rents and annuities providing stipends for chantry-priests were transferred to the Crown, along with the funds of parish gilds and fraternities assigned to 'superstitious' purposes. The ultimate aim of this campaign was the total demolition of the intercessory structure.[34] To what extent, in reality, was it effectively implemented?

In the parishes of the south-west, the characteristic response seems usually to have been a dutiful – if unenthusiastic – conformity to official decrees. Wardens' accounts indicate that in most parish churches, the recitation of bede-rolls was obediently abrogated in 1548. At Stratton, for example, names ceased to be added to the roll, and payments to the vicar for reading it now came to an end.[35] Extant accounts record also an almost invariable cessation of masses for the dead at about the same time.[36] Even more remarkable was the alacrity with which parishes obeyed the official instructions for the dissolution of religious gilds. By 1550, these once-vital institutions appear to have been virtually eliminated from every parochial community for which accounts remain.

At Stratton, for instance, the stockwardens' account for 1547 (made on 1 January 1548) indicates the existence of gilds known as Allhallows, Our Lady and St George, Our Lady, St Andrew, St Thomas, St Armil, Christ, the Trinity, and the High Cross. The next account, made at the feast of St Andrew in 1548, records only four. By 1549, only the High Cross survived; and it, too, seems to have been suppressed thereafter. The last account of All Saints' gild at Launceston was compiled on All Saints' Day in 1548. The 'Brewers of the Processional Ale', who had organized rites at North Petherwin as well as selling bread and ale, similarly ended in 1548. More-bath lost its 'Young Men' and 'Young Women' at about the same time. Annual *diriges* for a fraternity at Woodbury ceased in 1548; and in 1550 the parish sold three ewes which had belonged to St Margaret's store. By 1549, the former complexes of 10 or 11 groups at Camborne and at Antony had dwindled to one and three respectively; and even these were soon to end.[37] The few groups that survived this deluge of destruction were invariably shorn of their 'superstitious' functions. At North Petherwin, for example, St Christopher's store had organized a regular *dirige*, mass and bede-roll. The store continued to exist throughout the reign of Edward VI, but from 1548 these activities disappeared entirely from its accounts; its traditional identity had been effectively effaced.[38]

The suppression of intercessory institutions was followed by the dispersal of their property. A single day – 25 February 1549 – saw the sale by the government of land belonging to a chantry at Beaford, of a house at Broadhempston that had maintained an anniversary, and of property at Exeter which had supported the singing of an antiphon in St Petrock's parish church, as well as the disposal of land at Ashburton which had belonged to the fraternity of St Lawrence.[39] Sometimes the former premises of a chantry were converted to non-religious use. St Nicholas' chapel at Looe, for example, became the hall of a secular gild.[40] Some, moreover, were subjected to physical attack. In 1549, following the dissolution of St George's gild at Lostwithiel and the cessation of its annual procession, *dirige* and feast, the gild's chapel in the parish church was deliberately 'defaced' by the townsmen. They acted on the orders of their mayor, Richard Hutchings.[41]

The general passivity of popular responses to this unprecedented assault upon the intercessory system is indicated also by surviving wills. Only 6 of the 30 testators in 1547 (20%) still thought it judicious to invest in prayer for the dead; the prevalent uncertainty is evident in the request of Peter

Amis of Lanlivery for a trental, 'if it may be'. Such investment, moreover, appears in no more than 3 of the 17 wills from 1548 (11%), and in only one of the 20 from 1549 (5%). The sole exception in the latter year was John Southwood of Hemyock, who on 10 March left 12d to a priest in return for his prayers.[42] Bequests to gilds, furthermore, are found in no more than 6 of the 77 wills from 1547–9 (8%). The import of these statistics is clear. As the Protestant proclivities of the Edwardian regime became increasingly explicit, testators grew correspondingly reluctant to risk investment in the traditional apparatus of intercession. A rising number, significantly, were beginning to divert their bequests towards the poor of this world instead.

For more than two years, until the summer of 1549, any attempts at resistance to this devastation of traditional religion seem to have been remarkably restricted in scale. They were limited to localities like Ashburton, where some of the inhabitants attempted with violence to prevent the confiscation of lands and market-tolls formerly owned by the gild of St Lawrence.[43] Most parishes, by contrast, seem to have submitted to the commissioners without overt dissent. Woodbury was again typical, dutifully sending its representatives to Exeter in 1547–8 'for the church lands',[44] while at Morebath the Three Men and the wardens rode to meet the commissioners at Tiverton 'to make an answer for chantry ground'. Nor should it be too readily assumed that even the Western Rebellion of June–August 1549 necessarily indicates a determination by the majority of West-Countrymen to restore the intercessions by force. It is true that the rebel articles declare that 'we will have every preacher in his sermon, and every priest at his mass, pray specially by name for the souls in Purgatory, as our forefathers did'. They demand also the confiscation of 'the half part of the abbey lands and chantry lands in every man's possession, howsoever he came by them', in order to finance the restoration of two establishments in each county 'for devout persons, which shall pray for the king and the commonwealth'.[45] Since, however, the articles were almost certainly formulated by the traditionalist priest who led the revolt, the extent to which they accurately represent the attitudes of the rebel rank-and-file must remain open to doubt. Cranmer told the rebel laymen that they had been deceived by their priestly leaders, 'which devised those articles for you, to make you ask you wist not what';[46] and it is certain that several of the insurgents' motives – notably their desire for plunder, their fear of taxation, and their bitter antagonism towards members of the gentry – were essentially secular rather than religious in nature. It is equally important to note the apparent failure of the rebellion to engage more than a relatively small minority of the regional population – an estimated 7000 out of perhaps 100 000 inhabitants of the south-west. The resigned conformity of Morebath seems to have been markedly more typical than the desperate resistance of Sampford Courtenay. At the same time, moreover, there were significant individuals and groups,

both within Exeter and beyond, who proved actively loyal to the Edwardian regime.[47]

The revolt's bloody defeat by Lord Russell, and the ensuing campaign of
fines, confiscations and executions, would appear in fact to have extinguished the last sparks of organized resistance to the assault upon intercessions. Certainly the official orders for the dismantling of altars, at
which prayers and masses for the dead had been offered, were implemented
with conspicuous compliance in most parishes for which accounts survive.
The parishioners of Woodbury, for example, pulled down their altars in
1550, paying James Croft 'for carrying out of the rubble of the altars', and
selling 'stones of the altars', as well as 'three broad stones that lay apon the
altars'. The wardens at Stratton paid for 'drawing down of the altars' in
1551, and sold 'stones of the altars' for 4s.4d, while at Dartmouth in 1552
old altar-stones were to be found lying out in the churchyard.[48] At the
same time, vast quantities of vestments and altar-plate, much of which had
been used in intercessory rites, were disappearing from the parish
churches, either by sale, by theft, or by official confiscation.[49] That the
prevailing popular attitude to this new wave of destruction was again
characterized by resignation and compliance is confirmed by the apparently total lack of resistance recorded in the surviving sources. It is also
revealing that, in the 32 wills made between January 1550 and July 1553,
there was not a single attempt to arrange intercessions in any form. Nor
was there even one recorded bequest to a religious gild. Gifts to the poor,
by contrast, were included in no less than 15 of the 32 wills.

IV

Was devotion to prayers for the dead eliminated permanently by the
Edwardian regime? Or could it revive and flourish in the more favourable
climate of Mary's reign? How effective, at local level, was the alleged
'restoration' of Catholicism in 1553–8?

There is no doubt that many subsidiary altars at which intercessions
had once been performed – like St Margaret's at Woodbury – were re-
erected by parishes within months of the queen's accession in July 1553.
Others, however, were restored only after considerable hesitation – until
1554–5 at Chagford and Braunton, for instance, and until 1555–6 at
Morebath – while in some parishes they may never have been restored at
all.[50] It is also suggestive that, of the 22 parishes for which accounts
survive, there is certain record of the revival of intercessory activity in
only 13. Again, moreover, the revival was not necessarily spontaneous. It
was deferred until 1555–6 at Exeter St Petrock and at Woodbury, until 1557
at Chagford, and until as late as 1558–9 at Exeter St John's Bow. In nine
parishes there is no evidence of intercessions at all. Equally notable is the
absence from all the accounts, with the sole exception of those for

Dartington, of payments to priests for the recitation of bede-rolls – a virtually ubiquitous feature of pre-Edwardian accounts. It would therefore appear that most communities never succeeded in reviving these prayers for the dead.[51]

Even more revealing is the light thrown by accounts upon the restoration of religious gilds. Of the 22 recorded parishes, not one seems ever to have approached the total of 9, 10 or 11 groups maintained by several pre-Edwardian communities. Only seven appear to have revived as many as two, three or four. Seven restored a single group, while the remaining eight seem to have restored none at all. Nor did the Marian gilds necessarily resume their pre-Edwardian functions. St Brannoc's at Braunton might buy 'vittle against St Brannoc's obit for the brother and sisters', hire a priest 'to come to say mass when our Ale was', and pay a man 'for going about the town the brotherhood day' to proclaim it;[52] but many of the revived gilds were little more than fund-raising agencies for the parish church. St Christopher's at North Petherwin, for example, failed to revive the *diriges*, masses and bede-roll readings that it had organized regularly until 1548. Nor do the accounts of the High Cross store at Stratton – formerly the organizer of a popular bede-roll – record a single new registration upon it in the reign of Mary.[53] When every allowance has been made for incompleteness, the unavoidable impression given by Marian accounts is that the restoration of intercessory institutions and activities was never, in reality, more than a very tentative and limited phenomenon.

This impression, moreover, receives substantial confirmation from contemporary wills. Prayers or masses for the dead had been endowed in 70 per cent of the wills from 1520–9, in 51 per cent of those from 1530–9, and in 33 per cent of those from 1540–6. Of the 60 wills from 1553–9 – that is, from Mary's accession to the Elizabethan injunctions – such bequests appeared in no more than 11 (18%). John Tuckfield, alderman of Exeter, might still in 1554 leave money to his apprentice, servants and maids, 'to pray for me', and Richard Friend of Ermington might still in 1557 endow a priest 'to sing for my soul and all my friends';[54] but even amongst testators, with their generally conservative tendencies, such confidence in the ancient modes of intercession was no longer common. Even more striking is the failure of all but one of the 60 testators to include bequests to religious gilds. The sole exception was Robert Easton of Chudleigh, who as late as April 1559 left 6s.8d to the local store of Our Lady.[55] This dramatic reduction of support for such institutions, which contrasts so markedly with their popularity on the eve of the Reformation, provides further substance for the conclusion that the Henrician and Edwardian upheavals had dealt the traditional piety a crushing blow – a blow from which it was never, even in the favourable circumstances of Mary's reign, to recover.

It was, therefore, a religious practice in unmistakeable decline that came under renewed and determined attack from the Elizabethan regime. The royal commissioners reached Exeter in September 1559 and, according to the contemporary Exonian John Hooker, 'did deface all the altars and monuments of idolatry, and forbade any more masses or popish services to be used'.[56] Once more the most frequent local response to official instruction seems to have been a dutiful conformity. The destruction of altars is recorded even in the accounts of villages that were relatively small and remote. Thus the parishioners of Coldridge sent representatives to meet the visitors at Barnstable, and then paid for 'ridding of the altars of the church'. Similarly at Woodbury, after the wardens' appearance before the visitors at Exeter, men were paid for pulling down St Margaret's altar, and for carrying away the stones.[57] Soon, moreover, the parish churches were to be stripped again of their vestments and plate.[58] In every parish for which relevant accounts survive, furthermore, prayers and masses for the dead appear totally to have ceased in 1559. By the 1560s, therefore, the ancient practices of intercession seem to have been well-nigh eradicated from the pattern of parochial religion.

Belief in Purgatory, inevitably, did not vanish overnight. Some testators, like William Spiring of Bradninch in 1560, would still arrange the disposal of their property 'for the wealth of my soul and all Christian souls'.[59] Such belief, nevertheless, could no longer be expressed in ritual performance. Of 90 testators from 1560–9, only one dared even to request the performance of intercession. This was William Turner of Cullompton, who in January 1561 still hoped for an annual dole to the poor on his burial-day, 'to pray for me and my father and mother and my two wives, Thomasine and Joan, and all Christian souls'.[60] At the same time, moreover, religious gilds were experiencing a further reduction both in number and in importance. Many of the groups revived under Mary were ended in 1559–60. In several parishes, including St Petrock's, St John's Bow, and St Mary Steps at Exeter as well as Ashburton, Crediton, Dartington, Kilmington and Woodbury, not one such gild appears to have survived into the 1560s.[61] Other communities rarely retained more than one or two, and even these had invariably been divested of their original intercessory functions. St Katherine at Chagford seems merely now to have raised money for the church by selling ale. The two groups dedicated to Sts John and George and St Brannoc at Braunton, though still dispensing food and drink to the poor on 'brotherhood day', no longer arranged their traditional intercessions. St Christopher at North Petherwin similarly survived into the 1560s, but its customary *diriges*, masses and bede-roll recitations had long since been abandoned.[62] It is scarcely surprising that such emasculated institutions were no longer able to attract the enthusiastic support of former years. Their wardenship now was often refused, as at Chagford and Chudleigh.[63]

More significantly, they failed to receive a single bequest in any of the 90 West-Country wills from this decade.

The conclusion to be drawn from the different types of surviving evidence is therefore relatively clear. Whatever the case in other regions, the impact of the Reformation upon intercessions in the south-west can in no way be dismissed as either 'restricted' or 'delayed'. On the contrary: the effects of official pressure upon this crucial component of the popular religion appears to have been increasingly noticeable at parish level from as early as the 1530s, and ultimately to have proved devastating. What is indicated by the statistics, as well as by evidence of a less quantifiable nature, is a fundamental reorientation of religious activity – a virtual eradication, within one life-span, of practices which had for generations lain close to the very heart of the popular piety.

V

Long-established patterns of religion were thus erased: by what were they replaced? Was the ancient enthusiasm for intercession transmuted into a corresponding acceptance of the 'Protestant' view of salvation? To what extent was the decline of the old ideology accompanied by a rise of the new?

There is no doubt that, even at relatively low levels of West-Country society, authentically Protestant attitudes to salvation were occasionally emerging in the Reformation decades. They received their clearest expression in the tracts written in 1547–9 by Philip Nichols, a young Devonian layman of comparatively humble social origins. Nichols rejected the entire concept of Purgatory as unscriptural. 'Christ speaketh not any one word of Purgatory – no, nor any place of all the scriptures, from the first word of *Genesis* to the last of St John's *Revelation*.' Equally characteristic of Protestant emphases was Nichols's confidence that believers are assured of an immediate passage to Heaven after death by the atoning work of Christ. Since the wicked proceed immediately to Hell, there is no need for a 'third place'. (One might equally claim a fourth place for the Devil, he argues; if God refuses souls entry into Heaven until they are cleansed of wickedness, may not Satan debar souls from Hell until they are purged of virtue?) Since Purgatory does not exist, prayers and masses for the dead are no more than fraudulent inventions of the priesthood, devised in order to increase its wealth and to maintan its ascendancy over 'simple consciences here, in this world'. 'As for matins-mumblers and mass-mongers, with *diriges* and trentals, with such superstitious prayers: the scripture speaketh not of them.'[64]

That Protestant views of the after-life were occasionally to be found at a relatively low social level in the mid-Tudor south-west is thus beyond dispute. The extent of their acceptance by the regional population at large, however, is markedly more problematic. One source of evidence is provided by the records of the Consistory Court at Exeter. Its act books and deposition books, which run intermittently from Henry VII to Elizabeth I, offer strikingly little indication of popular Protestantism in the diocese before 1570.[65] A similar impression is given by the Exeter episcopal registers for this period. John Atwill of Walkhampton might in 1506 dismiss bede-rolls as more effective in enriching clerics than in saving souls, and Otto Corbin at Exeter in 1515 might declare, 'I care not for my soul, so I may have an honest living in this world; and when ye see my soul hang on the hedge, cast ye stones thereto';[66] but the marked rarity of such cases again suggests that neither 'Lollard' nor 'Protestant' attitudes to salvation ever attracted widespread support in the region before 1570. The same conclusion is to be drawn from the records of other contemporary courts, some of which (notably Chancery and Star Chamber) dealt tangentially with religious affairs. The only court cases from this period to reveal unambiguously Protestant conceptions of the after-life are in fact the two recorded by John Foxe. The first concerns Thomas Benet, a private schoolmaster who was burned at the stake at Exeter in 1532; he reportedly accused the clergy of selling masses for souls in 'feigned Purgatory', and declared salvation to be dependent upon Christ's atonement rather than upon human achievement. The second case is that of Agnes Priest, an uneducated woman from near Launceston; she also was burned as a heretic at Exeter, in 1558. Agnes regarded trentals, *diriges*, soul-masses and purchased prayers as 'foolish inventions'; for, 'God's Son hath, by his Passion, purged all'. These are the sole instances of such belief to be recorded by the *Acts and Monuments* for the entire diocese in the Reformation decades.[67]

Further clues are provided by wills. Authentically Protestant formulae, expressing confidence in the soul's immediate passage to Heaven by virtue of Christ's atoning work, are conspicuously absent from all 30 West-Country wills with recorded formulae from 1520–9. Of the 30 with formulae from 1530–9, moreover, only two contain possible indications of such belief. The Cornishman William Nanfan avowed in 1536 that God would grant, 'after this present and miserable life, eternal life to all faithful souls in the joy everlasting', while John Forde of Ashburton in 1538 commended his soul 'to Almighty God and to his infinite mercy, trusting that by the merits of his Passion [I am] to have the fruition of his Godhead in Heaven'. Yet the Protestantism of even these two testators is doubtful: Forde in fact arranged prayers and masses for his soul in no less than 20 local churches.[68] Solifidian assertions, moreover, appear only once in the 21 wills with formulae from 1540–6, and only twice in the 16 from 1547–9. Two of these three testators – Nicholas Wise in 1540, and Richard Colwill under Edward VI – may not have been resident in the region, since Wise (despite his West-Country associations) requested burial at Shoreditch, and Colwill owned land both in Devon and outside. The only certain resident to express Protestant convictions in his will before 1550 is therefore John Bougin of Totnes. In 1548 he bequeathed his soul to God and his body to Christian burial, 'abolishing all feig[ned] ceremonies contrary to Holy Scripture, which is God's word and commandment'. Instead he arranged psalms, 'in the honour of God and with thanksgiving that it hath so pleased him to call me to his mercy and grace'.[69]

Only after the defeat of the Western Rebellion in 1549 – and after the replacement of the conservative John Veysey by the vigorously Protestant Miles Coverdale as bishop of Exeter in 1551 – did the pattern begin to change. Of 18 testators between January 1550 and July 1553, confidence in the sufficiency of Christ's atonement was expressed by six; namely John Harris, John Bond of Crediton, John Anthony of Dartmouth, William Amadas of Plymouth, and Philip Mayhew and John Hurst of Exeter. Thus Anthony, a merchant, bequeathed his soul to God in 1552, 'believing that by the merits of Christ's Passion [I am] to have remission of all my sins, and to be one of the same number that are elected to be with him in everlasting glory'; and Amadas, in June 1553, commended himself to Christ, 'in whom and by whom is all my whole trust of clean remission and forgiveness of my sins'.[70] Amadas himself was undoubtedly committed to Protestantism.[71] In five other cases, however, it is less clear that solifidian assertion reflects a personal conviction rather than a dutiful conformity to official norms. A high degree of conformism is certainly suggested by the rapidity with which such formulae ceased to appear after Edward's death: only 2 are found in 32 wills made between Mary's accession and Elizabeth's injunctions. Although Harry Reynold in 1554 required burial 'according unto God's holy word', and John Lane of Broadhembury in October 1558 declared himself 'perfect in mind and, trusting in Jesu, safe in soul', a clearly Protestant attitude to death seems to have been expressed only by two citizens of Exeter, namely John Drake (in 1554) and Griffith Meredith (in 1557). Drake, a merchant, proclaimed his 'faithful trust and hope in the infinite goodness of Almighty God, my Maker and Redeemer', and his expectation of eternal life 'after my departing out of this wretched and transitory life'. Meredith committed himself to God, 'trusting to be saved by the shedding of Christ's blood, and in all the merits of his Passion'.[72]

Even after the return of Protestant government under Elizabeth I, such statements of faith remained strikingly rare. Of 30 West-Country wills with recorded formulae from 1560–9, they appear in no more than 4. William Lake, a merchant of Plymouth, described himself in 1560 as a 'most miserable sinner', and asked God 'that the merits of thy son Jesus Christ may be a full redemption and satisfaction for the trespasses that I have done or committed since I came into this wretched world, so that my most wretched soul may be saved amongst thy saints'. Joan Lake of Plymouth – possibly his wife – proclaimed in 1562 a similar confidence in salvation 'by no other means' than the Passion of Christ. In the same year a yeoman from Combe Pyne, John Helier, declared that he expected to receive, through Christ's work, 'the fruition of his Godhead in Heaven'. In 1566, finally, Robert Ebsworthy of Bridestow bequeathed 'my soul to God, and my body to the earth, and my sin to the Devil, desiring God for Christ's sake to forgive them'.[73] Such declarations would seem still to have been uncommon at the popular levels of West-Country society. Most of the extant wills from this decade are suggestively silent about the fate of the testator after death.

What conclusions are to be drawn from the available evidence? Protestant views of the after-life were undoubtedly beginning to attract support from at least some members, both male and female, of the lay population below the level of the gentry. Though found in some rural communities, this support appears to have been strongest in the larger towns, particularly Exeter and Plymouth; here the literacy required for Bible-reading was relatively common, Protestant preaching was comparatively frequent, and trade-links with Protestant London were often strong. By 1570, nevertheless, it was still limited to a relatively small proportion of the regional population. The traditional apparatus of intercession had been progressively dismantled, and was now beyond repair; but in the minds and hearts of most West-Countrymen it had yet to be replaced by an enthusiastic commitment to the new and alien doctrine of justification by faith alone. In reality, it seems more often to have been replaced by uncertainty, confusion, and indifference to the officially sanctioned forms of religion. In their campaign to suppress the ancient piety, the agents of Reformation had achieved substantial success; but the substitution of an alternative spirituality was proving to be a separate and a markedly more difficult problem.

Notes

1 A.G. Dickens, *Lollards and Protestants in the Diocese of York, 1509–1558* (1959).
2 C. Haigh, *Reformation and Resistance in Tudor Lancashire* (1975).
3 R. Whiting, 'Abominable Idols: images and image-breaking under Henry VIII', *Journal of Ecclesiastical History* January 1982.]
4 G. McN. Rushforth, 'The Windows of the Church of St Neot, Cornwall', *Exeter Diocesan Architectural and Archaeological Society Transactions* (1927).
5 J. Prince, *Worthies of Devon* (1701), 324, 325.
6 DC 2864 (bede-roll, late-fifteenth century).
7 PRO, Chancery, Early Proceedings (C 1), 900/34,35 (1533–8).
8 DRO, 745C (service-book, late-medieval), p. 3.
9 J. Foxe, *Acts and Monuments* (1583), Ii, p. 1039.
10 This and all subsequent references to wills (unless otherwise indicated) relate to the author's analysis of (a) 177 wills from 1520–69, as preserved in PRO, Prerogative Court of Canterbury, Wills (PROB 11), and (b) 221 testamentary abstracts from 1520–69, as preserved in DRO, Moger Abstracts of Devon Wills (47 typescript

volumes); Devon and Cornwall Record Society Library, Exeter, Oswyn Murray Abstracts of Wills (39 typescript volumes), and C. Worthy, *Devonshire Wills: A Collection of Annotated Testamentary Abstracts* (1896). The 221 abstracts are summaries of the originals; the 177 wills are complete copies. The testators came from a wide range of parishes, both urban and rural.

11 PRO, Prerogative Court of Canterbury, Wills (PROB 11), 21, fo. 18*v*; 23 fo. 71; 24, fo. 10.

12 PRO, Prerogative Court of Canterbury, Wills (PROB 11), 20, fo. 229*v*; 21, fos. 128, 202*v*; 22, fos. 8, 302; 24, fo. 10.

13 PRO, Prerogative Court of Canterbury, Wills (PROB 11), 20, fos. 229, 229*v*; 23, fo. 29; 24, fo. 10; DRO, Moger Abstracts of Devon Wills, 19, Thomas Hamlyn, 1526.

14 C. Henderson, *Essays in Cornish History* (1935), 75–9; DRO, Chagford CWA, 1500–30, *passim*; BL Additional MS 32243, Stratton High Cross wardens' accounts, 1512–30, *passim*; (CRO), North Petherwin CWA, fos. 14, 22*v*, 32*v*, 38*v*, etc.

15 BL Additional MS 32243, Stratton High Cross wardens' accounts, 1512–30, *passim*: CRO, North Petherwin CWA, fo. 38*v*, etc; Henderson, *Essays*, 75–9; DRO, Chagford CWA, 1500–30, *passim*; R. Carew, *Survey of Cornwall* (1811 ed.), 322–323; PROC, Exchequer, Court of Augmentations, Proceedings (E 315), 122/15–28.

16 A. Hanham (ed.), *Churchwardens' Accounts of Ashburton, 1479–1580* (1970), xii–xv; DRO, Chagford CWA, 1500–30, *passim*; BL Additional MS 32243, Stratton High Cross wardens' accounts, 1512–30, *passim*; BL Additional MS 32244, Stratton Stockwardens' accounts, 1532 *et seq.*; CRO, Camborne CWA, 1535 *et seq.*; J.E. Binney (ed.), *The Accounts of the Wardens of the Parish of Morebath, 1520–73*, (1904) *passim*; Devon and Cornwall Record Society Library, Exeter, transcript, South Tawton CWA, 1524, *et seq.*; ERO, Winkleigh CWA, 1519 *et seq.*; transcript in the possession of Mr F.L. Harris, Antony CWA, 1538 *et seq.*; CRO, North Petherwin CWA, *passim*.

17 PRO, Prerogative Court of Canterbury, Wills (PROB 11), 19, fo. 208; 22, fo. 191*v*; 23, fo. 54; DRO, Moger Abstracts of Devon Wills, 19, Thomas Hamlyn, 1526.

18 PRO, Prerogative Court of Canterbury, Wills (PROB 11), 27, fo. 69*v*; 29, fo. 201; 31, fo. 44.

19 PRO, Preorogative Court of Canterbury, Wills (PROB 11), 25, fo. 280*v*; 26, fo. 76.

20 PRO, Preorogative Court of Canterbury, Wills (PROB 11), 26, fo. 79*v*.

21 PRO, Prerogative Court of Canterbury, Wills (PROB 11), 25, fo. 227*v*.

22 PRO, Star Chamber Proceedings, Henry VIII (STAC 2), 25/80, 142; PRO, Chancery, Early Proceedings (C 1), 781/26 (1533–8); 786/54 (1533–8); 930/1 (1533–8).

23 PRO, Star Chamber Proceedings, Edward VI (STAC 3), 2/20; 7/45; PRO, Chancery, Early Proceedings (C 1), 959/35–7 (1538–44); 976/32, 33 (1538–44); 986/44 (1538–44); 1042/7–9 (1538–44); 1200/10, 11 (1547–51).

24 DRO, Consistory Court Book 778, *sub* 12 January 1533/4, 17 March 1533/4; PRO, Chancery, Early Proceedings (C 1), 1029/46–50 (1538–44); 1162/52 (1544–7); 1185/31 (1547).

25 L.S. Snell (ed.), *The Chantry Certificates for Cornwall* (1953) pp. 21, 27, 42, 53; L.S. Snell (ed.), *The Chantry Certificates for Devon and the City of Exeter* (1961), xxii, 41.

26 Snell, *Cornwall*, 34, 48, 50; Snell, *Devon*, xxi, xxii, 23, 24. For Trotte, see also above, n. 5.

27 ERO, Exeter St John's Bow CWA, *passim*. Hanham, *Churchwardens' Accounts*, *passim*. DRO, Chagford CWA, *passim*. CRO, St Thomas-by-Launceston CWA, *passim*. DRO, transcript, Broadhempston CWA, *passim*. Binney, *Accounts*, *passim*.

28 DRO, Chagford CWA, *passim*. CRO, Camborne CWA, *passim*. BL Additional MS 32244, Stratton Stockwardens' accounts, 1541, 1542, *et seq*. ERO, Woodbury CWA, 1543 *et seq*. CRO, North Petherwin CWA, *passim*. Hanham, *Churchwardens' Accounts*, *passim*. Devon and Cornwall Record Society Library, Exeter, transcript, South Tawton CWA, *passim*.

29 Binney, *Accounts*, 73; transcript in the possession of Mr F.L. Harris, Antony CWA, 69–86 (*c*. 1543–5); BL Additional MS 32243, Stratton High Cross wardens' accounts, 1540–6.

30 G.H. Cook, *The English Mediaeval Parish Church*, (1954), 261.
31 G.W.O. Woodward, *The Dissolution of the Monasteries* (1966), 171, 172.
32 ERO, Woodbury CWA, 1546.
33 PRO, Chancery, Early Proceedings (C 1), 601/1 (1529–32); 631/4 (1529–32); 1228/63 (1547–51); Snell, *Cornwall*, 28, 53, 54; Snell, *Devon*, xxi, xxii, 25.
34 Cook, *Parish Church*, 262.
35 BL Additional MS 32243, Stratton High Cross wardens; accounts, 1547, 1548, *et seq*. The abnormal number of registrations in 1547 (20) may represent a panic-reaction to the advent of Protestant government; they were certainly the last at Stratton.
36 E.g. ERO, Exeter St Petrock CWA; ERO, Exeter St John's Bow CWA; DRO. Exeter Holy Trinity CWA; Hanham, *Churchwardens' Accounts, passim*. CRO, St Thomas-by-Launceston CWA; BL Additional MS 32244, Stratton Stockwardens' accounts; ERO, Woodbury CWA.
37 BL Additional MS 32244, Stratton Stockwardens' accounts, 1547, 1548, 1549; BL Additional MS 32243, Stratton High Cross wardens' accounts, 1549; CRO, St Thomas-by-Launceston CWA, 1548; CRO, North Petherwin CWA, fos. 28, 28*v*; Binney, *Accounts, passim*. ERO, Woodbury CWA, 1548, 1549, 1550; CRO, Camborne CWA, *passim*. transcript in the possession of Mr F.L. Harris, Antony CWA, *passim*.
38 CRO, North Petherwin CWA, fos. 3, 30–2. The erasure of the word 'bede-roll' from the 1548 account indicates its suppression in that year.
39 *Calendar of the Patent Rolls, Edward VI* (1924–9), II, 259.
40 C. Henderson, *Cornish Church Guide* (1925), 126.
41 PRO, Exchequer, Court of Augmentations, Proceedings (E 315), 122/15–28; above, n. 9.
42 PRO, Prerogative Court of Canterbury, Wills (PROB 11), 32, fo. 15*v*; DRO, Moger Abstracts of Devon Wills, 39, John Southwood, 1549.
43 PRO, Star Chamber Proceedings, Edward VI (STAC 3), 2/14.
44 ERO, Woodbury CWA, 1548, Binney, *Accounts*, 159.
45 BL, Royal MS 18 B XI, 'An Answer to the Articles'.
46 J. Strype (ed.), *Memorial of Archbishop Cranmer* (1848), II, 502, 503.
47 R. Whiting, 'The Reformation in the Sough-West of England', unpublished PhD thesis, Exeter University, 1977, 197–201; A. Fletcher, *Tudor Rebellions* (1973), 48–63.
48 DRO, Episcopal Registers, Veysey (RE XV), fos. 119*v*, 120; ERO, Woodbury CWA, 1550; BL Additional MS 32243, Stratton High Cross wardens' accounts, 1551; ERO, Dartmouth CWA 1552 (and page following).
49 Whiting, 'Reformation', 202–4.
50 ERO, Woodbury CWA, 1554; DRO, Chagford CWA, 1555; CRO, Braunton CWA, 1555; Binney, *Accounts*, 189.
51 Intercessions recorded: ERO, Exeter St Petrock CWA; ERO, Exeter St John's Bow CWA; DRO, Exeter Holy Trinity CWA; J.R. Chanter and T. Wainwright (eds.), *Reprint of the Barnstaple Records*, (1900), I, 212, 213; DRO, Chagford CWA; DRO, Crediton CWA; CRO, St Thomas-by-Launceston CWA; transcript in the possession of Mr F.L. Harris, Antony CWA; DRO, Braunton CWA; ERO, Dartingon CWA; Binney *Accounts*, 175–202, *passim*. CRO, North Petherwin CWA; ERO, Woodbury CWA. Intercessions not recorded: ERO, Exeter St Mary Steps CWA; Hanham *Churchwardens' Accounts*, 128–141, *passim*. CRO, Camborne CWA; ERO, Dartmouth CWA; BL Additional MS 32243, Stratton High Cross wardens' accounts; DRO, Coldridge CWA; R. Cornish (ed.), *The Churchwardens' Accounts of Kilmington, 1555–1608* (1901), *passim*. J Phear (ed.), 'Molland Accounts', *Transactions of the Devonshire Association* (1903), *passim*. Devon and Cornwall Record Society Library, Exeter, transcript, South Tawton CWA.
52 DRO, Braunton CWA, 1555–9. Cf. DRO, Chagford CWA; CRO, St Thomas-by-Launceston CWA; transcript in the possession of Mr F.L. Harris, Antony CWA; CRO, North Petherwin CWA; ERO, Woodbury CWA.
53 CRO, North Petherwin CWA, fos. 3*v*, 4; BL Additional MS 32243, Stratton High Cross wardens' accounts, 1553–9.

54 PRO, Prerogative Court of Canterbury, Wills (PROB 11), 39, fo. 203; DRO, Consistory Court Book 855A, fos. 311v, 312.
55 DRO, Moger Abstracts of Devon Wills, 13, Robert Easton, 1559.
56 ERO, Book 51 (John Hooker, Commonplace Book), fo. 352.
57 DRO, Coldridge CWA, 1560; ERO, Woodbury CWA, 1559.
58 Whiting, 'Reformation', 212, 213, 224, 225.
59 PRO, Prerogative Court of Canterbury, Wills (PROB 11), 50, fo. 152v.
60 PRO, Prerogative Court of Canterbury, Wills (PROB 11), 44, fo. 159v.
61 ERO, Exeter St Petrock CWA; ERO, Exeter St John's Bow CWA; ERO, Exeter St Mary Steps CWA; Hanham, *Churchwardens' Accounts*, 141–166, *passim*. DRO, Crediton CWA; ERO, Dartington CWA; Cornish, *Kilmington, passim*. ERO, Woodbury CWA.
62 DRO, Chagford CWA, 1560–70; DRO, Braunton CWA, 1560–70; CRO, North Petherwin CWA, fos. 4, 4v.
63 DRO, Chagford CWA, 1560–70; ERO, Chudleigh CWA, 1561.
64 BL, Royal MS 18 B XI, 'An Answer to the Articles', fos. 25–26; BL Reading Room 4404 B 61, P. Nichols, *A Godly New Story* (1548), 47.
65 DRO, Consistory Court Books 41, 775, 776, 777, 778, 779, 854 (I,II), 854A (I,II), 855, 855A, 855B, 856.
66 DRO, Episcopal Registers, Oldham (RE XIII), fos. 144v, 145, 179v–181.
67 Foxe, *Acts and Monuments*, II, 1039, 2050–2052.
68 PRO, Prerogative Court of Canterbury, Wills (PROB 11), 26, fo. 79v; 27, fo. 4v.
69 PRO, Prerogative Court of Canterbury, Wills (PROB 11), 28, fo. 149; F. 44 Alen; Devon and Cornwall Record Society Library, Exeter, Oswyn Murray Abstracts of Wills, 3, John Bougin, 1548. For the Protestant minority under Edward VI, Whiting, 'Reformation', 182.
70 PRO, Prerogative Court of Canterbury, Wills (PROB 11), 33, fo. 155; 34, fos. 154v, 225; 35, fo. 169; 36, fo. 20v; 44, fo. 274.
71 For his sponsorship of Protestant preaching, Whiting, 'Reformation', 74.
72 PRO, Prerogative Court of Canterbury, Wills (PROB 11), 37, fos. 144, 178; 41, fo. 243; 42A.
73 PRO, Prerogative Court of Canterbury, Wills (PROB 11), 45, fo. 60v; 46, fos. 128v, 258v; 48, fo. 459v.

6

The local impact of the Tudor reformations

RONALD HUTTON

In recent years, our understanding of the Tudor religious changes has been considerably increased by local studies, each concerned with a particular city, county or region and employing a range of different sources for the task.[1] This essay is concerned instead with one of the principal varieties of material used in such studies, the accounts kept by parish churchwardens, and attempts to make a national survey. By taking the surviving accounts

Reprinted from C. Haigh, ed. *The English Reformation Revised* (Cambridge, 1987).

from across the whole of the country, with supporting information from visitation returns, sermons, official correspondence and literary sources, it is possible to examine issues which cannot be considered convincingly in local studies, and so to offer a different perspective from earlier work on the subject.

Most of the churchwardens' accounts are incomplete, and several of those surviving give mere annual totals of income and expenditure without individual entries. In large part these faults are the work of time and personal inclination respectively, but they also reflect the tensions prevailing in the period as detailed sets of accounts often break off or become summary (infuriatingly) as the religious changes commence. Contentious items were erased as regimes and policies altered. Thus, of the 198 sets used for this study, being the great majority of those extant,[2] only eighteen cover *all* the years between 1535 and 1570 in detail.[3] Furthermore, they are geographically limited. The third of England north of the Trent is reflected by only a thirteenth of the accounts, and the four northernmost counties and the whole of Wales have yielded only one set each. The total represents about two per cent of the parishes of the age.

Nevertheless, the value of such a survey ought to be considerable. The accounts provide our principal evidence for the ritual and ornamentation employed in parochial worship. The sample collected reflects communities of all sizes, terrains and economies, scattered widely across the southern two-thirds of England with a few examples from other regions. A systematic exploitation of this source might at least extend the debate over the English Reformation.[4]

One immediate conclusion results from the study: that whether or not the English and Welsh were Protestant at specific points of the Tudor period, they certainly were *governed*. A crucial aspect of the religious changes was that churchwardens had repeatedly to receive or attend upon representatives of Crown, bishops and archdeacons, who instructed and cross-examined them. The churchwardens of Yatton in north Somerset had to attend visitations at Chew Magna in 1547–8, Bedminster and Wells in 1548–9, and Axbridge and Wells in 1549–50. In the single financial year 1550–1, the wardens of Stoke Charity, in the Hampshire downs, had to report twice to royal commissioners and once to the archdeacon. The villagers of Great Packington, Warwickshire, succeeded in preserving their rood loft intact for a year after Queen Elizabeth ordered such lofts to be cut down; then they were faced by a furious representative of the local archdeacon, and it was removed immediately.[5] Such typical examples indicate the considerable degree of enforcement which Church and State put behind their policies. Whether or not the Reformation came from 'above' or 'below', the presence of external authority was something with which most local people had to reckon in these years.

Another immediate impression is gained from the accounts: the consensus of recent historians, that pre-Reformation religion was a flourishing faith, is amply confirmed. For the years 1500–35, the entries record continual embellishment: churches were enlarged, rood lofts built or redecorated, windows reglazed, side altars added, new images of saints bought and existing ones decorated more richly, obits, lights and guild chapels multiplied, and additional rituals, popular customs and dramatic productions were instituted. Too often, the Church of the early Tudors is spoken of as a static entity, whether healthy or ailing. It is important to stress that many of the decorations and activities outlawed during the various Reformations had been present for only a generation, and that parish religion in 1530 was an intensely dynamic and rapidly developing phenomenon. From the churchwardens' accounts, one has the impression that to the average parishioner what was most disturbing about the local church was the chance that it might become too over-decorated to allow of further elaboration.[6] The remainder of this essay will be devoted to explaining, chronologically, what happened instead.

The first great acts of the Henrician Reformation, the establishment of the royal supremacy, the Injunctions of 1536 and the dissolution of the religious houses, made little discernible impact upon *parish* religion. The payment of Peter's Pence vanished punctually from all sets of accounts, while an occasional parish church benefited from the dissolution of a nearby monastery. The record scoop was at Halesowen, where the rood, organ, images and pictures were obtained from the abbey.[7] The first great alteration in local worship was made by the Injunctions of 1538, which instructed each parish to purchase a Bible; to extinguish all lights in the church except those on the altar, in the rood loft and before the Easter sepulchre; to remove any images which had been 'abused with pilgrimages or offerings'; to regard the surviving representations of saints simply as memorials and to be prepared for the removal of more later; and to reject the veneration of relics. The last direction affected only those few parishes which had relics to venerate, in our sample Halesowen and All Saints, Bristol, where they were promptly delivered to the bishop for destruction. The single positive Injunction, to buy a Bible, was also the most widely flouted, for most of the accounts in the sample do not record a purchase by the end of 1540. Of those which do, the majority derive from London and diocesan capitals, though a few rural communities did comply.[8]

The greatest consequence of these Injunctions for parish churches, however, was the snuffing out of the lights. In most a candle had been kept burning constantly before the image of a favourite saint, supported by special collections. Some had as many as thirteen such votive lights, while in arable districts of East Anglia and the east Midlands a 'plough light' had been maintained to bring blessings upon tillage. It was paid for by a gathering made on Plough Monday, the second after Epiphany, each year, solicited by the youth of the community going from door to door dragging a plough.[9] When the Injunction against them was published, all such candles were apparently promptly extinguished in the parishes in the sample.[10] In a few,[11] the Plough Monday collection went on, the proceeds going to the general church fund, but elsewhere, if it continued, it ceased to relate to religious matters. The Injunctions had achieved in this case an effect which the Protestant reformers were later to make general: the dissociation of many folk rituals from formal religion. The sample covering 1538 represents none of the rural parishes of the north, nor any in Wales. But, given that it includes some of the more remote parts of southern and central England, the acquiescence in the royal will is striking, especially as it was not imposed by visitors and commissioners with the thoroughness of later changes.

None of the accounts record the removal of images, for most of those associated with pilgrimage were housed in their own shrines. But the Injunctions had a tremendous effect of a different kind: after 1538 only one *new* image was erected in any of the parishes in the sample, until the Marian reaction.[12] This probably resulted from the threat to existing statues and pictures which one Injunction had made. It probably also signified that if saints were henceforth to be regarded only as good human beings, rather than as powerful intercessors whose presence was in some fashion embodied in their images, then parishioners were just not so interested in them. This latter explanation is also suggested by the decline in the number and importance of parish guilds which followed the Injunctions. These fraternities, supernatural insurance schemes whereby members paid a subscription in life to ensure prayers for their souls, may well have suffered from Protestant criticism of the doctrine of Purgatory; but Purgatory was upheld by the Act of Six Articles in 1539. Instead, it may be significant that most guilds had taken a patron saint, and the attack upon these intercessors may have weakened belief in the efficacy of the organisations. Certainly, those which collapsed fastest tended to be those dedicated to minor saints.[13] Thus, to an almost uncanny degree, the Henrician Reformation had inflicted effective blows upon a flourishing popular religion. The only part of the Injunctions commonly ignored was that which Protestants had hoped would supply a faith to replace that demolished: the order for the purchase of parish Bibles.

During the remainder of Henry's reign, some minor reforms were made in religion. One resulted from a royal proclamation of 1541,[14] ordering churchwardens to obtain a Bible or pay fines: under this pressure, virtually all parishes in the sample obeyed within three years, though a few took longer.[15] Between 1542 and 1545 also, a majority of the churches in the sample acquired the new processional in English, the first break in the monopoly of Latin in services.[16] Yet when the London parishes are excluded, the majority almost vanishes, and it is probably misleading.

Some country churches *did* obtain the processional, and some in London did not, but most of the parishes which failed to make the purchase were in remoter provinces, and the small number of accounts surviving from such communities produces an imbalance in the picture. Overall, the pattern indicates once more the limited interest in the positive aspects of Reformation unless parishes were coerced. In 1541 another proclamation carried the negative process further by abolishing the custom whereby children were dressed as saints or prelates, adding interest to certain feasts and another means by which money could be collected for pious purposes. The most celebrated of these figures was the Boy Bishop, who had officiated in certain cathedrals, religious houses and parish churches during the Christmas season. Prohibition was a marginal change in habits of popular piety, for the great majority of parishes had never introduced the custom and it had reached its peak of popularity a generation earlier. In those places where it still endured, it was terminated promptly in obedience to the royal will.[17]

Apart from the alterations enforced by law, however, the surviving accounts show that most of the rituals and ornaments of the 1520s remained in English churches in Henry VIII's last years. The images of saints were washed, utensils, banners, veils and vestments mended or replaced, and endowed obits sung for the dead. Six churches in the sample sold some service equipment,[18] but those things that went were usually old and certainly second-best, and such sales to raise ready cash had been made before.

The dramatic changes began with Henry's death in January 1547. It was marked by obsequies on a scale far greater than those accorded his two successors, and indicates something of the impact he had made on his subjects' imagination. Parishes in London, Leicester, Cambridge, Norfolk, Worcester, Salisbury and Devon held diriges and dead-masses for him. The corporations of Shrewsbury and Norwich paid for such services, the latter placing 120 candles and six escutcheons around the catafalque.[19] During the first seven months of Edward VI's reign, in the 'ritual half' of the Christian year, the old ceremonies were carried out as before, but there were a few signs of change. The wardens of St Botolph, Aldgate, bought six books of psalms in English, though the curate refused to use them. Those of another London parish removed all images, including the rood, and painted texts from Scripture on the walls, but were rebuked by the Privy Council after a protest by the bishop and the Lord Mayor. Images were apparently broken at Portsmouth.[20] Against such incidents must be set the number of provincial churches which continued to invest in the old order, replacing the cords which drew up rood cloths and lenten veils, buying new altar cloths and vestments, mending the rood or rood loft and painting banners.[21] A Radnorshire man even set up alabaster stelae in his church carved with scenes from the life of Becket, the saint proscribed ten years before.[22]

It was in this context that the government of Protector Somerset issued its Injunctions on 31 July. They ordered the destruction of all 'shrines', paintings and pictures of saints and all images which had been offered to or had candles burned before them; limited the lights in the church to a couple upon the high altar; forbade processions in or around the church when mass was celebrated; and repeated the instruction to purchase the Bible and added one to buy the *Paraphrases* of Erasmus. To enforce these, the realm was divided into six circuits, Archbishop Cranmer and the Privy Council naming from four to six visitors for each. All the men chosen were either Protestants or reliable servants of the regime: a carefully selected handful of activists. Their activity is recorded in all the surviving accounts during the rest of the year and the next, including those for Lancashire and Cumberland. It was frequently felt heavily. Some Salisbury churchwardens had to produce two bills for the visitors, one certifying the condition of the church before their coming and the other detailing the changes that had been made since. Yorkshire and Somerset parishes had to return a second bill after their first was rejected, while one in Shropshire had to send in eight bills. At Hull, the visitors broke the statues in the church in person. At St Paul's Cathedral, they destroyed most of the images in September, and pulled down all the remainder two months later, at night to avoid a commotion. They generally made wardens present evidence upon oath, and sometimes summoned other parishioners in addition, to obtain alternative information.[23]

Even while the visitation was proceeding, government policy evolved. In September 1547, in response to uncertainty on the part of the corporation of London, the Privy Council reaffirmed that images which had not been cult objects could remain – unless the priest, the churchwardens *or* the visitors decided upon their removal.[24] On 6 February a royal proclamation forbade four important ceremonies of the old Church: the blessing of candles at Candlemas, ashes upon Ash Wednesday and palms upon Palm Sunday, and the adoration of the rood upon Good Friday, popularly called 'Creeping to the Cross'.[25] Two weeks later, the council ordered the removal of *all* remaining images from churches, on the grounds that their continued presence was causing dispute and disorder.[26] In the autumn of 1547, two acts of Parliament had carried the Reformation further, one instructing that the laity should take communion in both kinds, and the other decreeing the seizure by the State of the endowments of chantries, religious guilds and perpetual obits, on the grounds that the doctrine of Purgatory was false.

The impact of this campaign upon the parish records is profound, but blurred by the fact that few accounts dated individual items, so that the precise chronology of change is usually irrecoverable. Two parishes show unmistakable evidence of Protestant zeal: Rye, where the images were removed before September 1547 and called 'idols', and St Botolph Aldgate, where the congregation got rid of their curate in October after a fierce tussle with the Lord Mayor, and adopted an English service.[27] All observers agree that images were cleared from the churches of London by the end of that year,[28] and the surviving accounts bear this out. The process seems an orderly one, the statues and panes of glass being removed by workmen paid by the wardens rather than shattered privately. It was a very formal sort of iconoclasm. In the provinces it was virtually complete by the end of 1548, in most cases as a consequence of the royal visitation, and in the autumn of 1547 the Privy Council punished two cases of resistance, at St Neots and High Wycombe.[29] The last recorded clearances of images took place at St Dunstan, Canterbury, in 1549, and at Worfield, Shropshire, and Ashburton, Devon, in 1549–50. The surviving Lancashire account does not mention the removal of images by name, but after the visitation the wardens sold much brass, pewter, and iron, which probably marks the same process. The surviving account from York records that the statues were taken away in 1547, and the curate of a living near Doncaster stated firmly that all in the county were plucked down early in 1548.[30] At Stratton, Cornwall, the rood and 'pageants' were removed in 1548, replaced during the rebellion of 1549, and then taken down again.[31] Thus it looks as if the campaign against representations of saints had triumphed all over England within about three years. In the same period, most of the churches in the sample were reglazed and coated with white lime on the interior, almost certainly to obliterate images in stained glass and wall-paintings. In seventeen parishes out of the ninety-one in the sample for these years, the rood lofts themselves, upon which some of the principal images had stood, were demolished. No provision for this had been made in the official instructions: in some of the urban parishes reforming zeal seems an obvious reason, but some of the provincial demolitions remain mysterious.[32]

The same success attended the government's action against chantries, gilds and obits. For this task it employed county commissions, numbering between five and thirteen and mixing officials of the Court of Augmentations with local gentry. More than the visitors, therefore, they represented action by the central government through a filter of provincial notables. But the contrast can be exaggerated, for these men were not a cross-section of shire leadership but individuals hand-picked for the job. How much sensitivity they displayed in preserving the educational and charitable functions of the institutions they dissolved varied from county to county, but all worked with remarkable speed and efficiency. They began their surveys in February 1548 and the expropriations after Easter.[33] All the obits and almost all the gilds vanish from the surviving accounts during that year, and the last gild is mentioned at Stratton in 1549. In the same period the common custom of tolling bells for the repose of all souls in Purgatory upon the evening of All Saints' Day died out in every parish in the sample. All that was left of the great number of institutions and rituals concerning the dead was the occasional burning of candles at the burial of a parishioner.[34]

All the four ceremonies prohibited by the government in February 1548 were forsaken that year in every church in the sample. With them went others of universal importance: the burning of a paschal candle from Easter Eve until Ascension Day, and the blessing of new fire and the hallowing of the font upon Easter Eve.[35] Many churches in large towns had adopted the ritual of carrying the consecrated host beneath a canopy in procession upon Corpus Christi Day. Although not specifically forbidden by statute or proclamation, this had incurred the bitter hostility of Protestants, who regarded it as idolatry, and had ceased everywhere by 1548.[36] Another rite not specifically condemned by the government was that of lodging the host in an Easter sepulchre upon Good Friday and 'resurrecting' it upon Easter Day. This was attacked by Archbishop Cranmer in his visitation articles of 1548, and by lesser prelates thereafter.[37] Despite the fact that all the parishes in the sample, save some small rural communities, had practised this ceremony in the mid-1540s, its survival is only recorded in one place from 1549 until the death of Edward.[38] Yet another very common ritual, especially in urban churches, had been the reading or singing of the Passion upon Palm Sunday, often by performers in costume. This was apparently forbidden by nobody, but by 1549 it survived in only two parishes in the sample, and it ended in that year.[39] All these ceremonies were formally legal but disliked by Protestants: it is unclear whether they were forsaken because they were denounced by royal or ecclesiastical visitors, or whether the proscription of related rites caused their spontaneous abandonment in a mood of confusion and disorientation.

With these ecclesiastical rituals crashed a whole world of popular custom which had been associated with the parish church. In communities across most of southern England, the principal source of parish funds had been the holding of church ales by the wardens, usually in Whitsun week. During the mid-1540s such ales were regular occurrences in seventeen parishes in the sample, but after 1549 they continued in only five of these.[40] Some reason for this decline is provided by the chance survival of one document:[41] a letter from the royal visitors of the West Country in 1547, forbidding such ales upon the grounds of the 'many inconveniences' arising from them. The choice of a practical rather than a religious objection to the custom is significant, for the charge of 'inconvenience' was to be levied at such popular gatherings repeatedly over the next hundred years. Already, the alliance between Protestant Reformation and the regulation of folk recreations in the name of order had been formed. That this was the attitude of most, but not all, of the sets of visitors is suggested by the fact that four of the five parishes was apparently more lenient.

Almost certainly as part of the same process, the remaining Plough Monday gatherings vanish from the sample after 1547. In 1547–8 Wandsworth parish sold its maypoles, and the great pole which had stood in Cornhill was hacked to pieces in 1549 after a Protestant preacher called it an idol.[42] Another item which vanished from the accounts after 1547–8 was 'hocking', the collection of money, on the Monday and Tuesday after Easter Week, by gangs of men or women who captured members of the opposite sex in the street and made them pay forfeits.[43] With this disappeared the mysterious 'hognels' or 'hogglers', groups of parishioners who went about in the winter season apparently collecting for parish funds.[44] The Injunctions of 1547 only forbade the holding of processions about church and churchyard, and need not have halted the most important processions of all, those around the parish in Rogation Week with cross and banners to ask blessings upon it. Yet in each parish in the sample this custom also lapsed in 1547–8.[45] Still another casualty was the habit of decking churches, like private houses, with greenery at certain feasts: thus those of London were festooned with holly and ivy at Christmas, box on Palm Sunday and birch at Midsummer. Such trappings were abandoned in every community represented by the accounts before the end of 1548. Like so many of the rites and customs described above, they were not specifically prohibited in Injunctions, acts of council or visitation articles, but could be subsumed under the general headings of 'superstition' or 'idolatry'.

Alongside this immense process of demolition, the reformers laboured to inculcate their new faith, but with much less success. In 1547 the government sponsored the publication of the *Book of Homilies*, sermons on key topics and doctrines which could be read by a clergy incapable of preaching. During the reign of Edward, this was purchased by only nineteen out of the ninety-one parishes in the sample,[46] and the majority of those which did not obtain the volume were precisely those provincial or rural communities where the priest would most need it. The government had more success with the English translation of Erasmus's *Paraphrases*: of the parishes in the sample, forty-one had bought it before the end of 1548, and another twelve by the end of Edward's reign. How far this lively but scholarly work was read or understood by parishioners is, however, a different matter, and some of the entries recording the purchase do not encourage optimisim. In the accounts of Yatton, Somerset, the book is called 'The Paraphrases and Erasmus', in those of St Dunstan, Canterbury, 'Parasimus', and in those of Sheriff Hutton, Yorkshire, 'Coloke of Herassimus'.[47] Of the sample, twenty parishes employed the cruder but probably effective educational technique of having texts from Scripture painted upon the walls, the rood loft or a cloth hung from the loft. The greatest positive step taken by the regime was the publication of the first Book of Common Prayer, prescribed by the parliamentary Act of Uniformity of 1549. With this legal provision behind it, the book was obtained by *every* parish in the sample by the specified date, Whit Sunday 1549. In December of that year, however, a royal proclamation complained that many priests were failing to use it, and attempted to eliminate competition by ordering the delivery of old service books to the bishops for destruction.[48] Seventeen parishes in the sample obeyed, and most of the remainder combined compliance with the spirit of the order with fund-raising, by selling off the volumes condemned. Hence, whatever priest or congregation may have thought of it, the Protestant service seems to have been conducted across most, and perhaps all, of the realm by 1550.

The regime of Protector Somerset has been regarded by Protestants at the time, and historians since, as relatively moderate and willing to compromise in the work of reform. Yet its impact was devastating: the great majority of the decorations and rites employed in and around English churches in early 1547 had gone by late 1549. As far as the churchwardens' accounts tell the story, all that the succeeding 'radical' administration of Northumberland had to do was to 'mop up' by revising the Prayer Book, replacing the altars with communion tables and confiscating the obsolete church goods. The new service was introduced in every parish in the sample within the prescribed period in 1552–3, and the other reforms were just as thoroughly carried out, although over a longer period. In fourteen parishes in the sample, altars were removed under Somerset, apparently a token of local Protestant zeal: a third of these were in the capital, but nine counties are also represented.[49] In April 1550 Nicholas Ridley, the new Bishop of London, instituted a campaign to take down the rest, and by the end of the year this had happened – not merely in every church in his diocese for which accounts survive, but in all those in the sample from Bristol and some from a range of shires including Devon, Worcestershire and Yorkshire.[50] Thus, when in November the Privy Council wrote to the bishops that most of the altars in the country had been taken down, and that the remainder should now be removed to avoid disputes,[51] they could have been exaggerating only slightly, if at all. The order, doubtless driven home by the ecclesiastical visitations recorded in the accounts, was complied with by virtually all the remaining parishes in the sample within the year: only Thame, in Oxfordshire, managed to postpone the work until December 1552.[52]

The Privy Council had been interested in the fate of church goods since 1547, when it ordered the bishops to ensure that inventories were made in each parish. In 1549, complaining of sales and misappropriations, it instructed sheriffs and justices to take fresh inventories, retaining copies, and to prosecute those who had disposed of equipment. Three years later, commissioners were appointed to repeat this process, and in January 1553 another set of commissions was issued with instructions to seize all the surviving goods except linen, chalices and bells. Plate, money and jewels were to be sent to London, while robes, cloths and base metals were sold locally and the proceeds sent up.[53] The activities of the bishops are mostly lost in the usual entries of reports to ecclesiastical visitations, but all the accounts register the activities of the county commissioners. Those of 1552–3 were, like the men who dissolved chantries and gilds, local worthies selected for their obedience or enthusiasm, and they did their work well. The churchwardens of Harwich had their initial inventory rejected, and the acceptance of their second was postponed until the whole commission was present. The vicar of Morebath, Devon, was interrogated four times over. After visiting the commissioners for the North Riding five times and writing to them once, the wardens of Sheriff Hutton had to attend the Council of the North to obtain a stay of confiscation of some of their church goods.[54] The parish accounts also show that the government's fear of disposal and misappropriation was justified, for sixty-nine of the ninety in the sample record the sale of ornaments and vestments between 1547 and 1552. The majority of sales had occurred in London and the neighbouring counties, both more Protestant and, arguably, more conscious of a need to profit from the goods before the government did. The sums raised were often comparatively large, such as the £32 from one sale at St Stephen Walbrook or £42.9s at the other City church of St Alphege, London Wall. Yet they often represented only a percentage of the goods' original value, a glaring case being at St Lawrence, Reading, where the gilding of just two tabernacles in 1519 had cost £1 but all the tabernacles and some other fittings were sold in 1547 for 2s.8d.[55] Clearly, many parishes were determined to turn the religious changes to financial advantage, and almost certainly were hurrying to sell their goods before confiscation set in.

A sample of the surviving visitation returns and church court records for Edward's reign bears out the impression left by the accounts. In Kent in 1548 people from three parishes were accused of having failed to deface images removed from churches, and one rector summoned for having continued the ceremonies of paschal candle and sepulchre at Easter. In late 1550, before altars were proscribed by the Privy Council, members of fourteen Kentish parishes were in trouble for not destroying them with sufficient speed and two priests were excommunicated till this was done, while seven priests were accused of having kept old service books. In Lancashire in 1552, four parishes admitted to having failed to remove altars, and in Wiltshire in 1553, one parish confessed to having an altar. In the archdeaconry of Norwich in 1549, none of the thirty-one parishes admitted to preserving images, tabernacles or the old cermonies. In the diocese of Ely during the whole of Edward's reign, visitations aroused some concern about the quality of the clergy and their performance of the Protestant service, but none about the adaptation of the churches for Protestant worship.[56] For Wales there exist no such records, but evidence of a sort is provided by the lament of a Glamorgan poet written near the end of the reign, describing the churches as universally empty of altars, roods, pyxes and holy water stoops.[57] Such sources reinforce the impression of compliance with the reforms and (in the case of Kent) of the ruthlessness with which the Protestants who had taken over the ecclesiastical machinery would enforce that compliance, running ahead of declared government policy.

Long before Edward's commissioners had completed the task of turning obsolete church goods into public money, the goods had ceased to be obsolete. The king was dead, Mary on the throne, and the Reformation halted and then reversed. The new monarch took power in July 1553, and decreed a temporary toleration of both creeds. In December Parliament repealed the reforming statues of Edward's reign and restored the service of 1546, and the queen ordered every parish to build an altar, obtain a cross, and hallow ashes on Ash Wednesday, palms on Palm Sunday and water on Easter Eve. In March she issued Injunctions for the restoration of all processions and all 'laudable and honest ceremonies'.[58] The fact that most wardens did not date individual entries vitiates attempts to assess the choices of parishioners and priests during the period of 'liberty' from July to December, but there are some indications. At Stratton, Cornwall, vestments were repurchased, a canopy for the sacrament made and tapers bought as soon as Mary took power. The wardens of Stanford-in-the-Vale, Berkshire, sold the communion table with a reference to the past 'wicked time of schism'. At Harwich the high altar was made, and at Halse, Somerset, the mass restored, by October. In the London church of St Dunstan-in-the-West both altar and old service were back before the end of September.[59] These hints bear out the picture presented by the literary sources,[60] of a slight spontaneous revival of Catholicism in the capital and a more pronounced one in the provinces. It was a distinctly more impressive anticipation of policy than Edward's Reformation had received in early 1547, but the Protestants in those months, unlike the Catholics in late 1553, had had no legal freedom to act.

Once the administrative machinery had been captured by the proponents of Counter Reformation, it was worked with all the vigour that Protestants had given it. Metropolitan, episcopal and archidiaconal visitations and royal commissioners passed through the provinces, and wardens were constantly returning inventories and statements to them. In December 1553 the Privy Council imprisoned a Maidstone man who had sponsored a petition for Protestantism in his parish, while in March it made four Essex gentry give bonds to erect altars in their respective churches. The wardens of one London parish, St Pancras Soper Lane, were ordered by Cardinal Pole's commissioners in 1555 not merely to rebuild a rood loft but to make it five feet long, with images, and to complete the work in six weeks. Those of another, St Botolph Aldgate, imposed a rate to raise money for extensive rebuilding, on the command of Bishop Bonner. The metropolitan visitors instructed those of St Neots in 1556 to rebuild every

altar which had stood in their church in King Henry's time, within one
month. Those of Bromfield, Essex, were excommunicated in 1558 because
their church contained no images, while during two months in 1554 the
wardens of Harwich had to return three successive bills to the queen's
commissioners.[61]

Accounts survive from 134 parishes in the sample for Mary's reign, and
show a considerable homogeneity in the process of Catholic restoration.
By the end of 1554, all had rebuilt a high altar, and obtained vestments and
copes, some or all of the utensils and ornaments of the mass (crucifix, holy
water stoop, chalice, pyx, pax, patten, sacring bell, chrismatory, cruets,
censers and candlesticks) and some or all of the necessary books (a mass
book, processional, psalter, manual, coucher, hymnal, antiphonal, legend,
breviary and grail). During the remainder of the reign, they added to this
equipment, and most acquired a rood with flanking figures of Mary and
John, some images or paintings of saints, a side altar, rood lights, and altar
cloths, rood hangings, banners and a canopy. All those parishes which had
removed their rood lofts under Edward now rebuilt them. Where the
purchase of items is not recorded, this may often mean that they were
brought out of hiding, and the frequent entries for mending old ornaments
bears this out. In many parishes, a wooden crucifix was bought at first, to
be replaced by a silver or gilded one, and the rood, Mary and John painted
on a cloth until carved wooden figures could be paid for. The process
slackened only slightly after the first year, and most of the parishes in the
sample were carrying out further embellishments until the moment of
Mary's death. The majority of these acquisitions were compulsory: the
high altar and mass were prescribed from December 1553, while rood lofts,
and the rood, Mary and John that they carried, were necessary by 1555 and
images of patron saints of parishes by 1556.[62] Yet most of the parishes in the
sample decorated their churches more than the legal minimum required.

All this activity posed a serious financial problem: the meagre expenses
of Reformation had easily been covered by selling church goods, but
restoration cost a great deal. The Privy Council ordered ten of Edward's
commissions to return to parishes those ornaments they had received
which were as yet intact, but this procedure was of benefit to only three
of the churches in our sample.[63] In nineteen cases, the accounts record that
parishioners presented the parish with goods (in many cases probably
bought from it under Edward) or money to obtain them.[64] (On the other
hand, records of church courts under Mary abound with suits against
people who failed to disgorge ornaments or cloths when pressed to do
so.[65]) In many churches items were apparently brought out of store. But the
accounts make it clear that the great bulk of the work of restoration had to
be paid for, by rates and compulsory gatherings among the congregation
or from accumulated funds. A multiplicity of local solutions was found: at
South Littleton in Worcestershire, for example, the priest agreed to pay for

the necessary books on being given the right to cull and sell the pigeons which lived in the steeple.[66] The financial problem amply explains why the process of restocking the churches was so gradual, and more so in rural parishes where the Reformation had presumably taken least hold. It is small wonder that in every case the new decorations and utensils were less imposing and expensive than those disposed of under Edward.

The restoration of ritual was fairly complete. Every church in the sample readopted the paschal candle, the blessing of new fire and the hallowing of the font, while the Easter sepulchre reappeared in the same proportion of churches (the great majority) where it had existed before the Reformation. The blessing of palms and reading of the Passion of Palm Sunday,[67] the hallowing of candles at Candlemas,[68] 'Creeping to the Cross',[69] the Corpus Christi processions,[70] the Boy Bishop[71] and the ringing of bells upon All Saints' Day[72] feature as often in the Marian accounts as before the Reformation. Celebrations of the reconciliation of England to the Papacy are mentioned in only three cases,[73] probably an accurate reflection of the traditional lack of interest of most parishioners in the distant pontiff. Customs connected with the parish church, such as ales,[74] Hocktide gatherings,[75] Plough Monday collections,[76] the hognels or hog-glers,[77] May games,[78] Rogationtide processions[79] and decking of churches with plants, underwent a complete revival, becoming as common as they were in the last years of Henry VIII. Most of these activities were not encouraged by the Marian regime, and in 1555 the Privy Council forbade all May games in Kent on the grounds that 'lewd practices' of 'vagabonds and other light persons . . . are appointed to be begun at such assemblies'.[80] Clearly, the popular culture associated with the old Church retained considerable ebullience, and the impulse to regulate it more severely in the name of public order crossed the confessional divide.

Amid such enthusiastic revival, it is interesting to note what was *not* restored under Mary. The abiding casualties of the preceding Reformation seem to have been the cult of the saints and the provision for souls in Purgatory. Only one set of accounts, from Prescot, Lancashire, records the purchase of more than three images, other than those of the rood loft. Most wardens only obtained those made compulsory, the loft statues and that of the patron of the parish. Where one or two more were added, they tended to be those of the Virgin or the better-known Apostles rather than of saints who had inspired local cults before the Henrician attack. Only at Prescot, again, do lights seem to have been burned before any images, save those upon the high altar or rood loft, and private donations of statues or pictures, or embellishments to those existing, appear in only five sets of accounts (out of the 134).[81] Only four parishes in the sample definitely rebuilt more than two of the side altars at which saints had been honoured,[82] in contrast to the large number found in pre-Reformation churches, especially in towns. A small minority of the parish guilds and fraternities which had flourished in the early 1530s were restored, and most of these were the 'high' guild or store of their communities, unconnected with a particular patron, or dedicated to the Virgin. Nor does it appear that all those revived had intercessory functions, some now being fund-raising organisations.[83] In contrast with the almost ubiquitous references in pre-Reformation accounts to obits, bede-rolls, dead-masses and burial rites employing a cross and tapers, these forms of intercession for indivi-dual souls feature in only thirty-two of the Marian accounts in the sample.

Such alterations should not be over-emphasised. After all, the work of centuries could not be repeated in five years. The attention of resources of devout parishioners would be employed under Mary in restoring the essential (and compulsory) trappings of Catholic worship. Perhaps the absence of an obvious Catholic successor to the throne in the event of Mary's demise discouraged individual investment in ornaments, rituals and fraternities. Yet the continuity with the decline of both these great forms of belief during the later years of Henry is striking. Had devotion to personal patron saints and conviction of the need to secure prayers for the repose of one's soul been as strong as they had obviously been in the 1520s, they should have left more impression on the accounts. The hiatus of Edward's reign might even have added urgency to the need to express them. But Marian Catholicism seems both less 'personalised' and less 'localised' than the faith of the old Church.

Visitation records, again, bear out the picture of restoration presented by the accounts. In Wiltshire in 1556, only two parishes admitted to having no altars and two others to lacking a rood, Mary and John. In Lancashire in 1554, only one of thirty-one churches and chapels visited had no altar, one no images and seven no ornaments; by 1557, three out of thirty-four had less than the full complement of books and ornaments, and all had altar and images. Under Elizabeth, when exaggeration would have been politic, out of 153 Lincolnshire parishes, only four claimed to have had no rood under Mary, one no side altars, eight no vestments, ten no candle-sticks and five no mass books. Of 242 Somerset parishes visited in late 1557 and early 1558, twenty-one admitted to having no pyx, six to having no rood, twenty-two to having no Mary and John, two to having no rood loft and one to having no crucifix. The slowest progress was recorded in Kent. There, thanks to a mixture (impossible to quantify) of more thorough reformation, more widespread Protestantism and more searching visita-tion, in 1557 out of 243 parishes, forty-five had no holy water stoops, fifty-three no rood light, twenty-two no rood, sixty no crucifix, forty-three no candlesticks, fifty-three no pyx, forty-seven no high altar and ninety no side altars, while sixty-one lacked some of the necessary books.[84] All told, however, it was not a bad achievement for so few years. Putting the whole body of evidence together, it looks as if, had Mary reigned for as long as Elizabeth did, the religion of her realm would have been emphatically

Catholic, but still rather different from that of her grandfather's: more uniform in its patterns of piety, more subject to direction from the centre, much less remarkable for local and personal cults. It would not have been just the old Church revived, but neither was the Counter-Reformation Church upon the Continent, and the differences were more or less the same in the European case as those suggested here for England.

The death of Mary in November 1558 put religion into limbo yet again. A proclamation by Elizabeth in December ordered that the existing rites be continued pending a settlement, save that the Creed could be pronounced in English. When private persons attacked fittings, vestments and books in a church in Sussex and one in London, the Privy Council ordered their punishment. Not until April 1559 did Parliament pass a statute prescribing use of a new Protestant liturgy, by Midsummer Day, with the ornaments and vestments which had been legal in 1548, unless the queen directed otherwise.[85] It is thus hardly surprising to find that the Catholic rituals were maintained in virtually every church in the sample until after Easter 1559. Only at Rye, a strong centre of Edwardian Protestantism, was any spontaneous move made towards reform, when the wardens removed the altars before Easter. By contrast, some parishes in early 1559 behaved as if Mary's religion was going to endure, such as St Andrew, Canterbury, where the crucifix was mended, Marston, Oxfordshire, where a bequest was made to purchase one, and Ludlow, where a new canopy was made for the host.[86]

In July, Elizabeth issued a set of Injunctions and a set of commissions for a visitation to enforce them. The Injunctions promised a Protestant Reformation rather more moderate than that of Edward: they instructed parishes to obtain the Bible and the *Paraphrases*; forbade processions on a practical ground – that they caused parishioners to compete acrimoniously for places, but exempted those of Rogationtide provided that they were a mere beating of parish boundaries without cross and banners; left the decision between an altar or a communion table to the parish or to the visitors; and ordered the destruction of monuments 'of feigned miracles, pilgrimages, idolatory and superstition' while not specifically forbidding the retention of images.[87] This impression of compromise is contradicted by the nature and work of the royal visitors. On paper they numbered 125, divided between six circuits, and included many peers and leading gentry. In practice, the majority of these notables failed to serve, and the work was apparently done in each area by four or five individuals, mostly lawyers or clerics. They were led by men who had been in exile during Mary's reign, and represented some of the most determined Protestants in Elizabeth's realm.[88] It is thus not surprising that, in the bulk of the 127 sets of accounts in the sample surviving wholly or partly for the first twelve years of her reign, the arrival of the Injunctions and visitors is followed promptly by the removal of altars and images.

The 1559 visitors were as exacting as any of the previous royal and ecclesiastical enquiries. Several sets of churchwardens had to re-submit reports to them, and those of Steeple Ashton, Wiltshire, had to attend them six times and to hand in bills thrice.[89] In London the commissioners produced a trail of bonfires of roods and images, and sometimes of vestments, cloths, Easter sepulchres, banners and ornaments as well. At Exeter they forced the citizens who had most venerated the images under Mary to throw them into the flames.[90] At Yatton, Somerset, the wardens begged for a reprieve for their church's Mary and John, to no avail.[91] The temper of the queen's agents may well have been summed up by a sermon delivered by one of those in the northern circuit, Edwin Sandys, glorifying his monarch for defacing 'the vessels that were made for Baal', breaking down 'the lofts that were builded for idolatory' and demolishing 'all polluted and defiled altars'.[92] Like Edward's government, Elizabeth's had been restrained in its declarations, ruthless in its actions.

In fact, the impression of a clean sweep given in Sandys's sermon is fallacious, and Elizabeth's Reformation seems to have been rather slower and less effective than Edward's had been. At Crediton, Devon, the priest was still blessing Candlemas candles in the year after the visitation and the smashing or burning of most of his church's ornaments. In two York churches, the altars were taken down only in 1561, and the images remained in one of these until 1562.[93] The altars survived at Wing, Buckinghamshire, Stanford-in-the-Vale, Berkshire, and Worfield, Shropshire, until 1561, at Stoke Charity, Hampshire, till 1561–2, at St Mary-at-Hill, Chester, until 1562, and at Thame, Oxfordshire, until 1564. At Morebath, Devon, the high altar was simply covered with a board.[94] In most of these cases, the authorities had to exert considerable pressure to secure compliance – but secure it they did. The Elizabethan ecclesiastical visitation and court records bear out this picture. In Kent by 1569 the process of reformation had been very effective, leaving only a few holy water stoops and one crucifix undefaced. In the Norwich diocese in that year the physical changes were also more or less complete, though the bishop had great trouble stopping parishes ringing bells on All Saints' Day. In Essex in 1565–6 one church still had an altar, and two still had images. In Lincolnshire, 153 parishes claimed in 1566 to have removed all trappings of Catholic worship, but the process had taken the full seven years, and the altars and images were still in place at Belton-in-Axholme until just before the account was rendered. The metropolitan visitors of the diocese of Lichfield in 1560–1 had to order wardens from at least four Staffordshire villages to destroy altars. A church in Holderness in 1567 had retained altars and images, and another its images. Statues of saints survived in several Lancashire churches in 1563–4, and one altar remained until 1574. In 1567 the Bishop of Bangor reported that he had recently found, in this most remote and mountainous of all dioceses, images with candles burned before them, altars, and relics which were carried in processions at feasts: a cross-section of all the structures and ceremonies condemned by Protestants since 1538.[95]

This was still a relatively rapid and complete destructive reformation, and if comparable records had survived for the north and North Wales from Edward's reign, they would probably show at most the same degree of conformity. But when evidence is available for comparison, the reforms of 1559 appear to have been delayed and resisted to a somewhat greater degree than those of 1547–50. Four reasons may account for this: that the early Elizabethan machinery of enforcement was weaker than that of Edward; that Mary's regime had left Catholicism a stronger faith than before; that after the reversal of 1553 parishioners were reluctant to destroy their churches' fittings until a Protestant succession to the throne was secured; and that the ability of the Tudor State to make its subjects alter their religious habits on demand had slightly declined. There is no evidence in favour of the first of these, and much against, but the relative importance of the remaining three cannot be determined from the sources employed in this study. The case of rood lofts, however, indicates that the last two may have been the most significant.

The Protestant objection to the lofts was that articulated by Sandys: their purpose had been to support images, to which they might function as memorials. It is likely that, once stripped of statues, their religious significance for most parishioners was minimal, but they were large and beautiful structures upon which much money and pride had been lavished. In 1560 the new Bishop of London, Edmund Grindal, encouraged the Protestant parishioners of St Michael le Quern to insist on the demolition of theirs. This course was taken by their fellow believers in nearby St Mary Woolnoth,[96] and in the same year by most of the other city parishes in the sample and nine in the provinces, almost all of these being either in towns or in East Anglia.[97] In October 1561, using the now traditional excuse for a further step in reform, Elizabeth ordered that to prevent contention all remaining lofts were to be cut down to the beam.[98] This direction was followed within the year in most of the remaining southern and midland parishes in the sample, and in a few in the north also, but there are signs of considerable reluctance. In seven cases the accounts record serious pressure exerted by diocesan officials to secure compliance, and in three of these the parishioners were excommunicated.[99] In the province of York, most of the parishes in the sample ignored the order, until in 1570–1, in the aftermath of the Revolt of the Earls and the translation of Grindal to York, a comparable effort of enforcement was mounted.[100] During the next two decades, most visitations resulted in the discovery and destruction of one or two more lofts, and many parishes, either from choice or coercion, further cut down the remnants of theirs.[101] Even so, pre-Reformation rood lofts, apparently unrestored, exist today at North Weald, Essex, and in three churches in Somerset, five in Wiltshire, three in Yorkshire and ten in Wales, and more were removed during the last century. They illustrate the extent to which a community could resist relatively peripheral aspects of the Reformation if it were very determined and very lucky. By contrast, only one pre-Reformation rood, Mary and John survives in an English or Welsh church (at Betws Gwerffyl Goch, near Corwen), and not a single stone altar.

Nor did popular pastimes succumb to Elizabeth's Reformation as completely as to Edward's. Most of the parishes in the sample which held church ales under Mary continued to do so into the new reign. The same is true of May games, while Hocktide gatherings went on in three parishes in the sample,[102] hognel or hoggler collections in three,[103] and Plough Monday collections in two others.[104] Decking of churches with vegetation ceased in most parishes in the mid-1560s, but continued in three of the sample much later.[105] All this argues for some restrictive impact upon traditional festivities by the early Elizabeth reformers, and certainly the drives for reformation of religion and of manners were frequently to be associated later in the reign (and ever since). But the contrast with the almost total collapse of the same customs in 1547–8 is still marked, and puzzling.

As in the reign of Edward, the positive aspects of the Reformation are less apparent in the accounts than the negative. Certainly, virtually all those in the sample record the new Prayer Book within a year of its issue, and most of those in the sample record seem to be incomplete. But only thirty-three of the 127 enter the purchase of a new Bible, while two payments for mending an old one suggest that an unknown number were brought out of hiding. The *Paraphrases* were definitely obtained by twenty-six parishes, and, again, may have been restored to others by private hands, while the purchase of the revised *Book of Homilies* appears in twenty-three sets of accounts. The erection of a board written with the Ten Commandments is recorded for thirty-four parishes in the sample. The probability that the Bible and *Paraphrases* were restored informally to churches makes it difficult to compare the success of Edward's regime in propagating Protestant views with that of Elizabeth during its first six years; however, in both cases it can be said that the removal of Catholic decorations was more easily achieved than the substitution of Protestant texts. At the visitation of Kent during 1569, no parish admitted to preserving an altar, image or rood loft, but forty of the 169 returns recorded the absence of either the Bible or the *Paraphrases*:[106] and this was the most perfectly reformed county of the decade, and one with good visitation records.

To conclude: the evidence of the churchwardens' accounts bears out the assertions of Dr Haigh and Professor Scarisbrick, that the great majority of the English and Welsh peoples did not want the Reformations of Henry,

Edward and Elizabeth. Catholic practices retained their vitality in the parishes until the moment they were proscribed, and there were few anticipations of official instructions. Indeed, the accounts suggest that Tudor parishioners were reluctant to implement any religious changes. If it be asked then why they got them, the answer is that they were forced to conform. The machinery of coercion and supervision deployed by the government was so effective that for most parishes passive resistance was simply not an option. When active resistance was employed, by the Pilgrims of Grace, the western rebels of 1549 and the followers of the Northern Earls, it proved disastrous. The absence of comparable violent opposition to Mary's religious policy argues for its relative popularity, the rebellion of Wyatt being far less clearly related to religious developments than were the conservative risings. Yet it is arguable from the accounts that her counter-reform, too, would not have achieved as much as it did without considerable pressure by the authorities. Furthermore, these records testify to the power of the Tudor regime to compel the minds of its subjects as well as their bodies. It appears that the English and Welsh of the early sixteenth century had a limited capacity to sustain any beliefs attacked both by leading churchmen and by the Crown. They had great difficulty in digesting Protestantism, but they lost faith in precisely those aspects of the Pre-Reformation Church which had been most dynamic, most personal and most localised. There are signs by the accession of Elizabeth of a slight growth in reluctance to comply with each new royal demand, but it cannot be proved that this was any more than the parochial equivalent of war-weariness, rather than heightened religious belief.

In essence, churchwardens' accounts suggest that the English Reformation has been treated too much as a confessional struggle and not sufficiently as an episode in the history of the secular British polity. The association had been there from the beginning, for Christianity was after all imposed in these islands by a series of royal decisions. In this sense the Protestant Reformation was indeed a harking back to the primitive Church, though not in the way that the reformers intended.

Notes

1 During the ten years before writing, the principal examples have been C. Haigh, *Reformation and Resistance in Tudor Lancashire* (Cambridge, 1975); F. Heal, 'The Parish Clergy and the Reformation in the Diocese of Ely', *Proceedings of the Cambridge Antiquarian Society*, LXVI (1975–6), pp. 141–63; P. Clark, *English Provincial Society from the Reformation to the Revolution* (Hassocks, 1977), and 'Reformation and Radicalism in Kentish Towns', in *The Urban Classes, the Nobility and the Reformation* (German Historical Institute, 1979); D. Palliser, *Tudor York* (Oxford, 1979), Chapter 9; R. Whiting, 'The Reformation in the South-West of England' (University of Exeter PhD thesis, 1977), 'Abominable Idols', *J.E.H.*, XXXIII (1982), pp. 30–47, and 'For the Health of My Soul', *Southern History*, v (1983), pp. 69–94

(*see* Reading 5 above); A.M. Johnson, 'The Reformation Clergy of Derbyshire', *Journal of the Derbyshire Archaeological and Natural History Society*, C (1980), pp. 49–63; G. Williams, 'Wales and the Reign of Mary I', *Welsh History Review*, X (1980–1), pp. 334–58; E. Sheppard, 'The Reformation and the Citizens of Norwich', *Norfolk Archaeology*, XXXVIII (1981–3), pp. 44-55; and G. Mayhew, 'The Progress of the Reformation in East Sussex', *Southern History*, V (1983), pp. 38–67.

2 For reasons of space, a full list of the accounts used cannot be given here.

3 St Lawrence, Reading; Stratton; St Mary-on-the-Hill, Chester; St Michael, Oxford; Thame; Holy Trinity, Chester; Great Witchingham; St Margaret, Westminster; St Martin-in-the-Fields; Worfield; Leverton; Morebath; Ashburton; St Petrock, Exeter, Badsey; Boxford; St Mary, Bungay; and Wing.

4 Recently fuelled not only by the works quoted in n.1, but by J.J. Scarisbrick's general survey, *The Reformation and the English People* (Oxford, 1984).

5 Bishop Hobhouse, *Churchwardens' Accounts* (Somerset Record Society, 1890), pp. 160–2; J.F. Williams, *Early Churchwardens' Accounts of Hampshire* (1913), p. 79; Warwickshire R.O., DR 158/19, p. 10.

6 R. Hutton, *The Rise and Fall of Merry England* (Oxford, 1994), Chapter 2.

7 F. Somers, *Halesowen Accounts* (Worcestershire Historical Society, 1957), p. 78. Sherborne also obtained an image, from Cerne Abbey: Dorset R.O., P155/CW/19.

8 St Margaret, Westminster; St Martin-in-the-Fields; St Lawrence Pountney; St Mary Magdalen Milk Street; All Hallows Staining; St Petrock, Exeter; St Dunstan, Canterbury; Great Dunmow; Dartmouth; Yatton; All Saints, Bristol; Sheriff Hutton; and Thame did. Wing; St John, Peterborough; Leverton; Morebath; Cratfield; Bethersden; St Michael, Oxford; Ashburton; Badsey; Halesowen; Sherborne; Holy Trinity, Chester; Stratton; Culworth; Swaffham; and Boxford did not.

9 Mentioned in the accounts of St John, Peterborough; Leverton; Sutterton; Wigtoft; Great Witchingham; Great St Mary, Cambridge; Shipdam; St Mary, Bungay; Holy Trinity, Bungay; Brundish; and Denton. Boxford and Cratfield had the collection but no light.

10 The 'stock' light was still burning at St Thomas, Salisbury, in 1546–7, but may have stood on the altar or rood loft: H. Swayne, *Accounts of St. Edmund and St. Thomas Salisbury* (Wilts. Record Society, 1896), p. 274. In 1542 a gift was made for St Giles's light to the university church at Cambridge, but there is no mention of the light itself: J. Foster, *Accounts of St. Mary the Great* (Cambridge Antiquarian Society, 1905), p. 98. In 1546–8 a St Mary candle was burned at Prescot, Lancashire, but this seems to have stood in for the paschal candle made in every church for Easter: F. Bailey, *Prescot Churchwardens' Accounts* (Lancashire and Cheshire Record Society, 1953), pp. 24–7.

11 Boxford; Swaffham; Tilney; Brundish; Cratfield.

12 St Lawrence, Reading, had an image of Jesus glued to a desk in 1541, but this may have been a repair: C. Kerry, *History of the Municipal Church of St Lawrence, Reading* (1883), p. 32. So the only certain exception is the erection of a St Clement at St Nicholas, Bristol, in this same year: E. Atchley, *Transactions of the St Paul's Ecclesiological Society*, VI (1906), p. 62.

13 The guilds and their history have been well treated by Whiting, 'For the Health of my Soul' (*see* Reading 5 above), and Scarisbrick, *Reformation*, Chapter 2, and the south-western sources used by Dr Whiting are by far the best parish records for this sort of institution. I differ from him only in suggesting that prayers for the dead and saints may have been closely inter-related.

14 P.L. Hughes and J.F. Larkin, eds., *Tudor Royal Proclamations* (New Haven, 1964), 1, no. 200.

15 Like Cratfield (1547), Tarring (1547), St Peter-in-the-East, Oxford (1545–6); and St Mary Woolnoth (1545–6).

16 Bramley; Yatton; St Margaret, Westminster; St Michael Spurriergate, York; St Andrew, Lewes; Ashburton; Badsey; St Martin Outwich; Stogursey; St Nicholas, Bristol; Long Sutton; St Martin, Oxford; St Mary, Bungay; All Hallows Staining; St Dunstan-in-the-West; and St Mary Magdalen Milk Street bought it. Boxford;

Crondall; St Michael, Worcester; Morebath; Leverton; Ludlow; Thame; Woodbury; St Mary Woolnoth; and St Michael Le Quern apparently did not.

17 Evidence for the period 1530–41 survives from Boxford, Sherborne and St Andrew, Lewes. The proclamation is in Hughes and Larkin, *Proclamations*, I, no. 202.

18 St Lawrence, Reading; Great St Mary, Cambridge; North Elmham; St Martin Outwich; St Mary Woolnoth; and Tarring.

19 St Michael, Worcester; St Martin, Leicester; Great St Mary, Cambridge; Mickfield; Ashburton; St Thomas, Salisbury; North Elmham; Wandsworth. C. Wriothesley, *A Chronicle of England*, ed. W.D. Hamilton (Camden Society, 1875), I, p. 181; H. Owen and J.B. Blakeway, *A History of Shrewsbury* (London, 1875), I, p. 341; Blomefield, *The County of Norfolk* (London, 1806), III, pp. 216–17.

20 Guildhall R.O., MS. 9235/1, 17 July 1547; *A.P.C.*, II, pp. 25–6; *The Letters of Stephen Gardiner*, ed. J.A. Muller (Cambridge, 1933), pp. 273–6.

21 E.g. Halesowen; Ludlow; Winterslow; Stratton; Thame; Great Hallingbury; Christ Church, Bristol; Wandsworth; Marston; St Mary-on-the-Hill, Chester; Bletchingley; Ashburton.

22 B.L. Add. MS. 25460, fo. 70 (deposition by New Radnor parishioners).

23 The visitors are discussed in W.K. Jordan, *Edward VI: The Young King* (London, 1968), pp. 163–6. Details of their activities are in Swayne, *St Edmund and St. Thomas*, pp. 274–5; Somerset R.O., D/P/ban. 4/1/1, year 1546–7; H. Walters, 'Accounts of Worfield', *Transactions of the Shropshire Archaeological and Natural History Society*, VII (1903–9), p. 239; J. Purvis, 'Sheriff Hutton Accounts', *Yorkshire Archaeological Journal*, XXXVI (1944), p. 184; G. Hadley, *History of Kingston-upon-Hull* (Hull, 1788), pp. 88–9; R. Howlett, ed., *Moumenta Franciscana* (Rolls Series, 1882), pp. 214–15; Wriothesley, *Chronicle*, II, p. 1; C.B. Pearson, 'Accounts of St Michael, Bath', *Somersetshire Archaeological and Natural History Society Proceedings*, XXVI (1877–80), p. 118.

24 Corporation of London R.O., Journal 15, fo. 322, and Letter Book Q, fos. 210V and 214.

25 E. Cardwell, *Documentary Annals of the Reformed Church of England* (Oxford, 1844), I, p. 42.

26 J. Strype, *Ecclesiastical Memorials* (Oxford, 1822), II (ii), p. 125.

27 East Sussex R.O., Rye Corporation Records 147/1, fo. IIIV; Guildhall, R.O., MS. 9235/1, 5 Oct.-23 Dec. 1547.

28 *Calendar of State Papers, Spanish*, IX, p. 148; *Monumenta Franciscana*, II, pp. 214–15; Wriothesley *Chronicle*, II, p. 1.

29 *A.P.C.* II, pp. 140–1, 147.

30 J. Cowper, 'Accounts of St. Dunstan', *Archaeologia Cantiana*, XVII (1886–7), pp. 111–12; A. Hanham, *Accounts of Ashburton* (Devon and Cornwall Record Society, 1970), p. 124; Walters, 'Worfield', p. 114; Bailey, *Prescot*, pp. 25–7; B.I.Y., PR Y/MS. 3, fo. 217v; A.G. Dickens, 'Robert Parkyn's Narrative', *E.H.R.*, LXII (1947), p. 66.

31 B.L., Add. MS. 32243, fos. 48–9.

32 Boxford, 1547; St Ewen, Bristol, 1547–8; Morebath, 1551; St Martin, Leicester, 1548–9; Wandsworth, 1548–9; Rye, 1547; Badsey, 1552–3; St Martin-in-the-Fields, 1552–3; St Michael, Cornhill, 1548; Banwell, 1548; St Mary Redcliffe, Bristol, 1550; All Saints, Bristol, 1549–50; St Nicholas, Bristol, 1548; Tilney, 1548; St John Bow, Exeter, 1549; South Littleton, 1552–3; St Michael, Gloucester, 1550–1; St Mary-at-Hill, London, 1547–8.

33 W.K. Jordan, *Edward VI: The Threshold of Power* (London, 1970), Part VI; C.J. Kitching, 'The Chantries of the East Riding', *Yorkshire Archaeological Journal*, XLIV (1972), pp. 178–85; N. Orme, 'The Dissolution of the Chantries in Devon', *Transactions of the Devonshire Association*, CXI (1979), pp. 75–123; Scarisbrick, *Reformation*, Chapter 6.

34 At Wandsworth.

35 The last in the sample to use them being Ludlow and Prescot, at Easter 1549.

36 Recorded in 1545–7 at St Dunstan, Canterbury; Holy Trinity, Chester; Ashburton;

Sherborne; and all the Bristol and London churches in the sample. The decline of the rite in London is chronicled in *Monumenta Franciscana*, II, pp. 217, 220, 228.

37 Cited in A. Heales, 'Easter Sepulchres', *Archaeologia*, XLII (1867), p. 304.

38 At Minchinhampton in 1551 (printed in Heales, 'Easter Sepulchres', p. 304).

39 St Lawrence, Reading, and St Nicholas, Bristol.

40 Boxford; Wing; Crondall; Morebath; Yatton; Ashburton; Worfield; St Michael, Oxford; Sherborne; Halse; Ilminster; Marston; Pyrton; Norton-by-Daventry; Thame; Winsford. The last five were those where ales survived.

41 Historical Manuscripts Commission, *Dean and Chapter of Wells MSS*, II, pp. 264–5.

42 C. Davis, 'Accounts of Wandsworth', *Surrey Archaeological Collections*, XV (1900–2), p. 90; J. Stow, *A Survey of London* (ed. C.L. Kingsford, 1908), p. 144.

43 Like the Boy Bishop, this was in decline by the 1540s, when it features in the accounts from Wing; St Andrew, Canterbury; St Thomas, Salisbury; St Lawrence, Reading; and Thame.

44 Recorded in the mid-1540s at Hawkhurst; Wandsworth; Bletchingley; Banwell; Chagford; and Nettlecombe.

45 It was particularly important at Christ Church, Bristol; St Ewen, Bristol; St Michael, Oxford; St Thomas, Salisbury; Holy Trinity, Chester; Long Sutton; and in the London parishes in the sample. Robert Parkyn noted that it ceased generally in Yorkshire after 1549; Dickens, 'Narrative', p. 67.

46 By Bramley; St Ewen, Bristol; St Martin, Leicester; Pyrton; Yatton; Wandsworth; Tarring; St Andrew Hubbard; St Edmund, Salisbury; St Mary, Dover; Thame; Great Hallingbury; Crediton; All Hallows Staining; St Margaret Pattens; St Alphage London Wall; St Botolph Aldgate; St Dunstan-in-the-West; St Lawrence Pountney.

47 Hobhouse, *Churchwardens' Accounts*, p. 161; Cowper, 'St Dunstan', p. 111; Purvis, 'Sheriff Hutton', p. 185.

48 Hughes and Larkin, *Proclamations*, I, no. 353.

49 St Benet Gracechurch; St Lawrence, Reading; Wimborne Minster; Rye; St Andrew Hubbard; St Michael Cornhill; Winterslow; Holy Trinity, Chester; Holywell; Harwich; Tilney; St John Bow, Exeter; St Botolph Aldgate; and St Stephen Walbrook. In addition, the altars at St Leonard, Eastcheap, were broken up by private persons in October 1548: Corporation of London R.O., Letter Book Q, fo. 250v; Repertory 11, fo. 473v.

50 Boxford; Wing; St Nicholas, Warwick; St Martin, Leicester; Yatton; Banwell; Halesowen; St Mary, Devizes; Sheriff Hutton; Louth; St Mary, Bungay; Woodbury; St Michael, Bath.

51 A.P.C., III, pp. 168–9.

52 Oxfordshire R.O., Par. Thame b. 2, p. 104.

53 All entered conveniently in W. Page, ed., *Inventories of Church Goods* (Surtees Society, 1896), pp. xii–xv.

54 Essex R.O., T/A/122/1, fos. 32–3; J.E. Binney, *Accounts of Morebath* (Exeter, 1904), p. 175; Purvis, 'Sheriff Hutton', p. 187.

55 Guildhall R.O., MS. 59312, years 1549–50, and MS. 1432/1, fo. 101; Kerry, *St Lawrence*, p. 68.

56 Haigh, *Lancashire*, p. 144; C.E. Woodruff, 'Original Documents', *Archaeologia Cantiana*, XXXI (1915), pp. 95–105; Wiltshire R.O., Salisbury Diocesan Records, Detecta Book I, fos. 106–35; Norfolk R.O., ANW 1/1; Cambridge University Library, EDR B12/3.

57 G. Williams, 'The Ecclesiastical History of Glamorgan, 1527–1642', in G. Williams, ed., *Glamorgan County History*, IV (1974), pp. 218–19.

58 Strype, *Memorials*, III (i), p. 34; Hughes and Larkin, *Proclamations*, I, nos. 390, 407.

59 B.L. Add. MS. 32243, fo. 53; W. Haines, 'Accounts of Stanford', *The Antiquary* (1888), p. 118; Essex R.O., T/A/122/1, fo. 62; Somerset R.O., D/P/hal. 4/1/4, fo. 21; Guildhall R.O., MS. 2968/1, year 1552–3.

60 *The Diary of Henry Machyn*, ed. J. Nichols (Camden Society, 1848), p. 42; C.H. Cooper, *Annals of Cambridge* (Cambridge, 1842), III, p. 82; Dickens, 'Narrative', p. 80; *Narratives of the Days of the Reformation*, ed. J.G. Nichols (Camden Society,

1859), p. 81; *Monumenta Franciscana*, II, pp. 242–7; Wriothesley, *Chronicle*, II, pp. 101–5.

61 *A.P.C.*, IV, pp. 375, 411; J.P. Malcolm, *London Redivivum* (London, 1802), II, p. 169; Guildhall R.O., MS. 9235/1, year 1554–5; H. Pollard, 'Cardinal Pole's Visitation', *Transactions of the Cambridgeshire and Huntingdonshire Archaeological Society*, IV (1915–30), pp. 81–7; Essex R.O., D/P 248/5/1, p. 6, and T/A/122/1, fo. 71.

62 Wriothesley, *Chronicle*, II, pp. 105, 131, 134.

63 Prescot; Ashburton; and All Saints, Bristol. The council orders are in *A.P.C.*, IV, pp. 338, 344, 348, 354–5, 360–1, 371, 376; V, pp. 112–13; VI, pp. 267–8.

64 Morebath; Great Dunmow; Eltham; Stanford-in-the-Vale; Wandsworth; St Petrock, Exeter; St Botolph, Aldgate; St Martin, Leicester; St Nicholas, Warwick; St Martin-in-the-Fields; St Mary-at-Hill; Banwell; Halesowen; St Mary-on-the-Hill, Chester; Shipdam; Crediton; Woodbury; St Dunstan-in-the-West; and Tintinhull.

65 E.g. Woodruff, 'Original Documents', pp. 107–10.

66 Worcestershire R.O., 850/1284/1, p. 12.

67 At St Benet Gracechurch; St Andrew, Canterbury; Chagford; St Martin-in-the Fields; St Peter Cheap; St Matthew Friday Street; St Michael Cornhill; Ludlow; Thame; Coldridge; All Hallows Staining; St Margaret Pattens; St Alphage London Wall; Halse; St John, Bristol; St Botolph Aldgate; St James Garlickhithe; St Dunstan-in-the-West; St Mary Woolnoth; and St Peter Westcheap.

68 At Strood; Bethersden; St Andrew, Lewes; Mere; Thame; Holy Trinity, Cambridge; Swaffham; Crediton; Woodbury; All Saints, Bristol; St Mary Woolnoth; and Bridport.

69 Recorded at Great St Mary, Cambridge; Tarring; and St Thomas, Salisbury. Wriothesley, *Chronicle*, II, p. 105, states that it was universally restored in London.

70 Recorded at Holy Trinity, Chester; Wing; Strood; Lambeth; Wandsworth; Ashburton; Louth; Ludlow; St Mary, Dover; St Mary, Bungay; Holy Trinity, Cambridge; and in all the Bristol and London accounts.

71 At St Mary-on-the-Hill. Machyn, *Diary*, pp. 77–8, 121, 160, and Stow, *Annals*, pp. 121, 160, agree that most other London parishes revived the custom.

72 At St John, Peterborough; Strood; Stanford-in-the-Vale; Bethersden; Ashburton; Long Sutton; Thame; St Mary, Bungay; Swaffham; Tilney; Dartington; Woodbury; Christ Church, Bristol; All Saints, Bristol; St Botolph Aldgate; St Mary Woolnoth; and St Michael le Quern.

73 Stanford-in-the-Vale; Sheriff Hutton; and South Littleton.

74 Recorded in Mary's reign at Crondall; St John, Winchester; St Nicholas, Warwick; Morebath; Yatton; Stanford-in-the-Vale; Marston; Pyrton; Thame; St Michael, Oxford; Ashburton; Badsey; St Edmund, Salisbury; Mere; St Mary, Dover; Sherborne; Woodbury; and Halse.

75 At St Andrew, Canterbury; Bramley; Stoke Charity; St John, Winchester; St Lawrence, Reading; St Michael, Oxford; Lambeth; St Edmund, Salisbury; and St Thomas, Salisbury.

76 At Leverton; St Mary, Bungay; Holy Trinity, Bungay; and Swaffham.

77 At Molland; Ashburton; Launceston; Banwell; Coldridge; Winkleigh; Minchinhampton; Halse. Curiously, while thriving in the west under Mary, they do not seem to have reappeared in the south-east.

78 At Crondall; St John, Winchester; St Lawrence, Reading; and Thame.

79 At Holy Trinity, Chester; Snettisham; St Martin, Leicester; Strood; Lambeth; Wandsworth; St Edmund, Salisbury; St Thomas, Salisbury; Ludlow; Mere; Long Sutton; Melton Mowbray; St Michael, Bath; and all Bristol and London parishes in sample.

80 *A.P.C.*, V, p. 151.

81 St Nicholas, Warwick; Morebath; St Botolph Aldgate; St Martin, Leicester; and St Martin-in-the-Fields.

82 St Lawrence, Reading; St Mary, Devizes; St Dunstan-in-the-West; Prescot.

83 Whiting, 'For the Health of My Soul', pp. 82–3 (*see* Reading 5 above); Scarisbrick, *Reformation*, pp. 36–8.

84 Wiltshire R.O., Salisbury Diocesan Records, Detecta Book 2, fos. 1–21; Haigh, *Lancashire*, p. 202; E. Peacock, *English Church Furniture* (London, 1866), *passim*; Somerset R.O., D/D/Ca/27; *Archdeacon Hapsfield's Visitation, 1557*, ed. L.E. Whatmore (C.R.S., LXV–VI, 1950–1).

85 Hughes and Larkin, *Proclamations*, I, no. 451; A.P.C., VII, pp. 76–7; *Statutes of the Realm*, IV (i), pp. 355–8.

86 East Sussex R.O., Rye Corporation Records, 147/1, fo. 154v; C. Cotton, 'Accounts of St. Andrew', *Archaeologia Cantiana* (1917–22), p. 51; F. Weaver and G. Clark, *Churchwardens' Accounts* (Oxfordshire Record Society, 1925), p. 22; T. Wright, *Ludlow Churchwardens' Accounts* (Camden Society, 1869), p. 92.

87 Hughes and Larkin, *Proclamations*, I, no. 460.

88 W.P. Haugaard, *Elizabeth and the English Reformation* (Cambridge, 1970), pp. 136–8; Wriothesley, *Chronicle*, II, p. 145; G. Williams, 'The Elizabethan Settlement', in *Welsh Reformation Essays* (Cardiff, 1967), pp. 141–53.

89 Wiltshire R.O., 730/97/1, year 1559.

90 Machyn, *Diary*, pp. 206–9; Wriothesley, *Chronicle*, II, p. 146; Devon R.O., Exeter Corporation Records, John Hooker's Commonplace Book, fos. 352–3. The accounts for St Andrew, Holborn, make clear that the immolation of the rood, Mary and John was on the direct orders of the visitors: Malcolm, *Londinium Redivivum*, II, pp. 186–7.

91 Hobhouse, *Churchwardens' Accounts*, pp. 170–1.

92 E. Sandys, *Sermons*, ed. J. Ayre (Parker Society, 1841), p. 250.

93 Devon R.O., 1660A/PW1/V, years 1559, 1560; B.I.Y., MS. Y/MCS 16, pp. 43–65, and R.XII Y/HTG 12, p. 13.

94 Buckinghamshire R.O., PR/234/5/1/, years 1561–2; Haines, 'Stanford-in-the-Vale', p. 168; Williams, *Early Churchwardens' Accounts*, p. 87; Walters, 'Worfield', p. 134; Cheshire R.O., St Mary-on-the-Hill, year 1562; Oxfordshire R.O., Par. Thame b. 2, p. 160; Binney, *Morebath*, pp. 210, 238.

95 Essex R.O., D/AEA/23 and D/AEV/1; Peacock, *Church Furniture, passim*; A. Hussey, 'Archibishop Parker's Visitation 1569', *Home Counties Magazine*, VI (1904), pp. 109–14; Norfolk R.O., VIS/1/1569; L.J.R.O., Lichfield Diocesan Records, B/V/1/3; B.I.Y., IR. VI. A.2; Haigh, *Lancashire*, pp. 114, 210–20; P.R.O., S.P. 12/4/27.

96 Guildhall R.O., MS. 2895/1, fo. 169; MS. 1002/1, fo. 99.

97 St Peter Westcheap; St Stephen Walbrook; St Mary Magdalen Milk Street; St Mary Woolchurch Haw; St Dunstan-in-the-West; St Botolph Aldgate; St Margaret Moses (at command of Lord Mayor); St Andrew Hubbard; St Benet Gracechurch; Boxford; St Martin, Leicester (on orders of mayor); Halesowen; Holy Trinity, Coventry; Thame; Chelmsford; Bromfield; Heybridge; and Tilney.

98 W.H. Frere, *Visitation Articles and Injunctions* (Alcuin Club Collections, 1910), III, pp. 108–10.

99 Stoke Charity; Stanford-in-the-Vale; Prescot; Great Packington; Worfield; Stratton; and Cornworthy. Excommunication was employed at the last three places.

100 See Holy Trinity, Chester; Holy Trinity Goodramgate, York; Masham; and Sheffield.

101 A typical example being Ashburton, where the loft was 'pulled down' in 1563–4, 1571–2 and 1579–80. Five other Devon parishes made further reductions in the 1570s, and the pattern holds for other counties.

102 Bramley; St Edmund, Salisbury; and St Thomas, Salisbury.

103 Molland; Launceston; and Minchinhampton. They were active at Dursley, Gloucestershire, until 1626: Gloucester R.O., P124/CW/2/4.

104 Leverton and St Mary, Bungay.

105 St Ewen, Bristol; Lambeth; and St Dunstan-in-the-West.

106 Hussey, 'Archbishop Parker's Visitation', *passim*.

7

Iconoclasm in England: official and clandestine

MARGARET ASTON

Iconoclasm was a feature of the English Reformation from its very beginning.[1] It recurred intermittently and sporadically, from the 1530s to the 1640s, and made an important contribution to events at each significant phase of settlement. The influence of iconoclasts in England is comparable with that of iconoclasts abroad, but reflects the peculiar nature of English reform, which was both tightly controlled from the centre and also upsetting in its switchback course. The removal and return of images, and the prolonged process of attrition that bore on some categories of imagery, caused individuals to express themselves through iconoclasm much longer than was the case in most continental centres of reform.[2]

The work of European iconoclasts stood throughout as an inspiration – or deterrent – to the complete clearance of all imagery from all churches. There were individuals who looked ahead, even under Henry VIII, to the ultimate iconoclastic position that was reached a century later. But official policy moved in effect by stages, proscribing a wider range of imagery as time went on, with the result that iconoclastic reformers, jumping ahead to deal with further categories of idols, vented their dissatisfaction by acts of demonstrative destruction. Breaking an image might be a way of stealing a march on hesitant or procrastinating magistrates. Officials and policy-makers, iconomachs themselves, were repeatedly at odds with more radical iconoclasts. Iconoclasm, always declaratory of Reformation on the move, itself declared divisions in the movement of reform. It raised in an acute manner the question of authority.

The eradication of idols presented many reformers with their Catch 22. One could not achieve a purified rite while churches still flaunted traces of idolatry. But to sweep away all the trappings of idols and false worship without first securing the hearts and minds of believers might jeopardize the reforming process. Luther, faced by the hasty iconoclasm of Karlstadt and the 'Heavenly Prophets', saw this clearly. Until the idols of the mind had been dealt with, it was pointless (as well as dangerous) to start demolishing external idols. In Strasbourg Capito said much the same

Reprinted from Clifford Davidson and Ann Eljenholm Nichols, eds *Iconoclasm vs. Art and Drama* (Kalamazoo, 1989).

thing. The suppression of idols (which meant all sorts of objects regarded as sacred) before preaching had implanted the true faith would, he said, offend weak consciences and invite a reaction against reform.[3]

On the other hand, independent zealots found the destruction of images a useful lever to promote or accelerate reform. To demolish images – or to clear a church of sculptures, paintings, and reredoses – was a declaratory act of faith which presented a physical rupture with the past. It could amount to a challenge to cautious or conservative authorities who were proving dilatory over the implementation of doctrinal change. Another catch situation was created, for to replace the ousted images in such circumstances would itself inevitably be contentious, while to acquiesce amounted to capitulation.

We can see a kind of counterpoint developing between the private and public destoyers: between the official, publicized, propagandist acts of iconoclasm, and the spontaneous, clandestine, illicit breakings or burnings undertaken by private groups or individuals. Strange though it may now seem, the public iconoclastic spectacle became part of the repertoire of government propaganda almost as soon as Henry VIII decided, under Thomas Cromwell's guiding hand, to sponsor the process of reform. The nearest modern equivalent that comes to mind is the breaking up of statues and ripping down of photo portraits that has taken place in this century at changes in Eastern bloc regimes. But that is not an exact parallel, for the statues of Stalin (for example) were of recent vintage, and even those who erected them were familiar with the language of the image-breakers and the vulnerability of public icons of this kind. Reformation iconoclasts, on the other hand, though they likewise destroyed for the end of *renovatio*, were employing a method that, being known at the time only as a proscribed activity, was quite novel as a government procedure. Its very adoption declared such magistrates to be reversing the world they were changing.

The spectacular burning or dismemberment of idols served the purpose of winning support for religious change by calling crowds to witness the ritual dismissal of rejected cult objects. Corporately venerated objects were corporately eliminated. Iconoclasm was a social process, designed to give group solidarity to the inauguration of doctrinal change. But as all recent advocates or perpetrators of such deeds had been condemned or burned as heretics, it must have appeared to some observers that their world was veritably turning upside down. For some that would naturally not have been unwelcome. Individuals were ready to take their cue, and there were various occasions on which government iconoclasm was imitated or followed by illegal acts of destruction. The motives were doubtless mixed, ranging from conscience-stricken new belief to revenge on failed intercessors, youthful pranks or drunken demonstrations, and conscious efforts to challenge authority.

Only a few years before Henry VIII's volte-face, steps were taken to counter some quite daring acts of clandestine iconoclastic destruction. It was probably in 1522 that Cardinal Wolsey and John Longland, bishop of Lincoln, together issued an indulgence promising pardons to all those who contributed to the restoration of the church of Rickmansworth in Hertfordshire, which had been badly damaged by nocturnal arson. 'Wretched and cursed people cruelly and wylfully set fyre upon all the ymages and on the canape that the blessyd sacrament was in', and also set light to the church vestry, with the result that this building with all the ornaments in it and the chancel were burned. These undercover culprits remain unknown, though it seems quite probable that they were Lollards, or at any rate were in some way caught up in the recent anti-heretical proceedings that had disturbed the entrenched communities in the neighbouring Chiltern Hills.[4]

More Deeds of this kind are reported to have taken place early in the following decade, when the likelihood of continental inspiration of some kind is greater though still not explicit. According to John Foxe, many images were 'cast down and destroyed in many places' in 1531–2.[5] In fact, the examples he cited were all in one area in Essex and Suffolk, from Ipswich and several villages around Colchester. The incident to which this report was attached, described in graphic detail that had been given to the martyrologist by one of the participants, belonged to the same region. This was the burning of the rood of Dovercourt, a village in Essex just south of Harwich – an episode dated by Foxe to 1532. Like the Rickmansworth incident, it was carried out under cover of darkness, though in this case the perpetrators were caught.

The Dovercourt image was revered for miraculous powers, which according to Foxe (whose evidence obviously leaves something to be desired) included the ability to prevent anyone shutting the church door. The four men who set out to disprove this 'idol', including Foxe's narrator who was called Robert Gardner, came from the villages of Dedham and East Bergholt some ten miles and more away to the west at the head of the Stour estuary. They were favoured by a 'sondrous goodly night, both hard frost and fair moonshine' for their exploit – as well as by the fact that there was no need to break into the church, since local belief was such that nobody dared to shut its door. The mere ability to remove the rood and to carry it a quarter of a mile away 'without any resistance of the said idol' seemed itself to negate its repute, but the marauders left nothing to chance and made a bonfire of the vanquished carving before returning home. Within six months, according to Foxe's circumstantial account, three of these offenders were indicted for felony and hanged. Only Robert Gardner managed to escape.[6]

But the tale does not end here, for Foxe also tells us of the involvement of another man, a cleric. This was Thomas Rose, rector of Hadleigh, a village in Suffolk, about eight miles north-west of Dedham and East

Bergholt. Rose was a convinced supporter of reform who survived various troubles, including two flights abroad under Henry VIII and several examinations and another exile under Mary, to see his own life story published by Foxe in Elizabeth's reign, by which time he was well into his seventies, though still active as a preacher at Luton in Bedfordshire. Nearly half a century earlier, Rose's sermons at Hadleigh had attracted attention for their vehemence against images, and among those he inspired to plot destruction were the four Dovercourt iconoclasts. After their successful mission they handed over the coat that had been on the rood to Thomas Rose, and he duly proved his own convictions by burning it.[7]

Although, according to Foxe (who remains our sole source for these events), the four iconoclasts refused to implicate Rose, he did not escape scot-free. He had enemies at Hadleigh who complained in high places with the result that he was examined before the Council and imprisoned in Bishop Longland's house for several months. It was thanks to Cranmer that Thomas Rose's fortunes improved. After Cranmer's consecration in March 1533, the offender was moved to the custody of the archbishop at Lambeth, a change which may be ascribed to the fact that his living belonged to the patronage and immediate jurisdiction of the archbishops of Canterbury. This connection may also have helped to get Thomas Rose reinstated in his living, and in March 1534 Cranmer wrote to the parishioners of Hadleigh suggesting that they should let bygones be bygones and forget their old grudge against their rector.[8]

The Dovercourt affair took place at an interesting moment. While from May 1532 steps were being taken towards the unilateral action that would cut the knot of the king's divorce, there was little to indicate that Henry might be ready to support the image-breakers. All iconoclasts, still suspect and subject to the ancient proscription of church law as dangerous heretics, acted perforce by subterfuge. Anxiety about the heretical dimensions of the case against church images was increasing (witness the expanded 1531 edition of Thomas More's *Dialogue Concerning Heresies*), and in the minds of conservatives the aspirations of native critics were conflated with the challenge of continental reformers. A sermon delivered some time before 1534 by Henry Gold, vicar of Hayes in Middlesex, warned against the dangerous teaching of Karlstadt as the source of such horrific deeds as the recent burning of a crucifix.[9] Old Lollard objections to images and pilgrimages entered a new domain. Whatever the persuasions of those who attacked images, they would be judged at the bar of a new set of expectations, and by 1532 texts of continental reformers dealing with this topic had reached England.

If theology of some kind, at some remove, lay behind the Dovercourt destruction, it is difficult to say whose it was. What had Thomas Rose been reading? We do know of someone he had almost certainly been hearing. Thomas Bilney, whose opposition to images was one of the salient features of his teaching, had preached at both Ipswich and Hadleigh in 1527. And, according to reports of a sermon given in London, he had called for the destruction of images: 'as Ezechias distroyed the brasen serpent that Moyses made by the commanndement of God, even soo shuld kynges and prynces now a dayes dystroy and burne the Images of saynts sett upp in churches and other placys'.[10] The questions Bishop Tunstall prepared for examining Bilney and Thomas Arthur included one on whether it was more Christian to remove images of saints from churches than to permit them to remain to be gilded and honoured.[11] Bilney and Arthur recanted and abjured in 1527. But Bilney, after rethinking his position, was burned at the stake in Norwich in August 1531.

It seems not impossible that there was a connection of some kind between Bilney and this batch of East Anglian image-breakers. The link is established in one case. In 1533 two shoemakers of Eye in Suffolk (about twenty miles north of Ipswich) were examined and abjured certain heresies, including refusal to worship cross or crucifix. One of them, Robert Glazen, was alleged to have said that if he had the rood of Eye in his yard he would burn it. He confessed that the source of his views was a sermon preached by Thomas Bilney at Hadleigh in 1527.[12] Did Bilney's execution provoke some of his followers into demonstrations of support for his views? Is it possible that the Dovercourt bonfire was some kind of riposte, as the Rickmansworth blaze some ten years earlier may have been related to the local executions of Lollards? Such questions must be rhetorical, but we can be sure that the iconoclasts' psychology was complex. Combining with the conscious determination was a heady mixture of derring-do, personal loyalties and frustrations, and the intoxicating excitement of an illicit nocturnal fire.

The situation changed dramatically at the time of the Dissolution. Well before the second set of royal injuctions was issued in the autumn of 1538, the country as a whole had become alerted to the threat (or promise) of royal iconoclasm. Monastic dissolutions were accompanied by the suppression of cult images – parochial as well as conventual.[14] And those for whom the suppression of idolatry was an urgent priority saw to it that the reduction of celebrated 'idols' – that is, images that had been pilgrimaged and offered to – received the maximum publicity in their demise. Ritual disproofs of venerated statues, until recently so dangerous an undertaking, now became government stunts, part of an official campaign of propaganda and credal engineering.

In July 1538 there was a public bonfire at Chelsea of the celebrated Virgin statues from Walsingham and Ipswich and of other images collected for this purpose, which (duly denuded of their jewels and ornaments) were burned at the direction of Thomas Cromwell 'because the people should use noe more idolatrye unto them'.[15] Earlier in the same year another event of the same kind had attracted a good deal of notice and aroused the hopes of reformers abroad. This was the ceremonial destruction of the rood from the Cistercian house of Boxley in Kent that took place at St Paul's on Sexagesima Sunday (also St Matthias's Day), 24 February. It was a carefully stage-managed event, undoubtedly contrived to focus attention on the reformist cause. For though the numbers of pilgrims to Boxley were on the decline by the 1530s, it was a well-known centre beside the route to Canterbury. Henry VIII offered half a mark to the Rood of Grace soon after his accession, and the papal legate Lorenzo Campeggio stopped off for a night at Boxley on his way to London in 1518. The abbey's miraculous crucifix was (or had been) capable of responding physically to the entreaties of ailing supplicants. It could turn its eyes and move its lower lip, and may have been one of those jointed figure carvings (examples of which still survive abroad) which were able to move like puppets.[16]

It was as a puppet that the Rood of Grace was publicly exposed. After an initial disparaging display on market-day at Maidstone, for the benefit of Kent locals, the rood was taken up to London for ritual disproof at the most public of all England's pulpits. Bishop Hilsey of Rochester preached an edifying sermon at Paul's Cross, thundering against the blasphemous and fraudulent deceptions of images. He made full use of the set piece placed before his congregation by demonstrating the cords and devices of the revered crucifix as he denounced the manipulations of the 'engines used in old tyme' in this image. The climax was dramatic:

> After the sermon was done, the bishopp tooke the said image of the roode into the pulpitt and brooke the vice of the same, and after gave it to the people againe, and then the rude people and boyes brake the said image in peeces, so that they left not one peece whole.[17]

According to another contemporary, John Finch, who delightedly reported the rood's unmasking to a correspondent in Strasbourg,

> after all its tricks had been exposed to the people, it was broken into small pieces, and it was a great delight to any one who could obtain a single fragment, either, as I suppose, to put in the fire in their own houses, or else to keep by them by way of reproof to such kind of imposters.[18]

A second iconoclastically disposed bishop, Hugh Latimer, then made his contribution to the occasion. He carried a small statue to the door of St Paul's and 'threw [it] out of the church, though the inhabitants of the country whence it came constantly affirmed that eight oxen would be unable to remove it from its place'.[19] This was probably the diminutive figure of St Rumwold, which had also formed part of the devotions at Boxley.[20]

Euphoric reports such as Finch's radiated exaggerated expectations. The self-conscious theatricality of the occasion, so obviously framed to impress the 'simple people', can scarcely have had the instant success that he and others claimed. If some were already conscious that credulity was exploited by clerical manoeuvres (and a London crowd was likely to include such sceptics), one or two iconoclastic demonstrations were not going to bring a harvest of converted ignoramuses to condemn the clergy as 'mere conjurors' working despicable trickery on the people. The unprecedented nature of the events must have taken some members of Hilsey's congregation by surprise. It was indeed intended to be a ceremony that shocked by deliberate reversal of ancient assumptions. Latimer, chucking the sculpture out of the cathedral, was providing an ocular demonstration of the emptiness of its supposedly miraculous powers – just as the men who burned the Dovercourt rood had erased a spiritual claim together with a physical object. Throwing the image out of the church, out of a consecrated building into the open space outside, was also a symbolic action that stood for the process Hilsey was advocating. It was a matter of desanctification, or repositioning the central sanctum of the holy.[21] Idolatry would not be eradicated from believers' devotions until the images they misused had been removed from sacred places and tested in the world as the Boxley rood had been put to the test; images that had proved false must be put where they belonged and profaned in the most profane of secular places.

Native pride and sense of possession apart, it may be that the sheer act of removing the cult image from the place where it had stood time out of mind, shattered its miraculous power just as devastatingly as its physical breaking. Local beliefs bonded to localized saints, attaching the special mana of a venerated relic or icon to a specific location. Holy images, like the bodily remains of holy persons, were believed to have evinced their supernatural power by choosing their place of abode and rendering their removal impossible. Just as St James the Great or St Edmund had, through the miraculous journeying or immovability of their mortal remains, identified their final resting-places, so – according to the Kent legend reported by William Lambarde – the Boxley rood, made by a skilful carpenter to help pay his ransom, had originally arrived in this village as the result of its own extraordinary horse-ride from Rochester.[22]

We should be chary of taking at face value the reformers' triumphant claims about the delighted reaction of crowds who saw holy images being execrated and destroyed. The true (and surely mixed) feelings about these events may be largely a matter of surmise, but one man who made known his grief at the treatment of the Boxley rood was a London curate, Edward Laborne. He went on record for passing remarks about the example of St Augustine, who had not been against converting the English with 'a crosse of wode and a picture of christe', and in whose time 'so wyse men were as now be'.[23] If it was the unscripted illiterate whose misuses of imagery the literate were bothered about, by definition we only know half the story.

Some believers might well have been fearful of participating in the dismemberment of holy statues, and maybe it is significant that on two of
these occasions at St Paul's, Wriothesley reports 'the boys' as doing the
breaking.

Would the demonstration of the rood's engines' necessarily have undermined people's feelings for it? Mechanical imagery of this kind was not out
of the ordinary, and if the locals at Boxley prided themselves on having the
handiwork of a specially ingenious craftsman, there were plenty of other
such clever devices to be seen in pageants and plays and ceremonial. Some
of these were quite sophisticated, and must have added spectacularly to the
illusions of dramatic performances. In 1433, the York Doomsday pageant,
for which the affluent Mercers were responsible, included, besides 'A cloud
and ii peces of Rainboe of tymber Array for god' and a heaven with red and
blue clouds, an iron swing or frame pulled up with ropes 'that god sall sitte
vppon when he sall sty vppe to heuen'. A cloud machine of this kind would
also have made it possible to execute the stage direction of the York
Transfiguration play: 'Hic descendunt nubes. Pater in nube.' At Lincoln
Cathedral a contraption with cords enabled the dove of the Holy Ghost to
descend at Pentecost. And, not far from Boxley, the Canterbury pageant of
St Thomas (which came to an end about the same time as the Rood of
Grace) had a mechanical angel which – though perhaps less cunning than
the golden angel that had bent down to offer the crown to Richard II in his
coronation pageant – was nevertheless a moving figure. In 1515–16 a penny
was spent 'for wyre for the vyce of the Angell', and two pence 'for candell
to lyght the turnying of the vyce'.[24]

Popular experience of dramatic imagery was not divorced from the
experience of statues of the saints in churches. Remembering this must
caution us against falling in too readily with the cause-and-effect scepti-
cism presented by the iconoclasts. John Hoker of Maidstone reported
hearty laughter in the market-place of his town when the Rood of Grace
went on show. But laughter had not been alien to the devotions at Boxley
where the alternating weight and weightlessness of St Rumwold caused
merriment among visitors, seeing 'a great lubber to lift at that in vayne,
whiche a young boy or wence had easily taken up before him'. Not all
laughter was derisive, and not all illusions were to be equated with delu-
sion. Those who watched a Resurrection play, or a carved Christ being
elevated from an Easter Sepulchre on Easter Day, could both revere the
miraculous and respect the limitations of physical enactment. But representation itself became different for those who tended to see the suspen-
sion of disbelief as akin to submission to misbelief.[25]

Iconoclastic demonstrations were to become familiar. But how would
they have presented themselves at this time to those (the majority of
believers) who did not share John Finch's views? What points of reference
were there for such image-breaking? It may help somewhat to redress the

imbalance in contemporary reporting if we consider the contexts in which the 'simple believer' might hitherto have encountered the phenomenon of iconoclasm.

In the first place he or she knew – or should have known – that breaking images and crosses was a most serious offence, subject to the severest penalties of church law. According to the sentence of the great curse, solemnly pronounced to parishioners four times a year, 'Alle arn acursed . . . that robbyn, brekyn, or brennyn, holy cherche violently, or chapel, or place relygyous, or othere placys halwyd or privylegyd, or brekyn crosses, awterys, or ymagys, in dyspyght and vyolens'.[26] Anyone who lived within range of Rickmansworth or Dovercourt would have known the grave consequences of breaking this law, and as recently as 1529 the sanction of secular authority supplemented the ancient provision when the Reformation Parliament excluded those who pulled down crosses in highways from its general pardon.[27]

There were depictions which showed the terrible punishments that fell on those who transgressed in this way. England has nothing quite so dramatic as the early sixteenth-century Florentine painting of the execution of Antonio di Giuseppe Rinaldeschi, delineated hanging from a window of the Bargello while angels and devils contended over the fate of his soul. Rinaldeschi's crime was the blasphemy of throwing horse dung at a painting of the Virgin.[28] A comparable scene appears among the late fifteenth-century paintings of miracles of the Virgin in Eton College Chapel and the Lady Chapel of Winchester Cathedral. There (illustrating a story in Vincent of Beauvais' *Speculum historiale*) a perfidious soldier, shown throwing a stone at a statue of the Virgin, is immediately struck dead while the image miraculously bleeds.[29] Divine and human law alike imposed the severest penalties on those who attacked images.

There was, on the other hand, a context in which image-breaking was recognized and legitimate. This too was representd in contemporary art forms, which must have made it relatively familiar to believers.[30] The utter destruction, by supernatural or divinely aided human agency, of the idols of the heathen was a recurring theme in the lives of saints. It was recounted in sermons, and it seems safe to assume that it also featured in the drama of the saints. 'Then thay turnet hom to the mawmetes that weron yn the tempull, and commawndet the fendes that weron yn hom forto come out, and schow hom to the pepull, and then plucke the ymages al to powdyr; and soo thay dyd.'[31] Mirk's *Festial* thus described the action against Persian idols by Sts Simon and Jude. The destruction of idols was also part of the story of St George.

Likewise Saynt George and Saynt Sebastian
Despising ydoles which courtes used then,

Suffered harde death by manifolde torment
For love and true fayth of God omnipotent.[32]

Though it is as a dragon-killer that St George is chiefly remembered, he
was celebrated by Alexander Barclay and others as a 'most stronge con-
founder of fals ydolatry'. The second part of St George's life in the *Golden
Legend* was taken up by the tale of how he refused to sacrifice to idols as
commanded by the emperor, the climax of which is God's dramatic answer
to the saint's prayer: a descent of fire from heaven, which destroys the
pagan temple, with all its idols and priests. Barclay's version of Mantuan's
life (which was published by Richard Pynson in 1515) gave a full account of
this episode, 'and howe at the prayers of saynt George the great temple of
the Idollys brast in sonder and sanke into the erth with horryble noyse and
murdre of paynyms'.[33]

Whether or not this scene featured in plays of St George, it was certainly
recounted from the pulpit and appears, for instance, in an address for St
George's day in the early fifteenth-century *Speculum sacerdotale*.[34] The
saint's arraignment for denouncing pagan idolatry was also one of the
twelve images illustrating his life in a window at St Neot in Cornwall.[35]
Long after the Reformation, fossilized references to St George's prowess
against idols remained embedded in the chivalric farrago of his chapbook
fame. The destruction of 'each Idol God' during his mission to Persia
appears in *The Life and Death of the Famous Champion of England, St.
George* collected by Samuel Pepys, which had some relationship with the
Mummer's Play story of the saint, while another chapbook version of
about 1750 recounts that:

> As he went he could not forbear taking notice of the idolatry of the
> Persians, and at last his zeal for the service of Christ transported him
> so far, that he went into their temples, overthrew their images, &c.
> which caused the whole kingdom to rise in arms against him.[36]

There is an inherent probability that St George's iconoclasm featured in
the many dramatic forms in which his story was presented in the fifteenth
century, and a stage direction for a medieval French play shows the kind of
scene that could have been enacted: 'The dragon must come out of the idol
and not be seen again, and the idol must be broken in pieces by the son of
the said bishop.'[37]

Medieval England did not lack knowledge, then, of legitimate iconoclasm, but this belonged to a completely different world from that of the
images encountered in everyday devotions. Given the ancient separation of
these worlds – the world inhabited by familiar saints, and the alien world
of pagan cults – their sudden assimilation could only have been startling.
A capricious switch of royal policy abruptly inaugurated a whole new
outlook in which things formerly kept apart were suddenly associated.

The proscribed became legal: two kinds of imagery that had not previously been placed in relation to each other were, almost overnight, equated. Christian images of saints were regarded in the same light as pagan idols and were destroyed just as Christian saints had once destroyed idols of heathen gods. In March 1538, a royal candle was still burning before the image of Our Lady of Walsingham.[38] Four months later the revered statue went up in flames. It is not surprising that some of Henry VIII's subjects began to talk of him as a Lollard.[39]

The inauguration of this extraordinary reversal was given a great deal of publicity as plays, ballads, and sermons produced by Thomas Cromwell's circle hammered home the 'fantasies' and errors of England's idolatry. But the situation, despite all the attacks on new-style 'idols' that were openly chastized in 1538, was far from clear. For by no means all church images were condemned as idolatrous, and the government, in attempting to distinguish between those that were inadmissible (conceived to have spiritual powers) and those that were valid (as a means of instruction), certainly never intended that individual subjects should start taking initiatives on this matter.[40] This was, however, precisely what happened. The dangerous lead given by the official iconoclasts prompted some radicals to follow suit. Clandestine image-breaking was given a new spur.

Affairs in London illustrate very clearly this threatening interaction between officially sponsored destruction and imitative subversive reform. One incident in particular showed with immediate effect how government destruction could thrill individual enthusiasts. On 22 May 1538, three months after the breaking of the Boxley rood, the capital was treated to another iconoclastic spectacle. This was a double burning, designed to demolish two misbeliefs in one fire: support for papal authority, and trust in the miraculous powers of images. A large crowd, including various notables accommodated on a specially erected platform, was gathered on this day to listen to an edifying sermon preached by Hugh Latimer and to watch the simultaneous burning of the Observant Franciscan, John Forest – who had been confessor to Queen Catherine of Aragon, and was guilty of loyalty to the pope – and the large figure of St Derfel, extracted against strenuous local opposition from the village of Llandderfel in Wales, where he was credited with powers to save souls from hell and of whom it had been prophesied that he would one day set a forest on fire.[41]

There was another aspect of this *auto-da-fé* which would not have been lost on those who saw heresy and orthodoxy changing places. Friar Forest, who was about sixty-eight when he died, was the first person to be burned as a heretic, as well as executed as a traitor, for believing in the church of Rome and upholding the authority of the pope.[42]

The morning after this event, 23 May, the parishioners of St Margaret Pattens in the city of London woke up to discover that their church's rood had been broken to pieces in the night. This was done, according to

Wriothesley, by 'certeine lewde persons, Fleminges and Englishe men, and some persons of the sayd parishe'.[43] The rood may have been specially vulnerable because it had been placed in a tabernacle in the churchyard while the church was being rebuilt, offerings to the rood being allocated to the new work, which had at this time progressed as far as the steeple. As one of the more famous images in London, it had for some while been the butt of denigration and suspect invective. For instance, among the charges reported by Foxe as being brought in 1529 against William Wegen, priest of St Mary at Hill, was 'that he being sick, went to the Rood of St Margaret Pattens; and said before him twenty Paternosters; and when he saw himself never the better, then he said, "A foul ill take him, and all other images".' A few years later Jasper Wetzell of Cologne added his voice to such domestic dissent: 'being at St. Margaret Pattens, and there holding his arms across, he said unto the people, that he could make as good a knave as he is, for he is but made of wood'.[44]

Some of the iconoclasts were caught and brought to book. The same day, Thursday 23 May, recognizances were taken from eight men – all of different trades – in the court of the aldermen to which they bound over. The eight, associated 'by theyre owne confessyon', with twenty more (unnamed), and with James Ellys, pewterer, and John Gough, stationer, 'assembled togyther late yn the nyght tyme yester nyght last past pulled downe ther the Roode at Saynt Margaret Paten'. The accused were not without defence. They said that according to Mr Edward Crome's report the bishop of Worcester (Hugh Latimer) believed it to be Cromwell's will that the said image should be removed.[45]

If the blend of native and imported dissent had been undermining the repute of the rood for some while, there was also a spearhead of underground reforming initiative contributing to its demise. For the stationer named in this list had long been helping to publicize the evangelical case. John Gough was a publisher with a consistent record of sponsoring reforming books. He had been in trouble for such during the previous decade, and – particularly interesting in the context of the St Margaret Pattens affair – he may have had a hand three years before this event in the production of the first book that openly canvassed the cause of iconoclasm in English: a translation of Martin Bucer's *Das einigerlei Bild*. Given what we know of the background to all these events, it is scarcely surprising that the accused iconoclasts pleaded the belief that Cromwell had ordered the removal of the rood.[46]

The effects of these affairs were felt far afield. Five months later, in the autumn of 1538, Cromwell was sent a letter from Lifton in Devon, written by William Dynham, gentleman. It reported a conversation that had taken place at a supper party at the priory of St Germans in Cornwall, during which Alexander Barclay, the poet and ex-Benedictine, had been unwise enough to suggest that the removal of images was getting out of hand. 'I thinke menne are to besye in pullinge downe of Ymages, without especiall commanundement of the Prynce', he said. Dynham, who was keen to expose Barclay's 'kankrid harte', egged him on. 'I knowe none them pulled downe but sutche as Idolatrye was commytted unto', he replied, adding provocatively that there was much scriptural support for such action. The example of St Margaret Pattens came up, adding to the heat of the argument, since Dynham advanced the view that although these icono-clasts were 'some what dispraised', they had a godly end in view and their doings were therefore tolerated. Barclay demurred. He suggested contrari-wise that the serious fire that had taken place in the parish after the rood-breaking, burning many tenements and some people, represented divine vengeance for a great offence.[47]

The official policy regarding the reform of images at this time was dangerously ambiguous. The second set of royal injunctions, issued the day before Dynham wrote his letter, marked the advent of authorized iconomachy in every parish subject to the supreme head (in theory). For the first time there was an open assault on images and pilgrimage as unscriptural, superstitious and idolatrous; and for the first time parish clergy were instructed to take down images. This order was, however, limited to a particular category of images. It was those that (in the words of Injunction 7) were 'abused with pilgrimages or offerings' which, for the avoidance of idolatry, the clergy were 'to take down and delay'. The pro-blems were: how to decide – and who would decide – when an image was abused and, if the word *delay* meant simply to bear away, what suitable redress was there when enthusiasts took the injunction to mean not simply removal but also destruction?[48]

The months and years that followed showed that the iconoclastic refor-mers had opened up quite a hornet's nest. If on one side it seems remark-able that central government directive could erase with such speed so much ancient observance and ritual, there are, on the other side, plenty of examples of local controversies. Taking down an image was not the same at all as destroying it, and action of either sort might be challenged under the existing law. Although activists, especially those in dioceses whose bishops were iconoclastically inclined (or ready to let the image-reformers take over), could take advantage of the lack of clarity in the new law, they might find themselves up against vociferous resistance. At Salis-bury, quite a stir resulted from the officious attempt by the city's under-bailiff, John Goodall, to prevent worshippers in the cathedral from kneel-ing before and kissing an image of Christ on Easter Day, 1539.[49] In Cranmer's own diocese considerable differences of opinion over interpre-tations of the 1538 injunctions were revealed by the inquiries set in train by the Prebendaries Plot of 1543, and, while two of the archbishop's deputies seem to have been earnestly bent on curtailing idolatry, others were busy opposing the removal of images. For instance, one Bartholomew, surgeon, was alleged to have said to Cranmer's apparitor, William Burges, 'Thou art he that would have pulled down our St. George, but your master lyeth by the heel, and we have showed the taking down therof to the King's Council and were bid set it up again'.[50] In some cases images removed for alleged abuse were indeed subsequently reinstated. The rector of Milton near Canterbury, it was said,

> had in his church . . . an image of St. Margaret, to which was a common pilgrimage, and caused it to be taken down. And upon St. Margaret's day last past Mr. John Crosse, sometime cellarer of Christchurch, came to the same church and did set the same image again with a garland of flowers on the head of it, and did strowe the church and said mass there.[51]

Such were the dangers of dicing with these differences of opinion that the authorities themselves sometimes went clandestine. In September 1547, when Edward VI's council was increasingly worried by disputes over the removal of images, the London authorities directed each alderman 'in the moste secrette discrete and quyette manner he can devyse', to visit the parish churches in his ward with the incumbent and churchwardens, and having 'shutt the churche doores' so that no crowds could gather, to make a record of the images – which were offered or prayed to and which not, who had taken them down and what became of them, what misdemeanours had been committed in this process, and what images still remained.[52]

On two occasions when images were removed from St Paul's, the risk of disturbance in the city was obviated by taking action overnight. The famous rood at the north door of the cathedral, together with the image of St Uncumber, were taken down by the dean of St Paul's (acting on orders sent through the mayor, Sir Richard Gresham) on the night of 23 August 1538.[53] Likewise in November 1547, when the royal visitors – anticipating the action that in the rest of the country took place the following year – were pulling down all images in London's parish churches, the works in St Paul's were undertaken by night. This proved difficult, and there was an accident as the large rood in the centre of the cathedral was dismantled in the darkness. The labourers let the great cross fall to the ground, killing one or two workmen and hurting others. Naturally there were those who drew a moral like Alexander Barclay's: God had spoken.[54]

Waverers and opposers of this kind were answered by another iconoclastic display. Ten days after the accident over the rood, a sermon and demonstration at Paul's Cross on the first Sunday in Advent (27 November 1547) announced to the capital – and to the rest of the kingdom – that the young king was taking up the mantle of Josiah that had been donned by his father in 1538. The sermon was preached by Bishop Barlow of St David's (who had his own iconoclastic record), and he had exemplary specimens on hand to drive home his moral. In front of his pulpit was exhibited an image of Our Lady which the clergy of St Paul's had vainly tried to conceal from the royal visitors. Barlow also had a jointed Easter Sepulchre figure of Christ, which likewise may be assumed to have been familiar to a number of his auditors. The moral was double; 'the great abhomination of idolatrie in images'; and the great sin of harbouring idols. To those of Barlow's mind, there was a world of difference between removing images from churches and destroying them. Idolatry could only be defeated by annihilation. 'After the sermon the boyes brooke the idolls in peaces.'[55]

Henry VIII, sensing the perils of Cromwellian policy, had retreated in the 1540s from the spectacular iconoclasm of 1538. Reform of images continued, but the supreme head, who did not see eye-to-eye with his archbishop on this score, was readier to complete the termination of major pilgrimage shrines than to undertake the eradication of idolatry desired by a number of his subjects. Some of these evangelicals went abroad when the brakes were applied at the execution of Cromwell. Others found ways of continuing to work for the cause on their own. One such was William Forde who, as usher of Winchester College between *c.* 1543 and 1547, managed – not without personal cost – to execute an iconoclastic manoeuvre in the college chapel. The story was recorded for John Foxe by John Louth, archdeacon of Nottingham (d. 1590). Forde, who was himself a scholar at Winchester in the 1530s, returned as usher in his early twenties, having been converted into a 'greate enemye to papisme' while at Oxford.

> Ther was many golden images in Wykam's colleage by Wynton. The churche dore was directly over agaynste the usher's chamber. Mr. Forde tyed a longe coorde to the images, lynkyng them all in one coorde, and, being in his chamber after midnight, he plucked the cordes ende, and at one pulle all the golden godes came downe with *heyho Rombelo*. Yt wakened all men with the rushe. They wer amased at the terryble noyse and also disamayd at the greevous sight. The corde beinge plucked harde and cutt with a twytche lay at the church doore.

Forde, naturally, was suspect. He was found in bed, but that scarcely absolved him. After doing this good turn to his *alma mater*, his life was made a misery. He was railed at by masters and scholars, and mugged at night in the town, though (according to a Catholic reporter) he did succeed in converting the head boy.[56]

The iconoclastic purges carried out under the direction of royal visitors early in the reigns of Edward VI and Elizabeth I swept away much of what reformers objected to as idolatrous 'popish peltry'. And at Elizabeth's accession, when the restored roods and saints' images of the intervening Catholic years challenged the indignation of returned exiles, Londoners again witnessed ceremonial public image-burnings not unlike those of

1538. By the time of the issue of the Second Book of Homilies in 1563, with its long tripartite homily expounding the intolerable dangers of allowing any images to be set up publicly in churches, it might seem as if the iconoclasts had run their course.

> Alas, gossip, what shall we now so at church, since all the saints are taken away, since all the goodly sights we were wont to have are gone, since we cannot hear the like piping, singing, chanting, and playing upon the organs, that we could before.[57]

Churches surely looked bare, empty, denuded – 'scoured of such gay gazing sights', as the homilist, here rebuking the 'unsavoury' objections of tattling wives, scathingly put it. What remained for the iconoclasts to reform – apart from the fond memories and hoarded relics of the unconverted?

But the see-saw balance between public destruction and private enthusiasm was by no means over. Regional diversity apart, there still remained a range of objects that for long tested the initiative of committed purifiers. The imagery of church windows, crosses in churchyards and other public places, maypoles, and organs, were all grist to the iconoclastic mill. We can briefly see how this process continued by looking at the development of cross-breaking.

Disputes over the use of the cross took place on various levels during the reign of Elizabeth. Besides all the controversy aroused by the use of the sign of the cross in baptism, there was a campaign of attrition against the freestanding crosses in churchyards and other public places. Such monuments were defaced or destroyed officially on the grounds that they were sources of idolatry. For instance, in October 1571 rural deans in the diocese of York were ordered 'to se that no reliques of crosses remayne in any churche or chaple yard within there severall Deanryes'. Seven years later reports in the diocese of Chester suggest considerable lack of uniformity, some parishes still having their churchyard crosses while in others these had been reduced to stumps or headless monuments.[58] Discrepancies of this kind maddened the purists, and a number of open-air crosses were defaced or felled by individuals who took the law into their own hands.

At Durham, Neville's Cross was destroyed by nocturnal iconoclasts in 1589. This 'most notable famous and goodly large cross' had been erected to commemorate the victory of 1346 at which the Scots had lost to Lord Neville and the English their celebrated black rood, and its carvings included a Crucifixion as well as the four evangelists and Neville's arms. It apparently remained intact until thirty years after Elizabeth's accession when 'in the nighte tyme the same was broken downe and defaced'.[59]

Other less conspicuous activists went to work on parish crosses. In 1603 charges were brought in the quarter sessions at Chester against a group of offenders in Bishop Vaughan's diocese. Seven men were accused, and confessed that they had one Sunday thrown down with staves a stone cross standing in the churchyard of Wharton, Cheshire, and the same night two of them had broken panels of glass representing St Andrew and Lazarus in the chancel window at Tarvin some ten miles away. These nocturnal iconoclasts were the servants of John Bruen, who earned praise for his reform of 'painted puppets and popish idols' in the church at Tarvin. Doubtless it was the example set by this leading light of the godly in Cheshire that was being followed.[60]

Particularly celebrated examples of cross-breaking were those of Banbury and Cheapside. There could hardly be a more focal Puritan centre than Banbury (whose fame became linked with its cross), but even here iconoclasm was divisive and its proponents, aware of the contentiousness of the issue, tried to present the town with a *fait accompli*. Two stonemasons were set to work to hew down the Banbury High Cross at first light on the morning on 26 July 1600. This dawn endeavour was halted by a townsman who disliked the project, and before long a crowd of over a hundred had assembled, demonstrating for and against the work. There were enough supporters to see the demolition work completed, but also enough opponents to result in a case against a clique of the town's aldermen being taken to Star Chamber.[61]

The example of Cheapside Cross is illuminating. As one of the best-known crosses in the country, cherished and restored by generations of Londoners and a focal point in all city processions, it long withstood a battery of objections. This central public monument came to be viewed by some as the central idol in the land, and there were voices calling for its reform more than two generations before this was finally accomplished. One such advocate made known his view of the matter in a very well-read text.

The *Short Catechism for Householders* by John More and Edward Dering, issued in many editions between 1572 and 1634, was one of the more influential texts of its kind in the period. Edward Dering wrote the preface to this *Brief and necessary instruction, very needful to be known of all householders*, invoking readers to purification from 'the idolatrous superstition of the elder world'.[62] It was the world of popular literature he specifically had in mind: the dangerous 'spiritual enchauntmentes' and 'dreames and illusions' of the past that readers found in the tales of Robin Hood, Bevis of Hampton, and Arthur of the Round Table as well as saints' lives and satanic texts 'Hell had printed' – the chapbooks stocked by peddlers and chapmen alongside more edifying texts: those 'pleasant histories' which, as Margaret Spufford has shown, perpetuated the old world of monks and friars and priests with a timeless disregard for the changes effected by the Reformation.[63] We have seen how St George lived on in this literature, attached to some of the assumptions of medieval iconography. Dering's solution was simple. All such books, with songs and sonnets, fables, and tragedies, should be burned as publicly as possible in London's main thoroughfare so that (as he put it) 'the chiefe streete might be sanctified with so holy sacrifice. The place it selfe doth crave it, and holdeth up a gorgeous Idoll, fyt stake for so good a fire.'[64] A bonfire of vanities at Cheapside Cross: Dering's wish was to be granted, but not during his lifetime.

Whatever the inspiration on Dering's readers there were individuals who tried to do something about the egregious idol, Cheapside Cross. The first serious attempt took place in 1581. John Stow described what happened one midsummer under cover of darkness:

> The 21 June in the night, certaine young men, drawing ropes thwart the streete, on both sides the Crosse in Cheape, to stop the passage, did then fasten ropes about the lowest Images of the said Crosse, attempting by force to have plucked them downe, which when they could not doe, they plucked the picture of Christ out of his mothers lap, whereon he sat, and otherwise defaced her, and the Images by striking off their armes.[65]

Despite the issue of a proclamation offering a reward for identification of the offenders, these iconoclasts were not discovered. But the matter was taken to the highest authority. On 4 July the city aldermen appointed a committee who were forthwith to 'conferre togeather and consyder what course ys best to be taken concerninge the repayringe of the great crosse in Cheapesyde'. They were to take advice from the bishop of Salisbury or some other learned divine on the repairs and also 'for thanswearynge of her majesties commaundement in that behalfe'. Five days later a deputation of aldermen had to keep a Sunday morning appointment at court 'touchinge the crosse in Cheapesyde'.[66] The queen was evidently concerned about the state of the city monument, though Stow's account suggests that it was a long time before some perfunctory restoration to the damaged Virgin and Child was completed.

The city authorities were in no hurry to improve their ancient monument, and differences of opinion between them and Queen Elizabeth became all too clear at the turn of the century. The removal of the cross at the top of the Cheapside monument, on the grounds of its dangerous state of decay, led to troubles over its replacement. Bishop Bancroft thought that a cross should be put back, and he had the queen behind him. Others, who had the support of the vice-chancellor of Oxford, George Abbot, were wholly opposed to this and thought that a religiously neutral object, such as a pyramid should be placed there instead. In the end, Cheapside Cross got back its cross, despite the iconomachs' learned censures. But only twelve days afterwards the nocturnal iconoclasts struck again, once more defacing Virgin and Child.[67]

Crosses and crucifixes were very much in the news after the opening of the Long Parliament – thanks in part to their increased visibility in the 1630s. Crosses came under attack from many directions, and the monument in Cheapside became the topic of a small library of pamphlets in 1642–3. Most of them aimed at its demise, and it comes as no surprise to find that the final destruction of the cross was the work of private as well as public iconoclasts. In January 1642 surreptitious image-breakers launched a new attack, scaling the iron railing that had enclosed the monument since 1603 and breaking several statues, including the figure of Christ. After this, trained bands were set to keep nightly watch on the cross, though it was clear to some that it could not last long.[68] Its obsequies were penned and published. The end came on 2 May 1643 when, with an attendant force of mounted horse and foot companies, with drums beating and trumpets sounding, in the presence of a huge crowd of spectators, Cheapside Cross was finally hauled to the ground. A print by Wenceslaus Hollar commemorated this dramatic occasion, and play was made with the coincidence of date with the Invention of the Holy Cross (3 May) in the Catholic calendar.[69] It was an event comparable with the scenes of 1538. Once again, despite the alteration of circumstance and the changed conception of the source of idolatry – Rome – spectacular official iconoclasm was a great propagandist rite of dismissal. The vanquishing of the 'idol' was a declaratory ceremony designed to sweep idolators into the purified space created by the destroyers.

Ironically – and somewhat inconsistently, given their own view that God was no respecter of places – the iconoclasts dedicated the site of the demolished idol to further ceremonies of the same kind. Hollar delineated the burning of the Book of Sports 'in the place where the Crosse stoode' beneath his etching of its destruction. Both in 1644 and 1645, on days of public thanksgiving, ceremonial bonfires of popish books, pictures, and crucifixes took place on the empty site of Cheapside Cross.[70] Edward Dering would have been delighted.

Extremist purifiers, aiming to free believers from the religious clutter that had endangered their forebears, found spiritual meaning in blank walls and silence. The militant iconoclasts who, in the course of a century, managed to annihilate so much of England's artistic heritage, in the shape of religious sculpture, painting, stained and painted glass, organs, bells, plate, and vestments, may only have been a small minority of activists. Their influence was none the less for that. As Sir Thomas Gresham's agent reported of the destruction in Antwerp on the night of 20–21 August 1566, it was incredible that 'so few pepell durst or colde do so much'.[71] Overnight image-breaking by the few could alter the course of reform and affect the future beliefs of the many. Such actions played a critical part in the politics of reformation, and through this physical alteration, separating the faith from so much familiar scenery, Christians were ushered into a reshaped spiritual world. God was to be heard, not seen. In learning to live by the Word, people gradually learned to find in their Bibles the compensation for that huge deprivation of their century, the enforced withdrawal of the 'goodly sights' that had accumulated over generations. Many had regrets, but those schooled in the meaning of defilement increasingly found themselves at home in their bared and whitened churches. Some felt cleansed and were thankful, even able, like a preacher to Parliament in 1645, to echo the Elizabethan homilist:

> I am glad for my part, they are scoured of their gay gazing, and I marvelled a great while since, how, and why the Organs grew so many and blew so loud, when the very Homilies accused them for defiling God's house.[72]

Notes

1 Earlier versions of this paper were delivered in 1980 at the London University Seminar of Michael Hunter and Bob Scribner, and in 1984 at Keith Thomas's graduate seminar in Oxford. I am grateful for the comments offered on both occasions.
2 For the continental experience, see Carlos M.N. Eire, 'Iconoclasm as a Revolutionary Tactic: the Case of Switzerland 1524–1536', *Journal of the Rocky Mountain Medieval Renaissance Association*, 4 (1983), pp. 77–96, and *War Against the Idols: The Reformation of Worship from Erasmus to Calvin* (Cambridge, 1986).
3 René Bornert, *La réforme protestante du culte à Strasbourg au XVIe siècle (1523–1598): approche sociologique et interprétation théologique* (Leiden, 1981), p. 88, considering this danger of creating 'un blocage contre la réforme', cites Capito's *Was man halten und antwurten soll* (of October 1524).
4 The indulgence which vividly describes this event survives in a single copy in the BL (STC, 14077 c. 68), and is printed in facsimile in K.W. Cameron, *The Pardoner and his Pardons: Indulgences Circulating in England on the Eve of the Reformation* (Hartford, CT, [1965]), p. 49.
5 John Foxe, *The Acts and Monuments*, (*A & M*), ed. J. Pratt, 3rd ed. (London: G. Seeley, 1853–68), iv, p. 707.
6 *A & M*, iv, pp. 706–7.
7 *A & M*, viii, pp. 581–90. This account was first published in the 1576 edition of the *Acts and Monuments*. In 1538 Thomas Rose made a name for himself as a reformer. He received a handsome testimonial (sent to Cromwell, whose chaplain he was, according to Foxe) for a preaching tour in Lincolnshire, and was invited to preach in London, where it became known that Mass was being celebrated in English at his old parish of Hadleigh. *LP*, xiii, pt. 1, nos. 704, 1492, pp. 267, 552; *Wriothesley's Chronicle*, ed. W.D. Hamilton (Camden Soc., n.s. 11, 20, 1875–77), i, p. 83; Susan Brigden, *London and the Reformation* (Oxford, 1989), pp. 235–6.
8 Diarmaid MacCullouh, *Suffolk and the Tudors: Politics and Religion in an English County, 1500–1600* (Oxford, 1986) pp. 155, 159, 161, 163; John F. Davis, *Heresy and Reformation in the South-East of England, 1520–1559* (London, 1983), pp. 111–12; *Miscellaneous Writings and Letters of Thomas Cranmer*, ed. Edmund Cox (Parker Soc., Cambridge, 1846), p. 280; John Strype, *Memorials of Archbishop Cranmer* (Oxford, 1848–54), ii, pp. 369, 374–76; Jasper Ridley, *Thomas Cranmer* (Oxford, 1962), pp. 88–89. Possibly Rose was placed in the bishop of Lincoln's custody at the time of Warham's death; despite Foxe's report, (*A & M*, viii, p. 582), he seems to have regained the living at Hadleigh for a time.

9 *LP*, vii, no. 523, pp. 208–09: PRO, SP6/1, no. 14, fo. 64r; Brigden, *London and the Reformation*, p. 215. The development of the case against images in this decade is examined in Margaret Aston, *England Iconoclasts*, i, (Oxford, 1988), chap. 5.

10 Foxe, *A & M*, iv, p. 627, appendix vi (unpaginated), from Reg. Tunstall, Guildhall Library, London, MS 9531/10, fo. 133 v; Davis, *Heresy and Reformation*, p. 49. Bilney denied the charge as worded (*negat ut ponitur*).

11 Foxe, *A & M*, iv, appendix vi; Reg. Tunstall, fo. 133 v.

12 Davis, *Heresy and Reformation*, p. 83; Davis, 'The Trials of Thomas Bylney and the English Reformation', *Historical Journal*, 24 (1981), p. 785.

13 Foxe's phrase for the Dovercourt iconoclasts, *A & M*, iv, p. 706.

14 Recent helpful discussions of these events include Robert Whiting, 'Abominable Idols: Images and Image-breaking under Henry VIII', *Journal of Ecclesiastical History*, 33 (1982), pp. 30–47; Whiting, *The Blind Devotion of the People: Popular Religion and the English Reformation* (Cambridge, 1989); Ronald Hutton, 'The Local Impact of the Tudor Reformations,' in *The English Reformation Revised*, ed. Christopher Haigh (Cambridge, 1987), pp. 114–38 (*See* Reading 6 above).

15 *Wriothesley's Chronicle*, i, p. 83.

16 BL, MS Add. 21, 481, fo. 10 v, records under 29 July 1509: 'Item for the kinges offring at the Roode of grace 6s. 8d'. See also BL, MS Harl. 433, fo. 293; *Letters and Papers*, ii, pt. 2, no. 4333, p. 1336 (Campeggio, on this first visit to England, stayed at Boxley on the night of Monday, 26 July, having spent the weekend seeing the sights of Canterbury); Ronald C. Finucane, *Miracles and Pilgrims: Popular Beliefs in Medieval England* (London, 1977), pp. 208–10. I have benefited from the critical assessment of J. Brownbill, 'Boxley Abbey and the Rood of Grace', *The Antiquary*, 7 (1883), pp. 162–65, 210–13. The movements attributed to the rood grew in the telling.

17 *Wriothesley's Chronicle*, i, pp. 75–76. Wriothesley reports that the image 'was made of paper and cloutes from the legges upward; ech leeges and armes were of timber', and it seems that during Hilsey's sermon it was placed where his auditors could inspect it for themselves. The account sent to Cromwell by his agent Geoffrey Chambers, who arranged the exposure of the rood at Maidstone, two miles away, described 'certen ingynes and olde wyer, wyth olde roton stykkes in the backe of the same', which (like Wriothesley) does not suggest recent use. *Original Letters Illustrative of English History*, ed. H. Ellis (London, 1824–46), iii, pt. 3, pp. 168–69.

18 *Original Letters Relative to the English Reformation*, ed. H. Robinson (PS, Cambridge, 1846–47), ii, p. 607. Finch's report (unlike Wriothesley's) was far from first hand; he had the news from a German merchant who had English contacts. Other such accounts also stressed popular indignation against the impostures of monks and priests. See *Original Letters*, ed. Robinson, ii, pp. 604, 609–10, for those of William Peterson and Nicholas Partridge, sent respectively to Conrad Pulbert and Bullinger; for John Hoker of Maidstone's rhetorical letter to Bullinger, see Gilbert Burnet, *The History of the Reformation of the Church of England*, ed. N. Pocock (Oxford, 1865), vi, pp. 194–5; see also the account given by Henry VIII's representatives to the Marquis of Berghen *LP*, xiii, pt. 2, no. 880, p. 366. On John Finch of Billericay, see C.H. Garrett, *The Marian Exiles* (Cambridge, 1938), p. 153, postulating a possible connection with John Finch, a tiler of Colchester, who abjured Lollard heresies, including 'that no maner of worship ne reference oweth to be do to ony ymages', in 1431; *Heresy Trials in the Diocese of Norwich, 1428–31*, ed. Norman P. Tanner (Camden Soc., fourth ser., 20, 1977), pp. 181–89, esp. p. 185.

19 *Original Letters*, ed. Robinson, ii, p. 607; cf. p. 609.

20 William Lambarde, *A Perambulation of Kent* (London, 1576), pp. 181–89, gives a disparaging account of the practices at Boxley, including the deceptions of the image of St Rumwold, 'a preatie shorte picture of a boy sainct . . . small, hollow, and light' in itself, but capable of being fixed immovably in place by means of a wooden pin. Lambarde (b. 1536) had no first-hand knowledge, but based his report on what was 'yet freshe in mynde to bothe sides'.

21 A. van Gennep, *The Rites of Passage* (London, 1977), pp. 113–14. For examples of evangelical desecration of the previously holy by ritual inversion in profane space,

see R.W.. Scribner, 'Ritual and Reformation', in *Popular Culture and Popular Movements in Reformation Germany* (London, 1987), pp. 103–22.

22 Lambarde, *Perambulations in Kent*, pp. 182–85. On 'automobile' relics, see Stephen Wilson, *Saints and their Cults* (Cambridge, 1985), pp. 11, 41, 69.

23 He was curate of St Benet, Gracechurch Street, and the parishioners who accused him of preaching contrary to the injunctions surmised that he made the remark about Augustine because 'it grevede hym to see the Rode of Ungrace with soche other not with out good consideracyon broken in peces of late at paules and abolisshede', *LP*, xiii, pt. 1, no. 1111, pp. 406–07; PRO E 36/120, fo. 214; SP 1/132, fo. 218 r; Brigden, *London and the Reformation*, pp. 281–2.

24 *York*, ed. Alexandra F. Johnston and Margaret Rogerson, Records of Early English Drama (Toronto, 1979), i, p. 55; *The York Plays*, ed. Richard Beadle (London, 1982), p. 196; *Records of Plays and Players in Lincolnshire, 1300–1585*, ed. Stanley J. Kahrl, Malone Soc. Collections, 8 (1974), pp. xiii–xiv, 26–27; *Records of Plays and Players in Kent, 1450–1642*, ed. Giles E. Dawson, Malone Soc. Collections, 7 (1965), pp. 192–93.

25 See notes 18 and 20 above, for Hoker and for Lambarde on St Rumwold. For an example of an Easter Sepulchre image, see above p. 181; Pamela Sheingorn, '"No Sepulchre on Good Friday": The Impact of the Reformation on the Easter Rites in England', in *Iconoclasm vs. Art and Drama*, ed. C. Davidson and A.E. Nichols (Kalamazoo, MI, 1989), pp. 145–63. Jonas Barish, *The Anti-Theatrical Prejudice* (Berkeley and Los Angeles, 1981), considers the growth of suspicions of the theatre in England; see also Clifford Davidson, '"The Devil's Guts": Allegations of Superstition and Fraud in Religious Drama and Art during the Reformation', in *Iconoclasm vs. Art and Drama*, pp. 92ff.

26 *Jacob's Well*, ed. Arthur Bradeis (EETS, o.s. 115, 1900), p. 16. For the church's ruling on publication, see William Lyndwood, *Provinciale, (seu constitutiones Angliae)* (Oxford, 1679), p. 355.

27 Stanford E. Lehmberg, *The Reformation Parliament, 1529–1536* (Cambridge, 1970), p. 91; *Statutes of the Realm*, iii, p. 283; 21 Henry VIII, c. I, vii.

28 Samuel Y. Edgerton, Jr, *Pictures and Punishment: Art and Criminal Prosecution during the Florentine Renaissance* (Ithaca and London, 1985), pp. 47–58, and the same author's 'The Last Judgment as Pageant Setting For Communal Law and Order in Late Medieval Italy', in *Persons in Groups: Social Behavior as Identity Formation in Medieval and Renaissance Europe*, ed. Richard C. Trexler, Medieval and Renaissance Texts and Studies, 36 (Binghamton, NY, 1985), pp. 89–90.

29 M.R. James and E.W. Tristram, 'The Wall Paintings in Eton College Chapel and in the Lady Chapel of Winchester Cathedral', *Walpole Society*, 17 (1928–29), pp. 1–43, esp., for this scene, pls. xiv, xxi. In both cases the source is given in the accompanying inscriptions, that at Eton reading 'Qualitas ymago filii beate virginis a perfidis percussa sanguinem dedit. Vincentius'; for the story, 'De imagine que percussa sanguinem reddidit,' see *Speculum historiale fratris Vincencii ordinis predicatorum* ([Strasbourg], 1483), i, book viii, c. cx. The two series of paintings are related. For a sermon by the Durham Benedictine Robert Rypon, countering the Lollard case against images and the early iconoclastic example of Epiphanius, see G.R. Owst, *Literature and Pulpit in Medieval England* (Oxford, 1961), pp. 139–40.

30 An apocryphal scene in the life of Christ which was frequently depicted in medieval art (and which allowed artists to express their ideas of pagan idols) was a miracle that took place on the Flight into Egypt: as Christ and his parents entered an Egyptian city, all the idols fell and broke (fulfilling a prophecy of Isaiah). This story, deriving from the *Liber de infantia* or *Gospel of Pseudo-Matthew*, passed into popular sources including the *Golden Legend* and the *Meditations on the Life of Christ* attributed to St Bonaventure, and was illustrated in many places, including church windows (Great Malvern still has an example) and Bible pictures. On this topic see now Michael Camille, *The Gothic Idol* (Cambridge, 1989), pp. 1–7 (on idols of Egypt); M.R. James, *The Apocryphal New Testament* (Oxford, 1953), p. 75; Gordon McN. Rushforth, *Medieval Christian Imagery as Illustrated by the Painted Windows of Great Malvern Priory Church, Worcestershire* (Oxford,

1936), p. 287; Sandra Hindman, *Text and Image in Fifteenth-Century Illustrated Dutch Bibles* (Leiden, 1977), pp. 55–56, fig. 21.

31 John Mirk, *Festial*, ed. Theodor Erbe (EETS, e.s. 96, 1905), pt. I, p. 265.

32 *The Eclogues of Alexander Barclay*, ed. Beatrice White (EETS, o.s. 175, 1928), p. 100.

33 Jacobus de Voragine, *The Golden Legend* (Westminster: [William Caxton], 1483), fos. clvi v–clvii v; *Three Lives from the Gilte Legende*, ed. Richard Hamer, Middle English Texts, 9 (Heidelberg, 1978), pp. 65–74; *The Life of St. George by Alexander Barclay*, ed. William Nelson (EETS, o.s. 230, 1955), pp. 12–13, 90, 106; STC, 22,992.1.

34 *Speculum sacerdotale*, ed. Edward H. Weatherly (EETS, o.s. 200, 1936), pp. 129–33. This account reverses the *Golden Legend* order and places the burning of the idols before the dragon-killing; see p. 130 for St George's prayer at which 'there come downe a fyre fro heuen and sodeynly brande the temple with alle the godis and the maistris'.

35 Gordon McN. Rushforth. 'The Windows of the Church of St. Neot, Cornwall', *Exeter Diocesan Architectural and Archaeological Society Transactions*, 15 (1937), pp. 175–76, p. xlvi.

36 *The Life and Death of St. George, The Noble Champion of England* (London, [1750?]), p. 13. For the Pepys text (of which there were several editions between 1660 and 1689, his being possibly of 1685), I cite the copy in the Pepys Library, Magdalene College, Cambridge (Penny Merriments, ii (6), p. 123), on which see Margaret Spufford, *Small Books and Pleasant Histories* (London, 1981), pp. 227–31. I am most grateful to Margaret Spufford for lending me a xerox of this chapbook. St George's image-breaking also featured in a work which was in print for the best part of a century after its first appearance in 1596. In Richard Johnson's *The Most Famous History of the Seven Champions of Christendome* (London, 1608), p. 23, the Persians' solemn sacrifice to their pagan gods 'so mooved the impatience of the English Champion, that he tooke the ensignes and streamers whereon the Persian Gods were pictured, and trampled them under his feete'.

37 Lynette Muir, 'The Saint Play in Medieval France', in *The Saint Play in Medieval Europe*, ed. Clifford Davidson, Early Drama, Art and Music, Monograph Ser., 8 (Kalamazoo, 1986), p. 159. The idol in this Bourges *Actes des apôtres* was capable of special trick effects. Cf. Clifford Davidson, 'The Middle English Saint Play', in *The Saint Play in Medieval Europe*, pp. 37, 40, 48, on the possible dramatic role of idols in English plays of Sts Eustace, Lawrence and Catherine. Destruction of the entire pagan temple with its idol of 'mament' is one of the spectacular effects of the Digby *Mary Magdalene*; see *The Late Medieval Religious Plays of Bodleian MSS Digby 133 and e Museo 160*, ed. Donald C. Baker, John L. Murphy, and Louis B. Hall, Jr (EETS, 283, 1982), p. 76. The destruction by fire that would have been called for in this scene was also encountered in dramatic presentations of Doomsday; see *Coventry*, ed. R.W. Ingram, Records of Early English Drama (Toronto, 1981), p. 230, including a 1565 payment at Coventry for 'Settynge the worldes on fyre'.

38 LP, xiii, pt. 2, no. 1280, pp. 529, 535; Finucane, *Miracles and Pilgrims*, p. 205. Cf. LP, ii, pt. 2, pp. 1442, 1449, and BL, MS Add, 21,481, fos. 23 v, 51 r, 52 v, for earlier payments of the king's candle and his priest singing before Our Lady of Walsingham (costing £4.13s.4d. and £10 a year respectively) and for the king's offerings there in 1520.

39 LP, vi, no. 1255, p. 514, for the views of Richard Panemore (1533) on Latimer's reported preaching that church images should be pulled down and that the *Ave Maria* was no prayer; J.F. Davis, 'Lollards, Reformers and St. Thomas of Canterbury', *Birmingham Historical Journal*, 9 (1963), p. 13.

40 Aston, *England's Iconoclasts*, i, pp. 225–36, attempts to explain the situation at this time rather more fully than was done by John Phillips, *The Reformation of Images: Destruction of Art in England, 1535–1660* (Berkeley and Los Angeles, 1973), pp. 58–62.

41 *Wriothesley's Chronicle*, i, pp. 79–81; *Hall's Chronicle* (London, 1809), pp. 825–26; *Original Letters*, ed. Ellis, iii, pt. 3, pp. 194–95; cf. i, pt. 2, pp. 82–83.

42 *Wriothesley's Chronicle*, i, pp. 78–79; *LP*, xiii, pt. 1, no. 1043, p. 385; Ridley, *Thomas Cranmer*, pp. 160–61.

43 *Wriothesley's Chronicle*, i, p. 81; John Stow, *A Survey of London*, ed. C.L. Kingsford (Oxford, 1905), i, pp. 209–10.

44 Foxe, *A & M*, v, pp. 28, 32. The king offered 6s.8d to the rood in 1511; *LP*, ii, pt. 2, p. 1449; BL MS. Add. 21, 481, fo. 52 v.

45 Corporation of London Rec. Office, Repertory 10, fo. 34 v: 'as they say M'Cromer reportyd by the report of yᵉ bysshopp of Worceter that yᵉ lorde prevy seales [commaundet?] that yᵉ seid Image shuld be removyd'. I owe this reference to Susan Brigden, *London and the Reformation* (Oxford, 1989), pp. 290–1. The matter was of immediate concern to the court of aldermen, who, as patrons of the living, had two months earlier presented John Grene. He held St Margaret Pattens until July 1542, when he resigned (Repertory 10, fos. 25 v, 267 v; cf. *LP*, xiii, pt. 1, no. 866, p. 319; PRO, SP 1/131/242, for a John Grene who petitioned Thomas Wriothesley for advancement to a living, having failed in his expectation of promotion through service to Chancellor Audley).

46 The outcome of these proceedings is not known, but Gough was very much in business a few years after and was imprisoned in the Fleet for printing seditious books in 1541; see Margaret Aston, *Lollards and Reformers: Images and Literacy in Late Medieval Religion* (London, 1984), pp. 229–30, 242, 251, and *England's Iconoclasts*, p. 203.

47 *Original Letters*, ed. Ellis, iii, pt. 3, pp. 112–15. This letter was dated 12 October; *LP*, xiii, pt. 2, no. 596, p. 232. Barclay, who had preached the previous day in honour of the Virgin, was under pressure from Dynham who was determined to exploit the situation. Stow, *Survey of London*, i, pp. 209–10, reports the fire in the parish of St Margaret Pattens on 27 May 1538: 'amongst the basket-makers, a great and sudden fire happened in the night season, which within the space of three hours consumed more than a dozen houses, and nine persons were burnt to death there'.

48 There is a problem over the meaning of the word 'delay', for which the OED and MED do not give obvious analogous examples, the temporal meaning of the word (related to the Latin *differre* and English *defer*) being dominant. Ann Nichols suggests that since 'delay' and 'defer' could be used synonymously with the sense of 'postpone' (OED gives an example from John Palsgrave's *Lesclarcissement de la Langue Francoyse* [1530], 'I delaye one, or deferre hym, or put hym backe of his purpose'), possibly 'delay' could be used synonymously for 'defer' in the meaning of 'to put on one side, set aside' (OED cites Lydgate, *Minor Poems*: 'Grace withe her lycour cristallyne and pure / Defferrithe vengeaunce off ffuriose woodnes'). The word 'defer' with this obsolete non-temporal sense of set aside, carry down, convey away, was synonymous with another obsolete form 'delate' (derived from the Latin *deferre*). An example cited in the MED of the verb 'delaien' used in this same sense is the Wycliffite Bible's translation of Psalm 21:20 (*Tu autem Domine ne elongaveris auxilium tuum a me*) as 'But thou, Lord, delaie not thin help fro me'. It seems likely that the injunction's 'delay' bore such a meaning (*elongare*, to remove, make distant), and this interpretation is supported by the proclamation of November 1538 against Becket imagery, ordering it to be 'put down and avoided' from churches. See *Visitation Articles and Injunctions of the Period of the Reformation*, ed. W.H. Frere and W.M. Kennedy, Alcuin Club Collections, 14–16 (1910), ii, p. 38; *Tudor Royal Proclamations*, ed. Paul L. Hughes and James F. Larkin (New Haven and London, 1964–69), i, p. 276; Aston, *England's Iconoclasts*, i, p. 227.

49 Aston, *England's Iconoclasts*, i, pp. 230–2. Possibly this image, which held the host, was an Easter Sepulchre image: cf. H.J. Feasey, *Ancient English Holy Week Ceremonial* (London, 1897), pp. 134–37, and Pamela Sheingorn, *The Easter Sepulchre in England*, Early Drama, Art, and Music, Reference Ser., 5 (Kalamazoo, MI, 1987), pp. 58–59.

50 *LP*, xviii, pt. 2, no. 546, p. 295.

51 *LP*, xviii, pt. 2, p. 297. On John Crosse, see Emden (O), *1501 to 1540*, p. 153. For

affairs in Kent at this time, see Michael L. Zell, 'The Prebendaries' Plot of 1543: A Reconsideration', *JEH*, 27 (1976), pp. 241–53; Peter Clark, *English Provincial Society from the Reformation to the Revolution: Religion, Politics and Society in Kent, 1500–1640* (Hassocks, 1977), pp. 38–66.

52 Corporation of London Record Office, Repertory 11, fo. 349.

53 Brigden, *London and the Reformation* (Oxford, 1989), pp. 10, 291; PRO, SP1/135, fo. 247; *LP*, xiii, pt. 2, no. 209, p. 81; *Wriothesley's Chronicle*, i, p. 84. A call for this action was sent to Cromwell a month earlier by George Robinson, who in a letter of 16 July described how he had visited St Paul's: 'I went to powlles where I ffound sent Uncombre stonddyng in hyr old place and state with hyr gay gowne and sylver schews on and a woman kneelying beffore hyr at xi of the cloke.' It was for the king to be Josiah and take all such images away. *LP*, xiii, pt. 1, no. 1393, p. 515; PRO, SP1/134, fo. 183r.

54 *Chronicle of the Grey Friars of London*, ed. J.G. Nichols (Camden Soc., 1852), p. 55; *Wriothesley's Chronicle*, ii, p. 1.

55 *Wriothesley's Chronicle*, ii, p. 1; Millar MacLure, *The Paul's Cross Sermons, 1534–1642* (Toronto, 1958), pp. 40–1; Sheingorn, *The Easter Sepulchre*, p. 61. The second of these images belonged to the execrated class of moving figures, like the Boxley one: 'the resurrection of our Lord made with vices, which putt out his legges of sepulchree and blessed with his hand, and turned his heade'. See also Sheingorn, '"No Sepulchre on Good Friday"', pp. 152–4.

56 *Narratives of the . . . Reformation*, ed. J.G. Nichols (Camden Soc., 77, 1859), pp. 29–30; Emden (O), *1501 to 1540*, pp. 208–9; Nicholas Sander, *Rise and Growth of the Anglican Schism*, trans. D. Lewis (London, 1877), pp. 207–8. 'Golden Gods' (a scriptural phrase) would have been especially provocative.

57 *Certain Sermons or Homilies to be read in Churches* (Oxford, 1844), p. 311, from the Homily of the Place and Time of Prayer.

58 *Tudor Parish Documents of the Diocese of York*, ed. J.S. Purvis (Cambridge, 1948), pp. 177, 202.

59 *Rites of Durham*, ed. J.T. Fowler (Surtees Soc., 107, 1903), pp. 27–8. This regretful account, outspoken in its condemnation of the 'lewde and contemptuous wicked persons' responsible for this deed, was written about 1593, and gives a full description of the cross.

60 R.C. Richardson, *Puritanism in North West England* (Manchester, 1972), pp. 122–23, 158. (Since there is no Warton within range of Tarvin, I have taken the reference on p. 123 to relate Wharton, Cheshire.)

61 P.D.A. Harvey, 'Where was Banbury Cross?', *Oxoniensia*, 31 (1966), pp. 83–106; William Potts, *Banbury Cross and the Rhyme* (Banbury, 1930); *A History of the County of Oxford*, ed. Alan Crossley, Victoria History of the Counties of England (London, 1972), x, pp. 7–8, 23, 98.

62 *A briefe & necessary Instruction, Verye needefull to bee knowen of all Housholders* (London, 1572), sigs. Aii r–Aiii r. On this work (*STC*, 6679–6682.3, 6710.5–6724.5), see Patrick Collinson, *Godly People: Essays on English Protestantism and Puritanism* (London, 1983), pp. 297–98, 321–22.

63 Spufford, *Small Books and Pleasant Histories*, pp. 219–20, 240–1, 250–1. Dering's proscribed books would have included lives of St George like those mentioned above.

64 *A Briefe & necessary Instruction*, sig. Aiii (with reference to the 'zealous Ephesians' of Acts 19).

65 John Stow, *Annales, or, A Generall Chronicle of England* (London, 1631–32), p. 694; cf. Stow, *Survey of London*, ed. Kingsford, i, p. 266, and ii, p. 331, which records the lowest tier of images as including the Resurrection, the Virgin Mary, and King Edward the Confessor.

66 Corporation of London Record Office, Repertory 20, fo. 216.

67 Stow, *Survey*; ed. Kingsford, i, pp. 266–67; [G. Abbot], *Cheapside crosse censured and condemned* (London, 1641); *Acts of the Privy Council of England*, n.s. 1542–1631 (London, 1890–1964), xxx, p. 27, and xxxi, p. 44.

68 *The crosses case in Cheapside* ([London], 1642), pp. 1–2; *CSPD, 1641–43*, i, p. 274.

69 John Vicars, *A Sight of ye Transactions of these latter yeares* (London [1646]), p. 21;
     True information of the beginning and cause of all our Troubles (London, 1648), p.
     17; Richard Pennington, *A Descriptive Catalogue of the Etched Work of Wenceslaus
     Hollar, 1607–1677* (Cambridge, 1982), p. 75 (no. 491a).
70 Vicars, *A Sight*, p. 21; Bulstrode Whitelocke, *Memorials of the English Affairs*
     (Oxford, 1853), i, pp. 326, 482.
71 J.W. Burgon, *The Life and Times of Sir Thomas Gresham* (London, 1839), ii, p. 139;
     cf. ii, p. 137.
72 Thomas Thorowgood, *Moderation Justified, and the Lords Being at Hand
     Emproved* (London, 1645), p. 16; quoted by R.W. Ketton-Cremer, *Norfolk in the
     Civil War* (London, 1969), p. 262.

8

Mary

EAMON DUFFY

A convincing account of the religious history of Mary's reign has yet to be
written. More than any other period of Tudor history, the five years from
her accession to her death have been discussed in value-laden terms which
reveal the persistence of a Protestant historiography, authoritatively shaped
by John Foxe, which still hinders a just assessment of the aims and the
achievements of the Marian church. The phrase most commonly used to
describe the religious policy of the reign, the 'Marian reaction', reveals
more about the assumptions of those who use it than about the objectives
of the churchmen to whom it is applied. The limitations and presupposi-
tions of this historiographical tradition can be seen in its most distinguished product, A.G. Dickens's account of the English Reformation.[1]
Dickens devotes twenty-nine pages to the reign: six of them discuss (and
emphasize) adverse public reaction to aspects of Mary's rule, especially her
marriage to Philip II. Eight pages are devoted to the Protestant martyrs, six
pages to the Protestant minorities who continued to practise their religion
during the reign. Only two and a half pages are allocated to a discussion of
the positive impact of the Marian church, and the religious attitudes of the
broad majority of the nation who accepted and welcomed the return of
traditional religion. This brief section is, moreover, entirely confined to the
north of England, and therefore makes no use of the most important piece
of evidence we have for the objectives, methods, and effectiveness of the
Marian church, the returns of Archdeacon Nicholas Harpsfield's visitation
of Kent in 1557, surely the most searching visitation carried out in any

Reprinted from Eamon Duffy, *The Stripping of the Altars: Traditional Religion in England
1400–1580* (New Haven, 1992).

diocese in the Tudor period. In his discussion of Marian use of the press Dickens does not even mention the most characteristic and impressive product of the Marian church's desire to re-educate the nation in the fundamentals of Catholicism, Bonner's *Profytable and necessary doctryne*, and the thirteen *Homilies* compiled by his chaplains, John Harpsfield and Henry Pendleton, usually bound with it, despite the fact that Cardinal Pole in 1556 required every parish priest in England to acquire and preach from this book.

For Dickens the Marian church was, like its queen, 'the prisoner of a sorrowful past',[2] unable to generate policy or initiate reform, just as she was unable to produce an heir. Miserably failing to rise to the polemical challenge set by the 'formidable army of talent' among the Protestant exiles, the regime was trapped in religious and cultural sterility. Instead of creative instruction there were only 'the ceaseless processions made by government order round the streets and churches of London'. Mary and her clergy failed to discover the Counter-Reformation, and, lacking a 'programme of reconversion', had nothing to offer except an unpopular mixture of nostalgia for an irrecoverable past and a version of persecuting Catholicism tainted by association with Spain, certainly nothing which might have evolved into 'a broadly acceptable English Catholicism'.[3]

There is something intrinsically problematic about the notion of a Marian failure to 'discover' the Counter-Reformation, not least because, as yet, there was little that could be called the Counter-Reformation to be discovered. In 1553 the Council of Trent still had much of its most important work to do. Suspended in 1552, it was not to reconvene till both Mary and Pole had been dead for more than three years. When it did so it was to frame what is arguably its most important decree, on the establishment of seminaries, on the model mapped out for Marian England by Pole in 1555.[4] Indeed, the religious priorities in evidence in the attempts to re-establish Catholic belief and practice in Mary's reign closely parallel much that is often thought to be most characteristic of the Counter-Reformation. The leaders of the Marian church did in fact possess a realistic set of objectives, based on a shrewd and fundamentally sound assessment of the impact of reform on the broad mass of the population. Far from pursuing a programme of blind reaction, the Marian authorities consistently sought to promote a version of traditional Catholicism which had absorbed whatever they saw as positive in the Edwardine and Henrician reforms, and which was subtly but distinctively different from the Catholicism of the 1520s. Their programme was not one of reaction but of creative reconstruction, and they did not jettison all that had been done since 1534. The restoration in March 1554 of the ritual calendar as it had been after and not before Henry VIII's prunings is significant, and entirely characteristic.[5] The regime preserved and sought to build on much that had been produced by the reforms of the previous two reigns, and in its teaching did not flinch from adapting and repossessing for Catholic orthodoxy even language reminiscent of Cranmer's communion service.

There is, moreover, considerable evidence that the religious programme of the Marian church was widely accepted, and was establishing itself in the parishes. The Marian visitations have been quarried, even by comparatively sympathetic historians like Philip Hughes, for signs of turmoil and failure. Harpsfield's visitation of Kent in 1557 put the most Protestant county in England under a microscope, and in the process it certainly revealed just how much needed to be done before the restoration of Catholicism was complete. But the returns also reveal the startling extent to which the depredations of the Edwardine regime had already been repaired, and the herculean efforts being made by clergy, wardens, and parishioners to reconstruct the ritual and sacramental framework of traditional religion.[6]

Nor was the effort to reconstruct traditional religion confined to the parish church. Those who have criticized the Marian regime's use of the printing-press have neglected one aspect of the publishing history of the reign which is crucial to any adequate understanding of the religious programme of the Marian church. Thirty-five editions of the Sarum primer survive from Mary's reign, and four of the York primer, compared with a total of seventeen from the reign of Edward. Most of the Marian primers were produced between 1555 and 1558, fifteen editions surviving from 1555 alone. This rate of production swamps that of any earlier period. Quite apart from the demand for Catholic prayer books to which their sheer number testifies, the Marian primers themselves throw a flood of light on the religious priorities of the reign. Over half of the Marian primers printed in England came from a single publisher, John Wayland, or his assigns. The Wayland primers had a distinctive character and content, and carried the regime's stamp of approval. Wayland's first primer in 1555 claimed on its title page to have been 'newly set forth by certayne of the cleargye with the assente of the moste reuerende father in god the Lord Cardinall Pole hys grace: to be only used (al other sette apparte) . . . according to the Quenes hyghnes letters patentes', and his priviliged status as Crown patentee was reiterated in successive editions.[7] While they did not in fact command an effective monopoly of the market, his primers clearly represent the religion approved for lay use in Mary's church, and, as we shall see, their character and content disposes decisively of any idea that that religion was merely reactionary or represented an unreflecting return to the pattern which had prevailed before the break with Rome.

Religious priorities in Marian England

Queen Mary was proclaimed in London on 19 July, and in most of the north by St Mary Magdalene's day, 22 July. It was at once clear that Catholicism would be restored, and some communities proceeded to Counter-Reformation without tarrying for any. At Melton Mowbray the altar stones were put back up immediately, in order to sing Mass and *Dirige* for the king who had put an end to the Mass and prayer for the dead.[8] Robert Parkyn reported that in 'many places of the realme' the Catholic gentry commanded the clergy to sing Mass once more 'with a decentt ordre as haithe ben uside beffore tyme'. But since 'ther was no actt, statutte, proclamation or commandementt sett furthe for the sayme', many clergy 'durstt not be bolde to celebratte in Latten, thowghe ther hertts was wholly enclynede thatt way'.[9] Parkyn was a convinced papalist who had nevertheless conformed under Henry and Edward, and would do so again under Elizabeth. His testimony to both the inclinations of the majority of the clergy and their reluctance to take any initiative without the sanction of 'actt, statutte, proclamation or commandementt' demonstrates the extent to which the Tudor state had succeeded in calling its clergy to heel. But all uncertainty evaporated on 18 August, when the queen issued a proclamation making clear her own desire for the restoration of Catholicism, permitting the practice of both religions till such time 'as further order by common assent may be taken'. She called for national unity, and forbade religious disputation and name-calling or the publication of religious satire or controversy.[10]

This proclamation opened the floodgates of Catholic restoration: less than a week later, on St Bartholomew's Day, 24 August, 'the olde service in the lattin tongue with the masse was begun and sunge in Paules in the Shrowdes . . . and likewise it was begun in 4 and 5 other parishes within the cittie of London, not be commaundement but of the peoples devotion.'[11] By the beginning of September

> ther was veray few parishe churches in York shire but masse was song or saide in Lattin . . . Holly breade and holly watter was gyven, altares was reedifide, pyctures or ymages sett upp, the crosse with the crucifixe theron redye to be borne in procession . . . and yitt all thes cam to passe with owtt compulsion of any actt, statutte, proclamation or law.[12]

It was not of course plain sailing everywhere. London divided on the issue, and elsewhere the presence of strong reformed influences held back the tide of restoration. The Protestant propagandist, John Bland, was challenged by his churchwarden, John Austen, the leading traditionalist in his Kentish parish of Adisham, as early as 3 September. Austen denounced both Bland

and his clerk as 'heretic knaves' who 'have deceived us with this fashion too long'. Yet despite the swell of traditionalist feeling in the parish the 1552 communion service went on being used till the end of November, triggering a series of confrontations, priest against churchwardens, in which the communion table was repeatedly dismantled and re-erected. The issue was finally resolved on Holy Innocents Day 1554, the parish's patronal festival, when, because their own priest would not celebrate the old services, they hired a neighbouring traditionalist to come and sing matins, Mass, and evensong for them. The vicar tried to preach against transubstantiation at the Mass, but was pulled down by the parishioners, led by Austen, imprisoned in a side chapel, and subsequently arrested and taken to Dover for trial, and to his eventual terrible death by fire.[13]

The years of schism had left rifts, in many communities, which ran far deeper than any mere intellectual disagreement. The deputation which appeared before Archdeacon Harpsfield in 1557 to represent the Kentish parish of Brookland included John Knell, almost certainly the son of William Knell, the yeoman of Brookland who had been executed in 1539 for speaking against the supremacy. Also in the deputation was William Warcop, one of those who had informed against him.[14] Religious division was worse in Kent than in any other part of the country outside London, but Mary and her bishops were well aware of the tensions and divisions in parishes everywhere, and were convinced, as Henry had been convinced, that disputation was no way to resolve them. At the heart of the Marian regime's 'failure' to promote a controversial pamphlet war was a considered distrust of the social and religious effects of what Mary's first proclamation called 'the playing of interludes and printing of false fond books, ballads, rhymes and other lewd treatises' meddling in 'question and controversy touching the high points and mysteries of Christian religion'.[15] In the time of schism, Bonner wrote in the preface to the *Profytable and necessary doctryne*:

> Pernicious, and euylle doctryne was sowen, planted and set forth, sometymes by the procedyng preachers sermons, somtymes by ther prynted treatyses, sugred all ouer with lose libertye, (a thing in dede most delectable and pleasaunt unto the fleshe and unto al unruly persons) sometimes by readyng, playing, singing, and other like meanes and new devises, by reason wherof great insolency, disordre, contention, and moch inconvenience, dayly more and more, dyd ensue, to the greate dishonour of God, the lamentable hurte, and destruction, of the subjectes, and the notable reproach, rebuke and slaunder of the hole realme.[16]

The blustering scurrilities of Bale or Becon did not seem to the Marian authorities the best model for establishing truth and stabilizing the religious life of the people, for such 'pernicious and hurtful devices' could only engender 'hatred among the people and discord among the same'.[17] Satire and burlesque are commonly the weapons of those who seek to assail the established order, wedges hammered into the wall to create or exploit a breach. This was how the bishops perceived the position of Protestant controversialists, striving by fair means or foul to shake the religious convictions of centuries. It was the Protestants who needed to make an impression, and who sought to deploy the belly-laugh and the jeer to make their points. The bishops believed that what they needed to do was not to contribute to, but to quieten the babble of alehouse debate. Their objective was to re-establish the order and beauty of Catholic worship and the regular participation of the people in the sacraments, and to underpin it by a regular and solidly grounded pattern of parochial instruction, which would repair the damage of the schism.

This preference for the beauty of holiness over the cut and thrust of debate was not, in any straightforward way, a rejection of the value of scripture-reading or preaching, though there were those, like Gardiner, who were gloomy about the likely impact of either. As we shall see, the Marian church sought to ensure regular parochial preaching and followed Cranmer's precedent in preparing a set of homilies to be used by 'insufficient' preachers. Though the Bibles as well as Erasmus's paraphrases were collected up from the churches during the Marian visitations, Bible-reading or the possession of Bibles was never condemned by the regime. Protestant versions of the Bible were suspect, not English Bibles as such. Pole, as a member of the evangelically minded *Spirituali* of Cardinal Contarini's circle, had a deep sense of the value of scriptural preaching and expounded the Bible daily to his own household. A new English translation of the New Testament was one of the projects agreed and begun at Pole's legatine synod at the end of 1555.[18] But he abhorred religious argument and the spirit of self-sufficiency which he believed indiscriminate Bible-reading by lay people was likely to encourage. Better for the people to absorb the faith through the liturgy, to find an attentive and receptive participation in the ceremonies and sacraments of the Church the grace and instruction on which to found the Christian life. This was the true Catholic way, the spirit of the *parvuli*, the 'little ones' of Christ, for whom penitence, not knowledge, was the true and only way to salvation. The object of preaching and teaching was not to impart knowledge, but to cause the people to lament their sins, seek the healing of the sacraments, and amend their lives. As he told the citizens of London, speaking of the Protestant desire to 'cleave to Scrypture',

The whiche only desyre of ytselfe beynge good, yet not takynge the right waye to the accomplishing of the same, maketh many to falle into heresyes, thinkynge no better nor spedyer waye to be, for to come to the knowledge of God and his law, than by readynge of books, whereyn they be sore deceyved. And yet so yt be done yn his place, and wyth right order and circumstance, yt helpethe muche.[19]

Pole, a true Augustinian, did not think of the ceremonies of the Church as an end in themselves. The true light and life of the soul 'the Spirite of God gyvythe, neyther the ceremonyes whiche the heretykes doe rejecte, nor yet the Scrypture whereunto they doe so cleve'. Yet, he insisted,

> the observatyon of ceremonyes, for obedyence sake, wyll gyve more light than all the readynge of Scrypture can doe, yf the reader have never so good a wytt to understand what he readeth, with the contempt of ceremonyes. But the thynge that gyveth us the veraye light, ys none of them both; but they are most apte to receyve light, that are more obedyent to follow ceremonyes, than to reade.

There could hardly be a more decisive rejection not only of Protestanism, but even of any radical Erasmianism which exalted the text over symbolic or ritual gesture. It was not, however, an obscurantist or ritualist position. It had impeccable precedent in sixteenth-century English Catholic teaching, and much the same emphasis expressed in similar terms can be found in John Fisher's Good Friday sermon of the Crucifix. For Pole the restoration of ceremonies, including the 'endless procession' which have so exasperated historians, was important because participation in Catholic ceremony was symbolic of acceptance of the grace of God in the Church, and of attentiveness to the truths of God there proclaimed: 'of the observation of ceremonyes, begynnethe the verye educatyon of the chylderne of God; as the olde law doyth shewe, that was full of ceremonyes, whiche St Paule callythe *pedagogium in Christum*'. This was a message he read not only in scripture and the tradition of the Church, but in the recent history of England. As God made ceremonies the beginning of the good education of his children,

> so the heretykes makythe this the fyrste poynt of theyre schysme and heresyes, to destroye the unyte of the chyrche by contempte or change of ceremonyes; whiche semyth at the begynnynge nothinge. As yt semyd nothinge here amongste you to take awaye holy water, holy breade, candells, ashes, and palme; but what yt came to, you saw, and felt yt.[20]

In this emphasis on the positive value of ceremony and scarament, Pole and his colleagues, so often accused of lacking a grip of the realities of mid-Tudor England, were certainly more closely in touch with the feelings of the laity at large than were the reformers. Resentment and rejection of ritual change had lain close to the heart of both the Pilgrimage of Grace and the Western Rebellion, but it was not only in the dark corners of the land that men and women felt that the repudiation of time-honoured

ceremonies was symptomatic of more profound and more drastic disconti-
nuities. Procession, pax, holy bread, and holy water were the formal
expressions of the identity of the parish, and the rituals in which peck-
ing-order and precedence were manifested or negotiated. Repudiation of or
abstention from such rituals might be a manifestation of the repudiation of
neighbourly charity and the unity of the community. Ceremonies which, to
the reformers, were unchristian or idolatrous, were somewhere near the
centre of things in the religious and communal instincts of the people. The
parishioners of Stanford in the Vale dated the 'wicked time of schism' not
from Henry's reign, but from 1547, when 'all godly ceremonyes and good
usys were taken out of the Church'.[21] Three years before Mary's accession
John Ponet complained bitterly of the universal grumbling against the
reform, as men said to one another 'Believe as your forefathers have
done before you . . . follow ancient customs and usages.'[22] In re-establish-
ing the old ceremonial the Marian church was not engaged in irrelevant
antiquarianism, but playing one of its strongest cards.

Not that the Marian authorities were unaware of the need to teach the
people once more to appreciate and value the ceremonies which had been
proscribed by Cranmer and the Council under Edward. Behind the repudiation of ceremonial by the reformers lay a radically different conceptual
world, a world in which text was everything, sign nothing. The sacramental universe of late medieval Catholicism was, from such a perspective,
totally opaque, a bewildering and meaningless world of dumb objects and
vapid gestures, hindering communication. That spirit of determined non-
comprehension was very much in evidence in Marian England. It had been
the lifeblood of Lollardy, and had been enormously encouraged by the
spread of reformed teaching and practice. On Palm Sunday 1556 Laurence
Burnaby, a parishioner of Brampton in the diocese of Lincoln, cried out
when the vicar smote the door with the foot of the processional Cross and
the choir sang 'let him enter, the King of Glory', 'What a sport have we
towards. Will our vicar ronne at the quintine with God Almightie?'[23]

Accordingly, it was realized that any secure restoration of Catholicism
must be based on a long-term process of catechesis which would enable lay
people to understand and benefit from the ceremonies of the Church.
Bonner, who set the pattern here for the rest of the Marian episcopate,
required his clergy regularly to 'declare, set forth, and instruct the people
the true meaning of the ceremonies of the Church'. So holy bread was to

> put us in remembrance of unity. . . like as the bread is made of many
> grains, and yet but one loaf, and . . . to put us also in remembrance
> of the housel . . . which the people in the beginning of Christ's
> Church did oftener receive than they do use now in these days to do.

Similarly, the bearing about of the pax on Sundays was to be explained as a
reminder of the peace which Christ left his disciples, 'but also of that

peace, that Christ by his death purchased for the people'. In addition, four times a year the clergy were to preach longer sermons in which they declared to the people

> the signification and true meaning of all other laudable and godly ceremonies used of old time in this Church of England to the best of their power, in such sort, that the people may perceive what is meant and signified by the same, and also know and understand how and in what manner they ought to use and accept them for their own edifying.[24]

The precedent for such explanations was of course Henrician. It had been enjoined in the Ten Articles, and Latimer had adapted medieval materials to provide similar 'declarations' for his diocese.[25] 'Declaration' of the ceremonies had been a much contested point in the early 1540s, traditionalist clergy frequently refusing to make any such declaration and emphasizing instead the apotropaic character of sacramentals. On the other hand, 'declaration' had been one of the devices by which Henrician conservatives like Tunstall and Bonner had staved off the demise of the sacramentals and 'laudable ceremonies' whose abolition Cranmer and others sought. The 'Rationale of Ceremonial' (c. 1540) was the most sustained example of that policy, and some of the model 'declarations' Bonner provided for his clergy to use in Mary's reign closely resemble sections of the Rationale. The Marian church's adoption of the policy of declaration therefore demonstrates not only an awareness of a real pastoral need, but a willingness to absorb the lessons of the past, even when it meant canonizing methods developed in schism, and distancing itself, if only by silence, from the apotropaic understanding of the use of sacramentals.

There were in fact many aspects of the Henrician and Edwardine religious changes which the Marian church sought to preserve, from the provision of registers of births, deaths, and marriages, and a church chest, to an emphasis on basic religious instruction in English. Bonner also ordered his priests to preach quarterly sermons, 'to wit on the Sunday or solemn feast', recapitulating the essentials of the faith – the Creed, the Commandments, the avoidance of the seven deadly sins, the obligations of the seven works of mercy, and the seven sacraments. Pole required the clergy to preach every holy day, and before every sermon plainly to recite 'and diligently teach' the Lord's Prayer, the Hail Mary, the Creed, and the Ten Commandments in English, 'exhorting their parishioners to teach the same likewise to their children at home'. Unlearned clergy 'being no preachers', were to apply themselves to the study of holy scripture, and to give an annual account of their progress in study to their bishops. In the meantime, they were to be sure to catechize the 'youth of the parishioners'.[26] Addressing herself to the problem of clergy unable to preach,

Mary required each of her bishops to set out 'an uniform order . . . by homilies . . . for the good instruction and teaching of the people'. This, the expedient devised by Cranmer for a non-preaching clergy, was to elicit from Bonner in 1555 one of the most remarkable books of the reign, a neglected masterpiece of Tudor catechesis, *A Profytable and necessary doctryne, with certayne homelies adioyned . . . for the instruction and enformation of the people.*[27]

The *Profytable doctryne* is a vividly written exposition of the fundamentals of the faith, structured round the Apostles' Creed, the Ten Commandments, the seven deadly sins, the seven sacraments, the Lord's Prayer, and the Hail Mary. It was therefore intended to supply the parish clergy with the material they needed to fulfil the catechetical programme which Bonner had enjoined on them. Remarkably, Bonner took the *King's Book* of 1543, round which the traditionalists had rallied in the last year's of Henry's reign, as the framework on which he and his chaplains built the book. By preserving as much as he could of the *King's Book* he ensured a continuity of tone between the doctrine taught under Mary and that 'observed and kept in the latter time of King Henry the Eighth', an important factor in the retention of public confidence. This was a crucial perception. Traditionalists in Edward's reign had rallied round the *King's Book*, and however defective it might appear to the eyes of Marian orthodoxy, it could not lightly be set aside. In fact, however, the *Profytable doctryne* is an incomparably better catechetical tool than the rather lack-lustre *King's Book*. Not only was much in the later book new – the entire section on the seven deadly sins, on the Hail Mary, the treatment of the Second Commandment with its apparent prohibition of images, and the article of the Creed which dealt with 'The Holy Catholic Church' – but even those sections which retained much of the substance of the *King's Book* were sharpened and turned to account on behalf of the new regime. One of the central concerns of the *Profytable doctryne* was to reaffirm the centrality of the Church in every aspect of the Christian life, and in dozens of additions, large and small, this message was hammered home. So, at the end of the section on the third article of the Creed, 'which was conceived by the holy Ghost', Bonner introduces a striking quotation from Augustine, making the point that 'Christe is borne of a virgin that we mighte be borne of the wombe of the Churche being a vyrgyn'. The discussion on the Church in the ninth article of the Creed now included an extended quotation from Augustine on the unity of the Church, designed to strike an English reader by its applicability to the schism:

Take away, saith he . . . the beame of the sonne from the body of the sonne, the unitie of the lyght, can not suffer no division: break a boughe from the tree, the bough so broken, can floryshe and budde no more: cut of the river from the spring, the ryver so cut of, dryeth up.[28]

In the exposition of the way in which the Commandments were to be kept, Bonner introduced a passage from II Maccabees 7 – 'We are ready rather to die, then to breake or transgresse the lawes of God which oure fathers kepte' – and added:

> But of late dayes, in the tyme of our pestiferous scisme, the new broached brethren, rather woulde tumble to hel headlonge, then they would doo as the catholyke Churche from Chrystes tyme hetherto hath done, concernynge the lawes of God, and the rytes of the sayde catholyke churche.[29]

Nor did Bonner hesitate to wrench the reformers' weapons from their hands and turn them on them. The invocation of the Lollard tradition as offering a witness against Catholic error even before the Reformation was a favourite controversial ploy by reformers. In the newly composed section on images, Bonner cited in support of his position a Lollard version of the Commandments, made 'almost eight score yeare agone . . . even in time of heresye', thereby playing Lollards against Protestants. He included in his text an offer to show the original manuscript to 'any well dysposyd persons who shall desyre it'.[30] The *Profytable doctryne*, however, is much more than an attempt to score debating points against the reformers. It is a comprehensive and theologically skilful textbook, far more richly supported with quotations from scripture and the Fathers than the *King's Book*, yet not clogged with technical terms or an excess of learning. Generous quotation from and exegesis of key passages from the New Testament, such as the story of the Annunciation, must have been particularly valuable to parish priests of limited learning. Bonner's book successfully provided both an exposition of the essentials of Christian catechesis and an easily accessible collection of controversial and hortatory material designed to impress on the people the evils of the schism and the privileges of the restoration of Catholic communion.

Alongside the *Profytable doctryne* and designed to supplement it, was published a set of thirteen *Homilies*, largely the work of Bonner's chaplains, John Harpsfield and Henry Pendleton. Most of these were concerned with the great controversial topics raised by the schism and its aftermath – the nature and authority of the Church, the place of the papacy, the presence of Christ in the Sacrament of the altar. But several of the *Homilies* deal with more fundamental issues: the creation and fall, the nature of Christ's redeeming work, and two, on the comparatively uncontroversial topics of the misery of mankind and charity, were slightly revised versons of the *Homilies* of those titles from Cranmer's book. Their adoption into the Marian *Homilies* is remarkable, and another example of the regime's willingness to absorb and use whatever remained of value in the Edwardine reform. The homily 'On the miserie of all mankynde', in particular, is striking for its uncompromising Christocentricity, couched in language which, to listeners accustomed to six years of Cranmer's prayer book, must have been inescapably reminiscent of the theology and even the phrasing of the prayer of consecration:

> He is that hyghe and everlastynge priest, whyche hathe offred him selfe to God, when he instituted the sacrament of the Aultar, and once for all, in a bloody sacrifyce, doone upon the crosse, with which obla-tion, he hath made perfect for evermore, theim that are sanctifyed. He is the mediatoure, betweene God and man, which payed our raunsome to God, wyth hys owne bloude, and wyth that, hath cleansed us from synne.[31]

That emphasis on Christ and his Passion was a consistent characteristic of the Marian church. It goes a long way towards explaining the phrasing and theological ethos of many Marian wills, which have been taken to reflect Protestant leanings, but which find abundant justification in pas-sages of this sort, supplied to the Marian clergy for use in catechesis and preaching.

The *Profytable doctryne*, together with the accompanying *Homilies*, is well able to stand comparison not only with the *King's Book*, but with Cranmer's *Homilies*, which it equals in theological grip, and excels in liveliness and range of illustrative material. Its value was immediately recognized. Pole planned the production of a similar work for the whole of the country, but pending its production he ordered Bonner's book and the *Homilies* to be bought and preached from by the parish clergy through-out his metropolitan jurisdiction. The wardens of Morebath paid 2*s*.9*d* for their copy in 1556.[32] Bonner's book embodied much that was most central to the Marian regime, in particular its desire to maintain continuity with the Henrician past, but to reform the Henrician legacy into an orthodox Catholicism. Pole's legatine synod decided in December 1554 to produce a formulary of faith for the English Church: it is not without significance that the basis for the new formulary was to be the *King's Book*. The sections of the formulary were duly allocated, and work began. As with the proposed New Testament translation, nothing came of the scheme but Bonner's book indicates the sort of product which would have emerged. Nothing about it suggests an imaginative or controversial exhaustion. Only the death of the queen, and the Elizabethan rehabilitation and enlargement of Cranmer's collection, drove Bonner's work into an unde-served oblivion.[33]

The Marian primers

With the restoration of Catholicism, the reappearance of the traditional Sarum primer was a foregone conclusion. Henry's primer had run through more than two dozen editions, and had been used well into Edward's reign. Despite its very real reformed character, it preserved enough of the characteristics and materials of the traditional primers to be acceptable to conservative lay people, trained to pray on the old books, once the supply of these old books had been dried up by royal fiat. Successive editions of Henry's book had undergone some modification in Edward's reign, but the distinctive Edwardine primer, issued only in 1553, had effectively jettisoned every remaining link with the primers current before the break with Rome. It contained neither the Hours of the Virgin, the *Dirige*, the Commendations, nor the Psalms or prayers of the Passion. Instead it consisted essentially of prayer book matins and evensong, arranged with readings for the days of the week, and a large collection of 'Sundry Godly Prayers for Divers Purposes', including prayers for special classes and occupations of men – masters and servants, landlords and tenants, single men, wives, house-holders, and servants. Heavily didactic and penitential in tone, it is light years away from the traditional primers, and is an inescapably Protestant book.[34]

There was therefore a yawning gulf in the market which entrepreneurs rushed to fill on the accession of a Catholic queen. Printers in both London and France quickly produced editions of the traditional Sarum primer in Latin in 1554.[35] Freelance primers of this sort, in both English and Latin, were to continue to appear throughout Mary's reign, most of them printed in Rouen, but some of the best of them by the London-based Catholic printer, Robert Caley, who had worked in exile at Rouen during Edward's reign. Mary's government had no objection to the appearance of such primers, all of which were prefectly orthodox, but the regime was as alert as its predecessors to the importance of the primers for the settlement of religion, and in June 1555 there appeared the first edition of an officially approved primer, in English and Latin, published by John Wayland. Unlike Caley, Wayland was no exile for religion. He had functioned in London throughout the Edwardine period, had been the publisher responsible for Hilsey's *Manual*, and his assigns would later be responsible for the first Elizabethan primer. Presumably he was chosen to print the official Marian primer because of his proven reliability and established connections with government.[36]

Henry's primer had been, effectively, an act of state, as much an official product of reform as the English litany or the revised calendar. The precise status of the first Marian Wayland primer is less straightforward. It was backed up not by a royal proclamation forbidding subjects to use any other, but by letters patent from Philip and Mary, giving Wayland or his assigns exclusive rights to print all primers 'which by us our heirs, successors or by our clergy by our assent shall be authorised set forth and devised for to be used of all our loving subjects'.[37] Nevertheless, the description on the title page of the primer as 'An uniforme and Catholyke Prymer . . . newly set forth by certayne of the cleargye with the assente of the moste reuerende father in god the Lorde Cardinall Pole hys grace: to be only used (al other sette aparte) of al the kyng and Quenes maiesties louinge subiectes' clearly represented strong official endorsement of the book. Wayland produced at least ten other editions of this primer. All reiterated the royal grant of a monopoly on the printing of primers, but none of the subsequent editions carried the claim to be the one 'uniforme and Catholyke Prymer', or the reference to Pole's endorsement. It is clear that, provided the books concerned were clear of heresy, Mary's government did not seek to impose the stranglehold on devotional publishing that Henry's or Edward's Council had done. Nonetheless, there is no doubting the special status of the Wayland primers as an expression of the official religion favoured by the regime, and in fact they dominated the market, no other publisher producing so many editions of a single type.[38]

The Wayland primers follow the pattern of the reformed or rather modified Sarum primers current in the early 1540s, traditional in content but with the main text in English, and the Latin version confined to smaller print in the margins. They are sparingly and conventionally illustrated with large initials containing scenes from the life of Christ and traditional subjects such as David and Bathsheba at the beginning of the penitential Psalms. The *Dirige* has the image of Death with sceptre and pickaxe. The main contents are entirely traditional – the Little Hours of the Virgin, with the customary suffrages to the saints including Thomas Becket, the penitential Psalms, the litany, the *Dirige*, the Psalms of the Passion. Wayland put at the end of the book the 'Form of Confession' printed in some traditional primers in the 1530s, and the reappearance of this element of the Tudor primer after almost twenty years' absence was a notable indicator of the Marian church's strong emphasis on the value of the sacrament of penance. The primer also includes traditional devotional material like the 'Fifteen Oes', prayers to be used at the elevation, and St Bernard's verses.[39]

Despite the traditional contents, this section of the Wayland primer was strikingly different from the primers of the 1520s and early 1530s, for it lacks any indulgence rubrics and has none of the 'goodly painted prefaces' containing miraculous legends or promises so scorned by the reformers. The nearest the primer gets to any of these is the single sentence 'To our blessed Lady against the pestilence' before the hymn *Stella Coeli extirpavit*, an invocation to the Virgin against the plague. Moreover, the Wayland primer is almost entirely lacking in the elaborate affective prayers on the

Passion of Christ, and the many prayers to the Virgin, the saints, and the Blessed Sacrament which were so dominant a feature of the primers of the 1520s. Marian devotion is strongly present in the hymns and prayers of the Little Hours, of course, but it is not allowed to proliferate through the rest of the book. The elevation prayer provided is a translation of the *Ave Verum Corpus*; once again, the lush elaboration of the Eucharistic devotion of the earlier primers has been cut away. The book, while having all the warmth and tenderness innate in the Little Hours, prayers like the 'Fifteen Oes', and scriptural catenas like St Bernard's verses, is much more austerely and theologically 'correct' than the pre-Reformation books. This might be readily enough explained by the fact that Wayland's copy text was probably a primer produced for the English market at Rouen in 1536, in which this process of pruning had first been carried out. But the choice of the copy text is itself interesting. The Rouen primer of 1536 was the first straightforward translation of the Sarum primer, without the Protestant agenda evident in later reworkings. The Marian editor selected the most Catholic of the English primers available.[40] The sparer tone and less perfervid atmosphere of Wayland's primer therefore seems deliberate, and this is borne out by the fact that every other primer produced in Mary's reign, whether in English or Latin, shares the same silence about indulgences or miraculous legends. The wonder-world of charm, pardon, and promise in the older primers had gone for ever.

Yet more striking, however, are the non-traditional contents of Wayland's primers, the section of the book which displays most careful editorial treatment by the 'cleargy' spoken of on the title page. After the usual preliminaries of calendar and almanac, the primer has a series of prayers for each morning of the week, quite distinct from the liturgical prayers of the Little Hours. These morning prayers include Erasmus's famous 'O Lorde Jesus Christ, which art the bright sonne of the worlde, ever rising, never falling', and at least one, the prayer for Friday morning, was adapted from a traditional Latin prayer, *Piisime deus et clementissime pater.*[41] But most of them seem to have been composed specially for the book, and they illustrate the extent to which the clerical editors had absorbed the tone and style of mid-Tudor piety familiar from the prayers in Henry's primer. One of the most characteristic of these prayers is the long 'general morning prayer' into which is woven the Creed in English and the Lord's Prayer, combining devotion and catechesis. It also displays the striking emphasis on redemption through the Passion of Christ which we have already noted in the *Homilies*:

> Onely this is my comfort oh heavenlie father, that thou dyddest not spare thy onely derely beloved sonne . . . Wherefore through the meryte of hys most bitter death and passion, and thorough his innocent bloud shedyng, I beseche thee oh heavenly father that

thou wilt vouchsafe to be gracious and merciful unto me, to forgeve
and pardon me all my synnes, to lighten my heart with thy holye
spirite, to renue, confyrme, and strengthen me with a right and
perfect faythe, and to enflame me in love towardes the and my
neighboure, that I may hensforth with a willing and a glad hearte
walke as it be commith me, in thy most Godly and blessed comman-
dements, and so glorifie and prayse the everlastingly; and also that I
may with a free conscience and a quiet heart in all maner of temptat-
cions, afflictions, or necessities, and even in the very panges of death,
crie boldely and faythfully unto thee, and say: I beleve in God the
father almighty maker of heaven and earth.[42]

One final feature of the Wayland primers calls for comment. Just before
the 'Form of Confession' with which the book ends, the editors inserted
'Fyftie devoute prayers contayning severally what so ever is mete to be
prayed for, as by their tytles doth appere'. In fact there were more than
sixty of these prayers, and like the collection of morning prayers they are
printed in English only. They include characteristically Catholic elements –
prayers before and after reception of the Sacrament, and prayers for the
custody of the five bodily wits. There are also a number of prayers
traditionally found in pre-Reformation primers which had been edited
out of the books of the 1530s and 1540s, like the prayer of St Bede. But
the remarkable feature of these prayers is the fact that nearly two dozen of
them come from the collection of 'Godly Prayers' in Henry's primer, and
some of them are by Protestant authors like Wolfgang Capito and Thomas
Becon. Many of the prayers are scriptural paraphrases published by reformers like Taverner in the 1530s. The editor even retained the Protestant
rewriting of one of the most beloved Catholic prayers to the Virgin, the
Salve Regina, as a prayer to Christ, 'Hail heavenly kynge, father of mercy'.
These inclusions are deliberate, for the editor has not simply copied *en
bloc* from the king's primer to fill his space. About a third of the earlier
collection was omitted, some of them very evidently for their reformed
tone and content. It was not only Protestant prayers which suffered in this
purge. Vives's prayer agains the Devil survives. Erasmus's prayer for the
Church does not, while a number of those included have been reworked to
make them more securely Catholic, emphasizing ascetic or sacramental
elements, for example.[43]

Later editions of this primer add one further element, 'a playne and
godly treatise concerninge the Masse, and the blessed Sacrament of the
aulter, for the instruccyon of the unlerned and symple people'.[44] This brief
anonymous treatise, which was also published separately, appeared at the
end of at least three editions of Wayland's primer. Its title is somewhat
misleading, since, although it is clearly written, it makes some demands on
its readers, and was apparently aimed at intelligent middle-class lay

people, the citizens of London and other towns who formed the buying public for many of these primers.[45] The reformers in the 1530s, like William Marshall and John Hilsey, had included extended sections of polemical material attacking Catholic doctrine in their primers, and to that extent the Wayland ones followed their example. But the Protestant polemic had been incorporated into the text of the primer, mixing devotion with argument. This would have run counter to the whole spirit of the Marian reconstruction, and so the polemical material, more sober and reasoned in tone than Marshall's diatribes, comes in the form of a separate treatise at the end of the book. Nevertheless, its presence there indicates the sensitivity of the Marian authorities to the need to defend and explain the Catholic doctrine of the Real Presence and the Sacrifice, so often attacked in the previous two reigns, to the literate laity.

The Wayland primers are a remarkable and intelligent blend of old and new. In them both traditional and reformed materials have been pressed into service to a Catholicism in which the ancient pieties, to Sacrament and to saint, have their place, but where they are subordinated to a strong emphasis on the centrality of the Passion of Christ. The emergence of a genre of sober and scriptural prayers adapted to the daily circumstances of life, already evident in pre-Reformation writers like Whitford, but developed more fully by Protestant devotional authors like Taverner and Becon, has been accepted and assimilated. The new prayers in the Wayland primers show that the clerical editors were capable of producing impressive examples of their own. Once again, the application of the word 'reactionary' to this religion seems inappropriate, for the Wayland primers testify to the resilience, adaptability, and realism of the Marian attempt to restore Catholicism to the people. Professor Dickens has doubted whether the Marian Church seemed likely to evolve a distinctive and 'broadly acceptable English Catholicism'. On the contrary, that is precisely what is on display in these officially endorsed books.[46]

The programme in the parishes

The Marian authorities, in addition to the perennial task of teaching the fundamentals of the faith, were alert to the need for a programme of doctrinal instruction designed to combat heresy, to quicken zeal for the sacraments, and to encourage a loyalty to the Church and its traditions and rites. They were also concerned to promote a renewed and reformed Catholic devotion, which took account of the positive elements in the reformed piety of the 1540s, shorn of the excesses which had been a target of clerical purists even before the Reformation. The various episcopal and metropolitan injunctions concerning catechesis and preaching, Bonner's *Profytable and necessary doctryne*, and the Wayland primers, all of them ignored by most of those who have written about the Marian Church, are the concrete expressions of those objectives. A dimension of the Marian religious programme which has received more recognition, though usually adversely, is the reconstruction of the material and ritual structures of Catholicism in the parishes. This was where royal religious policy impinged most directly on the people, and it is in the effects of this parochial reconstruction that we can most clearly discern the responsiveness of the nation to the restoration of traditional religion.

The programme of practical reconstruction was, once again, mapped out by Bonner in the articles devised for the visitation of his diocese begun in the autumn of 1554, and in the Injunctions subsequently based on them.[47] Bonner's articles were adopted by other bishops as the basis of their own visitations, and were closely imitated in Pole's articles for his metropolitan visitation in 1556.[48] Bonner's programme was minutely detailed and dauntingly comprehensive. The articles and injunctions are heavily indebted not only to the legacy of medieval canons and visitation procedures, but to the royal and episcopal Injunctions produced since the commencement of the schism. The formidable apparatus of religious enforcement evolved within the reform was now to be turned against it.

Much in the articles replicates material found in every episcopal visitation of any period – queries about clerical residence, dress, diligence, and morals, the last issue being of course heightened and complicated by the need to separate married clergy from their 'concubines, or women taken for wives'. There were questions about the schoolmasters and midwives, about the practice of sorcery and the payment of tithes. But the main thrust of the articles was to tackle the legacy of the schism in all its dimensions. The best-known aspect of this is of course the search for heresy. Bonner wanted to know about the doctrine taught by the clergy, about the circulation of seditious or heretical books, about Protestant conventicles, about priests who administered any rites in English or held prayer book services in secret. He wanted to know the names of any of the laity who, at the sacring time 'do hang down their heads, hide themselves behind pillars, turn away their faces, or depart out of the church'. He asked about those who had eaten flesh on the traditional fasts or vigils. He asked for the names and addresses of any printers and booksellers who were circulating the prayer book or *Homilies*, or 'slanderous books, ballads or plays, contrary to Christian religion'. He also wanted to know of any lay people who expounded or declared scripture without episcopal permission, and any who 'murmured, grudged or spoke against' the Mass, the sacraments, or sacramentals such as holy bread, holy water, palms, ashes, or any 'laudable and godly ceremony', especially prayer for the dead, or who 'made noise, jangled, talked, or played the fool' in church in service time, or mocked or threatened priests when preaching or celebrating sacraments or sacramentals in the traditional forms. He asked for the names of any women who declined shrift and housel before a confinement, or who did not come to be churched afterwards. And he wanted to know of any lay people who tried to prevent the priest baptizing their children in the traditional way by immersion in the font, 'being yet strong, and able to abide and suffer it', seeking instead to have the child 'in the clothes, and only to be sprinkled with a few drops of water'.

In the detection of heresy, parochial conformity was crucial. Bonner wanted special vigilance to ensure that every parishioner confessed to their own curate in Lent and received the Blessed Sacrament at Easter. He wanted notification of any who refused to take part in parochial rituals like the procession on Sunday, the reception of holy bread or the kissing of the pax. Bonner even demanded to know whether any good singer, who had been a choir-man in Henry's or Edward's reign, now 'since the setting forth and renewing of the old service in the Latin tongue, absent and withdraw himself from the choir'. One imagines that this particular measure might have been counter-productive, and Henry Clerke, in trouble in the Lincoln diocese during Pole's metropolitan visitation in 1556 for singing the *Sursum Corda* in a pub, was probably one of these reluctant choristers.[49]

The articles and injunctions also addressed themselves to the physical aftermath of the schism. Texts or pictures painted on the walls and which 'chiefly and principally do tend to the maintenance of carnall liberty' by attacking fasting, clerical celibacy, the value of good works, or the veneration of the Blessed Sacrament, were to be blotted out. The Edwardine spoliation had stripped the churches of the essential ornaments used for Catholic worship; these were now to be replaced. Every church was to have a high altar of stone, covered with a properly consecrated altar-slab, and not the hastily pulled up grave-slabs which many churchwardens had set there in the first flurry of restoration. The parishioners were to provide forthwith all the books, vestments, and vessels needed for the services. The list is worth setting out at length, for it gives some idea of the sheer scale of the task the parishes now faced.

Every parish had to have the following: a holy water stoup and sprinkler set by the church door, a legend for the lessons at matins, an antiphoner, a gradual and a psalter for the musical parts of the service, an ordinal or 'pie' to guide the priest in the right performance of the services, a missal, a manual containing the occasional Offices like burials and baptisms, a processional, a chalice and paten and a set of cruets, a high Mass set of vestments for priest, deacon, and subdeacon, and a cope 'with all the appurtenances', altar frontals and hangings, three linen cloths, two for covering the altar and one for the priest's hands, three surplices and a rochet for the clerk, a processional Crucifix with candles, a cross to be carried before corpses, a censer and an incense boat, a bell to ring at the sacring, a pyx with 'an honest and decent cover' to reserve the Sacrament, a great veil to hang across the chancel before the altar in Lent, banners and handbells to carry in Rogation week, a holy water vessel to carry about, a great candlestick for the paschal candle, a font with a lockable cover, a chrismatory for the holy oils, and a large Rood and Rood-loft. There was also to be a lamp burning before the Blessed Sacrament.[50]

All these, of course, had been stripped out of the churches, many of them only a year before. The Edwardine commissioners had been instructed to leave in each church a cup, a bell, a covering for the table, and a surplice. Though many churches certainly held on to a good deal more, few, at any rate in Bonner's diocese, can have escaped without the confiscation of vital and expensive equipment; none in the south-east can still have had its images. Agitated deputations of wardens and parishioners lobbied Bonner to tell him that he was demanding the impossible, that all of this could not be provided quickly, but he remained adamant, and the surviving records of his visitation, and the glimpses of it we catch in Foxe, show him forcing the pace with all the vigour of his excitable temperament. He was assisted by one of the ablest figures in the Marian Church, his vicar-general Nicholas Harpsfield, who as Archdeacon of Canterbury in succession to Cranmer's brother Edmund was to carry out the exhaustive Canterbury visitation of 1557. London was to be Harpsfield apprenticeship.[51]

The London churchwardens who protested about Bonner's articles need not be suspected of doing so out of a Protestant desire to obstruct the reconstruction, though some certainly were sympathetic to the reform. Two things emerge with absolute clarity, not only from the evidence of the London visitation, but from churchwardens' accounts and visitation records from all over the country in the years from 1554 onwards. The first is the enormous financial and organizational strain the reconstruction put on parishes; the second is the energy and for the most part the promptness with which parishes set about complying. The work was to go on to the very end of the reign, and there were many parishes in which important items remained unprovided even in 1557 and 1558. But in most of these cases the slow pace of implementation seems to be due to financial or logistical difficulties, not Protestant resistance. The work of destruction could be carried out quickly and cheaply; rebuilding was another matter, not least because the financial returns of dispersal were entirely inadequate for the costs of replacement. St John's church in Winchester had sold off a hundredweight and a half of liturgical books as parchment waste in 1550, and had received nine shillings for them. To provide a single set of cheaply printed paper copies of the essential books required for the restored liturgy would have cost several times as much, always assuming that copies could be got, in competition with other churches.[52] A half-ton altar slab could be levered up and laid in the floor or smashed in hours, a gilded and carved Rood-loft with its images could be reduced to splinters or ashes in an afternoon. To replace such massive or elaborate structures, to commission, carve, set up, and decorate the images demanded resources of manpower, cash, and availability of craftsmen which parishes could not readily command. Yet command them they mostly did, and the implications of that costly compliance have not sufficiently been registered.

Ronald Hutton, after a recent survey of the 134 surviving sets of churchwardens' accounts for Mary's reign, concluded that there was 'a considerable homogeneity in the process of Catholic restoration'. By the end of 1554 all had rebuilt a high altar, obtained vestments and copes, some or all of the utensils of Catholic worship, and some or all of the books. During the rest of the reign this list was steadily added to, and most churches acquired a Rood with Mary and John, images of one or more saints, a side altar, Rood lights, banners, hangings, and a canopy for processions of the Blessed Sacrament. Though most of these items were compulsory, 'most of the parishes in the sample decorated their churches more than the legal minimum required'.[53] The progress of reconstruction at Stanford in Berkshire is fairly representative of this process. In the financial year 1553–4 the wardens recorded the last stage of the Edwardine dissolution, twenty pence for their expenses in carrying their church goods to Edward's commissioners. In the same year the Marian reconstruction begins, with payments for setting up the high altar, for watching the Easter sepulchre, and 'in expences goyng abroad to seke . . . the churche stuffe that was lackyng'. In 1554 they sold off a 'tabull wt a frame the whiche served in the churche for the comunion in the wycked tyme of sysme', and bought and had blessed two chalices, a pyx, and two corporases. Five loads of stone were bought for building the altars, and a painter was paid ten pence 'for payntting a lyttull Rode'. The wardens claimed six pence in expenses for a journey to Oxford 'to seeke bokes', and a carpenter was paid 3s.4d for erecting a lockable shrine or tabernacle on the altar, to keep the Blessed Sacrament in, Pole's legatine synod having decreed that this was the method of reservation to be followed. The financial pressures on them are confirmed by the fact that the pyx they provided was of pewter, as was their chrismatory. In the same year they bought the prayers to be said for the Pope, a whipcord and silk cover for the pyx, and some cords to draw up the trendle of lights before the Rood and the cloth which was drawn up before the Rood during the Palm Sunday liturgy. In 1555 they bought one volume of the breviary, a parchment processional, and 'an olde manuell in paper', both of these probably second-hand. They also traded in an old latten basin in part-exchange for a better one to be used for godparents to wash their hands at christenings. In 1556 the wardens travelled to Abingdon to commission a carved Rood, Mary, and John for the Rood-loft. The process of reconstruction was finished off in 1558 when they had a cross-shaped frame made to carry the candles during the singing of *Tenebrae*.[54]

Stanford was a traditionally minded community. The wardens seem to have dragged their feet about destroying their new Rood on Elizabeth's accession, and had to spend eight pence to certify their eventual compliance to the archdeacon. The parish was in trouble again in 1564 for carrying banners in Rogation week, and in 1566 for tolling the dead-bell all night on All Souls' Eve. They had started the reconstruction of the old religion in Mary's reign at once, by re-erecting their altars and resuming observance of traditional ceremonies like the sepulchre, and had thankfully sold off the Edwardine communion table. Yet the process of rebuilding took them four years, and there are signs of forced economy in much that they did. The parishes of Marian England were feeling the pinch, but they were spending substantially to re-equip themselves for Catholic worship.

The Crown and the bishops were well aware of these financial problems. The most obvious way of easing them was to recover as much as possible of the confiscated goods, many of them still in the hands of the commissioners or their delegates. The commissioners for the Weald of Kent were being hounded in 1556 for the return of goods to the churches in their remit, and were anxiously trying to recover them from the Crown officials to whom in turn they had surrendered them.[55] Pole and the other bishops instituted searches for withholders of church goods who had acquired them illicitly in Edward's reign. Though little plate appears to have been returned, many churches succeeded in securing some at least of their ornaments. Ashburton in Devon recovered its vestments and a cope, though they had to send wardens to London and Exeter to do so. The wardens of Prescot, Lancashire, recorded the outlay of thirty-one shillings in 1554 'in expences in the paroch besynes by the space of xxii days at Candlemas terme, for the obtaynynge of an indenture and oblygation that the churche and chappell goodes shuld be restored to that use wych they wher fyrst gyuen vnto'. The fact that there were no large expenditures for replacements over the next two years, only a number of minor repairs, suggests that they succeeded.[56] At Leverton in Lincolnshire the wardens spent two shillings in 1555 'for our horsse and or selfes when we sewed for the vestments' at Lincoln.[57]

Individuals who had acquired church goods were similarly pursued, and they or their executors were often successfully forced to regurgitate their gains or a cash equivalent. The parishioners of Luton pursued the heirs of a former churchwarden, Edward Crawley, for £6.13s.4d worth of goods which he had sold but not accounted for in Edward's reign; the executors gave the church ornaments to the value of the contested sum. The widow of a local gentleman who had acquired two chalices, a coat of crimson velvet 'called Jhus cope', an organ, assorted vestments, a bell, and a hundredweight of lead from the parish church of Houghton Conquest was forced or persuaded to carry out repairs and give vestments and ornaments to the value of £32.6s.8d.[58]

By no means all of this was enforced. Many individuals gave or sold back very cheaply the goods they had acquired. In some cases the returned goods were probably bought in the first place to preserve them, in others the buyers may have acquired them as a speculation, but either way, in 1554 and 1555 they came back. So at Ludlow Thomas Season was paid an earnest of 12 shillings against a sum of 26s.8d 'due to hym for 4 copes bought of hym and restored to the churche'.

Many who had acquired church goods in Edward's reign loaned them back to the churches. The parishioners of Cadney in Lincolnshire borrowed a vestment, a cope, an alb, a stole, a chrismatory, and much else from a local gentleman. The curate of Firsby loaned his parish all the liturgical books they needed, which he had probably bought in 1550. Sir James Bancroft loaned a vestment, a Mass book, and a pax to the parish of Gayton le Marsh. Stephen Bond loaned the parishioners of Greatford a pair of cruets and a pax.[59] Parishes with duplicate items might help out poorer communities. The parishioners of Saleby loaned a handbell to the parishioners of Beesby, though Saleby itself had borrowed a cope, a vestment, and a corporas cloth from assorted parishioners, and a Mass book and a manual from the vicar.[60] As might be expected, clergy were the commonest source of such loans. Many parishes were spared the expense of re-equipping themselves with vestments or books because their priest was willing to use his own personal property, as often as not acquired during the Edwardine spoliation.

These loans, whether from clergy or parishioners, might in due course become gifts. In 1556 Gilbert Pykeryng of Titchmarsh St Mary left his parish church 'the holle sute that I have of purpell velvet with all other things that they have of myn in the churche savyng the vestments with that belongs to the same'. In the following year Agnes Andrews left to her parish of Charlton a chalice, a Mass book, a cope, and 'all the vestments that I bought of the parishioners of Charleton'. And, tragically out of time, the parish priest of Ufford St Andrew in November 1558 left his parish 'the table (reredos) that standethe uppon the hygh aulter, a peyr of greate candlesticks, a masse boke, a processioners, and a manuell'.[61]

Parishes confronted with having to buy ornaments might do so by levying a cess on the householders, an expedient enforced by the authorities in Pole's diocese where other resources were not forthcoming. But gifts might also be solicited or volunteered. The wives of Morebath collected pennies, tuppences, and the occasional groat to buy Sir Christopher Trychay a new manual to baptize, marry, and bury with. The piety of Morebath or the eloquence of their vicar resulted in a series of such gifts. The young men and maidens raised 13s.10d 'voluntaryly' for the ceiling over the high altar, and Trychay recorded individual gifts as well – six shillings from Thomas Borrage to buy the Mass book, a box to put the Sacrament in from Richard Tywell, price 3s.4d, 6s.8d from Thomas

Stephens of Clotworthy for the Crucifix and the painting over the Sacrament, a pair of altar-cloths from John Norman at Court, nine shillings from Joan Morse and her son for the ceiling over St Sidwell's altar.[62]

In his visitation articles for London, Bonner had addressed this issue directly, and had instructed his archdeacons to see that clergy at deathbeds should put the sick person in remembrance 'of the great spoil and robbery that of late hath been made of the goods, ornaments and things of the Church', and exhort them to remember not only the poor, but also 'according to the old and laudable custom used in times past' to make some gift both to the mother church of the diocese and to the parish.[63] Giving of this sort to churches had of course totally collapsed in Edward's reign, and historians have been disposed to see the absence of any immediate resurgence in gifts to the Church in Mary's reign as an indication that parishioners' hearts were not in the restoration. The fact that in 1554 Bonner was actively encouraging gifts seems to sharpen this point, for it is certainly true that in some regions there is little evidence of large-scale giving of this sort till the last years of the reign. In Sussex, for example, a regular pattern of bequests to the Church does not seem to have re-established itself till 1557.[64]

This is certainly an issue which needs more regional study. There were counties where the laity does seem to have begun to endow parish churches through their wills more or less immediately. In Northamptonshire there are literally scores of such bequests in the wills of the Marian period, beginning in 1554 and becoming more common as the reign progressed: 'unto the reparacyon of my parishe churche ij sylke clothes to hange about the sacrament', 3s.4d to buy 'a boke called a manuell', 'to the settyng upp our ladye aulter 6d', 'a table cloth to ly uppon the hye awlter', 'my best wether shepe towardes the buying of ij handbelss for the . . . churche', 'to the byenge of a cope for the more honourable settynge forth of God's service'.[65] These bequests could be matched in many counties. Even in strife-torn Kent bequests to the parish churches for repairs, ornaments, and lights seem to have been beginning again in significant numbers from 1555. It does, however, seem clear that in few places, if any, did such bequests reach the levels achieved in the 1520s and 1530s, and nowhere did they displace the bequests to the poor which had become the dominant form of charitable giving under Edward.

It is tempting to see this failure of the older pattern to re-establish itself at pre-Reformation levels as a sign of the erosion of Catholic feeling and the spread of Protestant ideas. All the same, the temptation should be resisted. There were a number of reasons why Catholics should not have reverted to the older pattern. In the first place, the problem of the poor was worrying and more present in the public consciousness of mid-Tudor men and women than in earlier periods. Unease at the growth in the number of the poor was universal, and the draconian legislation of the mid-century

and the Elizabethan period is witness to the urgency of lay concern about
the problem of poverty. Poor relief was therefore both a meritorious work
of mercy and an urgent social necessity. The clergy themselves felt this.
Interestingly, between the drafting of his visitation articles, and the subsequent issuing of the Injunctions for London, Bonner changed the directions he gave to clergy about will-making among the laity. Where the
articles had highlighted the virtue of giving to the church, the Injunctions
stress only the need to remember the poor. The clergy were to 'induce them
to make their testament . . . and to remember the poor, and especially to
solicit for the maintenance of the hospitals of the city of London'.[66] Pole
himself may well have been responsible for this change. A product of the
Catholic reform movement in Italy, he had been deeply impressed by the
charitable works of the north Italian *scuoli* or lay confraternities, who
supported hospitals, lazar houses, and other good works for the poor. He
castigated Londoners bitterly for their indifference to the poor, contrasting
the cities of Italy with London, where there were not 'x places, neyther of
hospytalls, nor monasteryes yn the cyte, nor abowte the cyte; and yet for
you they maye dye for hunger'. Though he wished to see the restoration of
religious houses, the whole rhetorical weight of his treatment of the need
to give was on the needs of the poor: 'the doctryne of the chyrche ys the
doctryne of mercye and almes of God. Whyche mercye is receyved more
wyth comforte: but of them that use mercye, and gyve almes to other.'[67]
Accordingly, Pole's own metropolitian Injunctions required the clergy at
deathbeds to exhort the dying 'charitably to remember the poor, and other
deeds of devotion'.[68]

The Marian Church, then, despite the pressing needs of the parish
churches, actually continued the Edwardine policy of encouraging testators
principally to remember the poor in their wills, and did not press Bonner's
original policy of seeking to meet the expenses of reconstruction from
bequests. The re-establishment of the pattern of such bequests, therefore,
where it occurred, was not the result of pressure from above.

In any case, parishioners stretched to the limits by the immediate
demands of restoration in the parish churches, especially where these
were being met by compulsory cesses or levies, may well have felt that
they had done their bit while living. With the exception of small gifts to
lights, the custom of leaving gifts for ornaments in pre-Reformation wills
had rarely been designed to provide the routine expenses of the church:
these had been met by church ales, by revenue from lands and cattle and
buildings, by benevolences from gilds. Gifts in wills were in a sense a
manifestation of devotional luxury, the gilt on the gingerbread – a better
cope, a richer hanging, a new image. Even had Mary lived, it would have
been years before that situation could have been recreated, and the devotional point of the older practice, the performance of a gratuitous, super-
erogatory, devotional gesture, could be felt again. The will of George

Wryghte of Cobham in August 1555 stresses both that devotional drive and its limitations in the prevailing conditions in Marian England, when he directed that his executors should bestow five pounds of wax for a light

> When so ever any lighte shall fortune to be erected and sett upp before the Image or picture of Christ or in any other place to thonor and wourschipp of Chryst in memorye of his fyve woundes by which he suffired for me and all other beleving in hym.[69]

Two years later James Boswell of Sherburn asked his executrix to give 3s.4d to his parish church 'yf yt shall chance that ever saynt Antony light goo vpp and be founde agayne'. At Mary's accession, the lights before the images had been out for fifteen years, and few testators were willing to mortgage money on the uncertainties of their reintroduction. As parishioners, they shouldered the financial burdens of restoration with energy, even with enthusiasm; as testators they often left these things alone. There was a sense in which the devotional machinery of popular Catholicism had to be in place and working, up and running, before the old pieties could reassert themselves. And in any case, the destruction and robbery of sacred things had sent a deep shock through the devotional system of Catholic England; it is hardly surprising that confidence was slow to return in many places. Allen Wood, a yeoman from Snodland in Kent, left money for an annual obit, with candles and doles, but added that 'if the same obit by order of law be abrogated hereafter' then the money was to be distributed to the poor. This sense of the provisional character of all such obit arrangements was slow to disappear. In April 1558 Thomas Morritt of Sherburn made his will, bequeathing his soul to Almighty God, 'who shed his most pretious Bloyd and was Crucyfyed vpon the Crosse for the redemcion of me and all Synfull Creatours, to the blessed virgyn our lady Sanct Mary his mother and to all the Celestiall company of heaven'. He left five shillings to the Blessed Sacrament for tithes forgotten, and for the use of the parish church a rich collection of copes and vestments 'vpon this condicion. That yf it shall please the King and the Quenes maiestie and ther successors to call suche things into ther highenes possession as of late tyme haythe bene, then the said Copes, Vestments and Tunakles to remane to myne haires for ever.' Brian Bradforde of Stanley made a will bequething a chalice to Wakefield parish church,

> and also all such coipes vestements and other ornamenttes as I have remaininge in the said churche . . . to the mainteyninge of goodes services ther, so long as the lawes of this realme of England will permite and suffer the same to be used and occupied. Provided alwaies that yf yt shall fortune at any tyme herafter any law, ordinance or statute to be maid here within this Realme of England to the contrarie by reason whereof the said chalice, copes, vestments and

the other ornamentes maye not remayne to the vse afforesaid, that then and from thence forth I give and bequeth the same . . . vnto Robert Bradford my sone and his heires.

In the same way Arthur Dyneley of Swillington made a will in May 1558 providing for masses, *Diriges*, and a series of doles at month's mind and anniversary, 'Provyded alwayes that yf the laws of the realme do not permitte masse and dirige to be done, Then I wyll all the said money to be bestowed and gyuen vnto the poore'. Richard Malthous of Roclyff, leaving a set of vestments to the chapel of Sallay in August 1558, added the proviso that 'if the uses of vestments do cease in churches or chappells or if the said Chappell of Sallay be pulled downe' the vestments were to be restored to his wife and children. So soon before Mary's death such provisions have a prophetic note, but these men were expressing an unsettled feeling rooted in Edward's reign, not in any foresight about Elizabeth's. The spoliation, even by the spring of 1558, was 'of late tyme'. More time was needed before Catholic men could feel as confident as their fathers had done that gifts to God's glory in their parish church would actually be used to that end. The lack of such gifts in their old numbers reflects a failure of faith, not in the old ways, but in the constancy of councils and of kings.[70]

The visitation of Kent, 1557

The visitation of 243 parishes in Kent carried out by Archdeacon Nicholas Harpsfield in August and September 1557 offers us a detailed progress report of the Marian restoration in the county most devastated by the iconoclasm and upheaval of Edward's reign. Kent almost certainly had a greater proportion of committed Protestants than any other part of England outside London, a fact reflected in the numbers burned there.[71] In another sense, too, Kent was a burned-over district, where iconoclasm had been under way since the early years of the schism, and where Cranmer's encouragement and patronage had ensconced a large number of radical clergy in key positions. In Kent, therefore, the Marian regime was to encounter its toughest parochial challenge, and the visitation of Kent shows us the difficulties of the restoration at their most intense. Moreover, the visitation returns allow us to see a moving picture. Harpsfield meticulously recorded every dilapidation, every missing ornament, every breach of Injunction. Having done so, he gave detailed directions about what was to be done to remedy the defect, and the time allowed. Officials were later despatched back to the parishes to check whether the required work had been carried out or the required item supplied, and they occasionally made yet further visits, adding further notes or recording that the parish had finally complied. The returns therefore give us an unrivalled picture of the restoration in progress.[72]

The demands being made on Kentish parishes in 1557 were significantly greater than those on Londoners in 1554. In addition to all the accoutrements required by Bonner, Harpsfield was enforcing the building of at least two altars of stone in every church, a high altar and a side altar, each with its full complement of cloths, frontals, and curtains, a silk set for holidays, a cheaper set for workdays. There were also to be separate copes and Mass vestments for workdays and for holy days. There was to be a Rood light, which had to be of six or more tapers, depending on the size of the parish, there were to be a carved patron saint and a carved Rood with Mary and John, each of the figures at least five feet high. There was to be a register book and a wardens' account book, kept in a locked chest, and there was to be a full complement of grave-digging equipment, mattock, spade, and shovel. The altars themselves were inspected to see that the slabs for the *mensa* were properly consecrated: where gravestones had been used they were to be replaced with proper altar-slabs, and the archdeacon and his men scrutinized the floors of the church to see if any of the pre-Reformation altar-stones had been set into the ground; those that had were to be raised and reused or reverently stored. Where altar-stones had disappeared, the wardens were to insitute enquiries, trace them, and certify their whereabouts to the archdeacon. High altars which had been made too small for the proportions of the chancel were to be reconstructed on a larger scale.

There is difficulty about interpreting some items in the returns. Over 40 churches were told to 'paint' the Rood, Mary, and John. This is apt to mislead on several counts. Harpsfield was certainly not telling these parishes to put up a two-dimensional painting of the Rood. In the early stages of the restoration many parishes had stretched canvas over the tympanum above the Rood-loft, or whitewashed over the king's arms and scriptures already painted up there, and called in a local painter to fill the space with a painted Calvary; this arrangement actually survives at Ludham in Norfolk. But the bishops insisted that these paintings be replaced as soon as possible with carvings. Harpsfield rigidly enforced this ruling, making exceptions in only two cases. At Queenborough he noted that 'they haue no roode Marye nor John but of paynted clouthe for they say they neuer had other', and at Boughton Monchelsea there is a note that 'the Marie and John and the patrone of the church be not carved but painted', which suggests that they had a carved Rood imposed against the tympanum, the secondary figures being then painted in. Harpsfield or his officials use three terms about the Rood and other images – provide, paint, and set up. In some cases these are clearly different processes, as at River, where the wardens were instructed to set up the Rood, Mary, John, and the patron saint, 'and paint the same'. So it is difficult to be sure whether or not parishes asked to paint their Rood had an unpainted carving or were being told to get a carving. Some of the parishes so instructed definitely did possess the images themselves. At Harrietsham the wardens were instructed to 'painte the roode Marie and John with the patrone of the churche before Easter'; an official has added in the margin 'because they be grene'.[73] The churchwardens' accounts of Bethersden, where the archdeacon instructed them to paint the Rood and the patron 'decentlie', highlight the difficulties. The parish accounts record the purchase of the Rood, Mary, and John in 1557, along with a pax, a breviary, some candlesticks and a handbell. None of these items was recorded as missing at the visitation, so it seems likely that they were hurriedly purchased before the arrival of the visitors. There is a separate entry for the painting of the Rood after it had been fetched from the workshop at Ashford, and a number of expenses about the trip the wardens were forced to make to show the officials the new holy water pot, surplice, and processional cross they had been instructed to provide. It looks, therefore, as if the Bethersden requirement to 'paint' the Rood meant exactly that. If that is so, many or most of the churches told to 'paint' images may already have had them, but were being asked to colour them.[74]

Some of the same difficulties apply to the orders to set up stone altars. Philip Hughes calculated that forty-seven of the parishes 'had yet to find' high altars.[75] This is cetainly not so: many of the churches told to provide high altars simply had unsatisfactory ones, where the structure was made of wood or was badly built, or where the slab was a gravestone, or too small for the principal altar of the church. Only thirteen churches can be clearly identified as being without a stone high altar, and some of these had reasons the archdeacon was prepared to accept, as at Marden, where there were indeed many heretics but where the chancel was ruinous. The parish was told to erect a permanent altar when the necessary repairs had been completed. There is no suggestion in any of the parishes that there is not at least a wooden altar on which Mass was being said.[76]

Despite these problems of interpretation, the Kent returns make it clear that in virtually every parish by 1557 there was a high altar of stone, with the necessary altar furniture. There was at least one set of vestments, and in over 200 churches more than one. Almost all churches had missals, manuals, processionals, and breviaries, the crucial books for the basic celebration of the liturgy, though a few lacked choir books like the grail and antiphonary. Most churches had a christmatory for the holy oils, though some of these had clearly been through the wars in Edward's reign, and minor repairs such as the replacement of the pin on which the lid hinged are commonly demanded. Most churches had an Easter sepulchre, though not all had a decent frame to support the lights that burned before it. The commonest defect recorded was the absence of a lock and key for the font cover. Many churches were making do with one processional cross instead of the two required, and some of those, battered survivors from the

Edwardine spoliation, had lost the figure of Christ, or needed it fixing back. About half the churches lacked the full complement of towels, altar-cloths or frontals, though most had at least one of everything. There is no discernible pattern in the items missing, and little if anything that can be directly related to rejection of the rituals the objects were designed to serve. Thus forty-four churches lacked a pax, which in some cases might have reflected a dislike of the pax ritual; one of the signs of heresy Bonner required his officials to look for was abstention from the pax. But almost as many churches were short of grave-digging equipment, which can hardly be for ideological reasons, and fifty-nine churches had no register of births, deaths and marriages.

Perhaps more significant than any of the particular items lacking is the evidence the returns offer of prompt efforts to comply with the arch-deacon's requirements on the part of the parishes. Thus, over sixty churches were instructed either to supply, to paint, or to 'amend' the statue of their patron saint. Some were using pre-Reformation statues which had been damaged, and at Bonnington the scandalized archdeacon made the par-ishioners provide silk or linen clothing to cover their patron saint Rumwald, because their statue represented him as a naked boy.[77] It took two visits by officials to clothe St Rumwald, but only a dozen churches of the sixty with defective statues ultimately failed to carry out the improvements required, which does not suggest any widespread aversion to the veneration of images. Similarly, of the forty-four churches lacking a pax, only fourteen failed to provide one in the time allotted: since it was common practice before the Reformation to use a Gospel book as a paxbred, even these fourteen may have had a functioning pax ritual at their Masses.

There were of course, ample signs of heresy, and Harpsfield had clearly earmarked certain parishes for special scrutiny. At Elmstead, Capel le Ferne, Harstone, Hythe, St James's Dover, Littlebourne, and Bekesbourne the wardens were instructed to present any who did not carry and use their beads on Sundays and holidays, or who would not go in procession. At St James's Dover, where the scriptures had not yet been blotted out of the Rood-loft, the archdeacon noted that 'there be not iiijor besides women in the parishe that were bedes'.[78] At Chart, Sutton, Ulcomb, and several other parishes lists of singers who would not join the choir were compiled. Harpsfield paid particular attention to the need for preaching in such parishes, and the curates at Pluckley and Bekesbourne, both communities with dissidents in them, were rebuked for not providing sermons. At Sandhurst, Hawkhurst, Benenden, and Cranbrook the archdeacon ordered that the whole parish should be confessed before mid-Lent Sunday, then again in the later part of Lent, and a rota for every household was to be devised to see that all communicated. One member of every household was also to attend the processions on Wednesdays and Fridays. The curates had instructions to bury no one who had declined housel and shrift on their deathbeds, and to give Easter communion to no one who refused to creep to the cross. At Rolvenden, the archdeacon wanted the names of the men who had purchased the Bible and the paraphrases when the parish had sold them off. Heresy was therefore a real problem in some communities, and very much in the archdeacon's mind.

1557 was a year of burnings in Kent, in many of which Harpsfield was involved. But a study of the restoration of traditional religious practice is not the place for a survey of the pursuit of heresy, and I shall not attempt to consider the burnings here. This is neither to minimize their horror nor to suggest that they were without importance in the long-term reaction against the Marian reconstruction. There has indeed been a tendency in some recent writing about the Marian regime to play down their significance, on the grounds that the 300 or so deaths involved were insignificant in a society inured to frequent brutal executions for a whole range of crimes, and in comparison with the more draconian activities of the European Inquisitions. It is certainly true that early Tudor crowds turned out in large numbers to become spectators of the sport of burning Lollards or early Protestants, with little sign of sympathy or misgiving. One needs accordingly to be on guard against importing into the period twentieth-century revulsion at the very idea of torturing sincere and often outstandingly brave men and women to death for their religious convictions. Foxe's accounts of communal solidarity with the victims of the Marian burnings certainly cannot be taken at face value. The animosity of John Bland's parishioners towards their former vicar is eloquent testimony to the bitter legacy of schism. There were many communities with similar scores to be settled, and accusations of heresy might provide the materials of revenge.

Yet when all that is said, such attempts to soften the bleakest aspect of Mary's reign can be overdone. There had been burnings before, and in some regions, like the Chilterns or parts of East Anglia, burnings in substantial numbers. But England had never experienced the hounding down of so many religious deviants over so wide an area in so short a period of time. However eagerly the burnings were greeted or initiated in some communities, it is hard to believe that they were not often in the end self-defeating. They must often have aroused sympathy for their victims, though not necessarily support for those victims' opinions.

However that may be, this aspect of the Marian reconstruction made little impact on the visitation. Diocesan visitation was not the normal method for pursuing heresy, for which there was a separate commission. Presentments in the visitation were almost as much concerned with cunning women and conjurers, butchers who opened their shops during service times, and, perhaps most of all, those who acquired church property in the Edwardine spoliation. Harpsfield was not pressing those presented for suspected heresy too hard; he was primarily concerned to secure conformity. Margaret Geoffrie of Ashford, who had refused to venerate the Sacrament, was required on the following Sunday to

> sitte in the myddes of the chancell apon her knees havinge beades in her handes and devoutlie behaving her self and that at the tyme of the elevacion she shall devoutlie and reverentlie woorshipp the Blessed Sacrament and to make certificat thereof.[79]

Harpsfield was more flexible on this matter than on some less important issues, and he was clearly excercising some pastoral or prudential discretion, for he did not always insist on the element of public humiliation involved in this sort of gesture of recantation. The wife of Henry Baker of Stockbury was presented because she had stayed away from the ceremonies in her parish church on Holy Cross Day. On examination she admitted to having abstained from communion as well, though she made a satisfactory declaration of her belief in the real and substantial presence in the Sacrament of the altar. She was sentenced to go in procession the following Sunday, perform all the ceremonies reverently, and stand by while the vicar publicly declared her faith, and her negligence in not coming to church. However, 'because she did humbly submitte herself and acknowledged her fault' the archdeacon remitted her sentence, to spare her the public shame, instead warning the churchwardens in due course to provide a certificate of her good behaviour.[80]

Parishes which had had strongly Protestant clergy might of course retain strong Protestant minorities, but the legacy of a Protestant ministry might also be debts and resentment which served as a vaccine against the culprit's doctrines. John Austen had challenged John Bland in November 1554 with

> Master Parson . . . You know that you took down the tabernacle or ceiling wherin the rood did hang, and such other things: we would know what recompense you will make us. For the queen's proceedings are, as you know, that such must up again.[81]

Bland was ashes on the Kent wind by 1557, and the altar and the images stood again in his church, but his parishioners were still being pressed by the archdeacon to 'cause the bonde over the rood lofte to be caste in color'. At Lydden the parishioners told the archdeacon that their Edwardine vicar had 'spoyld the church' and 'dyd serve his hennes in the onle holliwater stock'. Parishioners sent scurrying round the countryside to recover altarstones or images disposed of by a Protestant vicar, or whose married priest had turned the parish candle-hearse into a cradle for his children, did not necessarily look back with longing to his ministry. And although heresy was clearly a serious problem in Kent, it is noteworthy that most of those detected in the visitation for suspicious beliefs or practices did in fact accept penance and conform. Fear certainly played its part in this, but so did the removal of the sources of Protestant teaching and the pressure of neighbours and custom. Many of those suspected were probably 'waverers and doubters' like the three parishioners of St Botolph's, London, during Bonner's visitation, who declared that 'before the Quenes reigne that nowe ys, they were mainteyners and favorers of suche doctryne, as then was putt forth, but not syns.'[82] And however unpopular the burnings were, it would be unwise to assume that all who disapproved of them, or showed sympathy with the victims, were Protestants. Neighbourhood was neighbourhood, however frayed by religious difference and the conflicts of the mid-century upheavals. Catholic stomachs too could turn at the smell of scorched flesh, but sympathy for a victim does not necessarily lead one to embrace the doctrine which brought them to the pyre. It is clear that in some communities parochial officials, like the constable or 'bosholder', were at best lukewarm in pursuit of suspect neighbours, but though the archdeacon's men were clearly well aware of this, there is no suggestion that they thought the parish officers themselves were suspect.[83]

There was certainly a whole range of pressing problems for the Church in Kent. The break with Rome had meant massive transfers of Church property and patronage, most of it into lay hands; as a result many chancels were desperately in need of repair, and there was a good deal of litigation about financial responsibility for the upkeep of buildings. The fact that the authorities in 1557 were still in hot pursuit of alienated church goods sold in the early 1540s says volumes about the difficulty of recovery. In most of this heresy was an irrelevance: what was at stake was property, as at Well, a hamlet in the parish of Ickham, where there was a chapel in which the parishioners had been accustomed to have a Mass in Rogationtide. But the farmer of the tithe, a local gentleman called Isaac, had let the chancel fall into ruin, had made hay-lots in the chapel, a workshop for a weaver, and a kennel for dogs, 'and there was such a savour of hogg skynned that no man could abide in the Chappell for stinck thereof'.[84] There were also severe problems of manpower. Sequestration of married clergy and the abolition of the chantries meant that many parishes lacked clergy, and in several cases Harpsfield had to make arrangements for parishioners to be allocated to attend services in neighbouring parishes, thereby creating problems of the wardens required to oversee regular participation.

Thus, although heresy did remain a formidable problem in some communities, the overall impression is one of successful if painful recovery, and of parishes doing what they could to meet the stringent requirements of the reconstruction. Bethersden, whose wardens had to troop back to Cranbrook to get a certificate for their new cross, surplice, and holy water pail, was not a recalcitrant community. Their accounts show steady expenditure from 1554 onwards to acquire all the essentials of Catholic worship. By the late summer of 1557, when they were in trouble with the archdeacon, they had simply not managed to get everything done. Indeed, improvization is more evident than resistance in these returns, like the parish of Longley, where they were using a wooden bucket to keep their holy water in, or Egerton, where they were required to buy a new pax immediately, 'bye cause they have none but a nakyd man with the xij sighnes aboute hym', or Charing, where they were using as a pax a small shield with a gentleman's arms on it, a miniature recapitulation of the dynamic of the English Reformation as a whole which the archdeacon was not prepared to tolerate. He demanded to know whose arms they were.[85]

Heresy apart, however, there were some signs in the visitation of real shifts in religious feeling. We should perhaps not attach as much weight as Philip Hughes did to the comparatively large number of parishes which had not yet got round to setting up the Sacrament. Of the thirty-six who had not done so before the visitation, all but seven complied in the time allowed, and the logistics of setting up the Sacrament may have had more to do with the delay than theology. But ninety-six parishes had no lamp burning before the Sacrament before the visitation, and the absence of these lights does perhaps suggest an erosion of traditional Eucharistic piety.

Perhaps more significantly, 116 churches, nearly half the parishes visited, had no side altar, and although all but thirty quickly supplied the omission, the initial fact is surely significant. Of course, the basic reason in most cases was certainly financial: most parishes were stuggling adequately to provide and adorn the high altar. In a sense, too, side altars were redundant in most churches in 1557. There simply were no longer the clergy to staff them, nor the numbers of Masses being said to make them necessary. But their absence signals the narrower devotional range of Marian Catholicism, a narrowing evident also in the fact that few gilds were re-established in Marian England. Where the parish was preoccupied with raising funds to equip its church for the basic round of services, the devotional elaboration of the gilds was an unaffordable luxury. The layman anxious to show his devotion now would find all the scope he required in the needs of his parish, and the demands of that solidarity were likely to override all others. But the absence of gild and chantry priests, and the altars they had once served, reduced and to some extent refocused the liturgical variety of the parish, as they certainly reduced the layman's control over daily worship. The daily Mass now in most communities was the one parish Mass, and laymen would no longer have the scope to develop or indulge devotional preferences for one Mass over another, one saint over another.

The only image in the nave of most churches now was the Rood, just as the only altar in many churches was the high altar. In Marian parish churches the sharpening of focus on the Crucifix was to a large extent a matter of simple economics. But whatever the reason, the fact was that the only representation of the Virgin in most churches would now be the weeping figure standing under the Rood, where once there might have been multiple images of Mary – the Pietà, the Mother of Mercy, Our Lady in childbed, the Madonna and Child. And the ranks of holy helpers who had once filled every angle of the chancel and presided over the altars were reduced now in most cases to one, or at most a couple. That fact alone would inevitably have an effect in reshaping lay perception of the role of Mary and the saints.

This narrowing of focus was not entirely a factor of the destruction of the old images. There is a deliberation and a consistency evident in the devotional policy being imposed by the archdeacon in the visitation. Where he required the provision of hangings or reredoses for altars, Harpsfield normally specified the imagery which was to adorn them, and it was, invariably, a picture of the Passion of Christ. Similarly, where paxes were lacking the parish was to provide one with a Crucifix embossed on it. These are obvious enough requirements, though pre-Reformation paxes, like pre-Reformation reredoses, often had other designs, such as the Lamb of God. Their imposition is nevertheless noteworthy. They should probably be seen as another dimension of that recasting of Catholicism in response to the reform, with a more marked or at any rate more self-conscious emphasis on the cross and redemption, which we have already identified as a feature of the devotional and doctrinal ethos of the regime. This was an aspect of the Counter-Reformation's deliberate redirection of the exuberant but sometimes unfocused piety of the pre-Reformation laity towards a more evangelical emphasis on Christ and his redemptive suffering, a feature of other parts of sixteenth- and seventeenth-century Catholic Europe as well as of Marian England. The historian of local religion in Philip II's Spain has noted precisely the same tendency by the religious authorities there to steer popular piety towards a more scriptually 'correct' devotional emphasis on Christ and his Passion, at the expense of some of the minor saints' cults of regional Spain. In this respect, as in others, Marian Catholicism was at one with the larger Counter-Reformation.

Notes

1 D. Loades, 'The Enforcement of Reaction 1553–1558', *Journal of Ecclesiastical History* XVI, 1965, pp. 54–66; A.G. Dickens, *The English Reformation* (1989), pp. 287–315, essentially reaffirming the emphases of his *The Marian Reaction to the Diocese of York*, Part I, *The Clergy* and Part II, *The Laity*, Borthwick Institute Publications, nos 11 and 12 (1957). In many ways the most satisfactory account of religion in Mary's reign is A.M. Bartholomew, 'Lay Piety in the Reign of Mary Tudor', Manchester MA Thesis, 1979.
2 Dickens, *English Reformation*, pp. 309–11.
3 Dickens, *English Reformation*, p. 315.
4 W. Schenk, *Reginald Pole, Cardinal of England* (1950), pp. 143–4; A.D. Wright, *The Counter Reformation* (1982), p. 154.
5 T[udor] R[oyal] P[roclamations, ed. P.L. Hughes and J.F. Larkin (1964)] II no. 407 (p. 37).

6 L.E. Whatmore (ed.), *Archdeacon Harpsfield's Visitation, 1557*, Catholic Record Society, XLV–XLVI (1950–1). The two volumes are continuously paginated, volume 1 ending at p. 173. Reference is by page number only.

7 I have not had access to the first edition, RSTC 16060, and I have used *The primer in Englishe (after the use of Sarum) with many godly and devoute prayers . . . Wherunto is added a plaine and godly treatise concerning the Masse . . . for the Instruccyon of the unlearned and symple people* (London, John Wayland 1555); RSTC 16063; Hoskins no. 211 (hereafter, Wayland *Primer*).

8 J.J. Scarisbrick, *The Reformation and the English People* (1984), p. 104.

9 'Robert Parkyn's Narrative', in A.G. Dickens, *Reformation Studies* (1982), p. 308.

10 *TRP*, II no. 390.

11 *Wriothesley Chronicle*, II p. 101.

12 'Robert Parkyn's Narrative', p. 309.

13 Foxe, *Acts and Monuments*, VII pp. 288–9.

14 *Harpsfield's Visitation*, p. 165.

15 *TRP*, II no. 390 (p. 6).

16 *A Profitable and necessary doctryne, with certayne homelies adioyned thereunto set forth by the reverende father in God, Edmonde byshop of London* (London, 1555). RSTC 3282, preface (unpaginated).

17 *TRP*, II no. 407 (p. 36).

18 R.W. Dixon, *History of the Church of England*, IV pp. 456–7.

19 J. Strype, *Ecclesiastical Memorials* (1816), III part 2, p. 503.

20 Strype, *Ecclesiastical Memorials*, III part 2, p. 502.

21 W. Haines (ed.), 'Stanford Churchwardens' Accounts 1552–1602', *The Antiquary*, 17 (1888), p. 70.

22 Duffy, *The Stripping of the Altars*, p. 469.

23 Strype, *Memorials*, III part 2, p. 392.

24 V[isitation] A[rticles and] I[njunctions of the Period of the Reformation, ed. W.H. Frere and W.M. Kennedy, 1908–10] II pp. 361–2.

25 *VAI*, II pp. 171–2.

26 *VAI*, II p. 402.

27 *TRP*, II no. 407 (p. 38).

28 The *Profytable and necessary doctryne* is unpaginated.

29 II Maccabees vii. 37 (Vulgate).

30 See Margaret Aston, 'Lollardy and the Reformation', in *Lollards and Reformers* (1984), pp. 219–42.

31 *Homilies seitte forth by the right reverend Father in God . . .* , RSTC 3285.4, fol. 12.

32 J.E. Binney (ed.), *The Accounts of the Wardens of the Parish of Morebath, Devon, 1520–1573* (Exeter, 1904) p. 189.

33 Dixon, *History of the Church of England*, IV p. 457.

34 The 1553 primer is printed in *The Two Liturgies . . . set forth by authority in the Reign of King Edward VI*, ed. J. Ketley, Parker Society (1844), pp. 357–484; see the discussion in H.C. White, *Tudor Books of Private Devotion* (1951), pp. 119–21.

35 E. Hoskins, *Horae Beatae Mariae Virginis, or, Sarum and York Primers* (1901), nos 203–5; RSTC 16058 and 16059.

36 H.S. Bennett, *English Books and Readers* (1970), I pp. 39, 180, 200.

37 Hoskins, p. 190.

38 RSTC nos 16060, 16063, 16064, 16065, 16066, 16077, 16079, 16080, 16082, 16084, 16084.5, 16085, 16086. The firm went on to produce the first Elizabethan primer.

39 This summary is based on RSTC 16063; Hoskins no. 215.

40 The Rouen primer and its derivatives are discussed in White, *Tudor Books of Private Devotion*, pp. 67–86.

41 Wayland *Primer*, sig. Bi ff.

42 Wayland *Primer*, 'a general morning prayer'.

43 There is a helpful discussion to which I am indebted in White, *Tudor Books of Private Devotion*, pp. 121–31; collation of contents in Hoskins, pp. 186–90.

44 It first appears in Hoskins, no. 211, RSTC 16063.

45 STC nos 16063–5.
46 Dickens, *English Reformation*, p. 315.
47 *VAI*, II pp. 330–59 (Articles), 360–72 (Injunctions).
48 Dixon, *History of the Church of England*, IV pp. 243–4; *VAI*, II pp. 401–8.
49 Strype, *Memorials*, III part 2, p. 404.
50 *VAI*, II pp. 365–6.
51 There is a good discussion of the visitation in G. Alexander, 'Bonner and the Marian Persecution', in C. Haigh, *The English Reformation Revised* (1987), pp. 157–75; see also M. Jagger, 'Bonner's Episcopal Visitation of London, 1554', *Bulletin of the Institute of Historical Research*, XLV (1973), pp. 306–11, and J. Oxley, *The Reformation in Essex to the Death of Mary* (1965), pp. 179–237.
52 J.F. Williams (ed.), *The Early Churchwardens' Accounts of Hampshire* (Winchester, 1913), p. 166. The wardens at Tilney paid 43 shillings to replace their books in 1554, A.D. Stallard (ed.), *The Transcript of the Churchwardens' Accounts of the Parish of Tilney All Saints, Norfolk 1443–1583* (London, 1922), p. 179.
53 R. Hutton, 'Local Impact', in C. Haigh (ed.), *The English Reformation Revised* (1987), p. 129 (*see* Reading 6 above).
54 Stanford Churchwardens' Accounts, pp. 117–20.
55 *Archaeologia Cantiana*, XIV (1882), pp. 321–2.
56 F. Bailey (ed.), *Prescot Churchwardens' Accounts*, Lancashire and Cheshire Record Society (1953), p. 30.
57 E. Peacock (ed.), 'Churchwardens' Accounts of Leverton', *Archaeologia* 41 (1867), p. 360.
58 *Bedfordshire Inventories*, ed. F.C. Eeles, Alcuin Club, 6 (1905), pp. 17–28.
59 Edward Peacock (ed.), *English Church Furniture, Ornaments and Decorations, at the Period of the Reformation. As Exhibited in a List of the Goods Destroyed in Certain Lincolnshire Churches AD 1566* (1866), pp. 83, 90.
60 Peacock (ed.), *English Church Furniture*, pp. 43–4.
61 'The Parish Churches and Religious Houses of Northamptonshire', *Archaeological Journal* 70 (1913), pp. 297, 417, 420.
62 Morebath Churchwardens' Accounts, pp. 182–3, 200–1.
63 *VAI*, II pp. 341–2.
64 G. Mayhew, 'Progress of the Reformation in East Sussex', *Southern History*, V (1983), pp. 53–5.
65 'Parish Churches of Northamptonshire', pp. 278, 296, 300, 301, 310, 317, 357, 410, 415, 428.
66 *VAI*, II p. 368.
67 Strype, *Memorials*, III part 2, p. 484, and cf. pp. 505–7.
68 *VAI*, II p. 403.
69 L.L. Duncan, 'Parish Churches of West Kent', *Transactions of the St Paul's Ecclesiastical Society*, III (1895), p. 247.
70 *Tudor Parish Documents of the Diocese of York*, ed. J.S. Purvis (1948), p. 142, *Testamenta Leodiensia*, ed. G.D. Plumb, Thoresby Society (1913–30), II pp. 121, 171–2, 256–8, 341–4: *Testamenta Cantiana: West Kent*, ed. L.L. Duncan (London, 1906), p. 71.
71 P. Clark, *English Provincial Society* (1977), pp. 98–106.
72 The Injunctions from the visitation have not been found, but the return of the officials to parishes is attested by later annotations on the return where the archdeacon's instructions have not been carried out, usually indicated by the word 'non' written above the relevant instruction; where the matter was subsequently set right, the 'non' is deleted, indicating a further scrutiny by the officials.
73 *Harpsfield's Visitation*, p. 225.
74 *Harpsfield's Visitation*, pp. 122–3 F.R. Mercer (ed.), *Churchwardens' Accounts at Betrysden*, Kent Records, (Ashford, 1928), pp. 107–15.
75 P. Hughes, *The Reformation in England* (1950–4), II p. 237.
76 *Harpsfield's Visitation*, pp. 190–4.
77 *Harpsfield's Visitation*, p. 264.
78 *Harpsfield's Visitation*, p. 53.

79 *Harpsfield's Visitation*, p. 118.
80 *Harpsfield's Visitation*, p. 244.
81 Foxe, *Acts and Monuments*, VII p. 289.
82 Alexander, 'Bonner', p. 169.
83 For example, at Marden; see *Harpsfield's Visitation*, pp. 190–4.
84 *Harpsfield's Visitation*, pp. 68–9; *Archaeologia Cantiana*, 31 (1915), p. 107.
85 *Harpsfield's Visitation*, pp. 171, 173.

OUTCOMES

Commentary

The Elizabethan Church settlement of 1559, or arguably the final promulgation of the Thirty-nine Articles in 1571, marks the terminal date of the English Reformation considered as an officially directed restructuring of doctrine and worship. But in terms of restructuring the religious beliefs of the mass of the English people, these dates more closely resemble starters' flags than finishing posts. In the two generations which followed, England would come to be identified, and would come to identify itself, as Europe's premier Protestant nation, a process that involved the long-term working-out of a number of momentous questions quite unresolved in 1559. How would the large number of 'Catholics' or 'traditionalists' be accommodated within an unequivocally Protestant church? How receptive would the bulk of the English people prove to be to the message of a now untrammelled Protestant evangelism? What would become of the drive for further Reformation in a Church which many of its leading clergy considered to be 'but half-reformed'?

In an extremely wide-ranging essay, Christopher Haigh touches on a number of these important themes, and consciously sets out to rock a number of historiographical boats. For Haigh the Reformation across much of England was quintessentially 'an Elizabethan event'. This might now be considered relatively uncontroversial (though see Reading 4), but to Haigh it was also pretty much a non-event. Despite the best efforts of a host of preachers and catechists, by the early seventeenth century it had become clear that the English 'could not be made Protestants'. Yet by a parallel process they had largely ceased to be Catholics. In contrast to the still-influential historiographical tradition which presents the efforts of Elizabethan seminary priests and Jesuits as crucial to the formation and survival of an English Catholic community, Haigh accuses them of throwing away opportunities and abandoning the great mass of conservative sympathizers to their fate. On this interpretation, the confessional struggle for the hearts and minds of the English people ended as something of a no-score draw. In many places the dominant religious ambience was a 'Parish Anglicanism' which sought consolation in the rites and ceremonies of the Protestant Church of England without internalizing any of its essential doctrines.

Judith Maltby's insistence (see Reading 10) that Haigh's 'Parish Anglicans' should be re-christened 'Prayer-Book Protestants' is more than a piece of terminological nit-picking: It suggests a fundamentally different set of criteria by which the success of the Reformation should be measured. In this interpretation, the defence of Prayer-Book ceremonies against 'Puritan' innovation need not indicate rearguard action by disgruntled 'church papists', but points rather to a genuine commitment to Cranmer's liturgy on its own terms by a generation who had known no other form of worship. Maltby sets herself the challenging task of elucidating something of the nature of religious 'conformity', an attitude of mind that by definition leaves few traces in the historical record. The usually fraught circumstances in which

Maltby's 'Prayer-Book Protestants' present themselves inevitably invites questions about how far such 'enthusiastic' conformists may be regarded as speaking for and on behalf of their silent neighbours. It is, however, hard to dissent from the observation that investigating the phenomenon of religious conformity deserves more takers from a historical community long obsessed with the pursuit of Puritans, recusants, heretics, witches and other sorts of deviants.

Both Haigh's approach to the impact of Reformation teaching in the parishes and Maltby's response to it address in their different ways the fundamental question of what, in the English context, we should consider to be characteristically and constitutively Protestant, of what a Protestant actually was. Reflection on these questions points the way to what has been termed a 'post-revisionist' approach to the study of religious culture in Elizabethan and early Stuart England. The readings by Patrick Collinson and Tessa Watt take us further into this muddy conceptual water. Like Margaret Aston (see Reading 7), Collinson places an iconoclastic impulse at the very heart of the English Reformation movement. But Collinson detects a profound cultural shift in the years around 1580 when an 'iconoclastic' urge to reform unacceptable images gave way to an 'iconophobic' rejection of the visual, dramatic and musical forms reformers had employed to their own advantage in the past (see Reading 3). This was a development so marked that it enables Collinson to speak of a 'second Reformation'. Arguably, the employment of this term is problematic – in the historiography of the European Reformation it is generally used to denote the attempted imposition of a Calvinistic Reform on top of a previous Lutheran one – but it does graphically convey the extent to which leading figures in the late Elizabethan Church, second-generation Protestants, were decidedly lacking in complacency, and feared for the integrity, if not the very survival of their cause. Among the 'godly' there seems to have been a clear sense that 'Reformation' (in the sense of re-ordering society to accord with the injunctions of God) could not stand still, but could only move on or slip back. In the light of research by Tessa Watt and others, Collinson himself might now accept that some aspects of his case are overstated.

Watt's analysis of the cheap religious literature likely to have been purveyed by rural pedlars in the late 1570s and early 1630s perhaps takes us as close as we are likely to get to a genuinely 'popular' religious outlook over the period during which the Reformation was in the process of 'bedding down', though we should remember that there is very little direct evidence for how purchasers of this material reacted to or understood its contents. Watt shares Collinson's insight that a distinct hardening of outlook is perceptible in the mid-Elizabethan period, as godly evangelists became increasingly distrustful of popular media for the dissemination of their message, but her focus on the extent to which (often illustrated) ballads were reprinted into the seventeenth century questions the degree to which this can be considered constitutive of a true 'cultural revolution'. In such texts 'traditional' religious concerns existed side by side with more self-consciously Protestant ones, but the Protestantism tended to be of an affective, non-dogmatic type. Here one notes a correspondence in important recent work by Ian Green on Elizabethan and early Stuart catechisms, which has stressed that in the best-selling items 'hard' doctrines like double predestination were conspicuously down-played.[1] Watt's perception that much of popular religious culture in this period is more usefully described as distinctively 'post-Reformation' than as thoroughly 'Protestant' is rapidly establishing a place for itself in the early modernists' lexicon. If it is the case that, almost in spite of its best intentions, the reformed Church of England sanctioned within its corporate life a considerable degree of continuity with the unreformed past, this may go some way to explaining its ability to win and retain the formal allegiance of the vast majority of the English people in the decades before the Civil War.[2] The comprehensiveness of the English Church and the diversity of religious outlook it admitted was, however, always as much a source of tension as it was a sign of success. There were in early seventeenth-century England a great many who knew themselves to be Protestants in a more precise and exclusive sense, and many of those who in the 1640s took up arms against their king did so because they perceived their Protestant birth-right to be in danger of imminent alienation. In that sense the 'outcome' of the English Reformation was far from settled in 1640.

Notes

1 Ian Green, "For Children in Yeeres and Children in Understanding": the Emergence of the English Catechism under Elizabeth and the Early Stuarts', *Journal of Ecclesiastical History,* 37 (1986), p. 406; *The Christians' ABC: Catechisms and Catechizing in England c. 1530–1740* (Oxford, Clarendon Press, 1996), pp. 356–86.
2 On this theme, see Eamon Duffy, 'Continuity and Divergence in Tudor Religion', in R.N. Swanson, ed. *Unity and Diversity in the Church, Studies in Church History* 32 (Oxford, 1996), pp. 171–205.

9

The Church of England, the Catholics and the people

CHRISTOPHER HAIGH

The puny mind of the historian, grappling with the almost infinite detail and complexity of the past, seizes with relief upon such simplifications as are to hand. Periodisation, the division of the past into manageable blocks for the purpose of study, is an essential, but dangerous, simplification. Our understanding of politics and religion in the sixteenth century has been bedevilled by the assumption that the period of 'the English Reformation' was definitively completed by 'the Elizabethan Settlement', leaving only the residual problem of those papists who did not realise that the Reformation struggle was over and they had lost. 1558–9 is too often regarded as a decisive turning point: students are expected to change their mentors (Elton give way to Neale), their organising concepts ('the Reformation' gives way to 'the origins of the Civil War'), and their categories – medieval obscurantism is dead, and we are in the exciting new world of 'the rise of Puritanism', 'the rise of the gentry', and 'the winning of the initiative by the House of Commons'.

But the ecclesiastical history of Elizabethan England is more profitably viewed not from the whiggish perspective of 'the causes of the Civil War', but as the second phase of a Reformation which was incomplete in two senses. First, though a political decision for Protestantism was taken in 1558–9, the form of that Protestantism remained uncertain and few believed that even the official, legal Reformation had come to a halt – while contemporaries were much less certain than some historians that the Reformation was irreversible and Protestantism safe. Second, although a *legislative* Reformation had taken place, there had, as yet, been only a very limited *popular* Reformation. Though there is a substantial body of opinion, led by Professors Dickens and Elton, which holds that Protestantism spread rapidly in early Tudor England, there is a growing 'slow Reformation' school, composed partly of historians who have conducted local studies of religious change. Protestantism *did* make early progress in towns such as Bristol, Colchester, Coventry, Ipswich and London, but elsewhere, and especially in the countryside, the reformist breakthrough came much later. In Cambridgeshire, Cornwall, Gloucestershire, Lancashire,

Reprinted from C. Haigh, ed. *The Reign of Elizabeth I* (Basingstoke, 1984).

Lincolnshire, Norfolk, Suffolk, Sussex and Yorkshire, the Protestant Reformation was an Elizabethan (and often mid-Elizabethan) event.[1] For much
of the reign of Elizabeth, the Church of England was a prescribed,
national Church with more-or-less Protestant liturgy and theology but
an essentially non-Protestant (and in some respects anti-Protestant) laity.
This essay explores some of the consequences of this discrepancy, and of
the competing evangelistic campaigns of Catholic and Protestant missionary clergy.

I

After the fluctuating religious policies of Elizabeth's predecessors, it is not
surprising that few expected the laws and injunctions of 1559 to constitute
a permanent 'settlement'. A little before Queen Mary's death, a Lancashire
JP had acknowledged 'that this new learning shall come again, but for how
long? – even for three or four months and no longer'. The Bishop of
Carlisle reported in 1562 that his people expected a change in religion
and prepared for it, and there were stories in Lancashire in 1565 that altars
and crucifixes were to be restored. There were persistent rumours of a
change of religion about 1580 (which led one candidate to postpone his
ordination, and a minister to shave off his beard in expectation of becoming a priest), and fears and hopes in the 1590s that the death of Elizabeth
would bring the restoration of Catholicism.[2] Clergy and parishioners were
therefore reluctant to remove altars and rood lofts, and deface images and
mass equipment. Most parishes yielded to pressure from the bishops:
churchwardens' accounts suggest that in most places altars and images
were displaced in 1559–60, and rood lofts taken down in 1561–2. But half
the churches of Lincolnshire kept their altars beyond 1562, and a quarter
kept their images, while there was local resistance to the removal of
'monuments of superstition' at Throwley and Elmstead in Kent, Writtle
in Essex, and Leigh and Wigan in Lancashire. Seventeen east Yorkshire
churches still had Catholic fittings in 1567, and in 1574 a score of Northamptonshire churches had the forbidden rood lofts. Even when the removal of
proscribed items from prominent places in churches was secured, it was
difficult to enforce their destruction or sale. Bishop Bentham complained
in 1560 that most Shropshire churches 'hath not only their altars still
standing, but also their images reserved and conveyed away, contrary to
the Queen's Majesty's injunctions, hoping and looking for a new day', and
in Sussex in 1569 there were 'images hidden up and other popish ornaments ready to set up the mass again'. The churchwardens of most
parishes did not sell their mass equipment and vestments until 1570–2,
and the wardens of Masham in Yorkshire finally disposed of their Catholic
vestments and altarcloths in 1595. Once in private hands, such items might
be kept for years in the hope that the mass would be restored, and five

parishioners of Kneesall in Nottinghamshire were in trouble for this in 1594.[3]

For a decade or more, the Church of England was a Protestant Church with many Catholic churches; for even longer, it was a Protestant Church with many Catholic, or at least conservative, clergy. In the diocese of Lincoln in 1576, 40 per cent of the ministers had been ordained before 1559, of the kind described by Anthony Gilby as 'old monks and friars and old popish priests, notorious idolators, openly perjured persons, halting hypocrites, manifest apostates'. Some conservatives conformed as cynically as Gilby claimed: the rector of Bilborough in Nottinghamshire acknowledged in 1577 'that he had given his faith unto the Church, and that faith that was lost he had given to his wife', and others made no secret of their hope that the mass would be restored. Several ministers provided the sacraments of the official Church in public and Catholic ones in private, and many more taught Catholic beliefs: some of those ordained under Elizabeth were also hostile to Protestantism, and in 1598 the parson of Barton-upon-Humber was teaching his people that there were seven sacraments and that the doctrines of Luther and Calvin were 'damnable, heretical and devilish'.[4] If the character of the clergy of the Church of England changed only slowly, as such conservatives died or were dismissed, the church services they provided conformed only gradually to the rubrics of the Book of Common Prayer. Throughout the 1560s and 1570s, the Church courts dealt with ministers who tried to 'counterfeit the mass', by muttering Latin prayers, facing east during the service, or raising the bread and wine in an 'elevation': in 1599, the vicar of Marston-upon-Dove in Derbyshire was still reading the service like a mass at an altar. The continuing use of communion wafers (prescribed by royal Injunctions), rather than ordinary bread (required by the Prayer Book), was one way in which parishes maintained continuity with the mass. References to 'singing cakes' in churchwardens' accounts suggest that at least a quarter of parishes used wafers in the 1560s, and, though there were attempts to suppress their use in the 1580s, there were parishes in Berkshire in 1584 and Hampshire in 1607 where the congregations refused to communicate except with wafers. The ecclesiological and liturgical rules of 1559 were thus implemented reluctantly, and often over ten or twenty years. In 1578 the parishioners of Weaverham in Cheshire were unusual only in the comprehensiveness of their disobedience:

They want [i.e. lack] a Communion Book, a Bible of the largest volume, the first tome of the Homilies. There is in the church an altar standing undefaced. There lacketh a linen cloth and a covering for the communion table, a chest for the poor and keeping of the register in. The parishioners refuse the perambulation. The people will not be stayed from ringing the bells on All Saints' Day. They frequent alehouses in service time. Great talking used in the church. No levying for the poor of the absents from the church. Morris dances and rushbearing used in the church. Jane, an old nun, is an evil woman and teacheth false doctrine. They refuse to communicate with usual bread. None cometh to the communion three times a year. They refuse to bring in their youth to be catechised. Crosses are standing in the churchyard.[5]

Under the tutelage of conservative clergy, the beliefs of the laity may have changed very little in the reign of Elizabeth. Preaching at Oakham in 1583, Thomas Gibson complained that by the influence of the old priests

the people are still in ignorance and blindness and kept still in their old and popish errors, received from their forefathers; they know not the use of the sacraments, or to what end they serve, they hold still their papistical transubstantiation: some say they receive their maker, other say 'they never heard what a sacrament meant'.

When, nearly a decade later, William Perkins listed 'these your common opinions' in an address 'to all ignorant people', he described a pattern of belief which also differed little from pre-Reformation popular Catholicism – little wonder that a Nottinghmshire man, required to recite his catechism in 1579, retorted that 'it is nothing but the old Christ in the Pope's time'. But where the Elizabethan church services were enforced in their entirety, there was a strong consciousness of change and a marked hostility to it. Francis Trigge objected in 1589 to the

weeping and bewailing of the simple sort, and especially of women. Who, going into the churches and seeing the bare walls, and lacking their golden images, their costly copes, their pleasant organs, their sweet frankincense, their gilden chalices, their goodly streamers, they lament in themselves and fetch many deep sighs, and bewail this spoiling and laying waste of the Church, as they think.

With a resentment of novelty came a nostalgia for the old: 'It was a merry world when the service was used in the Latin tongue', claimed an Essex man in 1581, and it was widely held that 'it was a good world when the old religion was, because all things were cheap'. Protestantism was blamed for high prices, bad weather, disease and threats from abroad; 'now we are in an evil way and going to the devil, and have all nations in our necks'.[6]

II

There was thus a substantial survival of conservative belief and practice in parishes served by ex-priests, and of conservative belief among the alien-ated anti-Protestants in parishes served by godly preachers. Those whose opinions were little influenced by the Elizabethan Reformation formed a reservoir of potential recruits for a separated Catholic Church, and even some ministers of the Church of England kept loyalty to Rome alive. In 1575 the curate of Guisborough 'did say that the Pope was and is head of the Church', and the vicar of Whalley, Lancashire, dismissed the English Church as 'a defiled and spotted Church', encouraging his parishioners to pray 'according to the doctrine of the Pope of Rome'. The vicar of Bonnington in Lincolnshire told his people in 1580 that they must make confession to Catholic priests, since only then could they be saved from damnation. Other clergy, perhaps more strong-minded than these, accepted the logic of such views and withdrew from the official Church, offering Catholic sacraments to the laity as recusant priests. By 1564, recusant priests were already working in the dioceses of Lichfield, Hereford, Worcester and Peterborough, and by 1571 there were thirty-eight such priests in Lancashire and a dozen more in Richmondshire and Claro: we know of seventy-five recusant priests who served in Lancashire in the reign of Elizabeth, and as many as 150 who worked in Yorkshire. Some of these men established themselves as domestic chaplains to the gentry, celebrating masses for their households and exercising little outside influence, but others, especially in the less well-governed areas of upland England, served unofficial congregations among their erstwhile parishioners or became itinerant priests to moorland hamlets.

It is difficult to asses the effectiveness of such priests, or to establish how many of the laity followed them into recusancy – or practised an ambidextrous religious life as 'church papists'. Neither the Privy council nor the bishops made sustained efforts to identify recusants until the late 1570s, and our evidence is very patchy. But, when rumour or crisis prompted more serious investigation, substantial numbers of recusants were often found. In 1567, when the Bishop of Chester was pressed into action by the Council, he discovered an established circuit of gentry houses in south-west Lancashire providing bases for at least seventeen mass priests, and a special visitation in 1571 found forty recusants among the gentry. When the fears which followed the papal bull of deposition in 1570 prompted a visitation of the archdeaconry of Norwich, Bishop Parkhurst found 180 recusants and non-communicants, and the Winchester consistory court dealt with 116 recusants and 128 non-communicants from Hampshire in 1570. In 1577, a hastily conducted national survey, which concentrated on gentlemen and known malcontents, listed 1500 recusants, and there were certainly many more, besides church papists: the 1577 list for Lancashire gives only forty-five names, but in 1578 304 Lancashire recusants were detected.[7] Twenty years after the accession of Elizabeth, therefore, the prospects for English Catholicism were good: within the framework of the Church of England, conservative opinion remained widespread and, apparently, intractable; outside, recusant priests and lay people had begun to organise an underground Church. It is true that the loyalty of mere conservatives to traditional belief and practice was conditional and partial, but they were at least potential full Catholics who might be won for recusancy by energetic proselytising. It is also true that as the recusant priests died off their opposition Catholic Church would collapse, unless they were replaced by new recruits. But both needs could have been met by the Catholic missionary enterprise mounted from the mid 1570s, which sent trained young priests to England for 'the preservation and augmentation of the faith of the Catholics'.[8]

III

The missionary effort of seminary priests and Jesuits has been regarded by most historians as a great success, which rescued English Catholicism from decline and preserved it against the persuasions of Protestant preachers and the persecutions of a ruthless regime. But it has already been suggested that conservative opinion had held up well in the first half of the Elizabethan period, and it will later be argued that the efforts of godly ministers created in the second half a small Protestant minority rather than a thoroughly Protestant nation. Protestant propaganda did little to limit the achievements of the missioners, and it may be that persecution was also less significant than has been supposed. Despite the horrific deaths and heavy fines inflicted upon some, the authorities of Church and state applied real coercive pressure only to a very few Catholics[9] – though the vicious Act of 1585 made the work of the priests more difficult and dangerous, at times of crisis and in better-governed districts. Although the mission was triumphant in the sense that it created the seigneurially structured form of Catholicism which was to survive in England, that form was not inevitable; in the sense that it failed to maximise the size and distribution of the potential Catholic community, the mission was a failure – albeit a heroic one.

The task of the missionary priests was to sustain and strengthen existing Catholic loyalties, but this they were unable to do, for two broad reasons.[10] First, from the earliest years of the mission there was a geographical maldistribution of clerical resources. After their training at Douai, Rheims or Rome, most priests came into England through ports such as Dover and Rye, and they tended to concentrate in the south-east, where Catholics were fewer and prospects less good. In 1580, half of the missioners were working in Essex, London and the Thames Valley, where only a fifth of detected recusants lived; the north, which had 40 per cent of detected recusants (and many more undetected) had attracted only a fifth of the priests. Robert Southwell complained in 1586 that 'the priests actually working in the harvest betake themselves in great numbers to one or two counties, leaving the others devoid of pastors'. By about 1590, there are signs of a glut of priests in Oxfordshire and actute shortages in the north. The Catholics of Malpas in Cheshire were able to attend only three masses in two years, a pair of lovers from Cleveland had to travel to Lincolnshire to find a priest to marry them and Richard Danby of Masham had to baptise his six children himself. While Catholic gentlemen in the Home counties, East Anglia and the Thames Valley might have resident chaplains, the people of the north and west were too often left to go to the devil – or the Church of England. Areas such as Cumbria and North Wales, where the prospects for Catholic survival and consolidation had seemed good until the 1580s, declined into gross superstition and conformism thereafter – probably because of insufficient priestly provision. Recusancy was expanding rapidly in the far north-west at least until 1589, but ten years later the Bishop of Carlisle reported that the recusant gentry were moving out of his diocese, and that the main problem he now faced was not Catholicism but the ignorance of the people owing to the deficiences of his own clergy.

The second reason for the relative failure of the Elizabethan Catholic mission was that scarce priestly resources were devoted disproportionately to the spiritual needs of the gentry. Since many of the Jesuits and seminary priests came from the gentry or were patronised by them, it is easy to see why this happened, while there were sound justifications for it in both practice and policy. The high risk of arrest in the well-governed parts of southern England and in scare periods such as the years following the Armada may have forced some priests to seek safety in the houses of prominent Catholics. Above all, the focus upon the gentry was quite deliberate, for both political and pastoral reasons: Catholic gentlemen would provide backing for any future restoration of the old religion, and it was hoped that the influence of Catholic landlords would keep their servants and tenants loyal to the Catholic faith. The leaders of the missionary effort, and especially the Jesuits, envisaged the construction of a separated recusant community in a seigneurial, rather than congregational, form. The clerical employment agency organised by William Weston in 1585–6 and supervised by Henry Garnet thereafter, sought to place incoming priests in the households of reliable Catholic gentry, where they often became family chaplains rather than district pastors.[12] Though some priests devoted themselves bravely and selflessly to the poor, there was an increasing emphasis upon work with the gentry. For four years William Anlaby worked on foot and in simple dress among the poor Catholics of Yorkshire, but in 1582, 'humbly yielding himself to the advice of his brethren', he bought a horse, improved his clothes, and turned his attention to the gentry of the south. When William Freeman arrived in England in 1587, he worked first, with 'weariness of body and sundry perils', among 'the meaner sort' in the west Midlands, until a Catholic gentlewoman took him in and made him tutor to her son.[13]

The consequence of this attention to the needs of the upper ranks was an inadequate provision for those of the lower orders. About 1590, the Jesuit Thomas Stanney was based with a gentry family in Hampshire and went on a circuit of local villages once a month. When asked to go out again to minister to poor Catholics, he replied that 'I had not been long since in those parts, where I was much fatigued with preaching, hearing confessions and administering the sacramens, the more because I was obliged to watch whole nights and to celebrate mass twice in the day, so that I had not, as yet, been able to recover myself'. 'Well, but Master', he was told by his guide, 'we still have a great many hungry souls that want bread, and there is no one to give it to them; we have many also that would be glad to shake off the yoke of bondage, heresy, and embrace the Catholic faith, and I can find none to help them and receive them into the Church. What then must I say to them?' This was a question to which the Catholic leadership had no answer: no doubt Stanney was doing his best, but he needed help, especially from priests without obligations to the gentry. In Suffolk in the 1620s a lay sister complained that there were too few priests, and that those available were too often prevented by their gentry hosts from working among the poor; she claimed it took six months to find a priest to receive three converts into the Church, and she had to travel twelve miles to get him. By then the disparity in provisions for gentry and the poor was clear and fixed: gentry families with chaplains had mass every day, but the poor had masses monthly.[14]

There was, therefore, a high risk of leakage from the Catholic community. In the Catholic heartlands of Monmouthshire, Herefordshire, Lancashire and the North Riding, social pressures might keep even neglected lay Catholics firm to their faith: in 1578 a man from Boroughbridge in north Yorkshire justified his recusancy on the grounds that 'he doth see that no such number now come to church as did in the time of Latin service', and in 1602 Lancashire Catholics explained their allegiance by saying, 'It is safest to do in religion as most do.'[15] But in most parts of England the inducement of social conformity worked in favour of attendance at the parish church, and the disciplinary mechanisms of the official Church pressed in the same direction: the hard core of recusants always had a penumbra of church papists, who might be seduced into abandoning their sometimes-tenuous Catholicism. Furthermore, there were parishes all over England and Wales which never received the attentions of recusant clergy or missionary priests, where conservative opinion survived, albeit in attenuated form, within the framework of the Church of England – with or without the support of like-minded ministers. The remainder of this essay explores the place of such conservatives and anti-Protestants within the Church of England. Could the energetic evangelism of godly ministers turn those who had been content to be Catholic under Mary (but would not disobey anti-Catholic laws under her sister) into believing Protestants?

And, if not, how would such 'mere conformists' fit into a Church whose ministers wanted an informed and activist laity and had little time for those

> that love a pot of ale better than a pulpit and a corn-rick better than a church-door; who, coming to divine service more for fashion than devotion, are contented after a little capping and kneeling, coughing and spitting, to help me to sing out a Psalm, and sleep at the Second Lesson, or wake to stand up at the Gospel and say 'Amen' at 'The Peace of God'; and stay till the banns of matrimony be asked, or till the clerk have cried a pied stray bullock, a black sheep or a grey mare, and then, for that some dwell far off, be glad to be gotten home to dinner.[16]

IV

Protestant ministers two generations after the accession of Elizabeth were conscious of the justice of the Catholic charge

> that we may have churches full of people but empty of sound Protestants: they will tell us in their books that a great part that are on our sides have no other motives to hold them there but only because they have been so born and bred, and received their religion as they do their inheritance, by descent and custom of the country, men whom decrees of Parliament and fear of laws keep with us, rather than any certain knowledge of the truth of our religion by the Scripture.

Their answer in the 1620s, as it had been in the 1560s, was preaching – preaching, and still more preaching. Professor Collinson has demonstrated with force and elegance how the provision of preaching improved over the reign of Elizabeth and after; but it is worth reminding ourselves how acute was the shortage at the beginning of the reign and how numerous were the gaps at its end. In the probably typical diocese of Peterborough, there were nine preachers for 285 parishes in 1560, and forty in 1576, though after a last-minute increase there were 144 by 1603. A series of surveys in 1586, admittedly compiled by critics of the bishops, suggests that only a fifth of parishes had preachers: in Surrey there were fifteen resident preachers, leaving 125 congregations 'altogether destitute of sufficient teachers'. In 1603 an investigation by the bishops showed that there were 4830 preachers in England for 9244 parishes, but in Staffordshire in the following year there remained '118 congregations which have no preachers, neither have had (for the most) now more than 40 years'.[17]

There was, by the middle of Elizabeth's reign, a preacher within reach of most villages, for the godly to go 'gadding' to his sermons; but the 'ungodly' would not 'gad', and the preachers must go to them. The system of quarterly sermons, by which churches which did not have their own preachers were to receive sermons from visitors every three months, seems to have been ineffective in many areas. Fifty-eight parishes in west Sussex had their quarterly sermons in 1579, but forty-six did not, and twenty-three parishes had sermons once a year or less frequently: at Barlavington and elsewhere, the churchwardens reported that they had no sermons, 'our parish being very small and not able to maintain the charge thereof'. In the diocese of York in 1575, 150 ministers were not providing sermons for their people, and the system was unsatisfactory in Oxfordshire in 1586. But, even where quarterly preaching did take place, the godly had little faith in its efficacy: 'Four sermons in the year are as insufficient ordinarily to make us perfect men in Christ Jesus . . . as four strokes with an axe are unable to fell down a mighty oak', it was said in 1585, and George Gifford thought even weekly sermons too few. In parishes without frequent preaching, it was claimed in 1588,

> what a pitiful thing it is to come into a congregation of one or two thousand souls and not to find above four or five that are able to give an account of their faith in any tolerable manner, whereby it might be said probably 'This is a Christian man, or he is a child of the church.'

'Wherefore (good brethren)', cried John More of Norwich, 'if ye will be saved, get you preachers into your parishes.'[18]

But, though the godly pleaded with the queen and the bishops for more preaching, their less-committed neighbours did not share their enthusiasm. A Northamptonshire woman complained in 1590 that 'Mr Sharpe and Mr Barebone had preached so long at Badby that they had brought all to nought, and that Welton was almost as bad. And that it was a merry world before there was so much preaching.' When John Bruen supplied preachers for Tarvin in Cheshire, they were 'much slighted by many, little regarded by the vulgar sort, much opposed by the popish and profane and too much undervalued by all'. Lengthy sermons were especially disliked: the people of Minsterworth in Gloucestershire complained in 1563 that their curate 'does weary the parish with overlong preaching', and the spokesman for the common man in a 1581 dialogue was told that 'if the preacher doth pass his hour bute a little, your buttocks begin to ache and ye wish in your heart that the pulpit would fall'. We may sympathise with Henry Hasellwood, of Coggeshall in Essex, called before the Church court in 1601 for standing in the churchyard during a sermon and throwing stones onto the church roof, 'to the great disturbance of the whole congregation'; he explained that 'he was at Mr Stoughton's sermon two hours and a half, and being urged to exonerate nature was compelled to go out of the church'. Sermons on moral reform seem to have pleased the godly but offended the rest: in 1592 an Essex man called his parson '"prattling fool" for preaching against drunkenness, saying moreover that he could, if he had authority, within a fortnight space make as good a sermon as he', and preachers against 'good fellowship' were widely unpopular – especially among innkeepers. In 1606 the vicar of Long Bennington, Lincolnshire, confessed that he had abandoned his attempts at moral reform because of the abuse he received from the parishioners.[19] Predestinarian preachers were also unpopular: 'they be over hot and severe, and preach damnation to the people . . . they meddle with such matters as they need not, as election and predestination'.[20]

If hostility to their preaching was a problem for godly ministers, sheer uncomprehending boredom in congregations was another. We should not suppose that Elizabethan church-goers sat in attentive rows, listening patiently to their preachers: they chattered, scoffed, squabbled and fought, and if the tedium grew unbearable they walked out. In 1592 eight Manchester parishioners were reported for walking out of sermons, eleven for talking in the churchyard during services, six for walking in the fields, and five for allowing drinking in their houses at service and sermon times. Sleeping during sermons may also have been common (eighteen were in trouble at Ramsey in 1597): the minister of North Colingham in Nottinghamshire told his people in 1598 'that some came to church more for a sleep than for the service of God, and other had more mind of going home to dinner than to hear God's word'. The noted Lancashire preacher John Angier complained later of parishioners sleeping in his sermons: 'some sleep from the beginning to the end, as if they came for no other purpose but to sleep, as if the sabbath were made only to recover that sleep they have lost in the week'. But Angier knew the preachers would have the last laugh: 'Hell was made for sermon-sleepers.' Although godly ministers had supposed early in the reign of Elizabeth that if the number of preachers could be increased their evangelistic campaign would be successful, there was a growing recognition later that sermons often did not work. 'We hear say that many painful preachers, both in towns and cities, exercising the word three or four times a week, yet do complain of the small profitting of the flock', lamented a petition to Parliament printed in 1585, and the position was much the same forty years later:

what excuse will they have who have been bred up in parishes that have had preaching almost time out of mind? Here one would think, in regard of time and means, men might be teachers rather than learners, but it is nothing so. Here also shall you meet with hundreds that shall need to be taught their very ABC in matters of religion: it is no marvel to see children or young men ignorant, when you shall have old men, 50, 60, yea 80 years old, whose grey hairs show that they have had time enough to learn more wit, yet in case to be set to school again . . . ask them the meaning of the articles of faith, of the petitions in the Lord's Prayer, or of other common points in catechism, and mark their answers, you shall see them so shuffle and fumble, speak half words and half sentences, so hack and hew at it, that you may almost swear they speak they know not what, of matters out of their element: though they be the wisest and craftiest-headed men in a parish, take them in other matters, yet in these things you would think verily they were born stark naturals and idiots.[21]

V

It was clear to the ministers, as it must surely be to historians, that the preaching campaign had produced only a small minority of godly Protestants, leaving the rest in ignorance, indifference or downright antipathy – 'Which cannot be imputed to the want of good preaching, but rather to the want of good hearing.' How could the people be brought to better hearing? After the first two decades of Elizabethan preaching, it was increasingly argued (especially by authors of catechisms) that the answer lay in regular catechising: 'The neglect of this duty in those ministers that be preachers is in very deed the cause why their preaching taketh so little effect amongst their parishioners', wrote a leading exponent of 'the profit and necessity of catechising, that is, of instructing the youth and ignorant persons in the principles and grounds of Christian religion'. The Royal Injunctions of 1559 required ministers to hold catechism classes in church for half an hour every holy day and every other Sunday, though the bishops soon increased the duty to an hour every Sunday, as well as holy days. But the task was widely neglected: of the west Sussex parishes which answered a question on catechising at the visitation of 1579, ten had classes, fifteen did not, and in four places the minister tried to hold classes but no one turned up. In Lancashire there was no catechising in seven churches in 1592, four in 1595, six in 1598, seven in 1601 and nine in 1604; in the diocese of Norwich in 1597 there was no catechising in seventy-eight parishes, and it was infrequent in fifteen more. The consequence in such parishes was, of course, ignorance: 'For the catechism', complained the parishioners of Eastergate in Sussex in 1579, 'we do think there be many cannot say it as it ought to be said, for lack of instructions.'[22]

The fault was not always the minister's: the churchwardens of Poling in Sussex reported in 1586, 'catechising given over in the default of parents and masters', who failed to send their young charges to classes. Though absence from classes was punishable, and though learning the catechism in the Book of Common Prayer was encouraged by excluding those who could not recite it from communion and refusing to allow them to marry or act as godparents, resistance was common: there were many more interesting things to do on Sunday afternoons. The minister of Woolavington in Sussex complained in 1579 that 'Graffham is a parish of great misrule upon sabbath days, dancing etc., whereto old and young of my parish go, so as I have seldom any at the catechism', and in 1590 a group of

Lancashire ministers reported that because of Sunday games and dancing 'the youth will not by any means be brought to attend the exercise of catechising in the afternoon, neither the people to be present at the evening service'. At Cromwell in Nottinghamshire in 1594, two men got into trouble for 'dancing and keeping of evil rule so near to the church' that their noise drowned the minister's catechising, and at Sheringham in Norfolk in 1597 it was reported that a fiddler regularly enticed the young from catechism.[23] The whole process of compulsory catechism and examination seems to have been much resented. Two Nottinghamshire men scoffed during catechism in 1579, and at Bloxham in Oxfordshire in 1584 a man refused to learn the catechism by heart on the grounds that he was able to read it. At Coggleshall in 1586, three truculent youths refused to recite the Ten Commandments during a catechism class, and one 'sat unreverently with his hat on his head, to the evil example of all the rest of that sort'. Testing that communicants could say the catechism before they were allowed to receive often caused trouble: sometimes it was simply one woman who refused to be examined, as at Broadchalke in Wiltshire in 1584; sometimes almost a whole congregation, as at an Essex parish in 1588. The minister of Hatfield Peverel was presented to the Bishop of London for nonconformity by parishioners who objected to the rigour of his examinations in 1585, and in another Essex village, Inworth, a man protested in 1592 that his minister 'asked me frivolous questions, as what should become of their bodies when they were in the grave, and whether all the world should be saved'.[24]

Although it is clear that catechising provoked hostility, the small numbers rejected from communion on grounds of ignorance suggest that the exercise was usually effective – the Prayer Book catechism was, after all, only a thousand words long, and the recitation of the Creed, Ten Commandments and Lord's Prayer posed no difficulty for those willing to learn. But the official catechism taught nothing that was specifically Protestant, and the godly ministers expected much more than rote learning of short formularies. To this end, about a hundred more demanding catechisms were published in the reign of Elizabeth, many of them in the 1580s, and the best-sellers, such as those by John More and Eusebius Pagit, went through more than a dozen editions each. The problems of teaching Protestant beliefs to ordinary people in simple form were recognised, and the authors of shorter catechisms criticised their rivals for using 'more words than can be carried in mind of the ignorant man'. Thomas Ratcliffe, minister at St Saviour's, Southwark, explained in 1592 that

I have brought the question and the answer to as few words as I could, and that for the ease of children and common people, who cannot understand or gather the substance of a long question or a long answer confirmed with many reasons.

Some ministers found that 'they cannot bring the unlearned in letters unto this knowledge', but Eusebius Pagit claimed he was able to teach his catechism to a whole household, including servants (except 'three or four whose capacity was but mean and simple'), in four months. But Pagit's catechism was, together with the Creed, Commandments and Lord's Prayer, about 3000 words long, broken up into short answers for ease of learning: two-thirds of the catechisms published were over 4000 words long, and often posed daunting tasks. Alexander Nowell's semi-official *Catechism or First Institution of Christian Religion*, described as 'being of a middle sort' and 'to be learned of all youth next after the little catechism' (i.e. after the Prayer Book catechism), asked 246 questions, was 15 000 words long, and was 115 pages in the pocket-edition – but it was reprinted eight times in the reign, and tens of thousands of young people must have suffered it.[25]

Pagit's catechising triumph took place in a private household, not in church, and he succeeded in four months by daily, not weekly, classes. Robert Cawdrey thought a child could learn the basic essentials of Protestantism in six months, but he expected family catechising three times a week, as well as the minister's Sunday classes. It was, indeed, often argued that catechising by the minister was worthless unless backed by further teaching at home:

> let the minister never so diligently catechise in the church, unless there be also a furtherance of his travail in several families at home, ere the next assembly all or most of the seed by him sowen before is gone, trodden under foot, or choked.

But most families, of course, did *not* have home catechising: Thomas Sparke thought in 1588 that only one household in a hundred had catechising, and that those who had were 'mocked at and derided as precise and curious fools'.[26] Large numbers of catechisms were published, and presumably sold, and certainly catechising was a feature of the life of the godly household – but there, if not exactly preaching to the converted, catechising was preaching to the children of the converted, and in the homes of the unconverted majority such worthy devotion was lacking. So preaching did not make Protestants unless backed by clerical catechising; the ministers' catechising did not make Protestants unless backed by family catechism; and only the godly Protestant minority catechised at home. It was almost impossible to break the circle.

Richard Greenham, rector of Dry Drayton in Cambridgeshire from 1570 to 1591, was an exemplary Protestant pastor. At Dry Drayton he preached six sermons a week (about 6000 in all), and catechised twice a week; he composed his own thoughtful and well-organised (but impossibly long) catechism; and his commonplace book shows him to have been a diligent visitor of the sick and a sympathetic comforter of troubled souls.

But after twenty-one years of exhausting effort he stumped off in disgust to London, because of 'the intractableness and unteachableness of that people among whom he had taken such exceeding great pains' – and an analysis of Dry Drayton wills suggest that his conclusion that he had, in all but a few families, failed, was just about right.[27] If Richard Greenham, of all men, in Cambridgeshire, of all counties, could not make committed Protestants of more than a tiny handful of his parishioners, then nobody could and the task was impossible. In Elizabethan conditions, with low levels of literacy and with the alehouse and the village green to distract the people from sermons and catechism, the English people *could not* be made Protestants – they could not be made to understand, accept and respond to the Protestant doctrines offered to them, justification by faith and pre-destination. A Kentish minister, Josias Nichols, told his readers in 1602 that

> I have been in a parish of 400 communicants, and marvelling that my preaching was so little regarded I took upon me to confer with every man and woman before they received the communion. And I asked them of Christ, what he was in his person; what his office; how sin came into the world; what punishment for sin; what becomes of our bodies being rotten in the graves; and, lastly whether it were possible for a man to live so uprightly that by well-doing he might win heaven. In all the former questions I scarce found ten in the hundred to have any knowledge, but in the last question scarce one, but did affirm that a man might be saved by his own well-doing, and that he trusted he did so live, and that by God's grace he should obtain everlasting life by serving of God and good prayers.

Nichols was testing if those parishioners were Protestants, and they were not. The sketches of 'the religion which is among the common sort of Christians, which may be termed the country divinity' provided by authors such as Cawdrey, Dent, Gifford and Perkins in the second half of Elizabeth's reign are impressively unanimous. 'Most men' believed in salvation by works, that they would earn places in heaven by charity and prayers:

> If a man say his Lord's Prayer, his Ten Commandments and his Belief, and keep them, and say no body harm, nor do no body harm and do as he would be done to, have a good faith God-ward and be a man of God's belief, no doubt he shall be saved without all this running to sermons and prattling of the Scripture.[28]

Worthy sentiment these may be, but, at the end of Elizabeth's reign, they are not Protestantism – and the godly ministers were still trying to crush them.

VI

The failure of Protestant evangelism in some parishes and among some people is, of course, only one side of the story. But the consequence of the two sides, of the fact that godly preaching created an activist Protestant minority and left the majority unmoved at best, and infuriated at worst, was trouble. It was a common accusation against godly ministers that their preaching was divisive. In a 1588 dialogue, an innkeeper complains of a preacher that 'He setteth men together by the ears, the town was never at quiet since he came, he teacheth such a doctrine as some do like and some not, so they fall at variance'; a critic of the preachers of Kent at about the same time asked, 'Hath not Minge brought Ashford from being the quietest town of Kent to be at deadly hatred and bitter division?', and claimed that other ministers had divided Chart, Tenterden, Cranbrook and elsewhere, while Nichols did 'offend all the congregations where he cometh'. In Essex, too, the ministers provoked clashes between 'the godly people' and 'the profane multitude' in about a dozen parishes between 1582 and 1591; the town of Maldon was riven, at least between 1584 and 1595, by disputes between the godly followers of George Gifford and a 'multitude of papists, heretics, and other enemies to God and her Royal Majesty'. At Rochdale in 1585 and Peasmarsh, Sussex, in 1588, communities were split into godly supporters of activist preachers with strong views on morals and sabbath observance, and hostile parties led by local alehouse-keepers.[29] Such parochial conflicts often polarised between the church on the one hand and the alehouse and village green on the other: the godly of King's Langley, Hertfordshire, petitioned in 1593–4 for the suppression of Ellis Coggdell's alehouse, where there had been dancing and drinking during evening prayer. At Hayley in Oxfordshire in 1596, Simon Wickins was 'requested by the youth to brew some ale, and thereby he had resort into his house upon a sabbath day, and had a minstrel, so that the youth did not repair unto the church at evening prayer'; in the same year Nicholas Hargreaves, of Newchurch in Pendle, was presented 'for playing upon organs in the house and drawing people from evening prayer upon the sabbath'.[30]

Some of the fiercest conflicts took place in the 1580s, when godly ministers and town corporations tried to suppress maypoles and May Day dancing. At Lincoln in 1584–5 there was a struggle for power between the godly party, who sought to impose strict controls on alehouses and sabbath observance, and a rival group who espoused the cause of maypoles and May festivities. At Shrewsbury in 1588, the maypole was put down by the magistrates and resistance by the Shearmen's Guild led to a number of imprisonments. There was trouble at Banbury over maypoles in both 1588 and 1589, with street demonstrations and counter-demonstrations in 1589, and disputes continued over Whitsun ales and morris dancing: the

Privy Council had to intervene to ensure order was restored. When the Mayor of Canterbury forbade the maypole in 1589, the disaffected organised a protest morris dance outside his house.[31] The attempts of the godly to control the behaviour of their fellows led to the accusation that they were 'busy controllers': 'I perceive you are one of those curious and precise fellows, which will allow no recreation. What would ye have men do? – we shall do nothing shortly.' The godly were 'Scripture men' and 'precise fools', 'no Protestants but pratlingstants, that use to tell lies'. 'A shame take all professors, cried an Essex woman in 1591, 'for they are all dissemblers and liars'; in 1599 a Chipping Ongar man was reported as 'a railer of our minister and most of the inhabitants who profess religion, calling them all heretics, hypocrites, such as he hath ever and in every place detested, clowns, etc.'[32]

Committed Protestants and their ministers were often the butts of coarse jokes and abuse, which mocked their claim to be 'godly'. At Rayleigh in Essex in 1589, the customers at an alehouse acted out a scene in which they impersonated the vicar, churchwardens and 'honest men of the parish'; Eve Tilie, of Yatton Kennell in Wiltshire, was 'a maker of rhymes and lewd songs' in 1599, who mocked her honest neighbours 'to the grief and disquietness of some of the better sort of people within the same parish'. The parish clerk of Winwick in Lancashire was 'generally noted to gibe and mock the ministers of the word', and his favourite trick was to give the names of men and women who disliked each other to the curate to read out as marriage banns, to the confusion of the curate and the amusement of the congregation. Married ministers and their wives were especially likely to be attacked; abuse of married clergy at the beginning of Elizabeth's reign occasions no surprise, but it is striking how widespread this remained later. Richard Fox, a Nottinghamshire man, thought in 1584 that 'it was never a good world since priests were married, and called the vicar's wife of Gringley "painted stock". Also he said that priests' calves and bishops' calves would overrun the realm.' Two years later, a woman of Seamer in north Yorkshire agreed: 'it was never a good world since ministers must have wives'. In 1592 John Mous, of Little Stambridge, Essex, was in trouble for 'using bad speeches towards the minister, and for reporting in the presence of many persons of good credit that all priests wives are whores and their children bastards', and a Sussex woman claimed in the following year 'that all priests wives were counted trulls'.[33]

Such cases as these may be no more than examples of the perpetual conflict between the Church and the world, the godly and the reprobate. But sometimes issues of principle, and religious principle at that, were at stake: some communities were not just divided over maypoles and ale; they were divided over church services and beliefs. At East Hanningfield in Essex in the 1580s, there were two religious groups: the godly, called 'saints and scripture men' by their opponents, met in conventicles, and the rector refused to give communion to the rest of the parish, who trooped off to West Hanningfield to receive the sacrament there. At Kinston-upon-Thames in 1586, the minister and 'the children of God' formed an exclusive sect, and 'If any will not join with them, they will not cease to slander him in most spiteful and ungodly manner, reporting him either to be a papist, an atheist, of the Family of Love, or one that hath no religion, or raise some evil slander against him'; the rejected sought revenge by accusing the godly of unorthodox opinions. Divisions in religion may have been involved in the conflicts over the maypole at Banbury in 1589. Sir Francis Knollys claimed that John Danvers, who had led the defence of ales and maypoles, 'leaned passionately to the strict observance of the ceremonies of the Book of Common Prayer'; but Anthony Cope, a leader of the anti-maypole group, had presented the presbyterian 'bill and book' to Parliament in 1587. When Thomas Bracebridge, who had encouraged the attack on maypoles, was deprived of the vicarage of Banbury for non-conformity, ninety-five fellow-citizens petitioned Burghley in his defence in 1590, but there were significant absentees from the list of his supporters. Ten years later, the godly group, who had attacked maypoles and backed Bracebridge, threw down the market crosses in Banbury and nearly provoked a riot: their opponents claimed that the strict godly regime which had been imposed on the town had driven the country people to use other markets. At Preston Capes, in Northamptonshire, there were also long-lasting religious disputes. The struggles between the nonconformist vicar, John Elliston, and those whom he branded as 'blasphemers of God's name, profaners of the sabbath', in 1584–5 centred on the vicar's attempts to force even adults to attend catechism classes, and his opponents' attempt to force him to wear the surplice, baptise with a cross, and church women after childbirth. Through the 1590s, the next incumbent, Robert Smart, was regularly presented by parishioners for his nonconformity; in 1603 he was briefly suspended for flagrant disregard of the Prayer Book rubrics; and in 1604 he refused to give communion to those who insisted on kneeling for it. By 1604 there was a liturgical stalemate in Preston Capes and the neighbouring parish of Woodford Halse: in both the minister would give communion only to those who would stand, but some of the parishioners would receive only if they were permitted to kneel.[34]

A common theme in these conflicts is the demand for liturgical conformity, an insistence by some parishioners that their ministers should perform the Prayer Book ceremonies in full. In 1574, a group from Cirencester refused to receive communion because it was not administered according to the Book of Common Prayer, and in 1583 a gentleman from Doddinghurst in Essex asked his minister to follow the Prayer Book; in return, he was abused in sermons. We have already noted the demand for surplice, cross and churching at Preston Capes in 1584–5, and there were

similar troubles at Flixton in Suffolk in 1588–90: there some of the congregation followed the services in their Prayer Books to try to keep the
vicar to the rubrics, but he retorted that 'they which would have service
said according to the Book of Common Prayer are papists and atheists'.
Historians too frequently use presentments of minister for nonconformity
as evidence for widespread hostility to surplices and ceremonies; but many
of them were rather pleas for conformity, efforts to force ministers to
supply in full the restricted ceremonial endorsed in 1559, for omission
of ceremonies was often unpopular and provocative. In 1597 the churchwardens of St Cuthbert, Thetford, complained that a woman had prevented their minister using the sign of the cross at a baptism, 'thereby
giving great offence to many those inhabitants of Thetford then and there
present'. In 1598 and 1601 it was complained that the vicar of Leyland in
Lancashire did not use the cross in baptism, 'wherefore many of the
parishioners do cause their children to be baptised at other churches';
the same was happening at Poulton in 1604, and at Kirkham in 1605,
where sixty-one families were in trouble for having their children chris-
tened away from their parish church.[35] Perhaps we have heard too much of
'sermon-gadding' by the godly, and should be more sensitive to 'sacrament-gadding' by the rest!

VII

In some parishes the opponents of the godly were clearly the profane, but
those who defended ceremonies against the godly can hardly be called 'the
ungodly'. Despite the risk of anachronism, they may properly be spoken of
as 'parish anglicans' – 'anglicans', because of their stress on the Prayer
Book and insistence that 'there is as good edifying in those prayers and
homilies as in any that the preacher can make'; and 'parish' because of
their emphasis on the harmony and vitality of the village unit, at play and
at worship. Their model minister was not the divisive godly preacher, but
(to the fury of those who damned him as a 'dumb dog') the pastor who
read services devoutly, reconciled quarrellers in his parish, and joined his
people for 'good fellowship' on the ale bench.[36] These 'parish anglicans'
and their favoured clergy had not been moved by the evangelistic fervour of
the Protestant Reformation – indeed, in the sense that they knew little of
doctrine and rejected justification by faith and predestination, they were
not Protestants at all. But, despite some similarity between their views and
those of their pre-Reformation forebears, they were no longer Catholics:
they had been neglected by the missionary priests, and they attended the
services of the Church of England and demanded obedience to its liturgy.
Those (or the children of those) who had reluctantly surrendered Catholic
ritual in the 1560s now expected from their ministers as much ceremony as
the Church of England would sanction. Although theirs was a residual

religion, and they were the spiritual leftovers of Elizabethan England, they should not be dismissed as 'mere conformists', for in their defence of ceremonies and festivities they formed a factor to be reckoned with. Indeed, it was their demand for some ritual in their services which made possible – even made necessary – the drive for liturgical uniformity carried out by Whitgift and Bancroft. Later, their kind would provide the parochial foundations upon which the Laudian Church was built, and a considerable body of support for Caroline ceremonialism and Arminian doctrine. But that is an unfashionable argument, and must be pursued elsewhere.

Notes

1 C. Haigh, 'The Recent Historiography of the English Reformation', *HJ*, xxv (1982) 995–1007; D.M. Palliser, 'Popular Reactions to the Reformation during the Years of Uncertainty 1530–70', in *Church and Society in England: Henry VIII to James I*, ed. F. Heal and R. O'Day (1977) pp. 35–56.

2 H.N. Birt, *The Elizabethan Religious Settlement* (1907) p. 311; University of Durham Department of Palaeography and Diplomatic, Durham Probate Records 1596, will of James Nelson (I am grateful to Dr K. Wrightson for mentioning this document to me and providing a copy); *The Seconde Parte of a Register*, ed. A. Peel, 2 vols (Cambridge, 1915) ii, 166; F.G. Emmison, *Elizabethan Life: Disorder* (Chelmsford, 1970) p. 58; W. B.[urton], *The Rowsing of the Sluggard* (1595) p. 27.

3 References to churchwardens' accounts are based on a study of almost 100 sets of Elizabethan accounts, from most parts of England, *English Church Furniture*, ed. E. Peacock (1866), *passim* (Lincs); Birt, *Elizabethan Religious Settlement*, pp. 428–9; R.F.B. Hodgkinson, 'Extracts from the Act Books of the Archdeacons of Nottingham', *Transactions of the Thoroton Society*, xxx (1926) 26–7.

4 *The State of the Church in the Reigns of Elizabeth and James I*, ed. C.W. Foster, Lincoln Record Society XXIII (1926) 457; *A Parte of a Register* (Middelburg, 1593) p. 62; R.F.B. Hodgkinson, 'Extracts from the Act Books of the Archdeacons of Nottingham', *Transactions of the Thoroton Society*, xxix (1925) 40; H. Hajzyk, 'The Church in Lincolnshire, c. 1595–c. 1640' (University of Cambridge PhD thesis, 1980) p. 422.

5 For a few examples of 'counterfeiting', etc., see W.H. Hale, *A Series of Precedents and Proceedings* (1847) pp. 152, 153; F.G. Emmison, *Elizabethan Life: Morals and the Church Courts* (Chelmsford, 1973) p. 195. R. Clark, 'Anglicanism, Recusancy and Dissent in Derbyshire, 1603–1730' (University of Oxford DPhil thesis, 1979) pp. 108–9; Wilts CRO, Diocese of Salisbury, Bishops' Records, Detecta Book 5, fo. 9; *A Hampshire Miscellany: Metropolitical Visitation of the Archdeaconry of Winchester, 1607–1608*, ed. A.J. Willis (Folkstone, 1963) pp. 10, 34–5, 41; K.R. Wark, *Elizabethan Recusancy in Cheshire*, Chetham Society (1971) p. 16.

6 T. Gibson, *A Frutifull Sermon* (1584) sig. D; W. Perkins, *The Workes*, I (Cambridge, 1612) sig. A2; Hodgkinson, 'Extracts from the Act Books', *Transactions of the Thoroton Society*, xxix, 35; F. Trigge, *An Apologie or Defence of our Dayes* (1589) pp. 24, 32, 35; Emmison, *Disorder*, p. 48; R. Greenham, *The Workes*, 3rd edn (1601) pp. 425–6.

7 *Archbishop Grindal's Visitation, 1575*, ed. W.J. Sheils, Borthwick Texts and Calendars (1977) p. 56; C. Haigh, 'The Continuity of Catholicism in the English Reformation', *P & P*, XCIII (1981) 41–53.

8 *Letters and Memorials of Fr Robert Persons, SJ*, ed. L. Hicks, Catholic Record Society XXXIX (1942) 319–21. For a much less optimistic version of early Elizabethan

Catholic history, see the formative article by A.G. Dickens, 'The First Stages of Romanist Recusancy in Yorkshire, 1560–1590', *Yorkshire Archaeological Journal*, xxxv (1941) esp. 157–8, 180–81; J. Bossy, *The English Catholic Community, 1570–1850* (1975) esp. pp. 4–5, 11–12, 106–7, 147. For a balanced assessment, see A. Dures, *English Catholicism 1558–1642* (1983) pp. 3–8, 18–19.

9 See, for example, F.X. Walker, 'The Implementation of the Elizabethan Statutes against Recusants, 1580–1603' (University of London PhD thesis, 1961) *passim*; C. Haigh, *Reformation and Resistance in Tudor Lancashire* (Cambridge, 1975) pp. 202–94; R.B. Manning, *Religion and Society in Elizabethan Sussex* (Leicester, 1969) pp. 14–33, 129–50.

10 I here follow the argument elaborated in C. Haigh, 'From Monopoly to Minority: Catholicism in Early Modern England', *TRHS*, 5th ser., xxxi (1981) 129–47, where full references and supporting detail can be found. Cf. Dures, *English Catholicism*, pp. 20–6.

11 *Unpublished Documents Relating to the English Martyrs*, ed. J.H. Pollen, Catholic Record Society v (1908) 309; Haigh, 'Continuity', 59–62; *CSPD*, 1598–1601, p. 362.

12 Haigh, 'Monopoly to Minority', 136–43.

13 R. Challoner, *Memoirs of Missionary Priests*, ed. J.H. Pollen (1924) p. 232; *Unpublished Documents*, pp. 347–8.

14 Challoner, *Memoirs*, pp. 595–6; M.C.E. Chambers, *The Life of Mary Ward*, ii (1885) 28, 35; Haigh, 'Monopoly to Minority', 143.

15 Borthwick Institute, York, HC.AB 9, fo. 164v; W. Harrison, *A Brief Discourse of the Christian Life and Death of Mistris Katherine Brettargh* (1602) sig. N.

16 N. Breton, *A Merrie Dialogue betwixt the Taker and Mistaker* (1603) pp. 12–13.

17 W. Pemble, *The Workes*, 3rd edn (1635) p. 567; *Seconde Parte*, ii, 88, 94; R.G. Usher, *The Reconstruction of the English Church*, 2 vols (New York, 1910) ii, 241; A. Peel, 'A Puritan Survey of the Church in Staffordshire in 1604', *EHR*, xxvi (1911) 352.

18 West Sussex RO Ep.1/23/5, *passim*; *Archbishop Grindal's Visitation*, p. vi; *Seconde Parte*, ii, 130–42; *A Parte of a Register*, pp. 216, 305; G. Gifforde, *A Briefe Discourse of Certaine Points of the Religion which is among the Common Sort of Christians which may bee Termed the Countrie Divinitie* (1598 edn) p. 70; J. More, *Three Godly and Fruitful Sermons* (Cambridge, 1594) p. 69.

19 W.J. Sheils, *The Puritans in the Diocese of Peterborough*, Northants Record Society xxx (1979) 45; W. Hinde, *A Faithfull Remonstrance of the Holy Life and Happy Death of John Bruen* (1641) pp. 83–4; C.W. Field, *The State of the Church in Gloucestershire, 1563* (Robertsbridge, Sussex, 1971) p. 15; Gifforde, *Briefe Discourse of Certaine Points*, p. 41; Emmison, *Morals*, p. 116; Hale, *Series of Precedents*, p. 208; *A Parte of a Register*, p. 362; Hajzyk, 'Church in Lincolnshire', p. 160.

20 Gifforde, *Briefe Discourse of Certaine Points*, pp. 38, 121; A. Dent, *The Plaine-Man's Path-way to Heaven*, 21st edn (1631) pp. 289–90.

21 C. Haigh, 'Puritan Evangelism in the Reign of Elizabeth I', *EHR*, xcii (1977) 47–8; Hodgkinson, 'Extracts from the Act Books', *Transactions of the Thoroton Society*, xxix, 52; *A Parte of a Register*, p. 208; Pemble, *Workes*, pp. 558–9.

22 Haigh, 'Puritan Evangelism', 47; R. Cawdrey, *A Short and Fruitfull Treatise of the Profit and Necessitie of Catechising*, 2nd edn (1604) p. 36; West Sussex RO Ep. 1/23/5, fo. 32 and *passim; Bishop Redman's Visitation, 1597*, ed. J.F. Williams, Norfolk Record Society xviii (1946) 17–18.

23 West Sussex RO Ep. 1/23/7, fo. 13v, Ep. 1/23/5, fo. 23v; 'State Civil and Ecclesiastical of the County of Lancaster', ed. F.R. Raines, *Chetham Miscellanies*, Chetham Society, old ser., xcvi (1875) 2; Hodgkinson, 'Extracts from the Act Books', *Transactions of the Thoroton Society*, xxix 36; *Bishop Redman's Visitation*, p. 79.

24 Hodgkinson, 'Extracts from the Act Books', *Transactions of the Thoroton Society*, xxix, 35; *The Archdeacon's Court; Liber Actorum, 1584*, ed. E.R. Brinkworth, Oxfordshire Record Society (1942) p. 159; Emmison, *Morals*, pp. 101, 118; Wilts CRO, Diocese of Salisbury, Bishops' Records, Detecta Book 5, fo. 35; *The Presbyterian Movement in the Reign of Queen Elizabeth*, ed. R.G. Usher, Camden Society, 3rd ser., viii (1905) 71; *Seconde Parte*, ii, 31.

25 T. Ratcliffe, *A Short summe of the Whole Catechisme* (1619 edn) Epistle dated 1592, sig. A3; [E. Pagit], *Short Questions and Answeares, Conteyning the Summe of Christian Religion* (1583 edn) sig. A3.

26 Cawdrey, *Short and Fruitfull Treatise*, pp. 23, 99; T. Sparke and J Seddon, *A Catechisme, or Short Kind of Instruction* (Oxford, 1588) pp. 1, 28, 55.

27 S. Clarke, *A General Martyrology* (1677 edn) pp. 12–15; M. Spufford, *Contrasting Communities* (Cambridge, 1974) pp. 327–8.

28 J. Nichols, *The Plea of the Innocent* (n.p., 1602) pp. 212–13; Cawdrey, *Short and Fruitfull Treatise*, pp. 87–9, 94, 117–18; Dent, *Plaine-Man's Path-way*, pp. 17, 25, 28, 237–8, 252–3, 264, 265, 271, 273, 278, 284; Gifforde, *Briefe Discourse of Certaine Points*, pp. 9, 69–70, 95, 116–17; Perkins, *Workes*, I, sig. A2. The final quotation is from Dent, *Plaine-Man's path-way*, p. 25.

29 *A Parte of a Register*, p. 362; *Seconde Parte*, I, 238; W. Hunt, *The Puritan Moment: The Coming of Revolution in an English County* (Cambridge, MA, 1983) pp. 146–7, 153–4; Haigh, 'Puritan Evangelism', 57; J.J. Goring, 'The Reformation of the Ministry in Elizabethan Sussex', *Journal of Ecclesiastical History*, XXXIV (1983) 359.

30 *Hertfordshire County Records: Notes and Extracts from the Sessions Rolls*, ed. W.J. Hardy (1905) I, 18; Bod. Lib., Oxford Diocesan Papers, d. 5, fo. 60v; Haigh, 'Puritan Evangelism', 53.

31 C. Hill, *Society and Puritanism in Pre-Revolutionary England*, paperback edn (1969) pp. 178–9 and refs; A. Beesley, *The History of Banbury* (1841) pp. 242–4, 615–16; *CSPD 1581–90*, pp. 586, 601, 602, 605; *APC, 1588–9*, p. 202; P. Clark, *English Provincial Society from the Reformation to the Revolution* (Hassocks, Sussex, 1977), p. 157.

32 Gifforde, *Briefe Discourse of Certaine Points*, pp. 2–3, 4, 45, 74; Dent, *Plaine-Man's Path-way*, pp. 24, 273; Hale, *Series of Precedents*, pp. 168, 221–2; Emmison, *Morals*, p. 215.

33 Hale, *Series of Precedents*, pp. 196–7; Wilts CRO, Archdeaconry of Wiltshire, Visitation Detecta Book 1586–99, fo. 172; Hodgkinson, 'Extracts from the Act Books', *Transactions of the Thoroton Society*, XXIX, 42: Emmison, *Morals*, p. 215; Manning, *Religion and Society*, p. 173.

34 P. Collinson, *Godly People: Essays on English Protestantism and Puritanism* (1983) p. 11; *Seconde Parte*, II, 44; Beesley, *Banbury*, p. 615; *Banbury Corporation Records: Tudor and Stuart*, ed. J.S.W. Gibson and E.R.C. Brinkworth, Banbury Historical Society XV (1977) 59–60; P.D.A. Harvey, 'Where was Banbury Cross?', *Oxoniensia*, XXXI (1966) 87, 93–4, 101–5; Sheils, *Puritans*, pp. 37, 68–9, 131; *Seconde Parte*, II, 291–6.

35 *The Commission for Ecclesiastical Causes within the Diocese of Bristol and Gloucester*, ed. F.D. Price, Bristol and Glos. Archaeological Society, Records Section, X (1972) 65; Emmison, *Morals*, p. 77; M. Spufford, *Small Books and Pleasant Histories* (1981) p. 34; *Bishop Redman's Visitation*, p. 69; Cheshire CRO, EDV 1/12a fo. 96, 1/12b fo. 122, 1/13 fo. 198v, 1/14 fos 186–7.

36 Gifforde, *Briefe Discourse of Certaine Points*, pp. 1–3; Cawdrey, *Short and Fruitfull Treatise*, pp. 79–80; *Seconde Parte*, II 165–9. For examples of parishioners following such 'pot companions' in preference to godly preachers, see *Seconde Parte* I, 160–1, 163; Emmison, *Disorder*, pp. 190–1. For a sympathetic presentation of the model, see the 'Patron for Pastors' in L. Wright, *A Summons for Sleepers* (1589) esp. pp. 49–51.

10

'By this book': parishioners, the Prayer Book and the established Church

JUDITH MALTBY

Moreover, by this book are priests to administer the sacraments, by this book to church their women, by this book to visit and housle the sick, by this book to bury the dead, by this book to keep their rogation, to say certain psalms and prayers over the corn and grass, certain gospels at crossways, etc. This book is good at all assaies [on every occasion]; it is the only book of the world.

Henry Barrow, *A Brief Discoverie*, 1590.[1]

I

The Protestant separatist Henry Barrow, assessing the religious health of the people after the Reformation, censured English parishioners for their over-attachment to the rites and ceremonies of the reformed Church of England. Historians, by contrast, have largely ignored the conformist element within the established Church. A generation of local studies inspired by Patrick Collinson's magisterial *Elizabethan Puritan Movement* (1967) have concentrated on those who failed to conform to the national Church, including Roman Catholics and Protestant separatists, but above all on nonconformist puritans who remained within the Church but refused to conform to many of its lawful practices. No doubt this is primarily a matter of sources: as John Morrill has rightly commented, 'religious commitment is best observed in conditions of persecution'. In the all too elusive world of the early Stuart parish, individuals who failed to conform and were prosecuted for it left behind more evidence of their activities than those who did conform. But a less respectable reason may also be suggested. Much of the work on religion at the local level rests on the belief that nonconformists took their faith more seriously than men and women who conformed to the lawful worship of the Church of England. It is not the intention here to challenge the view that puritanism is best understood as an active and legitimate strand within the established Church, but rather to endorse it. Such a view provides the necessary

Reprinted from Kenneth Fincham, ed. *The Early Stuart Church* (Basingstoke, 1993).

corrective to the 'Anglican vs. puritan' antithesis which has so bedevilled our understanding of early modern English Christianity. Rather, the assumption challenged here is that 'puritanism' had a monopoly on all that could be considered genuine, vigorous or successful in the Church of England: the flattering view that the godly present of themselves, that 'perception, realistic enough, that as sincere and genuine rather than merely conformable protestants they were thin on the ground'.[2] Identification of 'successful' movements in contemporary Christianity, or in the history of the Church, is a notoriously subjective exercise.

Meanwhile, many social historians, following Keith Thomas's *Religion and the Decline of Magic* (1971), hold a general view that conformity had little or no impact on the lives of ordinary people. For the mass of the population, especially the poor, any contest between the underworld of magic and folk religion and Christian orthodoxy led to the latter's quick retreat from the field. England was a society of 'two cultures' – popular and élite – and they were relatively self-contained with little cross-fertilisation. As Keith Wrightson has remarked: 'the truly godly commonly found themselves in a minority. For many of their neighbours church attendance remained a gathering of neighbours rather than an intensely spiritual experience.' Among much social history, as in the field of ecclesiastical history, the verdict of the self-validating 'godly' on the quality of the religious experiences of those outside their fellowship, 'the multitude', has been too readily accepted. Between those interested only in the puritan agenda for the Church, and those assuming the lack of importance of conventional religion in the lives of ordinary women and men, the question of the importance of the conforming majority has scarcely been raised.[3]

An exception must be made for work of Christopher Haigh. He has broken rank with the dominant interest in puritanism and attempted a more integrated view of English Christianity. He has questioned the effectiveness of preaching as the best instrument for inculcating sophisticated Protestant theology among the people and drawn our attention to the role of liturgy as a means of importing, through repeated words and actions, the basic tenets of the reformers. More recently he has argued: 'In some parishes the opponents of the godly were clearly the profane, but those who defended ceremonies against the godly can hardly be called "the ungodly".' Dr Haigh's analysis of 'parish Anglicans' (the term he prefers) takes some far more controversial turns, however. He has suggested that parochial support for the lawful liturgy and ceremonies directed by the rubrics of the Book of Common Prayer should be seen as residing in a constituency abandoned to their fate by the failure of the Roman Catholic mission priests. These men and women are rather unhappily but memorably described by him as the 'spiritual leftovers of Elizabethan England'. The continued authorisation and use of some pre-Reformation practices no more invalidates the label 'Protestant' in England than it does for many areas of the Lutheran Reformation where, by Genevan standards of reform, an unjustified number of pre-Reformation ceremonies were retained as well. Dr Haigh, like many of the historians he is critical of, allows 'Geneva' to fix the goal posts of Protestantism.

Even more doubtful is his assertion that these 'spiritual leftovers' formed the natural constituency for the controversial Laudian innovations of the 1630s. It seems reasonable to conclude that such Prayer Book Protestants did provide local backing for drives for liturgical conformity under Archbishops Whitgift and Bancroft, for example. After all, quite often, the fact we know about the presence of nonconformity is due to the diligence of the supporters of the Prayer Book through the presentations they made in ecclesiastical courts. But it shall be argued here that rather than forming a natural constituency for Laudianism, the descendants of these 'spiritual leftovers' helped to provide opposition to Laudian reforms: the policy of Thorough was perceived by them as an attack on parochial Prayer Book Protestantism.[4]

II

In 1604 fifteen articles were addressed to Bishop Richard Vaughan of Chester by parishioners at Manchester against their curate Ralph Kirk. Among other charges, it was alleged that Kirk had failed to wear the surplice, use the cross in baptism and administer communion according to the canons. We might be tempted to regard this as simply an example of pressure from the authorities for presentments resulting in a detailed series of accusations. In fact, closer inspection reveals much about the parishioners' own beliefs and concerns. Several of them wanted the sign of the cross to be made over baptised infants and 'pestered' Kirk to do this. So much so, that he started to insult the parents: 'he asketh them whether they will have a black, a red, or blue, or a headless cross and such other contemptuous words'. He was clearly no wit. Others were angry that Kirk had attempted to eliminate lay participation at morning prayer as directed by the Prayer Book.

> For the manner of morning prayer whereas divers of the parish, who have been used to help the parish clerk, to read verse for verse [i.e. to make the responses] with the curate for forty years last past and more. . . . The said Ralph Kirk hath of late times not permitted them to do so.

The parishioners claimed that Kirk had received a special monition from the chancellor of the diocese, ordering him to allow the people to make the accustomed and set responses of the Prayer Book service. Not only did Kirk fail to conform to the order but it would appear that the spark which escalated the conflict to the level of formal legal proceedings was precisely Kirk's behaviour on this point. The collegiate Church at Manchester has been described as a conservative institution; its fellows in particular were slow to adapt to religious changes of the mid-Tudor period. In 1571, one fellow attempted to make the Prayer Book eucharist as much like the pre-Reformation mass as he could. Have we therefore discovered some of Dr Haigh's 'spiritual leftovers'? I think not. The laity were rarely expected to make the Latin responses in the medieval mass; that they should was, for English Christians, an innovation of Archbishop Cranmer's liturgical reforms.[5]

The evidence from Manchester in 1604 of an informed and articulate group of conformist laity, demanding worship according to the Book of Common Prayer and willing to go to law to discipline their minister, is a pattern we find repeated elsewhere time and again. It is clear that many parishioners wanted the set order of prayers observed. William Hieron of Hemingby in Lincolnshire omitted set prayers and even rejected the idea of them, 'being as he [sees] . . . them a few dead lines', complained the articles against him presented towards the end of the sixteenth century. In 1602 the churchwardens of Kimcoate, Leicestershire presented their minister for not reading the whole of the Common Prayer: 'in many things he breaketh the order of the Church and the Book of Common Prayer'. Parishioners at Husband's Bosworth wanted the entire Prayer Book service and complained in 1603 that the curate Mr Hall was not reading the whole service, which indicates that at least some of the laity there knew what the order of the service should be. In 1639 parishioners in Tarporley, Cheshire, could tell that their curate John Jones was omitting the Ten Commandments from the communion service 'and other parts of divine service contrary to law and to the contentment of your ordinary and scandal of well affected people'. In fact, not only did some laity know what the order of service should be, but some of them brought their own books to follow it in. In 1590 Thomas Daynes, vicar of Flixton in Suffolk was deprived of his living in the consistory court in a case in which all the witnesses against him were parishioners. In addition to his predictable failure to use the sign of the cross in baptism, allow godparents, wear the surplice, church women, or pray for the queen as supreme governor of the Church of England, he rebuked his flock and called them 'papists and atheists' for bringing their Prayer Books to church in order to see if he was observing the lawful services. Daynes declared from the pulpit that 'his parishioners were papists and that they would rather . . . hear mass . . . than to hear the word of God truly preached'. He reproved his congregation 'for looking in their books' and said 'that they which would have service said according to the Book of Common Prayer are papists and atheists'. Knowledge of the liturgy and the desire for it to be properly performed was not exclusively a concern of pre-Reformation churchgoers or Roman Catholics.[6]

It is worth considering whether the attitudes revealed in these cases reflect more accurately the preferences of 'church papists' than 'Prayer Book Anglicans'. Professor Collinson has recently argued for the former interpretation; that objections to puritan practices came from semi-conforming Catholics as a way presumably to antagonise their godly ministers. The conservatism of the Manchester clergy early in Elizabeth's reign has already been remarked upon. There were, however, numerous presentments for Protestant noncomformity in Manchester and its dependent chapelries throughout our period. The choice of a Protestant liturgy does seem a curious weapon for 'church papists' to use; early in Elizabeth's reign conservatives in Manchester did their best to undermine the new Prayer Book. The vicar of Flixton, of course, claimed his accusers were papists, but we should exercise some restraint in readily accepting his version of events. 'Church papists' who not only attended the parish church but made use of the ecclesiastical courts and owned their own copies of the Book of Common Prayer seem an improbable combination. Smearing one's opponents with the damaging stain of popery, whether sincerely or as a deliberate libel, was hardly unknown in the early seventeenth century. Although he was accused of many things, few historians accept the charge against Archbishop Laud of crypto-popery made by some contemporaries. The Earl of Clarendon's observation that some of the so-called 'Calvinian faction' called 'every man they do not love, papist' is a warning worth bearing in mind.[7]

General support for the lawful liturgy also extended to the central sacramental acts of the Christian religion and its rites of passage. Repeated complaints were voiced about the failure to administer communion. In 1628 the inhabitants of the chapel of Bruera in Cheshire alleged that through the neglect of their minister they were being excluded from the sacramental life of the Church. The sincerity of the chapelry inhabitants about their desire to receive the communion was verified by one Edward Haydocke. He deposed that he had served the cure for many years for an annual stipend of £5. He read divine service and arranged yearly at Easter for another minister in priest's orders to celebrate the eucharist, 'this deponent being but a deacon'. The inhabitants of Bruera chapelry, according to their deacon of many years, *did* repair to receive the sacrament. So their feeling of being deprived seems to be genuine, rather than acting as a pretext to persecute an unpopular local clergyman.[8]

Not only is there evidence that the laity wanted communion services, but they often wanted to communicate themselves and in a certain manner. Feelings could run high on this matter, as Bishop Thomas Morton of Chester observed in 1618, 'some will receive the sacrament at the hands only of the conformable, and some only of unconformable' ministers.

Historians of local studies, however, have placed so much emphasis on either the priest who withheld the sacrament from parishioners who knelt, or members of the laity who refused to kneel at all, that the existence of parishioners who insisted on kneeling in the face of clerical criticism has been essentially ignored. William Hieron, for example, had such retrogrades in his flock, who complained that 'he hath refused to minister the communion to such as kneel until he hath lifted them up with his hands and then delivered them the sacrament'. He also railed against those who knelt at the Lord's Prayer. In the early 1640s, the parishioners of Tarporley battled with their rector Nathaniel Lancaster and his curate John Jones, through the Church courts, Quarter Sessions and by petitioning the king and the House of Lords. In their petition to the king, forty-five subscribers complained that Lancaster and Jones:

> called your petitioners dogs . . . in the pulpit who will not be conformable to his orders, nor will he suffer any of the parishioners to receive the communion at the feast of Easter, neither will they according to the ancient order of our Church of England prescribed in the Book of Common Prayer.

Lancaster also used an unlawful catechism and refused to admit any (including adults and especially 'old persons') to communion who refused to be instructed by an unauthorised catechism. When one John Walley petitioned against Lancaster in Quarter Sessions, he lamented the passing of 'many orders and customs which we have had in former times . . . [and are] now taken from us'. One of these customs was receiving at the communion rails: 'the rails before our communion table are cast aside'. It would be mistaken, however, to see this as an expression of 'popular Laudianism' as described by Dr Haigh. A plan for Tarporley Church dating from perhaps 1613 shows that the holy table stood behind rails even then, but was free-standing in the chancel. The distinction between approved rails that had existed before the onset of Laudian innovations and 'popish' rails imposed by the policy of Thorough was one made by contemporaries and endorsed in legal decisions in the House of Lords in the early 1640s.[9]

There is evidence that visiting the sick with communion was still desired after the Reformation. On one occasion a number of parishioners at Hemingby in Lincolnshire sent for Hieron on behalf of a bedridden man who desired 'to reserve the sacrament for the strengthening of his faith'. The vicar responded to this request by saying 'let him live by the strength of the last [communion], I do not mean to make a popish matter of it'. One of the 'many orders and customs which we have in former times' to be taken away by Nathaniel Lancaster at Tarporley, complained layman John Walley, was that there was now 'no visiting of the sick, nor any communion to them'. This was a far cry from what George Herbert advised in ministering to the sick or distressed. The country parson 'fails not to afford his best comforts, and rather goes to them than sends for the afflicted, though they can, and otherwise ought to come to him'. In ministering to the sick, Herbert urged the use of auricular confession, admonitions to charitable works and the administration of the eucharistic sacrament, stressing how 'comfortable and sovereign a medicine it is to all sin-sick souls, what strength and joy and peace it administers against all temptations, even to death itself'. Some parish priests and lay-people did match Herbert's high standards. A case from St Bridget's parish in Chester in 1612 tells of a minister, Mr Evans, encouraging a parishioner recovering from a long illness, Thomas Marsland, to prepare himself to attend holy communion the following day. If he was still too ill to come to church, however, the priest offered to bring communion to his house. Marsland was reluctant to take the sacrament 'for there was some thing [that] troubled him in [his] mind'. Evans expressed perfectly proper Prayer Book Protestantism: the minister giving warning of holy communion so that preparation can be made by the communicants as well as a willingness to visit the sick with the sacrament. Marsland, too, responded in a way thought proper for a lay person by the Prayer Book, that those too troubled in their conscience to receive holy communion should seek out a 'discreet and learned minister of God's Word' for pastoral advice.[10]

Conforming parishioners also wanted baptism, and like holy communion, they often wanted it performed lawfully. The rector of Folkingham had by his prolonged absences, complained the churchwardens, caused grief to some parents and exposed their children to danger. While Hoskins was away, parents were forced to walk two miles to the next parish in order to have their infants baptised, 'to their parents' grief and danger and peril to their infants'. This same charge was made against Lancaster and Jones in Tarporley: parents of young children complained that they were forced to travel several miles to a neighbouring parish in order to procure infant baptism or baptism with the Prayer Book ceremonies.[11]

Parental grief and anger could be great when a child died unbaptised. Conflict of this sort had a long history at Bunbury in Cheshire. In 1611 the vicar Richard Rowe was presented, not only for not making the sign of the cross in baptism, but that he 'refuses to baptise any but on the sabbath or holy day although it be in danger of death'. In 1626, it was charged against John Swan:

that you have . . . divers times or at least once . . . refused to baptise one or more child or children being in danger of death although you had notice of the same, in so much that they have died without that holy sacrament of baptism from you.

The long-suffering parishioners of Ellington in Huntingdonshire accused their parson Anthony Armitage in 1602 of refusing to baptise a child on a week day, which later died unbaptised.

> [Armitage] did refuse to baptise the child . . . in the week day, being made privy by the said Morley [the father] and other ancient women of the parish that the child was very weak and in peril of death, in so much the child died without baptism to the great grief of the parents.

The refusal to baptise on a week day is often seen by historians as an indication of puritan sentiments in a minister, reflecting the desire to discourage any magical connotations that the ceremony might have left to their 'semi-pagan' or 'crypto-papist' congregations. The model conformist parson George Herbert supported the view that baptism was ideally a *public* not a *private* sacrament. However, under such conditions as described concerning Francis Morley's child, Herbert, as a pastor, made exception – as did the Common Prayer Book.

> The pastors and curates shall oft admonish the people that they defer not baptism of infants any longer than the Sunday or other holy day next after the child be born, unless upon a great and reasonable cause be declared to the curate, and by him approved. And also they shall warn them, that without great cause and necessity they baptize not children at home in their houses.

Rowe and Swan may well have been acting from one sort of theological conviction. But was Anthony Armitage's action – or lack of it – the result of conviction or negligence? We do not know. It has been maintained that to puritan clergy baptism did not convey grace but marked admission to the congregation of Christ; to such clergy the death of an unbaptised child 'was not a catastrophe'. It is suggested here that to some parents the death of their unbaptised child was 'a catastrophe'; the Church court records testify to the 'great grief of the parents'.[12]

If omitting the sign of the cross in the baptismal rite can be taken as evidence of puritanism, may not reiterated insistence by individuals upon the ritual be taken as evidence that some parishioners desired the lawful ceremonies prescribed in the Prayer Book?[13] The parishioners of Anthony Armitage complained that he omitted the sign of the cross as well as the set prayer that went with the action. All the deponents in this case, who had information to contribute on this particular, confirmed it. Tempers apparently ran hot on this question. A yeoman, Richard Price, related that his child had been one of those the vicar had refused to cross 'and this deponent found fault with it'. Francis Morley, the father of the child who had died without baptism, described the disagreement between Armitage and Price more strongly and said they were 'at controversy because Armitage . . . would not sign it with the sign of the cross'. Perhaps Morley and

Price felt the same as George Herbert, and thought 'the ceremony not only innocent, but reverend'.[14]

Prayer Book Protestants wanted their dead buried properly, reverently and with the rites authorised by the established Church. In the various sets of articles arising out of the disputes at Tarporley, there are several concerned with proper burial. It was complained that Lancaster would not 'execute the holy order of the Church in burial'. He would not meet the corpse at the churchyard gate, nor permit mourners to come into the church, nor 'prayer among the congregation that come with the dead' – all ceremonies directed by the Prayer Book rubrics. Lancaster even struck a man as he tolled a bell for a passing soul, as had been directed in visitation articles for the diocese. John Swan of Bunbury also refused to meet the corpse at the churchyard gate, or use the Prayer Book rite.

> Neither did you meet the said corpse [and bring it] into the church-yard and church, nor read the usual prayers and service (appointed for the burial of the dead) when you went to accompany the same to the grave, but only carried the service book under your arm.

At the neglected chapelry of Bruera (1628), it was complained that no provision for decent burial had been made by the vicar of St Oswald's.[15]

Improperly conducted funerals were a point of great contentiousness between parishioners at Ellington in Huntingdonshire and the minister Anthony Armitage. They felt that the vicar did not 'perform his duty in the burial of the dead'. Only the previous Saturday before these articles were preferred, Armitage had gone to Huntingdon at the time arranged for the funeral of Mary Hale. He did not return until dusk, having kept the mourners and 'the whole parish also' apprehensively waiting for two hours inside the church, where they had moved to await their pastor's arrival. When he returned, Armitage refused to say the service until the people had moved the corpse outside; though by then it was so late 'that he could scarce see to read prayers', complained one parishioner. Once hustled out of the church (according to the Prayer Book the burial service should begin outside in the churchyard), the frustrated mourners apparently decided to bury their neighbour properly and carried her body all the way back to the churchyard gate where, again according to the Prayer Book's rubrics, the officiating priest was required to meet the corpse. But Armitage, the sub-scribers lamented, refused at any time to meet the body at the churchyard gate and the burial of their neighbour Mary Hale was no exception.[16]

The evidence for Armitage's shocking behaviour at the funeral of Mary Hale is largely supported in the depositions of witnesses made in this case. Several deponents claimed that once the vicar had finally arrived, he had refused to 'read prayers' before the actual interment; probably meaning that he left out the part of the service which was to be read by the priest as the body was moved from the churchyard to the grave. The tailor John Tall

added that Armitage had also refused 'to meet the corpse of one Richard
Gates his wife late of Ellington deceased'. Parishioners also saw the duty of
presiding at holy burial as one most desirably exercised by someone in holy
orders; indeed this is what the Prayer Book directed. John Tall had such
additional cause for grievance with Armitage, besides the vicar's treatment
of his neighbour's deceased wife. Tall's child and the child of a neighbour
Christopher Brit, were buried by the parish clerk, even though Armitage
was resident in Ellington. [Armitage] being at home his self, but [he]
appointed the clerk of the parish to put them into the earth very unde-
cently and undutifully, contrary to the order of the Book of Common
Prayer.' At Macclesfield in 1604 the curate had been illegally dismissed
by the mayor and replaced by one Francis Jackson, who was not only a
nonconformist but also, it was claimed, not even ordained.

> [Jackson has taken upon himself] to exercise the office of the minister
> or curate there, wherein the said Francis Jackson being a mere lay-
> man, hath taken upon him publicly to read divine service [and] to
> bury the dead. . . .

Jackson was not thought a 'sufficient' minister by the inhabitants of
Macclesfield because he was not in holy orders.[17]

Cases such as these raise some serious doubts about descriptions of
attitudes towards death in early modern England. It has been argued that
the rejection of ceremonies at funerals was not just a 'puritan' concern but
becoming standard among many 'orthodox Anglicans' as well by 1640.
Keith Thomas describes a growing indifference towards the dead in post-
Reformation England among the 'truly religious', due to the Protestant
doctrine of election.

> Whereas medieval Catholics had believed that God would let souls
> linger in purgatory if no masses were said for them, the protestant
> doctrine meant that each generation could be indifferent to the
> spiritual fate of its predecessor. . . . This implied an altogether
> more atomistic conception of the relationship which members of
> society stood to each other.

The 'problem' that the preciser sort of Protestants perceived with the
religious inclinations of their neighbours was not, in fact, one of indifference towards Prayer Book ceremonies and folk customs at funerals. The
separatist Henry Barrow strongly condemned the enthusiasm of the common people for the funeral ceremonies contained in the Prayer Book.
Indeed the detailed list of ritual transgressions which the Tarporley parishioners complained of for burials of kin and neighbours by their ministers; the dogged persistence with which the parishioners of Ellington
carried about the body of their dead neighbour Mary Hale in an attempt
to secure the lawful and conformable ceremonies due her; the anger and

discomfort expressed by the fathers, John Tall and Christopher Brit, over the irreverent interments of their children; or the concern at Macclesfield that Christian burial was an office best performed by a clerk in holy orders; suggests that they failed to hold an 'altogether more atomistic conception' of their relationships to each other in the family and the village community. Moreover, it appears that these parishioners were expressing that very 'solidarity' with their neighbours which has been linked to the 'hotter sort of Protestant'.[18]

It is worth noting that an absent feature of these cases, and most court cases concerning overtly religious matters, is any hint as to what understanding of grace was held by the participants. People certainly objected to being labelled unregenerate from the pulpit by their clergy, as was the case with the parishioners of William Hieron of Hemingby, whom he likened to 'thieves in gaol'.

> . . . and in the pulpit [Hieron] divideth his authority thus, having one or two that he thinketh assent his novelties. He pointeth unto them, I speak to you regenerate, and turning his body countenance and hand to the rest of the parishioners he sayeth, I speak to you also.

That the people of Hemingby objected to Hieron's remarks is hardly surprising, regardless of whether they as individuals chose to emphasise divine initiative or human response as the key to salvation. Whether laypeople who presented their clergy for nonconformity were more likely to be Calvinist or Arminian seems to me to be an unanswerable question: the evidence for any direct connection does not exist. There is no doubt, especially in the early decades of the seventeenth century, that in Parliament and the universities differences over how grace operates in the world were hotly disputed. In the parish, however, the *hows* of worship, perhaps more than the *whys* of worship, were what concerned many lay people, and perhaps even most clergy as well. It would be as mistaken to see such an attitude as shallow or unsophisticated as to paint the theological debates in the universities and Whitehall as obscure or élitist. It may mean that disagreements over the outward expressions of religious belief have a clarity and immediacy for the life of a community absent in many soteriological debates. 'Faith apart from works', after all, 'is dead' (James 2.17).[19]

III

Church court records provide one source for understanding Prayer Book Protestantism; a second source are the petitions, nearly two dozen in number, produced in support of the liturgy and episcopacy between 1640 and 1642. The growing perception that the Church of England was 'in danger' is a marked feature of conformist thought on the eve of the

Civil War. The Short and Long Parliaments provided a two-fold opportunity for the airing of grievances in religious and civil matters, as well as the means to seek their redress. Perhaps it is surprising in retrospect but the early months of the Long Parliament witnessed a degree of unity on religious matters. It was a shared hostility to Thorough, however, which provided the sense of unity of purpose; once the destruction of the Laudian ascendancy over the English Church was underway, cracks began quickly to appear. The series of Root and Branch petitions against episcopacy and proposals in the House of Commons of radical change in the government and worship of the Church of England rallied conformist Protestants in defence of the lawful liturgy.[20] Their petitions provide little support for Dr Haigh's view that they had welcomed the ceremonial innovations of Archbishop Laud in the 1630s. Huntingdonshire conformists, for example, agreed that recent corruptions had been allowed in the Church but suspected that many of the petitions calling for reform 'under [the] colour of removing some innovation, lately crept into the Church and worship of God, and reforming some abuses in the ecclesiastical courts' intended rather the destruction of the reformed Church of England.

> [These petitions] which we conceiving and fearing not so much to aim at the taking away of the said innovations, and reformation of abuses, as tending to an absolute innovation of Church government and subversion of that order and form of divine service, which hath happily continued among us, ever since the Reformation of Religion.

Petitioners from Somerset agreed and called for the 'condign punishment' of those responsible for introducing recent corruptions into the government and worship of the established Church.[21] In contrast both to the Laudians and to the rooters, the conformist petitioners looked favourably back to the 'Church of Elizabeth and James', rejecting innovations of the 1630s and proposals for reform in 1640–2 alike.

Pro-Church petitions were sometimes the result of proddings and encouragement by an MP who used the petition to back his support of the established Church in Westminster, which may have been the case with Sir Ralph Hopton in Somerset. Conversely, as in Herefordshire and Cornwall, the unreceptiveness of a county's representatives could spur conformists in the provinces to petition as a way of circumventing their obstructive or apathetic MP and making their views known. Great importance was placed by the Commons' leaders of all complexions on the role of petitions.[22]

The gentry appear to have dominated the drafting and organising of petitions. Assizes and Quarter Sessions – the natural gathering places of a county's élites – formed the obvious places for the hatching of petitions. This is well illustrated in Gloucestershire, Cornwall, Kent and Somerset, for example.[23] Furthermore, although the pro-Church petitions obviously shared common concerns, by and large these are expressed with individuality, indicating local rather than centralised composition. This is in marked contrast to the Root and Branch petitions which were often formulaic and followed a lead set by interests in Westminster. The textual similarity of the Root and Branch petitions was ironically noted by the royalist poet Abraham Cowley: 'Petitions next for every town they frame,/ To be restor'd to those from whom they came,/The same style all and the same sense does pen,/Alas, they allow set forms of prayer to men'. In some cases there is no evidence to suggest that Root and Branch petitions were ever circulated in the county before being presented in Westminster. The most obvious instance of this was in Cheshire, where the rooters simply doubled the numbers claimed by the petition for upholding episcopacy. Divisions in county communities over the future of the religious settlement often followed older established lines of rivalry between leading families, as in Cheshire, Herefordshire and Nottinghamshire. But mutual concern over the future of the Church of England could also occasion the laying aside of old differences, as in the case of the alliance of two former election rivals, Sir Roger Twysden and Sir Edward Dering in Kent.[24]

As striking as the evidence for the local composition of and initiative for the pro-Church petitions is the fact that the prime movers and drafters were overwhelmingly members of the laity. The clergy have left little evidence of their involvement in the initial stages. Parochial ministers in particular, however, did play an important role in 'getting hands'; the crucial next stage in a petition's life, as in Devon, Suffolk, Lincolnshire and Cheshire. Bearing in mind the dominant role of the laity in the conformist petitions, the level of support for the clergy expressed in them is all the more striking. Several petitions included calls for the better financial provision for parochial clergy, cathedrals and universities. The importance of preaching was sometimes linked with the importance of the sacramental ministry: a juxtaposition which should warn us against creating simple antitheses. Gloucestershire conformists strongly endorsed the Book of Common Prayer and episcopal government but maintained that no one should 'be enjoined to frequent his own parish church [unless] . . . there be in it a . . . preaching minister'. Equally the level of positive support for the clergy – though never at the abrogation of the laity's responsibilities – should urge us to a more nuanced consideration of the complex relations between clergy and laity than the treatment of 'anticlericalism' as a historical phenomenon has often allowed.[25]

Support for the Prayer Book was expressed with varying intensity and for a variety of reasons in the pro-Church petitions. Some petitions, stressing obedience to the law, called for the enforcement of conformity to the lawful liturgy and ceremonies until Parliament should make legal provision otherwise. Dissent in religion was, after all, disobedience from the law. But the clause often used, 'until such alteration be made', might just as well

reflect confidence that Parliament would uphold the Elizabethan settlement, rather than a thoroughgoing Erastianism. People in the provinces in
1641–2 had even less notion about where reform was heading than did
Members in Westminster. It seems clear that many MPs in 1641 did not
support radical reform of the national Church. Concern for the fate of the
Prayer Book 'swayed a majority of the House by the end of August, and
was strong enough to move men as zealous as William Strode, Serjeant
Wilde and John Crewe' away from the Parliamentary cause.[26]

But the Book of Common Prayer was also defended on far less expedient
grounds. Some petitions, like those from Staffordshire and Huntingdonshire presented the liturgy as the chief force for engendering the Reformation in the previous century. In this view the Prayer Book provided the
spiritual equivalent for the nation of regular exercise and a balanced diet:
its continued use ensured a 'continuous reformation' and kept the
Church of England 'healthy'; its regular use was the greatest guarantee
of a Church free from popery and schismatic heresies. Petitioners for the
Church expressed as well the conviction that the Prayer Book even aided
their worship of God. Cheshire conformists thought the Book of Common Prayer was viewed by the people

> with such general content, [and] received by all the laity, that scarce
> any family or person that can read, but are furnished with the Books
> of Common Prayer; in the conscionable use whereof, many Christian
> hearts have found unspeakable joy and comfort; wherein the famous
> Church of England our dear mother hath just cause to glory: and
> may she long flourish in the practice of so blessed a liturgy.

The fact that conformists could attach 'sacred value' to their worship was
reinforced by the sense of outrage expressed when Prayer Book services
were profaned or interrupted. Petitioners from Cornwall condemned 'irreverent vilifiers of God's house', while from Southwark some conformists
complained of the 'insolent carriage' of some clergy and laity during the
time of divine service:

> some [of them] calling the doctrine and discipline of our Church
> cursed, others refusing to read the Book of Common Prayer, enjoined
> by statutes, others calling it popish, others behaving themselves most
> unreverently at those prayers, or standing without the church till they
> be done, refusing to join with the congregation, in those prayers.

A sense of anger at the violation of sacred time and sacred place is
expressed in a number of pro-Church petitions. Such behaviour in church
was described by the Cheshire petitioners as 'sacrilegious violences . . .
upon divers churches'.[27] That the word 'sacrilege' was used is surely
significant and telling. The fact that some contemporaries were unable
to recognise any 'sacred value' in Prayer Book worship does not mean that

we cannot now recognise such feelings among men and women who did conform.

IV

It is now appropriate to turn to one of the most difficult questions concerning support for the lawful liturgy and polity of the Church of England: what can be said, if anything, about the different sections of society from which the established Church attracted loyalty and even, perhaps, affection? Or, as opponents maintained, were supporters and subscribers for the Church most often drawn from 'gullible labourers': '. . . hedgers at the hedge, ploughmen at the plough, threshers in the barns'?[28]

Material from Church court cases of the sort already discussed does provide occasional impressionistic evidence of the social spread of adherents of Prayer Book Protestantism; the wide range of persons who could and did organise to present clergy who failed to perform their ministerial obligations faithfully according to the Book of Common Prayer. Legal proceedings were initiated and supported by individuals across a wide sweep of the social spectrum: from gentlemen and yeomen to husbandmen and day labourers; women and men; those who could sign their names and those who made their marks. The active supporters of the proceedings on behalf of the much put upon parishioners of Anthony Armitage in Ellington, Huntingdonshire, ranged widely in terms of their social standing. Thirteen of the deponents against their minister included one gentleman, one yeoman, two labourers (one of whom was a woman), three tailors, one draper, three husbandmen, one 'sheerman' and one whose occupation was unstated. Seven or eight of them, that is over half, made their marks at the end of their depositions.[29] Court material such as that discussed above and evidence provided by the subscribers to the Cheshire petition for the Prayer Book suggests that support for the Church of Elizabeth and James came from a cross-section of English society. It was not 'determined' by social or economic standing.

Although a great many petitions were produced in 1640–2 in support of the Book of Common Prayer and episcopacy, few survive with the schedules of subscribers. Not only did Cheshire produce two pro-Church petitions, one for episcopacy in February 1641 and one for the Prayer Book in December 1641, but the schedules of subscribers for both survive, providing roughly 6000 names for the former and 9000 names for the latter.[30] These schedules of names, when compared with economic documents relating to the same locality, provide an almost unique opportunity to build a profile of the social and economic composition of supporters of the established Church. The subscribers to the petition for the Prayer Book will be examined here, as they relate directly to the concerns of this essay.

There is not space here to describe in detail the methodological concerns underpinning the analysis. In the end, it was possible to match five of the sixty-three identifiable localities to complementary extant church rates for the years 1640–2. The choice of the five communities was dictated entirely by the serendipity of identification and survival of church rates and subsidy returns. Happily, however, the five communities – Tilston, Frodsham, Wilmslow, Marbury and Middlewich – provide a reasonable geographic spread across the county.[31]

An obvious question to ask is what proportion the subscribers to the Common Prayer petition formed out of the overall adult male population in the five localities? The rate of subscription varied from 69 per cent for Wilmslow to 27 per cent for both Frodsham and Tilston; Wilmslow was in fact the only community in which the rate of subscription among adult males reached over 50 per cent. How many of the subscribers were eligible to pay the church rates? Using data from 1640–2 the results range from 49 per cent of subscribers in Tilston to just 18 per cent in Frodsham. In all five communities less than half of the subscribers were economically significant enough to contribute to one of the humblest forms of taxation in the early seventeenth century, the church rates.

Another revealing source for the economic and social standing of subscribers are the subsidies imposed by central government on localities throughout the period of the Personal Rule. However, these subsidies were even more élitist than Ship Money, affecting only the most substantial members of the gentry and they throw a light on a handful of the most economically and socially substantial of the potential subscribers for the petition to uphold the Prayer Book.[32]

The most important question raised by this information is how genuine are the signs of support expressed for the Prayer Book? To put it bluntly, were those who made their marks or signed their names simply caving in to pressure from above when they subscribed for the liturgy? It is argued here, based on the evidence from four parishes and one dependent chapelry, that the subscriptions for the Prayer Book represent a 'free-will offering'.

To begin with the male groups of those presumably most susceptible to 'social control': men receiving poor relief, those too economically insignificant even to be rated, and men rated for one shilling or less. Taking the five communities together there are no clear trends of subscribers to non-subscribers; both groups appear to spread evenly across these economic categories. This is also true of the middling sort – the type of individuals who largely filled parish office. Again, those paying the subsidy were also fairly evenly divided.

Out of a group of five communities it is hard to generalise about the degree of influence exercised by the clergy. In three out of the five, the petition enjoyed support from the clergy: Frodsham (27%), Tilston (27%) and Wilmslow (69%). But there are no clear patterns. In Frodsham, where the vicar Rowland Heywood and his curate and parish clerk subscribed and where the incumbent was later ejected with great bitterness during the Civil War, 27 per cent of adult males subscribed. Whereas in Tilston, which also had a subscription rate of 27 per cent, the minister Essex Clark continued to serve the living until his death in 1654. The rector of Wilmslow, Thomas Wright, appears to have been a responsible and resident pastor and much regarded by his parishioners. In March 1645 when Sir William Brereton ejected Wright from his living with the use of Parliamentary troops, the rector's neighbours rescued him from their hands and spirited him away. Such local regard may account for the high subscription rate of 69 per cent but even a popular cleric like Wright did not absolutely control the religious sensibilities of his churchwardens, or even those receiving poor relief. The chapelry of Marbury produced a subscription rate of 29 per cent – a rate similar to Tilston and Frodsham – without any apparent lead from the minister, one Thomas Orpe. Perhaps most striking of all is that Middlewich, with its notable nonconformist lecturer Thomas Langley and incumbent Robert Halliley, nevertheless produced a subscription rate of 41 per cent of adult males in favour of the Book of Common Prayer.[33]

It is by examining the allegiances of parish officers that a pattern may be suggested. In Tilston, Wilmslow and Middlewich there was strong support among officers and leading parishioners for the Prayer Book petition. In Frodsham they were fairly evenly divided. Only in Marbury was there a clear majority of officers and leading parishioners who did not subscribe. Marbury at 29 per cent is perhaps the strongest case of all for viewing the petition as an expression of individual consciences given the absence there of strong support from the gentry, clergy or church officers. In short, support for the lawful liturgy as expressed by signatures and marks on a petition appears to cut across the social spectrum of all five communities.[34] Several other questions need now to be briefly considered.

First of all, how is one to interpret *non*-subscription for the Prayer Book? Given that the Cheshire Root and Branch petition was never actually circulated in the county before being presented at Westminster – in sharp contrast to the petitions for episcopacy and liturgy – it is hardly surprising that no schedules of subscribers survive which would have allowed the comparison of places and individuals. Furthermore, we are left with a problem of interpretation that more usually dogs studies of conformity: is *failure* to subscribe an indication of opposition or apathy to the established Church? How do we judge the silence of the historical record? We may, however, be more sure of the *positive* nature of those who did subscribe as a legitimate expression of committed conformity.

Secondly, the historiographical questions concerning social control are put in a new light. Bearing in mind that it has only been possible to analyse five communities (although the five localities include 917 individuals), nevertheless there was a tendency for the Prayer Book petition to enjoy support from the lay officers of the parish. But this support does not appear to have had a direct effect on the rate of subscriptions. These are just the sort of men who are often presented as the agents of the 'reformation of manners' and 'preciser Protestantism'. It is suggested here, however, that such men could equally be agents for committed conformity, supporting the established Church not passively but actively. The men who held parish office, who signed the memoranda authorising rates, were individuals of local lay leadership and influence. That leadership, however, could be just as much for the maintenance of the religious settlement as for its reconstruction or complete transformation. For example, over a third of the parish officers in nine Cambridgeshire parishes put their weight behind a petition against Bishop Wren in particular, and episcopal government in general, in 1640–1. The men (and sometimes the women) who filled parish offices were, perhaps more than the clergy, the 'natural' local Church leaders. Their expressions of religious commitment could be on behalf of the established Church as against it, as the evidence from Cheshire and Cambridgeshire illustrates. Nevertheless, ordinary parishioners, even the poor, were capable of what appears to be a free expression of their own religious commitment. Even with strong local lay leadership generally only a minority of adult males subscribed. The Cheshire petition for the Book of Common Prayer reinforces the evidence from the Church courts that conformity was as 'sincere and genuine' a strand in parish religion as puritanism.[35]

V

We need to be more critical concerning the 'godly's' assessment of the quality of the religious lives of their conforming neighbours. Nonconformist innovations could drive people out of church as well as conformity to the Book of Common Prayer. Petitioners from Manchester complained of Ralph Kirk's innovations, 'whereby he hath driven a great number from the service of God'.[36] The godly were not always consistent about the multitude. Richard Baxter's famous description in his autobiography of a religiously and morally lazy Church of England in the 1620–30s should be weighed against another description of his on the religious activities of the people during the Commonwealth.

> The profane, ungodly, presumptuous multitude . . . are as zealous for crosses, and surplices, processions and perambulations, reading of a gospel at a cross way, the observation of holidays, and fasting days, the repeating of the litany, or the like forms in the Common Prayer, the bowing at the naming of the word Jesus (while they reject his worship), the receiving of the sacrament when they have no right to it, and that upon their knees, as if they were more reverent and devout than the true laborious servants of Christ; with a multitude

of these things which are only the tradition of their fathers; I say, they are as zealous for these, as if eternal life consisted in them.[37]

Even critics of the Church of England at times acknowledged the existence of enthusiasm for its worship and corporate liturgical life, however misguided they felt that support and affection to be. The time has come for historians of the Tudor–Stuart Church to acknowledge it as well. As to whether conformist enthusiasm was misplaced or not is a question which deserves greater even-handedness than it has received from historians heretofore.

Notes

1 Henry Barrow, *A Briefe Discoverie of the False Church* in *The Writings of Henry Barrow 1587–1590*, ed. Leland Carlson (1962), p. 362.

2 John Morrill, 'The Church in England in the 1640s', *Reactions to the English Civil War 1642–1649*, ed. J. Morrill (1982), p. 91; Patrick Collinson, 'A Comment: Concerning the Name Puritan', *JEH*, 31 (1980). For the 'Anglican vs. puritan' approach see Patrick Collinson, *The Puritan Character: Polemic and Polarities in Early Seventeenth-Century English Culture* (Los Angeles, 1989), p. 27. For his more favourable view of popular religion elsewhere, see *The Religion of Protestants* (Oxford, 1982), ch. 5.

3 Keith Wrightson, *English Society 1580–1680* (1982), p. 213, see also pp. 206–21; Keith Thomas, *Religion and the Decline of Magic* (New York, 1971), ch. 6, esp. pp. 159–66. For challenges to the 'economic determinist' view of religious identity see Margaret Spufford, *Contrasting Communities: English Villagers in the Sixteenth and Seventeenth Centuries* (Cambridge, 1974), ch. 13, and Collinson, *The Religion of Protestants*, ch. 5. For a sensitive treatment of issues of conformity, see Spufford, 'Can We Count the "Godly" and the "Conformable" in the Seventeenth Century?' *JEH*, 36 (1985); and Martin Ingram, *Church Courts, Sex and Marriage in England 1570–1640* (Cambridge, 1987), pp. 94, see also ch. 3 *passim*.

4 Christopher Haigh, *Reformation and Resistance in Tudor Lancashire* (Cambridge, 1975), pp. 306–7; 'The Church of England, the Catholics, and the People', *The Reign of Elizabeth I*, ed., C. Haigh (1984), pp. 206–9, 211, 217–19 (*see* Reading 9 above); Ian Green, 'Career Prospects and Clerical Conformity in the Early Stuart Church', *P and P*, 90 (1981), pp. 111–12. See also Haigh's stimulating article 'The Recent Historiography of the English Reformation', *The English Reformation Revised*, ed., C. Haigh (Cambridge, 1987).

5 CRO, EDC.5/1604 misc. (Manchester); Haigh, *Reformation and Resistance*, pp. 209, 214, 217, 218–19, 220; see F.R. Raines *The Rectors of Manchester and Wardens of the Collegiate Church* (Chetham Society, v. vi, 1885); *The Fellows of the Collegiate Church of Manchester* (Chetham Society, xxi, 1891); R.C. Richardson, 'Puritanism in the Diocese of Chester to 1642' (University of Manchester PhD thesis, 1969), pp. 55–61. For more of Kirk's activities see R.C. Richardson, *Puritanism in North-west England: a Regional Study of the Diocese of Chester to 1642* (Manchester, 1972), pp. 23, 27, 29, 40, 41, 81, 185.

6 LAO, 58/1/5; Ch. P/6 fol. 27; 58/2/67; C.W. Foster, *The State of the Church in the Reigns of Elizabeth and James I as Illustrated by Documents Relating to the Diocese of Lincoln* (Lincoln Record Society, xxiii, 1926), pp. 217, 290; CRO, EDC.5/1639/129; *The Book of Common Prayer 1559*, ed. John Booty (Washington, DC, 1976), pp. 248–9. All references to the Prayer Book are taken from this edition. Nesta Evans, 'The Community of South Elmham, Suffolk, 1550–1640' (University of East Anglia MPhil thesis, 1978), pp. 170–1; Claire Cross, 'Lay Literacy and Clerical Misconduct

in a York Parish during the Reign of Mary Tudor', *York Historian* (1980), pp. 10, 12, 14. That ordinary villagers were willing and able to use both the ecclesiastical and the secular courts to present their grievances in the early modern period has been demonstrated for an Essex community. See Keith Wrightson and David Levine, *Poverty and Piety in an English Village: Terling, 1525–1700* (New York, 1979), pp. 113–14.

7 Professor Collinson cites in support of the 'church papist' argument the example of Wye in Kent, where parishioners objected to the puritan practices of the vicar. Wye probably had the highest number of recusants in East Kent. He does not say, however, what percentage of the population were recusant or whether any of those presented for their Catholicism were involved in the presentations against the minister. Patrick Collinson, 'Shepherds, Sheepdogs, and Hirelings: the Pastoral Ministry in Post-Reformation England', *The Ministry: Clerical and Lay*, eds W.J. Sheils and Diana Woods (*Studies in Church History*, 1989) 208n. 74, see also pp. 207–11; Richardson, 'Puritanism in Chester', pp. 55–68; Earl of Clarendon, *Selections from the History of the Rebellion and The Life by Himself*, eds G. Huehens and H.R. Trevor-Roper (Oxford, 1978), p. 103.

8 CRO, EDC.5/1628 misc. (Bruera Chapelry, St Oswald, Chester).

9 Thomas Morton, *A Defence of the Innocencie of the Three Ceremonies of the Church of England* (1618), p. 44. The rubrics direct: 'Then shall the minister receive the communion in both kinds himself . . . and after to the people in their hands kneeling', *1559 BCP*, pp. 263–4. See also Spufford, 'Can We Count the "Godly"?'. LAO, 58/1/5; BL, Add. MSS 36913, fo. 140. See also CRO, QJB 1/6/87v–88; QJF 71/ 4/23–4; EDC.5/1639/129; Haigh, 'The Church of England', p. 219 (*see* Reading 9 above); CRO, EDP.263/5; James Hart, 'The House of Lords and the Reformation of Justice 1640–1643' (University of Cambridge PhD thesis, 1985), pp. 99–105, 121, 225–6, 231. I am grateful to Dr Hart for bringing these cases in the Lords to my attention.

10 LAO, 58/1/5; CRO, QJF 71/4/23; George Herbert, *A Priest to the Temple*, ed. Edward Thomas (London, 1908), p. 246; CRO, EDC.5/1612 misc. (St Bridget's, Chester); *1559 BCP*, p. 257.

11 LAO, 69/1/23; 69/1/14; 69/2/15; CRO, QJF 71/4/24. Dr Haigh has commented on the neglect of 'sacrament-gadding' in contrast to 'sermon-gadding' in our view of post-Reformation lay religion. Haigh, 'The Church of England', p. 218 (*see* Reading 9 above).

12 Cited in Richardson, *Puritanism*, p. 28; LAO, 69/1/23; Herbert, p. 256; *1559 BCP*, p. 277. The Prayer Book also makes it clear that baptism normally should take place as part of the main worship on Sunday: 'And then the godfathers, godmothers, and the people with the children must be ready at the font either immediately after the last Lesson at Morning Prayer, or else immediately after the last Lesson at Evening Prayer, as the curate by his discretion shall appoint', *1559 BCP*, p. 270. It has been argued that high rates of infant mortality and particular views of providential theology made parents less bereaved at the deaths of their children than in the modern period. See Lawrence Stone, *The Family, Sex and Marriage in England 1500–1800* (1977), pp. 206–15. Arguing against this view are Linda Pollock, *Forgotten Children: Parent–Child Relations from 1500-1900* (Cambridge, 1983), pp. 124–8, 134–7, 140–2; Ralph Houlbrooke, *The English Family 1450–1700* (1984), pp. 202–7, 215–22. See also John Bossy, *Christianity in the West 1400–1700* (Oxford, 1985), pp. 14–19, 26–34, on baptism and death.

13 Failure to perform, or objections to the sign of the cross in baptism has been used as evidence of 'puritanism' in, e.g., Richardson, *Puritanism*, pp. 26–8, 79–80; Ronald A. Marchant, *The Puritans and the Church Courts in the Diocese of York 1560–1642* (1960), pp. 225–317, *passim*; W.J. Sheils, *The Puritans in the Diocese of Peterborough 1558–1610* (Northamptonshire Record Society, 30 1979), pp, 68, 69, 78, 84; Patrick Collinson, *The Elizabethan Puritan Movement* (1967), p. 367. Dr Haigh has emphasised the conformist element in disputes over the sign of the cross in baptism. Haigh, *Reformation and Resistance*, p. 306.

14 LAO, 69/1/14; Herbert, p. 256.

15 CRO, QJF 71/4/24. See the *Visitation Articles* for Chester diocese of Richard Vaughan (1604, no. 30) and Thomas Morton (1617, no. 40). See also Vernon Staley (ed.), *Hierurgia Anglicana* (3 vols, 1902–1904), ii, pp. 195–6; Claire Gittings, *Death, Burial and the Individual in Early Modern England* (1984), pp. 133–5. CRO, EDC.5/1630, misc. (Bunbury). There were sentences of scripture appointed to be read while the body was carried from the churchyard gate to the grave. *1559 BCP*, p. 309. CRO, EDC.5/1628 misc. (Bruera Chapelry, St Oswald's, Chester).

16 LAO, 69/1/24. 'The priests meeting the corpse at the church stile, shall say or else the priests and clerks shall sing, and so go either unto the church, or toward the grave "I am the resurrection and the life"', *1559 BCP*, p. 309.

17 LAO, 69/2/15; 69/1/23; see also 69/2/14; CRO, EDC.5/1604 misc. (Macclesfield). The churchwardens of Apethorpe, Northamptonshire, complained that they had no curate to perform clerical offices, so that 'for want of a priest, they have been compelled to bury the dead bodies themselves', neither had they service read, nor sermons preached. Cited in Sheils, *Puritans*, p. 91.

18 David E. Stannard, *The Puritan Way of Death: a Study in Religion, Culture and Social Change* (New York, 1977), pp. 101, 103–104; Thomas, *Decline of Magic*, p. 603; Barrow, *A Brief Discoverie*, p. 458; Collinson, *Movement*, pp. 370–1. See Natalie Zemon Davies's discussion of these in 'Some Tasks and Themes in the Study of Popular Religion', *The Pursuit of Holiness in Late Medieval and Renaissance Religion*, eds, C. Trinkaus and H. Oberman (Leiden, 1974).

19 LAO, 58/1/5. Nicholas Tyacke, *Anti-Calvinists: the Rise of English Arminianism c. 1590–1640* (Oxford, 1987).

20 *The Short Parliament Diary (1640) of Sir Thomas Aston*, ed. Judith Maltby (Camden Fourth Series, xxxv, 1988). William Abbott, 'The Issue of Episcopacy in the Long Parliament: the Reasons for Abolition' (University of Oxford DPhil thesis, 1981); John Morrill, 'The Attack on the Church of England in the Long Parliament, 1640–1642', *History, Society and the Churches: Essays in Honour of Owen Chadwick*, eds Derek Beales and Geoffrey Best (Cambridge, 1985), pp. 105–8 and *passim*; Anthony Fletcher, *The Outbreak of the English Civil War* (1981), esp. chs 3, 9.

21 John Nalson, *An Impartial Collection of the Great Affairs of State* (2 vols, 1682), ii. pp. 720–2, 726.

22 Nalson, ii, pp. 726–7; David Underdown, *Somerset in the Civil War and Interregnum* (Newton Abbot, 1973), pp. 22–8; John Webb, *Memorials of the Civil War* (1879), i, pp. 85–6; BL, Thomason Tracts E.150 (28), p. 41; Derek Hirst, 'The Defection of Sir Edward Dering, 1640–1641', *HJ*, 15 (1972), p. 193; Anthony Fletcher, 'Petitioning and the Outbreak of the Civil War in Derbyshire', *Derbyshire Archaeological Journal* (1973), pp. 33–44.

23 Gloucs. RO, D2510/13; BL, Thomason Tracts E.150(28), p. 41, Alan Everitt, *The County of Kent and the Great Rebellion* (Leicester, 1966), p. 92; Hirst, 'Defection', p. 201; David Underdown, *Revel, Riot and Rebellion: Popular Politics and Culture in England 1603–1660* (Oxford, 1985), p. 140; Fletcher, *Outbreak*, 194.

24 Abraham Cowley, *The Civil War*, ed. A. Pritchard (Toronto, 1973), p. 77; *CSPD*, 1640–41, p. 529; John Morrill, *Cheshire 1630–1660: County Government and Society during the 'English Revolution'* (Oxford, 1974), pp. 51–3; Fletcher, *Outbreak*, pp. 302–306.

25 *Buller Papers*, Buller Family (1895), pp. 31, 33–4; Clive Holmes, *Suffolk Committee for Scandalous Ministers 1644–1646* (Suffolk Record Society, 1970), pp. 54, 69; J.W.F. Hill, 'The Royalist Clergy of Lincolnshire', *Lincolnshire Architectural and Archaeological Society Reports and Papers* (ii, 1938), pp. 45, 49, 53, 54; BL, Add. MS 11055, fols 130v–131. Discussed in greater detail in chs 3 and 4 of my 1991 Cambridge PhD thesis.

26 Hirst, 'Defection', p. 206 n. 57.

27 Sir Thomas Aston, *A Collection of Sundry Petitions* (1642), p. 42; Nalson, ii, pp. 720–2, 758; BL, Thomason Tracts E.151(11), pp. 6–7.

28 *Buller Papers*, pp. 33–4.

29 LAO, 69/2/15.

30 HLRO, Main Papers, Feb. [27], 1640/1; 20 Dec. 1641.

31 The methods applied to produce the economic and population statistics presented here are fully discussed in ch. 5 of my Cambridge PhD thesis.

32 The Cheshire gentry, as in other parts of the country, appear to have developed a rota system among themselves for spreading out the burden of payment. Such a system helps to explain why most of the self-styled gentlemen among the subscribers fail to appear in the 1640–1 subsidies. Henry Best, *Rural Economy in Yorkshire in 1641* (Surtees Society, xxxiii, 1857), p. 87. Graham Kerby, 'Inequality in a Pre-Industrial Society: a Study of Wealth, Status, Office and Taxation in Tudor and Stuart England with Particular Reference to Cheshire' (University of Cambridge PhD thesis, 1983); Spufford, *Contrasting Communities*, pp. 233–4. Subsidies used: PRO, E179/85/135; E179/85/131; E179/85/136.

33 'Loans, Contributions, Subsidies, and Ship Money, Paid by the Clergy of the Diocese of Chester in the Years 1620, 1622, 1624, 1634, 1635, 1636, and 1639', ed. G.T.O. Bridgeman in *Miscellanies Relating to Lancashire and Cheshire* (Lancashire and Cheshire Record Society, xii, 1885), pp. 78, 92, 100, 115, 120; Frodsham: John Walker, *The Sufferings of the Clergy*, ed. and revised A.G. Matthews (Oxford, 1948), p. 91; G. Ormerod, *History of Cheshire* (3 vols, 1882), ii, p. 58; AO; Tilston: AO; Ormerod, ii, p. 697. Wilmslow: AO; Ormerod, iii, p. 595; J.P. Earwaker, *East Cheshire* (2 vols, 1877), i, p. 91, ii, pp. 91–3; *Minutes of the Committee for the Relief of Plundered Ministers* (Lancashire and Cheshire Records Society, xxviii, 1893), pp. 146–7. Marbury: AO; Walker, pp. 305, 306; Raymond Richards, *Old Cheshire Churches* (Didsbury, revised and enlarged edn, 1973), p. 227; William Urwick (ed.), *Historical Sketches of Nonconformity in Cheshire* (Manchester, 1864), p. 150. Middlewich: *Plundered Ministers*, pp. 173–4; Urwick, pp. 7, 62, 151, 164–7, 201, 213–14; Ormerod, iii, p. 185.

34 See ch. 5 of my Cambridge PhD thesis.

35 Margaret Spufford, 'Puritanism and Social Control?', *Order and Disorder in Early Modern England*, eds A. Fletcher and J. Stevenson (Cambridge, 1985), *passim*: *Contrasting Communities*, pp. 232–3, 267–71; 'Can We Count the "Godly"?', pp. 434, 437n. 20. Cf. Collinson, *Puritan Character*, p. 27.

36 CRO, EDC.5/1604 misc. (Manchester).

37 Richard Baxter, *The Saints Everlasting Rest* (1650), pp. 342, 344.

11

From iconoclasm to iconophobia: the cultural impact of the Second English Reformation

PATRICK COLLINSON

I

My title is sufficiently gnomic to call for some explanation, both with reference to my interest in iconoclasm and iconophobia, and in respect of those terms themselves. I have been typecast, or have cast myself, as a historian of Puritanism, but should prefer to be known (if at all) as a student

Reprinted from *The Stenton Lecture* (Reading, 1985).

of the secondary stages and processes of the Reformation in England. But what was the English Reformation: a social and cultural movement with the irresistible force of a river or an artificial and imposed act of state? Was it Reformation 'from below' or 'from above'? And when, give or take a decade or two, is the event, or rather process, supposed to have happened? One possibility is early Reformation from above, enforced by royal and parliamentary edict in the reigns of Henry VIII and Edward VI and not subsequently reversed or even reversible; another, early Reformation from below, precocious and popular and rooted in native dissent and lay, anticlerical sentiment. A further possibility is that the Reformation was an act of state which took effect only in the reign of Elizabeth: late Reformation from above; yet another, popular Reformation from below, late or even very late, the 'second Reformation' of my title, which was still looked for in the 1640s.[1] These are not mutually exclusive positions. It is possible, as Professor A.G. Dickens insists, to believe in Reformation from both above and below, indeed to recognise its essential and dialectical character as consisting of complex from-above and from-below interactions.[2] The early and late positions are perhaps harder to reconcile. Either one believes that the Reformation was irreversible at the time of Edward VI's death, in which case the Marian reaction was bound to fail and could never have had the quality of an English counter-reformation, or one doesn't.

My own reflections on this problem have been increasingly influenced by the recognition that in some senses English Protestantism regressed, becoming less not more popular in character, as we proceed from the mid-sixteenth to the early seventeenth century, and from a time when the Reformation was associated with novelty, youth, insubordination and iconoclasm (when indeed it was still a *protest*[3]) to the period of its middle age, when it was more obviously associated with the maintenance of the *status quo* than with subversion, with middle-aged if not middle-class preoccupations, and when its attacks on traditional culture met with widespread and popular resistance.[4] By the early seventeenth century, the cause of preachers, religious publicists and social controllers often no longer pretended to be the popular cause to which it had aspired in earlier years. I am far from suggesting that the Protestant scheme of salvation and all that went with it had been universally understood or that it received massive support in the opening stages of the Reformation process (except perhaps in London and some parts of East Anglia, Essex and Kent, and especially in the cloth towns); or that there were more Protestants in England in 1550 than there were to be in 1600 or 1620. That would be absurd. But the martyrologist John Foxe had filled out his scenes with a cast of thousands, 'a great many', 'a multitude', 'all the faithful people', his rhetoric crediting the people with an inspired common sense grounded in fundamental honesty. Early Protestant propaganda took up the tradition of Piers Plowman and Luther's Karsthans in casting the common man as a centre of right-thinking theological gravity, exposing the sophistical and false learning of a corrupt clergy.[5] But as we travel forward fifty years, this character gives way to ignorant opponents of the Gospel like Atheos in George Gifford's caustic dialogue *The Country Divinity* and the plebeian in Arthur Dent's *Plain Mans Path-way* who says 'Well, I cannot read, and therefore I cannot tell what Christ or Saint Paul may say.'[6]

Early seventeenth-century preachers were not always hostile to the ignorant poor. Some expressed pity and evangelical concern,[7] but rarely admiration. Foxe's inclusive rhetoric was now inverted, to exclude from the Church of God in the most proper sense a host of papists, 'atheists' and other enemies, from the merely 'carnal' to the actively malignant. A favourite scriptural *topos* for voicing concern about the rotten state of the visible Church was the Parable of the Sower, in which only a little of the seed falls fruitfully on good ground; and the moral requires the preacher to blame the hearers, not the good seed or the sower, for the poor harvest which is gathered.[8] 'The multitude' now becomes a mostly pejorative term. The idea that Christ's true Church is 'a little flock' was integral to New Testament Christianity itself. But whereas some English authors applied the theme of the little flock to 'little England' in its cosmic struggle with the gigantic, foreign enemy of the popish Antichrist,[9] others complained of the grossly unequal balance of forces for and against true religion within England itself. Philip Stubbes in the *Anatomy of Abuses* (1583) is aiming at the majority of his own compatriots when he observes that 'the number of Christ his elect is but few, and the number of the reprobat is many; the way that leadeth to life is narrow, and few tread that path; the way that leadeth to death is brod and many find it.' It was to become a commonplace that in the visible Church the 'greater part' will normally be the 'worse part', the 'better part' the 'smaller part': one writer sugesting one in twenty 'Christians indeed' as a plausible ratio.[10]

This pessimistic rhetoric is admittedly double-edged, as well as having more of a conventional than an observational significance. It may be evidence of what it complains of, but it may equally well signify almost the reverse: the full internalisation and intensification of Protestant religious values, leading to heightened expectations and an aroused concern about alleged hypocrisy and carnality, and above all the sin of 'security'. But either way Protestantism became morally a more demanding religion, which is as much as to say that it became both inwardly and outwardly more repressive, less like a religion of liberation.

Seen in this context, Puritan Separatism articulated rejection of a false and ungodly communion with the ungodly or relatively irreligious multitude, its strongest motive a formal objection to the principle of an all-inclusive and mixed parochial Church. This objection was shared by the majority of Puritans, who witnessed against schismatic separation and insisted on the obligation of private Christians to continue to adhere to the public congregation. Indeed, those who remained part of the parish and declined to depart for Amsterdam practised, or at least preached, a form of social segregation which was more drastically divisive and stressful both for themselves and for society as a whole than ecclesiastical separation itself. Apart from participation in the communion of the parish one should have as little to do with the bulk of one's neighbours as possible. Unnecessary 'company keeping' and 'good fellowship' were vices. Neighbourhood was a hollow reed. There were no friends like the friends of one's soul.[11]

How are these negative imperatives to be accounted for? An easy answer would be to observe that seriously committed Christians are, as a matter of fact, always in the minority, so that these early seventeenth-century saints were merely responding to the reality of their situation. A rather more sophisticated answer would explore the consequences of internalising in social relations and experience a morally austere and demanding version of Christianity which turned the doctrine of election into a principle of invidious exclusion and stimulated an unrelenting warfare between the elect and the children of perdition, accentuating that mentality of opposites and contrary correspondences which was so prevalent in early modern England.[12] We should also have to give some weight to the legal insecurity experienced by Calvinist Protestants in a Church which was not modelled and disciplined according to their principles.

A distinctly *less* sophisticated explanation deals in crude social categories. The godly are said to have been more or less equivalent to the better sort in the sense of the more affluent, in contemporary diction those of 'ability', the 'civil sort'; not necessarily rich people but thriving, the successful yeoman farmer with access to buoyant markets and the capacity to accumulate capital, the 'industrious sort', to use a compelling phrase which Christopher Hill borrowed at a high rate of interest from the seventeenth century itself. For 'the multitude', read the rest, the mass of people depressed into poverty or near-poverty by demographic and economic pressures, a source of growing anxiety to their social betters. According to some historians, Puritanism or evangelical Protestantism in action was much the same thing as 'social control', a means of repressing the threatening and 'malapert' behaviour of what has been characterised as a kind of 'third world' existing in the entrails of Elizabethan England.[13] This is not all wrong by any means but nor can it be quite right. The religious and moral struggle was engaged *within* classes as well as *between* them. It was a relatively free option for the sons and daughters of Kentish yeomen, in about 1580, whether on Sundays they went out to sermons or to dances.[14] Both activities were fashionable. Both involved travel and some expenditure. The poor were probably effectively excluded from both. Young people were perhaps more likely to opt for dancing. After their mid-twenties, with the advent of marriage and the responsibilities of house-keeping, the attraction of the sermon might prove stronger, although middle-aged householders of means often acted as patrons of the Sunday dances, hiring the minstrels and paying for the beer. So I read the literature of complaint and the evidence of criminal proceedings in both ecclesiastical and secular courts. And perhaps more people went to both dances and sermons than these sources tend to suggest.[15]

II

So much is prolegomenon. Our subject properly concerns some cultural reverberations of the complex and even contradictory processes of the English Reformation. More than a hundred years ago, in his pioneering *History of the English People*, J.R. Green wrote a sentence which was profoundly true. All that follows merely elaborates and illustrates what Green wrote. Some time between the middle of the reign of Elizabeth and the meeting of the Long Parliament in 1640 the English became the people of a book, and that book was the Bible. 'No greater moral change ever passed over a nation.'[16] I believe that Green was quite correct in his dating. If anything I should be more precise, placing the moral and cultural watershed of which he wrote in 1580, or thereabouts.

　　Let us be more specific about the nature of the watershed. The first generation of Protestant publicists and propagandists, the Edwardian generation, made polemical and creative use of cultural vehicles which their spiritual children and grandchildren later repudiated, as part of their rather general programme of rejection. They wrote and staged Protestant plays. They sang Protestant songs and godly ballads to secular and popular tunes. And they made brilliant use of the graphic image, both to attack Catholicism and to commend their own religious convictions and values. These strategies constitute, for my purpose, what is meant by Iconoclasm. It is not what students of the great Iconoclastic Controversy of the eighth century understand by the term, nor yet what writers on Continental Protestant movements, especially in the Netherlands in 1565, mean by it. For the present purpose Iconoclasm implies a spirited attack, verbally violent or actually violent, on certain unacceptable images, but not the total repudiation of all images, which on my terms is Iconophobia. Indeed, Iconoclasm in this sense may imply the substitution of other, acceptable images, or the refashioning of some images for an altered purpose. It is hostile to false art but not anti-art, since its hostility implies a true and acceptable art, applied to a laudable purpose. As George Herbert asked: 'Is there in truth no beautie?'[17]

To return to our three cultural milieux. All three were familiar and traditional. Therefore those first-generation Protestant communicators who exploited them were in continuity and communication with the tradition, sharing common cultural ground with their Catholic opponents. This common ground ceased to exist round about 1580. So this significant cultural watershed occurred not between the last generation of traditional Catholicism and the first generation of Protestantism but between the first and second generations of Protestants. It divided the first and second Reformations.

A related theme concerns the changing attitudes of religiously minded Protestants to alehouses, inns and other places of popular resort. At first, they were at home in such places, where they argued points of theological difference with their opponents (the phenomenon called by contemporaries 'jangling'[18]) and engaged in mutual edification among themselves. In the 1530s that formidable and inventive figure Robert Wisdom exhorted his flock 'to take the scripture in their hands' when they met together at the alehouse on Sundays and holidays, 'and to talk, commune and reason of it'. When Bishop Bonner objected that this would lead to mishandling of Scripture by drunkards, Wisdom retorted that on the contrary the presence of the Bible would prevent people from getting drunk.[19] In Mary's days the Protestants of Colchester made their headquarters in the inns of the town, leading A.G. Dickens to remark that if the battle of Waterloo was won on the playing fields of Eton, the Reformation was won in the pubs of Colchester. In London, the secret Protestant congregation gathered at the Swan at Limehouse, the Kings Head at Ratcliffe, the Saracens Head at Islington. On one occasion the company of thirty consumed 'three or four pots of beer' – apparently each – before turning their attention to the sermon.[20]

As a place of 'common resort', associated with 'good fellowship', devout or merely respectable Elizabethan Protestants increasingly distanced themselves from drinking houses. According to one Puritan writer, anyone having a godly mind who entered such an establishment 'doth thinke he cometh into a little hell'. Clergymen who 'haunted' alehouses stood rebuked, not only by 'Puritans' but by the Royal Injunctions of 1559 and later by George Herbert in *The Priest to the Temple*. And the parochial clergy, all over Reformation and Counter-Reformation Europe, were as never before the representative and exemplary Christians. So religion and this most prevalent matrix for popular sociability and culture began to draw apart.[21] In 1569 there was 'talk had of Scripture' in an alehouse in East Kent. But at least one of those present thought it inappropriate to be 'talking of Scripture on the alebench'. Whether religion also began to abandon the more respectable urban inns to the variety of other and secular functions which these often large and elaborate establishments served is less certain. But here, in T.S. Eliot's famous phrase, was some dissociation of sensibility.[22]

One covert Protestant congregation gathered in an inn for the ostensible purpose of seeing a play.[23] It is well enough known that John Bale and other early Protestant clerical authors wrote under official patronage propagandist plays, adapting established theatrical conventions and devices for their own polemical purposes, which they shared with Thomas Cromwell and his men. A genre which first flourished under such regular auspices became a theatre of subversive protest in Henry VIII's last years, only to burst out with renewed confidence after the old king's death, when Gardiner and other conservative bishops were pilloried in 'all sorts of farces and pastimes'.[24] Such plays were anti-Catholic rather than positively Protestant, and it might be thought more difficult and certainly less entertaining to present in dramatic form the abstractions of Protestant soteriology. Yet the contrary is suggested by *Jacob and Esau*, of which the theme is predestination, and even more by Lewis Wager's play *The life and repentaunce of Marie Magdalene*.[25] This work is not widely esteemed as a major dramatic achievement. Yet it treats persuasively as well as didactically the evangelical themes of sin and redemption, carefully explaining that Mary's deliverance was by mere grace, appropriated by faith, not something merited by the moral strength of her own repentance.

But in this and other religiously motivated plays and interludes, for the most part composed by clergymen, such 'morality' coexists with the uninhibited employment of 'mirth', that is, of bawdry. No Miss World contest ever dwelt more lovingly on the vital statistics of the contestants than did Wager on the physical attributes of the stunning blonde, Mary Magdalene. And when his heroine responds to the 'prick of conscience', the Vice, characterised as Infidelitie, exclaims: 'Prick of conscience quod she? It pricketh you not so sore/as the yong man with the flaxen beard dyd I thinke' (II.11.1050–1). No godly preacher of the next generation could have tolerated such a scurrilous, nay 'filthy' libretto.[26]

It has sometimes been thought that such plays were never part of the active dramatic repertory, or no part of the Elizabethan repertory. But if *Marie Magdalene* was pre-Elizabethan, it was first printed in 1566. The first Elizabethan decade witnessed the publication of a whole cluster of Protestant moral interludes,[27] some written in earlier years, others originating at this time. Examples are *Nice Wanton*, *Lusty Juventus*, *The Disobedient Child* and *New Custom*. The same period saw the printing of the biblical plays *Virtuous and Godly Susanna* by Thomas Garter (a more skilful but also an even more prurient play than *Marie Magdalene*),[28] *Godly Queen Hester* (in truth a Henrician political satire), *Jacob and Esau* and *The Story of King Darius*. The conventions of these pieces are grounded in the tradition, partly of morality, partly of miracle plays. But they are distinctively Protestant and of their own time, not only in some theological undertones and overtones, but in identifying the vices with stock figures of popery and prelacy, so giving vent to anti-Catholic polemic, and in a characteristically Protestant modification of the prodigal son theme, dramatising the moral choices confronting Youth, poised between evil courses – idleness, pleasure, sexual incontinence – and good – obedience, education, religious seriousness.[29]

David Bevington (correcting Chambers) has demonstrated that these plays were not printed for the sole benefit of the Malone Society.[30] Some of them were primarily school plays. But their stage directions make clear that they were also considered suitable for performance by the early Elizabethan touring companies consisting of 'four men and a boy'. The casual evidence of Willis's *Mount Tabor*, describing fifty years after the event a moralistic interlude performed in Gloucester in the 1560s or early 1570s, strengthens the conviction that these pieces were the common stock-in-trade of provincial players for at least the first half of Elizabeth's reign.[31] And Wager's *Marie Magdalene* contains a reference to an audience which has paid for admission.[32]

This was a period when the traditional religious drama was still alive and comparatively well in many towns, notably Coventry, where in Mary's reign a Protestant prisoner and future martyr (he died in prison) had been allowed out of ward to play his part in the seasonal pageant of the Corpus Christi plays.[33] If that was inconsistent with a godly Protestant profession, John Careless went to his grave unaware of the fact. In the same city of Coventry the Corpus Christi cycle was only suppressed in 1579. So for twenty years it coexisted with the powerful preaching of the city's apostle and archdeacon, Thomas Lever. Did Lever attack the plays from the pulpit as the preachers inveighed against them at Chester? At Chester, York and Wakefield, the mysteries came to an end only in the mid-1570s; this, the time of Archbishop Grindal's presence in York, constituting the decisive cultural watershed for the North.[34] In the provinces, the anti-theatrical reaction was progressive and ultimately drastic. By the 1590s urban magistrates were shutting their gates against the licensed companies of travelling actors whose performances had begun to replace the traditional and indigenous plays: and it was soon standard practice to pay them to go away. This eventually happened in Stratford-upon-Avon, of all places. At Chester, citizens could be fined for going out of the city to witness such 'obscene and unlawful' entertainments. At Dorchester a truculent impresario who protested at a refusal to let his men perform was imprisoned for his pains.[35] A poem by John Kaye (or Key) of Huddersfield, dateable between 1576 and 1588, remarks: 'Now seinge that players doe not goe Abrode/Nor yet fine musicians we may not aforde. . . .'[36]

This is not the occasion to prise apart all the possible reasons for the violence of the mid-Elizabethan anti-theatrical reaction, a matter much debated by scholarship and exhaustively catalogued as early as 1633 in that vast encyclopedia of antipathy, Prynne's *Histrio-Mastix*, which digested, besides countless ancient authorities, 'above 150 moderne Protestant and

Popish writers of all sorts'.[37] Among the possible motives, arranged by different scholars in various hierarchies,[38] we have the objection to drama as pagan or even 'devilish' in origin, Sabbatarianism, concern for public health and order, dread of prodigality and idleness, an ever-increasing sensitivity to anything 'filthy', that is, suggesting and inciting sexual licence, the rejection of dramatic fictions as (in effect) lies, with a particular objection to the transvestite lie; and, most significantly for a discussion of incipient iconophobia, resistance to the theatrical appeal to what has been called 'the idolatrous eye'. 'For the eye', wrote Stephen Gosson, the playwright filled the stage with 'all manner of delights'. Anthony Munday concurred: 'There commeth much evill in at the eares, but more at the eyes . . . '[39] No doubt the commercial institutionalisation of the metropolitan theatre in the late 1570s was a catalyst. So too a related shift in the dramatic repertoire, away from improvement and towards the 'vain' entertainment of Italianate romances, and in the direction of the spectacles to which the demotic audience was susceptible.[40] Professor Ringler exaggerated only a little when he insisted that the metropolitan, literary onslaught on the theatre broke abruptly without much warning, and in 1577, as soon as the first public theatres opened their doors.[41]

What is most relevant to the present argument is the repudiation by these professional complainers not only of 'vain' and wanton plays but of all plays whatsoever, including religious plays and moralities. In 1551 the great German reformer Martin Bucer had observed (from his professorial chair in Cambridge) that

> for the making of tragedies the Scriptures constantly offer an abundance of material . . . For these stories are thickly packed with godlike and heroic people . . . Since all these qualities have wonderful power to strenghten faith in God, to arouse love and desire of God and to create and increase not only admiration of piety and justice, but also the horror of impiety and of the sowing and fostering of every kind of evil.

How much better to employ these sources rather than the profane literature of pagan poets![42] In a speech in Elizabeth's first parliament, Abbot Feckenham of Westminster could still take for granted the Protestant alliance of pulpit and stage when he attacked the 'preachers and scaffold players of this new religion'.[43] But by 1566 a note of defensiveness has crept into the Prologue to Wager's *Marie Magdalene*, if indeed it was not there already, since the Prologue, like the play itself, may have been Edwardian in origin: 'Doth not our facultie learnedly extoll vertue?/ Doth it not teache God to be praised above al thing?'[44] In Stephen Gosson's *School of Abuse* (1578) there is some ambivalence in the concession that there are such things as 'good plays and sweet plays', which Gosson specifies, including one of his own. But he no longer thinks them 'fit for every mans diet neither ought they commonly to be shown.' This connects with Thomas Norton, one of the authors of *Gorboduc*, but a main pillar of city government as well as the busiest of all Elizabethan MPs, who in 1574 condemned public theatre-going as 'unnecessary and scarcely honest'.[45] Presumably the fear was that a popular audience would enjoy the 'mirth' but miss the moralistic point of plays intended for improvement. These were transitional attitudes and Theodore Beza of Geneva was in the course of a similar transition when he wrote his biblical play *Abrahams Sacrifice* in 1550. In the Preface he admits to having altered 'some small circumstances' of the story for dramatic effect.[46] The thoroughly matured Beza would surely have condemned absolutely such artistic licence.

With no such reservations at all, Philip Stubbes in 1583 first distinguished between divine and profane plays and then proceeded to condemn the divine as the more intolerable of the two, since in such 'sacrilegious' performances the glorious majesty of God was handled 'scoffingly, flauntingly and jibingly'. This is reminiscent of the argument that white witches were worse than black witches, precisely because they pretended to do good by devilish means. As Prynne would later insist, 'the more elegant and witty therefore the Playes, the more dangerous and destructive are they'. Venomous pills must be coated with honey. 'The more witty and sublime their stile and manner, the more pernicious their fruites.' Stubbes wrote that the merits of Christ's passion were not available to be 'derided and jested at, as they be in these filthie playes and enterludes'. It was not lawful 'to mix scurrilitie with divinitie, nor divinitie with scurrilitie'. Applied to religious drama, this was already a commonplace. John Northbrooke, in no sense an original writer, had pronounced in 1577 that to perform 'histories out of the scriptures' was to mingle scurrility with divinity, or to eat meat with unwashed hands. 'Illotis Manibus' was one of Erasmus's *Adagia*, where the *topos* is related to those who handle theology in ignorance of the philological skills on which it depends. 'Truly *with hands and feet unwashed*, he is taking the most sacred thing of all, not to treat it, but to profane it, pollute it and do it violence.' This point is worth observation, since attitudes classified as 'Puritan' often represent the application of the message of Christian humanism, or 'Erasmianism'.[47]

If we consult the records of the last days of the old religious drama, we can easily see what Stubbes and Northbrooke found so objectionable, sensing the depth of the gulf now opening up between the old and the new religious sensibilities, the mimetic and didactic presentations of religious truth. In the Coventry accounts of the Cappers' Gild there are payments 'to pylatt iijs viijd'; 'Item, paid to God (evidently a smaller part) xvjd'; at Chester, the cost is recorded of the 'guildinge of little God's face'. In York the nuts customarily distributed in the annual procession of Yule and Yule's Wife (a frankly bawdy affair) were said to be 'in rememberance of that most noble Nut our saviour's blessed body'.[48] How many light years would one have to travel to escape from the notion that Christ's body could be suitably symbolised by a nut and to arrive at a typical Jacobean sermon! Stubbes thought that the opening words of St John's Gospel were a proof text against the religious drama: 'the word is God, and God is the word'. To *represent* the Word was to 'make a mocking stock of him' and to perpetrate a counterfeit.[49]

If it appears more difficult to understand why *Jacob and Esau* or the realisation of Christ in Wager's *Marie Magdalene* should have been considered 'filthy', we must appreciate that we are dealing with an objection to 'playing' rather than preaching the Gospel which was more profound than any quarrel with the wanton profanity of secular comedy. So it was that on the eve of its greatest achievements, the English theatre was not available as a medium to explore and present the drama of salvation, while it was left to Handel in the eighteenth century to exploit the dramatic potential of the Old Testament. Confronted with the argument of the devil's advocate, that plays are as good as sermons 'and that many a good Example may be learned out of them', Stubbes explodes: 'Oh blasphemie intollerable!'; and most significantly, he links his dismissal of this strategem with the doctrine that the number of Christ's elect is limited, the way of salvation strait and narrow. For those who could not discover God in his Word, expounded from the pulpit, it was just too bad.[50] At York, a future archbishop, Matthew Hutton, passed judgment on the fifteenth-century play known as the Creed Play: 'It was plausible 40 yeares agoe, and wold now also of the ignorant sort be well liked: yet now in this happie time of the gospell, I knowe the learned will mislike it and how the state will beare with it I knowe not.' And at Chester, a local worthy remarked that the only utility of the traditional plays was 'to showe the Ignorance of oure forefathers'.[51]

The pamphlet war of 1577 to 1583 did not put paid to biblical drama, and although the genre did shrivel away to almost nothing by 1600, Murray Roston is no doubt correct to insist that its final passing cannot be simply attributed to Puritan opposition. Lily Campbell showed that it was possible from Henslowe's Diary and other sources to compile a list of as many as fourteen late Elizabethan scripture plays, at least two of which were performed in the public theatres. But that merely served to keep the issue alive for a few more years. Even Thomas Lodge, who had written against Gosson and was co-author with Greene of a play about the adventures of Jonah, *A looking glasse for London and England* (performed 1592, printed 1594), wrote in 1596 that 'in stage plaies to make use of Hystoricall Scripture, I hold it with the Legists odious, and as the Councill of Trent did . . . I condemne it' – Lodge being some kind of Catholic.[52] The statute of 1605 which prohibited blasphemy on the stage (and defined blasphemy very broadly) was no doubt indicative of a rather general shift in public taste, extending to disapproval of 'playerly gestures' in the pulpit, which Prynne would condemn as 'altogether scandalous and unseemly for a Minister'. 'He is the best Minister who is most unlike a Player, both in his gesture, habit, speech and elocution.'[53]

This portion of the argument can be summarised as the changing history of the three Ps. Bishop Stephen Gardiner of Winchester had complained of his mishandling by Protestant dramatists (and the Protestant Prynne would later approve of his complaint and endorse it), leading Foxe in the *Book of Martyrs* to spin an alliterative phrase: 'Printers, Players and Preachers trouble Winchester'. Thirty years later, Gosson launched a vicious attack on 'Poets, Pypers and Players'. In 1610 William Crashaw rang a less felicitous variation when he defined the three great enemies of religion as 'the Devil, Papists and Players'.[54]

III

Moving on to another form of popular culture, the broadside ballad, we find a parallel sequence.[55] In the 1560s there was a flood of godly ballads, keeping company with the moralistic interludes. Indeed, there is a distinct affinity between the two enterprises in that both moral interludes and godly ballads usually conclude with the convention of a prayer for the queen and the state. But in the godly ballads there is a distinct absence of 'mirth', with the significant exception of the resonances of the tunes to which they were to be sung. The corpus includes anti-Catholic ballads, as much political as religious, ballads preserving the memory of the Marian martyrs, ballads exposing immorality such as *agaynste fornication etc a godly ballett* (Rollins 34, 1564–5) and ballads of hideous example in the spirit of the lost pamphlet *Judgement of God upon a periured person in Gunne Alley who ripped his belly*.[56] A ballad was printed within two days of the 1580 earthquake attacking the theatre with the refrain *Comme from the plaie comme from the plaie* (Rollins 327, 8 April 1580). There were ballads of scriptural and doctrinal exposition, such as the title *Approvynge by the scriptures that our salvation consesteth only in Christe, a godly new ballet* (Rollins 92, 1562–3), and ballads denouncing secular love ballads, such as Thomas Brice's *Against filthy writing and such like delighting* (Rollins 33, 1561–2) and *Reprovynge all reball sonnges* (Rollins 2277, 1563–4).

Such open attacks on secular balladry were rare. The more usual stratagem of the pedlars of moralities was parody, producing godly versions of popular songs to be sung to the same tunes. According to Hyder Rollins, the genre was made 'instantly popular' by the early Elizabethan parodic and loyal ballad *The countrye hath no pere*.[57] Virtually all successful ballads (and this was doubtless a tribute to their success) seem to have been given this treatment. We know of moralisations of *Go from my window, The hunt is up, John come kiss me now, Maid will you marry, Into a myrthful may morning* and *O sweete Oliver* (which is quoted in *As You Like It*). The hit song *Row well ye mariners* (William Pekering, 1565–6) provoked several moralised versions: *Row well ye maryners moralyzed* (1566–7, 3 editions), *Row well Godes maryners* (Alexander Lacey, 1567–8), *Row well ye Christes maryners* (also Pekering, 1567) (Rollins 2327–2333). Claude Simpson writes of 'the irresistible urge to appropriate its lilting line [the tune is lost] to moralizing purposes'.[58] The famous *Daunce and songe of deathe* (Rollins 480, 1568–9) beginning 'Can you dance the shaking of the sheets?' was evidently a moralisation of a lost ballad called *Dance after my pipe*. The tune is mentioned in the play *Misogonus* (1560). William Elderton's celebrated *Gods of love* (Rollins 987), for long known directly only from a snatch in *Much Ado About Nothing*, was twice parodied, as *The complaynte of a synner vexed with payne* (William Birch, Rollins 357) and as *The ioy of virginitie*, which occurs in the collection *A handeful of pleasant delites* (No 16). Elderton's *Pangs of love* was also twice parodied.[59]

In addition to these singles, there were albums, more ambitious collections of moralistic parodies, notably the Maidstone surgeon John Hall's huge compilation *The court of virtue* (1565), which confutes what Hall called those 'lecherous ballads', the verses of Wyatt and others contained in *The court of Venus*, and evidently employing the same music. There was another *Court of Venus moralized* by the industrious Thomas Brice.[60] Such parodies or 'counterfeits' were in an established tradition and were widely practised in Reformation Europe. In France Marguerite de Navarre rendered 'Sur le pont d'Avignon' as 'Sur l'arbre de la Croix'.[61] Among leading English reformers, Miles Coverdale, Thomas Becon and Robert Wisdom all in effect agreed with the nineteenth-century salvationist William Booth that there was no reason why the Devil should enjoy a monopoly of the best tunes.[62]

All this is well enough known to students of Elizabethan verse and to anyone who has investigated the history of the broadside ballads. But what has not been acknowledged, even by the principal authority, Hyder Rollins, is that the godly parodic ballad, like the Protestant moral interlude or biblical play, began to go out of fashion in the 1580s. I have made a rough and ready analysis[63] of ballad titles which works on a rather arbitrary definition of what constitutes a godly ballad and in most cases relies on a mere title in the *Stationers Register*, where the ballad itself is no longer extant. Nevertheless the analysis may have some impressionistic value. In the fourteen years 1559 to 1572, no less than 169 godly ballads were issued, 160 of them in the ten years 1562–1571; none at all between 1573 and 1576; and then only 63 in the eight years 1577–1584, 24 in the one year 1586, 21 in the nine years 1588–1595, and virtually none after 1595. The last notable moralistic retort to a hit song occurred in 1580, following the printing of *A newe northern dittye of the ladye Greene Sleves* (Rollins 1892).[64] Within a fortnight a licence was granted for *Green Sleeves moralized to the Scripture* (Rollins 1051). Other godly ballads proceeded to appropriate this immediately popular tune,[65] including *The godly and virtuous song and ballad* of the Marian martyr, John Careless, whom we have already met acting in the Coventry mystery plays.[66] This was hardly surprising. As ice-cream vendors know to our cost, the tune is hard to forget and in the age of the ballads no less than eighty distinct texts were set to it.[67]

But public taste was changing and by the 1590s it no longer seemed fitting to sing a religious lyric to such a melody. Thomas Nashe wrote disparagingly in *Have with you to Saffron-Walden* (1596) of 'such another device . . . as the godly Ballet of *John Carelesse*, or the Song of *Green sleeves moralized*'; while Mistress Ford in *The Merry Wives* (1600–01) (II.i.59–61) complains that Falstaff's words 'do no more adhere and keep place together than the hundred Psalms to the tune of Green Sleeves'.[68] When, in 1597, 'certain evil disposed persons' accused a Kentish vicar of leading his congregation in a rendering of the 25th Psalm to Green Sleeves, he brought a legal action against them for defamation of character.[69] By then the policy of musical parody may have been tacitly abandoned. It is significant that while the mid-sixteenth-century Scottish collection familiarly known as *The gude and godlie ballatis*, which contains several English parodies, was kept in print with editions of 1567, 1578, 1600 and 1621,[70] it has no English counterpart. In 1595 it was still possible to purchase a copy of the first and only edition of *The court of virtue* (1565), but that was hardly a mark of success.[71] The godly ephemera later collected by Pepys[72] were a different genre, chapbooks rather than broadsheets and not intended for singing.

Part of the reason for the abandonment by religious publicists of any attempt to compete in the popular market of broadside balladry (or, more realistically, the abandonment by ballad-mongers of the religious side of their trade) lay in the changing attitude of the godly towards the ballad singers. The war now declared against the minstrels was, if anything, even more total than that waged against stage players. In *The Anatomy of Abuses* Stubbes talks about dancing the wild morris through the needle's eye to Heaven and asks of the musicians: 'Who be more bawdie than they? Who uncleaner than they? Who more licentious and loose minded? Who more incontinent than they?'[73] The ordinary occupation of unattached and technically 'vagrant' minstrels was the accompaniment of country dances, and it was this which made them anathema in the eyes of the preachers and other complainers. In Kent the act books of the archdeacon's courts for the 1570s are replete with the prosecutions of minstrels alleged to have played in service time, drawing the youth away from church 'in heaps'. In 1578 the Canterbury preacher John Walsall carried his complaints up to London in a Paul's Cross sermon which fulminated against 'vaine fiddlers and vagabond pipers', and which was at once printed 'at the earnest request of certain godly Londoners and others'. Walsall put on one level the London players who drew larger audiences than the preachers and the country minstrels. Two years earlier, one of his clerical neighbours had complained of a musician who had lured away most of his congregation. 'By report he had more with him than I had at the church.'[74]

The crucial argument occurs in Thomas Lovell's versified *Dialogue between Custom and Veritie concerning the use and abuse of dauncing and minstrelsie* (1581), where Veritie denounces the minstrels for being all things to all men:

> Some godly songs they have: some wicked ballads and unmeet . . .
> For filthies they have filthy songs,
> for baudes lascivious rimes:
> For honest good, for sober grave
> songs, so they watch their time.

Lovell invokes the Epistle of James to condemn the chameleon-like adaptability of the musicians. Out of the same mouth ought not to proceed blessing and cursing.[75] This was to excoriate not only the country minstrels but ballad-mongers like William Elderton, who with his famous grog-blossom of a tippler's nose had no reputation for godliness but was content to supply the market for sacred as well as secular song, a lucrative strategy akin to the device known as 'flyting'.[76] Fifteen years later, the Suffolk preacher Nicholas Bownd took an even harder line against balladry in his *Doctrine of the Sabbath*. Bownd had heard that in the first age of the Protestant gospel, psalm-singing had almost driven out the singing of ballads. (Foxe was probably his source.) But now the tide was flowing in a contrary direction. At every fair and market the minstrels were singing and selling the ballads, which country people stuck on their walls for want of any other decoration. In Bownd's opinion, psalms and ballads could not possibly coexist. 'They can so hardly stand together.' And the suggestion that the ballad-mongers might be hired to sing the Psalms was dismissed out of hand. The 'singing men' were so notoriously ungodly that it would be better to stop their mouths altogether than to allow them to pollute such sacred songs.[77] This was to turn into a sour and negative complaint the positive aspiration of Miles Coverdale in the early English Reformation, combining elements of Erasmian and Lutheran idealism: 'Would God that our minstrels had none other thing to play upon, neither our carters and ploughmen other thing to whistle upon, save psalms, hymns and such godly songs as David is occupied withal!'[78]

What we are uncovering is a drastic separation of the sacred and the secular, and of two popular musical genres which began by being closely intertwined: balladry and psalmody. By 1600 Psalms invariably meant the Psalms of David, sung to their own sacred melodies. Although they might be used by godly people on all and any occasions, they were primarily intended for congregational singing, in church. But fifty years earlier the situation had been very different. Many of the so-called 'scripture songs' of the first age of the Reformation were not scriptural at all but, as we should say, protest songs: polemics against the Mass, or the faults of the clergy, or the folly of going on pilgrimage. Foxe preserved just such a song of fifty stanzas called *The fantasie of idolatry*, 'for posterity hereafter to understand what then was used in England'. The author was William Gray, who also wrote the popular secular ballad *The hunt is up*.[79] These pieces were sung anywhere *except* in church and they had no connection with congregational worship. In periods of persecution they were sung, loudly, by Protestant prisoners so that they could be heard on the street outside. In Essex they were performed at weddings, by what Foxe calls 'common singers against the sacraments and ceremonies'.[80] For example, in Mary's reign an apprentice to a Colchester minstrel was sent out to a country bridal feast to perform a repertoire of so-called 'scripture songs', which included *News out of London*, an attack on the Mass and the queen's 'misproceedings'.[81]

Nothing tells us more about the broad social and cultural bottom of the early Reformation than these scripture songs of the 1930s, 1940s and 1950s. They benefited from the patronage of Thomas Cromwell and the commercial investment of London printers. Solid citizens encouraged their apprentices 'to sing a song against the sacrament of the altar'. It was not beneath the dignity of the Oxford scholar Julins Palmer to be 'a jolly writer of three halfpenny books' and 'doggish rhymes'. In Worcester an eleven-year-old boy composed an anticlerical ballad called *Come down for all your shaven crown*, perhaps echoed in Elderton's anti-catholic Elizabethan ballad *Northumberlands newes*, with its refrain 'Come tumbling down, come tumbling down'.[82] By the 1580s there was little of this tradition left.

Musicologically, this seems to be what happened.[83] Both balladry and psalmody had evolved as popular adaptations of the music of the late Henrician and Edwardian courts and they shared the same tunes and the same metre. It is not clearly the case that psalmody was a secondary development. The close affinity of the two genres is implicit in the proposal of Sternhold and his continuators that their psalm settings should take the place of 'fayned rymes of vanitie', 'all ungodly songs and ballads'. William Baldwin's wish, expressed in the deciation to Edward VI of his metrical version of *The Ballads of Salomon* was: 'Would God that such songes myght once drive out of office the baudy balletes of lecherous love', an admonition repeated in John Day's title page to *The whole book of psalms*.[84] Here was antipathy but also affinity. Mid-Tudor Bibles naturally attributed to '*The Song of Solomon*' the title '*The Ballad of Ballads*'. As with Clement Marot's French Psalter, congregational use of the metrical

Psalms was a secondary development, an adaptation of music originally intended for private and domestic use. Stow's continuator Edmund Howes remembered in the 1630s that the Psalms had once been sung to 'galliards and measures'. 'Geneva Psalms' were sometimes called 'Geneva Jigs', implying that they were sung at a lively pace to instrumental accompaniment; and that they displayed rhythmical qualities in performance which are absent from the musical notation as printed.[85]

John Calvin was insistent that only the Psalms of David could be sung in church. He also ruled against the ecclesiastical use of 'chansons villains et impudiques', insisting that psalm singing should have the quality of 'poids et majesté', with the text enjoying precedence over the music.[86] In Elizabethan England, congregational psalm-singing, men and women singing together in unison, spread like a grass-fire.[87] This too was popular religion and, in a sense, popular culture, which would endure for three centuries. Although they probably had secular origins, the psalm tunes soon acquired the character of religious melodies sung on religious occasions by religious people: not so much protest songs as hymns. In practice, the repertoire of tunes may have been small, and very small in comparison with the thousand or so ballad tunes thought to have been published in the sixteenth and seventeenth centuries, over 400 of which survive or can be reconstructed.[88] And sung unaccompanied, in large and cavernous buildings, the psalm tunes slowed down. Nicholas Temperley has calculated that by the late seventeenth century the speed was as ponderous as two seconds or more to each note. By the time of John Playford's *Brief introduction to the skill of music* (1650s), psalm tunes were printed in minims and semibreves, songs and dances in crotchets and quavers. In 1619 George Wither wrote that to sing the Psalms to 'those roguish tones, which have formerly served for profane jigs' and to set the psalm tunes to profane words were two equally inadmissible procedures.[89]

IV

Not much space has been spared for my third topic, although it is awesome in scope and significance: pictorial art and its creeping disappearance as a means of communicating religious knowledge and arousing moral virtue – the iconophobia of our title according to a strict and narrow understanding of the term. Nothing demonstrates more forcefully the absolute refusal of so many late Elizabethan and Jacobean religious communicators to appeal to the senses and to popular taste than the pictures which are missing from their books, where you might expect to find them. And the implication is that they were deliberately restricting their appeal: or so one would have to conclude after reading Dr Scribner's account of the brilliant deployment of visual propaganda in the German Reformation.[90] We shall take no more than a few stabs at this large subject, excluding from consideration the sacred and moral emblematic picture and the more recondite *imprese*, a large omission but since our concern is primarily with popular culture one which will not wholly disable the argument. Nor are the remarks which follow intended to imply any disparagement of the (neglected) pictorial arts of Elizabethan and Jacobean England, especially as applied in a secular didactic context, decorative, ceremonial and heraldic. These works lent themselves to a form of appreciation best described as 'reading'. They were, as Dr Michael Leslie observes, pictures to be read.[91]

Among the Britwell Ballads in the Huntington Library there is a religious broadsheet of 1604 called *The map of mortality*. It is illustrated with a picture of Christ as the Good Shepherd with crown of thorns and nimbus, drawn in an appealing and vaguely mannerist style: something so rare and unusual for its period as to startle.[92] One reacts in the same way to Isaac Oliver's thoroughly un-English miniatures of Christ and of the Returned Prodigal of a few years later. Oliver, of course, was of French extraction and the only English painter of his generation who is known to have travelled in Italy. Jill Finsten writes of his 'sophisticated internationalism' and describes these little paintings, probably intended for the Catholic Queen Anne, as 'progressive and precocious'.[93]

In 1569 Stephen Bateman published *A christal glasse of christian reformation*, the declared purpose of which was to 'plainly shew unto all, the estates of every degree by order of picture and signification'. There are thirty pictures of vice, all realistic and representational in the manner of the illustrations to Foxe's *Book of Martyrs*. The pictures of virtue are fewer and express emplematic metaphors.[94] Forty years later Richard Bernard, a prolific clerical author who migrated from Nottinghamshire to Somerset and from a rather extreme, semi-separatist Puritanism to a more conformable position, published *Contemplative pictures with wholesome precepts*. But there *are* no pictures and Bernard's explanation is significant: 'These are certaine pictures [of God, Goodness, Heaven; the Devil, Badness, Hell] not Popish and sensible for superstition, but mentall, for Divine contemplation.'[95] The rejection of 'sensible' pictures as 'popish' was, in effect, to repudiate such images as falling foul of the Second Commandment, on which Calvin placed a distinct emphasis, insisting that it made idols and images effectively indistinguishable.

To be sure, Bernard's prose is so vivid, for example in his descriptions of the majesty of God[96] or in his characterisation of the Devil, that it might be thought that the reader would have no difficulty in forming his own mental images of these things, beside which any woodcut would be crudely inadequate. One recalls Erasmus's memorable remark in the *Paraclesis* that the *words* of the New Testament make Christ so fully present that 'you would see less if you gazed upon Him with your very eyes'; and also Sidney's suggestion in the *Defence* that the Psalms make you 'as it were, see

God coming in His majesty', for poems are 'speaking pictures', a figuring forth. *Ut pictura poesis.*[97] And there was no other legitimate way to envisage God, for as James I asked: 'How can we paint God's face when Moses, the man that ever was most familiar with God, never saw but his back parts?' When Richard Haydock in his anglicisation of Lomazzo's *Tratto dell'Arte* encountered the suggestion that the image of God the Father should be represented with perfect clear colours he remarked: 'And I [think] that he should not be Painted at all.'[98]

What do we know about the capacity to form mental pictures of some-one who has almost never seen an actual picture? What would our mind's-eye conception of Christ consist of if we had been totally isolated from the Christian iconographical tradition? The visual imagination of ordinary people in Jacobean England is not a very accessible subject. But let us remind ourselves that in principle and more often than not in fact the pictures with which pre-Reformation churchgoers had been familiar – the Trinity in the habitual form of the Father sustaining the Son with the Holy Spirit above in the form of a dove, Christ enthroned in judgment, not to speak of biblical and hagiographical narrative pictures – were now alto-gether destroyed or (as at Stratford-upon-Avon) slobbered over with white-wash. It has been almost a commonplace to observe that in Elizabethan England the image of the Virgin was replaced by that of the virgin queen in polite and even popular devotion. Perhaps it was so, in some sense. But in the churches eyes were drawn not to some idealised portrait of Elizabeth but to the potent, emotive but wholly abstract symbolism of the royal arms.

So much for church art. As for the schoolroom, Professor Höltgen has pointed out that the only picture which we can be certain penetrated the Elizabethan grammar school was the cut at the back of Lily's Grammar which showed three boys raiding a pear tree. When the young Henry Peachman was caught copying this picture he was severely punished, which did not prevent him from publishing, in due course, *Graphice, or the most auncient and excellent art of drawing* (1606): and before that recording the only known 'artist's impression' of a Shakespeare play in performance.[99]

It is a remarkable fact, like Sherlock Holmes's dog which did not bark, that most Elizabethan and Jacobean Bibles have no illustrations. John King remarks that the illustrated Bibles published in the reign of Edward VI have no successors: a pardonable exaggeration. They represent 'an anom-aly in the publication history of authorized editions'.[100] The youth in the interlude *The longer thou livest* earns a cheap laugh when he is handed a New Testament by Piety and begins to search for the non-existent pictures:

> God's santy, this is a goodly book indeed.
> Be there any saints in it and pilcrows?

But after turning a few leaves: 'Here is little good cheer.'[101]

But what, it may be asked, about all those brilliant, action-packed pictures in Foxe's *Book of Martyrs*, some of them prodigious pull-outs, which were reproduced from the same blocks right up to the 1630s, and thereafter continued in derivative and debased versions to enliven the dreariness of Sunday afternoons for generations of Protestant children, even into the present century? It is perhaps unlikely that such pictures would have been commissioned and executed if Foxe had been first published in the 1590s or early 1600s. There are no illustrations to Thomas Beard's *Theatre of divine judgments*, a collection of dramatic 'providences' which may appear to cry out for them. Foxe preserves a piece of mid-sixteenth-century Protestant aesthetic, fossil-like, into the altered cultural climate of the late sixteenth century and beyond.

By the 1620s and 1630s, with van Dyck in England and Rubens responding to English royal patronage, a contrary cultural tide was flowing with some strength, the artistic expression of the anti-Calvinist reaction we nickname Arminianism. By 1635 Francis Quarles's *Emblems and Hiero-glyphikes* contained a representation of God enthroned as *Amor Divinus*, taken from a Jesuit source without alteration. Only in the edition of 1643 was this popish image replaced with the acceptable Hebrew lettered device of the Tetragrammaton, word rather than image.[102] But that literally illustrates the extent to which English Arminianism repudiated the Reformation itself, putting this episode beyond consideration in an essay devoted to cultural modifications within Protestantism.

The argument in respect of the drama, music and graphic art has been one and the same. The primary thrust of Protestantism which came to fruition around 1550 was hostile to false art, images which were vehicles for false belief. But it devised its own mimetic programme, its own iconography, which had many points of contact and sympathy with inherited and traditional forms. In this sense the first Reformation was neither anti-art nor anti-popular. The secondary thrust gathering momentum around 1580 came close to dispensing with images and the mimetic altogether, while disparaging the tastes and capacities of the illiterate, the mass of the people. The Suffolk puritan saint John Carter may be allowed the last word in expressing the creeping ascetic totalitarianism which has been our theme. In expounding the Sermon on the Mount, Carter made this gloss upon Christ's own glossing of the Seventh Commandment. It condemned not only an idle and easy life, lascivious company, needless gadding, haunting of suspected houses and unreasonable meetings and revellings but these three things: 'Love-songs and Bookes, . . . filthy objects in Pictures, Playes, or whatever else stirreth up corrupt nature.' Before that is dismissed as an extreme and Puritanical attitude, we may note that the official *Homilies* of the Church of England declared that 'the seeking out of images is the beginning of whoredom'.[103]

Advice is one thing, practice another. The real extent of practical iconophobia in Jacobean England is unexplored and for the most part unexplorable. If the inventory of the household maintained at York by Henry Hastings, third earl of Huntingdon, means what it says, the earl had no pictures on his walls whatsoever: only maps, non-representational floral hangings, a table of the Ten Commandments in a frame and 'one table in a frame contayninge the cause of salvacion and damnation'.[104] These furnishings would have caused no offence to a Muslim of the Wahhabi sect. But Robert Dudley, earl of Leicester, Huntingdon's brother-in-law and political ally, possessed plenty of pictures and wall-hangings in a lavish Mannerist style,[105] while their contemporary, the politician Sir Thomas Smith, covered his walls at Hill Hall in Essex with two series of frescoes: the one depicting the legend of Cupid and Psyche, the other the Old Testament stories of King Hezekiah.[106] The Suffolk household of that exemplary godly magistrate Sir Robert Jermyn was well known to Nicholas Bownd, who wanted to stop the mouths of the singing men. And yet it accommodated George Kirby, Jermyn's music master, who published the first six-part madrigals in England, written for Jermyn's daughters.[107] The better documented evangelicals of the nineteenth century were variable in their practice with regard to such matters. Some read novels. Some did not. Some went to the theatre. Others abstained. Naturally preachers like Bownd found it easier to reprehend the musical tastes of the common people than those of Jermyn's daughters.

V

Why? It is certainly a difficult question and far from local, since as Peter Burke has shown in his *Popular Culture in Early Modern Europe* 'the triumph of Lent' was a nearly universal phenomenon. 'Puritan' may have some value as a description of John Carter's mentality and moral attiudes but it is of little explanatory use to say that English Protestanism had hardened into Puritanism. That is to play with words. Another phrase 'the reception of Calvinism' is more helpful. True, it implies a rather primitive notion of how ideas work in history, as if a certain dose of Calvin's divinity had been poured into so many receptive English bottles, while 'influence' is a word out of fashion among historians of the intellect. But it is undeniable that Calvin took a hard line on these matters. And if we appreciate that he was heating to a kind of maximum intensity layers of anti-sensualism, drawn from Plato, Augustine, St John Chrysostom and other Fathers, as well as from the humanists of his own century, Erasmus not least, then we should be unwise to underestimate Calvin's impact on a susceptible English moral consciousness. The unrelenting struggle against Catholicism must also be central to our understanding of the Protestant impact on culture. The drastic polarisation of the mind which tended to extrapolate popery from any trace of theological deviance or weakness made it hard to distinguish between acceptable and unacceptable images. Witness John Donne's confusion in *Satire III*:

> To adore, or scorn an image, or protest,
> May all be bad . . .

The attack on the theatre had a close affinity to the denunciation of Catholic worship as theatricality, just as the Puritan polemic against magic and witchcraft connected with rejection of the Mass as a kind of conjuring and necromancy. Before the Reformation it was sometimes sufficient for a layman to be found in possession of a book – any book – to be suspect of heresy. After the Reformation, pictures – almost any pictures – aroused suspicion of popery.[108] And, to be sure, pictures as household possessions were as rare as books had once been. Dr Susan Foister has found that of 613 inventories (from the Prerogative Court of Canterbury) compiled between 1417 and 1588 (and mostly Tudor) only 63 list pictures or other works of art; and that under Elizabeth there was a distinct 'tailing off' of pictures on religious subjects. 'It is clear that the majority of even the most prosperous classes in Tudor England did not own any paintings or sculpture at all . . .'[109]

The fathers ate sour grapes and the children's teeth were set on edge. By the time of the Civil War a thoroughly seasoned iconophobia could be provoked in Sussex by the contents of a Flemish bark which was stranded near Worthing. A scandalised parliamentary colonel, Herbert Morley, reported to the Speaker of the House of Commons the discovery on board of 'certain pictures which contain most gross idolatry', including a 'monstrous' image of the Trinity. Among these canvases, products of some Antwerp studio, was a painting of the betrothal of St Ursula, intended for a church in Seville. This was misconstrued as an allegorical representation of the Virgin, presiding over a ceremony in which Charles I was surrendering his sceptre to the queen and the pope. 'I look upon this picture as an hieroglyphic of the causes and intents of our present troubles', wrote Morley in despatching the offending object to London, where it went on exhibition in the Star Chamber.[110]

However, problems remain. As we have been taught the principles of Protestant poetics by Barbara Lewalski, Lily Campbell and John King,[111] the Reformation, even in its Calvinist expression, was not hostile to art, only to false and idolatrous art, 'men's fantasies'. There was scope for artistic sincerity. Lucas Schan's naturalistic representations of animals and birds in Conrad Gesner's *Historia Animalium*, some of them carefully coloured, were also Protestant art, in the tradition of Dürer's *De Symmetria*.[112] Then why was it inadmissible for so many second-generation Protestants to appeal directly to the eye with images bearing a literal resemblance to the biblical word, for example with a faithful likeness of Christ in portrait form; or by means of a dramatic realisation of a gospel story, like Lewis Wager's touching re-enactment of the scene in the house of Simon the Pharisee, when Mary Magdalene washed the feet of Jesus with her tears – virtually the last appearance of Christ on the English stage for 350 years? Why was the almost gnomic hermeticism of emblematic conceits lawful but naturalism not? This was as much to say that pictorial symbols were accessible only to literate cognoscenti, who had least need of them, in the way that truth had been concealed in parables, lest the vulgar should comprehend. It is not as if there was no established Protestant pictorial language, representing the humanity of Christ. Mid-Tudor Bibles contain plenty of such images. Francis Quarles's question of 1638 is very apt. Christ is presented in Scripture as Sower, Fisher and Physician. 'And why not presented so, as well to the eye as to the eare?' But this was written in justification of those 'silent parables', emblems.[113]

Consequently, those grappling with these problems suspect hidden depths, ironies, contradictions. It was not because Zwingli and Calvin were without a musical ear that Zwingli excluded music from worship altogether and that Calvin admitted it only under stringent conditions. Zwingli was a talented amateur musician and Calvin knew, doubtless from personal experience, that music had 'grande force et vigeur d'esmouvoir et enflamber le coeur des hommes.'[114] Protestants of this secondary generation were suppressing powerful appetites in themselves, appetites equated with sensuality, in Carter's words 'whatever stirreth up corrupt nature'. Of his part as a poet Theodore Beza wrote (in the words of his Elizabethan translator):

> For I confesse, that even of nature I have delighted in poetrie, and I can not yet repent me of it; nevertheless it greveth me right sore, that the little grace which God gave me in that behalfe, was imployed by me in such things as the very remembrance of them irketh me now at the hart.[115]

When all else fails, we reach for the psychologist, if only for the amateur psychologist lurking within each one of us. Some scholars, no less desperate than ingenious, have wondered whether the logocentric iconophobia of a reformer like Zwingli may not imply the dominance of the left hemisphere of the brain, the seat of language-related faculties, over the visual and musical faculties of the right hemisphere. I do not know what professional neurophysiologists and psychologists would make of that, or of the evidence which this essay has presented. But it does appear that the cultural impact of what looks almost like a second English Reformation resembles that famous day in Sweden when, at a certain signal, vehicles stopped driving on the left and changed to the right, so relatively sudden and drastic was the change.

Notes

1 Christopher Haigh, 'The Recent Historiography of the English Reformation', *Historical Journal*, xxv (1982), pp. 995–1007.

2 I refer to points made by Professor Dickens in conversation. However, the argument is everywhere implicit in his *The English Reformation* (1964) and in his contribution to *The Reformation Crisis*, ed. J. Hurstfield (1965).

3 Susan Brigden, 'Youth and the English Reformation', *Past and Present*, no. 95 (1982), pp. 37–67. (*See* Reading 3 above) Cf. N.Z. Davis, 'The Reasons of Misrule: Youth Groups and Charivaris in Sixteenth-Century France', *Past and Present*, no. 50 (1971), pp. 41–75, reprinted in N.Z. Davis, *Society and Culture in Early Modern France* (1975), pp. 97–123. Cf. also Janine Garrisson-Estèbe: 'Globalement, les nouvelles générations sont massivement présentes là, où la violence a parlé': *Protestants du Midi 1559–1598* (Toulouse, 1980), pp. 49–51.

4 Patrick Collinson, 'Popular and Unpopular Religion', chapter 5 of *The Religion of Protestants: the Church in English Society 1559–1625* (Oxford, 1982); David Underdown, *Revel, Riot and Rebellion: Popular Politics and Culture in England 1603–1660* (Oxford, 1985), pp. 44–105; Peter Burke, *Popular Culture in Early Modern Europe* (1978). Cf. Emmanuel le Roy Ladurie's shopping list of what was abusive in the perception of the Protestants of the Cévennes: 'The Mass, dancing, laughter, bowling and card playing, too long or too intimate bethrothals, the debaucheries of serving-girls, abortion, feminine vanities and masculine quarrels . . . ': *The Peasants of Languedoc* (1976), p. 170.

5 John N. King, *English Reformation Literature: Tudor Origins of the Protestant Tradition* (Princeton, 1982).

6 George Gifford, *A briefe discourse of certaine points of the religion which is among the common sort of christians which may bee termed the countrie divinitie* (1581); Arthur Dent, *The plaine mans path-way to Heaven* (1601), p. 30. An exception to prove the rule is John Comyns's sermon *The thankefull Samaritane* (1617), preached in Exeter Cathedral. Comyns thought that the poor and painful husbandmen commonly displayed more holiness and conscionable obedience than knights and gentlemen. 'The Mechanicall man is a better Christian than a Merchant man.' However, that the one healed leper who gave thanks should be a Samaritan was a paradox, and this led Comyns into these further paradoxes.

7 See Duffy, 'The Godly and the Multitude in Stuart England', *Seventeenth Century Journal* 1 (1986), pp. 31–49.

8 George Gifford, *A sermon on the parable of the sower* (1582); William Harrison, *The difference of hearers* (1613), discussed by Christopher Haigh in 'Puritan Evangelism in the Reign of Elizabeth I', *English Historical Review*, xcii (1977), pp. 30–58. Cf. Thomas Carew on 'The Little Flock of Christ' in *Certaine godly and necessarie sermons* (1603): 'The fault it . . . in the peoples hearts' (Sig. G). 'It seems by this parable that in the visible Church there are many more hypocrites than true Christians . . . Of this number [scil. of true Christians] there might peradventure be pointed out some one or two in this town, some two or three in that town, although we cannot see many' (Sig. H6).

9 John Norden, *A mirror for the multitude* (1586).

10 *Philip Stubbes's Anatomy of Abuses in England in Shakspere's Youth AD 1583*, ed. F.J. Furnivall (New Shakespeare Society, n.s.s. iv, vi, xii. 1877–82), p. 144; John Darrell, *A treatise of the Church written against them of the separation, commonly called Brownists* (1617), pp. 25, 28–9. Cf. the pessimism of Jeremy Corderoy in *A warning for worldlings* (1608).

11 This argument, which was deployed in my Birkbeck Lectures delivered in Cambridge in 1981, is further stated in my article, 'The English Convencticle', *Studies in Church History*, xxiii (1986), pp. 223–59.

12 Stuart Clark, 'Inversion, Misrule and the Meaning of Witchcraft', *Past and Present*, no. 87 (1980), pp. 98–127; Michael Hunter, 'The Problem of "Atheism" in Early

Modern England', *Transactions of the Royal Historical Society,* 5th ser. xxxv (1985), pp. 135–57.

13 These possibilities are explored, mainly on the basis of polemical and other literary evidence, in the writings of Christopher Hill; and, more recently and on a different basis, by Keith Wrightson, especially in Wrightson and David Levine, *Poverty and Piety in an English Village: Terling, 1525–1700* (1979), and in 'Aspects of Social Differentiation in Rural England 1580–1660', *The Journal of Peasant Studies,* v (1977). See also Peter Clark, *English Provincial Society from the Reformation to the Revolution: Religion, Politics and Society in Kent, 1500–1640* (Hassocks, 1977), '"The Ramoth-Gilead of the Good": Gloucester 1540–1640', in *The English Commonwealth, 1547–1640,* ed. P. Clark, A.G.R. Smith and N. Tyacke (Leicester, 1979), pp. 167–87 and *The English Alehouse 1200–1830* (1983). See the critical remarks of Margaret Spufford, 'Puritanism and Social Control?', in *Order and Disorder in Early Modern England,* ed. Anthony Fletcher and John Stevenson (Cambridge, 1985), pp. 41–57.

14 Collinson, *Religion of Protestants,* pp. 216–30.

15 For a particular attack on householders as patrons or 'bawds' of dancing, see Thomas Lovell, *A dialogue between custom and veritie concerning dauncing and minstrelsie* (1581).

16 J.R. Green, *History of the English People* (1876 edn.), p. 447.

17 A certain influence is exerted on these remarks and on much of what follows by Barbara K. Lewalski, *Protestant Poetics and the Seventeenth-Century Religious Lyric* (Princeton, 1979).

18 See *Tudor Royal Proclamations,* ed. Paul L. Hughes and James F. Larkin, i (New Haven, 1964), no. 186; and Henry VIII's last speech to Parliament of 24 December 1545: 'I am very sorry to know and hear how unreverently that precious jewel, the word of God, is disputed, rhymed, sung and jangled in every alehouse and tavern.' (J.J. Scarisbrick, *Henry VIII* (1968), p. 471.) Cf. the debate at the sign of the Bell in Northampton in 1538, reported by Margaret Bowker in *The Henrician Reformation: the Diocese of Lincoln Under John Longland 1521–1547* (Cambridge, 1981), pp. 166–7; and the Thaxted man who confessed that 'in Alehouses and other uncomelie and unmeate places' he had taken upon him to 'bable, talke and rangle of the Scripture which I understode not.' (John F. Davis, *Heresy and Reformation in the South-East of England, 1520–1559* (1983), p. 95.)

19 BL, MS. Harley 425, fols. 4–7. For the dating of Wisdom's narrative, see J.S. Bailey, 'Robert Wisdom Under Persecution 1541–1543', *Journal of Ecclesiastical History,* ii (1951).

20 William Wilkinson, *A confutation of certaine articles* (1579), reprinted, John Strype, *Annals,* II.ii (Oxford, 1824) pp. 282–3; *The Acts and Monuments of John Foxe,* ed. S.R. Cattley, viii (1839), pp. 458–60. Dickens's *bon mot* was proposed in an unpublished lecture (but see his *Reformation Studies* (1982), p. 507). Joyce Lewes of Lichfield drank a hearty breakfast on the morning of her martyrdom, sharing the cup with her friends, 'the women of that town', and pledging 'all them that unfeignedly love the gospel of Jesus Christ, and wish for the abolishment of papistry'. Later these women were prescribed penance 'for drinking with her'. (*Acts of Monuments,* viii. pp. 404, 429.)

21 *A dialogue concerning the strife of our Church* (1584), p. 6; *Documents Illustrative of English Church History,* ed. H. Gee and W.J. Hardy (1896), pp. 421–2; *The Works of George Herbert,* ed. F.E. Hutchinson (Oxford, 1941), p. 227; Clark, *The English Alehouse,* pp. 157–9.

22 Cathedral Archives and Library Canterbury, MS. X.8.8, fol. 349. I owe this reference to Dr R.J. Acheson.

23 *Acts and Monuments,* viii. p. 444.

24 Susan E. Brigden, 'The Early Reformation in London, 1520–1547', unpublished Cambridge PhD thesis (1977), pp. 302–4: *Acts and Monuments of John Foxe,* ed. S.R. Cattley, v (1838), p. 446. On Bale, see most recently King, *English Reformation Literature,* pp. 56–75 and *passim.*

25 *A newe mery and wittie comedie or enterlude newely imprinted, treating upon the*

historie of Jacob and Esau (licensed 1557/8, printed 1568, Malone Society reprint, 1956); Lewis Wager, *A new enterlude . . . entreating of the life and repentaunce of Marie Magdalene, not only godlie learned and fruitefull, but also well furnished with pleasaunt myrth and pastime* (1566; modern edn. ed. F.I. Carpenter (Chicago, 1904)). See King, *English Reformation Literature*, pp. 278–83.

26 Cf. the interlude by W. Wager (no relation), *The longer thou livest* (see following footnote) where (pp. 36–8 in Benbow edition) Incontinence tempts the young man Moros with talk of 'to kisse, to clip, and in bed to play/Oh with lustie girles to singe and daunce . . . Sometime you may have your choice of twenty.'

27 In chronological order of first publication: W. Wager, *The longer thou livest the more foole thou art* (*c.* 1559–68, written *c.* 1559); modern ed. R. Mark Benbow (Lincoln, Nebraska, 1967); *A newe interlude of impacyente poverte* (1560, written *c.* 1550); *A pretie new enterlude called Nice Wanton* (1560, written *c.* 1547–53); *Godly Queen Hester* (1561, written *c.* 1527); *A pretie new enterlude both pithie and pleasaunt of the story of Kyng Daryus* (1565); *An enterlude called Lusty Juventus* (1565); Thomas Ingelend, *A pretie and mery new enterlude called the Disobedient Child* (1569, written *c.* 1560); *A new enterlude no lesse wittie then pleasant entituled New Custome* (1573, written *c.* 1570); Thomas Garter, *The commody of the most vertuous and godlye Susanne* (licensed 1568–9, printed 1578; Malone Society reprint, 1937). (Dating from *The Revels History of the Drama in English* (1983), ii. *1500–1576*, corrected by King, *English Reformation Literature*.) See also Sylvia D. Feldman, *The Morality-Patterned Comedy of the Renaissance* (The Hague and Paris, 1970), Robert Potter, *The English Morality Play: Origins, History and Influence of a Dramatic Tradition* (1975), chapter 5 'Early Elizabethan Plays in the Morality Tradition'.

28 See the Prologue:

And though perchaunce some wanton worde doe passe which may not seeme,
Or gestures light not meete for this, your wisedomes may not deeme,
Accompt that nought delightes the heart of man on earth,
So much as matters grave and sad, if they be mixt with myrth.

Sensualitas says of Susannah: 'By God I would spend my best cote to fishe within her poole' (l. 427).

29 See especially *Nice Wanton*, *Lusty Juventus* and *The Disobedient Child*.

30 David Bevington, *From Mankind to Marlowe* (Cambridge, MA, 1962); E.K. Chambers, *The Elizabethan Stage*, i (Oxford, 1923), pp. 240–56. See also *The Revels History of the Drama*, which, like Chambers and many other writers, makes too absolute a watershed out of the royal proclamation of 16 May 1559 which prohibited the playing of interludes 'wherein either matters of religion or of the governance of the estate of the commonweal shall be handled or treated', which, in the manner of such proclamations, can only have taken temporary effect at best. (*Tudor Royal Proclamations*, ed. Paul L. Hughes and James F. Larkin, ii (New Haven, 1969), no. 458.)

31 Bevington, *Mankind to Marlowe*, pp. 13–14.

32 'Truely, I say, whether you geve halfpence or pence,/Your gayne shalbe double, before you depart hence.'

33 *R(ecords) of the E(arly) E(nglish) D(rama)*, iii. *Coventry*, ed. R.W. Ingram (Toronto, 1981), p. 207.

34 *REED*, I. *Chester*, ed. Lawrence M. Clopper (Toronto, 1979), pp. 109–17, 184, 197–9; *R of the EED*, II. *York*, i. ed. Alexander F. Johnston and Margaret Rogerson (Toronto, 1979), pp. 368–70, 378–9, 390–3; Harold C. Gardiner, *Mysteries' End: an Investigation of the Last Days of the Medieval Religious Stage* (New Haven, 1946), pp. 72–83; Patrick Collinson, *Archbishop Grindal 1519–1583: the Struggle for a Reformed Church* (1979), p. 203; David Palliser, *Tudor York* (Oxford, 1979), pp. 246–7.

35 *R.E.E.D. York*, pp. 481–2, 486; *Minutes and Accounts of Stratford-upon-Avon*, ed. E.I. Fripp, ii. *1566–1577* (Dugdale Society Pubns., iii. 1924), xxxvi. *R.E.E.D., Chester*, pp. 184, 292; Underdown, *Revel, Riot and Rebellion*, pp. 51–2.

36 Folger Shakespeare Library, MS. W.b.484, pp. 31–2. I owe this reference to Professor W. Ringler.

37 William Prynne, *Histrio-Mastix: the Players Scourge or Actors Tragedie* (1638), p. 701. See the collection of 'Documents of Criticism' in Chambers, *Elizabethan Stage*, iv. pp. 194–255.

38 William A. Ringler, 'The First Phase of the Elizabethan Attack on the Stage 1558–1579', *Huntington Library Quarterly*, v (1942), pp. 391–418; William Ringler, *Stephen Gosson: a Biographical and Critical Study* (Princeton, 1924); Chambers, *Elizabethan Stage*, i. pp. 242–56; Margot Heinemann, *Puritanism and the Theatre* (Cambridge, 1980); Jonas Barish, *The Antitheatrical Prejudice* (Berkeley and Los Angeles, 1981).

39 Stephen Gosson, *Playes confuted in five actions* (1582), Sig. E1; Anthony Munday, *A second and third blast of retraits from plaies and theaters* (1590), pp. 95–6. I owe this point to Dr Michael O'Connell of University of California, Santa Barbara.

40 Michael Hattaway, *Elizabethan Popular Theatre: Plays in Performance* (1982).

41 Ringler, 'The First Phase'. That there was some exaggeration in Ringler's argument is suggested by Edmund Grindal's letter as bishop of London to Sir William Cecil, 22 February 1563/4, in which he attributes a renewal of plague in London to the players, complains that 'God's word by their impure mouths is profaned and turned into scoffs' and recommends a proclamation to inhibit all plays for a year, 'and if it were for ever, it were not amiss.' (*The Remains of Edmund Grindal*, ed. W. Nicholson (Parker Society, Cambridge, 1843), pp. 268–9.)

42 Glynne Wickham, *Early English Stages 1300 to 1600*, i (1963), pp. 329–31.

43 *Proceedings in the Parliament of Elizabeth I*, i. *1558–1581* ed. T.E. Hartley (Leicester, 1981), p. 31.

44 Chambers, *Elizabethan Stage*, iv. p. 194.

45 Stephen Gosson, *The schoole of abuse* (1578), Sigs. C6^v–7^v; Chambers, *Elizabethan Stage*, iv. p. 273.

46 Theodore Beza, *A tragedie of Abrahams sacrifice*, tr. Arthur Golding (1577), Preface.

47 *Anatomy of Abuses*, pp. 140–3; Prynne, *Histrio-Mastix*, pp. 789–93; John Northbrooke, *A treatise wherein dicing, dauncing, vaine playes or enterluds with other idle pastimes etc. commonly used on the Sabboth day are reproved* (1577), (Shakespeare Society repr. 1843), p. 92; *Erasmus on his Times: A Shortened Version of the 'Adages' of Erasmus*, ed. M.M. Phillips (Cambridge, 1967), pp. 75–6.

48 R.E.E.D., *Coventry*, p. 150; R.E.E.D., *Chester*, p. 75; R.E.E.D., *York*, p. 361.

49 *Anatomy of Abuses*, p. 141.

50 *Anatomy of Abuses*, pp. 143–4.

51 R.E.E.D., *York*, p. 353; R.E.E.D., *Chester*, p. 248.

52 Murray Roston, *Biblical Drama in England from the Middle Ages to the Present Day* (1968), pp. 109–20; Lily B. Campbell, *Divine Poetry and Drama in Sixteenth-Century England* (Cambridge, 1959), pp. 238–60; Thomas Lodge, *A Defence of Poetry, Music and Stage-Plays*, ed. D. Laing (1853); Thomas Lodge, *Wits miserie, and the worlds madnesse* (1596), p. 40.

53 Prynne, *Histrio-Mastix*, p. 934. Cf. Collinson, *Religion of Protestants*, pp. 244–5.

54 *The Acts and Monuments of John Foxe*, ed. S.R. Cattley, vi (1838), p. 31; Gosson, *Schoole of Abuse*, Sig. D3; William Crashaw, quoted in H. Mutschmann and K. Wentersdorf, *Shakespeare and Catholicism* (New York, 1952), p. 102.

55 What follows is based on Hyder E. Rollins's listings in *An Analytical Index to the Ballad-Entries in the Registers of the Company of Stationers of London* (Studies in Philology 21.i, Chapel Hill, 1924); together with *The Roxburgh Ballads* (Ballad Society, 1869 etc), *The Bagford Ballads*, iv (Ballad Society, 1878), Hyder E. Rollins, *Old English Ballads 1553–1625 Chiefly from Manuscripts* (Cambridge, 1920), Hyder E. Rollins, *The Black-Letter Broadside Ballads* (P.M.L.A. xxxiv. 1919), *The Eving Collection of English Broadside Ballads in the Library of the University of Glasgow*, ed. John Holloway (Glasgow, 1971), *A Handfull of Pleasant Delights (1584) by Clement Robinson and Divers Others*, (ed.), Hyder E. Rollins (Cambridge, MA, 1924), *The Pack of Autolycus*, ed. H.E. Rollins (1972), *A*

Compendious Book of Godly and Spiritual Songs Commonly Known as 'The Gude and Godlie Ballatis' Reprinted from the Edition of 1567, ed. A.F. Mitchell (Scottish Text Society, xxxix. Edinburgh, 1897), *An Anthology of Popular British Ballad Poetry*, ed. V. de Sola Pinto and A.F. Rodway (1957); and the celebrated Britwell Ballads in the Huntington Library, examined in their originals but also reprinted in *Ballads and Broadside Chiefly of the Elizabethan Period*, ed. Herbert L. Collmann (Oxford, 1912). See also Claude M. Simpson, *The British Broadside Ballad and its Music* (New Brunswick, NJ, 1966).

56 Franklin B. Williams Jr, 'Lost Books of Tudor England', *The Library*, 5th ser. xxxiii (1978), p. 13. See Rollins 1335, *The judgment of God* (1580) and John Charnock's *The judgment of vyce* (Rollins 1337, 1565–6).

57 Rollins, *The Black-Letter Broadside Ballad*, p. 288.

58 Simpson, *The British Broadside Ballad*, pp. 615–19.

59 Rollins, *Old English Ballads*, pp. xxviii–ix; Hyder E. Rollins, 'William Elderton: Elizabethan Actor and Ballad Writer', *Studies in Philology*, xvii (1920), pp. 199–245; *A Handfull of Pleasant Delights*, p. 101. *The gods of love* was printed in *The Times* on 17 November 1958 from a MS. copy in the possession of James M. Osborn. (Simpson, *The British Broadside Ballad*, p. 260.) *The pangs of love* was parodied in *Knaw ze not God Omnipotent and Was not Salomon the King*, both in *Gude and Godlie Ballatis*. (Rollins, *The Black-Letter Broadside Ballad*, p. 288.)

60 John Hall, *The Court of Virtue* (1565), ed. Russell A. Fraser (New Brunswick, NJ, 1961). Four copies survive, all imperfect, that in the Huntington Library (complemented by the BL copy) providing the basis of this text. The surviving fragments of *The Court of Venus* are edited by Russell A. Fraser (Durham, NC, 1955). For Brice's moralisation, see Collmann, *Ballads and Broadsides*, no. 13. Hall also published *Certayne chapters taken out of the Proverbes of Salomon . . . translated into English metre* (1550) but the credit for this mostly belonged to Thomas Sternhold. 'A ballade againste nigardie and riches' with which Hall's *Proverbes* ends also occurs in the Catholic collection BL, MS. Add. 15225, fols. 7ᵛ–9ᵛ. In the preface to *Proverbes*, Hall displays the almost prurient fascination with vice which was characteristic of moral plagiarizers and writers of moral interludes, attacking 'these gygolat gerls' who dye their hair yellow and paint their faces.

61 H.P. Clive, 'The Calvinist Attitude to Music', *Bibliothèque d'Humanisme et Renaissance*, xx (1958), pp. 302–7.

62 Maurice Frost, *English and Scottish Psalm and Hymn Tunes c. 1543–1677* (1953).

63 The analysis is based on Rollins's *Analytical Index*, with the addition of certain ballads in the Huntington Library collections not included by Rollins.

64 The earliest reference to *Greensleeves* occurs in the *Stationers Register* for 3 September 1580, when Richard Jones was licensed to print *A newe northern dittye of the Lady Greene Sleves*. *Greene Sleves moralized to the Scripture* appeared on 15 September 1580.

65 They included *A most excellent godly new ballad: [shew]ing the manifold abuses of this wicked world, the intolerable pride of people, the wantonnesse [of] women, the dissimulation of flatterers, the subtility of deceivers, the beastlines of drunkards, the filthinesse of whoredome, the unthriftines of gamesters, the cruelty of landlords, with a number of other inconveniences.* (*The Pack of Autolycus*, no. 1.)

66 The connection with the *Song of John Careless* seems complex. *A godly and vertuous songe or ballade made by the constant member of Christe John Carelesse* (from which two lines are adapted in *King Lear*, I.iv.171–2) occurs in BL, MS. Sloane 1896, fols. 11–12ᵛ, and was printed by Miles Coverdale in *Certaine most godly, fruitful and comfortable letters* (1564) and often reprinted. In 1583 the 'tune of John Carelesse' was used for *A declaration of the death of Iohn Lewes, a most detestable and obstinate hereticke burned at Norwich the xviii daye of September 1583* and in 1586 another ballad was set to the same tune. (Rollins, *Old English Ballads*, no. 8.)

67 It seems to have been the third most popular Elizabethan hit tune, coming after 'Packington's Pound' and 'Fortune My Foe'. (Simpson, *The British Broadside Ballad*, pp. 564–70n; *A Handfull of Pleasant Delights*, p. 90n.)

68 Thomas Nashe, *Works*, ed. R.B. McKerrow (1915), iii. 104.
69 Cathedral Archives and Library Canterbury, MS.X.4.1 (i), fol. 51. I owe this reference to Dr R.J. Acheson.
70 *A Compendious Book*, pp. xxxiii–iv.
71 The evidence is in Maunsell's *Catalogue*. (*The Court of Virtue*, p. xiv.)
72 Margaret Spufford, *Small Books and Pleasant Histories* (1981), pp. 194–218.
73 *Anatomy of Abuses*, p. 171. For a more balanced view of the Elizabethan musical profession, see W.L. Woodfill, *Musicians in English Society from Elizabeth to Charles I* (Princeton, 1953).
74 See a number of cases from the *Acta* of the Canterbury Archdeaconry Court, including the case cited, in my *Religion of Protestants*, pp. 206–7. On minstrels and ballad singers and vendors as vagrants, see A.L. Beier, *Masterless Men: the Vagrancy Problem in England 1560–1640* (1985), pp. 97–8. John Walsall, *A sermon preached at Paules Crosse* (1578), Sigs. Eiii, Ev^v.
75 Lovell, *A dialogue between custom and veritie*.
76 Thomas Lodge wrote: '*Eldertons* nose would grin at them if they should but equall the worst of his Ballads.' (*Wits miserie*, p. 10.) And Thomas Nashe of a 'red nose Ballet-maker'. (*Works*, iii. p. 133.) See Rollins, 'William Elderton', Rollins, *Old English Ballads*, p. xviii. An example of Elderton's 'flyting' is his *Reprehension againste Green Sleves* (Rollins 2276, 13 February 1581.)
77 Nicholas Bownd, *The doctrine of the Sabbath* (1595), pp. 241–2.
78 Preface to Coverdale, *Goostly psalms and spirituall songs* (before 1539); quoted, Lewalski, *Protestant Poetics*, p. 33.
79 *Acts and Monuments*, v. pp. 404–9; Rollins, *Old English Ballads* , p. xi. For some French parallels, see Philip Benedict, *Rouen During the Wars of Religion* (Cambridge, 1981), p. 60, Donald Kelly, *The Beginnings of Ideology: Consciousness and Society in the French Reformation* (Cambridge, 1981), pp. 97–100.
80 *Acts and Monuments*, viii. p. 416, v. p. 445.
81 *Acts and Monuments*, viii. p. 578. In 1546 one Essex villager rebuked another for a song he had sung at a bridal feast, abusing the images of the saints as idols: 'Hunte, though thow be nowght thy selfe, entyce none oder man to be bad as thow arte.' (PRO, S.P. 1/130, fols. 151–2. I owe this reference to Dr Susan Brigden.) See a similar Essex case in G.R. Elton, *Policy and Police: the Enforcement of the Reformation in the Age of Thomas Cromwell* (Cambridge, 1972), p. 32.
82 *Acts and Monuments*, v. pp. 403, 445, viii. pp. 214, 554–5; *Letters and Papers of Henry VIII*, xviii (i), no. 447, p. 267; Huntington Library, Britwell Ballads no. 34 (HEH 18295).
83 My chief debt in what follows is to Nicholas Temperley, *The Music of the English Parish Church*, 2 vols. (Cambridge, 1979).
84 *Certayne Psalmes chosen out of the Psalter* (c. 1549), Sig. A3^r; William Baldwin, *Canticles or Balades of Salomon* (1549), Sig. A3^v; Temperley, *Music of the English Parish Church*, pp. 23, 37. See also Rollins, *The Black-Letter Broadside Ballad*, p. 259, King, *English Reformation Literature*, pp. 217–26, Hallett Smith, 'English Metrical Psalms in the Sixteenth-Century and their Literary Significance', *Huntington Library Quarterly*, ix (1940), pp. 249–71. Smith seems to me somewhat to underplay the denunciation by English psalmodists of 'ungodly songs and ballads'.
85 Temperley, *Music of the English Parish Church*, pp. 36, 63, 67, 34–5.
86 Clive, 'Calvinist Attitude to Music', pp. 86–7, 100–3.
87 The earliest references are in *The Diary of Henry Machyn*, ed. J.H. Nichols (Camden Society, xlii. 1848), p. 212, and *Zurich Letters*, ed. H. Robinson (Parker Society, Cambridge, 1842), p. 71.
88 Simpson, *The British Broadside Ballad*, p. xv.
89 Temperley, *Music of the English Parish Church*, pp. 57–71.
90 R.W. Scribner, *For the Sake of Simple Folk: Popular Propaganda for the German Reformation* (Cambridge, 1981).
91 Michael Leslie, 'The Dialogue Between Bodies and Souls: Picture and Poesy in the English Renaissance', *Word and Image*, i (1985), pp. 16–30. On Emblematics, see

Lewalski, *Protestant Poetics*, chapter 6, 'Protestant Emblematics: Sacred Emblems and Religious Lyrics'.

92 Huntington Library, Britwell Ballads no. 58, HEH 18319.

93 Jill Finsten, *Isaac Oliver: Art at the Courts of Elizabeth I and James I* (New York, 1981), i. p. 137, ii. p. 231.

94 Stephen Bateman, *A cristal glasse of christian reformation wherein the godly maye beholde the coloured abuses used in this our present tyme* (1569).

95 Richard Bernard, *Contemplative pictures with wholesome precepts* (1610).

96 Pages 5–6: 'The aziured skie his comely curtaine, his privie chamber, the place of unspeakable pleasure. His face is a flame of fire, his voice thunder, his wrath, dread and terrible horrour. If he meete his enemies, he rides upon the wings of the winde, his chariots are without number: he raineth upon them snares to entrap them, fire to devoure them, hailstones to kill them: he sends a smoak to smother them, a stormy tempest to terrifie them, the stincke of brimstone to annoy them and hote thunderbolts to shoote them thorow.'

97 Desiderius Erasmus, *Christian Humanism and the Reformation: Selected Writings*, ed. John C. Olin (New York, 1965), p. 106; Sir Philip Sidney, *An Apology for Poetry or The Defence of Poesy*, ed. G. Shepherd (Manchester, 1965), pp. 99, 101 and *passim*.

98 K.J. Höltgen, 'The Reformation of Images and Some Jacobean Writers on Art', in *Functions of Literature: Essays Presented to Erwin Wolff on his Sixtieth Birthday*, ed. U. Broich, T. Stemmler and G. Stratmann (Tübingen, 1984), pp. 126, 142.

99 Höltgen, 'Reformation of Images', p. 136; E.K. Chambers, 'The First Illustrations to "Shakespeare"', *The Library*, 4th ser. v (1925), pp. 327–9; J. Dover Wilson, 'Titus Andronicus on the Stage in 1595', *Shakespeare: A Documentary Life* (New York, 1975), pp. 122–3.

100 King, *English Reformation Literature*, pp. 127–8.

101 Wager, *The longer thou livest*, lines 469–70, 483.

102 Höltgen, 'Reformation of Images', pp. 127–9.

103 John Carter, *A plaine and compendious exposition of Christs Sermon on the Mount* (1627), p. 42; 'An Homily Against Peril of Idolatry', *Sermons or Homilies Appointed to be Read in Churches* (1811 edn.), p. 200.

104 Huntington Library, MS. HA Inventories Box 1, no. 1.

105 C.L. Kingsford, 'Essex House, Formerly Leicester House and Exeter Inn', *Archaeologia*, xxiii (1923), pp. 1–54.

106 Richard Simpson, 'Sir Thomas Smith and the Wall Paintings at Hill Hall, Essex: Scholarly Theory and Design in the Sixteenth-Century', *Journal of the British Archaeological Association*, cxxx (1971), pp. 1–20. (I owe this reference to Dr Michael Leslie.)

107 Patrick Collinson, *Godly People: Essays on English Protestantism and Puritanism* (1983), pp. 453–4.

108 Witness an inventory of things found in the house of Mrs Hampden of Stoke in Buckinghamshire on 27 January 1584, which included 'ii pictures upon parchment', 'a picture of Christe' and 'a picture of (as it is termed) the Judgment daye' – all of which were assumed to be incriminating. (PRO, S.P. 12/167/47.) In the same year, a search of the house of Roger Smyth, gentleman, in Holborn yielded 'xii prynted superstycous pictures' (PRO, S.P. 12/172/106), while in Paris Garden in Southwark a raid by the constables on the home of Hewghe Katlyn (again in 1584) uncovered 'certayne pictures . . . and on crucifix', which were delivered to the recorder of London. (PRO, S.P. 12/176/16.)

109 Susan Foister, 'Paintings and Other Works of Art in Sixteenth-Century English Inventories', *Burlington Magazine*, cxxiii (1981), pp. 273–82. I am grateful to Dr George Bernard for alerting me to Dr Foister's findings. Of course, as the preceding footnote tends to suggest, woodcuts and other prints were more prevalent than works of art of a kind and value which would lead to their inclusion in inventories, and to an extent which cannot now be known.

110 Charles Thomas-Stanford, *Sussex in the Great Civil War and the Interregnum 1642–1660* (1910), pp. 151–5. I owe this reference to Anthony Fletcher.

111 Lewalski, *Protestant Poetics*, Campbell, *Divine Poetry*, King, *English Reformation Literature*.
112 Richard Simpson, 'Smith and the Wall Paintings', pp. 6–7.
113 K.J. Höltgen, *Francis Quarles (1592–1644)* (Tübingen, 1978), p. 216.
114 Charles Garside Jr, *Zwingli and the Arts* (New Haven, 1966); Clive, 'Calvinist Attitude to Music', p. 86.
115 *Tragedie of Abraham*, Preface.

12

Piety in the pedlar's pack:
continuity and change, 1578–1630

TESSA WATT

Pedlars and ballad sellers had a reputation as 'masterless' men and women at the nether regions of society; often prosecuted as vagrants, and forced by economic hardship into petty crime.[1] Writers like Shakespeare and Robert Greene described pedlars who doubled as pick-pockets, while the record books show that real chapmen were indeed often accused of theft at fairs and markets.[2] Ballad sellers were not approved of by Protestant reformers like Nicholas Bownde, who considered the possibility of printing the psalms as broadsides, but rejected it on these grounds: 'Indeed, many of the common singing men are so ungodly, that it were better for them to leave their mouths stopped, then once to open them to pollute such holy and sacred songs.'[3]

However, despite this disapproval, and whether willingly or unwittingly, the pedlar of print could be a messenger bearing God's word into towns and villages across the country. Richard Baxter, who grew up in the village of Eaton Constantine in Shropshire, recorded how, around 1630, 'a poor pedlar came to the door that had ballads and some good books: and my father bought of him Dr Sibb's *Bruised Reed*'.[4] This book of sermons by the Puritan divine helped to strengthen the adolescent Baxter in his convictions, and gave him 'a livelier apprehension of the mystery of redemption'.

It is rare to find concrete references in this period to pedlars of print coming directly to the door, and to a small village such as Eaton Constantine. Ballad sellers appear most frequently in the court records of large cities such as Norwich, and they are often to be found at the major fairs.[5] However, we do know that in 1578 a pedlar in Cambridgeshire ventured

Reprinted from M. Spufford, ed. *The World of Rural Dissenters 1520–1725* (Cambridge, 1995).

several miles off the main road to the village of Balsham, where he sold 'lytle bookes' in the churchyard. One of these books was bought by 'a young barber-surgeon who does not appear to have been very prosperous, since he was also a patcher of old clothes, and swore on oath that he would be "worthe nothinge" if his debts were paid off'. His wares cannot have been very expensive; nor did the arrival of this itinerate bookseller, in itself, seem to cause any special remark.[6]

Did this pedlar's visit have anything to do with the presence of the Family of Love in Balsham, and did the 'little books' include the teachings of the Familist leader Hendrick Niclaes? In 1574, just a few years earlier, six Balsham yeomen confessed to holding private conventicles in their houses, and in 1580 four of them were imprisoned as members of the Familist sect.[7] A local leader of the sect in Wisbech owned over half a dozen books of Hendrick Niclaes's teachings, and other followers in the area must have had access to Familist writings.[8] Works which were printed at a Familist press in Cologne in this period included the cheapest and most portable of wares: a broadside of 1575 contains a blessing and grace to be said at table, and another offers an 'abc' for the Family's children.[9]

Our pedlar could have collected these broadsides from one of several booksellers in Cambridge, who were used to acquiring books published on the Continent for their scholarly clientele. The Cambridge stationer and bookbinder John Denys was apparently doing a brisk trade with the Continent, and in particular with the city of Cologne where the Familist works were printed. He died of 'plague' in 1578, the very same year our pedlar visited Balsham. His inventory of 1578 lists a copy of Avenarius's *Precationes* which was printed in Cologne in that same year of 1578.[10] Of course, the distribution of heretical works was not to be undertaken lightly, and it seems unlikely that an ordinary pedlar would wander the county carrying Familist broadsides to show to all and sundry. If our pedlar did distribute Niclaes's writings it would mean he had special connections with the Familist yeomen and was a regular and trusted supplier. If he did not, the Balsham sect may have got their books directly from a Cambridge bookseller, or perhaps from the London–Cambridge carrier. Certainly the Quakers of the seventeenth century used carriers to send their books, and in 1654 the Atherston–London carrier took the risk of carrying 100 copies of a Quaker pamphlet for distribution.[11] Or the Familists may have been served by a specialist pedlar of their own faith. The London stationer Michael Sparke remembered travelling around the country selling Roman Catholic books, during his apprenticeship between 1603 and 1610, and it may be that the Familists, too, had their own supplier who has escaped the record books.[12]

In the absence of further evidence it seems fair to assume that our Balsham bookseller was an ordinary petty chapman, possibly with a small but risky sideline feeding the Balsham Familists with seditious print. For our purposes, the crucial question is this: how did the wares of this chapman compare with those of Richard Baxter's pedlar in Shropshire some fifty years later? Were these men specialists in print, or did they sell books and ballads among other wares like cambrics and small courtship gifts, as did Shakespeare's Autolycus?[13] For now, we must leave the ribbons and gloves at the bottom of the pack, along with the merry chapbooks and bawdy ballads. In this essay, which must inevitably be speculative, I will describe a cross-section of the religious print which may have been carried by the petty chapman working in Cambridgeshire in the 1570s, and by his fellow-pedlar in Shropshire in the 1630s. Although publishers of the 1570s did produce a number of small and cheap books suitable for pedlars, as we shall see, the 1620s heralded an expansion at the bottom end of the publishing trade, and the rise of a whole new genre of chapbooks.

The pedlar working in Cambridgeshire would have had no shortage of potential suppliers of print, since the presence of the University in Cambridge attracted a number of booksellers. The village of Balsham lay some ten miles south-east of Cambridge, and could have been part of a circuit involving several days' walking. The inventory for John Denys shows that many of his books were Latin textbooks and other works for the members of the University, but that his shop also contained psalm books and prayer books suitable for ordinary householders, an assortment of pamphlets valued at as little as twopence each, and a dozen almanacs at a penny per copy.[14]

Assuming that the 'poor pedlar' of Shropshire was travelling on foot, without a horse, it seems likely that he worked a limited local circuit, centring on the town of Shrewsbury. The village of Eaton Constantine was only five miles from Shrewsbury, and well within half a day's walk. The pedlar could have collected his wares from a Shrewsbury bookshop on a sale-or-return basis, or may even have been in the bookseller's employ. By the late sixteenth century we know that the publisher Roger Ward stocked some 2500 books in his Shrewsbury bookshop; mostly catechisms, prayer books, Latin texts, sermons, psalters, and so on. At the cheap end of the market these included at least 225 copies of sermons, 69 unspecified 'bookes at pence', '22 Almanakes', '20 pictures not colored', and '1 Reame 6 quire ballates' (or about 650 broadsides), all of which might have been sent round to nearby villages with a pedlar.[15] Provincial booksellers like John Denys and Roger Ward may have had their own wares delivered to them by the Cambridge and Shrewsbury carriers, who could be found on Thursdays at specific inns in London, as listed in John Taylor's *Carriers Cosmographie*.[16] Both Cambridge and Shrewsbury were at the end of regular trade routes from the capital. For a carrier travelling by packhorse or waggon, Cambridge was five days' travel on the road north through Hertfordshire, while the journey to Shrewsbury would take two weeks on a route which led through Coventry and Birmingham.[17] The carriers were regularly entrusted with books and letters, and we know of at least one West Country carrier who transported cloth to London and returned to Stroud Water with psalters in the 1550s.[18] Our pedlars may have got their wares directly from the carriers, when London publishers 'sent' ballads and books to the country, specifically for sale by chapmen.

In the testimony of two London stationers brought before the High Commission in 1630, there is evidence of an established distribution system operating between London stationers and country chapmen. Accused of distributing a dangerous book, James Boler and Michael Sparke both claimed they were absent when copies of the book arrived at their London shops, and that their servants sent copies to country chapmen.[19] At Boler's house some forty copies were left with a female servant 'the one halfe whereof this examte servauntes before his coming home sent away to some Chapmen in the Country'. Michael Sparke's servants were said to have done the same with about forty copies, which 'they did in his absence send to divers of his chapmen in Oxford & Salisbury and other partes'. The fact that this was thought to be a reasonable line of defence indicates that 'sending away' books directly to country chapmen was a regular and common practice.

Finally, there were apparently large numbers of the London-based chapmen, including some 277 ballad sellers by 1641. Many were in the direct employ of the publishers, according to Henry Chettle's *Kind-Harts Dreame* (1593):

> no stationer, who after a little bringing them uppe to singing brokerie, takes into his shop some fresh men, and trusts his olde searvantes of a two months standing with a dossen groates worth of ballads. In which, if they proove thrifty, hee makes them prety chapmen, able to spend more pamphlets by the state forbidden then all the bookesellers in London.[20]

Even chapmen setting out from London could cover substantial distances. We have evidence of long-distance travel from cases in the Court of Requests from the 1590s, showing that chapmen from the midlands and south-west, as well as the home counties, were following regular trade routes to and from London. In 1595, a Leicester chapman had been bringing the wares of a London haberdasher to a local cordwainer for twenty years. A Nottingham chapman in the haberdashery trade owed £15 to his London supplier in 1608; while a chapman of Taunton in Somerset had, by 1623, run up a bill in silks worth some £120.[21] Long-distance travel was not only a way of life for these established chapmen with their regular suppliers and routes, but for the lesser classes of pedlars who were likely to fall foul of the vagrancy laws. A surviving 'register of passports' for vagrants apprehended in Salisbury includes 'Edward Kerbye, a balladseller, wandering' who had travelled from his 'home' in Holborne, London, in

1630. Four of the vagrants caught between 1598 and 1640 who were described in the register as 'chapmen' or 'petty chapmen' were also from the capital. Another London man, Walter Plummer of Southwark was stopped at Trowbridge Fair in 1620, 'carrying with him a store of ballads to sing in his travels'.[22]

Any certain knowledge about the suppliers of our chapmen in Cambridgeshire and Shropshire will probably remain elusive to the historian. However, with a knowledge of publishing in this period we can discuss some of the possible titles carried by these two pedlars, who were separated by a particularly interesting half-century in the development and expansion of the trade in cheap religious print.

Ballads

We are told by Baxter that the Shropshire pedlar carried broadside ballads, and it is likely that the Cambridgeshire pedlar of 1578 also carried this staple of cheap-print pedlars throughout the period.[23] Writing in 1595, Nicholas Bownde places the popularity of ballads in opposition to Protestant godliness: it is a disappointment to him that 'in the shops of artificers, and cottages of poore husbandmen . . . you shall sooner see one of these newe Ballades . . . than any of the Psalmes, and may perceive them to be cunninger in singing the one, than the other'.[24] However, an earlier generation of Protestant reformers, writing in the 1560s, 1570s, and 1580s, was happy to appropriate the ballad form and the ballad tunes for its own purposes, making no sharp break with pre-Reformation attitudes to traditional recreations. A study of ballad titles in the Stationers' Registers reveals an outpouring of 'moralizing' ballads, making up a full 35 per cent of ballads registered in the period 1560–88.[25] If he carried a representative cross-section, one in three of the ballads sold by our Cambridgeshire pedlar of 1578 would have dealt with a religious or moral theme.

The godly ballads which could have been hawked in the churchyard at Balsham in 1578 can be divided into four groups, reflecting the aims of Elizabethan Protestant reformers. The first and largest group was religio-political, attempting to galvanize support for the Protestant nation, against the papists at home and abroad. Our Balsham pedlar may have carried ballads like 'The cruel assault of Gods fort' (1560–1), a moralization of an earlier song 'Thassault of Cupide upon the fort where the louers hart lay wounded and how he was taken'.[26] John Awdeley's godly version began with Edward VI building a fort to shield God's truth, continued with a catalogue of the papists who besieged the fort in the Marian period, led by 'generall Gardner' and 'captain Boner'; and of the Protestants killed in defending the fort, the martyrs of 1555-6. The ballad ended, of course, with the Lord sending a new 'godly captaine', Elizabeth. Other ballads in the pack were the stories of individual martyrs, like the famous 'John Carelesse' taken from Coverdale, or the story of 'Anne Askew' adapted from Foxe.[27]

The second group of ballads in the pack were directed at the social reform which was meant to go hand in hand with religious reform. Our Elizabethan pedlar would have carried some of the diatribes which poured from the presses in the 1560s or 1570s, expressing the zeal of the new reformers for the transformation of society and its morals. The least imaginative were straightforward catalogues of social ills, from drunkenness to rent-racking, for which the nation could expect to receive collective punishment in the form of the plague and other disasters.[28] A group of apocalyptic ballads warned that the general Judgement Day was imminent, while another version of the alarum theme looked backward to the biblical examples of cities destroyed for their sin, from Sodom and Gomorrah to Jerusalem.[29]

The form of moral lesson which proved to be most palatable to ballad buyers was the aphoristic broadside, presenting a set of handy maxims for behaviour in everyday life, designed primarily to be implanted in the minds of the young. One organizing principle for the aphoristic ballad was the simple 'abc', each stanza beginning with a letter of the alphabet in order; a genre which grew, of course, out of the method by which most readers would have learnt their letters.[30] One of these broadsides would have been of particular interest to some of the householders of Balsham, the members of the Family of Love studied by Christopher Marsh. This broadside bore the initials of the Familist leader H[endrick] N[iclaes] and was printed in Cologne in 1575.[31] There is no tune, so the abc appears to have been intended for the wall rather than for singing:

A. Attend yee Youngones, and learne Understandinge.
B. Beare-favor to the Love, that she in you may have plantinge.
C. Com to the meekmynded Beeinge of Bounteousnesse.

There is a woodcut of schoolchildren in a classroom, and an introduction addressed to the Family's children warns them not to tackle great books 'er-ever yee have well exercised you in the A.B.C., and can perfectly spell all Woordes'. The broadside first appeared just three years before our pedlar was reported to be selling his wares in the Balsham churchyard.

Although most of the moralizing ballads emphasized collective repentance and outward behaviour, our pedlar could also have sold a third group of ballads presenting the more personal side of the Protestant message: the saving power of faith. The tone is positive, promising that the offer of grace is infinite and universal, if only the sinner will take the first step.[32] There is no promulgation of predestination in these ballads. One technique often used for this theme was the moral parody of the secular song, most often a love song, of which Christ becomes the object:

> Thou art my saviour sweete,
> foode and delight to me . . .
> To my tast, honnie sweete,
> to my eare, melodie . . . [33]

This song is based on 'Dainty come thou to me', rendered as 'Jesu come thou to me'. The central Protestant doctrine of justification by faith alone is made an encouraging proposition in these ballads.

Finally, the last group of ballads in our pedlar's pack tried to capture the people's imagination with scripture stories, in order to help effect the transition to a book-based religion. Early Elizabethan reformers like William Samuel had high hopes of replacing the old saints' lives and miracles with characters and events from the Bible:

> My mynd is that I wold have my contrey people able in a smale some to syng the hole contents of the byble, & where as in tymes past the musicians or mynstrells, were wont to syng fained myracles, saints lives, & Robin hode, in stede thereof to sing, undoutyd truthes, canonycall scryptures, and Gods doynges. [34]

The pedlar of the 1570s could have carried a whole stock of good stories from the Old Testament, some of which are obvious choices for their dramatic quality: Jonah and the whale, Abraham offering Isaac, Daniel in the lion's den, David and Goliath. Lesser-known episodes could be picked because of their relevance to contemporary concerns. The history of 'Manasses kynge of Juda', who brought punishment upon Jerusalem with his graven images and false altars, was an obvious lesson against popish idolatry. [35]

As well as Old Testament stories, the Elizabethan pedlar could have carried quite a variety of titles from the Gospels, especially songs making use of the parables. Ballads were registered on the fig tree and the grain of mustard seed, the ten servants and ten talents, the rich man and the unjust steward, and lessons from the sermon on the mount. [36] By setting them to popular tunes the reformers tried to give unlearned people direct access to the concepts of Christian faith and to provoke further interest in vernacular Bible reading: 'as the man that hearyth a parte of a story in the scryptures, & doth not knowe the hole: thys may move the hole to be red'. [37]

The range of ballads which could have been sold in the churchyard at Balsham in 1578 reflects the serious didactic purposes of the early Protestant reformers. By the time our Shropshire pedlar visited Richard Baxter's house in the 1630s, the situation had radically changed, and the ballad seller was no longer widely considered to be a potential tool of the Reformation. The writing of moralizing ballads had fallen out of fashion, as can be seen in the Stationers' Register entries. For the period 1560–88,

35 per cent of ballad titles were religious and moralizing; in 1588–1625 the figure drops to 19 per cent; and in 1625–40, to 9 per cent.[38] The decline may partly be attributed to a growing gap between what the reformers perceived to be 'godly' and 'ungodly' spheres of activity. This gap can be seen in Baxter's description of his village of Eaton Constantine, where the neighbours spent each Sunday dancing under a maypole near Baxter's house:

> So that we could not read the Scripture in our family without the great disturbance of the tabor and pipe and noise in the street. Many times I was inclined to be among them . . . But when I heard them call my father Puritan it did much to cure me and alienate me from them.[39]

Ballads, along with the dance tunes to which they were set, were no longer seen by reformers as potential routes to godliness: they had become part of those popular recreations which caused a keen sense of separation of 'the saints' from 'the rest'. The decline of the moralizing ballad can be attributed partly to the ballad's negative associations with bawdy lyrics, lascivious dancing and unsavoury pedlars, and partly to the growing success of the metrical psalms, which were taking over as the definitive godly songs by the seventeenth century.[40]

By the time of our Shropshire pedlar, then, only one in ten of the ballads registered each year were on religious themes. However, the proportion of godly ballads he carried in his pack was undoubtedly higher than this figure, which reflects only the new ballads being written, but not the republishing of old favourites. By 1624, six of the leading ballad publishers had collected together the copyrights to a stock of ballads, formed themselves into a syndicate called the 'ballad partners', and organized themselves for more efficient storage and distribution of the printed sheets. In 1624 they registered a large batch of 128 ballads, most of them old titles, of which a striking one third were still religious in subject matter.[41] These stock ballads tell us little about the situation at the cutting edge of Protestant reform, but perhaps much more about the impact of Protestantism on a wide public and about their religious tastes.

Many of the old titles registered by the 'ballad partners' in 1624 were reprinted again and again in turn by their trade descendants. These titles can be traced in the later bulk entries made for copyright purposes in 1656, 1675, and 1712, and still later in a catalogue of 1754.[42] From these sources, I have compiled a list of forty-six godly ballads of long duration on the market, of which forty-one can be shown to have lasted more than a quarter century, twenty-eight were sold over a half-century, and eleven of these survived a full century or more.[43] Of these 'stock' ballads, the majority (60%) can be shown to be of sixteenth-century origin. In other words, our Shropshire pedlar of the 1630s would have carried a number of the same titles sold by his colleague half a century earlier: ballads which had poured from the pens of the Elizabethan reformers, primarily before 1586.[44] The chapman who reached Richard Baxter's door would have carried a smaller selection of those ballads than our Elizabethan pedlar, selling only those which had proved their commercial success by the early decades of the seventeenth century.

The ballads in that Shropshire pack of the 1630s can give us some measure of how far Protestant goals were achieved in each of the four areas discussed above: politicized anti-Catholicism, social reform, personal salvation, and scripture stories. From the 'stock' of long-enduring titles we will examine in detail seven ballads which may be considered archetypical, each demonstrating a particular aspect of seventeenth-century piety. The pedlar's pack reflected a religious culture which was far from monolithic, showing a fragmentary reception of Protestant doctrine.

The first group of ballads, expressing sixteenth-century anti-Catholicism, did not in general survive into the seventeenth century. There is one notable type of exception: a group of four ballads on Protestant martyrs, of which three were female.[45] The human image of the martyr seems to have been worth a thousand arguments in the task of embedding anti-Catholic feeling in popular consciousness. These songs could have been bought and sung by the maypole dancers of Eaton Constantine for their gripping and tragic stories, regardless of religious content. As they entered into the ballad repertoire, however, they achieved the writers' aim of replacing Catholic saints with Protestant ones, amongst those readers and singers unlikely to have direct access to Foxe's great volumes.

The most successful ballad in this category, very likely to have found a place in the Shropshire pedlar's pack, was the story of the Duchess of Suffolk's exile during Mary's reign. It was adapted from Foxe by Thomas Deloney, set to the tune 'Queen Dido', and was still for sale in 1754.[46] In addition to the theme of a woman suffering for religion, there was the attraction of royalty travelling incognito, a popular ballad motif.[47] The duchess and her husband Bertie flee with their baby to Flanders, accompanied by just one nurse (who later runs away), and dressed as 'people poor'. Being refused shelter, and unable to speak the local language, they are forced to take refuge from the rain in a church porch. The interest of the story is in the temporary inversion of hierarchy:

> loe! here a princess of great blood
> doth pray a peasant for reliefe,
> With teares bedewed, as she stood,
> Yet few or none regards her griefe!

The heroine is thus incorporated into traditional ballad themes and conventions.[48] At the same time as Protestant historiography is popularized, much of the specific Protestant content and motivation is lost.

Not surprisingly, many of the second group of ballads, the moral dia-tribes of the Elizabethan reformers, did not survive to be sold by our pedlar of the seventeenth century. Accounts of the destruction of biblical cities did endure quite well, probably because they provided gripping stories, from which the warning to repent emerged secondarily as the moral. The *pièce de résistance* of this genre was 'Christ's teares over Jerusalem', an anonymous ballad based on Thomas Nashe's book of that name, and apparently first printed soon after the book's appearance in 1593.[49] The ballad succinctly combines a metrical paraphrase of Christ's prophecy of the destruction of Jerusalem, a brief but emotive description of the crucifixion and of Jerusalem's fall, and an account of plagues and punishments sent to contemporary England. Sensational details are highlighted:

> Yea, Dogs and Cats they eat, mice, rats and every thing,
> For want of food, 'their Infants young unto the Pot they bring'.

The successful narrative structure, probably the work of a London dra-matist, meant the survival of a ballad like 'Christ's teares' for over eighty years.[50]

Although there may have been room for the emotive piety of 'Christ's teares' in the pedlar's pack of the 1630s, the platitudes of the aphoristic ballads proved to be the most popular form of broadside morality. The archetypical ballad in this vein was 'Solomon's sentences', drawn from Ecclesiasticus but attributed to the wise king Solomon. It was first regis-tered in 1586, and remained in the ballad stock until at least 1675.[51] The gems of advice chosen by the ballad versifier as most applicable to his Elizabethan audience deal with financial matters, the raising of children, the running of a household. The advice is aimed at young males; the son in the ballad is warned in turn never to smile on his daughters, because they are prone to wantonness. Budding young householders are advised not to go to law with the magistrate and to pay their labourers promptly, imply-ing that at least in 1586 an audience of reasonably wealthy yeomen or tradesmen was expected. There is am emphasis on good works which must have appealed to the Pelagian tendency which, according to Richard Bax-ter, lingered on amongst the parishioners of rural England.[52]

From the practical morality of 'Solomon's sentences' we move to the more personal ballads appealing to the buyer's concern about his or her salvation. Making Christ the object of love songs like 'Dainty come thou to me' was a practice no longer in favour in the 1630s. However, the ballads of faith which did endure took the form of last dying speeches addressed to God: ballads which seem to have functioned as guides to the appropriate mental framework before death. The archetypical ballad of personal faith (surviving at least from 1624 to 1688) was attributed to a parish clerk: 'The earnest petition of the faithful Christian, being clerk of Bodnam, made upon his deathbed, at the instant of his transmutation.'[53]

The melody of 'The clarke of Bodnam' does not survive, but it was described as a 'sweet solemn tune' and may have imitated the toll of the passing-bell, as hinted in the text:

> Now my painful eyes lye rowling, and my passing-bell is towling,
> Towling sweetly, I lye dying, and my life is from me flying.

Ballads like 'The clarke of Bodnam' took a standard form: confession of complete unworthiness and repentance of sins, followed by prayers for grace, expressions of faith, and hope for reception in heaven. God, whether Father or Son, is a close and kindly figure: 'my loving Father sweet', 'blessed Son', 'sweet Jesus'.[54] They are thoroughly Protestant ballads, but there is no sense of a predestined elect. For the clerk, grace is a gift offered by Christ to all and available to the last minute:

> Yet though my sins like scarlet show, their whiteness may exceed the
> snow,
> If thou thy mercy do extend, that I my sinful life may mend.
> Which mercy, thy blest word doth say, at any time obtain I may.

Here there is little of the insistence on outward and life-long godliness found in many early seventeenth-century catechisms:

> Q. What if good workes be wanting?
> A. Then is iustifying Faith wanting whatsoever we professe.[55]

Whether or not the clerk of Bodnam would pass the most rigorous catechizing sessions of contemporary reformers, in his general effect he is undoubtedly the incarnation of a seventeenth-century godliness, the exemplary Protestant on his deathbed. But his was not the only approach to death available from the pedlar's pack of the 1630s. There was still a more traditional vision of damnation and salvation, descended from the art, drama, and song of pre-Reformation Catholicism, with little sign of any break. In more than half the stock ballads dealing with death, a retributive God is less interested in repentance and faith than in the preparation for salvation with good works, and the promise of Jerusalem is balanced (if not overshadowed) by the very real threat of hell-fire. If the ballad buyer found the Bodnam parish clerk too bland for his taste, he could choose a broadside of 'St Bernard's vision' (c. 1640), with a woodcut of demons prodding a naked body with pitchforks.[56] Here was a tiny fragment of the great medieval painting of 'The Doom' which had stood over the chancel arch in the parish church, now transferred to the cottage wall.

The ballad of 'St Bernard's vision' is a dramatization of the after-life, using a narrator who experiences a death-like state, but is then revived to tell the tale. This device came from a long tradition of clerical vision literature, made familiar to a wide audience through its influence on the paintings of 'The Doom'.[57] The first extant copy dates from c. 1640, and the ballad was one of only half a dozen seventeenth-century religious titles still available in Dicey's catalogue of 1754.[58] The ballad is subtitled 'A briefe discourse (dialogue-wise) betweene the soule and the body of a damned man newly deceased, laying open the faults of each other; with a speech of the divel's in hell'. The lugubrious tune 'Fortune my foe' is well suited to the wailing and groaning of the body and soul in their pain. The soul berates the body for its sins and pleasures which have brought them both to hell, 'where we in frying flames for aye must dwell'. 'St Bernard's vision' is a powerful argument for the continuity of a medieval religious outlook well into the early modern period.

This group of ballads passes on, almost unchanged, a centuries-old vision of the Last Judgement based on the individual's sins or merits in this life.[59] It is possible that the ballad buyers themselves did not always perceive a contradiction between this traditional scheme of salvation and current Protestant doctrine. It is quite possible that if a husbandman was of a mind to purchase a ballad about death, 'The clerk of Bodnam' might do just as well as 'St Bernard's vision', and our Shropshire pedlar probably sold both. The preoccupation with death, and the belief in a tangible heaven and hell, was an area of shared culture spanning the doctrinal rift between conformists and nonconformists, mainstream Protestants, and groups like the Familists or Quakers, even between Catholics and Protestants. The fear of death lay at the core of popular religion long before and long after the Reformation, and on this theme the ballads testify to just how little had changed.

The popularization of Scripture was one of the great aims of reformers at the time of our Balsham pedlar, as we saw, but the Old Testament ballads still on sale in the 1630s did not show the same breadth of themes and lessons. The most popular stories were those involving a beautiful young woman, shown to be either a paragon of virtue, or inconstant and deceitful, or unwittingly the cause of men's destruction. Ballads of 'Constant Susanna', Samson and Delilah, or David and Bathsheba came closest among the godly ballads to the narratives Child collected, and which we have come to think of as defining balladry.[60] The same ballad clichés were used: the 'maidens' are always 'fresh and gay', 'faire and bright'.[61] The opening of 'The story of David and Berseba' is similar in essence to that of 'Fair Margaret and Sweet William' and other 'traditional' ballads:[62]

> . . . It chaunced so, upon a day,
> the king went forth to take the ayre
> All in the pleasant moneth of May,
> from whence he spide a Lady faire . . .
> She stood within a pleasant Bower,
> all naked, for to wash her there;

> Her body, like a Lilly Flowere,
> was covered with her golden haire.[63]

The incorporation of this story into the body of 'folksong' was apparently successful, since the ballad, probably first registered in 1569–70, was still for sale in the Dicey catalogue of 1754.

Like the Old Testament ballads, songs based on the Gospels had narrowed in range between the 1570s and the 1630s. Of the many parable-ballads, only one remained in the pedlar's pack: the story of the prodigal son.[64] The ballad belongs with the stories of ungrateful children and mis-spent youth which were a continuing strand in popular balladry, like the 'Good fellows resolution' which became the well-known 'Wild rover'.[65] With this exception, the seventeenth-century ballad stock contains nothing of Christ's teachings, but moves back to basic events of his life and death which had been the central themes of pre-Reformation piety: the virgin birth, the passion, and resurrection.

The single most successful ballad from the Gospels was 'A new ditty, shewing the wonderfull miracles of our lord' (known by its first line 'When Jesus Christ was twelve'), which survived on the 'partners' stock-list of 1675, a century after its first registration.[66] In a jogging rhythm it describes how Christ turned the water into wine, fed the multitude with the loaves, raised Lazarus from the dead, healed the lepers, the lame, and the blind. This is a story to compete with any of the contemporary miracles described in the sensational news ballads:

> But yet for all these wonders great, the Jews were in a raging heat,
> Whom no persuasions could intreat, but cruelly did kill him.
> And when he left his life so good, the Moon was turned into blood,
> The earth and Temple shaking stood, the graves full wide did open.

'When Jesus Christ was twelve' is a succinct paraphrase of the plot-line of Christ's life, and may have performed a mnemonic function for its singers, like a musical catechism. However, it is devoid of any of the parables and teachings which the early Elizabethan gospellers had hoped to spread.

The general picture of popular piety gleaned from the godly ballads in our pedlar's pack of the 1630s is a conservative one. Religion is about the same fear of death and personal judgement which preoccupied medieval Catholics; it is about practical lists of good and bad behaviour; and about stories of miracles, a virgin birth, heroism, and even love and trickery. However, certain Protestant lessons, like the centrality of repen-tance, and the shift from Catholic saints to Protestant martyrs and Old Testament heroines, had apparently been absorbed by some of their buyers. The incorporation of Protestant aims into balladry created new archetypes: the brave Duchess of Suffolk; the wise king Solomon; the faithful clerk of Bodnam. Judging by their longevity, these new saints succeeded in populating the imagination of at least some of the readers and singers in seventeenth-century England.

Pictures

The sales appeal of the ballads was not only a matter of their content, but was also affected by their visual appearance. The broadsides carried by the pedlar in Cambridgeshire in the 1570s would have looked quite different from those sold by the Shropshire pedlar half a century later. The most striking change was the institution of woodcut pictures as a standard feature. Only one fifth of surviving sixteenth-century religious ballads are illustrated, while for the period 1600–40 more than five-sixths are illustrated.[67] There was also more of an attempt than in the sixteenth century to achieve some correlation between text and image.[68]

The increased importance of the woodcut pictures appears to have been closely linked to the development and specialization of the ballad trade in the early seventeenth century. The leading ballad publishers also began to put out large decorative woodcuts as a natural extension of their activities obtaining illustrations for their ballads. These included large poster-portraits of royalty and satirical prints, like 'Fill gut, & pinch belly' (1620), a picture of two monsters, 'one being fat with eating good men, the other leane for want of good women'.[69] One print which could have been carried by both our Cambridgeshire and Shropshire pedlars is a woodcut in the tradition of the 'Four Alls', which survives in a copy of *c.* 1580, and was still available in 1656.[70] This large woodcut (20 in × 14 in) is sloppily coloured in bright hues of blue, purple, orange, and brown, and depicts a bishop, king, harlot, lawyer, and 'country clowne', each with verses proclaiming their importance and power over the others. Of course, Death arrives with his spear to win the contest. The theme of death was common in pictures, as it was in the ballads, but it is a secularized vision, shorn of the spiritual dimension which had been present in medieval wall paintings and in the woodcuts of the *Ars Moriendi*: the angels and demons at the bedside, the weighing of souls, the intercession of the virgin, the divine judge.[71]

Contemporary 'iconophobia' seems to have limited the direct depiction of religious themes on these large woodcut pictures.[72] A Huguenot press in the Blackfriars produced Old Testament scenes and religious allegories, but appears to have avoided potentially idolatrous scenes like the crucifixion or nativity.[73] In the 1578 inventory of the Cambridge bookseller John Denys, a number of pictorial items are listed at the end: 'v other small pictures' (6*d*), 'a Rolle of the kynges' (6*d*), 'the storye of David' (6*d*), 'helias' (6*d*), 'the storye of Joseph' (7*d*).[74] A 'story' is a term normally used to describe a picture, and the 'stories' of David and of Joseph were almost certainly series of biblical pictures in the Blackfriars tradition.[75] However, the small number of pictures in stock, and the relatively high price of 6*d*, does not suggest that Denys was sending out great bundles of these pictures with chapmen like our Balsham pedlar.[76]

The most common form of printed decoration in humble households, according to contemporary accounts, was in fact the broadside ballad. Nicholas Bownde claims to have seen illiterate cottagers pasting up ballads in order to 'learne' them later: 'and though they cannot reade themselves, nor any of theirs, yet will have many Ballades set up in their houses, that so might learne them, as they shall have occasion'. In 1624 Abraham Holland mocked the habit in northern villages of sticking up ballads of Chevy Chase or the latest execution over the chimney. Ballads were also used to decorate public places: the standard decor of a country alehouse was 'a painted cloath, with a row of Balletts pasted on it'.[77]

The 'ballad partners' may have avoided religious themes in their large poster-size prints, but the woodcuts they used on their ballads tell quite a different story, testifying to a continued demand for pictures of Christ and other images which one might expect to be considered idolatrous.[78] It may be that the physical size of the pictures was a crucial factor: these small woodcuts of several inches square do not immediately suggest the act of adoration. Not all of the 'hotter sort of Protestants' were happy, however. In William Cartwright's *The Ordinary* (*c.* 1635), the puritan curate Sir Kit insults his companion, Rimewell the poet:

> Thou art a Lopaz; when
> One of thy legs rots off (which will be shortly)
> Thou'lt beare about a Quire of wicked Paper,
> Defil'd with sanctified Rithmes,
> And Idols in the frontispiece: that I
> May speak to thy capacity, thou'lt be
> A Balladmonger.[79]

As the reference to 'Idols in the frontispiece' suggests, even the crude little woodcuts, which ran like a frieze along the top of the ballad sheets, were the subject of criticism and controversy. A Quaker tract of 1655 later singled out ballad makers for special attack on account of the woodcuts:

> the Lord God of glory is arising, who saith, Thou shalt not make any Image of Male or Female, which you do amongst you, and are found upon your ballets, and so out of Gods councell, are amongst the heathen making Images.[80]

The continued use of traditional iconography on the ballads may at first have been partly a result of the economic advantages of using old sixteenth-century woodblocks. The discarded blocks acquired by the publishers were sometimes survivals from the pre-Reformation printing houses, like the cut of Christ and his disciples used by Richard Harper in the

1640s, once used by Wynkyn de Worde in 1506.[81] When the old blocks wore out and the publishers had scenes newly cut, they continued to cater to the demand for story-telling images, depicting simple and familiar scenes from the Gospels. 'The sinner's redemption' (1634?) carries a wood-cut of Christ between two labourers with hoes; 'The glorious resurrection' (1640?) shows him rising from the grave with the centurions leaping back in alarm.[82] Other broadsides depict the holy family on their flight into Egypt, and the virgin and child.[83] The most frequently used godly woodcut descended from the standard pre-Reformation image of Christ in Glory. On 'The sinner's supplication' (*c.* 1630) Christ blesses the ballad buyer from the starry vault, with palms raised in benediction and rays emanating from the clouds.[84] When this woodcut wore out the ballad partners had a copy cut, which survives on over a dozen ballads from the 1650s to 1680s: it had become a trademark recognizable to the godly-ballad buyer.[85]

The cottager who pasted a ballad like 'The sinner's supplication' on his wall apparently liked to have a figure of Christ to look at, even if only an awkward little woodcut Christ like this. And if some types of religious picture might cause suspicion of popery in a domestic setting, it was apparently a widespread practice to paste up ballads adorned with little woodcuts of the resurrection and the holy family. Recent arguments about the growth of 'iconophobia' have suggested that our pedlar of the 1630s was travelling in a world with a very limited range of religious images, compared with his predecessor of the 1570s.[86] However, the evidence of woodcut pictures, together with other media like wall painting and painted cloths, suggests that his visual universe had not changed so dra-matically.[87] The pedlar of Shropshire could still have carried quite a number of images, which helped the villagers who bought them to convert the words of the Protestant religion into visualized experience.

Little books

So much for single-sheet wares, but what of more substantial reading matter, the 'little books' sold in the Balsham churchyard? And what were the 'some good books' offered by the pedlar of Eaton Constantine, besides the one named title, Richard Sibbes' *Bruised Reed*? The book bought by Richard Baxter's father was probably the first edition of *The Bruised Reede, and Smoaking Flax*, a collection of sermons by the leading puritan divine, which was not itself very 'little' as books go.[88] Although printed in the very compact duodecimo format, it was a thick book of almost 400 pages, which would have cost 8*d* or 9*d* at the halfpenny per sheet prescribed by the Stationers' Company in 1598.[89] This would have been affordable to Baxter's yeoman father, but certainly not to all custo-mers along the pedlar's route.

Book prices must be set against a context of contemporary incomes. Keith Wrightson estimates a basic cost of subsistence of around £11–14 for a family in a normal year, while the wages of a labouring man might total only £9–10. Clearly there was little 'surplus' for luxuries like books and pamphlets. An early seventeenth-century husbandman with an arable holding of thirty acres might have £3–4 'surplus' after food, or an average of 14d to 18d a week.[90] At this level, our chapman would not be able to sell very many books at 9d, although he might do quite a good business in twopenny chapbooks. For this reason I will be concentrating on the very cheapest and 'littlest' books available in this period, examining the type of works which I believe would have been the main stock-in-trade of both our pedlars. However, as the presence of the *Bruised Reed* and one or two rare pedlar's inventories suggest, the pedlars also seem to have carried at least a few books we might describe as 'luxury' wares, for the wealthier households and better-educated readers along the route. The poor young packman, George Pool of Cumberland, was trudging up the hills with a few books worth 9d each, along with his haberdashery, when he died in 1695.[91]

Leaving George Pool's customers, along with Richard Baxter, to their 'good' but costly books, we will look for a cheaper form of chapbook which could have been sold to the same wide audience as the ballads. In the later seventeenth century, it is much easier to identify titles which were published specifically for sale by chapmen. Publishers advertised their trade-lists at the end of their own volumes: 'J. Back, at the sign of the Black Boy on London Bridge, furnisheth country chapmen or others, with all sorts of small books, ballads, and all other stationary-wares at reasonable rates.'[92] Collectors like Pepys and Wood bought these 'small merry books' and 'small godly books' directly from chapmen; and from these collections together with surviving publishers' inventories, Margaret Spufford has been able to reconstruct the chapbook trade of the late seventeenth century.[93]

Unfortunately booksellers before the 1650s did not print trade-lists in their books, nor have we found a chapman's or bookseller's inventory to shed light on distribution practices.[94] However, we do know that the chapbook trade after the Restoration was closely connected with the ballad trade, and that ballads were distributed in the countryside from the second half of the sixteenth century.[95] The ballad publishers apparently had direct access to a network of chapmen; at what point did they begin to distribute chapbooks along this network as well?

In order to trace the development of a specialized chapbook trade, I have examined the entire non-ballad output of eight leading ballad publishers, three from the late sixteenth century and five from the early seventeenth century.[96] I looked especially for the format which Pepys later bound together as 'penny merriments' and 'penny godlinesses': this standard 'penny' size format was twenty-four pages or less, in octavo or duodecimo. Pepys used the term 'penny' as a description of an unmistakable size and format, rather than a precise statement about price: in fact, from at least 1637, the standard price seems to have been twopence.[97] In addition to its cheapness (requiring only 1 to 1.5 sheets of paper), the 'penny' format was ideally designed for chapmen, who could have carried large numbers of these small books in their packs. This was to remain the standard format through the eighteenth and nineteenth centuries.[98] I have also looked for precursors of an assortment of longer works which Pepys called 'Vulgaria': these included twenty-four-page quartos called 'double-books' (costing 3*d* or 4*d*) and longer quartos called 'histories' (costing 6*d* or more).[99]

The full results of this investigation are published elsewhere.[100] The search yielded some three dozen extant 'penny books' of the early seventeenth century: not an enormous corpus, but (given the odds against their survival) enough to indicate the beginnings of a new genre. The 1620s was the decade in which the publishers organized themselves into a specialized syndicate for distribution of broadside ballads. The evidence also points to this as the period when ballad publishers began consciously to acquire the copyrights to these small books, which they could sell to the same wide market as their ballads.

What, then, of our Balsham pedlar in 1578, plying his wares before the development of this specialist trade? Since there was not yet a trade-list advertised specially for his purposes, he may have sold a whole range of books which could be described as 'little': that is, short, probably unbound, and light to carry. Many of these may have been 'merry' books such as the titles found in the library of Captain Cox the mason of Coventry, recorded in a letter of 1575.[101] Our Balsham pedlar might well have stocked *Adam Bell*, *The King and the Tanner*, and *The Fryar and the Boy*, all printed on just 1.5 to 2.5 sheets in quarto, and costing 1*d* or at most 2*d* at the normal rates per sheet.[102]

It is unlikely, however, that our Balsham pedlar sold only little books for entertainment and none for edification. In the late seventeenth century, although the proportion of new religious ballad titles had dropped, the new line of religious tracts made up no less than 32 per cent of the trade-lists of the 'small book' publishers.[103] One third of the ballads being published at the time of our Cambridgeshire pedlar were godly, and the total output of religious print remained very high throughout the period: 42 per cent of the STC works published in 1640 can be classified as religious.[104] If our pedlar's stock was at all representative, at least one in three of his 'little books' would have been godly ones.

Our chapman could have stocked up with these books at the shop of John Denys in Cambridge, who died in 1578, leaving over 759 volumes which are itemized in his inventory.[105] Most of these were specialized works for the University, many in Latin, but the presence of titles like

The Maner of Measurynge of All Maner of Lande suggests an audience
beyond the scholars in their college rooms.[106] There were a number of
books in English which were suitable for an ordinary lay audience and
valued at prices which would have been affordable to all but the poorest of
Cambridgeshire households. Twelve 'almanackes and prognostications' in
octavo were listed at only 1*d* each, while four copies of an account of the
voyage of 'captayne Furbisher' were also valued at 1*d* per copy.[107]

Apart from these, the majority of works at the bottom of John Denys's
price range were religious in content. Nine unbound copies of the 'psalmes
in meeter' were valued at 3*s*.6*d*, or just under 5*d* each: a reasonable price
for a staple of religious worship for godly Balsham householders at all
points on the Protestant spectrum. These psalm books were in the tiny 32°
format designed for carrying in the pocket, approximately 3 in × 2 in in
size, and could certainly have been described as 'little' books.[108] Another
religious handbook was the 'Right rule of godlie praiers', also in the
miniature 32°, valued at 1*s* for five copies, or just 2½*d* each. This was
probably *A Right Godly Rule; How All Faithfull Christians Ought to
Occupie and Exercise Themselves in their Dayly Prayers*, based largely
on prayers in the official primer of 1555, which were in turn the inheritance
of generations of Latin primers.[109] *A Right Godly Rule* offered short
prayers for each morning of the week, followed by more elaborate formulae
for specific occasions: 'in adversity', 'at the houre of death', 'before hee
goeth about any wordly busines'.

An alternative to this semi-official prayer book which may have been
carried by our Balsham pedlar was Edward Dering's *Godlye Private Praiers
For Householders in their Families*: the Cambridge bookshop contained
one copy valued at 2*d*, and another (presumably old or damaged) at only
1*d*. Dering provides for the same daily spiritual needs as other collections,
but his originality comes across in 'passages of honest puzzlement and even
wonder', and his Puritan convictions appear in prayers to 'roote out all
remnaunts . . . of idolatry'.[110]

Some of the pedlar's wares may have been educational tools for the
children of Balsham. A sixteenth-century Italian engraving shows a pedlar
with hornbooks hanging from his pack, and hornbooks would be reliable
wares for an English pedlar too, since every village would have children of
the age to learn their 'Christ cross row'.[111] For godly households with
older children and adults he may have stocked catechisms. Ian Green has
shown a barrage of alternative catechisms after 1570, reaching their first
peak in the 1580s, as many of the parish clergy began to expect more
knowledge from their catechumens than was found in the official Edwardian catechism. He identifies over 250 independent catechetical works:
with repeat editions, Green calculates that 'over three-quarters of a million
copies of these works were in circulation by the early seventeenth century,
in addition to perhaps half a million copies of the official forms'.[112] The

Cambridge bookshop in 1578 had seven copies of 'master moores cate-chismus', once again by Edward Dering, valued at 8*d* for the lot, or just over 1*d* each.[113] This catechism began with an ABC, and proceeded, in only three sheets octavo, with simple questions and answers on the Ten Commandments, the Creed, the two Sacraments, the role of good works and of prayer, the Lord's Prayer and finally a 'prayer contayning the summe and effect of this catechisme'.

As well as these educational tools, our pedlar may have sold a selection of short sermons and pamphlets which, if they came from John Denys's shop, tended to be 'Puritan' in bent. Three copies of 'master doctor fulkes sermone', probably *A Comfortable Sermon of Faith*, were valued at 4*d* all together.[114] For 2*d* you could have *A Conference Containing a Conflict had with Satan, wherein are Plainely Set Downe the True Markes and Tokens, whereby the Afflicted Conscience may Prove It Selfe, whether it be the Childe of God, or the Childe of Satan* (1577) by the Puritan divine Andrew Kingsmill. Readers worried about their sins are assured that their torment 'is the very token that you are Gods childe', for the reprobate take pleasure in their sinning, while only the blessed grieve for the wrongs they have done.[115] The neuroses of the godly about their salvation appear to have been good for the sale of cheap godly books in Cambridgeshire. Another work listed at 2*d* was Pierre de la Place, *A Treatise of the Excellencie of a Christian Man*, which included a discussion of how a man may know himself to be a Christian 'by the effects which the same spirit of God bringeth forth in him'.[116] For 2*d* you could also have Thomas Lever's *A Treatise of the Right Way from Danger of Synne* (1575), while for 3*d* or 4*d* the Cambridge shop stocked seven copies of Stephen Bateman's *The Golden Booke of the Leaden Goddes* (1577), which described heathen deities leading up to the greatest of 'leaden goddes', the Roman Catholic pope.

Clearly there were quite a number of suitable wares for our Balsham pedlar's pack in the bookshops of Cambridge, the city which served the area. We should not, however, rule out the possibility that he acquired wares directly from London. These could have included ballads, which notably do not appear in the surviving inventories of any Cambridge booksellers in this period, as well as other small pamphlets produced by the ballad publishers. Likely 'chapbooks' from these presses included little pamphlets like *An Epistle of the Ladye Jane to a Learned Man of Late Falne from the Truth of Gods Word* (ent. 1569–70), published by William Pickering.[117] Just as Anne Askew and the Duchess of Suffolk were popular balld heroines, stories of women suffering for their religion made good chapbook copy. Lady Jane's popularity was confirmed by the reprinting of this pamphlet in 1615, 1629, and 1636 by John Wright.[118] The dramatic narrative of a woman's martyrdom was used as a forum for a defence of Protestant doctrine and an anti-papist diatribe. The four discourses 'written with her own hands' included a catechism emphasizing that there were two Sacraments rather than seven, that the Eucharist was not the real body of Christ, and so on. The pamphlets of the sixteenth-century ballad publishers are, like their ballads, artifacts of early Elizabethan Protestantism, with its urgent need to convey reformed doctrine, the sense of the papist enemy not yet vanquished, and the mood of struggle, inspiration, and martyrdom.[119]

Leaving Balsham and our pedlar of the 1570s, it is likely that the Shropshire pedlar of the next century carried many of the same bread-and-butter staples of religious print – the primers, catechisms, and psalm books – acquired from a Shrewsbury bookshop. A book of 1635 was printed 'for William Millard, bookseller in Shrewbury', but unfortunately we know nothing more about Millard or his shop.[120] However, the 1585 inventory of an earlier Shrewsbury bookshop shows the quantity and variety of religious works which were readily available in that county long before the pedlar reached the Baxter's door.[121] Apart from a number of grammar-school texts, Roger Ward's stock was dominated by popular devotional manuals, including '60 prayer books', another '28 bookes of praier gilte', '13 primers', '41 psalters with psalmes', '41 Communion bookes with smale psalmes', and '42 singinge psalmes alone'. Catechisms were also stocked in large batches: 43 copies of 'pagettes catachismes', 27 of Edward Dering's catechism known as 'mores catachismes', 38 'nowells catachisms', 9 'Bezas catac[hisms]', another unspecified '83 catach[i]smes duble', and 25 of *The ABC with the Catechism*. Some of the Shropshire pedlar's 'good books' may have been cheap black-letter sermons: Roger Ward's stock included 90 sermons by unnamed authors valued at $2\frac{1}{2}d$ each, and another 93 at $3d$. (These entries are among the very few which include prices.) The large numbers of copies suggest that by the late sixteenth century this Shrewsbury bookshop was serving a wider catchment area than John Denys's Cambridge shop, and catering primarily to a lay rather than learned clientele.

Roger Ward's shop was the provincial outpost of his business in London, where he was notorious among stationers for his repeated book piracy. In 1582 he was hauled before the Court of Star Chamber for printing 10,000 copies of *The ABC with the Little Catechism*, which was the privilege of John Day. Ward admitted sending his servant John Legge to Shrewsbury with 1500 of these copies, which were then assembled in that town.[122] Clearly there was a large market for these basic educational tools in Shropshire. Ward was also asked how many he had 'sent out to be sold in the country'. Although he denied selling any copies to chapmen, his testimony contained a number of blatant falsehoods, and presumably there was good reason for the question to have been asked. Roger Ward was in trouble again in 1583 for printing 'the little primer and the usual psalter', and in 1582–3 he put out a pirated edition of 'Dentes Sermons', of which work forty-two copies are listed in his Shrewsbury inventory. This profitable tract was Dent's *Sermon of Repentaunce* (valued at 2*d* in the inventory of another bookseller in York) which had run to an impressive thirty-seven editions by 1638.[123]

Long-term best-sellers like Dent's suggest a degree of continuity in cheap religious print, but other 'little books' illustrate changes in both content and format by the seventeenth century. Roger Ward's Shrewsbury shop in 1585 contained '20 bookes of Robin consciens & suche', referring to a popular verse pamphlet of sixteen pages quarto, first registered to the ballad publisher John Awdeley.[124] The version of *Robin Conscience* which would have been carried by a sixteenth-century pedlar captures the flavour of Elizabethan Protestantism, presenting reformed ideas in a palatable narrative form. The godly Robin chastises his father Covetousnesse for extortion, his mother Newgise for vain apparel, and his sister Proud Beauty for her wantonness. But more than a morality tale, it is a Protestant manifesto, a conflict between old religion and new religion. The family swears 'By the Masse' while Robin urges them to 'have a respect unto Christ's Testament'. The vanity of his sister is associated with the vanity of Rome: her gold chains and embroidered hair are 'the decking and balming of proud living Idols'.[125] The father warns his son:

> By the masse, yf thou to the Scripture incline,
> Be sure that I wyll never do the pleasor
> Nor yet never helpe the, with none of my treasor.[126]

This paternal diatribe is described in the margin as 'the rebuke and admonicion of the generacyon of Satan'. As a generational conflict, with Protestant doctrine in the mouth of the son rebuking his parents, *Robin Conscience* supports the association of the mid-sixteenth-century Reformation with 'novelty, youth, insubordination and iconoclasm'.[127]

This is the pamphlet as it would have been sold by our pedlar of 1578, but our Shropshire chapman of 1630 would have carried a rather different version. In 1630, the ballad writer Martin Parker updated the tale for seventeenth-century tastes.[128] Gone is the Protestant content, gone is the generational conflict: in this story, morality is linked to social responsibility, as the 'Conscience' figure visits people from various walks of life and is turned away. The setting in named places around London ('Smithfield', 'Pye corner', 'Southwark') gives the moral a topical, contemporary feel; yet it is only in the country that 'Conscience' is finally welcomed. Not with the gentry or yeomanry (who refuse to give up their corn for the poor), but with the labourers:

> Mongst honest folks that have no lands,
> But get their living with their hands,
> These are his friends that to him stands,
> and's guiding.[129]

Martin Parker was the most popular and prolific of seventeenth-century ballad writers, and his involvement with these little books suggests they were aimed at the same public as the ballads. Indeed, the chapbook was sometimes merely a ballad text printed over a number of octavo pages, and sprinkled liberally with woodcuts.[130] There was a major change taking place in the 1620s and 1630s. The ballad publishers were collecting copyrights to small books which they could distribute to the same market as their ballads, and having these books printed in the 'penny' format (of twenty-four pages octavo or less) which was to become standard by the late seventeenth century. In doing so they did not think only of the dancers on the village green, but also of the sober godly readers like the Baxter family. The leading 'ballad partner', John Wright, was in fact far more involved in 'godly' books than 'merry' ones: we have only two surviving 'penny merriments' with his imprint, compared with five of a hybrid form I have called 'penny miscellanies', and a full dozen of what Pepys would call 'penny godlinesses'.

The 'penny miscellanies' were little collections of aphorisms, ranging from pure humour to pure moralizing and catechizing; most of the examples including a curious assortment of both, with no sense of incongruity. They would have sat well in the Shropshire pedlar's pack alongside ballads like 'Solomon's Sentences' and 'An Hundred Godly Lessons'. John Wright's surviving miscellanies were written by Nicholas Breton, and included *The Crossing of Proverbs* (1616), *The Soothing of Proverbs* (registered 1617), and *The Figure of Four* (1631), which parented a whole line of 'figures' of three, five, six, seven, and nine.[131] There were common sense sayings, practical advice, puns, and anti-female jokes: 'Three things will not prove well without beating: a Walnut tree, an Asse, and a Woman.'[132] But in all cases there was a large religious content too: not controversial doctrine, but simple injunctions for the daily living of a Christian life. Remember death, fear God, be sorry for your sins, avoid sloth and gluttony, be sober and chaste (especially if you are female). Most of this might have been written before the Reformation, although the writers sometimes incorporate the central position of faith in Christ, and, very rarely, a reference to the elect:

> The sweetnesse of this Name Jesus consists in three things: It is honey to the mouth, Melodie to the Eare, and joy to the Hearr [sic].

> The knowledge of God is threefold: Generall, Speciall, and Singular. Generall, as of the Philosophers: Special, as of the Christians: and singular, as of them that are blessed.[133]

These writers were poets, not preachers, and their little books may reflect the moderate religion of the majority of the literate public: those who would buy godly advice mixed with merry jests, but might not venture their 2*d* for a dose of the fire-and-brimstone found in the more puritanical 'penny godlies'.[134]

For those like the young Richard Baxter yearning for more fire in their faith, however, John Wright's trade-list included at least a dozen titles in 'penny book' size. These were largely the work of one author who appears to deserve credit, together with his publisher Wright, for the invention of the 'penny book' formula: John Andrews, 'Minister and Preacher of the word of God at Barricke Basset in the County of Wiltes'.[135] Another John Andrewes, a minister at St James Clerkenwell in Middlesex, gives us an idea of the reputation of our 'penny godly' author:

> For another there is, who writes both his Names as I do, and hath published divers Books, (as Petitions, Subpoena's, Christ-Crosses &c) . . . I doe hereby certifie thee, that I am not the man . . . for my part, howsoever I be the meanest among the many thousands that are called to the Sacred Priesthood; yet I may truly protest, that I never played the Circumforanean Theologaster: Istos enim Circulatores, qui Sacram Philosophiam honestius neglixissent, quam vendunt, semper exosus habui.[136]

In other words, by 1621 our Andrewes was known as a 'marketplace theologian' whose books were peddled around the countryside by chapmen of dubious character.

In his own works, our John Andrewes tells how he was called, late in life, from the profession of school teaching to become a minister. He had no regular living in Wiltshire: he was not the incumbent at Berwick Bassett, and must instead have been an occasional preacher or Puritan lecturer.[137] He claims to have lost 'to the value of three-score pounds by the yeare in spirituall livings within the Realme of Ireland', and hopes to relieve his family's impoverished situation by success with his books.[138] To this end he acts as his own part-publisher, printing one of his early works at his own cost, and taking over the distribution of two others, no doubt increasing his share of the profits.[139] However, Andrewes's little books were destined for life beyond the villages of Wiltshire, and it is quite likely that our Shropshire pedlar carried one or two of them in his pack. By the 1620s John Wright had begun to acquire the copyrights to distribute them along his ballad network, and they were selling so well that their author remarked on the phenomenon in 1630:

> whereas I have formerly published unto the view of the world, many small bookes for the setting forth of Gods glory. . . now seeing that my former bookes are so vendible, and so well likeing unto the

children of God, that in short time there have been divers impressions printed, I have therefore now set foorth another booke, intituled *Andrewes Repentance*.[140]

Andrewes's story is not unlike the pattern for later godly chapbook writers shown by Eamon Duffy: that is, ejected nonconformist ministers who turned to evangelical writing as a substitute for the usual pastoral duties.[141]

What were these small books which proved so 'vendible'? As Andrewes said himself, all were variations on the theme of 'repentance'.[142] Sometimes Andrewes focusses on the first step of repentance, the fire-and-brimstone 'alarum' to the unconverted sinner:

> Heare, oh therefore, heare all you that walke after the lusts of your owne hearts, and depart from Bethel the house of God, to starve your soules in Bethauen, the den of iniquity: It is sinne, oh! it is your unrepented sinne that drawes Gods anger towards you, that makes your eyes more dry than the stony rocke, and your hearts more hard than the Adament.[143]

But Andrewes dwells more often on the next step of the repentance process; offering encouragement to the penitent man who is already converted. If, says Andrewes, Satan shows you your sins and tempts you to despair, tell him 'Oh, thou hellish fiend, I say againe, Depart, I doe utterly defie thee, O take thy ugly sinnes againe, which thou hast caused me to commit; and lay them not unto my charge, for I am a member of my Lord and Saviour Jesus Christ.'[144]

Andrewes's style is always immediate and informal, and he includes himself as a companion in the reader's predicament. His books are notable for so often including his name in the title, as if for a loyal following waiting for his next 'penny godly' to appear. What kind of buyers was he appealing to? Andrewes himself gave some indication that he felt his audience would include those on the fringes of literacy; he addressed himself to hearers as well as readers: 'If thou dost reade or heare this worke . . . '; 'Gentle Readers, or Hearers, whosoever yee are, that are the Children of God'.[145]

The public for these little books did certainly include readers of at least gentry status, such as the Staffordshire lady, Frances Wolfreston. As well as Shakespearean quartos and other literary treasures, marked out with the inscription 'frances wolfreston hor [or her] bouk', Frances collected some fifty 'penny godlinesses'.[146] Those which bear a publication date number five from the 1640s (four of them by John Andrewes), eight from the 1650s, and twenty from the 1660s; a distribution which appears to reflect faithfully the snowballing growth of the trade.[147] However, Frances's copy of *A Golden Trumpet* gives an indication that not all of Andrewes's earlier readers were as well read and well off as herself: in 1648, the *Golden Trumpet* had reached its 'nine and twentieth Impression'.[148]

As well as the tracts of John Andrewes, our Shropshire pedlar may have carried other 'penny godlinesses' by the unknown 'George Shawe minister of Gods word', and a few titles by authors better known for more substantial works, like William Perkins.[149] His *Death's Knell or the Sicke Mans Passing-Bell*, which had reached its sixteenth edition by 1637, featured a title-page woodcut of a bed-side scene, with the skeleton figure of Death pulling at the rope of a bell.

At the cheapest end of the publishing trade, the key to survival was less often in finding new authors than in acquiring copyrights to old titles of proven popularity, and moving them into new formats. One piece of verse text illustrates well both the changes and the continuity between the eras in which our two pedlars plied their trade. 'The exhortacion of Robert Smith, unto his children, commonly set out in the name of maister Rogers' appeared in the 1563 edition of Foxe.[150] This was supposed to have been written in prison by the martyr Smith (d. August 1555), and brought to publication by Mathewe Rogers, with whose name the ballad became firmly associated. The popular title was simply 'Rogers Will'. The text was copied into numerous manuscripts of the period, and it became part of the long-enduring stock of godly ballads: both of our pedlars are likely to have carried it in broadside form.[151] It combined two of the most successful godly ballad formulas: the story of Protestant martyrdom and the parental advice ballad. It contained the usual predictable maxims to honour God and one's mother, give to the poor, beware lust, and (a small reminder of the situation in which it was composed) to 'abhore that arrant whore of Rome'. The bulk of the text might have been the advice of any parent to his or her children, but presumably the ballad gained weight from its origin in such spiritually significant circumstances:

> where I amonge myne Iron bands
> inclosed in the darke
> afewe dayes before my death
> did diddicate this warke.

In addition to the ballad, our pedlar of 1578 might also have carried 'Rogers Will' in the form of a 'litle booke' which was registered in 1577.[152] The work does not survive, but according to the detailed Stationers' Register entry, it contained four other godly texts, probably also in verse form: 'the complainte of veritye made by John Bradforde', 'the complainte of Raphe Allerton and others beinge prisoners in Lolers [Lollards?] Tower and wrytten with their bloude how God was their comforte', 'a song of Caine and Abell', and 'the saienge of Master Hooper that he wrote the night before he suffered upon a wall with a cole in the newe inne of Gloucester and his saienge at his deathe'. Here was, essentially, a miniature book of martyrs, of a portable size for both chapman and reader, and affordable to many readers for whom Foxe's great tomes would have been out of reach.

This book was not as 'little', however, as the 'penny godlinesses' which developed in the seventeenth century, which were usually the length of only one broadside ballad spread out over sixteen to twenty-four octavo pages. This is exactly what happened to the text of 'Rogers Will' when it got into the hands of the ballad partners Coules, Wright, Vere, and Gilbertson. When they were required to register their stock in 1656, their entry of 'ten little bookes' included the 'Exhortation that a Father Gave his Children' along with other familiar titles like 'Tom Thumb', '100 Godly Lessons', and 'Death's Knell'.[153] *The Exhortation that a Father Gave his Children* survives in a copy printed in 1648 for Francis Coules. Coules was in business from 1624 onwards, and this little book might well have been among the wares of our 1630 pedlar, in an earlier edition which does not survive.[154] The extant copy is just sixteen pages in octavo, with a scene of a martyr at the stake on the title page and back page. A number of generic woodcuts have been spread throughout: a king with his sceptre, a gentlewoman with feathered hat and fan, an old religious woodcut which may represent the coronation of the virgin. The text is exactly the same as that of the ballad.

The changing format of 'Rogers Will' demonstrates the development of the 'penny godliness', and a significant change in the cheap-print trade. At the same time, the longevity of the text itself indicates the conservative nature of much of popular piety. The successful chapbooks like 'Roger's Will', or ballads like 'The Duchess of Suffolk', probably survived because they could appeal to the dancers on the village green as well as to the Baxter family reading their Scripture. From his investigation of church courts in Wiltshire, Martin Ingram argues that respect for the church and Protestant values was not limited to the middle and upper strata of parish society, but 'probably applied also to many "honest householders" of the poorer sort, who had a definite, albeit modest stake in the community'.[155]

The pedlar's basic stock of cheap printed wares must have catered to this 'spectrum of unspectacular orthodoxy', within which most villagers fell. There were still variations and contradictions in these godly chapbooks and ballads, from the more traditional piety of 'St Bernard's Vision' to the greater emphasis on faith and the elect found in 'The Clerk of Bodnam' or John Andrewes's little repentance tracts. The resulting patchwork of beliefs may be described as distinctively 'post-Reformation', but not always thoroughly 'Protestant'. Piety retained a visual dimension, even if Christ in Glory was now banished to the tiny woodcuts along the top of a ballad. Religious emotion still attached itself to heroic archetypes, even if these were increasingly Protestant martyrs rather than Catholic saints. Morality still meant good neighbourly behaviour, and hell was still the same fiery place, a final threat as direct punishment for sins committed in this world.

As well as the popular ballads and chapbooks, our pedlars of Cambridgeshire and Shropshire must also have carried a number of books for the more serious students of religion, as the Baxters' purchase of 'Dr Sibb's *Bruised Reed*' suggests. The presence of large batches of inexpensive devotional manuals in provincial booksellers' inventories indicate that prayer books, psalm books, and catechisms were in demand throughout the country. Many of these could have been staples in the households of dissenters as well as mainstream Protestants. Members of the Family of Love, as Christopher Marsh has shown, participated in village life as constables, witnesses to wills, and even as churchwardens; they shared many values with other householders.[156] It seems unlikely that ordinary pedlars would carry the writings of Hendrick Niclaes or other proscribed works, unless they had already established special contacts with local members of the sect. However, the sale of sermons by William Fulke or Arthur Dent might well be the first step of conversion for rural readers, which could then lead to their involvement with local Protestants of the 'hotter sort', whether conformists or dissenters. We know how the printed word affected Sister Sneesby, a deaf old fen woman who was converted from her General Baptist beliefs to Quakerism by the reading of Quaker tracts.[157]

The possibility that the poor pedlar at the door could be an instrument of conversion was not lost on early Elizabethan reformers, who wrote broadside ballads urging the reform of society according to Protestant ideals. But if the pedlar of the 1570s was considered a potential agent of God's word, his descendant of the 1630s was widely reviled as belonging to a band of masterless men 'who neglect the sacred philosophy which they sell'.[158] The task of stocking the pedlar's pack was increasingly left to publishers like the 'ballad partners', who reprinted godly works with proven commercial appeal; and to ejected nonconformist ministers like John Andrewes of Wiltshire. The evangelical thrust was shifting from the ballads to the developing format of the penny chapbook. 'Marketplace theologians' like Andrewes no longer wrote ballads calling for widespread social reform, but instead published little repentance tracts aiming directly at the conversion of individuals.

The chapman, who no doubt weighed up with each step the value of every ounce in his pack, had to carry a basic stock of goods which would appeal to the widest audience: linens and haberdashery, simple luxuries, best-selling ballads and chapbooks, popular devotional manuals. The chapmen of the late seventeenth century were still carrying titles like *The Dying Man's Last Sermon*, *A Book of Prayer and Graces*, and *The Door of Salvation Opened*; in fact, a third of the chapbooks in their packs were apparently godly ones.[159] These little books could hardly have been worth their weight in gloves and ribbons if they did not sell. In the dissemination of religious ideas and beliefs, the petty chapman of rural England was undoubtedly an important agent, even if 'good books' were mixed together with bawdy ballads in the jumble of the pedlar's pack.

Notes

1 Ballad sellers and chapmen appear in the 'Register of Passports for Vagrants 1598–1669', in Paul Slack (ed.), *Poverty in Early Stuart Salisbury*, Wiltshire Record Society, 31 (Devizes, 1975).

2 William Shakespeare, *The Winter's Tale* (written 1610–11), IV.iii–iv. Robert Greene, *The Second Part of Conny-Catching* (1591). BL Harleian MS 6715, fol. 98v.

3 Nicholas Bownde, *The Doctrine of the Sabbath* (1595), p. 241.

4 R. Baxter, *Reliquiae Baxterianae* (1696), pp. 3–4.

5 David Galloway (ed.), *Records of Early English Drama. Norwich 1540–1642* (Toronto, 1984), pp. 115, 126, 141, 200–1, 237. Walter Plummer of Southwark was stopped at Trowbridge Fair in 1620, 'carrying with him a store of ballads to sing in his travels' (A.L. Beier, *Masterless Men: The Vagrancy Problem in England 1560–1640* (1985), p. 98).

6 Margaret Spufford, *Contrasting Communities: English Villagers in the Sixteenth and Seventeenth Centuries* (Cambridge, 1974), p. 208.

7 Christopher Marsh, 'The Gravestone of Thomas Lawrence Revisited (or the Family of Love and the Local Community in Balsham 1560–1630)' in M. Spufford (ed.), *The World of Rural Dissenters 1520–1725* (Cambridge, 1995), p. 214.

8 Spufford, *Contrasting Communities*, p. 208.

9 STC 18548.5, 'All the letters of the A.B.C. by every sondrye letter whereof, there is a good document set-fourth and taught, in ryme' ([N. Bohmberg, Cologne], 1575). STC 1858, 'A benedictie or blessinge to be saide over the table before meate and a grace or thankesgeevinge to be saide after meate' ([N. Bohmberg, Cologne], 1575).

10 E. Leedham-Green (ed.), *Books in Cambridge Inventories*, 2 vols. (Cambridge, 1986), I, pp. xviii–xix, 327.

11 Spufford (ed.), *The World of Rural Dissenters*, pp. 283, 285.

12 [M. Sparke], *A Second Beacon Fired by Scintilla* (1652), pp. 5–6.

13 Shakespeare, *The Winter's Tale*, IV.iii–iv. In *The Great Reclothing of Rural England: Petty Chapmen and their Wares in the Seventeenth Century* (1984), pp. 88–9, Margaret Spufford examines the items in Autolycus's pack, which included linen, cambrics, and lawns, haberdashery and small courtship gifts, as well as ballads.

14 Leedham-Greene (ed.), *Books in Cambridge Inventories*, I, pp. 326–40.

15 Alexander Rodger (ed.), 'Roger Ward's Shrewsbury Stock: An Inventory of 1585', *The Library*, 5th Ser., 13 (1958), pp. 252, 257, 259, 260, 267.

16 John Taylor, *The Carriers Cosmographie; Or a Briefe Relation of the Innes in and Neere London* (1637). In addition to the Cambridge 'carriers' there were also 'waggons or coaches', found on Thursdays and Fridays at the Black Bull in Bishopsgate Street.

17 Spufford (ed.), *World of Rural Dissenters*, pp. 38, 274, 276, 285–6.

18 See Thomas Seyver of Eastington, described by Michael Frearson in Spufford (ed.), *World of Dissenters*, p. 285.

19 W.W. Greg, *Companion to Arber. Being a Calendar of Documents in Edward Arber's Transcript of the Registers of the Company of Stationers of London 1554–1640* (Oxford, 1967), pp. 253–5. I am grateful to Michael Frearson for this reference. The book is identified by Greg as *Christ's Confession and Complaint* (pp. 70, 253).

20 Henry Chettle, *Kind-Harts Dreame. Conteinting Five Apparitions, with their Invectives against Abuses Raigning* (1593), sig. C2v.

21 PRO Req 2/259/64, Req 2/293/27, Reg 2/394/22. For further examples see Tessa Watt, *Cheap Print and Popular Piety, 1550–1640* (Cambridge, 1991), pp. 27–8.

22 Slack (ed.), *Poverty in Early Stuart Salisbury,* p. 58 and nos. 82, 152, 288, 476. Beier, *Masterless Men,* p. 98.

23 On the ubiquity of ballads see Watt, *Cheap Print,* pp. 11–13.

24 Bownde, *The Doctrine of the Sabbath,* p. 242.

25 See Watt, *Cheap Print,* pp. 42–9.

26 H.L. Collmann (ed.), *Ballads and Broadsides Chiefly of the Elizabethan Period . . . Now in the Library of Britwell Court* (1912), no. 3. *Tottel's Miscellany* (1557), ed. Edward Arber (1870), p. 172.

27 Miles Coverdale, *Certain Most Godly, Fruitful, and Comfortable Letters* (1564), pp. 634–8. 'John Carelesse' was registered as a broadside on 1 August 1586, amongst a re-registration of old stock. STC 853.5: 'A ballad of Anne Askew, intituled: I am a woman poor and blind' (1624?). Registered on 14 December 1624, but, once again, in a batch of ballads of much earlier provenance.

28 See Watt, *Cheap Print,* pp. 96–7.

29 For example, 'Of the horrible and wofull destruction of Sodome and Gomorra' (1570) in Joseph Lilly (ed.), *A Collection of 79 Black-Letter Ballads and Broadsides Printed in the Reign of Queen Elizabeth* (1867), p. 125; 'Of the horyble and woful destruction of Jerusalem' (1569?), in Collmann (ed.), *Ballads and Broadsides,* no. 5. For more information on apocalyptic ballads see Watt, *Cheap Print,* p. 97.

30 Spufford (ed.), *World of Rural Dissenters,* pp. 72 n. 250, 73.

31 STC 18548.5, 'All the letters of the A.B.C. . . . ' ([Cologne], 1575). Reprinted in John Holloway (ed.), *The Euing Collection of English Broadside Ballads* (Glasgow, 1971), no. 1.

32 In 'A christian conference between Christ and a sinner' Christ promises he will receive the sinner 'If once I do see thee be sory in heart' (William Chappell and J. Woodfall Ebsworth (eds.), *The Roxburghe Ballads,* 8 vols. (1871–97), III, p. 164).

33 'The sinner, dispisinge the world and all earthly vanities . . .' [ent. 1568–9?], in Hyder E. Rollins, *Old English Ballads 1553–1625* (Cambridge, 1920), p. 198.

34 William Samuel, *The Abridgement of Goddes Statutes in Myter* (1551), A2-A2v. Cited in John King, *English Reformation Literature: The Tudor Origins of the Protestant Tradition* (Princeton, 1982), p. 212.

35 Arber, I, p. 205 (1562–3), I, p. 378 (1568–9), II, p. 359 (1579–80), III, p. 486 (1611–12), I, p. 401 (1569–70).

36 Arber, I, p. 414 (1569–70), II, p. 376 (1580–1), II, p. 376 (1580–1), I, p. 415 (1569–70), I, p. 416 (1569–70).

37 Samuel, *The Abridgemente of Goddes Statutes in Myter,* A2-A2v.

38 See Watt, *Cheap Print,* pp. 42–9.

39 N.H. Keeble (ed.), *The Autobiography of Richard Baxter* (1974), p. 6.

40 See Watt, *Cheap Print,* pp. 55–73.

41 Arber, IV, pp. 131–2.

42 Ballad partners' entries for 1656 and 1675, in Eyre, II, pp. 36–7, 496–501. Entry to Thomas Norris and Charles Brown, 20 September 1712, reprinted in R.S. Thomson, 'The Development of the Broadside Trade and its Influence upon the Transmission of English Folksongs' (Cambridge, PhD, 1974), App. B. William and Cluer Dicey, *A Catalogue of Maps, Histories, Prints, Old Ballads, Copy-Books, Broadsheets and Other Patters, Drawing-Books, Garlands &c* (1754), reprinted in Thomson, 'Development of the Broadside Trade', App. C.

43 For a full list see Watt, *Cheap Print,* App. A.

44 For a list of 119 less successful religious ballads published before 1640, see Watt, *Cheap Print,* App. B.

45 'A godly and vertuous songe or ballade, made by the constant member of Christe, John Carelesse', in Coverdale, *Certain Most Godly, Fruitful, and Comfortable Letters,* pp. 634–8. 'A rare example of a vertuous maid in Paris . . . ', in Pepys Collection, Magdalene College, Cambridge, II, pp. 24–5. 'A ballad of Anne Askew,

intituled: I am a woman poor and blind', Manchester Central Library, collection of ballads, I, p. 54. 'The most rare and excellent history of the Dutchesse of Suffolkes calamity', in Chappell and Ebsworth (eds.), *The Roxburghe Ballads*, I, p. 287.

46 Pepys Collection, I, pp. 544–5. First printed in Thomas Deloney, *Strange Histories, of Kings, Princes, Dukes . . . With the Great Troubles of the Dutches of Suffolke* (1602). Taken from John Foxe, *Actes and Monuments* (1583 edn), II, pp. 2078–81.

47 See, for example, 'Kind Edward the Fourth and a Tanner of Tamworth', in F.J. Child (ed.), *The English and Scottish Popular Ballads*, 8 vols. (1882–98), no. 273.

48 For similar revelation scenes, see James Kinsley (ed.), *The Oxford Book of Ballads* (Oxford, 1982 edn), nos. 32, 47.

49 Pepys Collection, II, p. 6. It refers to the Armada which God sent against England 'of late', and to a recent plague, probably that of 1592.

50 On attribution of the ballad, see Watt, *Cheap Print*, p. 99 n. 98.

51 'A most excellent new dittie, wherein is shewed the sage sayings, and wise sentences of Salomon' (1586), in Collmann (ed.), *Ballads and Broadsides*, no. 84. Pepys Collection, II, p. 64.

52 Baxter commented on this Pelagian element amongst his parishioners (*Confirmation and Restauration, the Necessary Means of Reformation and Reconciliation* (1658), pp. 157–65). Discussed in Eamon Duffy, 'The Godly and the Multitude in Stuart England', *Seventeenth Century Journal*, 1, no. 1 (1986), p. 39.

53 Registered 1624. Chappell and Ebsworth (eds.), *The Roxburghe Ballads*, VII, p. 40. Pepys Collection, I, pp. 48–9.

54 'The sorrowful lamentation of a penitent sinner' [ent. 1624], in Chappell and Ebsworth, (eds.), *The Roxburghe Ballads*, VIII, p. 99; 'Clarke of Bodnam'.

55 James Balmford, *A Short Catechisme, Summarily Comprizing the Principal Points of Christian Faith* (1607), sig. A8v.

56 Chappell and Ebsworth (eds.), *The Roxburghe Ballads*, II, p. 491. Pepys Collection, II, p. 4.

57 A. Caiger-Smith, *English Medieval Mural Paintings* (Oxford, 1963), pp. 36, 31. The specific source was the supposititious 'Visio Sancti Bernardi', translated into English metre by William Crashaw in 1613 (*STC* 1908.5 to 1909.7).

58 William and Cluer Dicey, *A Catalogue of Maps, Histories, Prints . . .*, p. 65.

59 Only one of these afer-life ballads presents the Protestant message of the sinner saved by faith alone: 'A comfortable new ballad of a dreame of a sinner, being very sore troubled with the assaults of Sathan' (ent. 1624), Pepys Collection, I, p. 39. See Watt, *Cheap Print*, p. 112.

60 Child (ed.), *The English and Scottish Popular Ballads*.

61 Delilah in 'A most excellent and famous ditty of Sampson judge of Israell, how he wedded a Philistine's daughter' (?ent. 1564–4), Pepys Collection, I, p. 32.

62 Kinsley (ed.), *Oxford Book of Ballads*, nos. 44, 58.

63 'The story of David and Berseba' [?ent. 1569–70?], in Chappell and Ebsworth (eds.), *The Roxburghe Ballads*, I, p. 270.

64 'A new ballad; declaring the excellent parable of the prodigal child' [ent. 1570–1?], in Chappell and Ebsworth (eds.), *The Roxburghe Ballads*, I, p. 393.

65 'Good fellows resolution', discussed in Thomson, 'Development of the Broadside Trade', pp. 232–6.

66 Registered 11 September 1578. Andrew Clark (ed.), *The Shirburn Ballads* (Oxford, 1907), p. 103.

67 A similar trend can be confirn.ed for 'secular' as well as 'religious' ballads. Unfortunately, this change of visual appearance cannot be dated precisely because of a gap in the surviving broadsides: the sixteenth-century collections are mostly concentrated in the period from around 1550 to 1572, while the seventeenth-century collections do not begin in full force until 1624–5. For a list of surviving ballads, see Watt, *Cheap Print*, pp. 333–41.

68 See Watt, *Cheap Print*, p. 149.

69 See Watt, *Cheap Print*, Figs. 10 and 11 and pp. 143–6.

70 *STC* 6223. Thomas Warren re-registered the picture in 1656. (Eyre, I, p. 48.) The theme was known in France as 'Les Quatre Verités'. M. Dorothy George, *English*

Political Caricature to 1792. A Study of Opinion and Propaganda (Oxford, 1959), p. 9.

71 On woodcuts' depictions of death in the *Ars moriendi*, see Roger Chartier, *The Cultural Uses of Print in Early Modern France*, trans. Lydia C. Cochrane (Princeton, 1987), pp. 32–70.

72 On iconophobia see Watt, *Cheap Print*, pp. 131–40.

73 Giles Godet worked in England from the late 1540s to his death in 1571. Many of his blocks were still being used in 1656 by Thomas Warren. See Watt, *Cheap Print*, pp. 181–91.

74 Reproduced in Leedham-Green (ed.), *Books in Cambridge Inventories*, I, p. 338.

75 Susan Foister found that in the inventories of the prosperous classes a 'story' usually referred to a framed painting (Susan Foister, 'Paintings and Other Works of Art in Sixteenth-Century English Inventories', *The Burlington Magazine*, 123 (1981), p. 275).

76 Compare Charles Tias's 1664 stock, which contained pictures in 'reams' (Margaret Spufford, *Small Books*, pp. 91–101).

77 Bownde, *The Doctrine of the Sabbath*, p. 241. Abraham Holland in John Davies, *A Scourge for Paper-Persecutors, or Papers Complaint* (1624), sig. A2v of section by Holland. Wye Saltonstall, *Picturae Loquentes. Or Pictures Drawne forth in Characters. With a Poeme of a Maid* (1631), sig. E10v.

78 The 1584 inventory of Mrs Hampden of Stoke in Buckinghamshire included 'a picture of Christe' and 'a picture of (as it is termed) the Judgement daye', which were assumed to be incriminating (PRO, SP 12/167/47). Cited in Patrick Collinson, 'From Iconoclasm to Iconophobia: the Cultural Impact of the Second English Reformation', The Stenton Lecture 1985 (Reading, 1986), p. 37 n. 109 (*see* Reading 11 above), where two similar examples are noted.

79 *The Ordinary, a Comedy*, III.v. In *The Plays and Poems of William Cartwright*, ed. G. Blakemore Evans (Madison, 1951), p. 317.

80 This tract represents an extreme position against *any* images, not just religious images. However, it does illustrate the point that ballad woodcuts could give offence despite their relatively innocuous proportions, and that they were an ubiquitous form of image, worthy of attack (*A Declaration from the Children of Light*, cited in Hyder E. Rollins, *Cavalier and Puritan. Ballads and Broadsides Illustrating the Period of the Great Rebellion, 1640–1660* (New York, 1923), p. 68).

81 See Watt, *Cheap Print*, Fig. 19. Edward Hodnett, *English Woodcuts 1480–1535* (2nd edn, Oxford, 1973), no. 477, figure 46.

82 Chappell and Ebsworth (eds.), *The Roxburghe Ballads*, II, p. 486, I, p. 388. Reprinted in Watt, *Cheap Print*, pp. 170–2.

83 'Glad tydings from heaven' [*c.* 1630] in Roxburghe Ballads, BL, I, 134. The virgin and child woodcut is found on post-Restoration broadsides (e.g. Pepys Collection, II, pp. 27, 30), but appears to be of old stock.

84 'The sinner's supplication' [*c.* 1630], in Chappell and Ebsworth (eds.), *The Roxburghe Ballads*, II, p. 498. This Christ in Glory was a copy of an earlier woodcut used on a pamphlet of 1613, when it already contained several wormholes. See Hodnett, *English Woodcuts 1480–1535*, pl. 78. For similar images see figures 66, 117.

85 This copy from Pepys Collection, II, p. 13. Other copies are in Pepys Collection, II, pp. 28, 29, 47, 63; Wood Ballads, Bodleian Library, Wood. 401. (66), (160); Roxburghe Ballads, BL, II, pp. 141, 248, 422, III, pp. 371, 344.

86 Collinson, 'From Iconoclasm to Iconophobia', p. 841 (*see* Reading 11 above); restated in Patrick Collinson, *The Birthpangs of Protestant England: Religions and Cultural Change in the Sixteenth and Seventeenth Centuries* (New York, 1988), p. 117.

87 For a more detailed exploration of images in this period, see Watt, *Cheap Print*, pp. 131–216.

88 *STC* 22479. The first edition, published in 1630 (around the time of which Baxter writes), is available in a facsimile edition by the Scolar Press (1973) with an introduction by P.A. Slack.

89 Francis Johnson found that from about 1560 to 1635, prices for normal new unbound books stuck quite closely to this halfpenny per sheet (Francis R. Johnson, 'Notes on English Retail Book-Prices, 1550–1640', *The Library,* 5th Ser., 5 (1950), pp. 84, 93).

90 Keith Wrightson, *English Society 1580–1680* (1982), pp. 32–4.

91 Reference from Margaret Spufford.

92 Notice of 1686 in Margaret Spufford, *Small Books,* pp. 111–13.

93 *Small Books.*

94 John Andrews, bookseller of Pye Corner, appears to be the first to advertise chapbooks as a trade-list in the back of his books, in 1658–9 (see Watt, *Cheap Print,* p. 218).

95 See Watt, *Cheap Print,* pp. 11–30.

96 Richard Jones, William Pickering, and John Awdeley; John Wright, Henry Gosson, John Trundle, Francis Coules, and Francis Grove. See Watt *Cheap Print,* pp. 274–95.

97 Martin Parker describes his 'twopenny customers' in *Harry White his Humour* (1637). John Andrews, bookseller, lists seven books at 2d in the back of John Hart, *The Plain Mans Plain Path-Way to Heaven* (1659). Johnson, 'Notes on English Retail Book-Prices', pp. 89–90.

98 See descriptions of chapbook size in Harry B. Weiss, *A Catalogue of the Chapbooks in the New York Public Library* (New York, 1936), p. 3; Victor E. Neuberg, *The Batsford Companion to Popular Literature* (1983), p. 51.

99 Margaret Spufford, *Small Books,* pp. 130–1, 150–1.

100 Watt, *Cheap Print,* pp. 274–320 and Apps. H. to L.

101 Frederick J. Furnivall (ed.), *Captain Cox, his Ballads and Books; Or, Robert Laneham's Letter* (1871). Margaret Spufford, *Small Books,* pp. 51, 66, 77, etc.

102 See Watt, *Cheap Print,* Table 4. Reprints cost less than new books, an average of 1/3d per sheet. New pamphlets tended to be sold at a price of 1d per sheet, levelling off to the standard ½d at around four sheets (Johnson, 'Notes on English Retail Book-Prices', pp. 84, 93).

103 Margaret Spufford, *Small Books,* p. 197.

104 Calculated from figures given in Edith L. Klotz, 'A Subject Analysis of English Imprints for Every Tenth Year from 1480 to 1640', *Huntington Library Quarterly,* 1 (1938), p. 418.

105 Leedham-Green (ed.), *Books in Cambridge Inventories,* I, pp. 326–40.

106 'Serving of landes', valued at 8d, is identified by Elizabeth Leedham-Green as Richard Benese, *This Boke Sheweth the Maner of Measurynge of All Maner of Lande* (probably the edn of *c.* 1565). *Books in Cambridge Inventories,* I, p. 336.

107 STC 22265: Dionyse Settle, *A True Reporte of the Laste Voyage into the West and Northwest Regions, & c 1577 Worthily Atchieved by Capteine Frobisher* (1577).

108 A surviving copy of the Sternhold and Hopkins psalms in this format is *STC* 2449.5: *The Whole Booke of Psalmes, Collected into English Metre* (1577). A more prosperous yeoman could have bought a bound copy in various larger formats valued at 6d, 8d, or 10d in Denys's inventory.

109 STC 21446.7. The surviving copy dates from 1602, but the work was first registered to T. Marsh in 1562–3. The 1602 edition is 12.5 sheets in 16°, but the 32° edition may have been an abridged version. On the official primer, see Helen C. White, *The Tudor Books of Private Devotion* (Wisconsin, 1951), p. 125.

110 White, *Tudor Books,* p. 169. STC 6655 or STC 6685.5. Dering, *Godlye private praiers,* sig. C1.

111 In 1677 Robert Carr, chapman of Newcastle upon Tyne, had nineteen dozen hornbooks in his warehouse, at a halfpenny each or less. See Spufford (ed.), *World of Rural Dissenters,* p. 70.

112 Ian Green, '"For Children in Yeeres and Children in Understanding": The Emergence of the English Catechism under Elizabeth and the Early Stuarts', *Journal of Ecclesiastical History,* 37, p. 425.

113 Leedham-Green (ed.), *Books in Cambridge Inventories,* I, p. 335. Edward Dering,

A *Bryefe and Necessary Catechisme, very Needfull to be Knowne of All Housholders* (1577).

114 William Fulke, *A Comfortable Sermon of Faith, in Temptations and Afflictions* (1578 edn), a work of 3.5 sheets octavo.

115 Sig. C3.

116 Sig. D4v. This book should have been more expensive, at 8.5 sheets octavo. The twopenny copy may have been second hand.

117 *An Epistle of the Ladye Jane . . . Whereunto is Added the Communication that she had with Master Feckenham. Also Another Epistle to her Sister, with the Words she Spake upon the Scaffold. MDLIIII* [J. Day? 1554?]. Pickering's edition does not survive.

118 *STC* 7281. Wright's version was retitled *The Life, Death and Actions of the Lady Jane Gray. Containing Foure Discourses Written with her Owne Hands* (1615 etc.) and ran to three sheets in quarto.

119 For a more detailed account of these pamphlets, see Watt, *Cheap Print*, pp. 278–88.

120 John Terry, *The Defence of Protestancie* (1635 edn). See *STC* 'Index I. Printers and Publishers' (1991).

121 Rodger (ed.), 'Roger Ward's Shrewsbury Stock', pp. 247–68.

122 Cyril B. Judge, *Elizabethan Book-Pirates* (Cambridge, MA, 1934), pp. 49–50.

123 Rodger (ed.), 'Roger Ward's Shrewsbury Stock', pp. 259, 267. *STC* 6649.5. Robert Davies, *A Memoir of the York Press* (1868), p. 363.

124 Rodger (ed.), 'Roger Wards's Shrewsbury Stock', p. 252. *The Book in Meeter of Robin Conscience* [*c.* 1565?]. Another edition printed by Edward Allde [1590?]. Reprinted in W. Carew Hazlitt (ed.), *Remains of the Early Popular Poetry of England*, 4 vols. (1864–6), III, pp. 225–47.

125 *Robin Conscience*, original printed marginal notes, lines 296–300.

126 *Robin Conscience*, lines 71–3.

127 Collinson, 'From Iconoclasm to Iconophobia', p. 4.

128 *Robin Conscience, or, Conscionable Robin* (for F. Coules, 1635). Registered to M. Sparke, 20 April 1630.

129 *Robin Conscience*, p. 15.

130 For example, *The Pleasant and Sweet History of Patient Grissell* was first registered as a broadside in 1565–6 (Arber, I, p. 296), but around 1640 the ballad partner John Wright took the ballad and spread it out over 24 pages octavo, dividing the text into little chapters, adding a prose introduction and conclusion, and adorning it with seven woodcuts.

131 Anon., *The Figure of Three* (1636); Martin Parker, *The Figure of Five* (1645?); D.N., *The Figure of Six* (1652); Martin Parker, *The Figure of Seven* (1647); and Samuel Smithson, *The Figure of Nine* (1662). Later editions of these were included among Pepys's penny merriments.

132 Anon., *Figure of Three*, sig. B2.

133 *Figure of Three*, sig. A3.

134 On the moderate religion of 'honest householders' at all levels of society, see Martin Ingram, *Church Courts, Sex and Marriage in England, 1570–1640* (Cambridge, 1987).

135 John Andrewes, *Christ his Crosse* (1614). For a fuller account of John Andrewes see Watt, *Cheap Print*, pp. 306–11.

136 'I never played the marketplace theologian: I have always detested those pedlars who neglect the sacred philosophy which they sell.' Andrewes, *The Brazen Serpent: Or, the Copie of a Sermon* (1621), sig. A3.

137 Andrewes, *Christ his Crosse* (1614), sig. A4. Alexander B. Grosart (ed.), *Miscellanies of the Fuller Worthies' Library*, 39 vols. (Blackburn, 1868–76), II, 6.

138 *Andrewes Humble Petition* (for J. Wright, 1623 edn), sig. A4.

139 See verses at the back of *Christ his Crosse*, sig. L2v; a variation is repeated on the title page of *Andrewes Humble Petition* (1623 edn). The 1621 *Celestiall Looking-Glasse* was 'imprinted at my own cost and charges'.

140 *Andrewes Repentance* (1631 edn), sig. A2.

141 Duffy, 'The Godly and the Multitude', pp. 47–8.
142 *Andrewes Repentance*, sig. B1v.
143 *Andrewes Caveat to Win Sinners* (for J. Wright, 1631), sig. A6.
144 *Andrewes Repentance*, sig. A7.
145 *Humble Petition*, title page; *The Converted Man's New Birth* (1620), sig. A2.
146 Sale catalogue in BL: Sotheby C.S.413(3), 24 May 1856. For more on Frances Wolfreston see Watt, *Cheap Print*, pp. 315–17; Paul Morgan, 'Frances Wolfreston and "Hor Bouks": A Seventeenth-Century Woman Book-Collector', *The Library*, 6th Ser., 11 (1989), pp. 197–219.
147 A further dozen were listed in the sales catalogue as 'an one other', or titled but without date: most of these were lumped together with post-1660 books and probably date from that period. It is also very rare for a pre-1640 chapbook to have no date in the imprint.
148 This work was written before 1630 when its copyright was transferred to John Wright, but there are no surviving copies before 1641.
149 Watt, *Cheap Print*, pp. 311–15.
150 Foxe, *Actes and Monuments* (1563 edn), sigs. 3U$_2$–3U$_2$v.
151 'Mastare Rogers to his childerne', in MS Stowe 958; 'Mathewe Rogers to his childrine', in Cambridge University MS Ff.5.14. First registration probably the entry to William Pickering in 1564: 'An Instruction of a father to his cheldren' (Arber, I, p. 262). Entered as 'Rogers will' in 1624 (Arber, IV, p. 131).
152 It was entered on 14 October to John Arnold and then on 11 November to James Robotham, neither of whom appear to have been specialists in ballads or other cheap print (Arber, II, p. 319).
153 Eyre, II, p. 55.
154 The existing copy survives only because it was bought by the Staffordshire lady Frances Wolfreston, and preserved for 200 years by her descendants.
155 Martin Ingram, *Church Courts, Sex and Marriage in England, 1570–1640* (Cambridge, 1987), pp. 123–4, 94.
156 Spufford (ed.), *World of Rural Dissenters*, pp. 216–18.
157 Spufford (ed.), *World of Rural Dissenters*, p. 64.
158 Andrewes, *The Brazen Serpent*, sig. A3. The acquisition of paper wares to sell was sometimes the first recourse of the destitute. See Spufford, *World of Rural Dissenters*, p. 65.
159 Spufford, *Small Books*, pp. 197–201.

Index